Wonders

ELL Small Group Guide
Strategic Support for English Language Learners

Grade 1

Mc Graw Hill

mheducation.com/prek-12

Mc
Graw
Hill

Copyright © 2023 McGraw Hill

All rights reserved. No part of this publication may be reproduced or distributed in any form or by any means, or stored in a database or retrieval system, without the prior written consent of McGraw Hill, including, but not limited to, network storage or transmission, or broadcast for distance learning.

Send all inquiries to:
McGraw Hill
1325 Avenue of the Americas
New York, NY 10019

ISBN: 978-1-26-578144-6
MHID: 1-26-578144-3

Printed in the United States of America.

6 7 8 9 LMN 26 25 24 23   A

Contents

UNITS 1-2

ELL Small Group Planning vi
ELL Resources... vi
Understanding English Language Learner Levels........................... viii
Start Smart.. S2
Routines... S8
Planner... S10
Newcomers... S14

Unit 1 Reading/Writing 2–51
Week 1: Realistic Fiction 2
Week 2: Fantasy 12
Week 3: Fantasy 22
Week 4: Informational Text 32
Week 5: Fantasy 42

Unit 1 Summative Assessment 52–53

Unit 2 Reading/Writing 54–103
Week 1: Realistic Fiction 54
Week 2: Fantasy 64
Week 3: Informational Text 74
Week 4: Fantasy 84
Week 5: Informational Text 94

Unit 2 Summative Assessment 104–105

CONTENTS **iii**

Contents

UNITS 3-4

Unit 3 Reading/Writing 106–155
Week 1: Fantasy 106
Week 2: Drama 116
Week 3: Folktale 126
Week 4: Informational Text 136
Week 5: Informational Text 146

Unit 3 Summative Assessment 156–157

Unit 4 Reading/Writing 158–207
Week 1: Realistic Fiction 158
Week 2: Fantasy 168
Week 3: Informational Text 178
Week 4: Fantasy 188
Week 5: Informational Text 198

Unit 4 Summative Assessment 208–209

UNITS 5-6

Contents

Unit 5 Reading/Writing 210–259
Week 1: Fantasy 210
Week 2: Fantasy 220
Week 3: Biography 230
Week 4: Realistic Fiction 240
Week 5: Informational Text 250

Unit 5 Summative Assessment 260–261

Unit 6 Reading/Writing 262–311
Week 1: Fantasy 262
Week 2: Informational Text 272
Week 3: Realistic Fiction 282
Week 4: Realistic Fiction 292
Week 5: Informational Text 302

Unit 6 Summative Assessment 312–313

ELL Resources

A variety of resources will help English Language Learners meet grade-level expectations. The components scaffold instruction to tackle core content and leveled practice through integrated domains to help ELLs transition to more proficient levels of English.

Components	Differentiate: N = Newcomer B = Beginning I = Intermediate A = Advanced/Advanced-High AL = All Levels	Integrated Domains Reading Writing Listening Speaking	Available Digitally
ELL Small Group Guide • Literature Big Book • Shared Read • Anchor Text • Leveled Reader • Genre Passage • Writing	B, I, A	Reading, Writing, Listening, Speaking	●
Leveled Readers	AL	Reading, Writing, Listening, Speaking	●
Differentiated Genre Passages	AL	Reading, Writing, Listening, Speaking	●
ELL Differentiated Texts	B, I, A	Reading, Writing, Listening, Speaking	●
ELL Writing BLMs	AL	Reading, Writing, Listening, Speaking	●
Visual Vocabulary Cards	AL	Reading, Writing, Listening, Speaking	●

Components	Differentiate: N = Newcomer B = Beginning I = Intermediate A = Advanced/Advanced-High AL = All Levels	Integrated Domains 📖 Reading ✏️ Writing 👂 Listening 🎤 Speaking	Available Digitally
Newcomers • Newcomer Cards • Newcomer Teacher's Guide • Newcomer Online Visuals • Newcomer Interactive Games	N	📖 ✏️ 👂 🎤	●
Language Development Kit • Language Development Cards • Language Development Practice	B, I, A	📖 ✏️ 👂 🎤	●
Online Games	AL	📖 ✏️ 👂 🎤	●
Language Transfers Handbook	AL	📖 ✏️ 👂 🎤	●
Unit Assessment	B, I, A	📖 ✏️ 👂 🎤	●
Oral Language Sentence Frames	B, I, A	👂 🎤	●

ELL RESOURCES **vii**

Understanding English Language Learner Levels

The *Wonders* program provides targeted language support for all levels of English language proficiency. The English language learners in your classroom have a variety of backgrounds, each with different ethnic background, first language, socioeconomic status, quality of prior schooling, and levels of language proficiency. They bring diverse sets of academic knowledge and cultural perspectives that can enrich learning.

This overview is designed to help teachers determine the appropriate level of support for their English language learners and understand students' abilities depending on their language proficiencies. It is important to note that students may be at different levels in each language domain (listening, speaking, reading, and writing). Systematic, explicit, and appropriately scaffolded instruction helps English language learners attain English proficiency and meet the high expectations defined in English Language Arts standards.

BEGINNING

At this early stage of language development, students require significant language support. As they gain experience with English, support may become moderate or light for familiar tasks and topics.

The Student...

- recognizes English phonemes that correspond to phonemes produced in primary language;
- initially demonstrates more receptive than productive English skills;
- communicates basic needs and information in social and academic settings, using familiar everyday vocabulary, gestures, learned words or phrases, and/or short sentences;
- follows one- or two-step oral directions;
- answers *wh-* questions (who, what, when, where, why, which);
- comprehends words, phrases, and basic information about familiar topics as presented through stories and conversations;
- identifies concepts about print and text features;
- reads short grade-appropriate text with familiar vocabulary and simple sentences, supported by graphics or pictures;
- draws pictures and writes labels;
- expresses ideas using visuals and short responses.

INTERMEDIATE

Students require moderate support for cognitively demanding activities and light support for familiar tasks and topics.

The Student...

- pronounces most English phonemes correctly while reading aloud;
- communicates more complex personal needs, ideas, and opinions using increasingly complex vocabulary and sentences;
- follows multi-step oral directions;
- initiates and participates in collaborative conversations about social and academic topics, with support as needed;
- asks questions, retells stories or events, and comprehends basic content-area concepts;
- comprehends information on familiar and unfamiliar topics with contextual clues;
- reads increasingly complex grade-level text supported by graphics, pictures, and context clues;
- increases correct usage of written and oral language conventions;
- uses vocabulary learned, including academic language, to provide information and extended responses in contextualized oral and written prompts.

ADVANCED/ADVANCED HIGH

While the English language proficiency of students is advanced, some language support for accessing content is still necessary. If students are requiring little to no support, exiting them from the ELL designation should be considered.

The Student...

- applies knowledge of common English morphemes in oral and silent reading;
- communicates complex feelings, needs, ideas, and opinions using increasingly complex vocabulary and sentences;
- understands more nonliteral social and academic language about concrete and abstract topics;
- initiates and sustains collaborative conversations about grade-level academic and social topics;
- reads and comprehends a wide range of complex literature and informational texts at grade level;
- writes using more standard forms of English on various academic topics;
- communicates orally and in writing with fewer grammatical errors;
- tailors language, orally and in writing, to specific purposes and audiences.

UNDERSTANDING ENGLISH LANGUAGE LEARNER LEVELS

START SMART

Scaffolding the Literature Big Book: Units 1–3

Digital Tools

Children can access the Digital Resource Library for audio recordings of each **Literature Big Book.** The audio can be played on a page-by-page basis.

- Linguistically accommodated instruction for all levels offers access to the **Literature Big Books** and the **Paired Selections.**
- Prereading strategies enhance comprehension for children from different cultural backgrounds; prereading support includes preteaching the vocabulary, using visual and other resources, and providing a summary of the selection while showing photos or illustrations from the selection.
- The Interactive Question-Response routine with leveled prompts focuses on the meaning of the text.
- Oral language is developed through peer interaction.
- Targeted ELA academic language is reinforced through review and guided questions.
- Children have an opportunity to work independently and collaboratively on a variety of activities, including glossary building, role-plays, writing tasks, and peer-to-peer instruction. The routines help children take ownership of their language development.
- 🎧 Children can also listen to a digital recording of the selections to develop comprehension and practice fluency and pronunciation.

LESSONS 1-2 — READING • LITERATURE BIG BOOK • ACCESS THE TEXT — **WEEK 1**

LEARNING GOALS

We can understand what happens in a school as we listen to a story.

OBJECTIVES
Describe characters in a story, using key details.

Use illustrations and details in a story to describe its characters, setting, or events.

Retell stories, including key details, and demonstrate understanding of their central message or lesson.

Build on others' talk in conversations by responding to the comments of others through multiple exchanges.

LANGUAGE OBJECTIVES
Children will narrate, or tell, what happens in a school using key vocabulary.

ELA ACADEMIC LANGUAGE
- illustration
- Cognate: *ilustración*

MATERIALS
Literature Big Book, *This School Year Will Be the Best*, pp. 3-31
Visual Vocabulary Cards

DIGITAL TOOLS
🎧 Have children listen to the selection as they follow along to develop comprehension and practice fluency and pronunciation.
Use the online High-Frequency Words Activity for additional support.

This School Year Will Be the Best!

Prepare to Read

Build Background We are going to read a story about things that kids want to do at school during the year. Show the pictures on the cover and then ask children to share ideas about what they can do during the school year. *What do you want to do in school?* Model for children: *I want to play outside.* Have children repeat. Then have children talk about activities they want to do at school. Provide sentence frames. *I want to read _____. I want to _____.*

Focus on Vocabulary Use the **Visual Vocabulary Cards** to review the oral vocabulary words *learn* and *subjects*. As you read, use gestures and other visual support to clarify important story words, such as *hope, bring, take,* and *pet*. Say: *The word* hope *tells about something that I want to happen. Say the word* hope *with me.* Point to it in the text. Provide an example: *I hope to have sunshine today. What do you hope for?* I hope to make friends. I hope to have fun.

Summarize the Text Before reading, say the summary while pointing to the illustrations. *The story tells about the children's first day of school. We'll read about what the teacher and children wish for at school.*

Read the Text

Use the Interactive Question-Response Routine to help children understand the story.

Pages 3-9

Page 8 Read the text aloud. Point to the boy with his snake. *What is the boy's pet?* (a snake) *Is the boy happy?* (yes) *What is the boy doing?* (The boy is smiling.) Point to the boy under the desk and the teacher. *Are the boy and the teacher smiling? How do they look?* (No. They look scared.) Act out scared. *The pet snake makes the other children feel scared or nervous* (cognate: *nervioso*).

👥 *How do other children feel about the pet snake? Discuss with a partner.*

Beginning Point to the images of the children on page 8. Point to the boy with the snake. *Is the boy smiling?* Yes, the boy is smiling. *Are the other children smiling?* No, children are not smiling.

Intermediate Have partners point to the pictures as they respond. *What is the boy doing?* The boy is smiling. *Are the other children smiling?* No, children are not smiling. *Do the other children look scared?* Yes, the children look scared. *Do you have a pet?* (Answers will vary.)

Advanced/Advanced High Have partners give details. *What color is the snake?* The snake is purple. *Is it long or short?* The snake is long. *Where is the boy?* The boy is under a desk. *Do you have a pet?* (Answers will vary. Possible answers: I have a dog.)

Pages 12-21

Pages 14-15 Read the text aloud. Point to the children on the stage. *The children are in a play. They are wearing costumes. The children look like vegetables and fruits.* Encourage children to use circumlocution and non-verbal cues to ask questions about the illustration. Then restate their answers to clarify. Have them repeat after you. *Which vegetables or fruits do you see?* (tomato, apple, carrot) Point to pictures and say the words for children to repeat. *What are the children doing?* The children are dancing. Have children demonstrate dancing with you.

👥 *What are the children doing in the school play? Discuss with a partner.*

Beginning Point to the images of the children in the play. Help partners respond to the questions: *Are the children in a play?* Yes, the children are in a play. *What do the children look like?* The children look like tomatoes. *What are the children doing?* The children are dancing.

Intermediate Point to the boy dressed up as a carrot. *What vegetable is the boy in the play?* The boy is a carrot. *Does the boy look happy?* (no) *Why?* (Possible answer: The boy does not want to be a vegetable in the play.)

👥 **Advanced/Advanced High** Have partners compare the boy in the carrot costume with the other kids in the play. Point to the boy. *What does the boy hope for?* (Possible answer: The boy hopes he will not be a vegetable in the play.) *How does the boy look?* (Possible answer: The boy looks unhappy.) *What are the other children doing?* The other children are dancing. *How do they look?* They look happy.

Pages 22-31

Page 29 Read the text aloud. Point to the words "get to know" and say them aloud for children to repeat. *When you get to know someone, you learn about them.* Discuss examples, such as talking together. *What do you do to get to know a friend?* (Answers will vary. Possible answer: I play with my friend.)

👥 *How do you get to know about each other? Discuss with a partner.*

Beginning Review example for "get to know" with children to help them learn the phrase. *What do you do to get to know a friend?* I play with my friend.

Intermediate Help partners discuss to generate ideas for things they do to get to know their friends. *What do you do to get to know a friend?* I play/talk/read with my friend.

Advanced/Advanced High Help partners give details. *What do you do to get to know a friend?* I play with my friend in the park.

FORMATIVE ASSESSMENT

▶ **STUDENT CHECK-IN**
Have partners retell what the kids in the illustrations do at school. Then, have children reflect using the Check-In Routine.

Independent Time

Draw and Write Pair children of mixed proficiencies and have them discuss an activity they do with their friends. Then have them illustrate and write about one activity. Provide a sentence frame to help them write: *I ___ with my friend.* Have partners draw a picture and copy the sentence frame. Allow them to write what they can, help translate or elaborate, and then provide corrections as needed. Have partners present their drawings to the class using: *This is a picture of me and my friend. We are ___.*

Scaffolding the Shared Read

Wonders provides differentiated instruction for the Shared Read. Linguistically accommodated instruction for Beginning, Intermediate, and Advanced/Advanced High children offers access to the grade-level text.

- The Build Background section connects to the Essential Question and supports children from different cultural backgrounds.
- Prereading support includes preteaching the vocabulary, using visual and other resources, and providing a summary of the selection while showing photos or illustrations from the selection.
- The Interactive Question-Response routine with leveled prompts focuses on the meaning of the text.
- Oral language is developed through peer interaction.
- Targeted ELA academic language is reinforced through review and guided questions.
- Children have an opportunity to work independently and collaboratively on a variety of activities.
- 🎧 Children can also listen to a digital recording of the selections to develop comprehension and practice fluency and pronunciation.

AUTHOR INSIGHT

"Effective teachers understand that English Language Learners are studying complex concepts and processing new content in a new language. These children are capable of meeting high academic standards but require adjustments to the way instruction is presented. Their unique linguistic needs require that additional support be provided.

Linguistically accommodated instruction will result in greater participation in class and overall achievement."

—Dr. Jana Echevarria

Scaffolding the Anchor Text

START SMART

AUTHOR INSIGHT

"English Language Learners benefit from exposure to grade-level text and discussions to build language and literacy skills. Learning new information, words and concepts in a new language is challenging. English Language Learners need multiple exposures to new material and benefit from opportunities to practice interacting with it in authentic ways."

—Dr. Jana Echevarria

Wonders provides linguistically accommodated instruction for all levels to access the Anchor Text.

- Explicit instruction helps children read grade-appropriate content area text and comprehend increasingly challenging language.
- Instruction provides more support for English Language Learners to answer deep higher-level questions in the **Reading/Writing Companion.**
- Children benefit from multiple exposures to new material and opportunities to practice interacting with it in authentic ways.
- The Interactive Question-Response routine with leveled prompts focuses on the meaning of the text.
- Children reinforce skills and strategies and develop oral language by interacting with each other and practicing ELA academic language.
- Children can also listen to a digital recording of the selection to develop comprehension and practice fluency and pronunciation.
- Children have an opportunity to work independently and collaboratively on a variety of activities.
- 🎧 Children can also listen to a digital recording of the selections to develop comprehension and practice fluency and pronunciation.

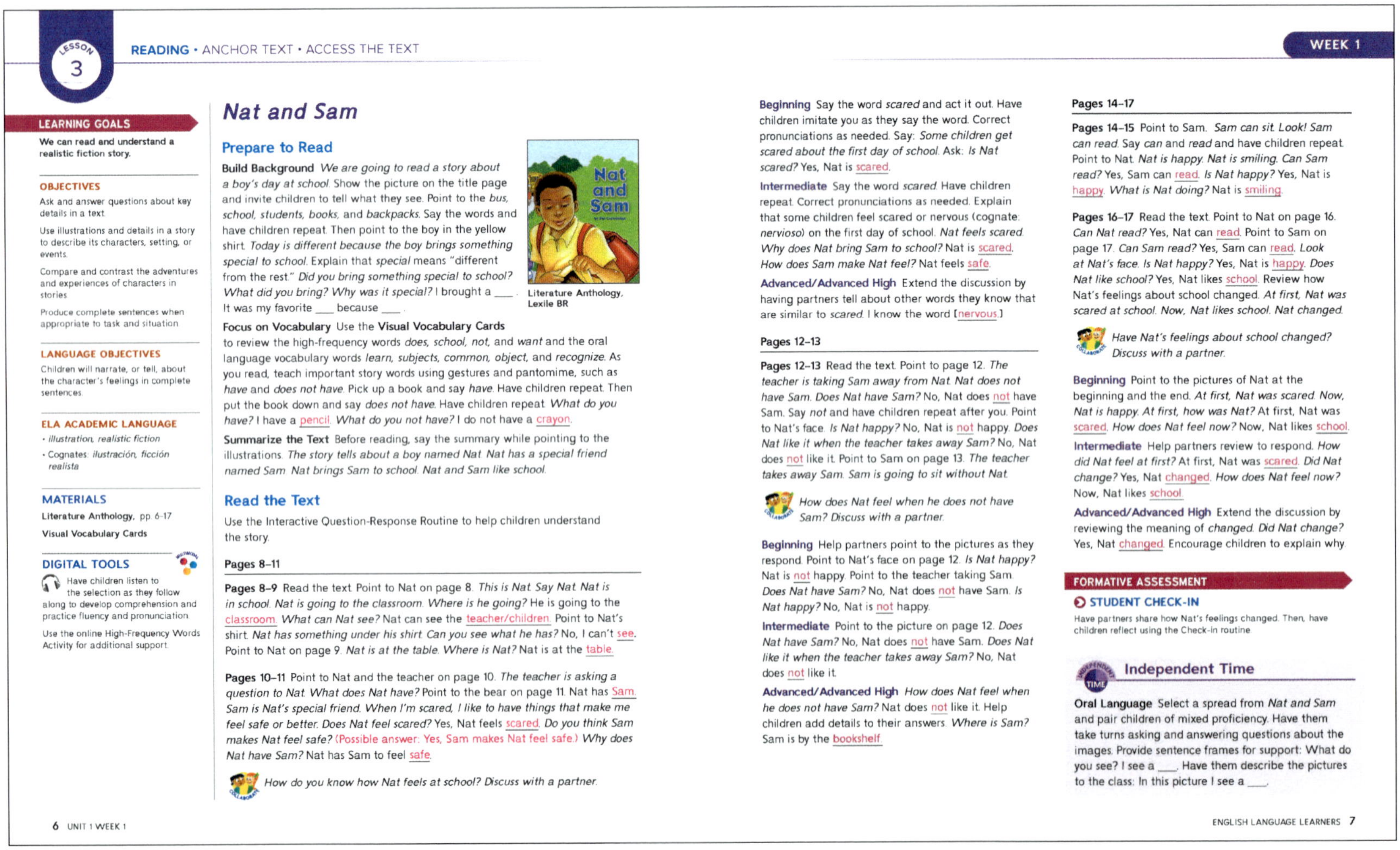

LESSON 3 — READING · ANCHOR TEXT · ACCESS THE TEXT — **WEEK 1**

Nat and Sam

LEARNING GOALS
We can read and understand a realistic fiction story.

OBJECTIVES
Ask and answer questions about key details in a text.
Use illustrations and details in a story to describe its characters, setting, or events.
Compare and contrast the adventures and experiences of characters in stories.
Produce complete sentences when appropriate to task and situation.

LANGUAGE OBJECTIVES
Children will narrate, or tell, about the character's feelings in complete sentences.

ELA ACADEMIC LANGUAGE
- illustration, realistic fiction
- Cognates: *ilustración, ficción realista*

MATERIALS
Literature Anthology, pp. 6-17
Visual Vocabulary Cards

DIGITAL TOOLS
Have children listen to the selection as they follow along to develop comprehension and practice fluency and pronunciation.
Use the online High-Frequency Words Activity for additional support.

Prepare to Read

Build Background *We are going to read a story about a boy's day at school.* Show the picture on the title page and invite children to tell what they see. Point to the bus, school, students, books, and backpacks. Say the words and have children repeat. Then point to the boy in the yellow shirt. *Today is different because the boy brings something special to school.* Explain that *special* means "different from the rest." *Did you bring something special to school? What did you bring? Why was it special?* I brought a ___. It was my favorite ___ because ___.

Literature Anthology, Lexile BR

Focus on Vocabulary Use the **Visual Vocabulary Cards** to review the high-frequency words *does, school, not,* and *want* and the oral language vocabulary words *learn, subjects, common, object,* and *recognize.* As you read, teach important story words using gestures and pantomime, such as *have* and *does not have.* Pick up a book and say *have.* Have children repeat. Then put the book down and say *does not have.* Have children repeat. *What do you have?* I have a pencil. *What do you not have?* I do not have a crayon.

Summarize the Text Before reading, say the summary while pointing to the illustrations. *The story tells about a boy named Nat. Nat has a special friend named Sam. Nat brings Sam to school. Nat and Sam like school.*

Read the Text

Use the Interactive Question-Response Routine to help children understand the story.

Pages 8–11

Pages 8–9 Read the text. Point to Nat on page 8. *This is Nat. Say Nat. Nat is in school. Nat is going to the classroom. Where is he going?* He is going to the classroom. *What can Nat see?* Nat can see the teacher/children. Point to Nat's shirt. *Nat has something under his shirt. Can you see what he has?* No, I can't see. Point to Nat on page 9. *Nat is at the table. Where is Nat?* Nat is at the table.

Pages 10–11 Point to Nat and the teacher on page 10. *The teacher is asking a question to Nat. What does Nat have?* Point to the bear on page 11. Nat has Sam. *Sam is Nat's special friend. When I'm scared, I like to have things that make me feel safe or better. Does Nat feel scared?* Yes, Nat feels scared. *Do you think Sam makes Nat feel safe?* (Possible answer: Yes, Sam makes Nat feel safe.) *Why does Nat have Sam?* Nat has Sam to feel safe.

How do you know how Nat feels at school? Discuss with a partner.

Beginning Say the word *scared* and act it out. Have children imitate you as they say the word. Correct pronunciations as needed. Say: *Some children get scared about the first day of school. Ask: Is Nat scared?* Yes, Nat is scared.

Intermediate Say the word *scared.* Have children repeat. Correct pronunciations as needed. Explain that some children feel scared or nervous (cognate: *nervioso*) on the first day of school. *Nat feels scared. Why does Nat bring Sam to school?* Nat is scared. *How does Sam make Nat feel?* Nat feels safe.

Advanced/Advanced High Extend the discussion by having partners tell about other words they know that are similar to *scared.* I know the word [nervous].

Pages 12–13

Pages 12–13 Read the text. Point to page 12. *The teacher is taking Sam away from Nat. Nat does not have Sam. Does Nat have Sam?* No, Nat does not have Sam. Say *not* and have children repeat after you. Point to Nat's face. *Is Nat happy?* No, Nat is not happy. *Does Nat like it when the teacher takes away Sam?* No, Nat does not like it. Point to Sam on page 13. *The teacher takes away Sam. Sam is going to sit without Nat.*

How does Nat feel when he does not have Sam? Discuss with a partner.

Beginning Help partners point to the pictures as they respond. Point to Nat's face on page 12. *Is Nat happy?* Nat is not happy. Point to the teacher taking Sam. *Does Nat have Sam?* No, Nat does not have Sam. *Is Nat happy?* No, Nat is not happy.

Intermediate Point to the picture on page 12. *Does Nat have Sam?* No, Nat does not have Sam. *Does Nat like it when the teacher takes away Sam?* No, Nat does not like it.

Advanced/Advanced High *How does Nat feel when he does not have Sam?* Nat does not like it. Help children add details to their answers. *Where is Sam?* Sam is by the bookshelf.

Pages 14–17

Pages 14–15 Point to Sam. *Sam can sit. Look! Sam can read.* Say *can* and *read* and have children repeat. Point to Nat. *Nat is happy. Nat is smiling. Can Nat read?* Yes, Sam can read. *Is Nat happy?* Yes, Nat is happy. *What is Nat doing?* Nat is smiling.

Pages 16–17 Read the text. Point to Nat on page 16. *Can Nat read?* Yes, Nat can read. Point to Sam on page 17. *Can Sam read?* Yes, Sam can read. Look at Nat's face. *Is Nat happy?* Yes, Nat is happy. *Does Nat like school?* Yes, Nat likes school. Review how Nat's feelings about school changed. *At first, Nat was scared at school. Now, Nat likes school. Nat changed.*

Have Nat's feelings about school changed? Discuss with a partner.

Beginning Point to the pictures of Nat at the beginning and the end. *At first, Nat was scared. Now, Nat is happy. At first, how was Nat?* At first, Nat was scared. *How does Nat feel now?* Now, Nat likes school.

Intermediate Help partners review to respond. *How did Nat feel at first?* At first, Nat was scared. *Did Nat change?* Yes, Nat changed. *How does Nat feel now?* Now, Nat likes school.

Advanced/Advanced High Extend the discussion by reviewing the meaning of *changed. Did Nat change?* Yes, Nat changed. Encourage children to explain why.

FORMATIVE ASSESSMENT

STUDENT CHECK-IN
Have partners share how Nat's feelings changed. Then, have children reflect using the Check-In routine.

Independent Time

Oral Language Select a spread from *Nat and Sam* and pair children of mixed proficiency. Have them take turns asking and answering questions about the images. Provide sentence frames for support: *What do you see?* I see a ___. Have them describe the pictures to the class: *In this picture I see a ___.*

Using Leveled Readers

The Leveled Readers for English language learners are scaffolded versions of the On Level Readers. Children benefit from reading linguistically accommodated text with the same genre focus and essential question as the other main selections.

- The Build Background section connects to the Essential Question and supports children from different cultural backgrounds.
- Prereading support includes preteaching the vocabulary, using visual and other resources.
- The Interactive Question-Response routine is chunked by section and focuses on the meaning of the text.
- Fluency is reinforced through teacher modeling.
- For the Build Knowledge: Make Connections activity, children work collaboratively to connect with ideas they have read in other selections.
- After working through the ELL version, some children may be ready to move on to the On Level text successfully.
- Children can also listen to a digital recording of the selections to develop comprehension and practice fluency and pronunciation.
- As an option, teachers can read aloud the text as children follow along.

AUTHOR INSIGHT

"Teachers must apply a wide range of effective scaffolding strategies to help ELLs process text at higher and higher levels of complexity and accelerate the development of their English proficiency. Leveled readers with linguistically accommodated texts that also share the same genre, vocabulary, and topic as the main selection have the potential to offer just the right level of ELL support and challenge."

—Dr. Josefina V. Tinajero

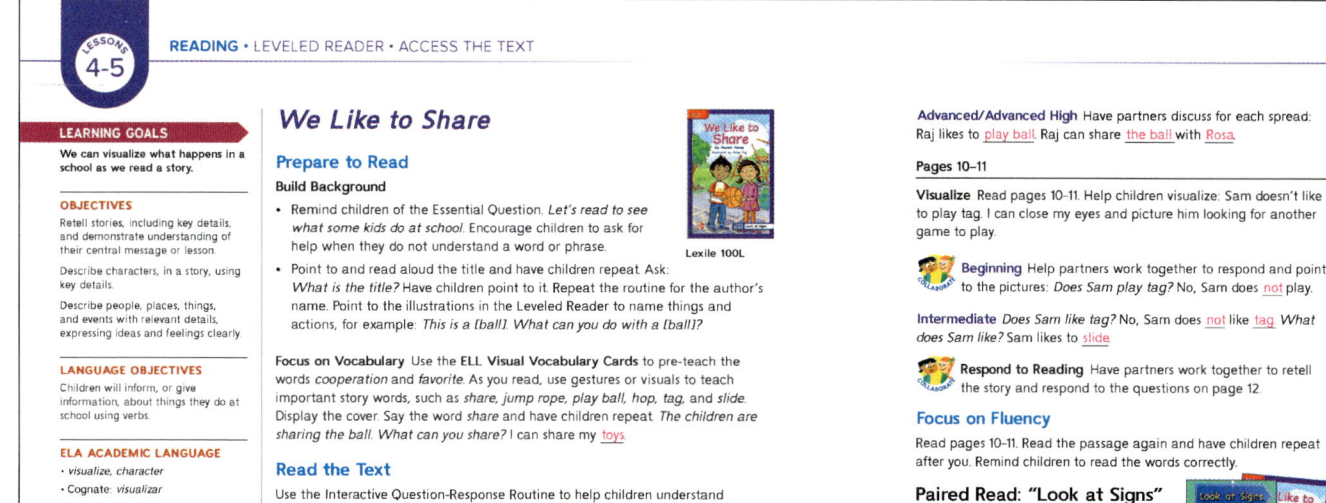

START SMART

Using Differentiated Genre Passages: Units 4–6

AUTHOR INSIGHT

"The attributes that make text especially complex for ELLs include unfamiliar words and phrases, the complexity of the syntax, the number of referential chains, and the amount of background knowledge required to understand the text. It is important for teachers to understand the attributes that make text complex for ELLs so that they can support ELLs in understanding complex text."

—Dr. Diane August

Genre Passages are online digital leveled texts with the same genre focus and Essential Question as the Shared Read and Anchor Text. The ELL Genre Passage lessons provide linguistically accommodated instruction for all levels and reinforce and apply the reading skills and text features of each genre.

- The Build Background section connects to the essential question and supports children from different cultural backgrounds.
- Prereading support includes preteaching the vocabulary, using visual and other resources.
- The Interactive Question-Response routine is chunked by section and focuses on the meaning of the text.
- The Respond to Reading questions focus on the text features, text structure, author's purpose, and/or comprehension skill and fluency.
- For the Build Knowledge: Make Connections activity, children work collaboratively to connect with ideas they have read in the other selections.
- The lesson provides opportunities for children to move to the next leveled passage.

Writing

Wonders provides differentiated instruction to support targeted sections of the daily core writing activities.

- The Actor/Action routine breaks down the modeled and interactive writing prompts to support understanding.
- Children work collaboratively to respond to the prompts and complete the writing activities in their **Reading/Writing Companion.**
- Daily scaffolded writing support is provided for all levels.
- The Independent Writing routine focuses on supporting children in accessing and retelling the anchor text, using text and picture evidence, analyzing the writing prompt, and completing My Writing Outlines.
- My Writing Outlines, created specifically to support English Language Learners, provide support that is gradually taken away through the course of the year. These outlines are then used to complete the activity in the Reading/Writing Companion.
- The self-selected writing activity focuses on revising the activity through teacher modeling and group as well as partner collaboration. The lesson provides an opportunity to review the weekly grammar skill.
- The **Language Transfers Handbook** and **Language Development Cards** provide additional grammar support.

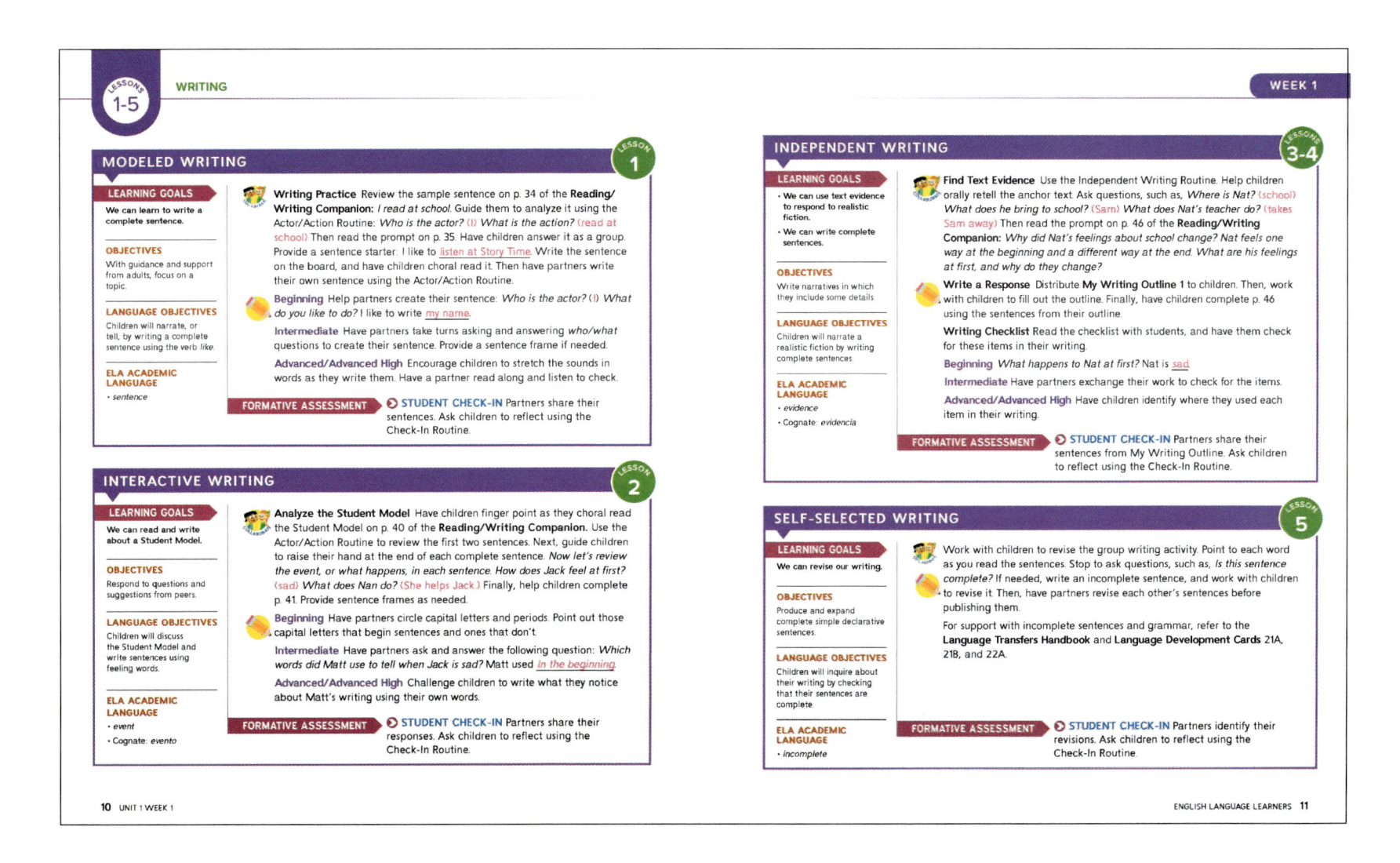

LESSONS 1-5 — WRITING — WEEK 1

MODELED WRITING (LESSON 1)

LEARNING GOALS
We can learn to write a complete sentence.

OBJECTIVES
With guidance and support from adults, focus on a topic.

LANGUAGE OBJECTIVES
Children will narrate, or tell, by writing a complete sentence using the verb *like*.

ELA ACADEMIC LANGUAGE
- sentence

Writing Practice Review the sample sentence on p. 34 of the **Reading/Writing Companion:** *I read at school.* Guide them to analyze it using the Actor/Action Routine: *Who is the actor?* (I) *What is the action?* (read at school) Then read the prompt on p. 35. Have children answer it as a group. Provide a sentence starter: *I like to* ___ *at Story Time.* Write the sentence on the board, and have children choral read it. Then have partners write their own sentence using the Actor/Action Routine.

Beginning Help partners create their sentence: *Who is the actor?* (I) *What do you like to do?* I like to write *my name.*

Intermediate Have partners take turns asking and answering *who/what* questions to create their sentence. Provide a sentence frame if needed.

Advanced/Advanced High Encourage children to stretch the sounds in words as they write them. Have a partner read along and listen to check.

FORMATIVE ASSESSMENT ▶ **STUDENT CHECK-IN** Partners share their sentences. Ask children to reflect using the Check-In Routine.

INTERACTIVE WRITING (LESSON 2)

LEARNING GOALS
We can read and write about a Student Model.

OBJECTIVES
Respond to questions and suggestions from peers.

LANGUAGE OBJECTIVES
Children will discuss the Student Model and write sentences using feeling words.

ELA ACADEMIC LANGUAGE
- event
- Cognate: *evento*

Analyze the Student Model Have children finger point as they choral read the Student Model on p. 40 of the **Reading/Writing Companion.** Use the Actor/Action Routine to review the first two sentences. Next, guide children to raise their hand at the end of each complete sentence. *Now let's review the event, or what happens, in each sentence. How does Jack feel at first?* (sad) *What does Nan do?* (She helps Jack.) Finally, help children complete p. 41. Provide sentence frames as needed.

Beginning Have partners circle capital letters and periods. Point out those capital letters that begin sentences and ones that don't.

Intermediate Have partners ask and answer the following question: *Which words did Matt use to tell when Jack is sad?* Matt used *In the beginning.*

Advanced/Advanced High Challenge children to write what they notice about Matt's writing using their own words.

FORMATIVE ASSESSMENT ▶ **STUDENT CHECK-IN** Partners share their responses. Ask children to reflect using the Check-In Routine.

INDEPENDENT WRITING (LESSONS 3-4)

LEARNING GOALS
- We can use text evidence to respond to realistic fiction.
- We can write complete sentences.

OBJECTIVES
Write narratives in which they include some details.

LANGUAGE OBJECTIVES
Children will narrate a realistic fiction by writing complete sentences.

ELA ACADEMIC LANGUAGE
- evidence
- Cognate: *evidencia*

Find Text Evidence Use the Independent Writing Routine. Help children orally retell the anchor text. Ask questions, such as, *Where is Nat?* (school) *What does he bring to school?* (Sam) *What does Nat's teacher do?* (takes Sam away) Then read the prompt on p. 46 of the **Reading/Writing Companion:** *Why did Nat's feelings about school change?* Nat feels one way at the beginning and a different way at the end. What are his feelings at first, and why do they change?

Write a Response Distribute My Writing Outline 1 to children. Then, work with children to fill out the outline. Finally, have children complete p. 46 using the sentences from their outline.

Writing Checklist Read the checklist with students, and have them check for these items in their writing.

Beginning What happens to Nat at first? Nat is *sad.*

Intermediate Have partners exchange their work to check for the items.

Advanced/Advanced High Have children identify where they used each item in their writing.

FORMATIVE ASSESSMENT ▶ **STUDENT CHECK-IN** Partners share their sentences from My Writing Outline. Ask children to reflect using the Check-In Routine.

SELF-SELECTED WRITING (LESSON 5)

LEARNING GOALS
We can revise our writing.

OBJECTIVES
Produce and expand complete simple declarative sentences.

LANGUAGE OBJECTIVES
Children will inquire about their writing by checking that their sentences are complete.

ELA ACADEMIC LANGUAGE
- incomplete

Work with children to revise the group writing activity. Point to each word as you read the sentences. Stop to ask questions, such as, *Is this sentence complete?* If needed, write an incomplete sentence, and work with children to revise it. Then, have partners revise each other's sentences before publishing them.

For support with incomplete sentences and grammar, refer to the **Language Transfers Handbook** and **Language Development Cards** 21A, 21B, and 22A.

FORMATIVE ASSESSMENT ▶ **STUDENT CHECK-IN** Partners identify their revisions. Ask children to reflect using the Check-In Routine.

Instructional Routines

The instructional routines provide carefully sequenced steps to scaffold instruction and allow children to focus on learning content. Once children are familiar with a routine, the teacher can use it to teach new skills and content efficiently.

Interactive Question-Response

This routine was designed to provide context and opportunities for English language learners to learn how information builds and connects and to focus on key concepts and vocabulary. The Access the Text lessons incorporate this routine in the instruction.

Read the Text in Chunks Read one section of text at a time so children can focus on the meaning of the text. For each text chunk:

- **Use Visuals and Text Features** Use headings to help children predict what the section will be about and images and other text features to aid children's comprehension.
- **Explain** As you read, explain difficult or unfamiliar concepts and words. Provide background and contextual knowledge as needed.
- **Ask Guiding and Supplementary Questions** Help children identify the most important information and details in the text chunk and understand how information builds and connects.
- **Scaffold Responses** Provide sentence starters/frames to help children express and communicate their ideas.
- **Reinforce Vocabulary** Reinforce the meaning and point out cognates and false cognates. Ask qustions that require children to use newly acquired vocabulary.
- **Retell** Have children retell the most important ideas in their own words.
- **Reinforce Skills and Strategies** Model using skills and strategies. Ask questions to help children apply the skills and strategies.

Vocabulary

Define/Example/Ask Routine Use this routine to help children learn unfamiliar, conceptually complex words they encounter in the texts. The **Visual Vocabulary Cards** provide this routine on the back of the card. Here is an example for *recent*.

1. **Define**: Recent *means something happened a short time ago. En español,* recent *quiere decir "reciente, ocurrido hace poco."* Recent *in English and* reciente *in Spanish are cognates. They sound alike and mean the same thing in both languages.*
2. **Example**: *Mary learns about recent events from the newspaper. En español: Mary se entera de los eventos recientes por el periódico.*
3. **Ask**: *What word is the opposite of recent?*

Cognates Help children transfer knowledge from their native language. Explain that cognates are in two different languages, but they look similar, sound similar, and mean approximately the same thing. Remind children to watch out for false cognates, which are words that sound the same and/or are spelled the same, but have different meanings, such as *pie/pie*.

Here is an example for the cognates *cat/gato*:

1. Display and say cognate word pairs and images.
2. Have a native Spanish speaker say *gato* and *cat*. Have other children echo.
3. Say sentences using the word, and have children echo after you or have partners say sentences using the word.

Sentence Analysis

Actor and Action Help children focus on the structure of written language by using this routine with sample sentences. This routine is primarily used in the writing lessons to analyze the models but can be used any time to talk about the text and confirm understanding.

1. Sentences can have an actor and action or an object and a description.
2. Review definitions: the actor/action is a person or thing that a sentence is about and what the person/thing is doing; the actor/description is how a person, place, or thing can be described.
3. Read the sentence while pointing to each word.
4. Ask children to identify actor(s)/action(s) or the action/description.
5. Then ask follow-up tag questions with *why, what, when,* or *how.*

Independent Writing Routine Use this routine to support the independent writing in Lessons 3 and 4.

Find Text Evidence

1. Review comprehension of the story by helping children orally retell it. Use the images from the selection and ask guiding questions.
2. When children have finished, explain that they are going to write about the selection.
3. Read the prompt found in the **Teacher's Edition** or the **Reading/Writing Companion.** Reword the prompt, and use questions as well as images from the selection to ensure understanding.

Write to the Prompt

4. Display the sentence starters found in the **Teacher's Edition.** Tell children you will use these to help write about the selection. Ask a volunteer to retell the prompt in their own words.
5. Provide a question to help children orally answer the first sentence frame. Model completing the sentence frame on the board, and have children choral read the response. Repeat the routine for the remaining sentence frames.
6. Once completed, ask children to copy the sentences into their writer's notebook or **Reading/Writing Companion.**
7. Have partners work together to read their sentences and talk about them. Provide scaffolded instruction as partners work together to revise their sentences.

Teacher Response Techniques

Throughout the lessons, use these techniques to motivate children's participation and build oral fluency.

- **Wait for Responses** Provide enough time for children to answer a question or process their ideas to respond.

Depending on their levels of proficiency, give children the option of responding in different ways, such as answering in their native language that you can rephrase in English, or answering with nonverbal cues.

- **Revise for Form** Let children know that they can respond in different ways, depending on their levels of proficiency. Repeat the children's response to model the proper form. You can model in full sentences and use academic language.
- **Repeat** Give positive confirmation to the answers that each child offers. If the response is correct, repeat the response in a clear voice and at a slower pace to encourage others to participate.
- **Revise for Meaning** Repeating an answer offers an opportunity to clarify the meaning of a response.
- **Elaborate** If children give a one-word answer or a nonverbal cue, elaborate on the answer to model fluent speaking and grammatical patterns. Provide more examples, or repeat the answer using proper academic language.
- **Elicit** Prompt children to give a more comprehensive response by asking additional questions or guiding them to get to an answer.

Planner Units 1-3

WEEKS 1-5

Customize your own lesson plans at **my.mheducation.com**

Reading

20+ mins — **Reading Suggested Daily Time**

MATERIALS
- Literature Big Book
- Visual Vocabulary Cards
- Reading/Writing Companion
- Literature Anthology
- ELL Leveled Reader
- Online Differentiated Texts
- Online ELL Visual Vocabulary Cards

Literature Big Book

Literature Big Book
- Access the Text

Prepare to Read
- Build Background
- Vocabulary
- Summarize the Text

Read the Text

COLLABORATE Partner Work

COLLABORATE Independent Time

🎧 Listen Along to Text

Shared Read

Shared Read
- Access the Text

Prepare to Read
- Build Background
- Vocabulary
- Summarize the Text

Read the Text

COLLABORATE Partner Work

COLLABORATE Independent Time

🎧 Listen Along to Text

Writing

15+ mins — **Writing Suggested Daily Time**

MATERIALS
Modeled and Interactive Writing
- Reading/Writing Companion

Independent Writing
- Anchor Text
- Reading/Writing Companion
- ELL Independent Writing Resources BLMS

Self-Selected Writing
- Online Language Development Kit
- Online Language Transfers Handbook
- Writer's Notebook

Modeled Writing

Modeled Writing
Write About the Shared Read

COLLABORATE Partner Work

Interactive Writing

Interactive Writing
Write About the Shared Read

COLLABORATE Partner Work

Learning Goals

Specific learning goals identified in every lesson make clear what students will be learning and why. These smaller goals provide stepping stones to help children meet their reading and writing goals.

S10 PLANNER

Reading

Anchor Text

Anchor Text
- Access the Text

Prepare to Read
- Build Background
- Vocabulary
- Summarize the Text

Read the Text

COLLABORATE Partner Work

COLLABORATE Independent Time

🎧 Listen Along to Text

Additional Texts

Leveled Reader
- Access the Text

Prepare to Read
- Build Background
- Vocabulary

Read the Text

COLLABORATE Partner Work

COLLABORATE Apply Skill and Strategy

🎧 Listen Along to Text

Self-Selected Reading
- Leveled Reader Library
- Differentiated Texts

Writing

Independent Writing

Independent Writing
Write About the Anchor Text

Apply Conventions

COLLABORATE Partner Work

Independent Writing
Write About the Anchor Text

Apply Conventions

COLLABORATE Partner Work

Self-Selected Writing

Self-Selected Writing
Revise with Conventions

COLLABORATE Partner Work

Check-in Routine

The routine at the close of each lesson guides children to self-reflect on how well they understood each learning goal.
Review the lesson learning goal.
Reflect on the activity.
Self-Assess by holding up 1, 2, 3, or 4 fingers.
Share with your teacher.

PLANNER **S11**

Planner Units 4-6

WEEKS 1-5

Customize your own lesson plans at
my.mheducation.com

Reading

20+ mins Reading Suggested Daily Time

MATERIALS
- Literature Big Book
- Visual Vocabulary Cards
- Reading/Writing Companion
- Literature Anthology
- ELL Leveled Reader
- Online Differentiated Texts
- Online ELL Visual Vocabulary Cards

Shared Read

Shared Read
- Access the Text

Prepare to Read
- Build Background
- Vocabulary
- Summarize the Text

Read the Text
- COLLABORATE Partner Work
- COLLABORATE Independent Time
- 🎧 Listen Along to Text

Anchor Text

Anchor Text
- Access the Text

Prepare to Read
- Build Background
- Vocabulary
- Summarize the Text

Read the Text
- COLLABORATE Partner Work
- COLLABORATE Independent Time
- 🎧 Listen Along to Text

Writing

15+ mins Writing Suggested Daily Time

MATERIALS
Modeled and Interactive Writing
- Reading/Writing Companion

Independent Writing
- Anchor Text
- Reading/Writing Companion
- My Writing Outline BLMs

Self-Selected Writing
- Online Language Development Kit
- Online Language Transfers Handbook
- Writer's Notebook

Modeled Writing

Modeled Writing
Write About the Shared Read
- COLLABORATE Partner Work

Interactive Writing

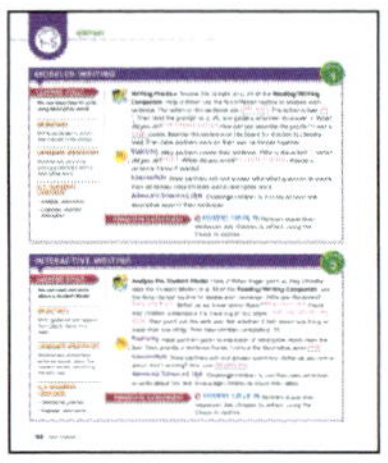

Interactive Writing
Write About the Shared Read
- COLLABORATE Partner Work

Learning Goals

Specific learning goals identified in every lesson make clear what children will be learning and why. These smaller goals provide stepping stones to help children meet their reading and writing goals.

S12 PLANNER

Reading

Additional Texts

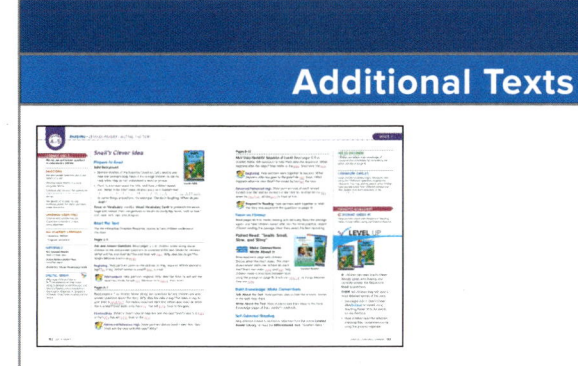

Leveled Reader
- Access the Text

Prepare to Read
- Build Background
- Vocabulary

Read the Text

COLLABORATE Partner Work

COLLABORATE Apply Skill and Strategy

🎧 Listen Along to Text

Self-Selected Reading
- Leveled Reader Database
- Differentiated Texts

Additional Texts

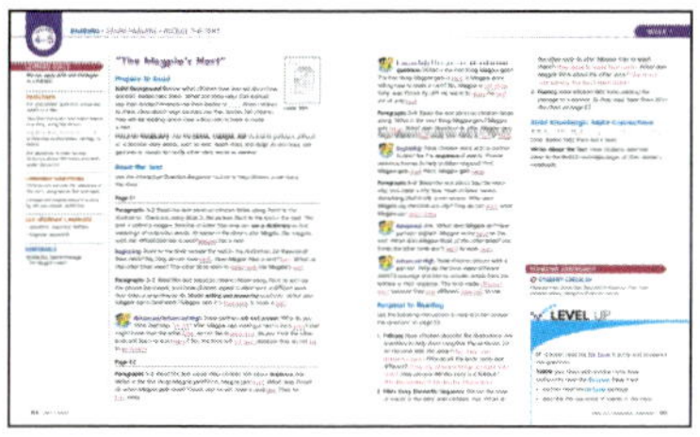

Genre Passages
- Access the Text

Prepare to Read
- Build Background
- Vocabulary

Read the Text

COLLABORATE Partner Work

COLLABORATE Apply Skill and Strategy

Writing

Independent Writing

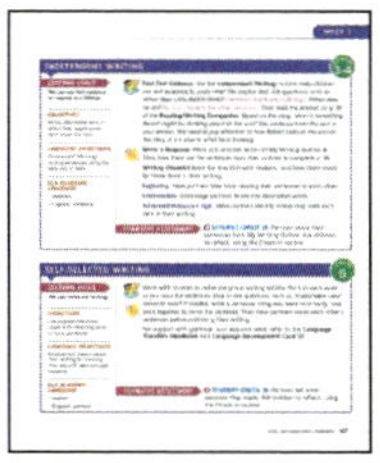

Independent Writing
Write About the Anchor Text

Apply Conventions

COLLABORATE Partner Work

Independent Writing
Write About the Anchor Text

Apply Conventions

COLLABORATE Partner Work

Self-Selected Writing

Self-Selected Writing
Revise with Conventions

COLLABORATE Partner Work

Check-in Routine

The routine at the close of each lesson guides children to self-reflect on how well they understood each learning goal.
Review the lesson learning goal.
Reflect on the activity.
Self-Assess by holding up 1, 2, 3, or 4 fingers.
Share with your teacher.

Supporting Newcomers

Components:
Using the Newcomer Kit

Use the online **Wonders Newcomer Components** for children with little or no English proficiency. These components provide newcomers with access to basic, high-utility vocabulary they can begin using right away and develop language skills to transition to the Beginning level of language proficiency.

Newcomer Cards

Each card introduces a topic through colorful visuals to stimulate conversation to help children develop oral language and build vocabulary.

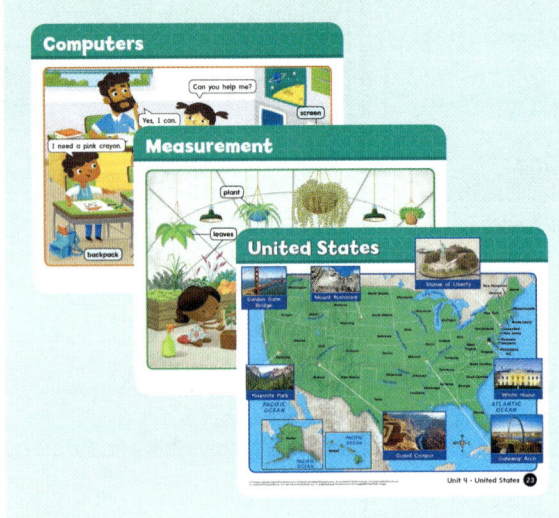

Newcomer Teacher's Guide

Provides three lessons for each Newcomer Card topic and student worksheets with reading and writing activities to help children transition into the English-speaking classroom.

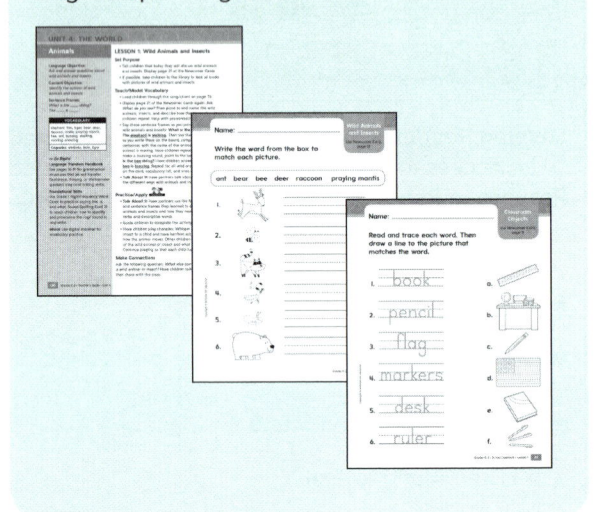

Suggested Planning:
4-Week Learning Blocks

Because newcomers can enter your classroom at any time during the year, the program is designed for flexibility with multiple entry-points for instruction:
- Use the Start Smart materials with new arrivals.
- The four units of instruction can be completed in any order, so new arrivals can join those who are already well underway.
- The Newcomer Teacher's Guide also provides songs and chants, reproducible manipulatives, conversation starters, and games.
- At the end of Start Smart and each unit, use the Progress Monitoring materials to measure children's progress.

UNIT 1: 4 WEEKS

Start Smart for new arrivals
- Alphabet
- Greetings
- Shapes and Colors
- Numbers

Unit 1: Life at School
- In the Classroom
- Computers
- A Day at School
- Calendar
- Weather

Materials
Newcomer Cards Start Smart, Unit 1
Newcomer Teacher's Guide
- Start Smart pp. 1–25
- Unit 1 pp. 26–57
- Optional Materials 154–T38
- Progress Monitoring T39–T45

Newcomer Visuals Start Smart, Unit 1
Newcomer Interactive Games

UNIT 2: 4 WEEKS

Start Smart for new arrivals
Unit 2: My Family and Me
- My Body
- Clothing
- Feelings
- My Family
- My Home

Materials
Newcomer Cards Start Smart, Unit 2
Newcomer Teacher's Guide
- Start Smart pp. 1–25
- Unit 2 pp. 58–89
- Optional Materials 154–T38
- Progress Monitoring T39–T45

Newcomer Visuals Start Smart, Unit 2
Newcomer Interactive Games

S14

Newcomer Visuals

Provide additional opportunities for vocabulary building and oral language development for each topic through prompts and words and phrases children can use.

Newcomer Interactive Games

Online Interactive Games provide independent practice to build vocabulary.

UNIT 3: 4 WEEKS

Start Smart for new arrivals
Unit 3: Community
- My Community
- Park
- Transportation
- Food and Meals
- Shopping

Materials
Newcomer Cards Start Smart, Unit 3
Newcomer Teacher's Guide
- Start Smart pp. 1-25
- Unit 3 pp. 90-121
- Optional Materials 154-T38
- Progress Monitoring T39-T45

Newcomer Visuals Start Smart, Unit 3
Newcomer Interactive Games

UNIT 4: 4 WEEKS

Start Smart for new arrivals
Unit 4: The World
- Measurement
- Animals
- Growth and Change
- United States
- My World

Materials
Newcomer Cards Start Smart, Unit 4
Newcomer Teacher's Guide
- Start Smart pp. 1-25
- Unit 4 pp. 122-153
- Optional Materials 154-T38
- Progress Monitoring T39-T45

Newcomer Visuals Start Smart, Unit 4
Newcomer Interactive Games

SUPPORTING NEWCOMERS 1

LESSONS 1-2

READING • LITERATURE BIG BOOK • ACCESS THE TEXT

LEARNING GOALS

We can understand what happens in a school as we listen to a story.

OBJECTIVES

Describe characters in a story, using key details.

Use illustrations and details in a story to describe its characters, setting, or events.

Retell stories, including key details, and demonstrate understanding of their central message or lesson.

Build on others' talk in conversations by responding to the comments of others through multiple exchanges.

LANGUAGE OBJECTIVES

Children will narrate, or tell, what happens in a school using key vocabulary.

ELA ACADEMIC LANGUAGE

- illustration
- Cognate: *ilustración*

MATERIALS

Literature Big Book, *This School Year Will Be the Best,* pp. 3–31

Visual Vocabulary Cards

DIGITAL TOOLS

Have children listen to the selection as they follow along to develop comprehension and practice fluency and pronunciation.

Use the online High-Frequency Words Activity for additional support.

This School Year Will Be the Best!

Prepare to Read

Build Background *We are going to read a story about things that kids want to do at school during the year.* Show the pictures on the cover and then ask children to share ideas about what they can do during the school year. *What do you want to do in school?* Model for children: *I want to play outside.* Have children repeat. Then have children talk about activities they want to do at school. Provide sentence frames: I want to read ____ . I want to ____ .

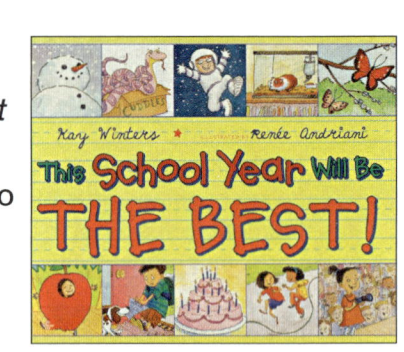

Literature Big Book

Focus on Vocabulary Use the **Visual Vocabulary Cards** to review the oral vocabulary words *learn* and *subjects*. As you read, use gestures and other visual support to clarify important story words, such as *hope, bring, take,* and *pet*. Say: *The word* hope *tells about something that I want to happen. Say the word* hope *with me.* Point to it in the text. Provide an example: *I hope to have sunshine today. What do you hope for?* I hope to make friends. I hope to have fun.

Summarize the Text Before reading, say the summary while pointing to the illustrations. *The story tells about the children's first day of school. We'll read about what the teacher and children wish for at school.*

Read the Text

Use the Interactive Question-Response Routine to help children understand the story.

Pages 3–9

Page 8 Read the text aloud. Point to the boy with his snake. *What is the boy's pet?* (a snake) *Is the boy happy?* (yes) *What is the boy doing?* (The boy is smiling.) Point to the boy under the desk and the teacher. *Are the boy and the teacher smiling? How do they look?* (No. They look scared.) Act out scared. *The pet snake makes the other children feel scared or nervous* (cognate: *nervioso*).

How do other children feel about the pet snake? Discuss with a partner.

Beginning Point to the images of the children on page 8. Point to the boy with the snake. *Is the boy smiling?* Yes, the boy is smiling. *Are the other children smiling?* No, children are not smiling.

Intermediate Have partners point to the pictures as they respond. *What is the boy doing?* The boy is smiling. *Are the other children smiling?* No, children are not smiling. *Do the other children look scared?* Yes, the children look scared. *Do you have a pet?* (Answers will vary.)

2 UNIT 1 WEEK 1

WEEK 1

Advanced/Advanced High Have partners give details. *What color is the snake?* The snake is purple. *Is it long or short?* The snake is long. *Where is the boy?* The boy is under a desk. *Do you have a pet?* (Answers will vary. Possible answers: I have a dog.)

Pages 12–21

Pages 14–15 Read the text aloud. Point to the children on the stage. *The children are in a play. They are wearing costumes. The children look like vegetables and fruits.* Encourage children to use circumlocation and non-verbal cues to ask questions about the illustration. Then restate their answers to clarify. Have them repeat after you. *Which vegetables or fruits do you see?* (tomato, apple, carrot) Point to pictures and say the words for children to repeat. *What are the children doing?* The children are dancing. Have children demonstrate dancing with you.

What are the children doing in the school play? Discuss with a partner.

Beginning Point to the images of the children in the play. Help partners respond to the questions: *Are the children in a play?* Yes, the children are in a play. *What do the children look like?* The children look like tomatoes. *What are the children doing?* The children are dancing.

Intermediate Point to the boy dressed up as a carrot. *What vegetable is the boy in the play?* The boy is a carrot. *Does the boy look happy?* (no) *Why?* (Possible answer: The boy does not want to be a vegetable in the play.)

Advanced/Advanced High Have partners compare the boy in the carrot costume with the other kids in the play. Point to the boy. *What does the boy hope for?* (Possible answer: The boy hopes he will not be a vegetable in the play.) *How does the boy look?* (Possible answer: The boy looks unhappy.) *What are the other children doing?* The other children are dancing. *How do they look?* They look happy.

Pages 22–31

Page 29 Read the text aloud. Point to the words "get to know" and say them aloud for children to repeat. *When you get to know someone, you learn about them.* Discuss examples, such as talking together. *What do you do to get to know a friend?* (Answers will vary. Possible answer: I play with my friend.)

How do you get to know about each other? Discuss with a partner.

Beginning Review example for "get to know" with children to help them learn the phrase. *What do you do to get to know a friend?* I play with my friend.

Intermediate Help partners discuss to generate ideas for things they do to get to know their friends. *What do you do to get to know a friend?* I play/talk/read with my friend.

Advanced/Advanced High Help partners give details. *What do you do to get to know a friend?* I play with my friend in the park.

FORMATIVE ASSESSMENT

▶ STUDENT CHECK-IN

Have partners retell what the kids in the illustrations do at school. Then, have children reflect using the Check-In Routine.

Independent Time

Draw and Write Pair children of mixed proficiencies and have them discuss an activity they do with their friends. Then have them illustrate and write about one activity. Provide a sentence frame to help them write: I ___ with my friend. Have partners draw a picture and copy the sentence frame. Allow them to write what they can, help translate or elaborate, and then provide corrections as needed. Have partners present their drawings to the class using: This is a picture of me and my friend. We are ___.

ENGLISH LANGUAGE LEARNERS 3

LESSONS 1-2

READING • SHARED READ • ACCESS THE TEXT

"Jack Can"

LEARNING GOALS

We can read and understand a realistic fiction story.

OBJECTIVES

Describe characters in a story, using key details.

Retell stories, including key details, and demonstrate understanding of their central message or lesson.

Build on others' talk in conversations by responding to the comments of others through multiple exchanges.

LANGUAGE OBJECTIVES

Children will narrate, or tell, what the characters can do using the verb *can*.

ELA ACADEMIC LANGUAGE

- realistic fiction
- Cognate: *ficción realista*

MATERIALS

Reading/Writing Companion, pp. 24–33

Visual Vocabulary Cards

DIGITAL TOOLS

Have children listen to the selection as they follow along to develop comprehension and practice fluency and pronunciation.

Use the online High-Frequency Words Activity for additional support.

Prepare to Read

Build Background Read aloud the Essential Question on page 24. Have children share what they can do at school. Use the illustrations on pages 24 and 25 to generate ideas. Point to and read aloud the title. *We are going to read about a boy named Jack.* Point to the picture of Jack. *This is Jack. Say the name Jack with me.* Point to Max. *This is Max. Max is Jack's friend. Say Max with me.*

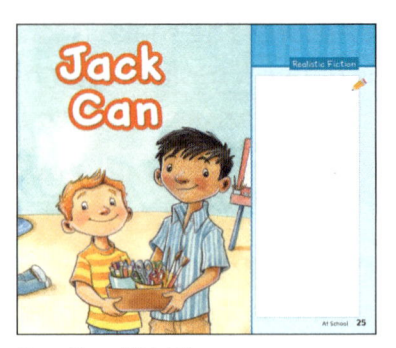

Reading/Writing Companion, Lexile BR

Focus on Vocabulary Use the **Visual Vocabulary Cards** to preteach the high-frequency words *does, school, not,* and *what* and the oral language vocabulary words such as *learn, subjects, common, object,* and *recognize.* As you read, use gestures and visual support to teach the important story words *crayons, paint, draw, board, reach,* and *stool.* Use the following routine for each new word: Point to the stool. Say the word *stool.* Have children point to the picture and repeat the word. *The girl is carrying a stool. What is the girl carrying?* Have children respond: The girl is carrying a stool.

Summarize the Text Before reading, say the summary and point to the illustrations. *This story tells about what Jack and Max can do at school.*

Read the Text

Use the Interactive Question-Response Routine to help children understand the story.

Pages 24–27

Pages 26–27 Read the text aloud as children follow. Point to the word *can* and say it aloud for children to repeat. *The word* can *means you are able to do something.* Provide an example: *I can walk.* Demonstrate the action. Have children give other examples of things they can do. Point to the word *can* and say the words aloud with children. Point to Max and ask: *Can Max draw? Yes, Max can* draw. Point to Jack and ask: *Can Jack paint? Yes, Jack can* paint.

What can Max do? What can Jack do? Discuss with a partner.

Beginning Use the pictures to review the words *draw* and *paint.* Point to the picture of Max and say: *Max can draw.* Have children repeat. *Can you draw?* (Yes/ No, I can/cannot draw.) Point to the word *can* and say it with children. Repeat the routine for Jack. Read aloud the text. Help partners ask and answer questions: *Can Max draw? Yes, Max can* draw. *Can Jack paint? Yes, Jack can* paint.

Intermediate Help partners give a more specific answer. *Can Max draw? Yes, Max can* draw. Point to Max's drawing. *What can Max draw? Max can draw a*

4 UNIT 1 WEEK 1

WEEK 1

boy. *Can Jack paint?* Yes, Jack can paint. *What can Jack paint?* Point to Jack's painting. Jack can paint a boy.

Advanced/Advanced High Help partners add details to their responses. Point to the drawing tools in the picture. *What does Max use?* Max uses a crayon. *What does Jack use?* Jack uses a brush. *What does Max draw?* Max draws a boy. *What does Jack draw?* Jack draws a boy. Point out that both Jack and Max draw pictures of themselves.

Pages 28–31

Page 29 Read the text aloud and have children follow along. Point to the word *not* and say it aloud for children to repeat. *The word* not *means you are unable to do something.* Provide an example by covering your eyes: *I can not see.* Read the text again. *What can Jack not do?* Jack can not paint. Help children practice using the word with examples, such as having them cover their ears asking: Can you hear?

Page 31 Read the text aloud and have children follow along. Point to the stool. *This is a stool. Say it with me.* Point to Nan. *What does Nan do?* Nan is carrying a stool. Remind children that the word *do* helps tell about an action. Ask volunteers to imitate writing and reading. Ask children: *What does [Sue] do?* Sue is reading. Sue is writing. Read the text aloud again. *What does Nan do?* Nan is carrying a stool.

What does Nan do? Discuss with a partner.

Beginning Guide partners to answer the question. Point to the stool. *This is Nan. Nan has a stool. Say* stool *with me. What is Nan doing?* Nan is carrying the stool. Have children repeat the word *carrying*. Correct pronunciations for *stool* and *carrying* as needed.

Intermediate Help partners give details on their answers. *What color is the stool?* The stool is green. *What does Nan do?* Nan is carrying the green stool.

Advanced/Advanced High Help partners elaborate on their answers. *Where is Nan carrying the stool?* Nan is carrying the stool to Jack.

Pages 32–33

Pages 32–33 Read the text aloud and have children follow along. Point to the word *help* and say it aloud and have children repeat after you. *Jack cannot write, so Nan helps Jack. She gave Jack a stool. Jack can write.* Read the text aloud again. *What can Jack do?* Jack can write. *Does Nan help Jack?* Yes, Nan helps Jack. *Does Jack like school?* Yes, Jack likes school. Help children extend their understanding by discussing why Jack likes school.

Can friends help you? Discuss with a partner.

Beginning Point to Jack and Nan and explain that Jack and Nan are friends. *Friends help each other. Does Nan help Jack?* Yes, Nan helps Jack. *Are Nan and Jack friends?* Yes, Nan and Jack are friends.

Intermediate Help partners give details on their answers. *What does Nan do?* Nan helps Jack. *What does Nan help Jack do?* Nan helps Jack write. *Are Nan and Jack friends?* Yes, Nan and Jack are friends.

Advanced/Advanced High Help partners elaborate on their answers. *What does Nan help Jack do?* Nan helps Jack write. *Does Jack like school?* Yes, Jack likes school. *Why?* Jack has friends.

FORMATIVE ASSESSMENT

STUDENT CHECK-IN

Have partners retell what the characters can do. Then, have children reflect using the Check-In Routine.

Independent Time

Oral Language *What do you do at your school?* Pair children of mixed proficiency. Have partners discuss what Max and Jack can do at school. Have them take turns asking and answering questions. Then have each pair tell the rest of the group. Provide sentence frames to help them: *What can Max/Jack do at school? Max/Jack can ___ at school. What can Jack not do? Jack can not ___. What does Nan do? Nan ___ Jack.*

ENGLISH LANGUAGE LEARNERS 5

LESSON 3

READING • ANCHOR TEXT • ACCESS THE TEXT

LEARNING GOALS

We can read and understand a realistic fiction story.

OBJECTIVES

Ask and answer questions about key details in a text.

Use illustrations and details in a story to describe its characters, setting, or events.

Compare and contrast the adventures and experiences of characters in stories.

Produce complete sentences when appropriate to task and situation.

LANGUAGE OBJECTIVES

Children will narrate, or tell, about the character's feelings in complete sentences.

ELA ACADEMIC LANGUAGE

- illustration, realistic fiction
- Cognates: *ilustración, ficción realista*

MATERIALS

Literature Anthology, pp. 6–17

Visual Vocabulary Cards

DIGITAL TOOLS

Have children listen to the selection as they follow along to develop comprehension and practice fluency and pronunciation.

Use the online High-Frequency Words Activity for additional support.

Nat and Sam

Prepare to Read

Build Background *We are going to read a story about a boy's day at school.* Show the picture on the title page and invite children to tell what they see. Point to the *bus, school, students, books,* and *backpacks*. Say the words and have children repeat. Then point to the boy in the yellow shirt. *Today is different because the boy brings something special to school.* Explain that *special* means "different from the rest." *Did you bring something special to school? What did you bring? Why was it special?* I brought a ___. It was my favorite ___ because ___ .

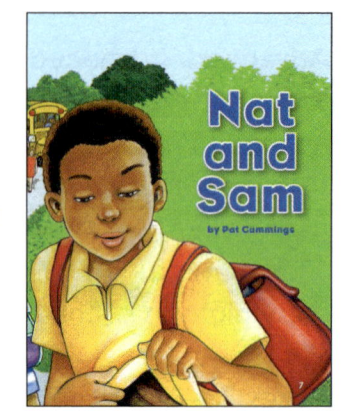

Literature Anthology, Lexile BR

Focus on Vocabulary Use the **Visual Vocabulary Cards** to review the high-frequency words *does, school, not,* and *want* and the oral language vocabulary words *learn, subjects, common, object,* and *recognize*. As you read, teach important story words using gestures and pantomime, such as *have* and *does not have*. Pick up a book and say *have*. Have children repeat. Then put the book down and say *does not have*. Have children repeat. *What do you have?* I have a pencil. *What do you not have?* I do not have a crayon.

Summarize the Text Before reading, say the summary while pointing to the illustrations. *The story tells about a boy named Nat. Nat has a special friend named Sam. Nat brings Sam to school. Nat and Sam like school.*

Read the Text

Use the Interactive Question-Response Routine to help children understand the story.

Pages 8–11

Pages 8–9 Read the text. Point to Nat on page 8. *This is Nat. Say Nat. Nat is in school. Nat is going to the classroom. Where is he going?* He is going to the classroom. *What can Nat see?* Nat can see the teacher/children. Point to Nat's shirt. *Nat has something under his shirt. Can you see what he has?* No, I can't see. Point to Nat on page 9. *Nat is at the table. Where is Nat?* Nat is at the table.

Pages 10–11 Point to Nat and the teacher on page 10. *The teacher is asking a question to Nat. What does Nat have?* Point to the bear on page 11. Nat has Sam. *Sam is Nat's special friend. When I'm scared, I like to have things that make me feel safe or better. Does Nat feel scared?* Yes, Nat feels scared. *Do you think Sam makes Nat feel safe?* (Possible answer: Yes, Sam makes Nat feel safe.) *Why does Nat have Sam?* Nat has Sam to feel safe.

How do you know how Nat feels at school? Discuss with a partner.

WEEK 1

Beginning Say the word *scared* and act it out. Have children imitate you as they say the word. Correct pronunciations as needed. Say: *Some children get scared about the first day of school.* Ask: *Is Nat scared?* Yes, Nat is scared.

Intermediate Say the word *scared*. Have children repeat. Correct pronunciations as needed. Explain that some children feel scared or nervous (cognate: *nervioso*) on the first day of school. *Nat feels scared. Why does Nat bring Sam to school?* Nat is scared. *How does Sam make Nat feel?* Nat feels safe.

Advanced/Advanced High Extend the discussion by having partners tell about other words they know that are similar to *scared*. I know the word [nervous.]

Pages 12–13

Pages 12–13 Read the text. Point to page 12. *The teacher is taking Sam away from Nat. Nat does not have Sam. Does Nat have Sam?* No, Nat does not have Sam. Say *not* and have children repeat after you. Point to Nat's face. *Is Nat happy?* No, Nat is not happy. *Does Nat like it when the teacher takes away Sam?* No, Nat does not like it. Point to Sam on page 13. *The teacher takes away Sam. Sam is going to sit without Nat.*

How does Nat feel when he does not have Sam? Discuss with a partner.

Beginning Help partners point to the pictures as they respond. Point to Nat's face on page 12. *Is Nat happy?* Nat is not happy. Point to the teacher taking Sam. *Does Nat have Sam?* No, Nat does not have Sam. *Is Nat happy?* No, Nat is not happy.

Intermediate Point to the picture on page 12. *Does Nat have Sam?* No, Nat does not have Sam. *Does Nat like it when the teacher takes away Sam?* No, Nat does not like it.

Advanced/Advanced High *How does Nat feel when he does not have Sam?* Nat does not like it. Help children add details to their answers. *Where is Sam?* Sam is by the bookshelf.

Pages 14–17

Pages 14–15 Point to Sam. *Sam can sit. Look! Sam can read.* Say *can* and *read* and have children repeat. Point to Nat. *Nat is happy. Nat is smiling. Can Sam read?* Yes, Sam can read. *Is Nat happy?* Yes, Nat is happy. *What is Nat doing?* Nat is smiling.

Pages 16–17 Read the text. Point to Nat on page 16. *Can Nat read?* Yes, Nat can read. Point to Sam on page 17. *Can Sam read?* Yes, Sam can read. *Look at Nat's face. Is Nat happy?* Yes, Nat is happy. *Does Nat like school?* Yes, Nat likes school. Review how Nat's feelings about school changed. *At first, Nat was scared at school. Now, Nat likes school. Nat changed.*

Have Nat's feelings about school changed? Discuss with a partner.

Beginning Point to the pictures of Nat at the beginning and the end. *At first, Nat was scared. Now, Nat is happy. At first, how was Nat?* At first, Nat was scared. *How does Nat feel now?* Now, Nat likes school.

Intermediate Help partners review to respond. *How did Nat feel at first?* At first, Nat was scared. *Did Nat change?* Yes, Nat changed. *How does Nat feel now?* Now, Nat likes school.

Advanced/Advanced High Extend the discussion by reviewing the meaning of *changed*. *Did Nat change?* Yes, Nat changed. Encourage children to explain why.

FORMATIVE ASSESSMENT

▶ STUDENT CHECK-IN

Have partners share how Nat's feelings changed. Then, have children reflect using the Check-in routine.

Independent Time

Oral Language Select a spread from *Nat and Sam* and pair children of mixed proficiency. Have them take turns asking and answering questions about the images. Provide sentence frames for support: What do you see? I see a ___. Have them describe the pictures to the class: In this picture I see a ___.

ENGLISH LANGUAGE LEARNERS 7

LESSONS 4-5

READING • LEVELED READER • ACCESS THE TEXT

LEARNING GOALS

We can visualize what happens in a school as we read a story.

OBJECTIVES

Retell stories, including key details, and demonstrate understanding of their central message or lesson.

Describe characters, in a story, using key details.

Describe people, places, things, and events with relevant details, expressing ideas and feelings clearly.

LANGUAGE OBJECTIVES

Children will inform, or give information, about things they do at school using verbs.

ELA ACADEMIC LANGUAGE

- visualize, character
- Cognate: *visualizar*

MATERIALS

ELL Leveled Reader: *We Like to Share*

Online Differentiated Texts, "We Can Bat"

Online ELL Visual Vocabulary Cards

DIGITAL TOOLS

Have children listen to the selection as they follow along to develop comprehension and practice fluency and pronunciation. Use Graphic Organizer 1: Character to enhance the lesson.

We Like to Share

Prepare to Read

Build Background

- Remind children of the Essential Question. *Let's read to see what some kids do at school.* Encourage children to ask for help when they do not understand a word or phrase.

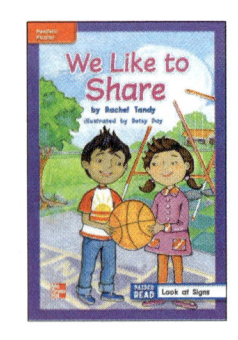

- Point to and read aloud the title and have children repeat. Ask: *What is the title?* Have children point to it. Repeat the routine for the author's name. Point to the illustrations in the Leveled Reader to name things and actions, for example: *This is a [ball]. What can you do with a [ball]?*

Lexile 100L

Focus on Vocabulary Use the **ELL Visual Vocabulary Cards** to pre-teach the words *cooperation* and *favorite*. As you read, use gestures or visuals to teach important story words, such as *share, jump rope, play ball, hop, tag,* and *slide*. Display the cover. Say the word *share* and have children repeat. *The children are sharing the ball. What can you share? I can share my toys.*

Read the Text

Use the Interactive Question-Response Routine to help children understand the story.

Pages 2–3

Read pages 2–3 as children follow along. Point to and say *jump rope, ball, swing*. Have children point to and repeat the words.

Beginning Help partners point to the pictures as they respond: *What is this? It is a ball. What do the kids like to do? The kids like to play.*

Intermediate Help partners respond: *What do the kids like to do? The kids like to play. Where do the kids play? The kids play at school.*

Advanced/Advanced High *Where do the kids play? The kids play at school. What do the kids play with? The kids play with a ball.*

Pages 4–9

Main Story Elements: Characters Read pages 4–5 as children follow along. Ask questions to help them describe the characters. Point to the jump rope. *What is this?* (jump rope) Point to Rosa. *Who is this?* (Rosa) *What does Rosa like to do? Rosa likes to jump rope.* Repeat the routine for pages 6–7 and 8–9.

Intermediate *What does Rosa like? Rosa likes to jump rope. Can Rosa share? Yes, Rosa can share.*

8 UNIT 1 WEEK 1

WEEK 1

Advanced/Advanced High Have partners discuss for each spread: Raj likes to <u>play ball</u>. Raj can share <u>the ball</u> with <u>Rosa</u>.

Pages 10–11

Visualize Read pages 10–11. Help children visualize: Sam doesn't like to play tag. I can close my eyes and picture him looking for another game to play.

Beginning Help partners work together to respond and point to the pictures: *Does Sam play tag?* No, Sam does <u>not</u> play.

Intermediate *Does Sam like tag?* No, Sam does <u>not</u> like <u>tag</u>. *What does Sam like?* Sam likes to <u>slide</u>.

Respond to Reading Have partners work together to retell the story and respond to the questions on page 12.

Focus on Fluency

Read pages 10–11. Read the passage again and have children repeat after you. Remind children to read the words correctly.

Paired Read: "Look at Signs"

Make Connections: Write About It

Echo-read each page with children. Discuss what each sign tells: *This is a stop sign. What does the sign tell us?* The sign tells us to <u>stop</u>. Help children make connections between texts using the question on page 15: Friends and signs <u>help</u> us at school.

Leveled Reader

Build Knowledge: Make Connections

Talk About the Text Have partners discuss how the activities in the texts are similar to or different from activities they like to do at their school.

Write About the Text Have students add their ideas to their Build Knowledge pages of their reader's notebooks.

Self-Selected Reading

Help children choose a fiction selection from the online **Leveled Reader Library,** or read the **Differentiated Text:** "We Can Bat."

FOCUS ON SOCIAL STUDIES

Children can extend their knowledge of how rules help us play by completing the social studies activity on page 16.

LITERATURE CIRCLES

Lead children in conducting a literature circle using the Thinkmark questions to guide the discussion. You may wish to discuss what children have learned about helping out at school from both selections in the Leveled Reader.

FORMATIVE ASSESSMENT

STUDENT CHECK-IN

Have partners share their Respond to Reading. Have children reflect using the Check-In Routine.

LEVEL UP

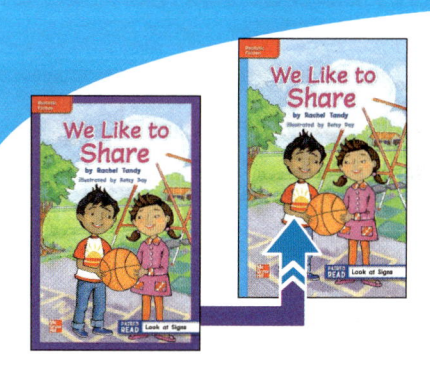

IF children can read *We Like to Share* **ELL Level** with fluency and correctly answer the Respond to Reading questions,

THEN tell children that they will read a more detailed version of the story.

- Use pages 2–3 of *We Like to Share* **On Level** to model using Teaching Poster 26 to list key details.
- Have children read the selection, checking their comprehension by using the graphic organizer.

ENGLISH LANGUAGE LEARNERS

LESSONS 1-5

WRITING

MODELED WRITING

LESSON 1

LEARNING GOALS

We can learn to write a complete sentence.

OBJECTIVES

With guidance and support from adults, focus on a topic.

LANGUAGE OBJECTIVES

Children will narrate, or tell, by writing a complete sentence using the verb *like*.

ELA ACADEMIC LANGUAGE

- sentence

Writing Practice Review the sample sentence on p. 34 of the **Reading/Writing Companion**: *I read at school.* Guide them to analyze it using the Actor/Action Routine: *Who is the actor?* (I) *What is the action?* (read at school) Then read the prompt on p. 35. Have children answer it as a group. Provide a sentence starter: I like to listen at Story Time. Write the sentence on the board, and have children choral read it. Then have partners write their own sentence using the Actor/Action Routine.

Beginning Help partners create their sentence: *Who is the actor?* (I) *What do you like to do?* I like to write my name.

Intermediate Have partners take turns asking and answering *who/what* questions to create their sentence. Provide a sentence frame if needed.

Advanced/Advanced High Encourage children to stretch the sounds in words as they write them. Have a partner read along and listen to check.

FORMATIVE ASSESSMENT ▶ **STUDENT CHECK-IN** Partners share their sentences. Ask children to reflect using the Check-In Routine.

INTERACTIVE WRITING

LESSON 2

LEARNING GOALS

We can read and write about a Student Model.

OBJECTIVES

Respond to questions and suggestions from peers.

LANGUAGE OBJECTIVES

Children will discuss the Student Model and write sentences using feeling words.

ELA ACADEMIC LANGUAGE

- event
- Cognate: *evento*

Analyze the Student Model Have children finger point as they choral read the Student Model on p. 40 of the **Reading/Writing Companion**. Use the Actor/Action Routine to review the first two sentences. Next, guide children to raise their hand at the end of each complete sentence. *Now let's review the event, or what happens, in each sentence. How does Jack feel at first?* (sad) *What does Nan do?* (She helps Jack.) Finally, help children complete p. 41. Provide sentence frames as needed.

Beginning Have partners circle capital letters and periods. Point out those capital letters that begin sentences and ones that don't.

Intermediate Have partners ask and answer the following question: *Which words did Matt use to tell when Jack is sad?* Matt used In the beginning.

Advanced/Advanced High Challenge children to write what they notice about Matt's writing using their own words.

FORMATIVE ASSESSMENT ▶ **STUDENT CHECK-IN** Partners share their responses. Ask children to reflect using the Check-In Routine.

10 UNIT 1 WEEK 1

WEEK 1

INDEPENDENT WRITING
LESSONS 3-4

LEARNING GOALS
- We can use text evidence to respond to realistic fiction.
- We can write complete sentences.

OBJECTIVES
Write narratives in which they include some details.

LANGUAGE OBJECTIVES
Children will narrate a realistic fiction by writing complete sentences.

ELA ACADEMIC LANGUAGE
- *evidence*
- Cognate: *evidencia*

Find Text Evidence Use the Independent Writing Routine. Help children orally retell the anchor text. Ask questions, such as, *Where is Nat?* (school) *What does he bring to school?* (Sam) *What does Nat's teacher do?* (takes Sam away) Then read the prompt on p. 46 of the **Reading/Writing Companion**: *Why did Nat's feelings about school change? Nat feels one way at the beginning and a different way at the end. What are his feelings at first, and why do they change?*

Write a Response Distribute **My Writing Outline 1** to children. Then, work with children to fill out the outline. Finally, have children complete p. 46 using the sentences from their outline.

Writing Checklist Read the checklist with students, and have them check for these items in their writing.

Beginning *What happens to Nat at first?* Nat is sad.

Intermediate Have partners exchange their work to check for the items.

Advanced/Advanced High Have children identify where they used each item in their writing.

FORMATIVE ASSESSMENT ▸ **STUDENT CHECK-IN** Partners share their sentences from My Writing Outline. Ask children to reflect using the Check-In Routine.

SELF-SELECTED WRITING
LESSON 5

LEARNING GOALS
We can revise our writing.

OBJECTIVES
Produce and expand complete simple declarative sentences.

LANGUAGE OBJECTIVES
Children will inquire about their writing by checking that their sentences are complete.

ELA ACADEMIC LANGUAGE
- *incomplete*

Work with children to revise the group writing activity. Point to each word as you read the sentences. Stop to ask questions, such as, *Is this sentence complete?* If needed, write an incomplete sentence, and work with children to revise it. Then, have partners revise each other's sentences before publishing them.

For support with incomplete sentences and grammar, refer to the **Language Transfers Handbook** and **Language Development Cards** 21A, 21B, and 22A.

FORMATIVE ASSESSMENT ▸ **STUDENT CHECK-IN** Partners identify their revisions. Ask children to reflect using the Check-In Routine.

LESSONS 1-2

READING • LITERATURE BIG BOOK • ACCESS THE TEXT

LEARNING GOALS

We can understand what happens in a city as we listen to a story.

OBJECTIVES

Describe characters and major events in a story, using key details.

Retell stories, including key details, and demonstrate understanding of their central message or lesson.

Build on others' talk in conversations by responding to the comments of others through multiple exchanges.

Ask and answer questions about key details in a text read aloud or information presented orally or through other media.

LANGUAGE OBJECTIVES

Children will narrate, or tell, the character's experiences around her city, using key vocabulary and simple sentences.

ELA ACADEMIC LANGUAGE

- author, illustrations, event
- Cognates: autor, ilustraciones, evento

MATERIALS

Literature Big Book, *Alicia's Happy Day,* pp. 2–26

Visual Vocabulary Cards

DIGITAL TOOLS

Have children listen to the selection as they follow along to develop comprehension and practice fluency and pronunciation.

Use the online High-Frequency Words Activity for additional support.

Alicia's Happy Day

Prepare to Read

Build Background *We are going to read a story about Alicia's birthday. Many good things, or events, happen on this day.* Show a picture of a birthday cake and talk about familiar events that happen on birthdays. *What happens on your birthday?* Model for children: *I have a birthday party.* Have children repeat. Then have children talk about good events that happen on their birthdays. Provide sentence frames: I have _____ . I see _____ .

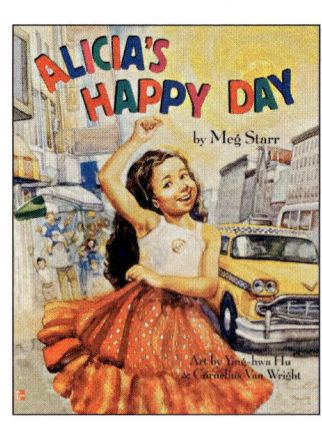

Focus on Vocabulary Use the **Visual Vocabulary Cards** to review the oral vocabulary words *city* and *country.* As you read, use gestures and other visual support to clarify important story words, such as *may, dance, give, decorate, sing,* and *laugh* (cognate: *decorar*). Say: *The word* may *in this story means "I wish, or hope, for something good to happen."* Point to *may* in the text and have children repeat the word. Provide an example: *May you have fun. What do you wish for? May friends* decorate *a cake. May friends* sing *"Happy Birthday" to you.*

Literature Big Book

Summarize the Text Before reading, say the summary while pointing to the illustrations. *Look at the illustrations. We see that Alicia lives in a city. This story tells about the happy day the author wants for Alicia. We'll read many wishes for Alicia on her birthday.*

Read the Text

Use the Interactive Question-Response Routine to help children understand the story.

Pages 2–11

Pages 4–5 Read the text aloud. Point to the name of the music store. *This is a music store named Casa Latina.* Point to the instruments. *The sign and the instruments help us know that Alicia is walking by a music store* (cognate: *instrumentos*). Gesture toward your ear. *What does Alicia har?* (Alicia hears salsa.) *Salsa is a kind of music* (cognate: *música*). Point to Alicia. *Is Alicia smiling?* Yes, Alicia is smiling. *What does Alicia start to do?* Alicia starts to dance.

What events have happened in Alicia's day so far? Discuss with a partner.

Beginning Point to the music store. *Does Alicia hear salsa?* Yes, Alicia hears salsa. Point to Alicia. *What does Alicia start to do?* Alicia starts to dance. *Is Alicia smiling?* Yes, Alicia is smiling.

12 UNIT 1 WEEK 2

WEEK 2

Intermediate Have children point to the music store. *What is the name of the music store?* The name of the store is Casa Latina. *What music does Alicia hear?* Alicia hears salsa. *What does Alicia start to do?* Alicia starts to dance. *Is Alicia smiling?* Yes, Alicia is smiling.

Advanced/Advanced High Have partners give details. *Where is Alicia?* Alicia is walking by a music store. *What is the name of the store?* The name of the store is Casa Latina. *Why does Alicia start to dance?* Alicia hears salsa music coming from the store. *How do you know hearing music is a good thing for Alicia?* (Possible answer: Alicia smiles and starts to dance.)

Pages 12–19

Pages 12–13 Read the text and point to the traffic sign in the illustration. Say: *Alicia and her mom are waiting to cross the street. What does the sign say?* (walk) Alicia and her mom can cross the street when the sign says "walk."

COLLABORATE *What are Alicia and her mom doing? Discuss with a partner.*

Beginning Help partners respond. Point to the traffic sign. *What are Alicia and her mom doing?* Alicia and her mom are waiting for the sign to say "walk." *Does the sign say "walk"?* Yes, the sign says "walk."

Intermediate Have partners point to the traffic sign. *What are Alicia and her mom waiting for?* Alicia and her mom are waiting to cross the street. *What does the sign say?* The sign says "walk." *Can they cross the street?* Yes, they can cross the street.

Advanced/Advanced High Have partners point to the word "walk" in the illustration. *What is Alicia looking at?* Alicia is looking at the sign. *Why is she smiling?* Alicia is smiling because the sign says "walk." *What will Alicia and her mom do now?* Alicia and her mom will cross the street.

Pages 20–26

Pages 20–21 *The author's wish starts on page 19: "May the orange lady give a ribbon of peel to you." The author continues her wish on page 20.* Read the text on page 20. Point to the man. Say: *The author calls this man the "Icey man." The Icey man sells ice cream.* Point to and say *ice cream* and have children repeat. *The author wishes for the Icey man to tell Alicia, "Helado de Coco for you." These are Spanish words for* coconut ice cream. *Say* coconut ice cream. *How does Alicia look?* (happy) Alicia looks happy and excited. *Does Alicia like coconut ice cream?* (yes)

COLLABORATE *What does the author wish for Alicia? Tell why the author wishes this. Discuss with a partner.*

Beginning Point to the Icey man. Help children respond. *What does the Icey man give Alicia?* The Icey man gives Alicia coconut ice cream. *Does Alicia like coconut ice cream?* Yes, Alicia likes coconut ice cream.

Intermediate Have partners point to the Icey man. *What kind of ice cream does the Icey man give Alicia?* The Icey man gives Alicia coconut ice cream. *Why does Alicia look happy?* Alicia likes coconut ice cream.

Advanced/Advanced High Have partners discuss what is happening in this scene. *Why does the author wish for Alicia to have coconut ice cream?* Alicia really likes coconut ice cream. It makes her birthday special. *What kind of ice cream do you like on your birthday?* (Answers will vary.)

FORMATIVE ASSESSMENT

▶ STUDENT CHECK-IN

Have partners discuss three things Alicia did throughout the story. Then, have children reflect using the Check-In Routine.

Independent Time

Ask and Answer Questions Pair children of mixed proficiencies and have them discuss the author's wishes for Alicia and what they like to do on their own birthdays. Have them take turns asking and answering questions. Then have each pair tell the rest of the group. Provide sentence frames to help them: *What is one wish for Alicia?* May you ___. *What do you like to do on your birthday?* I like to ___. *What do you wish for your partner's birthday?* May you ___.

ENGLISH LANGUAGE LEARNERS 13

READING • SHARED READ • ACCESS THE TEXT

LESSONS 1-2

LEARNING GOALS

We can read and understand a fantasy story.

OBJECTIVES

Retell stories, including key details, and demonstrate understanding of their central message or lesson.

Ask and answer questions about key details in a text.

Use illustrations and details in a story to describe its characters and setting.

LANGUAGE OBJECTIVES

Children will discuss characters' actions in different settings of the story, using simple sentences and key vocabulary.

ELA ACADEMIC LANGUAGE

- *fantasy, setting, characters*
- Cognate: *fantasía*

MATERIALS

Reading/Writing Companion, pp. 58–67

Visual Vocabulary Cards

DIGITAL TOOLS

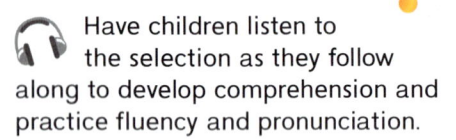

MULTIMODAL

Have children listen to the selection as they follow along to develop comprehension and practice fluency and pronunciation.

Use the online High-Frequency Words Activity for additional support.

"Six Kids"

Prepare to Read

Build Background *We are going to read a fantasy story called "Six Kids." A fantasy story can have animal characters that act like people. The six kids in this story are chicks.* Point to the chicks on pages 58–59. *Chicks are young chickens. Say* chickens*. Chickens live on a farm.* Point to the farm. *Say* farm. *The setting of this story is a farm.* Point to the cows. *Cows live on a farm. Say* cows. Point to the barn. *This is a barn. Say* barn.

Reading/Writing Companion, Lexile 250L

Focus on Vocabulary Use the **Visual Vocabulary Cards** to preteach the high-frequency words *down, out, up,* and *very* and the oral language vocabulary words *city, country, bored, feast,* and *scurried.* As you read, use gestures and visual support to teach the important story words, such as *shovel, watering can, water, garden, hill, blueberries,* and *pond.*

Summarize the Text Before reading, say the summary and point to the illustrations. *This story tells what six chicks do on a farm.*

Read the Text

Use the Interactive Question-Response Routine to help children understand the story.

Pages 60–67

Pages 60–63 Read the text aloud as children follow. Help children participate in the shared reading. Point to the word *dig* and say it aloud for children to repeat. Provide an example as you act out the action: *The kids dig with shovels.* Point to the watering can. *This kid has a watering can. Water is coming out. Where do the kids live?* (on a farm) *Farms have gardens. A garden needs water. The kids are digging a* garden. Point to the picture on page 63. *What do the kids do now? They go* down *a hill.*

COLLABORATE *What do the six kids do? Discuss with a partner.*

Beginning Point to the kids digging and say: *The kids dig.* Have children repeat. *Do the kids dig?* Yes, the kids dig. Then point to the kids on the hill. *Do the kids go up or down?* The kids go down.

Intermediate Help partners give more specific answers. *Do the kids dig?* Yes, the kids dig. *What do the kids dig?* The kids dig a garden. *Do the kids go up or down?* The kids go down. *What do the kids go down?* The kids go down a hill.

14 UNIT 1 WEEK 2

WEEK 2

Advanced/Advanced High Help partners add details. Point to the kids with shovels. *What kinds of tools do these kids use?* The kids use shovels. *What are the kids doing?* The kids are digging a garden. *Where do the kids carry their tools?* The kids carry their tools down a hill.

Pages 64–65

Pages 64–65 Read the text aloud and have children follow along. Point to the word *pick*. Say it aloud while acting out picking berries. Have children repeat: *pick*. Point to the blueberries. *The six kids pick blueberries. What do the six kids do?* The six kids pick blueberries. Point to the kids eating and playing. *Some kids eat blueberries. Some kids play. The kids are very blue. What color are the kids?* (blue) *This is a problem.*

What happens to the kids? Discuss with a partner.

Beginning Guide children to answer the question. Point to a kid picking blueberries. *Do the six kids pick?* Yes, the six kids pick. *Are the kids very blue?* Yes, the kids are very blue.

Intermediate Help partners give details. *What do the six kids do?* The six kids pick blueberries. *What happens to the kids?* The kids are very blue.

Advanced/Advanced High Help partners elaborate. *What happens to the six kids?* The six kids pick blueberries and get very blue. *Why are the kids very blue?* The kids are very blue because they eat blueberries and play with them.

Pages 66–67

Pages 66–67 Read the text aloud and have children follow along. Point to the word *dip* and say it for children to repeat. *The six kids are very blue, so they take a dip in the pond.* To take a dip *means "to jump into the water for a quick swim." Do the kids have fun?* Yes, the kids have fun. Point to the kids on page 66. *Are the six kids very blue now?* No, the kids are not very blue now. *The water makes the six kids clean.* Point to the word *fix*. *The water fixes the problem.* Point to the clean kids again. *Do the six kids like the farm?* Yes, the six kids like the farm.

Why do the kids like the farm? Discuss with a partner.

Beginning Point to the six kids in the pond, and remind children that the six kids were very blue from the blueberries. Help children respond. *What do the six kids do?* The kids dip. *Do the six kids have fun?* Yes, the six kids have fun. *Do the six kids like the farm?* Yes, the six kids like the farm.

Intermediate Help partners give details in their answers. *How do the six kids get clean?* The six kids dip in the pond. *Why do the six kids like the farm?* The six kids have fun on the farm. *Do the six kids play in the water?* Yes, the six kids play in the water.

Advanced/Advanced High Help partners elaborate on their answers. *Why do the six kids like the farm?* The kids like the farm because they have fun on the farm. *How do the six kids have fun on these pages?* The six kids dip in the pond and play in the water.

FORMATIVE ASSESSMENT

STUDENT CHECK-IN

Have partners retell three activities that the six kids do in the story. Then, have children reflect using the Check-In Routine.

Independent Time

Write and Draw Pair children of mixed proficiencies and have them discuss the six kids' activity that they think is the most fun. Use **Oral Language Sentence Frames**, page 3, Offering Opinions, to support children as they discuss their opinion with a partner. Then provide this sentence frame: The six kids ___. Have partners copy the sentence frame and draw a picture to go with it. Allow children to write what they can. Help translate or elaborate and then provide corrections as needed. Have partners present their pictures to the group.

ENGLISH LANGUAGE LEARNERS 15

LESSON 3

READING • ANCHOR TEXT • ACCESS THE TEXT

LEARNING GOALS

We can read and understand a fantasy story.

OBJECTIVES

Use illustrations and details in a story to describe its characters and setting.

Retell stories, including key details, and demonstrate understanding of their central message or lesson.

Describe people, places, things, and events with relevant details, expressing ideas and feelings clearly.

LANGUAGE OBJECTIVES

Children will narrate, or tell, the character's actions using words of movement and key vocabulary.

ELA ACADEMIC LANGUAGE

- illustration, relevant details, author
- Cognates: *ilustración, detalles relevantes, autor*

MATERIALS

Literature Anthology, pp. 26–39

Visual Vocabulary Cards

DIGITAL TOOLS

Have children listen to the selection as they follow along to develop comprehension and practice fluency and pronunciation.

Use the online High-Frequency Words Activity for additional support.

Go, Pip!

Prepare to Read

Build Background *We are going to read a fantasy story. A fantasy story has characters and events that are not real. Its characters can be animals.* Point to pages 26–27 and say: *The title of this story is* Go, Pip! Have children tell what they see. Help children identify the squirrel, park, tree, cart, and umbrella. Point to the squirrel. *This is Pip. Pip is a squirrel. Where is Pip? Pip lives in a park. What is Pip looking at? Pip is looking at a cart.* Provide sentence frames: The cart has _____ . The cart can _____ .

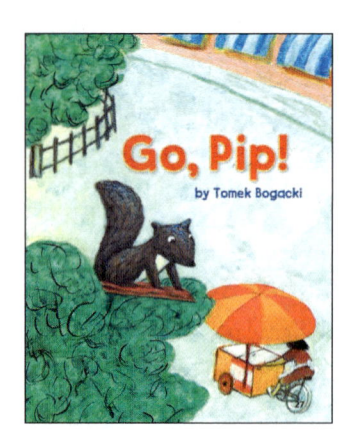

Literature Anthology, Lexile 30L

Focus on Vocabulary Use the **Visual Vocabulary Cards** to preteach the high-frequency words *down, out, up,* and *very* and the oral language vocabulary words *city, country, bored, feast,* and *scurried.* As you read, teach important story words using gestures and pantomime, such as *excited, look up, look down, big, building,* and *fit.* Look up at the ceiling and say: *I'm looking up.* Have children repeat: *look up.* Look down at the floor: *I'm looking down.* Have children repeat: *look down.*

Summarize the Text Before reading, say the summary while pointing to the illustrations. *The story tells about a squirrel named Pip. Pip lives in the park. One day Pip goes into the city.*

Read the Text

Use the Interactive Question-Response Routine to help children understand the story.

Pages 28–31

Pages 30–31 Read the text aloud. Point to Pip. *In the picture on page 29, Pip is jumping from the tree to the umbrella. On page 30, Pip is on the umbrella. The woman drives the cart out of the park. Where is the cart going?* The cart is going into the city. Point to the group of people. *The people see Pip riding on the umbrella. What do the people do?* The people wave to Pip. *What does Pip do?* Pip waves. *Pip is excited. How do you know Pip is excited?* (The picture shows what Pip is doing.)

What does the illustration show you about Pip? Discuss with a partner.

Beginning Say the word *excited* and act it out. Have children say and act out the word. Correct pronunciations as needed. Say: *Some children are excited in a new place.* Ask: *Does Pip look excited to be out?* Yes, Pip looks excited. *Does Pip wave?* Yes, Pip waves. *Will Pip see the city?* Yes, Pip will see the city.

16 UNIT 1 WEEK 2

WEEK 2

Intermediate Ask children to repeat the word *excited*. Say: *Some children are excited in a new place.* Point to the picture. Ask: *Does Pip look excited?* Yes, Pip looks excited. *Why?* Pip will see the city. *What does Pip do?* Pip waves at the people.

Advanced/Advanced High Have partners discuss: *How does Pip look?* Pip looks excited. *How do you know?* Pip waves when the people wave. *Why is Pip excited?* Pip knows he will see many places in the city.

Pages 32–37

Pages 32–33 Read the text. Explain that the illustrations and text give relevant details. Point to the map. *Pip has a map. Say* map. *The map shows places in the city.* Point to the tall building. *The building is a place in the city. The picture of this building helps me understand the author's words, "It is very big."* Point to page 33. *Now Pip is on top of the building. Pip has binoculars. Binoculars make things look bigger. What does the author say Pip can do?* Pip can look down.

Does Pip want to see new places? How do you know? Discuss with a partner.

Beginning Help children respond. Point to page 32. *Does Pip have a map?* Yes, Pip has a map. *The map shows new places. Does Pip want to see a very big building?* (yes) *Does Pip look up or down?* Pip looks up. Point to page 33. *Can Pip look down at new places?* Yes, Pip can look down.

Intermediate Point to page 32. *What does the map show?* The map shows new places. *Where does Pip look?* Pip looks up at a very big building. Point to page 33. *Why is Pip on the building?* Pip wants to look down at places in the city.

Advanced/Advanced High Have partners retell this part of the story. Pip looks at a map to find new places. Pip looks up at a very big building. Pip wants to see more new places. Pip goes to the top of a building and looks down at the city.

Pages 38–39

Pages 38–39 Read the text. Help children use inferential skills. Point to page 38. *After Pip sees many places, Pip sees the cart. The author asks, "Where will Pip go?" The author gives the answer on page 39: Pip will go home. Where will Pip go?* Pip will go home.

Why is Go Pip! *a good title for the story? Discuss with a partner.*

Beginning Help children respond. *Does Pip go home?* Yes, Pip goes home. *What does Pip show friends?* Pip shows the map. *Why is* Go Pip! *a good title?* Pip likes to go out.

Intermediate Help partners add details. *Where does Pip go?* Pip goes home to the tree. *What does Pip do at home?* Pip shows the map. *Why is* Go Pip! *a good title?* Pip goes to new places and has fun.

Advanced/Advanced High *What does Pip do?* Pip jumps on the cart and goes home. *Why is* Go Pip! *a good story title?* Pip goes out of the park and sees many places in the city. Then he goes home.

FORMATIVE ASSESSMENT

STUDENT CHECK-IN

Have partners discuss places that Pip visited throughout his adventure. Then, have children reflect using the Check-In Routine.

Independent Time

Draw and Write Pair children of mixed proficiencies. Have them discuss their favorite places in *Go, Pip!* Provide a sentence frame for support: I like ___. Have partners draw their favorite place and then describe it to the group. This picture shows ___.

ENGLISH LANGUAGE LEARNERS 17

LESSONS 4-5

READING • LEVELED READER • ACCESS THE TEXT

LEARNING GOALS

We can visualize what happens on a trip to the city as we read a story.

OBJECTIVES

Describe characters and settings in a story, using key details.

Retell stories, including key details, and demonstrate understanding of their central message or lesson.

Build on others' talk in conversations by responding to the comments of others through multiple exchanges.

Describe people, places, things, and events with relevant details, expressing ideas and feelings clearly.

LANGUAGE OBJECTIVES

Children will narrate, or tell what the characters do around the city, using the verbs *can, do, go, see,* and *like*.

ELA ACADEMIC LANGUAGE

- *visualize, fantasy*
- Cognates: *visualizar, fantasía*

MATERIALS

ELL Leveled Reader:
A Trip to the City

Online Differentiated Texts,
"I Can Go"

Online ELL Visual Vocabulary Cards

DIGITAL TOOLS

Have children listen to the selection as they follow along to develop comprehension and practice fluency and pronunciation. Use Graphic Organizer 1: Character to enhance the lesson.

A Trip to the City

Prepare to Read

Build Background

- Remind children of the Essential Question. Then say: *Let's read to see what a city is like in this fantasy story.* Explain that a fantasy story can have animal characters. Tell children to ask for help when they do not understand a word or phrase.

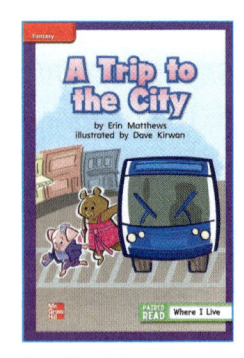

Lexile BR

- Point to and read aloud the title for children to repeat. Ask: *What is the title?* Have children point to it. Repeat the routine for the author's name. Point to the illustrations to name things and actions: *This is a [store]. We [shop in a store].*

Focus on Vocabulary Use the **ELL Visual Vocabulary Cards** to preteach the words *shopping* and *trip*. As you read, use gestures or visuals to each important story words, such as *see, pink, eat,* and *sit*. Display the cover. Say *trip* and have children repeat. *Pig and Bear go on a shopping trip to the city. Where do you go on a shopping trip?* I go to the city.

Read the Text

Use the Interactive Question-Response Routine to help children understand the story.

Pages 2–3

Read pages 2–3 as children follow along. Point to and say *bus, street, stores,* and *shopping.* Have children point to and repeat the words.

Beginning Help partners point to the picture on page 3 as they respond. *What is this?* This is a store. *Will Pig and Bear go shopping?* (yes)

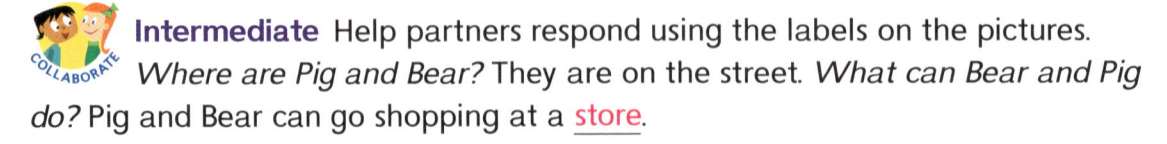

Intermediate Help partners respond using the labels on the pictures. *Where are Pig and Bear?* They are on the street. *What can Bear and Pig do?* Pig and Bear can go shopping at a store.

Advanced/Advanced High Have partners use the pictures and labels to respond. *Where can they go shopping?* They can go to a store.

Pages 4–9

Main Story Elements: Characters Read aloud as children follow along. Ask guiding questions. Point to the sign. *What is this?* (a sign) *What does Bear look at?* Bear looks at a pink hat. *Where is Bear?* (a hat store) Repeat with question about Pig.

Beginning *Does Bear look at a pink hat in the store?* Yes, Bear looks at a pink hat. *Does Pig look at a green hat?* Yes, Pig looks at a green hat.

18 UNIT 1 WEEK 2

WEEK 2

Intermediate *What does Bear look at in the hat store?* Bear looks at a pink hat in the hat store. Repeat the question about Pig.

Advanced/Advanced High Have partners retell: Bear and Pig see a hat store. Bear looks at a pink hat while Pig looks at a green hat.

Pages 10–11

Visualize Read pages 10–11. Help children visualize: *I can close my eyes and picture Bear pointing to the sign. She knows they can go eat there.*

Beginning Point to page 10. *Does Bear see a sign?* Yes, Bear sees a food sign. *Can Pig and Bear eat?* Yes, Pig and Bear can eat.

Intermediate Ask and answer: What does Bear see? Bear sees a food sign. What can Pig and Bear do? Pig and Bear can sit and eat.

Respond to Reading Have partners work together to retell the story and discuss the questions on page 12.

Focus on Fluency

Read pages 10–11 and have children echo-read with proper phrasing. Remind them to pause at the end of each sentence.

Paired Read: "Where I Live"

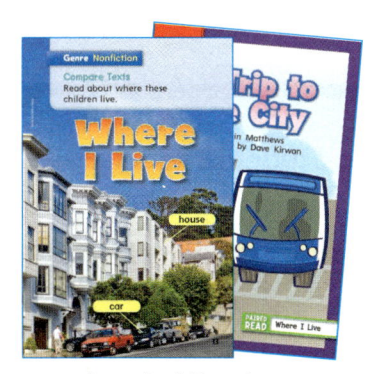

Make Connections: Write About It

Echo-read each page with children. Discuss places: *This is a playground. Where do you go to play?* I go to a playground, too. Help children make connections between texts: In *A Trip to the City,* the city has buildings. The city does not have a chicken.

Leveled Reader

Build Knowledge: Make Connections

Talk About the Text Have partners discuss how the places people live in the texts are similar to or different from where they live.

Write About the Text Have students add their ideas to their Build Knowledge pages of their reader's notebooks.

Self-Selected Reading

Help children choose a fiction selection from the online **Leveled Reader Library,** or read the **Differentiated Text:** "I Can Go."

FOCUS ON SOCIAL STUDIES

Children can extend their knowledge of what it is like where people live by completing the social studies activity on page 16.

LITERATURE CIRCLES

Lead children in conducting a literature circle using the Thinkmark questions to guide the discussion. You may wish to discuss what children have learned about different places from both selections in the Leveled Reader.

FORMATIVE ASSESSMENT

STUDENT CHECK-IN

Have partners share their Respond to Reading. Have children reflect using the Check-In Routine.

LEVEL UP

IF children can read *A Trip to the City* **ELL Level** with fluency and correctly answer the questions,

THEN tell children that they will read a more detailed version of the story.

- Use pages 5–9 of *A Trip to the City* **On Level** to model using Teaching Poster 26 to list key details.

- Have children read the selection, checking their comprehension by using the graphic organizer.

ENGLISH LANGUAGE LEARNERS 19

LESSONS 1-5

WRITING

MODELED WRITING

LESSON 1

LEARNING GOAL
We can learn how to write a sentence with descriptive details.

OBJECTIVES
With guidance and support from adults, focus on a topic.

LANGUAGE OBJECTIVES
Children will inform, or give information, by writing a complete sentence using the verb *like*.

ELA ACADEMIC LANGUAGE
- details
- Cognate: *detalles*

Writing Practice Review the sample sentence on p. 68 of the **Reading/Writing Companion**: *I ride bikes with my friends*. Guide children to analyze it using the Actor/Action Routine: *Who is the actor?* (I) *What is the action?* (ride bikes with my friends) Read the prompt on p. 69, and ask children to answer it as a group using the routine. Provide a sentence frame: I like to go to the park with friends. Write the sentence on the board for children to choral read. Then ask children to write their own sentence.

Beginning Help partners write their sentence using the routine. *Who is the sentence about?* (I) *What do you like to do?* I like to play ball.

Intermediate Have partners take turns asking and answering *who/what* questions to create their sentence. Help children add a descriptive detail.

Advanced/Advanced High Challenge children to include a descriptive detail and to check that the first word of the sentence is capitalized.

FORMATIVE ASSESSMENT → **STUDENT CHECK-IN** Partners share their sentences. Ask children to reflect using the Check-In Routine.

INTERACTIVE WRITING

LESSON 2

LEARNING GOAL
We can read and write about a Student Model.

OBJECTIVES
With guidance and support, respond to questions and suggestions from peers.

LANGUAGE OBJECTIVE
Children will discuss the Student Model and write sentences using descriptive details.

ELA ACADEMIC LANGUAGE
- details, word order
- Cognate: *detalles*

Analyze the Student Model Have children finger point as they choral read the Student Model on p. 74 of the **Reading/Writing Companion**. Use the Actor/Action Routine to review the first sentence. Ask questions to help children identify descriptive details: *Where do the kids live?* (on a farm) *How many kids are there?* (six) Then help children complete p. 75.

Beginning Ask partners to point to the capital letters in the text and describe what they see at the beginning of each sentence: Sasha used a capital letter at the beginning of each sentence.

Intermediate Have partners ask and answer questions about the student model. Provide a sentence frame: The descriptive detail is six.

Advanced/Advanced High *Did Sasha put her words in an order that makes sense?* Have them write an original sentence about what they notice.

FORMATIVE ASSESSMENT → **STUDENT CHECK-IN** Partners share their responses. Ask children to reflect using the Check-In Routine.

20 UNIT 1 WEEK 2

WEEK 2

INDEPENDENT WRITING

LESSONS 3-4

LEARNING GOAL

We can use text evidence to respond to a fantasy story.

OBJECTIVES

Write narratives in which they include some details.

LANGUAGE OBJECTIVES

Children will explain by writing sentences using descriptive details.

ELA ACADEMIC LANGUAGE

- evidence
- Cognate: *evidencia*

Find Text Evidence Use the **Independent Writing Routine**. Help children orally retell the anchor text. Ask questions, such as, *Is Pip an animal or a person?* (an animal) *What kind of animal is he?* (a squirrel) *Where does he live?* (a park in the city) *Where does he go?* (a street) Then read the prompt: on p. 80 of the **Reading/Writing Companion:** *How does Pip feel about his neighborhood? Let's look at the text and pictures that show what Pip sees and how he reacts.*

Write a Response Distribute **My Writing Outline 2** to children, and display it on a smartboard. Then, work with children to fill out the outline. After they have completed their outline, have children complete p. 80 using the sentences from their completed outline.

Writing Checklist Read the checklist with children, and have them check for these items in their writing.

Beginning *What does the word Pip begin with?* (capital *P*)

Intermediate Provide the following word bank: *big, busy, far*. Have partners work together to add these descriptive details to their sentences.

Advanced/Advanced High Have children identify where they used each item in their writing.

FORMATIVE ASSESSMENT

▶ STUDENT CHECK-IN Partners share their sentences from My Writing Outline. Ask children to reflect using the Check-In Routine.

SELF-SELECTED WRITING

LESSON 5

LEARNING GOAL

We can revise our writing.

OBJECTIVES

Print all upper- and lowercase letters.

LANGUAGE OBJECTIVES

Children will inquire about their writing by checking that sentences have the correct word order.

ELA ACADEMIC LANGUAGE

- publish
- Cognate: *publicar*

Work with children to revise the group writing activity. Point to each word as you read the sentences. Stop to ask questions, such as, *Are the words in this sentence in the correct order?* If needed, write a sentence with the words out of order, and work with children to revise it. Then, have partners revise each other's sentences before publishing them.

For support with grammar and word order, refer to the **Language Transfers Handbook** and **Language Development Card** 21B.

FORMATIVE ASSESSMENT

▶ STUDENT CHECK-IN Partners identify their revisions. Ask children to reflect using the Check-In Routine.

LESSONS 1-2

READING • LITERATURE BIG BOOK • ACCESS THE TEXT

LEARNING GOALS

We can understand what happens with a pet as we listen to a story.

OBJECTIVES

Retell stories, including key details, and demonstrate understanding of their central message or lesson.

Use illustrations and details in a story to describe its characters and setting.

Identify words and phrases in stories or poems that suggest feelings or appeal to the senses.

Ask and answer questions about key details in a text read aloud or information presented orally or through other media.

LANGUAGE OBJECTIVES

Children will discuss the character's feelings and actions, using feeling and action words.

ELA ACADEMIC LANGUAGE

- fantasy, text, illustrations
- Cognates: *fantasía, texto, ilustraciones*

MATERIALS

Literature Big Book, *Cool Dog, School Dog,* pp. 4–32

Visual Vocabulary Cards

DIGITAL TOOLS

Have children listen to the selection as they follow along to develop comprehension and practice fluency and pronunciation.

Use the online High-Frequency Words Activity for additional support.

Cool Dog, School Dog

Prepare to Read

Build Background *We are going to read a fantasy story about a dog. A fantasy story is a made-up story. It has characters, settings, and events that are not real.* Point to the picture of the dog on the cover. Ask: *What is this animal? It is a dog. Dogs can be pets. A pet is an animal that lives with a family. People like their pets. I have a [cat]. Do you have a pet?* Provide sentence frames: *I do/do not have _____ . I see _____ . This story is a fantasy because _____ .*

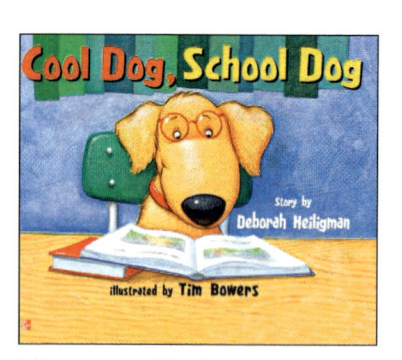

Literature Big Book

Focus on Vocabulary Use the **Visual Vocabulary Cards** to review the oral vocabulary words *care* and *train*. As you read, use gestures and other visual support to clarify important story words, including some phrases used to describe Tinka. For example, explain that *sun dog* is another way to say that Tinka likes to be outside. *Run-and-run-and-run dog* tells us that Tinka likes to run. Use the illustrations to help children understand other ways Tinka is described, such as the picture on the page with the text that calls Tinka *a cry dog*.

Summarize the Text Before reading, say the summary while pointing to the illustrations. *The story is about a pet dog that leaves home to go to school. We'll read about why the dog goes to school and what happens at school.*

Read the Text

Use the Interactive Question-Response Routine to help children understand the story.

Pages 4–13

Page 10 Read the text aloud. *The text says* Tinka is a groan dog, a moan dog, a hates-to-be-alone dog. *Groan and* moan *are sounds people make when they are sad.* Model making each noise for children. *Is Tinka sad?* Yes, Tinka is sad.

Does Tinka like to be alone? How do you know? Discuss with a partner.

Beginning Point to the picture of Tinka. Explain that Tinka is in the house. *Tinka is alone. Does Tinka look happy or sad?* Tinka looks sad. *Does Tinka groan and moan?* Yes, Tinka groans and moans.

Intermediate Have partners respond by describing Tinka's problem. *Does Tinka like to be alone?* No, Tinka hates to be alone. *How does Tinka look?* Tinka looks sad. *What does Tinka do?* Tinka groans and moans.

22 UNIT 1 WEEK 3

WEEK 3

Advanced/Advanced High Have partners give details when describing Tinka's problem. *Why is Tinka sad?* Tinka is sad because she is alone. *How do you know Tinka is sad?* Tinka groans and moans. *What do you think Tinka likes to do?* (Possible answer: Tinka likes to be with people.)

Pages 14–23

Pages 18–19 Read the text aloud. *The text says* Tinka is a vroom dog, a boom dog. Have children repeat the sounds *vroom* and *boom*. *What makes those sounds?* (a car) *Yes, Tinka runs like a fast car.*

What does Tinka do at school? Discuss with a partner.

Beginning Point to the picture of Tinka running. *Tinka is running. Tinka is making papers fall.* Have children repeat. Help partners respond to the question: *What is Tinka doing?* Tinka is running. Tinka is making papers fall.

Intermediate Preteach the following terms: *fast, knocks over, papers,* and *chairs.* Then have children ask and answer with a partner: What happens when Tinka goes to school? Tinka runs fast. Tinka knocks over chairs. Tinka makes papers fall.

Advanced/Advanced High Have partners answer the question about what Tinka does and then add details about people's reactions: *Are the children surprised or mad?* The children are surprised. *How will the teacher feel when she sees Tinka?* The teacher will be mad.

Pages 24–32

Pages 24–25 Read the text aloud. Point to the children. *The children plead for Tinka to come help them read. Plead means "to ask."* Repeat: *plead. The teacher thinks about her answer. What do you think the teacher will say?* (Possible answer: "Yes.")

What do the children want Tinka to do? Discuss with a partner.

Beginning Have children repeat: *books, read, plead.* Help partners respond to the questions. *What do the children have?* The children have books. *What do the children want Tinka to do?* The children want Tinka to read with them.

Intermediate Help partners respond to the questions. *What do the children want Tinka to do?* The children want Tinka to come and read with them. *Why do the children want Tinka to read with them?* They think Tinka can be a good dog.

Advanced/Advanced High Have partners discuss what the children want Tinka to do and then answer these questions with details. *Would you want Tinka to help you read at school?* (Answers will vary.) *Do you think Tinka will be good if she stays?* Yes, Tinka will be good if she sits with the children to read. Tinka likes to be with people.

FORMATIVE ASSESSMENT

▶ STUDENT CHECK-IN

Have partners discuss how Tinka felt and what she did throughout the story. Then have children reflect, using the Check-In Routine.

Independent Time

Oral Language Pair children of mixed proficiencies, and have them take turns asking and answering questions about what is happening in the illustrations on each page of the story. Provide sentence frames for support. Does Tinka look happy or sad? Tinka looks ___. What is Tinka doing? Tinka is ___. How do the children look? The children look ___. How does the teacher look? The teacher looks ___.

ENGLISH LANGUAGE LEARNERS

READING • SHARED READ • ACCESS THE TEXT

LESSONS 1-2

LEARNING GOALS

We can read and understand a fantasy story.

OBJECTIVES

Retell stories, including key details, and demonstrate understanding of their central message or lesson.

Compare and contrast the adventures and experiences of characters in stories.

Ask and answer questions about key details in a text.

LANGUAGE OBJECTIVES

Children will discuss what the characters can do using the words *can* and *can not*.

ELA ACADEMIC LANGUAGE

- fantasy, relevant details
- Cognates: *fantasía, detalles relevantes*

MATERIALS

Reading/Writing Companion, pp. 92–101

Visual Vocabulary Cards

DIGITAL TOOLS

Have children listen to the selection as they follow along to develop comprehension and practice fluency and pronunciation.

Use the additional grammar song.

Grammar Song

"A Pig for Cliff"

Prepare to Read

Build Background *We are going to read a fantasy story. Fantasy stories have characters that could not be real.* Point to and read the title. *We are going to read about Cliff and his pet.* Point to the picture of Cliff on the bike. *This is Cliff. Say* Cliff *with me. This is Cliff's new pet. The new pet is a pig. Say* pig *with me. The pig's name is Slim. Say* Slim *with me.*

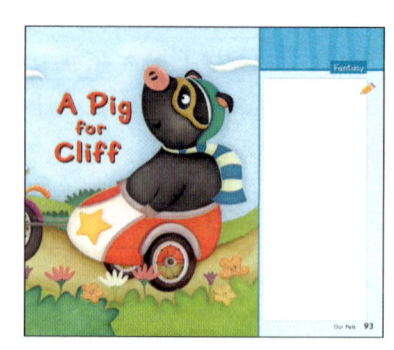

Focus on Vocabulary Use the **Visual Vocabulary Cards** to preteach the high-frequency words *be, come, good,* and *pull* and the oral vocabulary words *care* and *train*. As you read, use gestures and visual support to teach the important story words *swing, house, black, fit, door, break, fall, slip,* and *muddy*. Point to the swing, and say the word *swing*. Have children point to the swing and say *swing. The tree has a swing. What does the tree have?* Have children respond: The tree has a swing.

Summarize the Text Before reading, say the summary and point to the illustrations. *This story tells about Cliff. Cliff has a pet pig. We will read about what happens when Cliff is with his new pet pig.*

Reading/Writing Companion, Lexile 280L

Read the Text

Use the Interactive Question-Response Routine to help children understand the story.

Pages 94–97

Pages 96–97 Read the text aloud as children listen actively. Point to the phrase *can not fit*, and say it aloud for children to repeat. Point to the picture on page 88 and explain: *Slim can not get in the house. Slim can not fit! Slim is too big.* Point to Slim. *Can Slim fit in?* No, Slim can not fit in. Point to page 97. *Cliff is pulling on Slim's leg. Cliff says, "Come out, Slim!" What does Cliff say?* (Come out, Slim!)

COLLABORATE *What problem does Cliff have? Discuss with a partner.*

Beginning Use the pictures to review the words *very big, can not,* and *fit*. Help children respond using the words. *Is Slim very big?* Yes, Slim is very big. *Can Slim fit?* No, Slim can not fit.

Intermediate Help partners give a more specific answer about the problem. *Can Slim go in the house?* No, Slim can not go in the house. *Can Slim fit in the door?* No, Slim can not fit in the door. *Why can't Slim fit in the door?* Slim is too big.

Advanced/Advanced High Help partners elaborate. *What is the problem?* Slim is too big to fit in the door. *What does Cliff do?* Cliff tries to push Slim in the house. Then Cliff tries to pull Slim out.

24 UNIT 1 WEEK 3

WEEK 3

Pages 98–99

Page 98 Read the text aloud, and help children listen actively. Point to the word *Slam! Slam is the sound something heavy can make when it falls.* Provide an example by showing a heavy book. Say: *This book is heavy.* Drop the book. Point to the broken swing. *The swing breaks. Do Cliff and Slim fall? Yes, Cliff and Slim fall.* Read the text again. *What can Cliff not do? Cliff can not sit with Slim. Cliff and Slim are too heavy for the swing.*

What happens when Cliff and Slim sit on the swing? Discuss with a partner.

Beginning Help children respond to the questions. *Where do Cliff and Slim sit? Cliff and Slim sit on the swing. Does the swing break? Yes, the swing breaks. Do Cliff and Slim fall? Yes, Cliff and Slim fall.*

Intermediate Help partners give details in their answers. *Who sits on the swing? Cliff and Slim sit on the swing. What happens? The swing breaks, and Cliff and Slim fall. Why does the swing break? Cliff and Slim are too heavy to sit on the swing.*

Advanced/Advanced High Help partners elaborate on their answers. *The swing breaks when Cliff and Slim sit on it. Cliff and Slim fall off the swing. Cliff and Slim are too heavy.* Then have partners answer this question: *Does Cliff think the swing will break when he sits on it? No, Cliff looks very surprised.*

Pages 100–101

Pages 100–101 Tell children to look for relevant details in the illustrations and text. Read the text aloud. Point to the word *pull,* and say it aloud. Have children repeat. Point to the picture. *This hill is muddy.* Have children repeat: *muddy. Cliff can not go up the muddy hill, but Slim can. Cliff is holding Slim's leg, and Slim is pulling Cliff. Does Slim help Cliff go up the hill? Yes, Slim helps Cliff go up the hill.* Point to and say the word *good.* Have children repeat. *Is Slim a good pet? Yes, Slim is a good pet.*

Why is Slim is a good pet? Discuss with a partner.

Beginning Pantomime a pulling action to review the word *pull.* Say the word *pull,* and have children repeat. Have children point to details in the picture as they respond. *Does Slim help Cliff? Yes, Slim helps Cliff. What does Slim do? Slim pulls Cliff up the hill.*

Intermediate Help partners give details in their answers. *What does Slim do? Slim pulls Cliff up the muddy hill. Why does Cliff say Slim is a good pet? Slim helps Cliff go up the hill.*

Advanced/Advanced High Help partners elaborate on their answers. *Why does Cliff say that Slim is a good pet at the end of the story? Cliff can not go up the muddy hill, but Slim pulls/helps Cliff.*

FORMATIVE ASSESSMENT

STUDENT CHECK-IN

Have partners retell what each character in the story can and cannot do. Then have children reflect, using the Check-In Routine.

Independent Time

Ask and Answer Questions Pair children of mixed proficiencies. Have partners discuss how Slim helps Cliff. Then have children tell how a family member, or even a pet, helps them. Have them take turns asking and answering questions. Then have each pair tell the rest of the group. Provide sentence frames to help them: How does Slim help Cliff? Slim helps Cliff ___. How does your [pet/mom/dad] help you? My ___ helps me ___. [It/She/He] helps me by ___.

ENGLISH LANGUAGE LEARNERS **25**

LESSON 3

READING • ANCHOR TEXT • ACCESS THE TEXT

LEARNING GOALS

We can read and understand a fantasy story.

OBJECTIVES

Ask and answer questions about key details in a text.

With prompting and support, read prose and poetry of appropriate complexity for grade 1.

Build on others' talk in conversations by responding to the comments of others through multiple exchanges.

LANGUAGE OBJECTIVES

Children will narrate, or tell, what the characters in the story do, using words of movement and key vocabulary.

ELA ACADEMIC LANGUAGE

- fantasy, illustration, author
- Cognates: *fantasía, ilustración, autor*

MATERIALS

Literature Anthology, pp. 48–61

Visual Vocabulary Cards

DIGITAL TOOLS

MULTIMODAL

Have children listen to the selection as they follow along to develop comprehension and practice fluency and pronunciation.

Use the online High-Frequency Words Activity for additional support.

Flip

Prepare to Read

Build Background *We are going to read a story about a special pet.* Show the picture on pages 50–51, and invite children to tell what they see. Point to the *girl, backpack, dinosaur,* and *school.* Say the words, and have children repeat. Point to the dinosaur again. *The special pet is a dinosaur named Flip. Can a dinosaur be a pet in real life? No. I know this story is a fantasy because a dinosaur cannot be a pet in real life. In this story, the pet dinosaur walks to school with a girl.* Provide sentence frames: The girl owns the _____ . The girl walks to _____ .

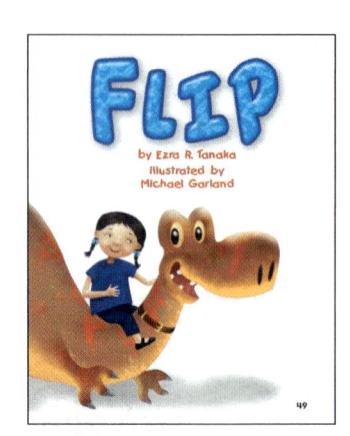

Literature Anthology, Lexile 30L

Focus on Vocabulary Use the **Visual Vocabulary Cards** to review the high-frequency words *be, come, good,* and *pull* and the oral language vocabulary words *care, train, companion, groom,* and *popular.* As you read, teach important story words, such as *class,* using gestures and pantomime. *In the story, Flip and the girl go to class. Class is the room at school, or classroom, where you learn.* Pantomime *listening, clapping, reaching,* and being *mad.* For *plan,* tap your head and look thoughtful, saying *I have a plan.*

Summarize the Text Before reading, say the summary while pointing to the illustrations. *The story is about a pet dinosaur named Flip. Flip's owner is a girl. Flip gets into the girl's school. Flip surprises the kids and the teacher.*

Read the Text

Use the Interactive Question-Response Routine to help children understand the story.

Pages 50–55

Pages 54–55 Read the text. *Pets can not go to school, but Flip gets in.* Point to the picture on page 54. *Now Flip and the girl are in class. The girl thinks that she can get into trouble. You can get into trouble in school if you do something that makes the teacher mad.* Point to the sentence *Be good, Flip!* and have children repeat it. *The girl tells Flip to be good. Do you think Flip listens to the girl?* No, Flip does <u>not</u> listen. Point to page 55. *Look at the illustration. Is Flip painting? Yes, Flip is <u>painting</u>. What are the kids doing?* The kids are painting too. Point to the picture of the mess and say: *Flip is making a mess! Say mess. Are the kids making a mess too?* (yes) *Are the children having fun with Flip?* (yes)

Why does the girl tell Flip to be good? Discuss with a partner.

26 UNIT 1 WEEK 3

WEEK 3

Beginning Help children respond. *Look at the words. What does the girl tell Flip? "Be good." Should Flip be in school?* (no) *Look at the picture on page 55. Does Flip listen?* No, Flip does not listen. *Do Flip and the kids make a mess?* Yes, Flip and the kids make a mess.

Intermediate Help partners ask and answer questions. *Why does the girl tell Flip to be good?* Flip should not be in school. *Look at the picture on page 55. Does Flip listen?* No, Flip does not listen. Flip and the kids make a mess.

Advanced/Advanced High Help partners ask and answer questions with details. *Why does the girl tell Flip to be good?* Flip should not be in school, and Flip does not know how to act in class/school. *What does the picture on page 55 tell you?* Flip and the kids have fun making a mess with paint.

Pages 56–59

Pages 58–59 Read the text. Point to the picture on page 58. *Miss Black has a problem. Miss Black wants to put a word card on the board.* Pantomime reaching as you say: *Can Miss Black reach the top?* No, Miss Black can not reach the top. Point to and reread page 59. *What do you think Flip's plan is?* (Answers will vary. Example: Flip is tall. Flip will help Miss Black.)

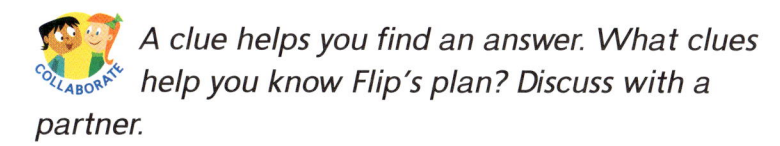

A clue helps you find an answer. What clues help you know Flip's plan? Discuss with a partner.

Beginning Point to page 59. *The words say Flip has a plan. What does Flip see?* Flip sees Miss Black. *Can Miss Black reach the top?* No, Miss Black can not reach the top. *Is Flip tall?* Yes, Flip is tall. *What can Flip do?* Flip can reach.

Intermediate Point to the words on page 59. Help partners respond. *What problem does Flip see?* Miss Black can not reach the top. *Why can Flip help?* Flip is tall. Flip can help Miss Black reach the top.

Advanced/Advanced High Help partners elaborate. Flip sees that Miss Black can not reach the top of the board. This is a problem. Flip knows he is taller than Miss Black and can help Miss Black reach.

Pages 60–61

Pages 60–61 Read the text. *Flip carries Miss Black to the board. Miss Black can reach the top. What does the class do?* The class claps. *When Flip made a mess, the teacher was mad. Now, Miss Black tells the kids that Flip can come back. Miss Black looks happy. The author says Flip is glad. Glad is another word for happy. Is Flip happy too?* Yes, Flip is happy too.

Look at the author's words. Why does Miss Black change her mind? Discuss with a partner.

Beginning Help children respond. *Does Flip help Miss Black?* Yes, Flip helps Miss Black reach the top. *Is Miss Black mad?* No, Miss Black is not mad. *What does Miss Black say?* Miss Black says Flip can come back.

Intermediate Point to the words on page 61. Help partners respond. *What do the kids ask?* "Can Flip come back?" *What does Miss Black say?* Flip can come back. *Why does Miss Black change her mind?* She is happy that Flip helps her.

Advanced/Advanced High Have partners respond with details. *How is Miss Black different now?* Miss Black is not mad at Flip. *What words help you know she changes her mind?* (Flip can.) *Why does Miss Black change her mind?* Flip helps Miss Black reach the top of the board.

FORMATIVE ASSESSMENT

▶ STUDENT CHECK-IN

Have partners retell one good thing and one bad thing that Flip does in the classroom. Then have children reflect, using the Check-In Routine.

Independent Time

Draw and Write Pair children of mixed proficiencies. Have them each draw their pet or a pet they would like to have. Have partners describe their pets to each other and then write a sentence or two about their pets. Provide sentence frames for support: The pet I like is ___. This pet ___. Then have children present their pet pictures to a classmate.

ENGLISH LANGUAGE LEARNERS 27

LESSONS 4-5

READING • LEVELED READER • ACCESS THE TEXT

LEARNING GOALS

We can visualize what happens at a pet show as we read a story.

OBJECTIVES

Retell stories, including key details, and demonstrate understanding of their central message or lesson.

Use illustrations and details in a story to describe its characters, setting, or events.

Describe people, places, things, and events with relevant details, expressing ideas and feelings clearly.

LANGUAGE OBJECTIVES

Children will discuss what the characters have and can do, using key vocabulary.

ELA ACADEMIC LANGUAGE

- *visualize*
- Cognate: *visualizar*

MATERIALS

ELL Leveled Reader: *Pet Show*

Online Differentiated Texts, "Pet at School"

Online ELL Visual Vocabulary Cards

DIGITAL TOOLS

Have children listen to the selection as they follow along to develop comprehension and practice fluency and pronunciation.
Use Graphic Organizer 2: Characters, Setting, Events to enhance the lesson.

Pet Show

Prepare to Read

Build Background

- Remind children of the Essential Question. *Let's read to find out what makes pets special. This is a fantasy story with animal characters.* Encourage children to ask for help when they do not understand a word or phrase.

- Point to and read aloud the title, and have children repeat. Ask: *What is the title?* Have children point to it. Repeat the routine with the author's name. Point to the illustrations to name pets, things, and actions; for example: *This is a [bike]. This is a [monkey]. The [monkey rides a bike].*

Focus on Vocabulary Use **ELL Visual Vocabulary Cards** to preteach the words *perform* and *talent*. As you read, use gestures or visuals to teach important story words, such as *be careful, ends, all,* and *win*.

Lexile 20L

Read the Text

Use the Interactive Question-Response Routine to help children understand the story.

Pages 2–5

Read pages 2–3 as children follow along. Point to and say *teacher, kids, excited, plan, talent show, iguana,* and *bird* for children to repeat. Repeat for pages 4–5.

Beginning Help partners point to the pictures. *Do the kids look excited?* Yes, the kids look excited. *What do the kids have?* The kids have pets.

Intermediate *How do the kids look?* The kids look excited. *What are the kids planning?* The kids are planning a talent show for pets.

Advanced/Advanced High *What are the kids talking about?* The kids are making plans for a pet talent show. *Why are the kids excited?* The kids are excited because their pets can be in the talent show.

Pages 6–9

Main Story Elements: Characters, Setting, Events Read as children follow along. Ask guiding questions as you point to the pets. *Who are they?* (pets) *What do they do?* (bird sings, iguana plays the drums) *What event is this?* (the pet talent show) Point to the plug. *The drums are loud.* Say *loud. What does the llama do?* The llama pulls the plug. Repeat the routine for pages 8–9.

Intermediate Have partners discuss: *Are the drums loud?* Yes, the drums are loud. *What does the llama do?* The llama pulls the plug.

28 UNIT 1 WEEK 3

WEEK 3

Advanced/Advanced High *Are the drums too loud?* (yes) *How do you know?* The kids cover their ears. The llama pulls the plug.

Pages 10–12

Visualize Read pages 10–11, and help children visualize: *I can close my eyes and picture the mouse performing while the class claps.*

Beginning *Do the kids clap?* Yes, the kids clap. *Do all the pets win?* Yes, all the pets win. *What do the pets have?* They have ribbons.

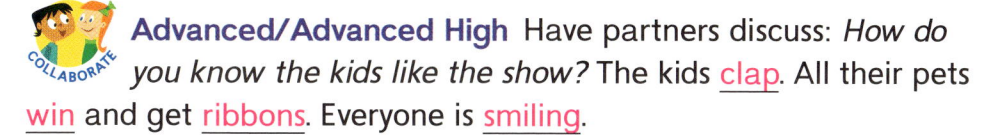

Advanced/Advanced High Have partners discuss: *How do you know the kids like the show?* The kids clap. All their pets win and get ribbons. Everyone is smiling.

Respond to Reading Have partners work together to retell the story and respond to the questions on page 12.

Focus on Fluency

Model reading pages 8–9, and have children repeat. For more practice, record children reading the passage, and then have them select the best recording.

Paired Read: "Love That Llama"

Make Connections: Write About It

Echo-read each page with children. Discuss llamas. *What are llamas like?* Llamas are smart/shy. Help children make connections between texts using the question on page 15: Pet llamas are shy.

Leveled Reader

Build Knowledge: Make Connections

Talk About the Text Have partners discuss how the pets in the texts are special.

Write About the Text Have students add their ideas to the Build Knowledge pages of their reader's notebooks.

Self-Selected Reading

Help children choose a fiction selection from the online **Leveled Reader Library** or read the **Differentiated Text:** "Pet at School."

FOCUS ON SCIENCE

Children can extend their knowledge of what pets need by completing the science activity on page 16. **STEM**

LITERATURE CIRCLES

Lead children in conducting a literature circle using the Thinkmark questions to guide the discussion. You may wish to discuss what children have learned about pets from both selections in the **Leveled Reader**.

FORMATIVE ASSESSMENT

STUDENT CHECK-IN

Have partners share their Respond to Reading. Have children reflect, using the Check-In Routine.

LEVEL UP

IF children can read *Pet Show* **ELL Level** with fluency and correctly answer the Respond to Reading questions,

THEN tell children they will read a more detailed version of the selection.

- Use pages 2–4 of *Pet Show* **On Level** to model using Teaching Poster 26 to identify key details.
- Have children read the selection, checking their comprehension by using the graphic organizer.

ENGLISH LANGUAGE LEARNERS

LESSONS 1-5

WRITING

MODELED WRITING

LESSON 1

LEARNING GOAL
We can write a sentence using details to tell about our ideas.

OBJECTIVES
With guidance and support from adults, focus on a topic.

LANGUAGE OBJECTIVES
Children will inform by writing a complete sentence using the verb *like*.

ELA ACADEMIC LANGUAGE
- details
- Cognate: *detalles*

Writing Practice Review the sample on p. 102 of the **Reading/Writing Companion**. Guide children to analyze the first part of the sentence using the Actor/Action Routine: *Who is the actor?* (I) *What is the action?* (like dogs) Repeat for the last part of the sentence. Point out that the word *because* links the two parts of the sentence. Then read the prompt on p. 103, and ask children to answer it as a group, using the routine. Finally, ask children to write their own sentence, providing one detail about the pet.

Beginning *What pet would you like? What do you like about that animal?* I like hamsters. Hamsters are soft.

Intermediate Have partners ask questions to elicit each part of the sentence: *What pet would you like? Why?* Provide a sentence frame.

Advanced/Advanced High Challenge children to include more than one descriptive detail about the pet they chose.

FORMATIVE ASSESSMENT ▶ **STUDENT CHECK-IN** Partners share their sentences. Ask children to reflect, using the Check-In Routine.

INTERACTIVE WRITING

LESSON 2

LEARNING GOALS
We can read and write about a Student Model.

OBJECTIVES
Write narratives in which they include some details.

LANGUAGE OBJECTIVES
Children will discuss the Student Model and inform by writing sentences using descriptive details.

ELA ACADEMIC LANGUAGE
- details
- Cognate: *detalles*

Analyze the Student Model Have children finger point as they choral read the Student Model on page 108 of the **Reading/Writing Companion**. Use the Actor/Action Routine to review the sentences. Then have children raise their hands when they hear a statement. Review descriptive details. *What does Marco tell us about Cliff's pet dog?* (He's new; he's furry; his name is Max.) Then help children complete page 109.

Beginning Help children identify Word Bank words in the last sentence.

Intermediate Have partners use this sentence frame to tell how Marco used details: Marco used the words new and furry to describe Max.

Advanced/Advanced High *What words did Marco use to describe his new pet?* Challenge children to write about Marco's writing, using their own sentences.

FORMATIVE ASSESSMENT ▶ **STUDENT CHECK-IN** Partners share their responses. Ask children to reflect, using the Check-In Routine.

WEEK 3

INDEPENDENT WRITING

LESSONS 3-4

LEARNING GOALS
We can respond to a fantasy story by extending the story.

OBJECTIVES
Write narratives in which they recount events in sequence.

LANGUAGE OBJECTIVES
Children will narrate by writing a sentence using verbs.

ELA ACADEMIC LANGUAGE
- *evidence*
- Cognate: *evidencia*

Find Text Evidence Use the Independent Writing Routine. Help children orally retell the anchor text using text evidence. Ask questions, such as, *What kind of pet is Flip?* (a dinosaur) *Where does Flip go?* (school/class) Then read the prompt on p. 114 of the **Reading/Writing Companion:** *Think about Flip. Write what might happen the next day when Flip goes to school.* We need to think about what Flip did on his first day of school.

Write a Response Distribute **My Writing Outline 3** to children. Then work with children to fill out the outline. Finally, have children complete p. 114 using the sentences from their outlines.

Writing Checklist Read the checklist with children, and have them check for these items in their writing.

Beginning *What do you have at the beginning of each sentence?* (a capital letter)

Intermediate Encourage children to add descriptive details.

Advanced/Advanced High Have partners identify where they used each checklist item in their writing.

FORMATIVE ASSESSMENT → **STUDENT CHECK-IN** Partners share their sentences from My Writing Outline. Ask children to reflect, using the Check-In Routine.

SELF-SELECTED WRITING

LESSON 5

LEARNING GOALS
We can revise our writing.

OBJECTIVES
Produce and expand complete simple interrogative sentences.

LANGUAGE OBJECTIVE
Children will inquire about their writing by checking that statements and questions are written correctly.

ELA ACADEMIC LANGUAGE
- *capitalization, punctuation*
- Cognates: *capitalización, puntuación*

Work with children to revise the group writing activity. Read the sentences, pointing to each word as you read. Stop to ask questions, such as, *Is this a statement or a question? How do you know?* If needed, write an incorrect statement or question, and correct it with children. Then have partners revise their writing together before they publish it.

For support with grammar and statements and questions, refer to the **Language Transfers Handbook,** and review **Language Development Cards** 21A and 22A.

FORMATIVE ASSESSMENT → **STUDENT CHECK-IN** Partners identify revisions they made. Ask children to reflect, using the **Check-In Routine.**

ENGLISH LANGUAGE LEARNERS 31

LESSONS 1-2

READING • LITERATURE BIG BOOK • ACCESS THE TEXT

LEARNING GOALS

We can understand how friends are around the world.

OBJECTIVES

Retell stories, including key details, and demonstrate understanding of their central message or lesson.

Ask and answer questions about key details in a text.

Ask and answer questions about what a speaker says in order to gather additional information or clarify something that is not understood.

Describe people, places, things, and events with relevant details, expressing ideas and feelings clearly.

LANGUAGE OBJECTIVES

Children will inform, or give information, about what friends do around the world, using key vocabulary and simple sentences.

ELA ACADEMIC LANGUAGE

- photographs
- Cognate: *fotografías*

MATERIALS

Literature Big Book, *Friends All Around*, pp. 2–24

Visual Vocabulary Cards

DIGITAL TOOLS

Have children listen to the selection as they follow along to develop comprehension and practice fluency and pronunciation.

Use the online High-Frequency Words Activity for additional support.

Friends All Around

Prepare to Read

Build Background *We are going to read a text about friends.* Show the picture of friends on the cover. Say: *The friends are in a circle. The friends are standing on a map. Are the friends smiling? Yes. Friends like to be together.* Model for children. *I dance with friends.* Have children repeat. Then have children talk about what they do with friends. *What do you do with your friends?* Provide sentence frames: I play with _____ . I _____ books with friends.

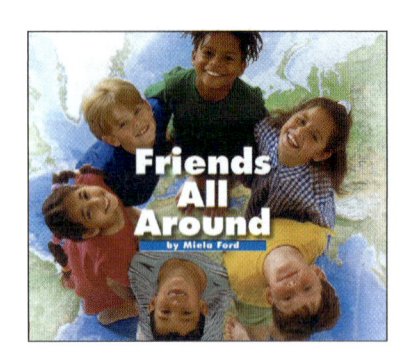

Literature Big Book

Focus on Vocabulary Use the **Visual Vocabulary Cards** to review the oral vocabulary words *cooperate* and *relationship*. As you read, use gestures and other visual support to clarify important story words, such as *share* and *ride*. Say: *Friends can share.* Point to *share* in the text. Provide an example: *Some friends share toys. What do you share with friends?* I share books with friends.

Summarize the Text Before reading, say the summary while pointing to the photos: *We are going to read about friends in many parts of the world. We'll read about what friends do together. We'll read about how friends get along too.*

Read the Text

Use the Interactive Question-Response Routine to help children understand the text.

Pages 2–15

Pages 4–5 Read the text aloud. Point to and read *together* and *each other*. Explain that these words have the same meaning: *with or as a group.* Point to the photo of the children planting. *Some friends are learning to plant together. What are the friends planting?* (a tree) Point to the photo of the girls. *Some friends teach each other. This girl teaches her friend about science.* Point to the larger photo. *The man shows the boy how he makes things. What do friends teach you?* (Answers will vary. Possible answer: Friends teach me to play a game.)

What do some friends do with each other? Discuss with a partner.

Beginning Point to the photo of the children on page 4. *Are the friends learning together?* Yes, the friends are learning together. *What are the friends learning?* The friends are learning to plant. Point to the photo of the girls on page 5. *Can the friends teach each other?* Yes, the friends can teach each other.

32 UNIT 1 WEEK 4

WEEK 4

Intermediate Have children point to the pictures as they respond. *What do the friends on page 4 do together?* The friends learn to plant a tree. *What do the friends on page 5 do?* One friend teaches another friend at school.

Advanced/Advanced High Have partners point to the photos as they give details. *What do the friends learn together and teach each other?* The friends learn to plant a tree together. The girl teaches her friend science. *What else can friends teach each other?* (Answers will vary. Possible answer: Friends can teach each other to make something.)

Pages 16–21

Page 16 Read the text aloud. Help children use visual support to enhance their understanding. Point to the Spain photo. *The girl jumps with a rope. Her friends hold the rope.* Point to the Greenland photo. *These friends jump with a rope too. Do you jump with a rope?* (Answers will vary.)

How do some friends jump? Discuss with a partner.

Beginning Point to the Greenland photo. *Do the friends have a rope?* Yes, the friends have a rope. *What are the friends doing with the rope?* The friends are jumping with the rope.

Intermediate Point to the photos on page 16. *What are the friends in both photographs doing?* The friends are jumping with a rope.

Advanced/Advanced High Have partners compare the photos on page 16. *How many friends jump with a rope in each photograph?* One friend jumps in Spain, but two friends jump in Greenland. *Does it look warm or cold in Spain?* It looks warm in Spain. *How does it look in Greenland?* It looks cold in Greenland.

Pages 22–24

Pages 22–23 Read the text aloud. Use texts to help children learn word meanings. Point to the phrase *get along*, and say it aloud for children to repeat. *Friends get along when they are happy together.*

Point to *argue* on page 24, and say it aloud for children to repeat. *Sometimes friends argue. They are not happy together. They don't like the same things.* Point to the photo. *Look at the children's faces. Do the friends get along?* (no)

When do friends get along, and when do friends argue? Discuss with a partner.

Beginning Help children respond to the questions. *When do friends get along?* Friends get along when they are happy together. *When do friends argue?* Friends argue when they are not happy together.

Intermediate Help partners generate ideas about getting along and arguing. *When do you and your friends get along?* We get along when we play/read together. *When do you and your friends argue?* We argue when we do not want to play/read the same game/book.

Advanced/Advanced High Have partners give details about when they get along and when they argue with a friend. (Answers will vary. Possible answer: My friend and I get along when we swing on the swings together. We argue when I want to run and my friend wants to play with a ball.)

FORMATIVE ASSESSMENT

STUDENT CHECK-IN

Have partners discuss activities from the text. Then have children reflect, using the Check-In Routine.

Independent Time

Write Pair children of mixed proficiencies, and have them describe what they and a friend do together. Provide sentence frames to help them: My friend and I ___ together. My friend and I ___ too. Allow them to write what they can. Help them translate or elaborate. Then have children present their sentences to partners.

READING • SHARED READ • ACCESS THE TEXT

LESSONS 1-2

LEARNING GOALS

We can read and understand a nonfiction text.

OBJECTIVES

Ask and answer questions about key details in a text.

Use the illustrations and details in a text to describe its key ideas.

Describe people, places, things, and events with relevant details, expressing ideas and feelings clearly.

LANGUAGE OBJECTIVES

Children will discuss what kids do to have fun, using key vocabulary and simple sentences.

ELA ACADEMIC LANGUAGE

- details, retell
- Cognate: *detalles*

MATERIALS

Reading/Writing Companion, pp. 126–135

Visual Vocabulary Cards

DIGITAL TOOLS

Have children listen to the selection as they follow along to develop comprehension and practice fluency and pronunciation.

Use the additional grammar video.

Grammar Video

"Toss! Kick! Hop!"

Prepare to Read

Build Background Read aloud the Essential Question. Have children share what they do together with friends. Use the photos throughout the selection to generate ideas. Point to and read the title. *We are going to read about kids playing.* Point to the photo on the opening page spread. *These kids are friends. The friends are playing a game together. Say* game *with me.* The game is called hopscotch. *On the other pages, we will see more ways friends play together.*

Reading/Writing Companion, Lexile 290L

Focus on Vocabulary Use the **Visual Vocabulary Cards** to preteach the high-frequency words *fun, make, they,* and *too* and the oral language vocabulary words *cooperate, relationship, deliver, chore,* and *collect.* As you read, use gestures and visual support to teach important words from the text, such as *friends, zip, toss, beach ball, soccer ball, kick, inside, blocks, doll, outside, hop,* and *flop.* Use the following routine for each new word: Point to the kids running on page 129. Say the word *zip*. Have children point to the photo and repeat the word. *The friends zip.* Zip *means "run fast." What do the friends do?* Have children respond: The friends zip.

Summarize the Text Before reading, say the summary, and point to the photos. *This text tells how friends have fun together.*

Read the Text

Use the Interactive Question-Response Routine to help children understand the text.

Pages 126–131

Pages 130–131 Read the text aloud as children follow. Point to the word *toss* on page 130. *The word* toss *means "throw."* Provide an example: *I toss the ball,* and demonstrate the action. Point to the kids in the photo, and ask: *Do the kids toss balls?* Yes, the kids toss balls. Repeat this routine for *kick* on page 131. Point out the word *too.* Explain that *too* means another activity. Have children repeat: *The kids toss. The kids kick too.* Help children name the colors they see on the soccer ball. (red, yellow, green, black, white)

How do the friends play together? Discuss with a partner.

Beginning Point to the photo of the kids tossing balls, and say: *The kids toss.* Have children repeat. Help partners respond: *Do the kids toss?* Yes, the kids toss. Repeat the routine for *kick,* helping partners respond: *Do the kids kick too?* Yes, the kids kick too.

34 UNIT 1 WEEK 4

WEEK 4

Intermediate Help partners give more specific answers as they point to the photos. *Do the kids toss?* Yes, the kids toss. *What do the kids toss?* The kids toss balls. *What do the kids on page 111 do?* The kids kick a ball too.

Advanced/Advanced High Help partners add details. Point to the beach balls in the photo. *What do the kids toss?* The kids toss beach balls. Point to page 111. *What do these kids do?* The kids kick a soccer ball too. *How is the soccer ball like the beach balls?* The soccer ball has many colors.

Pages 132–133

Pages 132–133 Read the text. Point to page 132. *The friends are having fun inside. Look at details in the picture. What do you see?* (blocks) *The friends are making a house out of blocks. What do you make out of blocks?* (Answers will vary. Example: tall buildings) Point to page 133. *The friends are making dolls out of socks and other items.* Point and say for children to repeat: *yarn, glue, socks, doll.* Ask: *What do the friends make?* The friends make dolls.

How do the friends have fun inside? Discuss with a partner.

Beginning Point to page 132, and have children respond: *Do the kids have blocks?* Yes, the kids have blocks. *Do the kids make a house?* Yes, the kids make a house. Point to the photo on page 133. *Do the kids make dolls?* Yes, the kids make dolls.

Intermediate Provide sentence frames. Have partners ask and answer: What do the three kids do together? The kids make dolls together. What do the two kids do? The kids make a block house.

Advanced/Advanced High Have partners ask and answer questions about the photos. What do the kids do/make? Some kids make a house out of blocks. Some kids make dolls out of socks and yarn.

Pages 134–135

Page 134 Read the text aloud, and have children follow along. Point to and say the words *hop* and *flop* for children to repeat. Point to the photo. *The friends are outside. Two kids are hopping. One kid is flopping, or falling. The kids are in big sacks.* Say *sacks. What do the kids do in the sacks?* The kids hop and flop.

How do the friends have fun outside? Discuss with a partner.

Beginning Have partners practice asking the question by repeating it after you: *How do the friends have fun outside?* Help partners respond: The friends hop in sacks. One friend flops. Do the friends have fun? Yes, the friends have fun. Have partners reverse roles for asking and answering.

Intermediate Help partners act the words *hop* and *flop. Use the pictures to retell how the friends have fun.* The friends have fun outside. They hop in sacks. One friend flops in his sack. The friends have fun together.

Advanced/Advanced High Have partners elaborate on their answers as they retell what the friends do. The friends hop in sacks on the grass. One kid flops to the ground. The friends all have fun together.

FORMATIVE ASSESSMENT

▶ STUDENT CHECK-IN

Have partners retell how the kids in the text like to have fun. Then have children reflect, using the Check-In Routine.

Independent Time

Ask and Answer Questions Pair children of mixed proficiencies. Have partners review and discuss the activities the friends in the story do together. Have partners take turns asking and answering questions while pointing to the pictures. Use **Oral Language Sentence Frames,** page 2, Asking and Answering Questions, to support children during this activity. Guide children to ask and answer questions about the friends in the text, using the sentence frames.

ENGLISH LANGUAGE LEARNERS **35**

LESSON 3

READING • ANCHOR TEXT • ACCESS THE TEXT

LEARNING GOALS

We can read and understand a nonfiction text.

OBJECTIVES

Use the illustrations and details in a text to describe its key ideas.

Ask and answer questions about key details in a text.

With prompting and support, read informational texts appropriately complex for grade 1.

Distinguish between information provided by pictures or other illustrations and information provided by the words in a text.

LANGUAGE OBJECTIVES

Children will explain what the two friends in the text do, using simple sentences and words of movement.

ELA ACADEMIC LANGUAGE

- photograph, author, relevant details
- Congnates: *fotografía, autor, detalles relevantes*

MATERIALS

Literature Anthology, pp. 68–81

Visual Vocabulary Cards

DIGITAL TOOLS

MULTIMODAL

Have children listen to the selection as they follow along to develop comprehension and practice fluency and pronunciation.

Use the online High-Frequency Words Activity for additional support.

Friends

Prepare to Read

Build Background *We are going to read a nonfiction text about two friends.* Show the picture on the title page, and invite children to tell what they see. Point to the girls, park, ball, and box. Say the words, and have children repeat. Then point to the girl with the ball. *This is Jill. What does Jill have? Jill has a ball.* Point to the other girl. *This is Pam. Pam has a box. Say* box. *The friends want to have fun together. They want to play games. Say* game. *A game is something you play or have fun doing. Do you like to play games with a friend?* Model answering, and have children repeat: *Yes, I like to play games with a friend.*

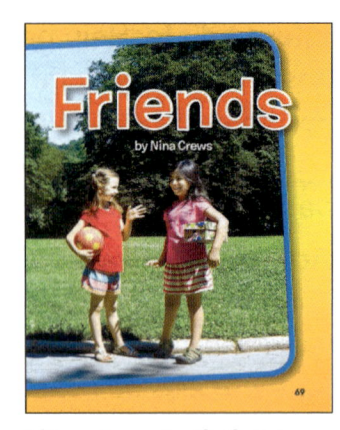

Literature Anthology, Lexile 60L

Focus on Vocabulary Use the **Visual Vocabulary Cards** to review the high-frequency words *fun, make, they,* and *too* and the oral language vocabulary words *cooperate, relationship, deliver, chore,* and *collect.* As you read, teach important words from the text, such as *play catch, play tag, quick, not as quick as,* and *plan,* using gestures and pantomime.

Summarize the Text Before reading, say the summary while pointing to the photographs. *The story tells about two friends named Pam and Jill. The friends play together.*

Read the Text

Use the Interactive Question-Response Routine to help children understand the text.

Pages 70–71

Pages 70–71 *Read the text. Look at page 70. The text says Pam and Jill are friends. I see in the photograph that Pam and Jill are playing together. The author says they play together a lot.* A lot *means "many times." Say* a lot. *Do you play with your friend a lot? Yes, I play with my friend* a lot. *I ask myself a question: What do Pam and Jill play? The photograph shows they are playing catch. The author says Pam and Jill toss a ball. When friends play catch, they toss a ball.*

How do you know what friends can do? How do the author's words help you? Discuss with a partner.

Beginning Point to the word *friends* on page 70. Help children respond: *Are Pam and Jill friends? Yes, Pam and Jill are* friends. Point to the photograph. *Do the friends play catch? Yes, the friends* play *catch. What do the friends toss? They toss a* ball.

36 UNIT 1 WEEK 4

WEEK 4

Intermediate Point to the first sentence on page 70. *What relevant detail do these words give about Pam and Jill?* Pam and Jill are friends. *Point to the second sentence. What does this text say about Pam and Jill?* They play a lot. *Point to the photo. The photo shows what they can play. What can the friends play together?* They can play catch.

Advanced/Advanced High Have partners ask and answer questions. *What is a relevant detail about Pam and Jill?* Pam and Jill are friends. *What do they do when they are together?* They play a lot. *What does the photo show they can do together?* (They can play catch.)

Pages 74–75

Pages 74–75 Read the text. Have children look for relevant details in the text and photos. Point to the photos. *Pam looks happy playing tag. Does Jill look happy?* (no) *Pam and Jill are friends, but they are different. Repeat: different. The text says Jill is not as quick as Pam. It says Jill is hot too. Does Jill like tag?* (no)

What do the photographs show you about Pam and Jill? Discuss with a partner.

Beginning Have children use the photos to confirm their understanding. *Is Pam smiling?* Yes, Pam is smiling. *Does Pam like tag?* Yes, Pam likes tag. *Is Jill smiling?* No, Jill is not smiling. *Is Jill quick?* No, Jill is not quick. *Does Jill like tag?* No, Jill does not like tag.

Intermediate Have partners use the photos to help them ask and answer questions: *What does Pam like?* Pam likes tag. *Does Jill like tag?* No, Jill does not like tag. *Why does Jill not like tag?* Jill is hot and not quick.

Advanced/Advanced High Help partners extend the discussion, using the photos. *Do you think Jill will stop playing tag?* Yes, Jill will stop playing tag. *Why?* Jill is hot, and she is not quick. *What do you think the friends will do?* (Answers will vary. Possible response: They will play a different game.)

Pages 76–79

Pages 78–79 Read the text. *Pam uses her plan. She brings a toy dog and a doll.* Point to and have children repeat: *dog, doll. Now Jill does not need to play tag. The friends can play something else. Something else means "a new thing." The text says Pam and Jill make up a game. When you make up a game, you think of a new game. Do you make up games with your friends?* (Possible response: yes)

Why does Pam have something else to do? Discuss with a partner.

Beginning Help children with responses. *Does Pam help Jill be happy?* (yes) *How does Pam help Jill?* Pam brings a dog and a doll. *What do Pam and Jill do together?* They make up a game.

Intermediate Help partners respond to the questions with details. *What does Pam bring?* Pam brings a dog and a doll. *What do Pam and Jill do?* They make up a game. *How does this help Jill?* Jill can stop playing tag.

Advanced/Advanced High Have partners work together to retell relevant details. Provide sentence frames: Pam and Jill make up a new game together. They use a dog and a doll from Pam's box. Pam's plan helps Jill not to be sad. I know Pam and Jill are having fun together because they are smiling.

FORMATIVE ASSESSMENT

STUDENT CHECK-IN

Have partners retell how Pam and Jill have fun together. Then have children reflect, using the Check-In Routine.

Independent Time

Oral Language Select a spread from *Friends,* and pair children of mixed proficiencies. Have partners take turns saying whether they like or do not like the activity on the spread and explain why they like/do not like it. Provide sentence frames for support. Do you like to ___? Yes/No, I like/do not like to ___. Have pairs retell to the group what their partner said. [Name] likes/does not like ___.

ENGLISH LANGUAGE LEARNERS **37**

LESSONS 4-5

READING • LEVELED READER • ACCESS THE TEXT

LEARNING GOALS

We can ask and answer questions about what friends can do together as we read a nonfiction text.

OBJECTIVES

Identify the main topic and retell key details of a text.

Ask and answer questions about key details in a text.

Describe people, places, things, and events with relevant details, expressing ideas and feelings clearly.

Produce complete sentences when appropriate to task and situation.

LANGUAGE OBJECTIVES

Children will discuss activities friends can do together, using the verbs *can, have, are,* and *like.*

ELA ACADEMIC LANGUAGE

- topic, relevant details
- Cognate: *detalles revelantes*

MATERIALS

ELL Leveled Reader: *Friends Are Fun*

Online Differentiated Texts, "Kids Have Fun!"

Online ELL Visual Vocabulary Cards

DIGITAL TOOLS

Have children listen to the selection as they follow along to develop comprehension and practice fluency and pronunciation. Use Graphic Organizer 3: Topic and Relevant Details.

Friends Are Fun

Prepare to Read

Build Background

- Remind children of the Essential Question. *Let's read to see what friends do together.* Encourage children to ask for help when they do not understand a word or phrase.

- Point to and read aloud the title, and have children repeat. Ask: *What is the title?* Have children point to it. Repeat with the author's name. Point to the photos in the **Leveled Reader** to name things and actions. For example: *This is [a game]. What can you do with [a game]?*

Lexile 100L

Focus on Vocabulary Use the **ELL Visual Vocabulary Cards** to preteach the words *friendship* and *together.* As you read, use gestures or visuals to teach important words from the text, such as *fun, help, make, share, big, little,* and *a lot of.* Display the cover. Say the word *fun,* and have children repeat. *The friends have fun. They hop in sacks. How do you have fun with friends? I [run] with friends.*

Read the Text

Use the Interactive Question-Response Routine to help children understand the text.

Pages 2–3

Ask and Answer Questions Read pages 2–3. Help children ask and answer questions about page 2: *Why are friends fun? Friends can run.*

Beginning Help partners point as they respond. *What are the friends doing?* They are running. *What can friends do?* Friends can run/hop.

Intermediate Help partners respond: *What can friends do?* They can run and hop. *What do friends like to do?* They like to play.

Advanced/Advanced High *What can friends do on the grass?* They can run and hop. *Why are friends fun?* They can run and hop together. They like to play.

Pages 4–9

Topic and Relevant Details Read pages 4–5. Ask guiding questions. *What is the topic of the text?* The topic of the text is fun things we can do with friends. *What is this?* (sand) *What are they making?* (a fort) *What is a relevant detail from the text?* Friends can make a fort with sand. Repeat the routine with other details.

Intermediate *What can friends do?* They can help you ride a bike. They can make a sand fort too.

38 UNIT 1 WEEK 4

WEEK 4

Advanced/Advanced High Have partners discuss each spread. Friends can help you <u>ride</u> a <u>bike</u> and <u>make</u> a sand <u>fort</u>.

Pages 10–12

Read pages 10–11 as children follow along. Point to the pictures, and say *cook* and *draw*. Have children repeat.

Beginning Help partners respond: *Do friends cook? Yes, friends <u>cook</u>. Do they have a lot of fun?* (yes) Can friends draw? Yes, they can <u>draw</u>.

Intermediate *Can the friends draw? Yes, they <u>can draw</u>. What can the friends draw?* They can draw a <u>flag</u>.

Respond to Reading Have partners work together to retell the story and respond to the questions on page 12.

Focus on Fluency

Read pages 8–9 aloud, and have children echo-read after you. Remind them to pause for punctuation.

Paired Selection: "I Like to Play"

Analytical Writing **Make Connections: Write About It**

Echo-read each page with children. Discuss what the narrator does with each friend: *What does the boy like to do with Sam?* He likes to <u>race</u>. Help children make connections between texts using the question on page 15: Friends have fun <u>running</u>. Friends have fun <u>making</u> sand castles and forts.

Leveled Reader

Build Knowledge: Make Connections

Talk About the Text Have partners compare the activities in the texts with activities they do with their friends.

Write About the Text Have students add their ideas to the Build Knowledge pages of their reader's notebooks.

Self-Selected Reading

Help children choose a nonfiction selection from the online **Leveled Reader Library** or read the **Differentiated Text:** "Kids Have Fun!"

FOCUS ON SOCIAL STUDIES

Children can extend their knowledge of what friends do when they play by completing the social studies activity on page 16.

LITERATURE CIRCLES

Lead children in conducting a literature circle using the Thinkmark questions to guide the discussion. You may wish to discuss what children have learned about friends from both selections in the **Leveled Reader**.

FORMATIVE ASSESSMENT

STUDENT CHECK-IN

Have partners share their Respond to Reading. Have children reflect, using the Check-In Routine.

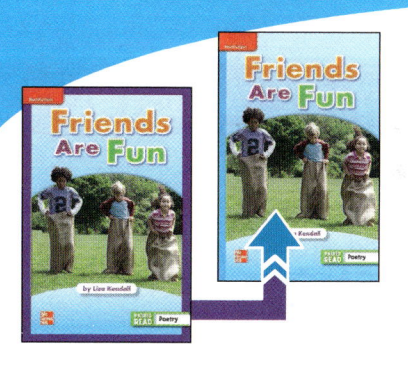

LEVEL UP

IF children can read *Friends Are Fun* **ELL Level** with fluency and correctly answer the Respond to Reading questions,

THEN tell children they will read a more detailed version of the selection.

- Use pages 2–3 of *Friends Are Fun* **On Level** to model using Teaching Poster 26 to identify the key details.

- Have children read the selection, checking their comprehension by using the graphic organizer.

ENGLISH LANGUAGE LEARNERS

LESSONS 1-5

WRITING

MODELED WRITING

LESSON 1

LEARNING GOALS

We can write details to tell more about a topic.

OBJECTIVES

Write informative texts in which they name a topic.

LANGUAGE OBJECTIVES

Children will inform by writing a sentence using a supporting detail.

ELA ACADEMIC LANGUAGE

- details
- Cognate: *detalles*

Writing Practice Review the sample on p. 136 of the **Reading/Writing Companion** by pointing to each word as children choral read. Help children analyze it using the Actor/Action Routine: The actor is "*I*". The action is *jump rope*. Discuss how *at lunch time* is a supporting detail. Then have children choral read the prompt on p. 137, and ask children to answer it as a group. Then ask children to write their own sentence using the Actor/Action Routine.

Beginning *Who is the actor? What is the action? What do you like to play? Who do you play with?* Provide a sentence frame.

Intermediate Have partners ask and answer *who/what* questions to create their sentence. Supply time phrases such as *every day* and *in the morning*.

Advanced/Advanced High Challenge children to include more than one supporting detail in their sentence.

FORMATIVE ASSESSMENT ▶ **STUDENT CHECK-IN** Partners share their sentences. Ask children to reflect, using the Check-In Routine.

INTERACTIVE WRITING

LESSON 2

LEARNING GOALS

We can read and write about a Student Model.

OBJECTIVES

Write informative texts in which they supply some facts about the topic.

LANGUAGE OBJECTIVES

Children will discuss the Student Model and inform by writing sentences about sentence types.

ELA ACADEMIC LANGUAGE

- prompts

Analyze the Student Model Have children finger point as they chorally read the Student Model on p. 142 of the **Reading/Writing Companion**. Read the first sentence. *Is this sentence an exclamation or an interjection?* (an interjection) *What does it end with?* (an exclamation point) Then review supporting details: *What do kids do?* (play ball, make houses and dolls) *Where do kids play?* (outside, inside) Then help children respond to the prompts on p. 143. Provide sentence frames as needed.

Beginning Help children point to the interjection and the exclamation: This sentence is an interjection/an exclamation.

Intermediate Ask partners to identify the end punctuation and types of sentences. Provide sentence frames as needed.

Advanced/Advanced High Challenge children to write about the text, using their own sentences. Encourage children to use supporting details.

FORMATIVE ASSESSMENT ▶ **STUDENT CHECK-IN** Partners share their responses. Ask children to reflect, using the Check-In Routine.

WEEK 4

INDEPENDENT WRITING
LESSONS 3-4

LEARNING GOALS
We can use text evidence to respond to a nonfiction text.

OBJECTIVES
Write informative texts in which they supply some facts about the topic.

LANGUAGE OBJECTIVES
Children will inform by writing a sentence using correct punctuation.

ELA ACADEMIC LANGUAGE
- text
- Cognate: *texto*

Find Text Evidence Use the Independent Writing Routine. Help children orally retell the anchor text. Ask questions, such as, *Who are the friends in this story?* (Pam and Jill) *What do they do first?* (toss a ball; hop.) When children have finished, explain that they are going to write about the story. Reread the prompt on p. 148 of the **Reading/Writing Companion**: *Why is Pam a good friend to Jill? The girls play a game, but there is a problem. Then Pam has an idea to do something different. What Pam does shows how she is a good friend.*

Write a Response Distribute **My Writing Outline 4** to children. Work with them to fill out the outline. After they have completed their outlines, have children complete p. 148, using the sentences from their completed outlines.

Writing Checklist Read the checklist with children, and have them check for these items in their writing.

Beginning Have partners track their words as they read their sentences.

Intermediate Encourage partners to use supporting details.

Advanced/Advanced High Have children add one more supporting detail and share it with a partner.

FORMATIVE ASSESSMENT ▶ **STUDENT CHECK-IN** Partners share their sentences from My Writing Outline. Ask children to reflect, using the Check-In Routine.

SELF-SELECTED WRITING
LESSON 5

LEARNING GOALS
We can revise our writing.

OBJECTIVES
Produce and expand complete exclamatory sentences.

LANGUAGE OBJECTIVES
Children will inquire about their writing and check for correct punctuation.

ELA ACADEMIC LANGUAGE
- publish
- Cognate: *publicar*

Work with children to revise the group writing activity. Read the sentences, pointing to each word as you read. Stop to ask questions, such as, *What punctuation do we use at the end of an interjection or exclamation?* (an exclamation point) If needed, write a sentence that is missing punctuation, and correct it with children. Then have partners work together to revise their writing before publishing it. Check they are using correct formatting.

For support with grammar, refer to the **Language Transfers Handbook,** and review **Language Development Cards** 22B and 23A.

FORMATIVE ASSESSMENT ▶ **STUDENT CHECK-IN** Partners tell what revisions they made. Ask children to reflect, using the Check-In Routine.

ENGLISH LANGUAGE LEARNERS **41**

READING • LITERATURE BIG BOOK • ACCESS THE TEXT

LESSONS 1-2

LEARNING GOALS

We can understand a text about how bodies move.

OBJECTIVES

Ask and answer questions about key details in a text.

Use the illustrations and details in a text to describe its key ideas.

Distinguish between information provided by pictures or other illustrations and information provided by the words in a text.

Ask and answer questions about what a speaker says in order to gather additional information or clarify something that is not understood.

LANGUAGE OBJECTIVES

Children will inform, or give information, about animals and what they can do, using words of movement and key vocabulary.

ELA ACADEMIC LANGUAGE

- illustration, nonfiction, ask, answer
- Cognates: *ilustración, no ficción*

MATERIALS

Literature Big Book, *Move!* pp. 2–32

Visual Vocabulary Cards

DIGITAL TOOLS

Have children listen to the selection as they follow along to develop comprehension and practice fluency and pronunciation.

Use the additional grammar video.

Grammar Video

Move!

Prepare to Read

Build Background *We are going to read a nonfiction text about animals and how they move.* Show the cover picture of the hopping rabbit. Say: *This is a rabbit. How does the rabbit move? The rabbit hops.* Then ask children to share ideas about animals. *What are some animals you know?* Model for children to repeat: *A cat is an animal.* Then have children talk about how animals move. Provide a sentence frame: *A cat ____ . A fish can ____ . A bird uses ____ .*

Literature Big Book

Focus on Vocabulary Use the **Visual Vocabulary Cards** to review the oral vocabulary words *physical* and *exercise*. As you read, use gestures and other visual support to clarify important words from the text, such as *walk, swing, swim,* and *dive.* Say: *These words tell how animals and people can move. Say the word* walk *with me.* Point to it in the text. Provide an example: *I* walk. *A dog* walks.

Summarize the Text Before reading, say the summary while pointing to the illustrations: *The text shows and tells about many animals. We'll learn about the different ways that animals move.*

Read the Text

Use the Interactive Question-Response Routine to help children understand the text.

Pages 2–9

Pages 4–5 Read the text aloud. Point to the gibbon on page 4. *What is this animal?* (a gibbon) *We saw the gibbon swinging on page 3. Can people swing?* (yes) *What is the gibbon doing now?* (walking) Point to the picture on page 5. *What is the jacana doing?* (walking) *The gibbon and the jacana are walking. Can people walk?* (yes) Point to the gibbon's feet. *The gibbon walks on its two back feet.* Point to the lily pad. *The jacana walks on lily pads that float on the water. What do you walk on?* (two feet on the floor/ground)

What do the gibbon and the jacana do? Discuss with a partner.

Beginning Point to the picture on page 4. *What can a gibbon do? A gibbon can* walk. Point to the picture on page 5. *What can a jacana do? A jacana can* walk. Point to the animals' legs. *Do the gibbon and jacana walk on two legs? Yes, they walk on two* legs.

42   UNIT 1 WEEK 5

WEEK 5

Intermediate Have partners respond to questions: *What do the gibbon and jacana do?* The gibbon and jacana walk. *How does a gibbon walk?* A gibbon walks on two back legs. *Where does the jacana walk?* A jacana walks on lily pads.

Advanced/Advanced High Help partners ask and answer: How can the jacana walk on lily pads? The jacana has long toes to help it walk on lily pads. How does a gibbon move through jungle trees? The gibbon uses its arms to swing through the trees.

Pages 10–21

Pages 10–11 Read the text aloud, beginning on page 9. Point to page 10. *What kind of animal is this?* (an armadillo) *We saw the armadillo swimming on page 9. Now the armadillo is leaping.* Leaping *means "jumping." Say* leaping. *Can people leap?* (yes) *The armadillo leaps when it is startled.* Startled *means "scared." Say* startled. Point to the picture on page 11. *What is this?* (a crocodile) *The crocodile leaps up to snag a meal. What will the crocodile snag?* (food)

When do the armadillo and the crocodile leap up? Discuss with a partner.

Beginning Point to the armadillo on page 10. *What is the armadillo doing?* The armadillo is leaping. *Is the armadillo happy or scared?* The armadillo is scared. Point to the crocodile on page 11. *What is the crocodile doing?* The crocodile is leaping. *Does the crocodile want to eat?* Yes, the crocodile wants to eat.

Intermediate Help partners point and respond: *What are the armadillo and the crocodile doing?* They are leaping. *Why does the armadillo leap?* The armadillo is startled/scared. *Why does the crocodile leap above the water?* The crocodile wants to snag/catch a meal.

Advanced/Advanced High Have partners compare the armadillo and the crocodile. Both leap up. The armadillo is startled, but the crocodile wants to eat.

Pages 22–32

Pages 22–23 Read the text aloud, beginning on page 21. Point to the picture on page 22. *What is this?* (a spider) *What does the spider do?*

Have children repeat: The spider floats. *The spider floats away on a thread. This thread of silk is from the spider's web.* Point to the picture on page 23. *What is this?* (a polar bear) *What does the polar bear do?* The polar bear floats. *The polar bear floats in the water. The water is dark and icy.* Icy *means* cold.

What do the spider and the polar bear do? Discuss with a partner.

Beginning Help partners point to the pictures as they respond. *Who floats?* The spider floats. The polar bear floats.

Intermediate Help partners ask and answer with details: *What does the spider do?* The spider floats on a thread of silk. *What does the polar bear do?* A polar bear floats in dark, icy water.

Advanced/Advanced High Have partners work together to use key details to answer additional questions: *Why does the spider float away?* It is very light. The wind makes it float. *Can the polar bear float away in the same way?* (no) *Why not?* The bear is too big to float in the air.

FORMATIVE ASSESSMENT

STUDENT CHECK-IN

Have partners explain how the animals in the text use their body parts to move. Then have children reflect, using the Check-In Routine.

Independent Time

Draw and Write Have children draw a picture of an animal and write about how they and the animal move in the same way. Provide a sentence frame to help them: A ___ leaps. I ___. Have children draw and copy the sentence frame. Allow them to write what they can, help translate or elaborate, and then provide corrections as needed. Have children present their drawings to the class, using: This is a picture of a ___. The ___ ___.

LESSONS 1-2

READING • SHARED READ • ACCESS THE TEXT

"Move and Grin!"

Prepare to Read

Build Background Read aloud the Essential Question on page 160. Have children share how they move. Use the photos on pages 160 and 161 to generate ideas. Point to and read aloud the title. Explain that *grin* is another word for *smile*. *We are going to read about how kids and their pets move.*

Focus on Vocabulary Use the **Visual Vocabulary Cards** to preteach the high-frequency words *jump, move, run,* and *two* and the oral vocabulary words *agree, difficult, exercise, exhausted,* and *physical*. As you read, use gestures and visual support to teach the important words from the text, such as *hop, swim, trot, grab, claw, leg, hand, arm, head,* and *foot*. Say the word *trot*. Have children point to the picture of the horse trotting on page 166 and repeat the word *trot*. *Trot means* run slowly. *The horse can trot. What can the horse do?* The horse can trot. (Cognate: *trotar*)

Summarize the Text Before reading, say the summary while pointing to the photos. *This story tells how some kids' pets can move. It tells how the kids can move, too.*

Reading/Writing Companion, Lexile 370L

Read the Text

Use the Interactive Question-Response Routine to help children understand the text.

Pages 162–163

Pages 162–163 Preview the possessive noun with an apostrophe. Hold up one of the children's books. *This is Mia's book.* Write the sentence *This is Mia's book* on the board and circle the 's. *In this story you will see an 's at the end of a kid's name. That will tell you who owns a pet.* Read the text aloud as children follow along. Remind children that *can* means you are able to do something. Point to the photo of the frog. *What kind of animal is this?* (frog) Point to the words *Scott's frog. This is Scott's frog. This is Scott. What can Scott's frog do?* Scott's frog can hop/jump. *Look at the frog's back legs. What helps the frog move?* (the frog's back legs) *What is Scott doing?* Scott is jumping/hopping. Point to the last sentence. *Say this text with me:* Scott can hop, hop, hop.

What can Scott's frog and Scott do? Discuss with a partner.

Beginning *What animal do you see?* I see a frog. *Can the frog hop?* Yes, the frog can hop. *Can the frog jump?* Yes, the frog can jump. *Can Scott hop and jump, too?* Yes, Scott can hop and jump, too.

LEARNING GOALS

We can read and understand a nonfiction text.

OBJECTIVES

Ask and answer questions about key details in a text.

With prompting and support, read prose and poetry of appropriate complexity for grade 1.

Ask and answer questions to help determine or clarify the meaning of words and phrases in a text.

Build on others' talk in conversations by responding to the comments of others through multiple exchanges.

LANGUAGE OBJECTIVES

Children will discuss, or talk about, what the people and animals in the text can do, using short phrases or sentences with the word *can*.

ELA ACADEMIC LANGUAGE

• apostrophe, essential question
• Cognates: *apóstrofo, esencial*

MATERIALS

Reading/Writing Companion, pp. 160–169

Visual Vocabulary Cards

DIGITAL TOOLS MULTIMODAL

Have children listen to the selection as they follow along to develop comprehension and practice fluency and pronunciation.

Use the additional grammar song.

🎵 Grammar Song

44 UNIT 1 WEEK 5

WEEK 5

Intermediate *What can Scott's frog do?* Scott's frog can hop and jump. *What can Scott do?* Scott can hop and jump. *What can Scott and his frog do?* Scott and his frog can hop and jump.

Advanced/Advanced High Have children work in pairs to discuss the photos and take turns asking and answering questions. *What can Scott and his frog do?* Scott and his frog can jump and hop. *How can Scott's frog jump and hop?* It can move its two back legs. *Do you think Scott likes to hop?* (yes) *Why?* (Possible answers: He looks happy hopping.)

Pages 164–167

Pages 164–165 Read the text aloud. Point to the photo on page 164. *What animal do you see?* I see a dog. *What can the dog do?* The dog can swim. Point to the words *a lot* in the text. *A lot* means "often or many times." When a dog swims, it kicks its two front legs. Ask children to point to the dog's front legs in the photo. Then turn to page 165. *This is Fran. The dog is Fran's dog. Does Fran swim a lot or a little?* (a lot)

What can Fran and her dog do? Discuss with a partner.

Beginning *What kind of animal is this?* (a dog) *What can the dog do?* The dog can swim. *Can Fran swim, too?* Yes, Fran can swim, too.

Intermediate *What can Fran's dog do?* Fran's dog can swim. *How does Fran's dog swim?* It kicks its two front legs. *What can Fran do?* Fran can swim, too. *Who swims a lot?* Fran and her dog swim a lot.

Advanced/Advanced High *What do you know about Fran's dog?* Fran's dog can swim a lot. It swims by kicking its two front legs. *What do you know about Fran?* Fran can swim a lot, too. *How does the text show that Fran swims a lot?* (The word *swim* is used three times.)

Pages 168–169

Pages 168–169 Read the text aloud and point to the crab. *This is a crab.* Point to a big claw and say: *The crab has a big claw. The crab can grab with the big claw. When you grab something, you take it fast.*

Model grabbing. *What can the crab do?* The crab can grab. Point to the photo of Skip. Have children point to their own hand, arm, head, leg, and foot as you say each label. Ask the question in the text: *What can Skip grab with?* (his hand)

What can Skip and Skip's crab do? Discuss with a partner.

Beginning *Can Skip's crab grab?* Yes, Skip's crab can grab. *Can Skip grab?* Yes, Skip can grab. *Can Skip grab with his hand or his claw?* (his hand) Have children point to the label *hand*.

Intermediate Have children say and act out *grab*. Have partners discuss pages 168–169: *What can Skip's crab do?* Skip's crab can grab. *What does Skip's crab grab with?* Skip's crab grabs with its big claw. *What can Skip do?* Skip can grab. *What does Skip grab with?* Skip grabs with his hand.

Advanced/Advanced High Have partners tell what Skip's crab and Skip can do. Then have partners discuss activities Skip can do using a labeled body part, such as: *Skip can hop with his legs.*

FORMATIVE ASSESSMENT

STUDENT CHECK-IN

Have partners retell what the people and animals in the text can do. Then have children reflect, using the Check-In Routine.

Independent Time

Ask and Answer Questions Pair children of mixed proficiency. Have partners look back at the selection to review the pets and their actions and take turns telling how each pet moves. Then have each pair tell the rest of the group. Provide sentence frames to help them: The ___ hops/swims/trots/grabs with its ___.

ENGLISH LANGUAGE LEARNERS **45**

LESSON 3

READING • ANCHOR TEXT • ACCESS THE TEXT

Move It!

Prepare to Read

Build Background *We are going to read about fun ways kids can move.* Pantomime several movements, such as running, jumping, and catching. *We use our bodies to move in lots of ways. We can use our legs to run. We can jump with our two feet. We can use our hands to catch and grab. We can do fun things. How can you move?* Model saying: *I can catch a ball with my two hands. What can you do with your two hands? I can catch/grab a ball with my two hands.*

Focus on Vocabulary Use the **Visual Vocabulary Cards** to review the high-frequency words *jump, move, run,* and *two* and the oral language vocabulary words *agree, difficult, exercise, exhausted,* and *physical.* As you read, teach important words from the text, such as *strong, fast, pick up, land, spin, hoop, hips,* and *tricks.* Pick up a heavy book and say: *My strong arms help me pick up this book. Do strong legs help you run?* (yes)

Summarize the Text Before reading, say the summary while pointing to the illustrations. *This text tells how we can move our bodies to do fun things like catching and swimming.*

Literature Anthology, Lexile 60L

Read the Text

Use the Interactive Question-Response Routine to help children understand the text.

Pages 86–89

Pages 86–87 Read the text. Point to the boy on page 86. *The boy is standing with his head down and legs up. This is called a* handstand. Have children repeat; handstand. *The boy does a handstand with his arms and hands.* Point to the girl on page 87. *What is this girl doing?* (running) *Which part of the body do you use to run?* (legs) *Strong legs help you run fast.*

Pages 88–89 Point to the girl on page 88. *What is this girl doing?* (jumping) *Is she having fun?* (yes) *How do you know?* She is smiling. *The author's words tell how she jumps: "I pick up my feet. I will land on the grass."* Explain that *land* means *to come down.* Point to the boy on page 89. *What is the boy doing? He is catching a* ball. Explain that another word for *catch* is *grab. What part of the body is the boy using? The boy is using two* hands. *The author's words tell how he catches. Say the author's words with me: "I use two hands. I can grab the ball."*

How do the children use their feet and hands? Discuss with a partner.

LEARNING GOALS

We can read and understand a nonfiction text.

OBJECTIVES

Ask and answer questions about key details in a text.

Know and use various text features to locate key facts or information in a text.

Ask questions to clear up any confusion about the topics and texts under discussion.

Produce complete sentences when appropriate to task and situation.

LANGUAGE OBJECTIVES

Children will discuss how the people in the text use their body parts to do different activities, using the verb *can.*

ELA ACADEMIC LANGUAGE

- author, label
- Cognate: *autor*

MATERIALS

Literature Anthology, pp. 86–93

Visual Vocabulary Cards

DIGITAL TOOLS

Have children listen to the selection as they follow along to develop comprehension and practice fluency and pronunciation.

Use the online High-Frequency Words Activity for additional support.

46   UNIT 1 WEEK 5

WEEK 5

Beginning Have children point to the girl's feet on page 88. *What can the girl do?* The girl can jump. *What does the girl pick up?* The girl picks up her feet. Have children point to the boy's hands on page 89. *What can the boy do?* The boy can catch. *Does the boy use one hand or two hands?* The boy uses two hands.

Intermediate Have partners point to appropriate parts of the pictures as they respond. *Look at page 88. What can the girl do with her feet?* The girl can jump. *How does the girl jump?* The girl picks up her feet. Then the girl will land on the grass. *Look at page 89. What can the boy do?* The boy can catch the ball. *How can the boy use two hands?* The boy can use two hands to grab the ball.

Advanced/Advanced High Have partners use the photos and text on pages 86 and 87 to discuss what helps the kids move. *What does the boy need to do a handstand?* The boy needs strong hands and arms to do a handstand. *What does the girl need to run fast?* The girl needs strong legs to run fast. Have partners discuss how the kids on pages 88 and 89 can jump and catch: The girl can jump high when she picks up her feet. The boy can catch when he uses two hands to grab the ball.

Pages 90–93

Pages 90–91 Read the text on page 90. *What can the boy do?* (swim) Point to and read the labels. *The text tells how he uses his arms and feet: What does the boy pull?* (arms) *What does the boy kick?* (feet) Read the text on page 91 and point to the hula hoop. *This girl has a hoop. Say* hoop. *She can spin the hoop. This means she can make the hoop go around and around.* Point to and say the label *hips* for children to repeat. *The girl moves her hips fast. This helps the hoop stay up and not fall. Can you spin a hoop?* (yes/no)

Page 92 Read the text. Explain that the word *tricks* in this text means "special ways of moving." Point out that the boy in the picture is upside down. *Where did we see another child who was upside down?* Encourage children to recall the handstand performer on the first page. *The boy's trick is putting his legs up. Can you do a trick?* (yes)

How do the labels help you know how the boy swims? Discuss with a partner.

Beginning Point to page 90. *What can the boy do?* The boy can swim. Have children point to the appropriate parts of the pictures as they respond. *Point to the* arms *label. Point to the boy's arms. Does the boy pull with his arms?* Yes, the boy pulls with his arms. *Point to the* feet *label. Point to the boy's feet. Does the boy kick with his feet?* Yes, the boy kicks with his feet.

Intermediate Have partners point to the appropriate labels as they respond. *What do the labels on page 90 tell you about the boy?* The labels are for arms and feet. The boy moves his arms and feet. This helps him swim.

Advanced/Advanced High Have partners explain the labels: These are the boy's arms and legs. These are the girl's hips. Then have them use the text on pages 90–91 to ask and answer questions using the question word *how:* How can the boy swim? He pulls with his arms. He kicks with his feet. How can the girl spin the hoop? She moves her hips fast.

FORMATIVE ASSESSMENT

▶ STUDENT CHECK-IN

Have partners retell three activities described in the text. Then have children reflect, using the Check-In Routine.

Independent Time

Draw and Write Have children draw and write about ways they can move. Provide sentence frames to help them write: I can ___. I move my ___ and ___ when I ___. Have children draw and copy the sentence frame. Allow them to write what they can, help translate or elaborate, and then provide corrections as needed. Have children present their drawings to the group, using: This is a picture of me. I can ___.

LESSONS 4-5

READING • LEVELED READER • ACCESS THE TEXT

LEARNING GOALS

We can ask and answer questions about how we can move as we read a nonfiction text.

OBJECTIVES

Ask and answer questions about key details in a text.

Identify the main topic and retell key details of a text.

Identify basic similarities in and differences between two texts on the same topic.

Ask questions to clear up any confusion about the topics and texts under discussion.

LANGUAGE OBJECTIVES

Children will inform, or give information, about how we can use our bodies for different activities, using the verbs *move* and *can*.

ELA ACADEMIC LANGUAGE

• nonfiction, relevant details
• Cognates: *no ficción, detalles relevantes*

MATERIALS

ELL Leveled Reader: *We Can Move!*

Online Differentiated Texts, "On the Move!"

Online ELL Visual Vocabulary Cards

DIGITAL TOOLS

Have children listen to the selection as they follow along to develop comprehension and practice fluency and pronunciation. Use Graphic Organizer 3: Topic and Relevant Details.

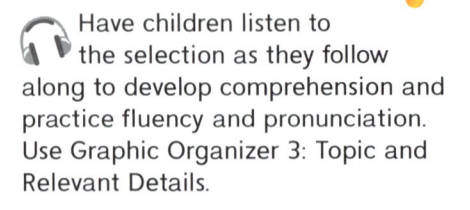

We Can Move!

Prepare to Read

Build Background

- Remind children of the Essential Question. *Let's read to see how the kids move their bodies. This text is nonfiction. It tells about real people.* Encourage children to ask for help when they do not understand a word or phrase.

Lexile 190L

- Point to and read aloud the title and have children repeat. Ask: *What is the title?* Have children point to it. Repeat the routine for the author's name. Point to the photos in the text to name actions and parts of the body, for example: *This boy [kicks]. What does he move to [kick]?*

Focus on Vocabulary Use the **ELL Visual Vocabulary Cards** to preteach the words *activity* and *energy*. As you read, use gestures or visuals to teach important words from the text, such as *body, martial arts, baseball, swing, bat, chase, soccer, uniform, [kick] hard, pool, roll, gymnastics,* and *mat*.

Read the Text

Use the Interactive Question-Response Routine to help children understand the text.

Pages 2–3

Read pages 2–3 as children follow along. *These pages show martial arts.* Point to and say *move, our bodies, help*. Have children point to and repeat the words.

Beginning Help partners point as they respond: *What can we move?* We can move our legs. *What can our legs do?* Our legs can kick.

Intermediate Ask partners to describe pages 2–3: *How can we move?* We can use our bodies. *How can our legs help us?* Our legs can help us kick.

Advanced/Advanced High Have partners discuss: *How can we move?* We can use our bodies. *How do our legs help us?* Our legs help us kick.

Pages 4–9

Topic and Relevant Details Read pages 4–5. Ask guiding questions. *What is the topic of the text?* The topic of the text is how our bodies help us move. Point to the *bat* label. *What is this?* (a bat) Point to the boy's arms. *What helps the boy swing?* (arms) *What is a relevant detail from the text?* We use our hands and arms to play baseball.

Beginning Help partners respond using the photos: *What is this?* This is a bat. *What can we do with our arms?* We can swing the bat.

48 UNIT 1 WEEK 5

WEEK 5

Intermediate Help partners ask and answer: What can we move? We can move our <u>arms</u> and <u>feet</u>. How do our arms help us? Our arms help us <u>swing</u>. How do our feet help us? Our feet help us <u>run</u>.

Pages 10–11

Ask and Answer Questions Read pages 10–11. Help children ask and answer questions: *This girl is in a gymnastics class.* What does the girl use? The girl uses a <u>mat</u>.

Intermediate *Where is the girl?* (on a mat) *What do we do on a mat?* We roll on a <u>mat</u>. *Do we move a lot?* Yes, we move <u>a lot</u>.

Advanced/Advanced High *Ask and answer:* What can we do in gymnastics class? We can <u>roll</u> on the <u>mat</u>. How else can you move? (Answers will vary.)

Respond to Reading Have partners work together to retell the story and respond to the questions on page 12.

Focus on Fluency

Read pages 8–9. Then reread them and have children echo-read after you. Remind children to read the words correctly.

Paired Read: "What's Under Your Skin?"

Make Connections: Write About It

Echo-read each page with children. Discuss bones and how they help you move. Help children make connections, using the question on page 15: The bones in my <u>legs</u> and <u>feet</u> help me move.

ELL Leveled Reader

Build Knowledge: Make Connections

Talk About the Text Have partners discuss how activities in the texts are similar to or different from how they move their bodies.

Write About the Text Have students add their ideas to the Build Knowledge pages of their reader's notebooks.

Self-Selected Reading

Help children choose a nonfiction selection from the online **Leveled Reader Library** or read the **Differentiated Text:** "On the Move!"

FOCUS ON SCIENCE

Children can extend their knowledge of how they move to play sports by completing the science activity on page 16. **STEM**

LITERATURE CIRCLES

Lead children in conducting a literature circle, using the Thinkmark questions to guide the discussion. You may wish to discuss what children have learned about how they move from both selections in the Leveled Reader.

FORMATIVE ASSESSMENT

STUDENT CHECK-IN

Have partners share their Respond to Reading. Have children reflect, using the Check-In Routine.

LEVEL UP

IF children can read *We Can Move!* ELL Level with fluency and correctly answer the Respond to Reading questions,

THEN tell children that they will read a more detailed version of the selection.

- Use pages 2–4 of *We Can Move!* On Level to model, using Teaching Poster 27 to list key details in the selection.
- Have children read the selection, checking their comprehension by using the graphic organizer.

ENGLISH LANGUAGE LEARNERS **49**

LESSONS 1–5

WRITING

MODELED WRITING

LESSON 1

LEARNING GOALS

We can learn how to use supporting details in our writing.

OBJECTIVES

Write informative texts in which they name a topic.

LANGUAGE OBJECTIVE

Children will inform by writing a complete sentence that includes a supporting detail.

ELA ACADEMIC LANGUAGE

- details
- Cognate: *detalles*

Writing Practice Review the sample on p. 170 of the **Reading/Writing Companion** by pointing to each word as children choral read. Guide children to analyze it using the Actor/Action Routine: *Who is the actor?* (I) *What is the action?* (kick the ball) *What is the supporting detail?* (with my foot) Then read the prompt on p. 171. Lead children to answer it as a group and then write it on the board for children to choral read. Then ask children to write their own sentence using the Actor/Action Routine.

Beginning Provide a sentence frame: I like to play soccer in my backyard.

Intermediate Have partners talk about their favorite sport by asking and answering *what/how/where* questions. Provide sentence frames if needed.

Advanced/Advanced High Challenge children to write a sentence that has two supporting details.

FORMATIVE ASSESSMENT ▸ **STUDENT CHECK-IN** Partners share their sentences. Ask children to reflect, using the Check-In Routine.

INTERACTIVE WRITING

LESSON 2

LEARNING GOALS

We can read and write about a Student Model.

OBJECTIVES

Write informative texts in which they supply some facts about the topic.

LANGUAGE OBJECTIVE

Children will discuss the Student Model and inform by writing a complete sentence using a supporting detail.

ELA ACADEMIC LANGUAGE

- details
- Cognate: *detalles*

Analyze the Student Model Have children finger point as they choral read the student model on p. 176 of the **Reading/Writing Companion**. Use the Actor/Action Routine to review the sentences. Have children look at the second sentence. *Point to the capital letter.* (I) *What is at the end of the sentence?* (a period) *What are the supporting details?* (strong, back) Then help children complete p. 177. Provide sentence frames as needed.

Beginning Have partners take turns identifying capital letters, periods, and spaces between words. Provide sentence frames: I noticed a capital *M*.

Intermediate Have partners point to a capital letter at the beginning and the period at the end to show an example of a sentence. Then provide a sentence frame: I noticed a capital letter and a period.

Advanced/Advanced High Challenge children to write their own sentences about what they noticed. Provide models as necessary.

FORMATIVE ASSESSMENT ▸ **STUDENT CHECK-IN** Partners share their responses. Ask children to reflect, using the Check-In Routine.

WEEK 5

INDEPENDENT WRITING
LESSONS 3-4

LEARNING GOALS
We can respond to a nonfiction text by extending the text.

OBJECTIVES
Write informative texts in which they provide some sense of closure.

LANGUAGE OBJECTIVES
Children will inform by writing sentences that include supporting details.

ELA ACADEMIC LANGUAGE
- *evidence, prompt*
- Cognate: *evidencia*

Find Text Evidence Use the Independent Writing Routine. Help children orally retell the anchor text, using text evidence. Ask questions, such as, *What can the girl do?* (jump) *What body part does she use?* (feet) *What does she do first?* (pick up her feet) Then read the prompt on p. 181 of the **Reading/Writing Companion**. *What's your favorite thing to do outside? Add a new page to the text. We need to think about an activity we like to do outside and then add supporting details that tell how we move.*

Write a Response Distribute **My Writing Outline 5** to children. Work with them to fill out the outline. After they have completed their outline, have children complete p. 181, using the sentences from their completed outline.

Writing Checklist Read the checklist with children and have them check for these items in their writing.

Beginning Provide sentence frames to help partners talk about their sentences: A supporting detail is I climb the steps with my feet.

Intermediate Have partners check for spaces between words and correct capitalization.

Advanced/Advanced High Have children identify where they used each checklist item in their writing.

FORMATIVE ASSESSMENT ▸ **STUDENT CHECK-IN** Have partners share their sentences from My Writing Outline. Ask children to reflect, using the Check-In Routine.

SELF-SELECTED WRITING
LESSON 5

LEARNING GOALS
We can revise our writing.

OBJECTIVES
Use end punctuation for sentences.

LANGUAGE OBJECTIVE
Children will inquire about their writing and check for correct punctuation.

ELA ACADEMIC LANGUAGE
- *punctuation*
- Cognate: *puntuación*

Work with children to revise the group writing activity. Point to each word as you read the sentences. Stop to ask questions, such as, *What punctuation do we use at the end of a statement?* (a period) If needed, write a sentence that is missing punctuation and revise it together. Then have partners revise each other's writing before publishing it.

For support with grammar, refer to the **Language Transfers Handbook** and review **Language Development Cards** 22B and 23A.

FORMATIVE ASSESSMENT ▸ **STUDENT CHECK-IN** Partners identify their revisions. Ask children to reflect, using the Check-In Routine.

ENGLISH LANGUAGE LEARNERS **51**

UNIT 1

Summative Assessment
Get Ready for Unit Assessment

Unit 1 Tested Skills

LISTENING AND READING COMPREHENSION	VOCABULARY	GRAMMAR	SPEAKING AND WRITING
• Listening Actively • Details	• Words and Categories	• Sentences	• Expressing Opinions • Presenting • Composing/Writing • Retelling/Recounting

Create a Student Profile

Record data from the following resources in the Student Profile charts on pages 356–357 of the Assessment book.

COLLABORATIVE	INTERPRETIVE	PRODUCTIVE

• Collaborative Conversations Rubrics
  • Listening
  • Speaking
	• Leveled Unit Assessment
	  • Listening Comprehension
	  • Reading Comprehension
	  • Vocabulary
	  • Grammar
	• Presentation Rubric
	  • Listening
	• *Wonders* Unit Assessment
		• Weekly Progress Monitoring
		• Leveled Unit Assessment
		  • Speaking
		  • Writing
		• Presentation Rubric
		  • Speaking
		• Write to Sources Rubric
		• *Wonders* Unit Assessment

The Foundational Skills Kit, Language Development Kit, and Adaptive Learning provide additional student data for progress monitoring.

Level Up

Use the following chart, along with your Student Profiles, to guide your Level Up decisions.

LEVEL UP	If **BEGINNING** level students are able to do the following, they may be ready to move to the **INTERMEDIATE** level:	If **INTERMEDIATE** level students are able to do the following, they may be ready to move to the **ADVANCED** level:	If **ADVANCED** level students are able to do the following, they may be ready to move to the **ON** level:
COLLABORATIVE	• participate in collaborative conversations using basic vocabulary and grammar and simple phrases or sentences • discuss simple pictorial or text prompts	• participate in collaborative conversations using appropriate words and phrases and complete sentences • use limited academic vocabulary across and within disciplines	• participate in collaborative conversations using more sophisticated vocabulary and correct grammar • communicate effectively across a wide range of language demands in social and academic contexts
INTERPRETIVE	• identify details in simple read alouds • understand common vocabulary and idioms and interpret language related to familiar social, school, and academic topics • make simple inferences and make simple comparisons • exhibit an emerging receptive control of lexical, syntactic, phonological, and discourse features	• identify main ideas and/or make some inferences from simple read alouds • use context clues to identify word meanings and interpret basic vocabulary and idioms • compare, contrast, summarize, and relate text to graphic organizers • exhibit a limited range of receptive control of lexical, syntactic, phonological, and discourse features when addressing new or familiar topics	• determine main ideas in read alouds that have advanced vocabulary • use context clues to determine meaning, understand multiple-meaning words, and recognize synonyms of social and academic vocabulary • analyze information, make sophisticated inferences, and explain their reasoning • command a high degree of receptive control of lexical, syntactic, phonological, and discourse features
PRODUCTIVE	• express ideas and opinions with basic vocabulary and grammar and simple phrases or sentences • restate information or retell a story using basic vocabulary • exhibit an emerging productive control of lexical, syntactic, phonological, and discourse features	• produce coherent language with limited elaboration or detail • restate information or retell a story using mostly accurate, although limited, vocabulary • exhibit a limited range of productive control of lexical, syntactic, phonological, and discourse features when addressing new or familiar topics	• produce sentences with more sophisticated vocabulary and correct grammar • restate information or retell a story using extensive and accurate vocabulary and grammar • tailor language to a particular purpose and audience • command a high degree of productive control of lexical, syntactic, phonological, and discourse features

LESSONS 1-2

READING • LITERATURE BIG BOOK • ACCESS THE TEXT

LEARNING GOALS

We can understand events on a farm as we listen to a story.

OBJECTIVES

Retell stories, including key details, and demonstrate understanding of their central message or lesson.

Use illustrations and details in a story to describe its characters and events.

Compare and contrast the adventures and experiences of characters in stories.

Describe people, places, things, and events with relevant details, expressing ideas and feelings clearly.

LANGUAGE OBJECTIVES

Children will explain the characters' ideas, using simple sentences.

ELA ACADEMIC LANGUAGE

- fiction, illustrations, characters
- Cognates: *ficción, ilustraciones*

MATERIALS

Literature Big Book, *Millie Waits for the Mail*, pp. 4–27

Visual Vocabulary Cards

DIGITAL TOOLS

Have children listen to the selection as they follow along to develop comprehension.

Use the additional grammar song.

🎵 Grammar Song

Millie Waits for the Mail

Prepare to Read

Build Background *We are going to read a story about a cow and a mail carrier. A mail carrier is a person who brings the mail to people in a community.* Preview the images in the text and then ask children to share what they know about mail carriers. *Have you seen a mail carrier in your community? What does the mail carrier do?* A mail carrier brings ____.

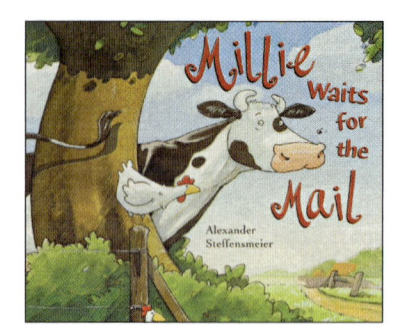

Literature Big Book

Focus on Vocabulary Use the **Visual Vocabulary Cards** to review the oral vocabulary words *occupation* and *community*. As you read, use gestures and other visual support to clarify important story words, such as: *deliver* and *package*. Show children a picture of a package and say: *This is a package. Say* package. *Who delivers a package?* A mail carrier delivers a package.

Summarize the Text Before reading, say the summary while pointing to the illustrations. *This story tells about a Cow named Millie. Millie loves to scare the mail carrier. One day the farmer and the mail carrier try to stop Millie.*

Read the Text

Use the Interactive Question-Response Routine to help children understand the story.

Pages 4–13

Pages 8–9 Read the text aloud. *Point to Millie. What is Millie?* (a cow) *What does Millie love to do?* Millie loves to scare the mail carrier. Act out *scared*. Then point to the mail carrier. *Is the mail carrier happy?* (No, he is not happy.)

Page 13 Read aloud the expression "felt so let down" and explain that it is an idiom that means "sad." Point to Millie's face. *Millie feels let down, or sad, when the mail carrier doesn't come. Tell your partner about a time you felt let down.*

What does Millie love most? Discuss with a partner.

Beginning Point to the image of the mail carrier on page 9. *What is Millie doing?* Millie is scaring the mail carrier. *Is the mail carrier smiling?* (no) *Does Millie like to scare the mail carrier?* (yes)

Intermediate Have partners use the pictures on pages 8–9 to respond. *What is Millie doing?* (scaring the mail carrier) *How does Millie scare the mail carrier?* (by shouting or yelling) *How does the mail carrier look?* (scared)

54 UNIT 2 WEEK 1

WEEK 1

Advanced/Advanced High Have partners work together to add details to their responses. *Why is this Millie's favorite time of day?* Millie can scare the mail carrier. *Does the mail carrier look scared? How do you know?* He drops his package. His face looks scared.

Pages 14–19

Page 16 Read the text aloud. Explain that the mail carrier wants Millie to stop scaring him. *Now he has an idea.* Point to the picture and ask: *What do you see?* (box, tape, scissors, the mail carrier) *The mail carrier is making a package. Who is the package for?* (the cow/Millie) *Why is the mail carrier making a package for the cow?* The mail carrier thinks she will like him. He thinks Millie will stop scaring him.

What is the mail carrier's idea? Discuss with a partner.

Beginning Point to the picture of the mail carrier. *What is the mail carrier doing?* He is making a package. *Who is the package for?* The package is for Millie/the cow.

Intermediate Have children give more specific answers. *What does the mail carrier say?* He says he will bring the cow a package. *What does the mail carrier think?* He thinks Millie will like him.

Advanced/Advanced High Have partners discuss the reasons for the mail carrier's actions. *Do you think Millie has ever received a package before?* (no) *Why does the mail carrier want to bring Millie a package?* The mail carrier wants Millie to like him. He wants Millie to stop scaring him.

Pages 18–27

Pages 20–21 Read the text. Clarify the meanings of expressions such as, *What on earth?* (an expression that shows surprise) and *heart dropped* (an expression that shows shock).

Pages 24–27 Read the text. *Look at this picture. Have we seen it before?* (yes) *When?* (at the beginning of the story) *What did Millie love to do then?* Millie loved to scare the mail carrier. *What does Millie love to do now?* Millie loves to deliver the mail.

How have Millie's feelings changed? Discuss your answer with a partner.

Beginning Point to the pictures of Millie on pages 9 and 27. *At the beginning of the story, Millie tried to scare the mail carrier. What is Millie doing now?* Millie delivers the mail. *Does Millie look happy?* Yes, Millie is happy.

Intermediate Help partners respond. *What did Millie do at first?* Millie scared the mail carrier. *What does Millie do now?* Millie delivers the mail. *Is Millie happy?* Yes, Millie is happy. *How do you know?* Millie is smiling.

Advanced/Advanced High Have partners discuss the reasons why Millie's feelings changed. Millie changed when the mail carrier brought her a package. Now Millie is happy to deliver the mail.

FORMATIVE ASSESSMENT

▶ STUDENT CHECK-IN

Have partners retell the mail carrier's idea. Then, have children reflect using the Check-In Routine.

Independent Time

Dialogues Pair children of mixed proficiencies and have them work together to write original dialogue for the event on pages 26–27 of the story. Provide examples of dialogue between the mail carrier and Millie or the farmer from other pages of the story, such as "This package is for *you*, you silly cow." If needed, provide children with dialogue sentence starters. Have children read aloud their completed lines of dialogue to the rest of the group. Encourage them to read the dialogue with appropriate expression and intonation.

ENGLISH LANGUAGE LEARNERS **55**

LESSONS 1-2

READING • SHARED READ • ACCESS THE TEXT

LEARNING GOALS

We can read and understand a realistic fiction story.

OBJECTIVES

Ask and answer questions about key details in a text.

Use illustrations and details in a story to describe its characters and setting.

Ask and answer questions to help determine or clarify the meaning of words and phrases in a text.

Produce complete sentences when appropriate to task and situation.

LANGUAGE OBJECTIVES

Children will narrate the character's trip to the library, using verbs, nouns, and simple sentences.

ELA ACADEMIC LANGUAGE

- realistic fiction, prediction, setting, retell
- Cognates: *ficción realista, predicción*

MATERIALS

Reading/Writing Companion, pp. 14–23

Visual Vocabulary Cards

DIGITAL TOOLS

Have children listen to the selection to develop comprehension and practice fluency and pronunciation.

Use the online High-Frequency Words Activity for additional support.

"Good Job, Ben!"

Prepare to Read

Build Background Read aloud the Essential Question on page 14. Have children share ideas about some jobs in the community. Use the illustrations throughout the text to help them generate ideas. Point to and read the title. *This story is about Ben and the people who work in his community. Who is in your community? What do they do?*

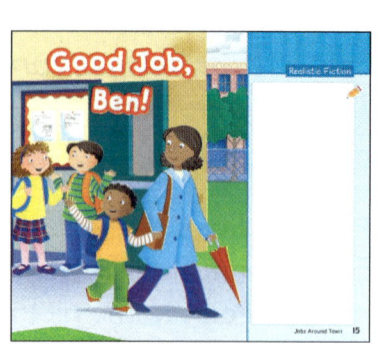

Focus on Vocabulary Use the **Visual Vocabulary Cards** to preteach the high-frequency words *again, help, new, there,* and *use* and the oral language vocabulary words *occupation, community, astonishing, equipment,* and *fortunately.* As you read, use gestures and visual support to teach the important story words *trip, block, cross, sniffs,* and *quick.* Say the word *cross* and point to the street on page 16. Have children point to the picture and repeat the word. *Ben and Mom want to cross. What do Ben and Mom want to do?* Have children respond: Ben and Mom want to cross.

Summarize the Text Before reading, say the summary while pointing to the illustrations. *This story tells about jobs in Ben's town. Let's read to learn about what people do in the community.*

Reading/Writing Companion, Lexile 130L

Read the Text

Use the Interactive Question-Response Routine to help children understand the story.

Pages 16–17

Pages 16–17 Read the text aloud. Point to the word *head* and have children repeat. *The phrase* head to *means* go to. *I can head to my home. I can head to school. Say* head to. *Where are some places you can head to?* I can head to the library. Have children give other examples of places they can head to. *Let's make a prediction about the places Ben and Mom might head to. Use the pictures to help you make a prediction.* Ben and Mom will head to a store.

What will Ben and his Mom do? Discuss with a partner.

Beginning Use the pictures to teach the words *get* and *bus.* Point to the picture of Ben and Mom and say: *Ben and Mom get on the bus.* Have children repeat. *What can Ben do?* Ben can get on the bus. Point to the word *town* in the text and say it with children. *Where can Ben go?* Ben can go into town.

Intermediate *Where can Ben and Mom go?* Ben and Mom can go into town. *How will Ben and Mom get to town?* Ben and Mom will take the bus.

56 UNIT 2 WEEK 1

WEEK 1

Advanced/Advanced High Have partners add details to their answers. *Where do Ben and Mom wait for the bus?* Ben and Mom wait on this block. *Where can Ben and Mom go?* Ben and Mom can go into town. *What kind of trip is this?* It is a big trip.

Pages 18–21

Pages 18–19 Read the text aloud and have children follow along. Point to the picture of the crossing guard on page 18. *A crossing guard is a job. The crossing guard can help Ben and Mom cross the street.* Point to the word *stop* and say it aloud. *This is the word* stop. *Let's say it together.* Have partners act out putting out their hands and saying, "Stop!" to each other. *The crossing guard says, "Stop" to Ben and Mom. She wants them to stop walking. What are Ben and Mom doing?* Ben and Mom are waiting to cross the street.

What jobs does Ben see? Discuss with a partner.

Beginning Have children use the words and pictures to tell what jobs Ben sees. Point to the men on page 19. *How many men does Ben see? Let's count the men.* Count from one to six. Ben sees six men. *What do the men do?* The men work. Explain the meanings of *drill, fix,* and *cracks* as necessary. Continue for the baker and the vet on pages 20–21.

Intermediate Guide children to answer the question by adding additional details to their answers. *What do the men do?* The men work. The men fix the street. Point to the rain. *The men work in the rain. Are the men wet?* Yes, the men are wet.

Advanced/Advanced High Have partners elaborate on their answers. *What job do the men do?* The men fix the street. *How do the men fix the street?* The men use a drill. *Why is it a "wet job"?* The men work in the rain.

Pages 22–23

Pages 22–23 Read the text aloud and have children follow along. Review the setting in the last part of the story. *Ben and Mom are at the library. The setting is the library.* Point to the building, librarian, and books as you say each word, and have children repeat. *We can get books at the library. Where is Ben?* Ben is at the library. *What can you get at the library?* I can get books. *A librarian helps Ben get books. Is Ben glad?* Yes, Ben is glad. *How do you know?* Ben is smiling.

What does Ben get? Discuss with a partner.

Beginning Point to the picture of Ben on page 23. *Where is Ben? Point to Ben.* Then point to the book in Ben's hands. *What does Ben have?* Ben has a book. *Say* book. *What does Ben get?* Ben gets books. *What can Ben do?* Ben can read.

Intermediate Have children add details to their answers. *What does Ben get?* Ben gets books. *What does Ben read?* Ben reads books on jobs.

Advanced/Advanced High Have children discuss with a partner: *What can Ben do?* Ben can read. *What does Ben read?* Ben reads books on jobs. *Why is it a "good job"?* Ben can read. Challenge children to look at the pictures on the books to discuss the kinds of books on jobs that Ben has.

FORMATIVE ASSESSMENT

❯ STUDENT CHECK-IN

Have partners retell different kinds of occupations that Ben saw during his trip to the library. Then, have children reflect using the Check-In Routine.

Independent Time

Ask and Answer Questions Pair children of mixed proficiencies. Have partners discuss the different jobs that Ben sees in his community. Have them take turns asking and answering questions. Then have each pair tell the rest of the group. Provide sentence frames to help them: *What jobs does Ben see?* Ben sees a vet. *What kind of job is this?* It is a pet job. *What other jobs does Ben see?* Ben sees a bus driver. *What kind of job is this?* It is a good job.

ENGLISH LANGUAGE LEARNERS 57

LESSON 3

READING • ANCHOR TEXT • ACCESS THE TEXT

LEARNING GOALS

We can read and understand a realistic fiction story.

OBJECTIVES

Retell stories, including key details, and demonstrate understanding of their central message or lesson.

Describe characters and major events in a story, using key details.

Build on others' talk in conversations by responding to the comments of others through multiple exchanges.

Ask questions to clear up any confusion about the topics and texts under discussion.

LANGUAGE OBJECTIVES

Children will narrate the characters' actions, using key vocabulary and simple sentences.

ELA ACADEMIC LANGUAGE

- illustration, details
- Cognates: *ilustración, detalles*

MATERIALS

Literature Anthology, pp. 6–19

Visual Vocabulary Cards

DIGITAL TOOLS

Have children listen to the selection as they follow along to develop comprehension and practice fluency and pronunciation.

Use the online High-Frequency Words Activity for additional support.

The Red Hat

Prepare to Read

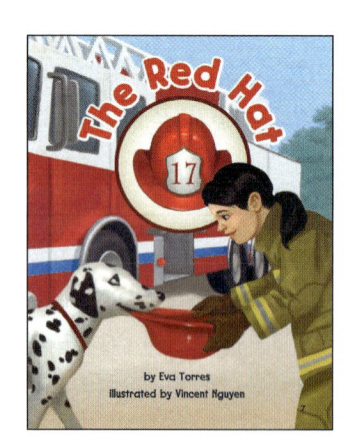

Build Background *We are going to read a story about a firefighter.* Break the word *firefighter* into two parts. Say the words *fire* and *fighter* as you point to each word, and have children repeat. Explain that *firefighter* means "a person who fights, or stops, fires." *Firefighters wear special clothes. These clothes help keep them safe. In this story, the firefighter wears a red hat.* Display the title page. Have children say and point to the red hat.

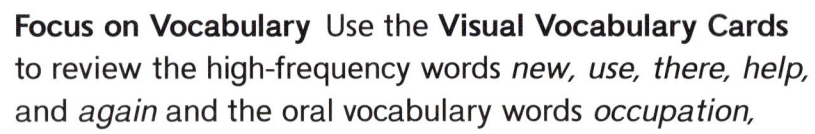

Focus on Vocabulary Use the **Visual Vocabulary Cards** to review the high-frequency words *new, use, there, help,* and *again* and the oral vocabulary words *occupation, community, astonishing, equipment,* and *fortunately.* As you read, teach important selection words using gestures and pantomime, such as *grabs* and *hops.* Grab an object and say *grab.* Have children repeat. *I can grab a pencil. What is something that you can grab?* I can grab a book. Repeat this routine with *hops.*

Literature Anthology, Lexile BR

Summarize the Text Before reading, say the summary while pointing to the illustrations. *This story is about Jen. Jen's job is to fight fires. Jen wears a special red hat at her job.*

Read the Text

Use the Interactive Question-Response Routine to help children understand the story.

Pages 8–13

Pages 8–9 Read the text. Point to Jen. *This is Jen. What does Jen get?* Jen gets a new red hat. Say *a lot* and review its meaning. Remind children that *a lot* is the opposite of *a little,* or not very much. *Will Jen use her new hat a lot?* Yes, Jen will use her new hat a lot.

Pages 10–13 Read the text. Help children retell the events on these pages using the words and pictures. Ask questions to help children retell the events: *Where is Jen?* Jen is in bed. Point to the bell above Jen's head. Say *bell. What does Jen hear?* Jen hears the bell. *What does Jen do?* Jen grabs her red hat. Jen gets down. *How can Jen help? Use the picture to help you answer.* Jen can put out the fire.

Why must Jen move fast? Discuss with a partner.

Beginning Have partners use the pictures on pages 12–13 to help them respond. *Does Jen hop on the truck?* Yes, Jen hops on the truck.

58 UNIT 2 WEEK 1

WEEK 1

Point to the fire on page 13. Say and point to the fire. *Why does Jen move fast?* There is a fire. *Can Jen help?* Yes, Jen can help.

Intermediate Point to the picture on page 12. *What does Jen do?* Jen hops on the truck. *Who moves fast?* Jen moves fast. *Why does Jen move fast?* Jen needs to get to the fire.

Advanced/Advanced High Have partners discuss the events on these pages: Jen hops on the truck. Jen goes! Jen moves fast. Jen can help put out the fire.

Pages 14–17

Pages 14–15 Read the text. Point to Jen on page 14, and then page 15. *The fire is out. Jen is wet. Why is Jen wet?* Jen put out the fire. Say *wet* and have children repeat. Point to Jen on page 15. *Jen plays. Who does Jen play with?* Jen plays with Matt and Jill. Point to the bell. *What does Jen hear?* Jen hears the bell.

Pages 16–17 Read the text. *Jen grabs her red hat. Jen goes.* Point to the picture of Jen climbing the ladder. *Jen climbs the ladder.* Act out the motion of climbing and have children do the same. Point to the ladder. *This is a ladder. What does Jen do?* Jen climbs the ladder. Jen will help.

How is Jen brave? Discuss with a partner.

Beginning Help partners respond: Point to Rex. *Where is Rex?* Rex is in the tree. *What does Jen do?* Jen climbs up the ladder. Jen gets Rex.

Intermediate Have partners add details to their answers. *What does Jen climb?* Jen climbs a ladder. *Is the ladder tall or short?* It is a tall ladder. *Is Jen scared?* Jen does not look scared.

Advanced/Advanced High Extend the discussion. Review the meaning of *brave*. *Is Jen Brave? Tell how you know.* Jen climbs a tall ladder. Jen helps Rex.

Pages 18–19

Pages 18–19 Read the text. Point to Jen on page 18. *Does Jen get Rex?* Yes, Jen gets Rex. Point to Jim and Rex on page 19. *Look at Jim's face. Is Jim happy?* (Yes, Jim is happy.) Point to Rex. *This is Rex. Look at Rex's face. Does Rex look happy?* Yes, Rex is happy. *Why is Rex happy?* Rex is safe. Jen helped Rex. Point to Jen's red hat on page 19. *What does Rex have?* Rex has a new red bed. *Show me Rex's bed. Say* new red bed.

Why does Jim say thank you to Jen? Discuss with a partner.

Beginning Have partners use the pictures to confirm their understanding. Explain that *glad* means *happy*. Smile to show that you are glad. Point to your smile. *I am glad. Say* glad. Point to Jim's face on page 19. *Look at the picture. Is Jim glad?* (yes) *Why is Jim glad?* Jen helped Jim.

Intermediate Have partners point to Jim and Jen. *What does Jim say to Jen?* Jim says thank you. *Why does Jim thank Jen?* Jen got Rex.

Advanced/Advanced High Help partners elaborate on their answers. *How does Jen help Jim?* Jen helps Jim get Rex. *Point to the people who are glad.* (Jen, Rex, Jim) *Why is Jim glad?* Jen saved Rex. *Why is Rex glad?* Rex has a new red bed.

FORMATIVE ASSESSMENT

❯ STUDENT CHECK IN

Have partners retell the two problems in the story and discuss how the characters fixed the problems. Then, have children reflect using the Check-In Routine.

Independent Time

Oral Language Select a spread from *The Red Hat* and pair children of mixed proficiencies. Have them take turns asking and answering *who, what, where,* and *when* questions using the images and text on the spread. Use **Oral Language Sentence Frames**, page 2, Asking and Answering Questions, to support children during this activity. Guide children to ask and answer questions about the characters, setting, and events using the sentence frames. If time allows, have children switch partners and repeat the activity using the images and text for a different spread.

ENGLISH LANGUAGE LEARNERS **59**

READING • LEVELED READER • ACCESS THE TEXT

LESSONS 4-5

LEARNING GOALS

We can make predictions about what happens in a realistic fiction.

OBJECTIVES

Describe characters, settings, and major events in a story, using key details.

Ask and answer questions about key details in a text.

Identify basic similarities in and differences between two texts on the same topic.

Ask questions to clear up any confusion about the topics and texts under discussion.

LANGUAGE OBJECTIVES

Children will narrate the story events using the verb *will*.

ELA ACADEMIC LANGUAGE

- realistic, predict
- Cognates: *realista, predecir*

MATERIALS

ELL Leveled Reader: *Ben Brings the Mail*

Online Differentiated Texts, "Bess Can Help"

Online ELL Visual Vocabulary Cards

DIGITAL TOOLS

Have children listen to the selection as they follow along to develop comprehension and practice fluency and pronunciation. Use Graphic Organizer 2: Character, Setting, Events to enhance the lesson.

Ben Brings the Mail

Prepare to Read

Build Background

- Remind children of the Essential Question. *Let's see what jobs need to be done in a community.* Encourage children to ask clarifying questions as needed.

- Point to and read the title and have children repeat. Then point to the picture of Ben. *This story is about Ben. Ben brings the mail. A person who brings the mail is called a mail carrier. What does Ben bring?* Ben brings the _____.

Lexile 70L

Focus on Vocabulary Use the **ELL Visual Vocabulary Cards** to preteach the words *delivery* and *neighborhood*. As you read, teach important story words, such as *letter, ad, box,* and *again*.

Read the Text

Use the Interactive Question-Response Routine to help children understand the story.

Pages 2–3

Main Story Elements: Character, Setting, Events Read pages 2–3. Help children identify the character, setting, and event. *What character do you see?* (Ben) *Where is Ben?* (in a street) *What is the setting?* The setting is a street.

Beginning Have children point to pictures as they respond: *Ben drives a special truck. Say and point to the* mail truck. *What is Ben holding?* Ben is holding mail.

Intermediate Have children talk to a partner about what they guess Ben will do next. *What will Ben do?* Ben will bring the mail to people.

Pages 4–7

Make and Confirm Predictions Have children make predictions about what Ben does. Read pages 4–7 as children follow along. Ask questions to help them confirm their predictions. Point to the letter on page 5. *What is this?* (a letter) Point to Miss Deb. *Who is this?* (Miss Deb) *What does Ben give to Miss Deb?* Ben gives Miss Deb a letter. Repeat this routine for pages 6 and 7.

Intermediate Have partners ask and answer questions. *What does Ben give Sam?* Ben gives Sam an ad. *Why will the ad help Sam?* Sam's bike is broken. *What does Ben give Meg?* Ben gives Meg a box.

Advanced/Advanced High Have partners discuss the different things a mail carrier can deliver. A mail carrier can deliver [letters, boxes, ads].

60 UNIT 2 WEEK 1

WEEK 1

Pages 8–11

Read pages 8–11 and have children follow along. Point to the pictures and say *mail box, Rex,* and *again.* Have children repeat.

Beginning Point to the pictures. *Does Ben give Rex mail?* No, Ben has no mail for <u>Rex</u>. *Will Ben come back again?* Yes, Ben will <u>come back</u>. Ben will have new <u>mail</u>.

Respond to Reading Have partners work together to retell the story and respond to the questions on page 12.

Focus on Fluency

Read pages 10–11. Then reread them and have children echo-read after you. Remind children to read the words correctly.

Paired Selection: "At the Post Office"

Analytical Writing — Make Connections: Write About It

Echo-read each page with children. Discuss what a postal worker does. *This is a postal worker. What does a postal worker do?* A postal worker sells <u>stamps</u>. Help children make connections between the two texts using the question on page 15. Ben and the postal worker help us with our <u>mail</u>.

Leveled Reader

Build Knowledge: Make Connections

Talk About the Text Have partners discuss why the jobs in the texts need to be done in a community.

Write About the Text Have children add their ideas to their Build Knowledge pages of their reader's notebooks.

Self-Selected Reading

Help children choose a realistic fiction selection from the online **Leveled Reader Library** or read the **Differentiated Text**, "Bess Can Help."

LITERATURE CIRCLES

Lead children in conducting a literature circle using the Thinkmark questions to guide the discussion. You may wish to discuss what children have learned about mail carriers from both selections in the leveled reader.

FORMATIVE ASSESSMENT

STUDENT CHECK-IN

Have partners share their Respond to Reading. Have children reflect using the Check-In Routine.

LEVEL UP

IF children can read *Ben Brings the Mail* **ELL Level** with fluency and correctly answer the Comprehension Check questions,

THEN tell children that they will read a more detailed version of the selection.

- Use pages 4–5 of *Ben Brings the Mail* **On Level** to model using Teaching Poster 28 to identify character, setting, and events.

- Have children read the selection, checking their comprehension by using the graphic organizer.

ENGLISH LANGUAGE LEARNERS

LESSONS 1-5

WRITING

MODELED WRITING
LESSON 1

LEARNING GOALS

We can learn to write a sentence about one idea.

OBJECTIVES

Write informative texts in which they name a topic.

LANGUAGE OBJECTIVES

Children will inform by writing a complete sentence using the phrase *want to be*.

ELA ACADEMIC LANGUAGE

- noun, idea
- Cognate: *idea*

Writing Practice Review the sample sentence on p. 24 of the **Reading/Writing Companion**. Guide children to analyze each part of the sentence using the Actor/Action Routine: *Who is the actor in this sentence?* (I) *What is the action?* (want to be a doctor) Then read the prompt on p. 25, and ask a volunteer to answer it. Write the sentence on the board for children to choral read. Have partners answer the prompt orally before writing their own sentence. Remind them to only give one idea.

Beginning *What do you want to be?* I want to be a teacher. Provide vocabulary as needed.

Intermediate Have partners take turns asking and answering questions to elicit their sentences: What do you want to be? I want to be a teacher.

Advanced/Advanced High Challenge children to identify the noun in their sentence. Encourage them to share their sentence with the group.

FORMATIVE ASSESSMENT ▶ **STUDENT CHECK-IN** Partners share their sentences. Ask children to reflect using the Check-In Routine.

INTERACTIVE WRITING
LESSON 2

LEARNING GOALS

We can read and write about a Student Model.

OBJECTIVES

Respond to questions and suggestions from peers.

LANGUAGE OBJECTIVES

Children will discuss the Student Model and write sentences using nouns.

ELA ACADEMIC LANGUAGE

- opinion, text
- Cognates: *opinión, texto*

Analyze the Student Model Have children choral read the Student Model on p. 30 of the **Reading/Writing Companion**. Review how *look* is used in the first sentence. Then guide children to notice a word that shows Eva's opinion. (fun) *Do you think Eva liked the story?* (yes) Have children check their answer using the last sentence. Then help them complete p. 31.

Beginning Guide children to point to nouns from the text. Then provide a sentence frame: I noticed the noun animals.

Intermediate Have partners take turns identifying nouns in the student model. Eva used the noun jobs. A job is a thing.

Advanced/Advanced High Challenge children to find words that show Eva's opinion, such as *fun, favorite,* and *recommend*.

FORMATIVE ASSESSMENT ▶ **STUDENT CHECK-IN** Partners share their responses. Ask children to reflect using the Check-In Routine.

62 UNIT 2 WEEK 1

WEEK 1

INDEPENDENT WRITING
LESSONS 3-4

LEARNING GOALS
- We can write an opinion about a realistic fiction story.
- We can write sentences with nouns.

OBJECTIVES
Write opinion pieces in which they supply a reason for the opinion.

LANGUAGE OBJECTIVES
Children will argue about a subject, or say why they like or dislike a subject, by writing sentences using nouns.

ELA ACADEMIC LANGUAGE
- opinion, clues
- Cognate: *opinión*

Find Text Evidence Use the Independent Writing Routine. Help children orally retell the anchor text. Remind them to look for clues in the story. Ask questions, such as: *What is Jen's new job?* (a firefighter) *What does she wear?* (a red hat) Then read the prompt on p. 36 of the **Reading/Writing Companion:** *Would you like to have Jen's job? Tell why or why not. We need to write our opinion about Jen's job and give a reason why.*

Write a Response Distribute **My Writing Outline 6** to children, and display it on a smartboard. Then, work with children to fill out the outline. After they have completed their outline, have children complete p. 36 of the Reading/Writing Companion using the sentences from their outline.

Writing Checklist Read the checklist with students, and have them check for these items in their writing.

Beginning *Point to a noun. Is it a person, place, or thing?* A tree is a thing.

Intermediate Guide children to notice that each sentence conveys an idea.

Advanced/Advanced High Have children identify where they used each checklist item in their writing.

FORMATIVE ASSESSMENT > **STUDENT CHECK-IN** Partners share their sentences from My Writing Outline. Ask children to reflect using the Check-in Routine.

SELF-SELECTED WRITING
LESSON 5

LEARNING GOALS
We can revise our writing.

OBJECTIVES
Use commas to separate single words in a series.

LANGUAGE OBJECTIVES
Children will inquire about their writing by checking that commas in a list are placed correctly.

ELA ACADEMIC LANGUAGE
- commas
- Cognate: *comas*

Work with children to revise the group writing activity. Point to each word as you read the sentences. Stop to ask questions, such as *This word is part of a list. Should a comma be here?* You may also write a sentence with a list of three items and no commas and correct the sentence together. Then, have partners revise each other's sentences before publishing them.

For support with grammar, refer to the **Language Transfers Handbook** and **Language Development Card** 1A.

FORMATIVE ASSESSMENT > **STUDENT CHECK-IN** Partners explain their revisions. Ask children to reflect using the Check-in Routine.

ENGLISH LANGUAGE LEARNERS 63

LESSONS 1-2

READING • LITERATURE BIG BOOK • ACCESS THE TEXT

LEARNING GOALS

We can understand what happens when three dassies build a home as we listen to a story.

OBJECTIVES

Retell stories, including key details, and demonstrate understanding of their central message or lesson.

Compare and contrast the adventures and experiences of characters in stories.

Identify words and phrases in stories or poems that suggest feelings or appeal to the senses.

Ask and answer questions about key details in a text read aloud or information presented orally or through other media.

LANGUAGE OBJECTIVES

Children will narrate the events of the story, using adjectives, and nouns.

ELA ACADEMIC LANGUAGE

- fantasy, predict
- Cognates: *fantasía, predecir*

MATERIALS

Literature Big Book, *The 3 Little Dassies,* pp. 3–32

Visual Vocabulary Cards

DIGITAL TOOLS

Have children listen to the selection as they follow along to develop comprehension and practice fluency and pronunciation.

Use the additional grammar video.

Grammar Video

The 3 Little Dassies

Prepare to Read

Build Background *We are going to read a story about animals called dassies.* Show the picture on the cover. *I know this is a fantasy because the dassies wear clothes. In this story, the three little dassies will leave home and find a new place in the desert. A desert is hot and dry.* Model for children: *It is time for the three little dassies to leave home.* Have children repeat. Then have children talk about what it is time for them to do. Provide a sentence frame: It is time for me to ____.

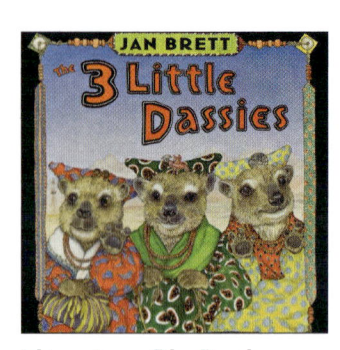

Literature Big Book

Focus on Vocabulary Use the **Visual Vocabulary Cards** to review the oral vocabulary words *shelter* and *materials*. As you read, use gestures and other visual support to clarify important story words, such as: *crowded, shivered, watching,* and *flap*. Say: *The word* shiver *means* shake when you are cold or afraid. *Say* shiver *with me.* Point to *shivered* in the text. Provide an example: *I shivered when I saw a spider. When did you shiver?* I shivered when I saw a snake

Summarize the Text Before reading, say the summary while pointing to the illustrations. *The story tells about three dassies that find their own place to live.*

Read the Text

Use the Interactive Question-Response Routine to help children understand the story.

Pages 3–5

Pages 4–5 Read the text aloud. Point to the dassies. *The dassies travel to the mountain. They are excited about this place. It is not crowded.* Point to the Agama Man. *The Agama Man says "welcome" from the scree. A scree is a group of stones.* Have children repeat *welcome. The Agama Man says that eagles live on the mountain.* Point to the eagles and say *eagle* for children to repeat. *Who lives on the mountain?* (eagles) *The text says that the dassies "shiver in the hot sun." Are they cold or scared?* (scared) *What are they afraid of?* (eagles)

What do the dassies think of this place? Discuss with a partner.

Beginning Review *crowded* and *eagles*. Point to the picture. *Is this place crowded?* No, this place is not crowded. *Do the dassies like the place?* (yes) *Do eagles live here?* Yes, eagles live here. *Do the dassies like eagles?* No, the dassies do not like eagles.

64 UNIT 2 WEEK 2

WEEK 2

Intermediate Have partners point to parts of the picture as they respond: *What is this place like?* It has a big mountain. It is not crowded. It has the Agama Man and eagles. *What do the dassies like?* They like that it is not crowded. *What do they not like?* They do not like that it has eagles.

Advanced/Advanced High Have partners give details. *Why do the dassies want to live here?* They like that it is not crowded. *What does the Agama Man say?* He says that a family of eagles lives here. *How do the dassies feel now?* They are scared of eagles.

Pages 6–19

Pages 16–19 Review pages 14–19. *What happens to Mimbi and Pimbi?* The eagle blows in their houses and drops them in the nest. *What are their houses made of?* (grass, sticks) Read the text aloud. *A shadow is a dark shape made when something blocks the light.*

Think about the events with two dassies. What do you predict will happen to Timbi? Discuss with a partner.

Beginning Help partners respond. *Does the eagle blow Mimbi's grass house in?* Yes, the eagle blows Mimbi's house in. *What happens to Pimbi's stick house?* The eagle blows Pimbi's house in. *Will the eagle blow in Timbi's stone house, too?* (Possible answer: no) *Will Timbi be safe?* (Possible answer: yes)

Intermediate Help partners ask and answer. *What does the eagle do to Mimbi's and Pimbi's houses?* He blows them in. *What will the eagle try to do with Timbi's house?* The eagle will try to blow in Timbi's house. *Will her stone house come down?* (Possible answer: no)

Advanced/Advanced High Help partners extend their predictions. *What will happen to Timbi?* The eagle will not be able to blow in Timbi's stone house and Timbi will be safe. *Do you think that the eagle will eat Mimbi and Pimbi?* (Possible answer: No, Mimbi and Pimbi can leave the nest when the eagle is away.)

Pages 20–32

Page 32 Confirm children's predictions about Timbi. Then read the text aloud. *This part of the book tells about real animals that live in Namibia. Where do real dassies live today?* (in stone houses) *Who helps look out for them?* (the agama men) *How do they spot eagles?* (black feathers)

How does the story change? Discuss with a partner.

Beginning Point to the picture. *Are these animals wearing clothes?* No, they are not wearing clothes. *Do they have names?* No they do not have names.

Intermediate *How are the dassies different in this picture?* They are not wearing clothes. *How is the text about these dassies different?* They do not have names. They do not talk.

Advanced/Advanced High *How is this page different?* (It is about real animals.) *What do you learn about real dassies, agama men, and eagles?* I learn that dassies live in stone houses, agama men watch the dassies, and eagles have black feathers.

FORMATIVE ASSESSMENT

STUDENT CHECK-IN

Have partners retell the dassies' problem and how the dassies found a solution. Then, have children reflect using the Check-In Routine.

Independent Time

Oral Language Pair children of mixed proficiencies. Have partners discuss what buildings the dassies have, and what each dassy's house is made of. Then have each pair tell the rest of the group. Provide sentence frames to help them: The three little dassies have ___. Mimbi's house is made of ___. Pimbi's house is made of ___. Timbi's house is made of ___.

ENGLISH LANGUAGE LEARNERS **65**

READING • SHARED READ • ACCESS THE TEXT

LESSONS 1-2

LEARNING GOALS

We can read and understand a fantasy story.

OBJECTIVES

Retell stories, including key details, and demonstrate understanding of their central message or lesson.

Use illustrations and details in a story to describe its characters, setting, or events.

Describe people, places, things, and events with relevant details, expressing ideas and feelings clearly.

LANGUAGE OBJECTIVES

Children will narrate the events of a story using singular and plural nouns.

ELA ACADEMIC LANGUAGE

- fantasy, characters, prediction
- Cognates: *fantasía, predicción*

MATERIALS

Reading/Writing Companion, pp. 48–57

Visual Vocabulary Cards

DIGITAL TOOLS

Have children listen to the selection as they follow along to develop comprehension and practice fluency and pronunciation.

Use the additional grammar video.

Grammar Video

"Cubs in a Hut"

Prepare to Read

Build Background Tell children that the story they will read is a fantasy. *This fantasy story has animal characters that talk.* Point to and read aloud the title. *We are going to read about three cubs.* Point to Gus. *The cub with a G on his shirt is Gus. Say the name* Gus. Point to Rus. *Rus has an R on his shirt. Say* Rus. Point to Bud on page 51. *This is Bud. What letter is on his shirt? The letter is ____. Say* Bud.

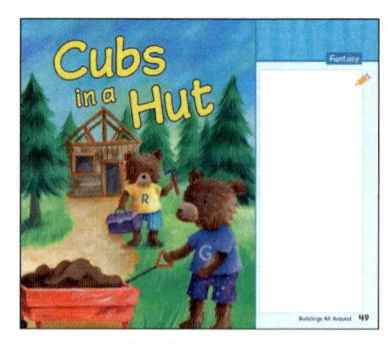

Reading/Writing Companion, Lexile 390L

Focus on Vocabulary Use the **Visual Vocabulary Cards** to preteach the high-frequency words *could, live, one, then,* and *three* and the oral language vocabulary words *shelter, materials, collapsed, furious,* and *refused.* As you read, use gestures and visual support to teach the important story words *stack, hammer, wheelbarrow, ladder, hut, drip,* and *wet.*

Summarize the Text Before reading, say the summary and point to the illustrations. *This story tells about how three bear cubs make a hut and then fix it.*

Read the Text

Use the Interactive Question-Response Routine to help children understand the story.

Pages 50–53

Pages 50–51 Read the text aloud as children follow along. *The cubs want to make a hut. A hut is a little house.* Point to the picture on page 51. *Look at the drawing. It shows the hut the bears want to build. What do the cubs get?* (a stack of sticks, mud, and grass)

Pages 52–53 Point to the picture on page 52. *Do the cubs make a hut?* (yes) *The picture shows a hut and tools.* Point to each tool as you say: *I see a hammer, a wheelbarrow, and a ladder.* Read the text aloud as children follow. Point to and say the phrase *a very good job* for children to repeat. *When we are happy with something we did, we say "We did a very good job."* Point to and say the words *move in* for children to repeat. *Move in means going to a place to live.* Point to the picture on page 53. *The cubs are moving in. They are putting in rugs and beds and lots of other stuff. What stuff do you see?* (a picture and a ball)

COLLABORATE *What do the cubs do with the new hut? Discuss with a partner.*

Beginning Use the pictures to review *move in, set up, rugs,* and *beds.* Point to the hut on page 52. *Do the cubs move in? Yes, the cubs* move in. *What do the cubs set up in the hut? They set up* rugs *and* beds.

66 UNIT 2 WEEK 2

WEEK 2

Intermediate Help partners give more complete answers. *What do the three cubs do with their hut?* They <u>move</u> in. They set up <u>rugs and beds</u>. They fill up the <u>hut</u> with lots of <u>stuff</u>, too.

Advanced/Advanced High Have partners elaborate on their answer. The cubs use a <u>hammer</u>, a wheelbarrow, and a <u>ladder</u> to build the hut. They are excited to <u>move in</u>. They set up <u>rugs and beds</u>. They fill up the hut with <u>lots of stuff</u>, like a picture and <u>a ball</u>.

Pages 54–55

Pages 54–55 Read the text. Point to the drops and the words *drip, drip, drip*. *These words tell how water sounds when it comes down.* Say *drip, drip, drip* for children to repeat. *I think it is raining outside. Water is coming in. It makes things wet. What gets wet?* Bud's <u>bed</u> and Gus's <u>head</u> get wet. *Are the cubs happy?* (no)

What happens in the hut? Discuss with a partner.

Beginning Guide partners to answer the question. Point to Bud's bed. *What happens to Bud's bed?* Bud's bed gets <u>wet</u>. *What happens to Gus's head?* Gus's head gets <u>wet</u>. *Is water dripping in the hut?* Yes, water is <u>dripping</u>. *Will the cubs fix it?* (Possible answer: yes)

Intermediate Help partners with responses. *What sound do the cubs hear?* (Drip, drip, drip!) *What does that sound mean?* Water is getting in the <u>hut</u>. *What happens to Bud and Gus?* Bud's bed <u>gets wet</u>. Gus's head <u>gets wet</u>.

Advanced/Advanced High Help partners ask and answer questions. *What happens one night?* Water <u>drips</u> in the <u>hut</u>. *What do the cubs do?* They get <u>up</u>. Bud yells that his bed <u>is wet</u>. Gus yells that his <u>head</u> is <u>wet</u>. *What does Rus think?* Rus thinks it is <u>not</u> fun to live in a <u>wet</u> hut.

Pages 56-57

Pages 56-57 Read the text and have children read along. Point to the picture. *It is raining. One cub has an umbrella. The cubs are on the roof.* Have children say *roof*. *They see the spot where rain comes in. They are fixing the roof.* Help children recall and confirm predictions they made. *I see tools they used to make the hut. What tools do you see?* (hammer, ladder) *I see boards, too.* Point to page 57. *What do the cubs do next?* They sleep in the <u>beds</u>. *Do they get wet?* No, they do <u>not</u> get wet. Point to and say the word *dry* for children to repeat. *Dry* means *not wet*. Point to and say the idiom *snug as a bug in a rug. This phrase means very comfortable.* Have children repeat it.

What do the cubs do? Discuss relevant details with a partner.

Beginning Point to page 56. *What do the cubs do?* They fix the <u>hut</u>. Point to page 57. *Is the hut wet or dry?* The hut is <u>dry</u>. *Do the cubs sleep?* Yes, they <u>sleep</u>.

Intermediate Help partners give details. *What do the cubs do about the dripping water?* They fix the <u>roof</u> of the hut. *What do the cubs do next?* They sleep in the <u>beds</u>. *Why can they sleep?* The hut is <u>dry</u>.

Advanced/Advanced High Help partners add details in their answer. *What do the cubs do about the dripping water?* The cubs climb a <u>ladder</u> to the roof. Next, they <u>see/spot/find</u> a hole. Then they use a <u>hammer</u> and boards to fix it.

FORMATIVE ASSESSMENT

STUDENT CHECK-IN

Have partners retell three tools the cubs used and how they used them. Then, have children reflect using the Check-In Routine.

Independent Time

Describe a Picture Select a spread from "Cubs in a Hut" for children to describe. Pair children of mixed proficiencies. Have them take turns asking and answering about images on the spread. Provide sentence frames for support: What do you see? I see a ___. Have partners describe the images to the group. In this picture, I see a ___. Use **Oral Language Sentence Frames**, page 6, Nouns/Noun Phrases, to help children extend or elaborate on their sentences.

ENGLISH LANGUAGE LEARNERS **67**

LESSON 3

READING • ANCHOR TEXT • ACCESS THE TEXT

LEARNING GOALS

We can read and understand a fantasy story.

OBJECTIVES

Compare and contrast the adventures and experiences of characters in stories.

Identify words and phrases in stories or poems that suggest feelings or appeal to the senses.

Build on others' talk in conversations by responding to the comments of others through multiple exchanges.

Produce complete sentences when appropriate to task and situation.

LANGUAGE OBJECTIVES

Children will narrate the characters' actions, using key vocabulary and simple sentences.

ELA ACADEMIC LANGUAGE

- predict, illustration, author
- Cognates: *predecir, ilustración, autor*

MATERIALS

Literature Anthology, pp. 26–43

Visual Vocabulary Cards

DIGITAL TOOLS

Have children listen to the selection as they follow along to develop comprehension and practice fluency and pronunciation.

Use the additional grammar song.

Grammar Song

The Pigs, the Wolf, and the Mud

Prepare to Read

Build Background *We are going to read a story about three pigs, a wolf, and the three pigs' house.* Show the picture on the cover and ask children what they see. Model for children: *The three pigs are making a mess.* Have children repeat. Point to the wolf. Tell children that this story is similar to a story they may have heard before: *The Three Little Pigs. Do you know this story?*

Focus on Vocabulary Use the **Visual Vocabulary Cards** to review the high-frequency words *could, live, one, then,* and *three* and the oral vocabulary words *shelter, materials, collapsed, furious,* and *refused.* As you read, teach important story words using gestures and pantomime, such as *mud.*

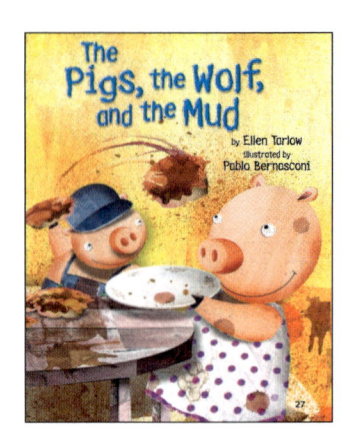

Literature Anthology, Lexile 320L

Summarize the Text Before reading, say the summary while pointing to the illustrations. *The story tells about three pigs that live in a mud hut. We'll read what happens when a wolf comes to their home.*

Read the Text

Use the Interactive Question-Response Routine to help children understand the story.

Pages 28–29

Pages 28–29 Read the text aloud. Point to the hut. *What does the illustration show?* (three pigs in a hut) *The hut is made of mud. Is your home made of mud?* (no) *The pigs live in the mud hut.* Point to the picture on page 29. *The mom pig is giving the boy pig a bath in mud. The mud is messy. Are the pigs mad?* (no) *The author tells us that pigs like a mess. Pigs think mud is fun!*

Why is the mud hut a good place for the pigs to live? Discuss with a partner.

Beginning Help partners point to the pictures as they respond. *Do the pigs look happy in the mud hut?* Yes, the pigs look happy. *Is mud messy?* Yes, mud is messy. *Do the pigs like mud?* Yes, the pigs like mud. *How do you know?* They are smiling.

Intermediate *What two things do the pigs like?* The pigs like mud and a mess. *How do the pictures tell you this?* The pigs look happy in the hut. *How do the words tell you this?* Pig Three yells "Mud is fun!"

Advanced/Advanced High Extend the discussion by having partners tell other words they know that describe mud. *I know the words dirty and sticky.* Have children use the words to tell why a mud hut is good for the pigs. (Possible response: The pigs like to be dirty and sticky.)

68 UNIT 2 WEEK 2

WEEK 2

Pages 30–37

Page 34 Read the text. Review that the wolf wants to eat the pigs. *The wolf huffs and puffs at the hut.* Huff and puff *is another way to say the wolf blows hard.* Point to the dust. *When the wolf huffs and puffs, mud flies and makes a mess.* Point to the word *"Yuck!"* The wolf says *"Yuck!"* We say yuck *when we do not like something.* Have children repeat *"Yuck!" Can the wolf huff and puff in mud?* (no)

Pages 36–37 Read the text. Point to the picture. *The wolf is kicking the hut. What is happening to the hut?* The hut is falling in. *Does the wolf look happy?* (no) *What word does the author have the wolf say again?* (Yuck!) *Do you think the wolf likes mud?* (no) *Do you predict that the wolf will eat the pigs?* (no)

Is the mud hut a bad place for the wolf to eat the pigs? Why or why not? Discuss with a partner.

Beginning Help partners point to the pictures on page 34 and pages 36–37 as they respond. *The wolf tries to make the hut fall two times. What happens to the wolf?* The mud gets on the wolf. *Is the mud messy?* Yes, the mud is messy. *Does the wolf want to be in the mud?* No, the wolf says "Yuck!"

Intermediate Help partners use pages 34 and 37 to respond. *What two things does the wolf say he cannot do?* He cannot huff or puff in mud. He cannot look at the mud. *Is the mud hut a bad place for the wolf?* Yes, it is a bad place for the wolf. He does not want to be in a messy place.

Advanced/Advanced High *Why does the wolf decide the mud hut is a bad place to eat the pigs?* When he blows on it or kicks it, the mud flies around and makes things messy. I know the wolf does not like the mud because he says "Yuck!"

Pages 38–41

Pages 40–41 Read the text. Have children repeat *could.* We sometimes use could *when we share ideas.* Point to the word *will.* Pig One says they will *use mud.* Point to the wolf. *The wolf is running away. What does the wolf say about the new mud hut?* (Yuck!)

Why is a new mud hut good for the pigs? Discuss with a partner.

Beginning Help partners recall how the pigs and wolf feel about mud. *Will the pigs like a new mud hut?* Yes, the pigs will like a new mud hut. *Will the wolf come to eat the pigs?* No, the wolf will not want to see mud.

Intermediate Help partners review. *How do the pigs feel about mud at the beginning?* They like it a lot. *Do they still feel the same way?* (yes) *Do you think the wolf will try to eat the pigs in the new hut?* No, the wolf does not like mud.

Advanced/Advanced High Help partners give several reasons why a mud hut will be good for the pigs. The pigs know mud is good for building. They think mud is fun. They like being messy. The wolf does not like mud. He will not come to eat them.

FORMATIVE ASSESSMENT

▶ STUDENT CHECK-IN

Have partners describe the differences between the pigs' first hut and the pigs' second hut. Then, have children reflect using the Check-In Routine.

Independent Time

Draw to Tell About a Story Pair children of mixed proficiencies and have them draw pictures to tell what the story is about. Provide sentence frames to help them talk and draw pictures. The story is about three___ and a ___. The three pigs live in a ___. The hut is made of ___. The wolf ___. The three pigs ___. Have children present their pictures to tell about the story to the group.

ENGLISH LANGUAGE LEARNERS **69**

LESSONS 4-5

READING • LEVELED READER • ACCESS THE TEXT

LEARNING GOALS

We can make predictions as we read a fantasy story.

OBJECTIVES

Retell stories, including key details, and demonstrate understanding of their central message or lesson.

Describe characters, settings, and major events in a story, using key details.

Ask and answer questions about key details in a text.

Identify basic similarities in and differences between two texts on the same topic.

LANGUAGE OBJECTIVES

Children will narrate the events of the story using key vocabulary.

ELA ACADEMIC LANGUAGE

- fantasy, prediction
- Cognates: *fantasía, predicción*

MATERIALS

ELL Leveled Reader: *Staying Afloat*

Online Differentiated Texts, "A Hut for Us"

Online ELL Visual Vocabulary Cards

DIGITAL TOOLS

Have children listen to the selection as they follow along to develop comprehension and practice fluency and pronunciation. Use Graphic Organizer 2: Character, Setting, Events to enhance the lesson.

Staying Afloat

Prepare to Read

Build Background

- Remind children of the Essential Question. *Let's read to see what a good boat is made of.* Encourage children to ask for help when they do not understand a word or phrase.

- Read aloud the title and have children repeat. Ask: *What is the title?* Have children point to it. Repeat the routine for the author's name. Tell children that this is a fantasy story. Point to the illustrations in the Leveled Reader to name things and actions.

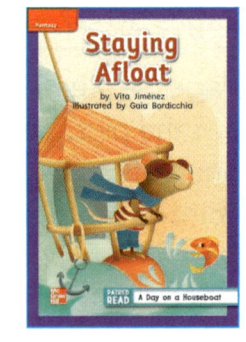

Lexile 10L

Focus on Vocabulary Use the **ELL Visual Vocabulary Cards** to preteach the words *construction* and *sink*. As you read, use gestures or visuals to teach important story words, such as *float, cardboard, hold,* and *wood*.

Read the Text

Use the Interactive Question-Response Routine to help children understand the story.

Pages 2–5

Main Story Elements: Character, Setting, Events Read pages 2–3. Help children identify character and setting. *Who is the character?* (Sam) *Where does Sam live?* Sam lives on a boat. *What is the setting?* (boat) The boat is the setting. We are going to read about what happens to Sam and his boat. These are the events.

Beginning Help partners point to pictures as they respond: *What is this?* It is a boat. *Can Sam's boat float?* Yes, Sam's boat can float.

Intermediate Help partners respond: *Where does Sam live?* He lives on a boat. *What can Sam's boat do?* His boat can float. *Where can he sit?* (on a deck)

Advanced/Advanced High Help partners ask and answer: *Who lives on a boat?* Sam lives on a boat. *What can Sam do?* He can sit on a deck. *What can his boat do?* It can float.

Pages 6–9

Make and Confirm Predictions Ask questions to help children make predictions. Point to Bob's boat. *Bob's boat is made of cardboard. Do you think Bob's boat will float?* (yes/no) Read page 8 and have children confirm their predictions.

Beginning *What do Sam and Bob do?* They jump in the boat. *Do waves jump in?* Yes, waves jump in. *Will Bob's boat float?* No, his boat will not float. *Will Sam help Bob?* Yes, Sam will help Bob.

70 UNIT 2 WEEK 2

WEEK 2

Advanced/Advanced High *What happens when Sam and Bob jump in Bob's boat?* Waves jump in. *What will happen next?* Bob's boat will sink. *What will Sam do?* Sam will help Bob.

Pages 10–11

Read pages 10–11 as children follow along. Point to pictures and say *plans* and *wood*. Have children repeat.

Intermediate Help partners respond. *What do Sam and Bob do now?* They make plans for a new boat. They make a good boat with wood.

Advanced/Advanced High Have partners describe the pictures. Sam tells his plans for a new boat. Sam and Bob use wood to make a boat.

Respond to Reading Have partners work together to retell the story and respond to the questions on page 12.

Focus on Fluency

Read pages 6–7. Have children echo-read. Remind them to read the words correctly. For more practice, record children reading the passage and have them select the best recording for you.

Paired Selection: "A Day on a Houseboat"

Analytical Writing **Make Connections: Write About It**

Echo-read each page with children. Discuss what each caption says you can do on a houseboat: You can sleep in the bedroom. Help children make connections between texts using the question on page 15. You and Sam can sit on a deck on a houseboat.

Leveled Reader

Build Knowledge: Make Connections

Talk About the Text Have partners discuss the buildings in the texts and tell if they have seen buildings like these before.

Write About the Text Have students add their ideas to their Build Knowledge pages of their reader's notebooks.

Self-Selected Reading

Help children choose a fiction selection from the online **Leveled Reader Library** or read the **Differentiated Text,** "A Hut for Us."

FOCUS ON GENRE

Children can extend their knowledge of the fantasy genre by completing the genre activity on page 16.

LITERATURE CIRCLES

Lead children in conducting a literature circle using the Thinkmark questions to guide the discussion. You may wish to discuss what children have learned about houseboats from both selections in the Leveled Reader.

FORMATIVE ASSESSMENT

▶ STUDENT CHECK-IN

Have partners share their Respond to Reading. Have children reflect using the Check-In Routine.

LEVEL UP

IF children can read *Staying Afloat* **ELL Level** with fluency and correctly answer the Respond to Reading questions,

THEN tell children that they will read a more detailed version of the story.

- Use pages 2–4 of *Staying Afloat* **On Level** to model using Teaching Poster 35 to identify character, setting, and events.
- Have children read the selection, checking their comprehension by using the graphic organizer.

ENGLISH LANGUAGE LEARNERS **71**

LESSONS 1-5

WRITING

MODELED WRITING

LESSON 1

LEARNING GOALS

We can learn to write a sentence with descriptive details.

OBJECTIVES

Write narratives in which they include some details.

LANGUAGE OBJECTIVES

Children will inform by writing a complete sentence using the verb *help*.

ELA ACADEMIC LANGUAGE

- detail
- Cognate: *detalle*

Writing Practice Review the sample on p. 58 of the **Reading/Writing Companion**. Guide children to analyze it using the Actor/Action Routine: *Who is the actor?* (I) *What is the action?* (helped my little brother) *What is the descriptive detail?* (with his homework) Then read the prompt on p. 59, and ask a volunteer to answer. Write the sentence on the board for children to choral read before writing their own sentence.

Beginning *Who is the actor?* (I) *Who did you help?* (my mom) *What did you do?* (bake a cake) Provide a sentence frame if needed.

Intermediate Have partners take turns asking and answering *who/what* questions to create their sentence. Provide a sentence frame if needed.

Advanced/Advanced High Challenge children to have more than one descriptive detail in their sentence.

FORMATIVE ASSESSMENT ➤ **STUDENT CHECK-IN** Partners share their sentences. Ask children to reflect using the Check-In Routine.

INTERACTIVE WRITING

LESSON 2

LEARNING GOALS

We can learn how to write a sentence with a descriptive detail.

OBJECTIVES

With guidance and support, respond to questions and suggestions from peers.

LANGUAGE OBJECTIVES

Children will discuss and write sentences about the Student Model, identifying singular and plural nouns.

ELA ACADEMIC LANGUAGE

- singular and plural nouns
- Cognates: *singulares, plurales*

Analyze the Student Model Have children finger point as they choral read the Student Model on p. 64 of the **Reading/Writing Companion**. Guide children to identify singular and plural nouns. *Clap once when you hear a singular noun, twice if it's plural.* Then review descriptive details: *How is the roof?* (leaky) *What other words can we use to describe the roof?* (yellow, grass) *What words can we use to tell about the cubs?* Then help children complete p. 65.

Beginning Ask partners to point to an example of a plural noun from the text. Then provide a sentence frame: I noticed the plural noun cubs.

Intermediate Have partners ask and answer questions: *What did you notice about Luis's writing?* Luis used descriptive details.

Advanced/Advanced High Challenge children to write about the text using their own sentences. Encourage them to share it with their group.

FORMATIVE ASSESSMENT ➤ **STUDENT CHECK-IN** Partners share their responses. Ask children to reflect using the Check-In Routine.

WEEK 2

INDEPENDENT WRITING
LESSONS 3-4

LEARNING GOALS

We can use text evidence to respond to a fantasy story.

OBJECTIVES

Write narratives in which they recount events in sequence.

LANGUAGE OBJECTIVES

Children will inform by writing sentences using text evidence.

ELA ACADEMIC LANGUAGE

- evidence
- Cognate: *evidencia*

Find Text Evidence Use the Independent Writing Routine. Help children orally retell the anchor text. Ask questions, such as: *Where do the pigs live?* (hut) *What does the wolf do?* (kicks the hut down) Then read the prompt on p. 70 of the **Reading/Writing Companion:** *Should the pigs be worried that the wolf will come back to bother them? Why or why not? We need to use text evidence to answer the question.* Display pp. 38-41 of the **Literature Anthology.** *What does the wolf think of mud?* (He does not like mud.) *What are the pigs using to build the new house?* (mud)

Write a Response Distribute **My Writing Outline 7** to children. Work with children to fill out the outline. After they have completed their outline, have children complete p. 70 using the sentences from their completed outline.

Writing Checklist Read the checklist with students, and have them check for these items in their writing.

Beginning Provide sentence frames to help partners talk about their sentences: I used the plural noun *pigs*.

Intermediate Encourage partners to use a descriptive detail.

Advanced/Advanced High Have parters identify where they used each checklist item in their writing.

FORMATIVE ASSESSMENT ▶ **STUDENT CHECK-IN** Partners share their sentences from My Writing Outline. Ask children to reflect using the Check-in Routine.

SELF-SELECTED WRITING
LESSON 5

LEARNING GOALS

We can revise our writing.

OBJECTIVES

Use singular and plural nouns with matching verbs in basic sentences.

LANGUAGE OBJECTIVES

Children will inquire about their writing by checking singular and plural nouns.

ELA ACADEMIC LANGUAGE

- singular, plural
- Cognates: *singular, plural*

Work with children to revise the group writing activity. Point to each word as you read the sentences. Stop to ask questions, such as, *Is this word a plural or singular noun? Should it have an s at the end?* If needed, write a sentence with a plural noun missing an *s* at the end, and revise the sentence together. Then have partners work together to correct each other's sentences before publishing them.

For support with singular and plural nouns and grammar, refer to the **Language Transfers Handbook** and **Language Development Cards** 1A, 2A, and 2B.

FORMATIVE ASSESSMENT ▶ **STUDENT CHECK-IN** Partners tell what revisions they made. Ask children to reflect using the Check-in Routine.

ENGLISH LANGUAGE LEARNERS

READING • LITERATURE BIG BOOK • ACCESS THE TEXT

LESSONS 1-2

LEARNING GOALS

We can understand information about animals as we listen to a text.

OBJECTIVES

Identify the main topic and retell key details of a text.

Describe the connection between two individuals, events, ideas, or pieces of information in a text.

Ask and answer questions about key details in a text read aloud or information presented orally or through other media.

Add drawings or other visual displays to descriptions when appropriate to clarify ideas, thoughts, and feelings.

LANGUAGE OBJECTIVES

Children will explain about different animals, using singular and plural nouns.

ELA ACADEMIC LANGUAGE

- nonfiction, compare
- Cognates: *no ficción, comparar*

MATERIALS

Literature Big Book, *Babies in the Bayou,* pp. 4–31

Visual Vocabulary Cards

DIGITAL TOOLS

MULTIMODAL

Have children listen to the selection as they follow along to develop comprehension and practice fluency and pronunciation.

Use the online High-Frequency Words Activity for additional support.

Babies in the Bayou

Prepare to Read

Build Background *We are going to read a nonfiction text about a place where animals live.* Display and say the title: *Babies in the Bayou,* and have children repeat. *The bayou is a place in the South of the United States. It has water and lots of plants and animals. The water in the bayou moves slowly.* Display the cover, and help children share what they see: *I see water and ____. I see baby ____.* Have children repeat: *I see alligators and ducks.*

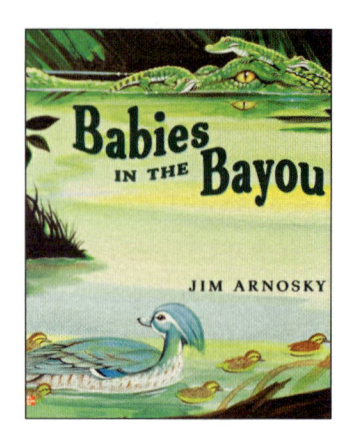

Focus on Vocabulary Use the **Visual Vocabulary Cards** to review the oral vocabulary words *habitat* and *depend.* As you read, use gestures and other visual support to clarify important selection words, such as *droops, wade, shallow, shepherds,* and *danger. The word* shallow *means "not deep." Say* shallow. *Provide an example: The water in the bayou is shallow. How is the water in the bayou?* It is shallow.

Literature Big Book

Summarize the Text Before reading, say the summary while pointing to the illustrations. *The story describes baby animals and their mothers in the bayou.*

Read the Text

Use the Interactive Question-Response routine to help children understand the text.

Pages 4–11

Pages 8–9 Read the text aloud. Point to the words *black and yellow tails. Point to the alligators' tails. What color is an alligator's tail?* (black and yellow) Point to the phrase *rows of sharp white teeth,* and guide children to point to the alligator's teeth. *Are your teeth like an alligator's?* (no) Point to the sleeping alligators. *What are these alligators doing?* They are sleeping. *Do they look like they are smiling?* (yes) *Where is their mother?* Their mother is in the water. *She is guarding them. Guarding means watching to see they are safe.*

Are baby alligators nice or scary? Discuss with a partner.

Beginning Point to the sleeping alligators. *What are the two baby alligators doing?* They are sleeping. Point to the alligator with its mouth open. *Is this alligator nice or scary?* It is scary. *Why?* It has sharp teeth.

Intermediate Have partners point to parts of the picture: *Do these two baby alligators look nice or scary?* They look nice. *Why?* They are smiling and sleeping. *How does the other baby alligator look?* It looks scary. *Why?* It has very sharp teeth.

74 UNIT 2 WEEK 3

WEEK 3

Advanced/Advanced High Have partners work together to compare alligators. *These baby alligators look* nice *because their mouths are* smiling. *This baby alligator and the mother look* scary. *This baby alligator has very* sharp teeth, *and the mother is very* big.

Pages 12–21

Pages 12–13 Read the text aloud. *These are baby raccoons. Say* raccoons. *Their tails are gray and black. The text says they have rings around their tails. Say* ring. *Point to a ring on a tail. Each ring looks like a ring on a finger.* Show a ring on a finger. Point to a raccoon's face. *What color is around the eyes?* (black) *The black part of their faces looks like a mask.* Show a mask or a picture of one. *What is their mom doing?* She is watching her babies.

How are these baby raccoons different from the baby alligators? How are they the same?

Beginning Help partners answer: *Are the raccoons' tails different from the alligators' tails?* Yes, their tails are gray and black. *The alligators' tails are black and* yellow. *Is the baby raccoons' mother near them?* Yes, their mother is near them. *Is the baby alligators' mom near them?* Yes, their mom is near them *too*.

Intermediate Help partners discuss: *How are the tails different?* The raccoons' tails are gray and black. *The alligators' tails are black and* yellow. *How are the mothers the same?* They watch their babies. *Do the raccoons and the alligators live in the same place?* Yes, they all live in the bayou.

Advanced/Advanced High Have partners compare tails, faces, and mothers: *Their tails have different* colors. *The raccoon's face has a black* mask. *Alligators have smiling mouths and sharp* teeth. *The mothers of both the raccoons and alligators stay with their* babies.

Pages 22–31

Pages 24-25 Read the text aloud. Point to the ducklings. *Ducklings* are baby ducks. *Say* ducklings. *The picture shows the ducklings in a row; they are next to each other. How many ducklings are in a row?* (six) *Follow* means "go after." *Do you follow someone?* (Yes, I follow my teacher.) Show a maze. *When you go through a maze, you have to turn and go different directions. Do you like to be in a maze?* (yes/no)

Point to the lily pads. Why does the text call the lily pads a maze? Discuss with a partner.

Beginning Point to the last duckling. *Can this duckling go down this way?* (no) *Why not?* A lily pad will stop the duckling. *Do you need to turn in a maze?* Yes, you need to turn. You need to go a different way.

Intermediate Point to the second duckling. *What will happen if this duckling turns here?* A lily pad will stop it. *What do you have to do in a maze?* You have to turn and go around things.

Advanced/Advanced High *What will happen if the second duckling turns to go up?* It will run into a lily pad. *Why are the lily pads a maze for the ducks?* The lily pads stop the ducks from going straight. They have to turn to go around the lily pads.

FORMATIVE ASSESSMENT

STUDENT CHECK-IN

Have partners retell characteristics and behaviors of three animals in the text. Then have children reflect, using the Check-In routine.

Independent Time

Create a Picture Glossary Pair children of mixed proficiencies, and have them create a picture glossary based on *Babies in the Bayou*. Have them draw and label pictures of the baby animals in the selection. Provide sentence frames to talk about them: Baby alligators have ___. Baby raccoons have ___. Baby turtles have ___. Ducklings ___. Their mother ___. Have partners present their picture glossaries to the group.

ENGLISH LANGUAGE LEARNERS 75

LESSONS 1-2

READING • SHARED READ • ACCESS THE TEXT

LEARNING GOALS

We can read and understand a nonfiction text.

OBJECTIVES

Identify the main topic and retell key details of a text.

Ask and answer questions to help determine or clarify the meaning of words and phrases in a text.

Ask questions to clear up any confusion about the topics and texts under discussion.

Produce complete sentences when appropriate to task and situation.

LANGUAGE OBJECTIVES

Children will inform about animals and their behavior, using singular and plural nouns and simple sentences.

ELA ACADEMIC LANGUAGE

- reread, inference
- Cognate: *inferencia*

MATERIALS

Reading/Writing Companion, pp. 82–91

Visual Vocabulary Cards

DIGITAL TOOLS

Have children listen to the selection as they follow along to develop comprehension and practice fluency and pronunciation.

Use the online High-Frequency Words Activity for additional support.

"The Best Spot"

Prepare to Read

Build Background Read aloud the Essential Question on page 82. Have children share what they know about places where animals live together. Use the images on pages 82 and 83 to generate ideas. Point to and read aloud the title. *We are going to read about animals that live in the forest.* Review that a forest has many tall trees. Point to the photo of the deer. *What kind of animal is this? It is a ____. Why is the deer standing on two legs? It is reaching to eat the leaves of a ____.*

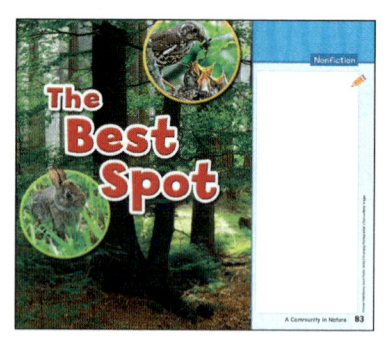

Reading/Writing Companion, Lexile 160L

Focus on Vocabulary Use the **Visual Vocabulary Cards** to review the high-frequency words *eat, no, of, under,* and *who* and the oral vocabulary words *habitat, depend, hibernate, tranquil,* and *tolerate*. As you read, use gestures and visual support to teach the important selection words *plant, bugs, trunk, ants, fox,* and *skunk*. Adapt the following routine for each word: Point to the plant on page 84. Say the word *plant*. Have children point to the photo and repeat the word. *A deer is eating a plant. What is the deer eating?* Have children respond: The deer is eating a plant.

Summarize the Text Before reading, say the summary and point to the photographs. *This nonfiction text tells about animals that live in the forest. It tells about their homes and what the animals do.*

Read the Text

Use the Interactive Question-Response routine to help children understand the text.

Pages 84–87

Page 86 Read the text aloud as children follow along. Point to the word *nest*, and say it aloud for children to repeat. *Birds live in a nest. They make their nests high up in the trees.* Point to the tall trees. Then point to the small photo. *The mom bird feeds her baby birds. She feeds them big bugs.* Have children say *feeds* with you. *What do the baby birds eat?* They eat bugs. Point to the word *Yum!* We say Yum! when we like the food we're eating. Do the baby birds like to eat bugs? (yes)

What is the mom bird doing? Discuss with a partner.

Beginning Use the photos to review *trees, birds,* and *bugs*. Point to the insect photo and say: *The mom bird gets bugs for her baby birds. Are the bugs big?* Yes, the bugs are big. *Where does the mom bird take the bugs?* She takes the bugs to the nest. *What is the mom bird doing?* She is feeding the baby birds the bugs.

76 UNIT 2 WEEK 3

WEEK 3

Intermediate Have partners answer questions: *Where is the nest?* It is up in the trees. *What kind of bugs does the mom bird get?* She gets big bugs.

Advanced/Advanced High Help partners elaborate as they ask and answer questions: *Where is the birds' home?* It is in a nest up high in the trees. *Why does the mom bird get big bugs?* She gets the bugs to feed her baby birds.

Pages 87–89

Page 88 Read the text aloud, and have children follow along. Point to the picture. *These ants live in the forest too. They pick up twigs. Twigs are small sticks. Ants pick up grass too. They zip in and out. Do they move fast or slowly?* (fast) *Do ants rest?* (no)

Page 89 Point to the label *Way In,* and have children follow the lines. *These are two ways the ants get into their home under the ground.* Point to the label *Ant Digging. Why do you think this ant is digging?* (to make the home bigger) Point to the *Queen Ant* label. *The queen ant lays eggs.* Point to the *Eggs* label. *These eggs will become baby ants.* Point to the *Food* label. *In how many rooms can ants find food?* (three)

COLLABORATE *What do ants do? Discuss with a partner.*

Beginning Guide partners to answer: Point to the ants with grass and twigs. *What do ants pick up?* They pick up twigs and grass. *Do ants dig too?* Yes, ants dig too. *Where do ants dig?* They dig in their home.

Intermediate Help partners ask and answer questions. Provide frames: *What do ants do outside?* They pick up twigs and grass. *What do ants do inside?* They dig. They find food. The queen ant lays eggs.

Advanced/Advanced High Help partners describe what ants do. Ants pick up twigs and grass. They zip in and out of their home. They dig new parts to make their home bigger.

Pages 90–91

Page 90 Read the text, and have children follow along. *Foxes live in the forest too.* Point to the word *stump. A stump is the part of a tree that is still in the ground after the tree is cut down. Where do the fox kits hop?* They hop on a stump. Point to the word *let. When a mom lets you do something, she says it is okay to do it. What does Mom fox let the kits do?* (run and jump) Point to *must. When you must do something, you need to do it. What do the kits need to do?* (eat) *The dad fox hunts. Hunts means "looks for." What do you think the dad fox hunts for?* (food) *He hunts at dusk. Dusk is when the sky is almost dark.*

COLLABORATE *What are kits? Discuss with a partner.*

Beginning Help partners point to the biggest fox. *Is this the mom fox or the kits?* It is the mom fox. Help children reread the text. *Do the kits hop?* Yes, the kits hop. *What else do the kits do?* They run and jump. *Are the kits the mom fox's kids?* Yes, the kits are her kids.

Intermediate Help partners reread the text and then make an inference: *What kinds of foxes does the text tell about?* (kits, Mom fox, Dad fox) *What do the kits do?* The kits hop and jump and run. *What are kits?* They are the kids of the mom fox and dad fox.

Advanced/Advanced High Help partners make inferences: The photo shows three small foxes with a big fox. The text says the mom lets the kits jump and run, and the dad hunts. The kits are the children of the mom and dad foxes.

FORMATIVE ASSESSMENT

❯ STUDENT CHECK-IN

Have partners provide descriptions for different animals in the text. Then have children reflect, using the Check-In routine.

Independent Time

Draw and Write Pair children of mixed proficiencies. Have children draw a picture of an animal that they have seen. Have partners name the animal they saw, where the animal lives, and what it does. Provide sentence frames to help them: I saw a ___. It lives in ___. It ___. Then have each pair present their animal pictures.

ENGLISH LANGUAGE LEARNERS 77

LESSON 3

READING • ANCHOR TEXT • ACCESS THE TEXT

LEARNING GOALS

We can read and understand a nonfiction text.

OBJECTIVES

Identify the reasons an author gives to support points in a text.

Ask and answer questions to help determine or clarify the meaning of words and phrases in a text.

With prompting and support, read informational texts appropriately complex for grade 1.

Ask questions to clear up any confusion about the topics and texts under discussion.

LANGUAGE OBJECTIVES

Children will inform about animals using verbs, singular nouns, and plural nouns.

ELA ACADEMIC LANGUAGE

- question mark, question, details
- Cognate: *detalles*

MATERIALS

Literature Anthology, pp. 48–59

Visual Vocabulary Cards

DIGITAL TOOLS

MULTIMODAL

Have children listen to the selection as they follow along to develop comprehension and practice fluency and pronunciation.

Use the additional grammar video.

Grammar Video

At a Pond

Prepare to Read

Build Background *We are going to read a nonfiction text about animals that live at a pond.* Show the photo on the title page, and invite children to tell what they see. Point to the ducks, flower, and water. Say the words, and have children repeat. Then point to the ducks again. Ask: *What do ducks do in the water?* Ducks ____ in the water.

Focus on Vocabulary Use the **Visual Vocabulary Cards** to review the high-frequency words *eat, no, of, under,* and *who* and the oral vocabulary words *habitat, depend, hibernate, tranquil,* and *tolerate.* As you read, teach important selection words using gestures and pantomime, such as *snack.*

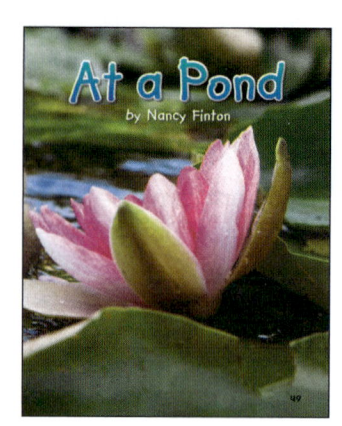

Literature Anthology, Lexile 190L

Summarize the Text Before reading, say the summary while pointing to the photographs. *This story tells about animals that live at a pond. The animals at a pond can be in the water, on land, or in the air.*

Read the Text

Use the Interactive Question-Response routine to help children understand the text.

Pages 50–51

Pages 50–51 Read the text. Point to and say *pond* for children to repeat. Point to the question mark on page 50. *This is a question mark. It shows a question. A question is what you ask to find out something. What is the author's question?* Who lives at the pond? *A pond has water. Say* water. *What is the question about water?* Who is under the water? Point to the land. *This is the land. Say* land. *Land is another word for* ground. *What is the question about land?* Who is on the land? Reread: *Who can fly to the pond? This question asks about animals that fly. Does the author answer the questions on this page?* No, the text says, "Let's see!"

Why does the author ask questions at the beginning of the text? Discuss with a partner.

Beginning Point to the word at the beginning of each question. *What is this word?* (Who) Reread the text on page 51 aloud. Point to the words *water* and *land. What places are these two questions about?* (water, land)

Intermediate Point to the first question on page 51. *What place does this question ask about?* It asks about the water. Point to the second question. *What place does this question ask about?* (the land) *What do these questions help you think about?* They help me think about animals under water and on land.

78 UNIT 2 WEEK 3

WEEK 3

Advanced/Advanced High Ask and answer: *What places do the questions on page 51 ask about?* (water, land, air) *In this text, does "who" ask about people or animals?* (animals) *How do you know?* (Possible response: People do not live in water.)

Pages 52–55

Page 54 Read the text. *Let's look at relevant details. This page tells what ducks do at a pond.* Point to the word *bill* and then to the duck's bill. *The duck's bill helps it eat. It dips its bill in the pond. What does the duck eat?* It eats bugs. Point to the large photo. *What are the ducks doing?* They are flying to the pond.

Page 55 Read the text. *This page tells what ducks do on land. The ducks make nests. What do they use?* (twigs and grass) *The ducks lay eggs. Where are the eggs?* (in a nest) Point to the question mark. *What is the question?* Who is in the eggs? Point to and say *Quack, quack, quack!* for children to repeat. *This is the sound ducks make.* Review that *ducklings* are baby ducks. *How many ducklings do you see?* (four)

Who is in the eggs? Discuss with a partner.

Beginning Reread page 55 for children. Guide them to the question mark and the word *Who.* Help them read the question: *Who is in the eggs?* Help children use the photo to answer: Ducklings are in the eggs. *What do ducks say?* (Quack, quack, quack!)

Intermediate Help partners respond. *What is the question?* Who *is in the eggs?* Can *you use the text to find the answer?* (yes) *Which words help?* (Quack, quack, quack!) *Can the photo help too?* (yes) *What does the photo show?* It shows ducklings.

Advanced/Advanced High Help partners explain the clues that can help them answer the question: The photo shows ducklings. The text shows the words *Quack, quack, quack!* The answer: Ducklings were in the eggs before they hatched.

Pages 56–59

Pages 56–57 Read the text. Point to page 56. *What is this page about?* (turtles) *Where can turtles be?* (on land and in water) *What do they do on land?* They rest in the sun. Point to page 57. *This page is about fish. Say* fish. *Can fish be on land?* (no) *What do fish and turtles do in water?* They swim. Point to and say *Gulp! Gulp is a sound made while eating. Say* gulp!

What does the author want to show you on these pages? Discuss with a partner.

Beginning Point to page 49. *What is the title?* (At the Pond) *Do the photos on pages 56 and 57 show a pond?* (yes) *What animal do you see and read about on page 56?* (turtles) *Which animal is on page 57?* (fish) *Do the text and photos show that the pond is home to turtles and fish?* Yes, the text and photos show the pond is their home.

Intermediate *Where are the animals on pages 56 and 57?* (at a pond) *What animals do the photos and text show?* (turtles and fish) *What home do the turtles and fish share?* Both turtles and fish live in a pond. This is what the author shows you.

Advanced/Advanced High Extend the discussion to include pages 58–59. *What does the author tell you about the animals on pages 56 through 59?* (All animals on these pages have the pond as their home.)

FORMATIVE ASSESSMENT

STUDENT CHECK-IN

Have partners provide descriptions about three animals at the pond and their kinds of movements. Then have children reflect using the Check-In routine.

Independent Time

Ask Questions Help children practice using *What, Where,* and *Who* questions about the selection. Pair children of mixed proficiencies. Provide sentence frames for support: What do you see on page [50]? I see ___. Who swims in a pond? ___ swim. Where do [frogs/turtles] rest? They rest ___. Have children share their questions and answers with the rest of the group.

ENGLISH LANGUAGE LEARNERS 79

READING • LEVELED READER • ACCESS THE TEXT

LESSONS 4-5

LEARNING GOALS

We can reread to understand a nonfiction text.

OBJECTIVES

Distinguish between information provided by pictures or other illustrations and information provided by the words in a text.

Identify the reasons an author gives to support points in a text.

Identify basic similarities in and differences between two texts on the same topic (e.g., in illustrations, descriptions, or procedures).

Describe people, places, things, and events with relevant details, expressing ideas and feelings clearly.

LANGUAGE OBJECTIVES

Children will discuss what meerkats do, using singular and plural nouns.

ELA ACADEMIC LANGUAGE

• reread

MATERIALS

ELL Leveled Reader: *Meerkat Family*

Online Differentiated Texts, "The Swamp"

Online ELL Visual Vocabulary Cards

DIGITAL TOOLS

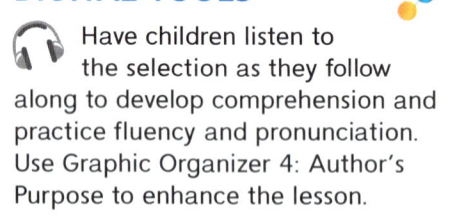

Have children listen to the selection as they follow along to develop comprehension and practice fluency and pronunciation. Use Graphic Organizer 4: Author's Purpose to enhance the lesson.

Meerkat Family

Lexile 170L

Prepare to Read

Build Background

- Remind children of the Essential Question. *Let's read to learn about where animals live together.* Encourage children to ask for help when they do not understand a word or phrase.

- Say the title, and have children repeat it. Point to the image of the meerkats on the cover. *This is a meerkat. Meerkats are small animals that live in families. Who is part of your family? My family is my ____ and ____ .*

Focus on Vocabulary Use the **ELL Visual Vocabulary Cards** to preteach the words *environment* and *survival*. As you read, use visuals or gestures to teach important selection words such as *fur, noses,* and *eyes*. Discuss the words *tail* and *ears*, using the photos on pages 4 and 6. Point to the meerkat's tail. *Do meerkats have tails?* Yes, meerkats have tails. Repeat this routine for *eyes*.

Read the Text

Use the Interactive Question-Response routine as you read.

Pages 2–5

Author's Purpose *Let's look at the text and photos to see whether the author's purpose for writing* Meerkat Family *is to inform, persuade, or entertain.* Read pages 2–5. Have children echo-read the labels with you. *How do the labels help us?* They give information about the photos.

Beginning/Intermediate Point to the bug. *What is this?* It is a bug. Point out the meerkat. *What is the meerkat doing?* The meerkat is eating. *What is the meerkat eating?* The meerkat is eating a bug.

Advanced/Advanced High *Look at the photo and text on page 5. What do meerkats eat?* The meerkats eat plants and small animals.

Pages 6–9

Reread Read pages 6–9 aloud. Ask guiding questions to help children identify the most important details. Point to the burrow on page 6. *This is a burrow. Where do meerkats live?* Meerkats live in burrows.

Intermediate Have partners reread each page to clarify information. *Where do meerkats live?* Meerkats live in burrows. *Where are burrows?* Burrows are under the ground.

Advanced/Advanced High *Where do meerkats live?* (in burrows) *What is a burrow like?* A burrow has many rooms. Burrows are cool.

80 UNIT 2 WEEK 3

WEEK 3

Pages 10–11

Read pages 10–11 as children follow along. Point to the photos, and say the words *adult*, *babies*, *hide*, and *safe*. Have children repeat.

Beginning Have partners talk about each page with a partner. *Who cares for meerkat babies?* (adults) *What do meerkat babies learn?* Meerkat babies learn how to hide.

Intermediate *What do babies learn?* They learn to hide. *Why do they hide?* They hide to be safe. They are safe with their families.

Author's Purpose *Did we learn something from reading this text? Or did the author try to persuade us to do something?* (We learned something.) *What did we learn?* (facts/information about meerkats) *Why did the author write* Meerkat Family? (to inform)

Respond to Reading Have partners work together to retell the selection details and respond to the questions on page 12.

Focus on Fluency

Read pages 10–11. Then reread them, and have children echo-read after you. Remind children to read the words correctly.

Paired Selection: "I Live in a House!"

Make Connections: Write About It

Echo-read each page with children. Discuss where the boy in the story lives.
People live in different places. Where does the boy live? The boy lives in a house. Help children make connections between the texts, using the question on page 15. Animals and people live in different places.

Leveled Reader

Build Knowledge: Make Connections

Talk About the Text Have partners discuss how the texts talk about where animals live.

Write About the Text Have students add their ideas to the Build Knowledge pages of their reader's notebooks.

Self-Selected Reading

Help children choose a fiction selection from the online **Leveled Reader Library** or read the **Differentiated Text,** "The Swamp."

🧪 FOCUS ON SCIENCE

Children can extend their knowledge of where animals live by completing the science activity on page 16. **STEM**

LITERATURE CIRCLES

Lead children in conducting a literature circle using the Thinkmark questions to guide the discussion. You may wish to discuss what children have learned about animal communities from both selections in the **Leveled Reader**.

FORMATIVE ASSESSMENT

▶ STUDENT CHECK-IN

Have partners share their Respond to Reading. Have children reflect, using the Check-In routine.

LEVEL UP

IF children can read *Meerkat Family* **ELL Level** with fluency and correctly answer the Respond to Reading questions,

THEN tell children they will read a more detailed version of the selection.

- Use pages 8–9 of *Meerkat Family* **On Level** to model using Teaching Poster 29 to identify the main topic and key details.

- Have children read the selection, checking their comprehension by using the graphic organizer.

ENGLISH LANGUAGE LEARNERS **81**

LESSONS 1-5

WRITING

MODELED WRITING

LESSON 1

LEARNING GOALS
We can focus on a topic when we write a sentence.

OBJECTIVES
Write informative texts in which they name a topic.

LANGUAGE OBJECTIVES
Children will inform by writing a sentence that focuses on a topic.

ELA ACADEMIC LANGUAGE
- topic

Writing Practice Review the sample on p. 92 of the **Reading/Writing Companion.** Guide children to analyze it using the Actor/Action routine: *Who is the actor in the sentence:* deer, plants, *or* forest? (deer) *What is the action?* (eat plants in the forest) Then read the prompt on p. 93, and ask children to answer it as a group. Write the sentence on the board for children to chorally read before writing their own sentence.

Beginning *Which animal is the actor in your sentence?* (turtles) *What is the action?* (eat fish) *What is the topic?* (turtles)

Intermediate Have partners ask and answer *who/what* questions to create sentences about their favorite animal. Provide sentence frames as needed.

Advanced/Advanced High Have partners exchange sentences and identify the actor, action, and topic of each sentence.

FORMATIVE ASSESSMENT ▶ **STUDENT CHECK-IN** Partners share their sentences. Ask children to reflect, using the Check-In routine.

INTERACTIVE WRITING

LESSON 2

LEARNING GOALS
We can read and write about a Student Model.

OBJECTIVES
Write informative texts in which they supply some facts about the topic.

LANGUAGE OBJECTIVES
Children will discuss and write sentences about the Student Model, identifying the topic.

ELA ACADEMIC LANGUAGE
- possessive
- Cognate: *posesivo*

Analyze the Student Model Have children chorally read the Student Model on p. 98 of the **Reading/Writing Companion.** Use the Actor/Action routine to review the first sentence. Check that children understand the possessive noun in the last sentence. *Whose favorite food is nuts?* (a squirrel's) Then ask, *What is the topic Ben wrote about?* (squirrels) *What is a detail about the topic?* (They are small and fluffy.) Then help children complete p. 99.

Beginning Have partners point to the capital letters and describe how they are used: Ben used a capital letter at the beginning of each sentence.

Intermediate Have partners identify the possessive noun and explain how they know: I noticed the possessive noun squirrel's. It has 's at the end.

Advanced/Advanced High Challenge children to describe details that tell more about the topic. *What did you learn about squirrels?* Have children write original sentences about what they noticed.

FORMATIVE ASSESSMENT ▶ **STUDENT CHECK-IN** Partners share their responses. Ask children to reflect, using the Check-In routine.

WEEK 3

INDEPENDENT WRITING

LESSONS 3-4

LEARNING GOALS

We can respond to a nonfiction text by extending the text.

OBJECTIVES

Write informative texts in which they provide some sense of closure.

LANGUAGE OBJECTIVES

Children will inform by writing complete sentences using possessive nouns.

ELA ACADEMIC LANGUAGE

- *possessive nouns*

Find Text Evidence Use the Independent Writing routine. Help children orally retell the anchor text. Ask questions, such as, *Where are the animals in this selection?* (a pond) *Who can be on land or in the water?* (frogs, turtles) Then read the prompt on p. 104 of the **Reading/Writing Companion:** *Write two more pages about one of the animals in* At a Pond. *Use the photos to help you.* Display p. 56 of the **Literature Anthology** to find more information about turtles. *Let's see if the photo can help.*

Write a Response Distribute My Writing Outline 8 to children. Work with children to fill out the outline. After they have filled in their outlines, have children complete p. 104 of the Reading/Writing Companion, using the sentences from their completed outline.

Writing Checklist Read the checklist with students, and have them check for these items in their writing.

Beginning Have partners check that their possessive noun ends in *'s*.

Intermediate Have partners ask: What is the most important idea? Which sentences tell more information about it?

Advanced/Advanced High Have partners identify where they used each checklist item in their writing.

FORMATIVE ASSESSMENT > **STUDENT CHECK-IN** Partners share their sentences from My Writing Outline. Ask children to reflect, using the Check-in routine.

SELF-SELECTED WRITING

LESSON 5

LEARNING GOALS

We can revise our writing.

OBJECTIVES

Use common, proper, and possessive nouns.

LANGUAGE OBJECTIVES

Children will inquire about their writing by checking that *'s* is used for possessive nouns.

ELA ACADEMIC LANGUAGE

- *publish*
- Cognate: *publicar*

Work with children to revise the group writing activity. Point to each word as you read the sentences. Stop to ask questions, such as, *Is this word a possessive noun? Should it have an 's at the end?* After making the necessary corrections, have partners work together to correct each other's sentences before publishing them. Have children check that they used the possessive form correctly.

For support with possessives and grammar, refer to the **Language Transfers Handbook** and **Language Development Card** 3B.

FORMATIVE ASSESSMENT > **STUDENT CHECK-IN** Partners tell what revisions they made. Ask children to reflect, using the Check-in routine.

ENGLISH LANGUAGE LEARNERS 83

READING • LITERATURE BIG BOOK • ACCESS THE TEXT

LESSONS 1-2

LEARNING GOALS

We can understand how people help in a community as we listen to a biography.

OBJECTIVES

Identify the main topic and retell key details of a text.

Describe people, places, things, and events with relevant details, expressing ideas and feelings clearly.

Distinguish between information provided by pictures or other illustrations and information provided by the words in a text.

Ask and answer questions about what a speaker says in order to gather additional information or clarify something that is not understood.

LANGUAGE OBJECTIVES

Children will discuss Martin Luther King Jr. using key vocabulary.

ELA ACADEMIC LANGUAGE

- biography, reread
- Cognate: biografía

MATERIALS

Literature Big Book, *The Story of Martin Luther King Jr.,* pp. 4–27

Visual Vocabulary Cards

DIGITAL TOOLS

Have children listen to the selection as they follow along to develop comprehension.

Use the online High-Frequency Words Activity for additional support.

The Story of Martin Luther King Jr.

Prepare to Read

Build Background *We are going to read a biography about Martin Luther King, Jr. A biography tells about a real person.* Show the picture on the cover. Say: *We celebrate Martin Luther King Jr. Day each year. Martin Luther King Jr. was an important leader in his African American community and in our country. A leader is a person who shows the way.* Model for children: *I am a leader when I teach. When are you a leader? I am a leader when I _____ a new student.*

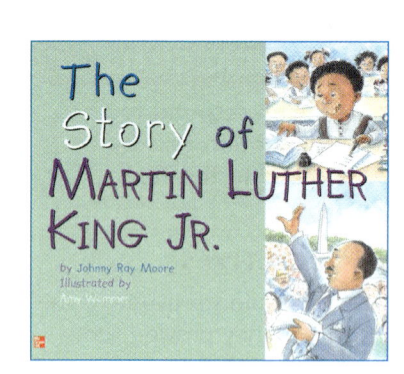

Literature Big Book

Focus on Vocabulary Use the **Visual Vocabulary Cards** to review the oral vocabulary words *leadership* and *admire.* As you read, use gestures and other visual support to clarify important selection words, such as *preacher, more, fair, unfair, old, serve, water fountain, white, colored,* and *angry.* The word *fair* means "treating all people the same way." *Unfair* means "not treating people the same." Say *fair* and *unfair.* Provide examples: *It is fair to let all kids play a game. What is unfair?* It is unfair to not let all kids play a game.

Summarize the Text Before reading, say the summary while pointing to the illustrations. *This true story tells about the life of Martin Luther King Jr. It tells about things he saw that he did not like. It tells how he made things more fair.*

Read the Text

Use the Interactive Question-Response routine to help children understand the text.

Pages 4–9

Pages 6–7 Read the text aloud. Point to Martin Luther King Jr. *This text is about Martin when he was a boy. The text tells us he was born in 1929. When was he born?* (1929) Point to the preacher. *This is Martin's father. Martin's father was a preacher. A preacher speaks to people in a church.* Point to Martin's mother. *Who was she?* She was a school teacher.

What can Martin learn from watching his father and mother? Discuss with a partner.

Beginning Point to Martin's father. *Is Martin's father preaching?* Yes, he is preaching. *Who do preachers speak to?* (people) *Where do preachers speak?* (at church) *What can Martin learn from his father?* He can learn to preach. Point to Martin's mother. *Martin's mother was a teacher. What can Martin learn from his mother?* He can learn to teach.

Intermediate Have partners point to the picture as they respond. *What is Martin's father doing?* He is preaching to a large group. *What can Martin learn*

84 UNIT 2 WEEK 4

WEEK 4

from him? Martin can learn to preach to a big group. *Who is sitting next to Martin?* (Martin's mother) *What can Martin learn from her?* (to teach people)

Advanced/Advanced High Have partners give details. *What can Martin learn from watching his parents?* He can learn to preach to large groups and teach. He can learn to be a leader too.

Pages 10–15

Pages 14–15 Read the text aloud. Point to the water fountain, name it, and have children repeat. Point to the sign. *The word* white *on the sign means only white people can drink here. Does Martin look happy?* (no) *He looks sad. The text says Martin has to find a sign that says "Colored." The word* colored *was used for* African Americans *at that time.*

Can Martin drink from the water fountain in the picture? Why or why not? Discuss with a partner.

Beginning Help partners respond: *What does the sign say?* (white) *Is Martin white?* No, he is not white. *Can he drink here?* No, he can not drink here. *What sign does he need to find?* (Colored)

Intermediate Point to the sign. *What does this sign mean?* White people can drink from the water fountain. *Can Martin drink from it?* No, he can not drink from it. *Why?* He is not white. *Is this fair?* (no)

Advanced/Advanced High Have partners explain what the sign means. *Who can drink from this water fountain?* A white person can drink from this water fountain. *Can Martin drink here?* No, he can only drink at fountains with the Colored sign. *Is this fair?* No, it is not fair.

Pages 16–27

Pages 20–21 Read the text aloud. *What is Martin doing in the picture?* (speaking to many people) Point to the words inside the quotation marks. *These are the words Martin Luther King, Jr. spoke. People still think about these words today.* Point to the word *dream. Here, a dream means something you want that is hard to get.* Point to *judged. It is not good to judge someone by how they look. That is unfair.*

Reread pages 16–17. What is Martin's dream for his community? Discuss with a partner.

Beginning Help children reread pages 16–17 and use details in the illustrations on pages 10–15 to answer questions. *What places were unfair to African Americans?* (old schools, restaurants, water fountains) *Does Martin want African Americans to [go to good schools]?* (yes)

Intermediate Have children ask and answer questions. Provide frames: What was unfair to Martin when he was a boy? He had to go to an old school. He could not eat at some restaurants or drink from some water fountains. What does Martin want in his speech? He wants people to treat African Americans fairly/in a fair way.

Advanced/Advanced High Have children retell what Martin wants as a child and what he wants in his speech. As a child, he wants to go to the best school, eat at any restaurant, and drink at any water fountain. In his speech, he wants white people to treat all African Americans fairly.

FORMATIVE ASSESSMENT

▶ STUDENT CHECK-IN

Have partners retell three things that upset Martin Luther King Jr. growing up. Then have children reflect, using the Check-In routine.

Independent Time

Draw and Share Pair children of mixed proficiencies. Have partners discuss the dreams they have to make people's lives better, and have each draw a picture of their dream. Then have each pair present their dream pictures to the rest of the group. Provide sentence frames to help them: I have a dream that ___.

ENGLISH LANGUAGE LEARNERS 85

LESSONS 1-2

READING • SHARED READ • ACCESS THE TEXT

LEARNING GOALS

We can read and understand a fantasy story.

OBJECTIVES

Use illustrations and details in a story to describe its characters.

Describe people, places, things, and events with relevant details, expressing ideas and feelings clearly.

Produce complete sentences when appropriate to task and situation.

LANGUAGE OBJECTIVES

Children will narrate the characters' problem and solution, using key vocabulary and simple sentences.

ELA ACADEMIC LANGUAGE

- fantasy, main character, retell
- Cognate: *fantasía*

MATERIALS

Reading/Writing Companion, pp. 116–125

Visual Vocabulary Cards

DIGITAL TOOLS

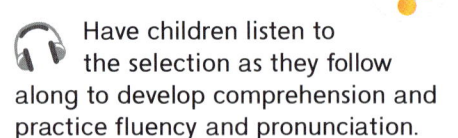

Have children listen to the selection as they follow along to develop comprehension and practice fluency and pronunciation.

Use the online High-Frequency Words Activity for additional support.

"Thump Thump Helps Out"

Prepare to Read

Build Background Point to and read aloud the title. *We are going to read a story about rabbits. This story is a fantasy. The animal characters in it talk and wear clothes. The main character's name is Thump Thump.* Say the name *Thump Thump.* The word *thump describes a sound.* Demonstrate this sound for children. Have children repeat the word *thump* and make their own thumping sound.

Reading/Writing Companion, Lexile 510L

Focus on Vocabulary Use the **Visual Vocabulary Cards** to review the high-frequency words *all, call, day, her,* and *want* and the oral vocabulary words *admire, leadership, connections, enjoy,* and *rely.* As you read, use gestures and visual supports to teach the important story words *sang, hit, got stuck,* and *rushed.*

Summarize the Text Say the summary, and point to the illustrations. *This story tells about a rabbit that thumps and helps his community.*

Read the Text

Use the Interactive Question-Response routine to help children understand the story.

Pages 118–119

Page 119 Read the text aloud, and have children follow along. Read the word *Hush!* and have children repeat it. *The word hush means "be quiet."* Provide an example: *I say Hush! when someone plays a song too loud. When do you say Hush!?* I say Hush! when someone talks too loud. The rabbits do not like the sound "one bit." When we say we do not like something one bit, we really do not like it.

What do the other rabbits want Thump Thump to do? Why do they want him to do that? Discuss with a partner.

Beginning Point to the picture, and ask: *Do the rabbits look happy or angry?* They look angry. Point to the words *Hush! Stop that.* Ask: *What do the rabbits say to Thump Thump?* (Hush! Stop that!) *Do the rabbits like the thumping one bit?* No, they do not like it one bit. *Is it too loud?* Yes, it is too loud.

Intermediate Help partners provide a more complete answer. *What do all the rabbits yell to Thump Thump?* They yell, "Hush! Stop that, Thump Thump!" *What do the rabbits want Thump Thump to stop doing?* They want him to stop thumping. *Why do they want Thump Thump to stop thumping?* It is too loud.

Advanced/Advanced High Help partners work together to tell about the problem. When Thump Thump thumps, the other rabbits get angry. They want Thump Thump to stop thumping.

86 UNIT 2 WEEK 4

Pages 120–121

Pages 120-121 Read the text aloud, and have children follow along. Point to the words *bang, crash,* and *clunk*. These are words that describe sounds. The rabbits hear these sounds when the bus hits a rock. *Do you think these sounds are loud or soft?* (loud) Say the sounds for children to repeat. Then ask: *What is the bus stuck in?* (mud) Point to the words *"Help us!"* on page 121. Have children repeat the words. *A little rabbit yells this. Do the big rabbits hear her?* (no)

What problems do the little rabbits have? Discuss with a partner.

Beginning Point to the rock. *What is this?* It is a rock. Point to the mud. *What is this?* It is mud. Point to the word *stuck*. *Does the bus get stuck?* Yes, it gets stuck. *Can the bus move?* No, the bus can not move. Point to the words *could not fix it*. *Could the little rabbits fix the bus?* No, the little rabbits could not fix it. Point to page 121. *Do the big rabbits help?* No, the big rabbits do not help.

Intermediate Help partners ask and answer: What does the bus hit? The bus hits a rock. Can the bus move? No, it can not move. Why can the bus not move? It is stuck in the mud. Can the little rabbits fix the bus? No, they can not fix it. What does one little rabbit do? She yells for help. Do the big rabbits help? No, the big rabbits do not hear her.

Advanced/Advanced High Have partners ask and answer. What is the problem? The bus can not move. What happens to the bus? The bus hits a rock. It gets stuck in the mud too. Can the little rabbits fix it? No, they can not fix it. How do they try to solve the problem? A little rabbit yells for help. The big rabbits do not hear her.

Pages 122–123

Pages 123–123 Read the text aloud, and have children follow along. Point to the word *overheard*. We overhear sounds that are loud. *Who overhears Thump Thump thumping?* (the big rabbits) Point to the word *rushed*. *Rush* means *"hurry"* or *"go fast."*

Pages 124–125 Point to the word *long*. The big rabbits want Thump Thump to thump loud and for a long time when a rabbit needs help. *Do the big rabbits like Thump Thump's loud thumping now?* (yes)

How does Thump Thump solve the problem? Discuss with a partner.

Beginning Point to Thump Thump on page 124, and ask: *What does Thump Thump do to help?* He thumps and thumps and thumps. *Do the big rabbits overhear him?* (yes) *What do the big rabbits do?* They come fast. *Do they fix the bus?* Yes, the big rabbits fix it.

Intermediate Help partners give details. *How does Thump Thump solve the problem?* He thumps a lot. The big rabbits hear him thumping loud. The big rabbits come fast/running. They fix the bus.

Advanced/Advanced High Help partners retell how the problem is solved. Thump Thump wants the big rabbits to help. He thumps loud many times to make the big rabbits hear him. The big rabbits hear thumping and rush to fix the bus. Then they ask Thump Thump to thump when any rabbit needs help.

FORMATIVE ASSESSMENT

STUDENT CHECK-IN

Have partners retell how the little rabbits' opinion of Thump Thump changes throughout the story. Then have children reflect, using the Check-In routine.

Independent Time

Ask and Answer Questions Pair children of mixed proficiencies, and have them practice using *what, who, where,* and *when* questions about the story. Provide questions and sentence frames. What happens to the bus? It gets stuck. When do the big rabbits come? When they hear thumping. Who thumps? Thump Thump. Where do the little rabbits go? They go home. Have partners share their questions and answers with the rest of the group.

LESSON 3

READING • ANCHOR TEXT • ACCESS THE TEXT

LEARNING GOALS

We can read and understand a fantasy story.

OBJECTIVES

Ask and answer questions about key details in a text.

Use illustrations and details in a story to describe its characters, setting, or events.

Identify who is telling the story at various points in a text.

Compare and contrast the adventures and experiences of characters in stories.

LANGUAGE OBJECTIVES

Children will discuss events in the story, using verbs with -ing.

ELA ACADEMIC LANGUAGE

- illustration, author, dialogue
- Cognates: *ilustración, autor, diálogo*

MATERIALS

Literature Anthology, pp. 64–79

Visual Vocabulary Cards

DIGITAL TOOLS

Have children listen to the selection as they follow along to develop comprehension.

Use the additional grammar video.

Grammar Video

Nell's Books

Prepare to Read

Build Background *We are going to read a story about an elephant who loves books.* Show the picture on the title page, and invite children to tell what they see. Point to the elephant, cat, dog, pig, bird, mice, books, plant, and table. Say the words, and have children repeat. *I see piles of books on the table.* Explain that a *pile* is a lot of things lying on top of each other. *How many books do you see in the pile of books under the elephant?* I see four books in that _____ . *How many piles of books do you see on the table?* I see _____ of books on the table.

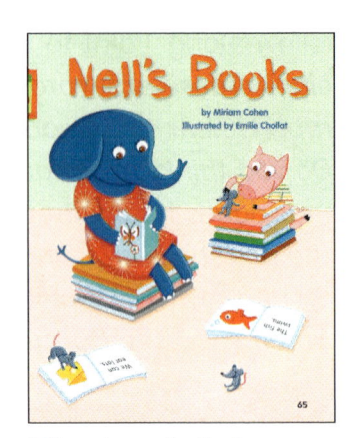

Literature Anthology, Lexile 200L

Focus on Vocabulary Use the **Visual Vocabulary Cards** to review the high-frequency words *all, call, day, her,* and *want* and the oral vocabulary words *admire, leadership, connections, enjoy,* and *rely.* As you read, teach important story words, such as *just* in the sentence "She just reads," using gestures and pantomime.

Summarize the Text Before reading, say the summary while pointing to the illustrations. *The story tells about an elephant named Nell and her friends. Nell likes to read a lot. She wants her friends to read too.*

Read the Text

Use the Interactive Question-Response routine to help children understand the story.

Pages 66–67

Page 66 Read the text. Point to Nell. *The elephant in the illustration is Nell. Say Nell. I see a tree and a house, so I know that Nell is outside. Where is Nell?* She is outside. *What is Nell doing?* (sitting in a chair, reading) Point to the piles of books. *Nell has lots of books near her. How many piles of books do you see?* (three) *How long does the author say Nell can sit and read?* (all day long)

Page 67 Point to the dog and the cat. *The picture shows Cat and Dog playing tennis. In the text, Cat and Dog ask Nell to play tennis with them. What do they want Nell to do?* They want Nell to play tennis with them.

How do you know that Nell likes to read a lot? Discuss with a partner.

Beginning *Does the picture show Nell playing?* (No.) *What is Nell doing?* Nell is reading. *Does the picture show lots of books?* Yes, the picture shows three piles of books. *What does Nell say?* "Shh! I am reading."

88 UNIT 2 WEEK 4

WEEK 4

Intermediate Point to the text on page 66. *How do you know Nell likes to read?* The text says, "She liked it a lot." *How does the picture show Nell reads a lot?* It shows piles of books.

Advanced/Advanced High Have partners give details from the text and picture. The text says Nell liked reading "a lot"; she "could read all day." The picture shows her holding a book with piles of books around her. It shows that she is not playing with Cat and Dog.

Pages 68–75

Pages 72–73 Read the text. Remind children that it is raining. *What is Nell doing?* (Nell is giving Dog a book.) *What does Dog say?* (Yuck!) *When do people say "yuck"?* (when they do not like something) *What does this tell you about Dog?* Dog does not like to read. Point to the picture on page 73. *What is Nell doing?* She is giving books to Cat and Pig. *What do Cat and Pig say?* (Ick!) Ick *means the same as* yuck. *Do Cat and Pig like to read?* (no)

Pages 74–75 Read the text. Point to the tent. *What is this?* (a tent) *Who is in the tent?* (Dog) *What is Dog doing?* Dog is reading. Point to and say *tub* for children to repeat. *Who is in the tub?* (Pig) Point to the flower pot. *This is a pot for a plant. Say* pot. *Who is in the pot?* (Cat) *Are Cat and Pig reading too?* (yes)

COLLABORATE *The friends' feelings about reading change. How do the illustrations help you know this? Discuss with a partner.*

Beginning Point to the pictures on pages 72 and 73. *Do the friends look happy when Nell gives them books?* (no) Turn the page. *What are the friends doing now?* They are reading. *Do they like to read now?* Yes, they like to read. *How do you know?* They are smiling.

Intermediate Point to the pictures on pages 72 and 73. *What do these pictures show?* Nell is giving the friends books. The friends do not look happy. *Do the friends like to read?* (no) *What does the picture on the next page show?* The friends are reading and smiling. *What does that tell you?* Now they like to read.

Advanced/Advanced High Help partners compare pictures on both spreads. On pages 72 and 73, the friends show they do not like to read. On pages 74 and 75, the friends are reading, and they are smiling.

Pages 76–79

Pages 76–77 Read the text. Point to the dialogue. *The sentences inside quotation marks tell the words characters say. This is a called a* dialogue. *What does Cat tell Nell?* "You can hand out books to all." *What does Nell say?* "That is just my wish."

COLLABORATE *Why did Nell's friends get her a truck? How does the dialogue help you know this?*

Beginning Help children reread the dialogue on page 77. *Do the friends want to help Nell?* Yes, the friends want to help Nell. *How do you know?* Cat says the truck can help Nell hand out books.

Intermediate Have partners ask and answer questions. Why do the friends give Nell the truck? They want to help her. How does the dialogue tell you this? Dog says they made the truck for her. Cat says the truck will help Nell hand out books.

Advanced/Advanced High Have children retell the parts of the dialogue that show why Nell's friends got her a truck. Dog tells Nell the friends got it for her. Cat tells her that now she can hand out books to all.

FORMATIVE ASSESSMENT

▶ STUDENT CHECK IN

Have partners retell how the characters discover a new hobby. Then have children reflect, using the Check-In routine.

Independent Time

Describe Pictures Select a spread from *Nell's Books*, and pair children of mixed proficiencies. Have them ask and answer questions about the image(s). Provide sentence frames: Who do you see? I see ___. What is [Name] doing? She/He is ___. Have pairs describe the picture to the group: In this picture I see ___. She/He is ___.

ENGLISH LANGUAGE LEARNERS **89**

LESSONS 4-5

READING • LEVELED READER • ACCESS THE TEXT

LEARNING GOALS

We can reread to understand a fantasy story.

OBJECTIVES

Describe characters, settings, and major events in a story, using key details.

Retell stories, including key details, and demonstrate understanding of their central message or lesson.

Identify basic similarities in and differences between two texts on the same topic.

Use illustrations and details in a story to describe its characters, setting, or events.

LANGUAGE OBJECTIVES

Children will narrate the characters' actions in the story, using common and proper nouns.

ELA ACADEMIC LANGUAGE

- characters, setting, events
- Cognate: *eventos*

MATERIALS

ELL Leveled Reader: *Squirrels Help*

Online Differentiated Texts, "A Fish Helps"

Online ELL Visual Vocabulary Cards

DIGITAL TOOLS

Have children listen to the selection as they follow along to develop comprehension and practice fluency and pronunciation. Use Graphic Organizer 2: Character, Setting, Events to enhance the lesson.

Squirrels Help

Prepare to Read

Build Background

- Remind children of the Essential Question: *Let's read to see how squirrels help out in their community.* Encourage children to ask for help when they do not understand a word or phrase.

- Read the title aloud for children to repeat. Repeat this routine for the author's name. Then say: *I know this story is a fantasy because it has animal characters that talk.* Point to the illustrations in the **Leveled Reader** to name things and actions, such as: *This is a [bag]. What can you do with a [bag]?*

Lexile 190L

Focus on Vocabulary Use the the **ELL Visual Vocabulary Cards** to preteach the words *helpful* and *prepare*. As you read, use gestures or visuals to teach important story words, such as *look for, nuts, shut, sad, thank you, winter,* and *spring.* Display the cover. Say the word *squirrels,* and have children repeat it. *The squirrels are looking for nuts. What other things do squirrels do?* Squirrels run up trees/run fast.

Read the Text

Use the Interactive Question-Response routine to help children understand the story.

Pages 2–5

Read pages 2–3 as children follow along. Point to and say *look for, nuts, all day,* and *bag.* Have children point to and repeat these words.

Beginning *What do the squirrels look for?* (nuts) *How many nuts does Sue have?* She has three nuts.

Intermediate Help partners respond: *What do the squirrels look for?* They look for nuts. *What does Sue have?* She has three nuts in a bag.

Advanced/Advanced High *How long do the squirrels look for nuts?* They look for nuts all day. *What is Sue's problem?* She has only three nuts in her bag.

Pages 6–9

Main Story Elements: Character, Setting, Events Read pages 6–7 as children follow along. Ask questions to help them describe characters. Point to the squirrels on page 6. *Who helps Sue?* (Tom) *What does he do?* Tom shows Sue a good spot. Sue will find lots of nuts there. *What does she say?* (Thank you.)

Beginning *What do Tom and Dad do?* They bring Sue to a good spot. *Does Sue find nuts?* Yes, Sue finds nuts. *What does Sue say?* She says, "Thank you."

90 UNIT 2 WEEK 4

WEEK 4

Advanced/Advanced High Have partners discuss how Sue thanks Tom on each spread. She says "Thank you" for helping her find nuts. In winter, she hangs a note that says "Thanks."

Pages 10–12

Reread Read pages 10–11 as children follow along. Help children reread if they do not understand the text. Point to the picture. *I see no snow here. It is not winter. It is spring.* Have children repeat *spring.*

Intermediate Have partners discuss: *What can Sue do?* She can help squirrels find nuts. *Where will they go?* They will go to the good spot.

Advanced/Advanced High *What happens in spring?* Squirrels look for nuts again. *How can Sue help?* She can show them the good spot.

Respond to Reading Have partners work together to retell the story and respond to the questions on page 12.

Focus on Fluency

Read pages 4–5. Then reread them, and have children echo-read after you. Remind children to read the words correctly.

Paired Selection: "Food Drive"

Analytical Writing — Make Connections: Write About It

Echo-read each page with children. Discuss food drives: *What does the sign say to do?* Bring all food to Room 4. Help children make connections between texts: The squirrels help others find nuts. The kids bring food to people.

Leveled Reader

Build Knowledge: Make Connections

Talk About the Text Have partners discuss how people help out in a community.

Write About the Text Have students add their ideas to the Build Knowledge pages of their reader's notebooks.

Self-Selected Reading

Help children choose a fiction selection from the online **Leveled Reader Library** or read the **Differentiated Text**, "A Fish Helps."

FOCUS ON GENRE

Children can extend their knowledge of the fantasy genre by completing the genre activity on page 16.

LITERATURE CIRCLES

Lead children in conducting a literature circle using the Thinkmark questions to guide the discussion. You may wish to discuss what children have learned about helping others in both selections in the **Leveled Reader**.

FORMATIVE ASSESSMENT

> **STUDENT CHECK-IN**

Have partners share their Respond to Reading. Have children reflect, using the Check-In routine.

LEVEL UP

IF children can read *Squirrels Help* ELL Level with fluency and correctly answer the Respond to Reading questions,

THEN tell children they will read a more detailed version of the story.

- Use pages 4–5 of *Squirrels Help* On Level to model using Teaching Poster 28 to identify character, setting, and events.

- Have children read the selection, checking their comprehension by using the graphic organizer.

ENGLISH LANGUAGE LEARNERS 91

LESSONS 1-5

WRITING

MODELED WRITING

LESSON 1

LEARNING GOALS

We can write a strong beginning sentence.

OBJECTIVES

Write informative texts in which they name a topic.

LANGUAGE OBJECTIVES

Children will inform by writing a complete sentence, using correct punctuation.

ELA ACADEMIC LANGUAGE

- punctuation
- Cognate: *puntuación*

Writing Practice Review the sample on p. 126 of the **Reading/Writing Companion**. Guide children to analyze it using the Actor/Action routine: *Who is the actor?* (I) *What is the action?* (have fun walking my dog) *With whom does the actor walk the dog?* (my mom) *When does the actor do this activity?* (every day) Then read the prompt on p. 127, and ask children to answer it as a group. Write the sentences on the board for children to chorally read before writing their own sentences. Have children point to the punctuation mark at the end of the sentences.

Beginning Provide a sentence frame: I like to play soccer with my friends.

Intermediate Have partners ask questions: *What do you like to do? Who do you do it with? How often do you do it?*

Advanced/Advanced High Challenge partners to tell why their sentences are a good beginning for a story.

FORMATIVE ASSESSMENT ▶ **STUDENT CHECK-IN** Partners share their sentences. Ask children to reflect, using the Check-In routine.

INTERACTIVE WRITING

LESSON 2

LEARNING GOALS

We can read and write about a Student Model.

OBJECTIVES

With guidance and support, respond to questions and suggestions from peers.

LANGUAGE OBJECTIVES

Children will discuss and write sentences about the Student Model, identifying parts of a story.

ELA ACADEMIC LANGUAGE

- nouns

Analyze the Student Model Have children chorally read the Student Model on p. 132 of the **Reading/Writing Companion**. Use the Actor/Action routine to analyze the first sentence. Then ask: *Who loves to dance?* (Danny the dragon) *Is the first sentence the beginning, middle, or end of the story?* (beginning) Finally, help children complete p. 133.

Beginning Have partners identify a proper noun in the Student Model. Provide a sentence frame: I noticed that Danny is a proper noun.

Intermediate Have partners talk about the beginning, middle, and end of Robert's story. Provide sentence frames, such as: I noticed Robert told Danny's name at the beginning.

Advanced/Advanced High Have partners discuss each part of the story. *Which part tells you Robert's opinion about Danny?* (the end) Have children write an original sentence about what they noticed.

FORMATIVE ASSESSMENT ▶ **STUDENT CHECK-IN** Partners share their responses. Ask children to reflect, using the Check-In routine.

WEEK 4

INDEPENDENT WRITING
LESSONS 3-4

LEARNING GOALS
We can respond to a fantasy story by extending it.

OBJECTIVES
Write narratives in which they use temporal words.

LANGUAGE OBJECTIVES
Children will narrate by writing complete sentences, using end punctuation marks.

ELA ACADEMIC LANGUAGE
- *characters*

Find Text Evidence Use the Independent Writing routine. Review the characters in the anchor text. Then help children orally retell the story. Ask questions, such as, *How do the animals feel when it rains?* (bored) *How does Nell help?* (She gives them books to read.) Reread the prompt on p. 138 of the **Reading/Writing Companion:** *Extend the story to tell what Nell might do next. Nell can take her books everywhere now. What might she do?* (share books with everyone)

Write a Response Work with children to fill out My Writing Outline 9. Then have children complete p. 138, using the sentences from their outlines.

Writing Checklist Read the checklist with students, and have them check for these items in their writing.

Beginning Have partners identify a proper noun in their stories: Nell is a proper noun. It begins with a capital letter.

Intermediate Have partners exchange stories and look for end marks: This sentence ends with a period. Have them identify common and proper nouns.

Advanced/Advanced High Encourage partners to describe in their own words what happens in the beginning, middle, and end of their stories.

FORMATIVE ASSESSMENT ▶ **STUDENT CHECK-IN** Partners share their sentences from My Writing Outline. Ask children to reflect, using the Check-in routine.

SELF-SELECTED WRITING
LESSON 5

LEARNING GOALS
We can revise our writing.

OBJECTIVES
Use common, proper, and possessive nouns.

LANGUAGE OBJECTIVES
Children will inquire about their writing by checking that their common and proper nouns are correct.

ELA ACADEMIC LANGUAGE
- *common and proper nouns*

Work with children to revise the group writing activity. Point to each word as you read the sentences. Stop to ask questions, such as, *What kind of noun is this?* (common/proper) *Should it begin with a capital letter?* Then have partners work together to correct each other's sentences. Tell them to check that their proper nouns are capitalized.

For support with nouns and grammar, refer to the **Language Transfers Handbook** and **Language Development Card** 1B.

FORMATIVE ASSESSMENT ▶ **STUDENT CHECK-IN** Partners identify their revisions. Ask children to reflect, using the Check-in routine.

ENGLISH LANGUAGE LEARNERS **93**

LESSONS 1-2

READING • LITERATURE BIG BOOK • ACCESS THE TEXT

LEARNING GOALS

We can understand how maps can help us as we listen to a story.

OBJECTIVES

Identify the main topic and retell key details of a text.

Know and use various text features (e.g., headings, tables of contents, glossaries, electronic menus, icons) to locate key facts or information in a text.

Ask and answer questions about key details in a text read aloud or information presented orally or through other media.

Ask questions to clear up any confusion about the topics and texts under discussion.

LANGUAGE OBJECTIVES

Children will discuss the details of various types of maps, using different types of nouns.

ELA ACADEMIC LANGUAGE

- realistic fiction, map
- Cognates: *ficción realista, mapa*

MATERIALS

Literature Big Book, *Me on the Map,* pp. 3–27

Visual Vocabulary Cards

DIGITAL TOOLS   MULTIMODAL

Have children listen to the selection as they follow along to develop comprehension and practice fluency and pronunciation.

Use the online High-Frequency Words Activity for additional support.

Me on the Map

Prepare to Read

Build Background *We are going to read a story about maps a girl makes. This story is realistic fiction. The girl is not real; the places are real.* Show the cover, and say: *This is a map.* Have children repeat. *What can a map show?* Model for children: *A map can show land and oceans.* Help children talk about what maps can show. Prompt, for example: A school map can show ____.

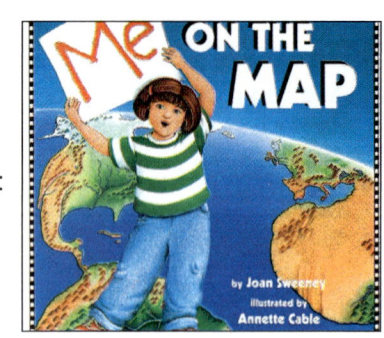

Literature Big Book

Focus on Vocabulary Use the **Visual Vocabulary Cards** to review the oral vocabulary words *locate* and *route*. As you read, use gestures and visual supports to clarify important story words, such as *street, town, state, country,* and *world. Our town is [Pebble Creek]. Say the word* town *with me.* Point to the word *town* on page 8 and to your town on a state map. Repeat this routine for the word *state*, using the text and map on page 13. Provide an example: *My town is [Pebble Creek]. My state is [Florida].* Have children repeat.

Summarize the Text Before reading, say the summary while pointing to the illustrations. *This story tells about a girl who shares her maps of where she lives.*

Read the Text

Use the Interactive Question-Response routine to help children understand the story.

Pages 3–7

Page 6 Read the text aloud. Point to the top picture. *This is a picture of the girl's house. Does it show the outside or inside of the house?* (outside) Point to the map. *The girl drew this map. It shows different rooms in the house.* Help children name the rooms on the map. Say: *The words* My Room *tell where the girl's room is. Point to the girl's room. Where is her mom and dad's room?* (across from her room) *Which room is next to her mom and dad's room?* (the bathroom)

COLLABORATE *What can you learn about the girl's house from her map? Discuss with a partner.*

Beginning Help partners point to and name each room on the map: *This is the [brother's room]. Which is bigger, the patio or the garage?* (the garage)

Intermediate Have partners take turns pointing to and naming rooms: *This is the [brother's room].* Ask: *Which is bigger, the girl's room or the mom and dad's room?* (mom and dad's room) *Which room is next to their room?* The bathroom is next to their room.

Advanced/Advanced High Have partners give details as they point: *This is the [living room]. It is [the biggest] room. This is the [patio]. It is next to the [garage]. This is the [girl's room]. It is across from the [mom and dad's room].*

94 UNIT 2 WEEK 5

WEEK 5

Pages 8–17

Pages 12–13 Read the text aloud. Point to page 12. *The picture shows the girl's country.* Have children say: *the United States of America. This is our country too.* Have children point with you. *I see a city. What does the city have?* (buildings) *I see the flag on the capitol. I see towns, farms, bodies of water, a desert, and hills.* Point to page 13. *This is a map of our country. It has all fifty states. The girl's state is Kansas. Kansas is in the middle of the country. Point to Kansas.* Name the states near it for children to repeat: *Colorado, Nebraska, Missouri, Oklahoma. Where is our state? Our state is near [state names].*

COLLABORATE *What can you learn about the girl's state and your state from the map? Discuss with a partner.*

Beginning Help partners point and respond. *Which state does the girl live in?* She lives in Kansas. *Which states are near Kansas?* (Colorado, Nebraska, Missouri, Oklahoma) *Is our state near Kansas?* (yes/no)

Intermediate *What is the girl's state?* Her state is Kansas. *Where is Kansas on the map?* It is near Colorado, Nebraska, Missouri, and Oklahoma. *What is near our state?* ([names of states near your state])

COLLABORATE **Advanced/Advanced High** Have partners ask and answer: *Where is Kansas located in our country?* It is in the middle of our country. It is near Colorado, Nebraska, Missouri, and Oklahoma. *Where is our state?* It is [location]. It is near [nearby states]. *How do we get to Kansas?* Go across [state names].

Pages 18–27

Pages 24-25 Read the text aloud. Point to and say *all over the world* for children to repeat. This means "all places in the world." *This map shows children on places where they live. The text says everybody has their own special place. Everybody* means "all people." Point to North America. *Is this our place on the map?* (yes)

COLLABORATE *How can you find your special place on the map? Discuss with a partner.*

Beginning Help partners reread pages 18–23. Then help them use what the girl finds to tell what they can find on each map. Provide this sentence frame for responding: I can find my country/state/town/street.

Intermediate Have partners reread pages 18–23. Then have them ask and answer: How do you find your country? I look at a map of the world. How do you find your state? I look at a map of my country. How do you find your town? I look at a map of my state. How do you find your street? I look at a map of my town.

Advanced/Advanced High Have partners reread pages 18–23 and then tell how to find your special place. Use a map of the world to find your country. Use a map of your country to find your state. Use a map of your state to find your town. Use a map of your town to find your street. Ask: *If you don't have a map of your house, what can you do?* (I can draw one.)

FORMATIVE ASSESSMENT

▶ STUDENT CHECK-IN

Have partners choose one of the maps in the story and discuss its qualities. Then have children reflect, using the Check-In routine.

Independent Time

Draw and Share Pair children of mixed proficiencies. Have partners each draw a map of their rooms, their homes, or their streets. Ask partners to discuss the words they will write to label their maps. Provide a sentence frame for support: I will write the word ___. Then have each pair present their maps to the rest of the group, using: This is a map of my ___. It shows ___.

ENGLISH LANGUAGE LEARNERS 95

READING • SHARED READ • ACCESS THE TEXT

LESSONS 1-2

LEARNING GOALS
We can read and understand a nonfiction text.

OBJECTIVES
With prompting and support, read informational texts appropriately complex for grade 1.

Know and use various text features (e.g., headings, tables of contents, glossaries, electronic menus, icons) to locate key facts or information in a text.

Use the illustrations and details in a text to describe its key ideas.

Build on others' talk in conversations by responding to the comments of others through multiple exchanges.

LANGUAGE OBJECTIVES
Children will discuss photographs and maps to identify places, using common and proper nouns.

ELA ACADEMIC LANGUAGE
• nonfiction, map, detail, question
• Cognates: *no ficción, mapa, detalle*

MATERIALS
Reading/Writing Companion, pp. 150–159

Visual Vocabulary Cards

DIGITAL TOOLS
Have children listen to the selection as they follow along to develop comprehension and practice fluency and pronunciation.

Use the additional grammar song.

🎵 Grammar Song

"Which Way on the Map?"

Prepare to Read

Build Background Read aloud the Essential Question on page 150. Use the image of the map on page 151 to help children generate ideas about what maps show. Then say: *We are going to read about how to use maps. We can look at a map to see places in a town.* Remind children of the meaning of *town*: *A town is a place where many people live. It also has stores. Say* town *with me.*

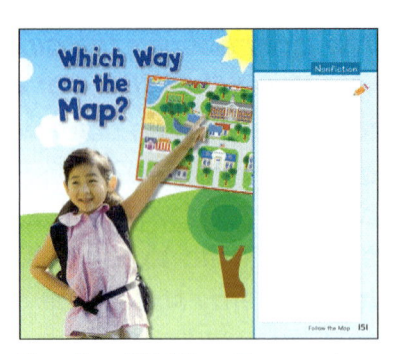

Reading/Writing Companion, Lexile 160L

Focus on Vocabulary Use the **Visual Vocabulary Cards** to review the high-frequency words *around, by, many, place,* and *walk* and the oral vocabulary words *locate, route, height, model,* and *separate.* As you read, use gestures and visual supports to teach important selection words *bricks, playground, lake, post office, mail box,* and *restaurant.*

Summarize the Text Before reading, say the summary, and point to the photos. *This text tells how two kids named Mitch and Steph look at a map of places in their town. The places include a school, a park, a post office, and a restaurant.*

Read the Text

Use the Interactive Question-Response routine to help children understand the text.

Pages 152–153

Pages 152–153 Read the text aloud as children follow along. Point to the words *big town,* and say: *These kids live in a big town. A big town has lots of places. Do you live in a big town?* (yes/no) Point to the map and the flashlight. *They have a map and a flashlight. The flashlight helps them read the map. Say* flashlight. Point to the map on page 153. *This map shows places in the town.* Point to the welcome sign. *The sign tells the name of the town. The name of the town is Chatham. What places do you see on the map of Chatham?* Help children name the places on the map. (Possible answers: lake, park, school, houses, market, city hall, bank, fire station, restaurant, store)

COLLABORATE *Why do Mitch and Steph look at a map of their town? Discuss with a partner.*

Beginning *Do Mitch and Steph live in a big town?* Yes, they live in a big <u>town</u>. *Are they walking around the town?* Yes, they are walking around the <u>town</u>. *What does the map show?* The map shows <u>places</u> in the town.

Intermediate Have partners ask and answer: *Where do Mitch and Steph live?* They live in a <u>big town</u>. *What does the map show?* The map shows each <u>place</u> in the town. *How can the map help Steph and Mitch?* It can help them find <u>places</u>.

96 UNIT 2 WEEK 5

WEEK 5

Advanced/Advanced High Help partners work together to add details: *Mitch and Steph look at a map because it shows them each place in their town. The map shows them how to walk from one place to another.*

Pages 154–155

Page 154 Read the text aloud. Point to the picture. *This is a big building. It is made of red bricks. The text does not tell us what this place is. It gives us a detail that helps answer a question. What is the question on this page?* (Which place is this?)

Page 155 Point to the word *spot*. *The text asks, "Can you spot it on the map?" The word* spot *means "find." Look at the picture on page 154. Do you see the same picture on the map?* (yes)

Which place does the text describe? Point to it on the map. Discuss with a partner.

Beginning Guide partners to answer: *Does this place have bricks or wood?* (bricks) *What color are the bricks?* They are red. *Do many children go here?* Yes, many children go here. *What is this place?* It is a school. *Point to the school on the map. Is the school on the map like the place in the picture?* (yes)

Intermediate Help partners give details. *How does this place look?* It is big. It has red bricks. *Who goes here?* Many children go here. *What is this place?* It is a school. *How do you know the school is on this map?* It looks like the big picture of the school.

Advanced/Advanced High Help partners elaborate: *What is this place?* It is a big school. *How do you know?* The text says many children go here. *How do you know where the school is on the map?* The red brick building on the map looks like the building on page 154.

Pages 156–159

Pages 156–157 Read the text aloud, and have children follow along. Point to the photo. *I see a bench near some grass.* Point to the bench. *The text says people chat on benches. Chat means "talk." I see a playground. The playground has slides. What will Mitch and Steph do at this place?* (run and play catch) *The text says this place is by a lake.* Point to the lake on the map. *Is this a fun place?* (yes)

Which place does the text describe? Where is it on the map? Discuss with a partner.

Beginning Guide partners to respond: *What do you see at this place?* (bench, slides, trees, grass) *Is this a fun place?* Yes, it is a fun place. *What is this place?* (a park) *Find the park on the map. What is by the park?* A lake is by the park.

Intermediate Help partners give details. *What does the text say people can do at this place?* People can chat on benches and run and play catch. *What is this place?* It is a park. *Where is the park on the map?* It is by a lake.

Advanced/Advanced High *What is this place?* (a park) *How do you know?* The picture shows a playground and a bench. The text says people run and play catch here. *Which details helped you find the park on the map?* (the playground, trees, and grass; the lake the text says is by it)

FORMATIVE ASSESSMENT

▶ STUDENT CHECK-IN

Have partners provide descriptions of places in the photographs or maps. Then have children reflect, using the Check-In routine.

Independent Time

Draw and Share Pair children of mixed proficiencies. Have them create a map showing three places. Have one partner describe a place without naming it. Have the other partner guess it. Provide sentence frames: My place has ___. People ___ here. What is it? Then have children present their maps to the group.

ENGLISH LANGUAGE LEARNERS

READING • ANCHOR TEXT • ACCESS THE TEXT

LESSON 3

LEARNING GOALS

We can read and understand a nonfiction text.

OBJECTIVES

Know and use various text features (e.g., headings, tables of contents, glossaries, electronic menus, icons) to locate key facts or information in a text.

Use the illustrations and details in a text to describe its key ideas.

Ask and answer questions about key details in a text.

Describe people, places, things, and events with relevant details, expressing ideas and feelings clearly.

LANGUAGE OBJECTIVES

Children will discuss places on maps, using location words, such as *by, to, on, next to,* and *from.*

ELA ACADEMIC LANGUAGE

- symbols, key, title
- Cognates: *símbolos, título*

MATERIALS

Literature Anthology, pp. 86–93

Visual Vocabulary Cards

DIGITAL TOOLS

Have children listen to the selection as they follow along to develop comprehension and practice fluency and pronunciation.

Use the online High-Frequency Words Activity for additional support.

Fun with Maps

Prepare to Read

Build Background *We are going to read a nonfiction text about maps. This text will tell us how to read a map. We will read map titles.* Point to the title. *On some maps we will see symbols. Symbols are small pictures that show where some things are on a map.* Point to the symbols on the map on page 91. Explain that the map's key is a list of all the symbols on the map. Have children repeat the words *symbols* and *key*. *What can a picture of food on a map be a symbol for? It can be a symbol for a _____ .*

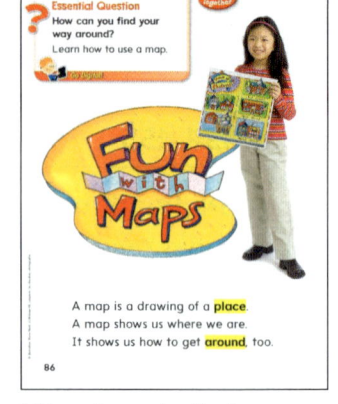

Focus on Vocabulary Use the **Visual Vocabulary Cards** to review the high-frequency words *around, by, many, place,* and *walk* and the oral vocabulary words *locate, route, height, model,* and *separate*. As you read, teach important selection words, such as *north, south, east,* and *west,* using gestures and pantomime. Point to the top of a map, and say *north* for children to repeat. Point to the bottom, and say *south* for children to repeat. Continue the routine for *west* and *east. Which direction is up?* (north) *Which is down?* (south)

Summarize the Text Before reading, say the summary: *The story tells about different kinds of maps. It tells about the key and symbols on a map too.*

Literature Anthology, Lexile NP

Read the Text

Use the Interactive Question-Response routine to help children understand the text.

Pages 86–89

Pages 86–89 Read the text. Point to the map. *This map shows Phil's room.* Point to and say *door* and *windows* for children to repeat. *What else do you see in Phil's room?* (bed, lamp, clock, rug) *What is the map's title?* (Phil's Room) Point to the map on pages 88-89. *What is the title?* (Town of Chatwell) Point to and say *streets* for children to repeat. *What is on this map?* (places in a town)

What kinds of places does the map show? Discuss with a partner.

Beginning Help partners read the map title on page 87: *Phil's Room. What is this a map of? It is a map of Phil's* room. *Does the title tell you this?* (yes) *Is this a big place or a small place?* (small place) Have partners point to the map title on pages 88–89 and say it: *Town of Chatwell. What does this title tell you? The map is of a* town *named Chatwell. Is this a big place or a small place? It is a big* place.

Intermediate Point to the title on the map on page 87, and help children read it. *What does the title tell you about the map? The map shows Phil's* room. *What is*

WEEK 5

in the room? (bed, chair, toy box) *Is the room small?* It is a small room. Point to the map title on pages 88–89, and help children read it. *What does this title tell you?* The map shows the town of Chatwell. *What else tells you the map shows a town?* The map shows streets and places. *Is a town a big place?* Yes, a town is a big place.

Advanced/Advanced High Have partners work together to tell about both maps: The title of this map is Phil's Room. It shows Phil's room. His room has windows, a door, a [bed], and [a toy box]. It is a small place. The title of this map is Town of Chatham. It shows buildings and streets. It is a big place.

Pages 90–93

Pages 90–91 Read the text. Point to the key. *This is a key. A key on a map has symbols that stand for real things on the map. The words tell what the symbols mean.* Point to and say the key's words for children to repeat: *pond, picnic tables, playground, baseball field, band shell,* and *snack bar. Do you see a pond on the map?* (yes) *Point to the pond.*

Pages 92–93 Read the text. Point to the word *imaginary. An imaginary place is not a real place.* Point to and say *Treasure Island* for children to repeat. *This map's details tell a story. What happens?* A pirate ship goes around a volcano to a cave to find gold.

Read the text. Point to the word *treasure. A treasure is worth a lot of money.* Point to and say the key's words for children to repeat: *pirate ship, cave, waterfall, volcano, cove, chest of gold.* Provide a visual of a chest of gold. *The X shows where the chest of gold is. Do you see a pirate ship on the map?* (yes) *Follow the broken lines. Where do the pirates go?* They go to the cave to get the chest of gold.

How does the map key help you understand the map? Discuss with a partner.

Beginning Help children match the key's symbols to the places on the Bell Park and Treasure Island maps. *Find the word playground. Do you see swings on the map?* (yes) *What does the swings symbol stand for?* (a playground) *Do the words and symbols in the key help you know what the places on the map are?* (yes/no) *Find the word pirate ship. Do you see a ship on the map?* (yes) *Point to the pirate ship. What does the ship symbol stand for?* (pirate ship) Continue with other places on the Treasure Island map.

Intermediate Help partners explain each map's key. *The Bell Park map key says a picture of swings means a playground.* The map shows a place with swings. That place is a playground. *How does a key help you read a map?* It shows what the symbols on the map mean. Continue with the Treasure Island map. *The Treasure Island map key says a picture of an X means a chest of gold. The map shows an X.* The X means treasure.

Advanced/Advanced High Have partners use each key to explain the maps. Examples: The Bell Park key says the water on the map is a pond. The Treasure Island key says the X on the map is a chest of gold. *How does the key help you?* It gives words for symbols so I understand the same symbols on the map. *How can you use the key?* I can use the key to find places on the map.

FORMATIVE ASSESSMENT

▶ STUDENT CHECK-IN

Have children select two places on one of the maps and discuss how to get to one place from the other. Then, have children reflect using the Check-In Routine.

Independent Time

Discuss a Map Pair children of mixed proficiencies, and have them discuss the Bell Park map. Have them take turns pointing to places and asking and answering questions. Provide sentence frames to support children's development of oral questions and responses: What does the picture of the ___ stand for? It stands for ___. Where can you go to ___? I can go to ___. Then have pairs each present one question and answer to the rest of the group. Encourage pairs to use content-area vocabulary in their questions and responses. Have partners help each other clarify pronunciations as needed.

ENGLISH LANGUAGE LEARNERS **99**

LESSONS 4-5

READING • LEVELED READER • ACCESS THE TEXT

LEARNING GOALS

We can reread to understand a nonfiction text.

OBJECTIVES

Identify the main topic and retell key details of a text.

Identify basic similarities in and differences between two texts on the same topic.

With prompting and support, read informational texts appropriately complex for grade 1.

Produce complete sentences when appropriate to task and situation.

LANGUAGE OBJECTIVES

Children will discuss the information on the maps using location words.

ELA ACADEMIC LANGUAGE

- nonfiction, topic, details
- Cognates: *no ficción, detalles*

MATERIALS

ELL Leveled Reader: *How Maps Help*

Online Differentiated Texts, "Use a Map"

Online ELL Visual Vocabulary Cards

DIGITAL TOOLS

Have children listen to the selection as they follow along to develop comprehension and practice fluency and pronunciation. Use Graphic Organizer 3: Topic and Relevant Details to enhance the lesson.

How Maps Help

Prepare to Read

Build Background

- Remind children of the Essential Question. *Let's read this nonfiction text to see how people find their way around a big park.* Encourage children to ask for help when they do not understand a word or phrase.

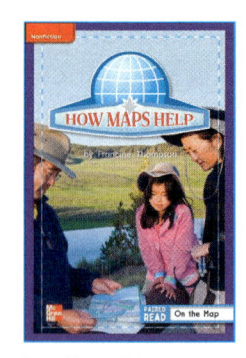

- Point to and read aloud the title, and have children repeat it. *What is the title?* Repeat the routine for the author's name. Point to the illustrations in the **Leveled Reader** to name things and actions, for example: *This is a picnic. What can you do on a picnic?* You can sit outside and _____ .

Lexile 60L

Focus on Vocabulary Use the **ELL Visual Vocabulary Cards** to preteach the words *direction* and *location.* As you read, use gestures or visuals to teach important selection words, such as *trail, picnic,* and *the way out.*

Read the Text

Use the Interactive Question-Response routine to help children understand the text.

Pages 2–3

Read pages 2–3 as children follow along. Point to the sign. *The sign tells the name of a park: Yellowstone National Park. What is the name of this park?* (Yellowstone National Park) *How can a sign help?* It can show the name of a park.

Beginning *Where is the family?* They are at a big park. *Where is the name of the park?* (on the sign) *What does the family need?* They need a map.

Intermediate Ask and answer: *What does the family need?* The family needs a map. *How does the sign help?* The sign shows the name of the park.

Pages 4–9

Reread Read pages 6–7. Point to and say *trail, mountain, pond, river,* and *North Entrance* for children to repeat. Help children reread if they do not understand. *You can look at the pictures to help you understand the information.*

Beginning *What does the family want to do?* They want to walk on a trail. *Look at the map. Point to a trail by a pond. Is it on the west side of the park?* (no)

Advanced/Advanced High Have partners ask and answer: *What does the family want to do?* They want to walk on a trail. *Where is Beaver Ponds Loop Trail?* (near the North Entrance)

100 UNIT 2 WEEK 5

WEEK 5

Pages 10–12

Topic and Relevant Details Read pages 10–11. Ask questions to help children describe relevant details. Have children repeat *This way out* and *parking lot* from the map.

Intermediate *What does the family want?* They want to go <u>home</u>. *What does the map show?* It shows many <u>ways</u> to the parking <u>lot</u>.

Advanced/Advanced High Have partners discuss how a map helps the family: The map shows them how to find <u>deer</u>, <u>trails</u>, <u>picnic</u> places, and the <u>way out</u>.

Respond to Reading Have partners work together to retell the story and respond to the questions on page 12.

Focus on Fluency

Read pages 10–11. Then reread them, and have children echo-read after you. Remind children to read the words correctly.

Paired Selection: "On the Map"

Analytical Writing — Make Connections: Write About It

Echo-read each page with children. *How does the bus get to E Street?* It goes north on Main <u>Street</u>. Help children make connections between texts: Maps show us where to <u>go</u> and how to get to a <u>place</u>.

Leveled Reader

Build Knowledge: Make Connections

Talk About the Text Have partners discuss how the maps in the texts can help someone get around.

Write About the Text Have students add their ideas to the Build Knowledge pages of their reader's notebooks.

Self-Selected Reading

Help children choose a nonfiction selection from the online **Leveled Reader Library** or read the **Differentiated Text**, "Use a Map."

🌍 FOCUS ON SOCIAL STUDIES

Children can extend their knowledge of maps by completing the social studies activity on page 16.

LITERATURE CIRCLES

Lead children in conducting a literature circle using the Thinkmark questions to guide the discussion. You may wish to discuss what children have learned about maps from both selections in the **Leveled Reader**.

FORMATIVE ASSESSMENT

▶ STUDENT CHECK-IN

Have partners share their Respond to Reading. Have children reflect, using the Check-In routine.

LEVEL UP

IF children can read *How Maps Help* **ELL Level** with fluency and correctly answer the Respond to Reading questions,

THEN tell children they will read a more detailed version of this selection.

- Use pages 5 and 7 of *How Maps Help* **On Level** to model using Teaching Poster 29 to list key details.

- Have children read the selection, checking their comprehension by using the teaching poster.

ENGLISH LANGUAGE LEARNERS

LESSONS 1-5

WRITING

MODELED WRITING

LESSON 1

LEARNING GOALS

We can learn how to write a supporting detail.

OBJECTIVES

Write informative texts in which they supply some facts about the topic.

LANGUAGE OBJECTIVES

Children will inform by writing a sentence, using a supporting detail.

ELA ACADEMIC LANGUAGE

- details, sentence
- Cognate: *detalles*

Writing Practice Review the sample on p. 160 of the **Reading/Writing Companion**. Guide children to analyze it using the Actor/Action routine: *What is this sentence about?* (my city) *What does the sentence tell about the city?* (It has a post office, Mark's Food Store, and a big, beautiful park.) Read the prompt on p. 161, and guide children to provide supporting details as they respond. Write the sentence, modeling how to separate each place name with a comma. Then ask partners to write their own sentences.

Beginning Help children choose a place for the first blank in this sentence frame: Rosewood Park *has a* slide *and* swings. *Is* Rosewood Park *a proper noun?* (yes)

Intermediate Have partners ask and answer questions to elicit the name of a place and things they see there.

Advanced/Advanced High Challenge children to add one more supporting detail to their sentences, such as a phrase to name the street.

FORMATIVE ASSESSMENT ▸ **STUDENT CHECK-IN** Partners share their sentences. Ask children to reflect, using the Check-In routine.

INTERACTIVE WRITING

LESSON 2

LEARNING GOALS

We can read and write about a Student Model.

OBJECTIVES

With guidance and support, respond to questions and suggestions from peers.

LANGUAGE OBJECTIVES

Children will discuss and write sentences about the Student Model, identifying an irregular plural noun.

ELA ACADEMIC LANGUAGE

- irregular plural noun
- Cognate: *plural*

Analyze the Student Model Have children chorally read the Student Model on p. 166 of the **Reading/Writing Companion**. Use the Actor/Action routine to review the first sentence. Then ask: *Can you find an irregular plural noun?* (children) *How do you know?* (It does not end with *-s* or *-es*.) Then help children complete p. 167.

Beginning Help partners identify a proper noun in the Student Model. Provide a sentence frame: I noticed the proper noun Chatham.

Intermediate Have partners look for supporting details. Provide sentence frames: Maria used a supporting detail *to tell more about* the map.

Advanced/Advanced High Challenge children to write original sentences telling what they noticed about Maria's writing.

FORMATIVE ASSESSMENT ▸ **STUDENT CHECK-IN** Partners share their responses. Ask children to reflect, using the Check-In routine.

WEEK 5

INDEPENDENT WRITING

LESSONS 3-4

LEARNING GOALS
We can use text evidence to respond to a nonfiction text.

OBJECTIVES
Write informative texts in which they supply some facts about the topic.

LANGUAGE OBJECTIVES
Children will explain what they learned about different kinds of maps, using text evidence.

ELA ACADEMIC LANGUAGE
- *details*
- Cognate: *detalles*

Find Text Evidence Use the Independent Writing routine. Help children orally retell "Fun with Maps." Ask questions, such as: *Which map has buildings and streets?* (the map of a town) *Which map has a key?* (the map of a park) Then reread the prompt on p. 171 of the **Reading/Writing Companion:** *Think about the different kinds of maps in the text. How can maps help us? The text has four different maps. Let's look at the text and images to see how each map helps us.*

Write a Response Work with children to fill out My Writing Outline 10. Then have them use the sentences from their outlines to complete p. 171.

Writing Checklist Read the checklist with students, and have them check for these items in their writing.

Beginning Have partners identify a supporting detail: Rooms in a house is a supporting detail.

Intermediate Challenge partners to add another supporting detail.

Advanced/Advanced High Have partners identify where they used each checklist item in their writing.

FORMATIVE ASSESSMENT → **STUDENT CHECK-IN** Partners share their sentences from My Writing Outline. Ask children to reflect, using the Check-in routine.

SELF-SELECTED WRITING

LESSON 5

LEARNING GOALS
We can revise our writing.

OBJECTIVES
Use singular and plural nouns with matching verbs in basic sentences.

LANGUAGE OBJECTIVES
Children will inquire about their writing by checking their irregular plural nouns.

ELA ACADEMIC LANGUAGE
- *nouns*

Work with children to revise the group writing activity. Point to each word as you read the sentences. Stop to ask questions, such as, *Is this a singular or plural noun? Is it a regular or an irregular plural noun?* Then have partners work together to correct each other's sentences. Tell partners to check for the correct spelling of their singular and plural nouns.

For support with grammar and plural nouns, refer to the **Language Transfers Handbook** and **Language Development Card** 3A.

FORMATIVE ASSESSMENT → **STUDENT CHECK-IN** Partners tell what revisions they made. Ask children to reflect, using the Check-in routine.

ENGLISH LANGUAGE LEARNERS 103

UNIT 2

Summative Assessment
Get Ready for Unit Assessment

Unit 2 Tested Skills

LISTENING AND READING COMPREHENSION	VOCABULARY	GRAMMAR	SPEAKING AND WRITING
• Listening Actively • Details	• Words and Categories	• Nouns	• Presenting • Composing/Writing • Supporting Opinions • Retelling/Recounting

Create a Student Profile

Record data from the following resources in the Student Profile charts on pages 356–357 of the Assessment book.

COLLABORATIVE	INTERPRETIVE	PRODUCTIVE

• Collaborative Conversations Rubrics
  • Listening
  • Speaking
	• Leveled Unit Assessment
	  • Listening Comprehension
	  • Reading Comprehension
	  • Vocabulary
	  • Grammar
	• Presentation Rubric
	  • Listening
	• *Wonders* Unit Assessment
		• Weekly Progress Monitoring
		• Leveled Unit Assessment
		  • Speaking
		  • Writing
		• Presentation Rubric
		  • Speaking
		• Write to Sources Rubric
		• *Wonders* Unit Assessment

The Foundational Skills Kit, Language Development Kit, and Adaptive Learning provide additional student data for progress monitoring.

Level Up

Use the following chart, along with your Student Profiles, to guide your Level Up decisions.

LEVEL UP	If **BEGINNING** level students are able to do the following, they may be ready to move to the **INTERMEDIATE** level:	If **INTERMEDIATE** level students are able to do the following, they may be ready to move to the **ADVANCED** level:	If **ADVANCED** level students are able to do the following, they may be ready to move to **ON** level:
COLLABORATIVE	• participate in collaborative conversations using basic vocabulary and grammar and simple phrases or sentences • discuss simple pictorial or text prompts	• participate in collaborative conversations using appropriate words and phrases and complete sentences • use limited academic vocabulary across and within disciplines	• participate in collaborative conversations using more sophisticated vocabulary and correct grammar • communicate effectively across a wide range of language demands in social and academic contexts
INTERPRETIVE	• identify details in simple read alouds • understand common vocabulary and idioms and interpret language related to familiar social, school, and academic topics • make simple inferences and make simple comparisons • exhibit an emerging receptive control of lexical, syntactic, phonological, and discourse features	• identify main ideas and/or make some inferences from simple read alouds • use context clues to identify word meanings and interpret basic vocabulary and idioms • compare, contrast, summarize, and relate text to graphic organizers • exhibit a limited range of receptive control of lexical, syntactic, phonological, and discourse features when addressing new or familiar topics	• determine main ideas in read alouds that have advanced vocabulary • use context clues to determine meaning, understand multiple-meaning words, and recognize synonyms of social and academic vocabulary • analyze information, make sophisticated inferences, and explain their reasoning • command a high degree of receptive control of lexical, syntactic, phonological, and discourse features
PRODUCTIVE	• express ideas and opinions with basic vocabulary and grammar and simple phrases or sentences • restate information or retell a story using basic vocabulary • exhibit an emerging productive control of lexical, syntactic, phonological, and discourse features	• produce coherent language with limited elaboration or detail • restate information or retell a story using mostly accurate, although limited, vocabulary • exhibit a limited range of productive control of lexical, syntactic, phonological, and discourse features when addressing new or familiar topics	• produce sentences with more sophisticated vocabulary and correct grammar • restate information or retell a story using extensive and accurate vocabulary and grammar • tailor language to a particular purpose and audience • command a high degree of productive control of lexical, syntactic, phonological, and discourse features

LESSONS 1-2

READING • LITERATURE BIG BOOK • ACCESS THE TEXT

LEARNING GOALS

We can understand measuring time as we listen to a poem.

OBJECTIVES

Retell stories, including key details, and demonstrate understanding of their central message or lesson.

With prompting and support, read prose and poetry of appropriate complexity for grade 1.

Build on others' talk in conversations by responding to the comments of others through multiple exchanges.

Produce complete sentences when appropriate to task and situation.

LANGUAGE OBJECTIVES

Children will narrate what can happen in different amounts of time, using key vocabulary and sentences.

ELA ACADEMIC LANGUAGE

- discuss, illustration
- Cognates: *discutir, ilustración*

MATERIALS

Literature Big Book, *A Second Is a Hiccup,* pp. 2–35

Visual Vocabulary Cards

DIGITAL TOOLS

Have children listen to the selection as they follow along to develop comprehension and practice fluency and pronunciation.

Use the additional grammar song.

Grammar Song

A Second Is a Hiccup

Prepare to Read

Build Background *We are going to read a poem about different units of time. A poem is like a song; it often has words that rhyme.* Display the cover and read the title. Pantomime a hiccup. *Does a hiccup last a long time? No, a hiccup only takes a second. A second is a way we measure time.* Ask children to tell what they know about time. Use a clock or calendar to help generate ideas such as *day, second, week, month*. Then have children tell what they can do in different units of time: *I can go to school and home in a _____. I can hop many times in a _____.*

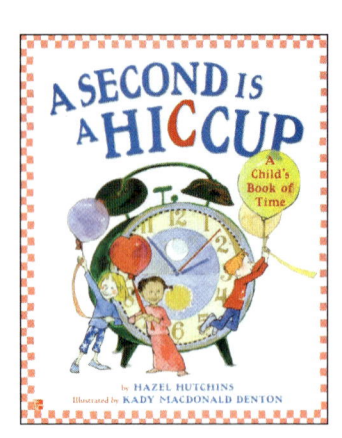

Focus on Vocabulary Use the **Visual Vocabulary Cards** to review the oral vocabulary words *immediately* and *schedule*. As you read, use gestures and visual support to clarify important words from the poem, such as: *sandy, tower, sprinkly, shower, fade, peek, seasons, laces,* and *float*.

Literature Big Book

Summarize the Text Before reading, say the summary while pointing to the illustrations. *The poem tells about what you can do in different units of time. We'll read about a second, a minute, an hour, a day, a month, and a year.*

Read the Text

Use the Interactive Question-Response routine to help children understand the poem.

Pages 4–17

Page 15 Read the text aloud. Point to the first image. *This is a clothes basket. What is the boy doing?* He is folding clothes. Point to the next image. *What is the girl doing?* She is drawing a picture. Point to the bottom row. *This girl has a hockey stick. What is she doing?* She is playing hockey. Point to the final image. *What are these children doing at school?* They are making a pot/bowl.

What kinds of days are there in a week? Discuss with a partner.

Beginning Point to the boy folding clothes. *Does the boy have a work day or a play day?* The boy has a work day. *Are the other children working?* No, the other children are not working. *Do the children in the last picture have a play day or a school day?* They have a school day.

Intermediate Have partners point to pictures as they respond. *What kind of day does this boy have?* He has a work day. *Which child has a home day?* (this girl) *What does she do on her home day?* She draws. *What kind of day does this girl*

106 UNIT 3 WEEK 1

WEEK 1

have? She has a play day. She plays hockey. *Who has a school day?* (these children) *What do they do?* They make a pot. *What is your favorite day?* My favorite day is a home day.

Advanced/Advanced High Have partners give details. *What might you do on home days?* On home days, you might paint or draw. *What might you do on play days?* On play days, you might play sports. *What is your favorite way to spend a play day?* On play days, I like to run outside.

Pages 18–23

Page 18 Read the text aloud. *How many weeks are in a month?* (four) Show a calendar to help children name this month. Then point to and say *rearrange* for children to repeat. Rearrange *means "change."* Point to the picture. *I see people in warm clothes. What do you see?* Two people are playing catch. A man is with his dog. The dog and a boy are looking at a ball. Two people are looking up at the moon.

What can change in a month? Discuss with a partner.

Beginning Discuss how *rearrange* means "reorganize." *What rearranges in a month?* Seasons rearrange. Review season words. *What season does the picture show?* (winter) *What will the next season be?* The next season will be spring.

Intermediate Point to the picture. *What in the picture changes in a month?* Caterpillars change in a month. *What does the text say often changes in a month?* Seasons change.

Advanced/Advanced High Help partners add details in their responses. Caterpillars change in spring. Seasons often change in a month, too. Winter can change to spring in a month.

Pages 24–35

Page 24 Read the text aloud. Point to the carousel. *What are the children doing?* (going in a circle) *A year is like a circle because it starts in one month and goes all the way around and back to the first month.*

Page 30 Read the text aloud. Point to the phrase *Linked together* and reread it aloud. *When two things are linked together, they are connected. When you link arms, you are connected.* Have children link arms to demonstrate. Have children share examples of other things that are connected. (knots, parts of a chain)

What are some important changes that happen within a year? Discuss with a partner.

Beginning Point to the baby. *Do babies learn to walk in a year?* Yes, babies learn to walk in a year. Point to the children. *What do bigger babies learn to do in a year?* Bigger babies learn to talk in a year.

Intermediate Help partners discuss to generate ideas for how things change in a year. *What are some important holidays that happen in a year?* Important holidays in a year are New Year's Day, the Fourth of July, and Memorial Day.

Advanced/Advanced High Help partners give details about themselves. *What are important ways you have changed in a year?* I can read and write better. I am taller. I have new friends.

FORMATIVE ASSESSMENT

> **STUDENT CHECK IN**

Have partners retell what can happen or change in different amounts of time. Then have children reflect using the Check-In routine.

Independent Time

Interactive Word Wall Pair children of mixed proficiencies and have them write the units of time on note cards and draw a picture for each one. Have pairs use their cards to create a word wall about time. Have partners explain their pictures to the rest of the group using: This is a [second]. You can ___ in a [second].

ENGLISH LANGUAGE LEARNERS 107

LESSONS 1-2

READING • SHARED READ • ACCESS THE TEXT

LEARNING GOALS

We can read and understand a fantasy story.

OBJECTIVES

Retell stories, including key details, and demonstrate understanding of their central message or lesson.

Describe characters, settings, and major events in a story, using key details.

Identify words and phrases in stories or poems that suggest feelings or appeal to the senses.

Build on others' talk in conversations by responding to the comments of others through multiple exchanges.

LANGUAGE OBJECTIVES

Children will narrate what the characters do, using time words and phrases.

ELA ACADEMIC LANGUAGE

- fantasy, predict, prediction
- Cognates: *fantasía, predecir, predicción*

MATERIALS

Reading/Writing Companion, pp. 14–23

Visual Vocabulary Cards

DIGITAL TOOLS

Have children listen to the selection as they follow along to develop comprehension and practice fluency and pronunciation.

Use the online High-Frequency Words Activity for additional support.

"Nate the Snake Is Late"

Prepare to Read

Build Background Read aloud the Essential Question on page 14. Have children share different ways they measure time. Use the illustrations on pages 14 and 15 to generate ideas. Point to the clocks. *Nate the Snake measures time with clocks. How do you measure time? I measure time with a _____.* Point to and read aloud the title. *This fantasy story is about a character named Nate. Who is the main character? The main character is _____.*

Reading/Writing Companion, Lexile 460L

Focus on Vocabulary Use the **Visual Vocabulary Cards** to review the high-frequency words *away, now, some, today, way,* and *why* and the oral vocabulary words *calendar, occasion, weekend, immediately,* and *schedule*. As you read, use gestures and visual support to teach important story words *8 o'clock, bath, nap, lane, pals,* and *grin*. Use the following routine for each new word: Point to the clock. Say: *It is 8 o'clock.* Have children point to the clock and repeat. *What time is it on this clock? It is* 8 o'clock.

Summarize the Text Before reading, say the summary and point to the illustrations. *This story tells what a snake named Nate does on his way to school. He thinks he has a lot of time, so he stops to do many activities.*

Read the Text

Use the Interactive Question-Response routine to help children understand the story.

Pages 16–19

Page 17 Read the text aloud as children follow along. *Nate says he has to be somewhere at half past ten. Another way to say* half past ten *is* ten thirty.

Pages 18–19 Read the text aloud as children follow along. *Nate thinks he has some time to spare.* Time to spare *means more time than we need. When we have time to spare, we are early, not late.* Point to the clock. *What time is it? It is* 8:30. Point to page 19. *Where is Nate now? He is in a* lake. *Do the frogs want to play with him?* No, *they hop* away.

Do you predict Nate will have time to spare? Discuss with a partner.

Beginning Point to the picture on page 19. To wade *means "to walk slowly in water." What is Nate doing? Nate is wading in the* lake. *Does Nate try to play? Yes, he tries to* play *with the* frogs. *It is 9 o'clock. Nate needs to be somewhere at 10:30. Will he be early? Yes, he will be* early./*No, he will* not *be* early.

108 UNIT 3 WEEK 1

Intermediate Help partners give more specific answers. *What does Nate do?* He stops to wade in the lake. He tries to play with the frogs. *Do you* **predict** *he will stop again?* Yes, I predict he will stop again. *Do you predict he will have time to spare?* No, I predict he will not have time to spare.

Advanced/Advanced High Help partners add details to their predictions. *Do you think Nate will arrive with time to spare?* No, I do not think he will arrive with time to spare. *What details make you think that?* He has already stopped one time, and I think he will stop again. I predict this will make him late.

Pages 20–21

Page 20 Read the text aloud. Point to the word *gaze* and say it for children to repeat. Gaze *means "to look at something for a long time." What does Nate gaze at after his nap?* He gazes at the clock. Have children point to the clock. *What is the time on the clock?* The time is 9:30. *Have you seen clocks on other pages in the story?* (yes)

Why is there a clock on every page of the story? Discuss with a partner.

Beginning Use visual support to guide partners. *Look at the illustration at the beginning of the story. What time is it at the beginning?* At the beginning, it is 8 o'clock. *What time is it when Nate leaves his house?* When he leaves, it is 8:30. *What is the time on page 20?* It is 9:30. *Does the time get earlier or later?* The time gets later.

Intermediate Help partners add details to their answers. *What do the clocks in the illustrations show us?* The clocks show that it's getting closer to 10:30. *What do you think the next clock will show?* I think the next clock will show a time past/after 10:30.

Advanced/Advanced High Help partners extend their thinking. *How would the story be different if it did not show clocks on every page?* If the story did not show clocks on every page, we would not know how close the time is getting to 10:30. We would not worry/think that Nate would be late.

Pages 22–23

Pages 22–23 Read the text aloud and have children follow along. Point to the word *dash* and say it for children to repeat. Dash *is another word for* hurry. Point to the building. *This is where Nate needs to be. Is Nate close to the building?* (yes) *What time is it?* It is 10:30. Point to the picture on page 22. *Nate arrives at the library. A library is a place that has lots of books. The time on the clock is 10:45. Is Nate late?* (yes) *Was your prediction correct?* (yes)

Why do you think Nate dashes up the lane? Discuss with a partner.

Beginning *If you dash, do you go fast or slow?* When you dash, you go fast. *When you are excited, do you go fast or slow?* When you are excited, you go fast. *Is Nate excited to go to the library?* Yes, he is excited.

Intermediate Help partners add details to their answers. *Do you think Nate is excited to go to the library?* (yes) *How do you know?* I think Nate is excited because he goes fast when he gets closer to the library.

Advanced/Advanced High Help partners work together to elaborate on their answers. *What else do you learn about Nate from his actions?* I know that he cares about his friends. He does not want them to wait.

FORMATIVE ASSESSMENT

▶ STUDENT CHECK IN

Have partners retell why Nate was late to story hour at the library. Then have children reflect using the Check-In routine.

Independent Time

Telling Time Ask children to think about what they do at different times each day. Have children create clocks. Pair children of mixed proficiencies and have them ask and answer questions about their schedules while showing times on their clocks. Have each pair share with the group. Use **Oral Language Sentence Frames,** page 7, Modifying to Add Details, for support as children talk about their daily schedules.

ENGLISH LANGUAGE LEARNERS **109**

LESSON 3

READING • ANCHOR TEXT • ACCESS THE TEXT

LEARNING GOALS

We can read and understand a fantasy story.

OBJECTIVES

Ask and answer questions about key details in a text.

Use illustrations and details in a story to describe its characters, setting, or events.

Compare and contrast the adventures and experiences of characters in stories.

Build on others' talk in conversations by responding to the comments of others through multiple exchanges.

LANGUAGE OBJECTIVES

Children will narrate the character's trip to school, using words that rhyme and key vocabulary.

ELA ACADEMIC LANGUAGE

- author, dialogue
- Cognates: *autor, diálogo*

MATERIALS

Literature Anthology, pp. 6–23

Visual Vocabulary Cards

DIGITAL TOOLS

Have children listen to the selection as they follow along to develop comprehension.

Use the online High-Frequency Words Activity for additional support.

On My Way to School

Prepare to Read

Build Background *We are going to read a story about what happens to a boy on his way to school.* Show the picture on the title page and invite children to tell what they see. Point to the *bus, ape, pig,* and *frogs.* Say the words and have children repeat. Then point to the ape driving the bus. *This is not a normal trip to school. Some strange things happen.* Explain that something that is *strange* is something you never or almost never see. *What is strange about this picture?* It is strange for an ape to _____ a _____. It is strange for a _____ to be on a bus.

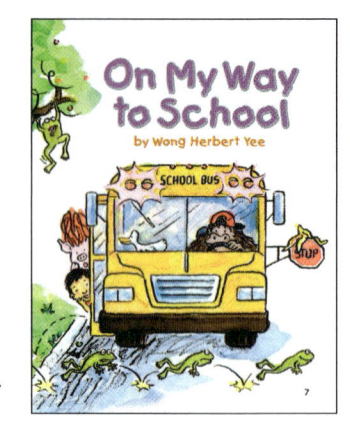

Literature Anthology, Lexile 330L

Focus on Vocabulary Use the **Visual Vocabulary Cards** to review the high-frequency words *away, now, some, today, way,* and *why* and the oral vocabulary words *calendar, occasion, weekend, immediately,* and *schedule.* Before reading the story, clarify vocabulary children will need for understanding. As you read, teach important story words, such as *wig,* using gestures and pantomime. Point to the wig on the pig's head. *A wig is like a hat, but it is made of hair. Who is wearing a wig?* The pig is wearing a wig.

Summarize the Text Before reading, say the summary while pointing to the illustrations. *The story tells about a boy's trip to school on a school bus. He gives some strange reasons for why he is late to school.*

Read the Text

Use the Interactive Question-Response Routine to help children understand the story.

Pages 8–13

Pages 10–11 Read the text. Point to the boy and pig running to catch the bus. *Where are the boy and pig going?* They are going to school. Point to page 11. *They see a trash truck that is out of gas. Who is on top of the truck?* Two apes and a duck are on top of the truck.

Pages 12–13 Read the text. Point to the apes. *What are the apes doing?* The apes are getting on the bus. *The boy says the apes and a duck sit with the rest of them. Who else is on the bus?* The boy, a pig, and the bus driver are on the bus. *The boy says, Apes made me late for school today! Why does the boy say this?* The boy says apes made him late because the bus stopped to let the apes on.

COLLABORATE *Who is telling the story? What clues does the author use to help you know? Discuss with a partner.*

110 UNIT 3 WEEK 1

WEEK 1

Beginning Reread the sentence *Apes made me late for school today.* Point to *me. Who is* me *in the story?* (the boy) Have children point to the boy on a previous page and complete the sentence frame. *Me is the* boy.

Intermediate Point to *Apes made me late for school today. Who is* me *in the story? Me is the* boy. *How else does the author tell you the boy is telling the story?* The author uses the word *I* and pictures of the boy.

Advanced/Advanced High Extend the discussion: *Why do you think the boy is telling the story?* The boy is telling the story to explain why he is late for school.

Pages 12–15

Pages 12–13 Read the text. *On page 13, the dog is slipping on banana peels. Who dropped the peels?* (the apes) Point to and say *slip, flip* for children to repeat. *Slip* and *flip rhyme. Rhyming words end in the same sounds. What words rhyme with* wig? (pig, big)

What feeling does the story have because of the rhyming words? Discuss with a partner.

Beginning Help partners read page 12 aloud. *Which words rhyme?* (bus, us) *Do rhyming words make a story funny?* Yes, they make a story funny.

Intermediate Have partners find the rhyming words. (bus, us; slip, flip; away, today) Have partners each read two lines. *Do rhyming words make this story funny or sad?* Rhyming words make it funny.

Advanced/Advanced High Have partners ask and answer: What feeling do the rhyming words give this story? They give it a silly/funny feeling.

Pages 16–21

Pages 16–17 Read the text. Point to page 16. *Who gets on the bus?* Frogs get on the bus. *Who else is there?* The boy, pig, apes, and duck are there. Point to page 17. *What happens next?* The frogs hop in the lake.

Pages 18–19 Read the text. Point to the pictures. *The boy tells what everyone does when they get off the bus. Where does the duck go?* The duck goes to get gas. *What do the apes do?* The apes fish and nap.

Pages 20–21 Read the text. Point to page 20. *Where are the boy and pig?* They are at school. Have children point to the crocodile. *Is the crocodile getting out?* (yes) Point to page 21. *The boy is telling his teacher all of the strange events that he says made him late.*

How do you know the boy made these things up? Discuss with a partner.

Beginning Display page 19. *Can ducks fly with big cans?* No, ducks can not fly with big cans. *Do apes fish?* No, apes do not fish. Display page 20. *Do crocodiles wear sunglasses?* (no) *Do these events tell you the boy made these things up?* (yes)

Intermediate Have partners review the events and then respond. *Could the events the boy tells Miss Blake really happen?* No, they could not really happen.

Advanced/Advanced High Have children extend their thinking. *How do you think Miss Blake will react to what the boy tells her? Tell why you say that.* I think Miss Blake will not believe the boy because what he says could not really happen. For example, [there is no such thing as a gumdrop tree].

FORMATIVE ASSESSMENT

▶ STUDENT CHECK IN

Have partners retell what kind of animals join the boy on the bus. Then have children reflect using the Check-In routine.

Independent Time

Write a Dialogue Have children imagine what Miss Blake says after the boy explains why he is late. Tell children that a dialogue is two or more people talking. Pair children of mixed proficiencies and have partners write a dialogue of what Miss Blake might say and what the boy might say. Then have children perform their dialogues. If children need support, provide sentence frame choices, such as:

Miss Blake: Are you sure that ___?
Boy: Yes, I am sure that ___. /Maybe I ___. Or:
Miss Blake: I see why ___. You ___.
Boy: Yes, ___./No, ___.

LESSONS 4-5

READING • LEVELED READER • ACCESS THE TEXT

LEARNING GOALS

We can make and confirm predictions as we read a fantasy story.

OBJECTIVES

Retell stories, including key details, and demonstrate understanding of their central message or lesson.

Describe characters, settings, and major events in a story, using key details.

Identify basic similarities in and differences between two texts on the same topic (e.g., in illustrations, descriptions, or procedures).

Build on others' talk in conversations by responding to the comments of others through multiple exchanges.

LANGUAGE OBJECTIVES

Children will explain how a calendar is useful, using time words such as *date, today, next,* and *soon*.

ELA ACADEMIC LANGUAGE

- confirm, events
- Cognates: *confirmar, eventos*

MATERIALS

ELL Leveled Reader:
Kate Saves the Date!

Online Differentiated Texts,
"Turtle Is Late"

Online ELL Visual Vocabulary Cards

DIGITAL TOOLS

Have children listen to the selection as they follow along to develop comprehension and practice fluency and pronunciation.

Use Graphic Organizer 5: Beginning, Middle, End to enhance the lesson.

Kate Saves the Date!

Prepare to Read

Build Background

- Remind children of the Essential Question. *Let's read to learn about different ways of measuring time.* Encourage children to ask for help when they do not understand a word or phrase.

- Read the title aloud and have children repeat. Point to the illustration on the cover. *What are the mice holding?* The mice are holding a ____. *What month does the calendar show?* The ____ shows the month of ____.

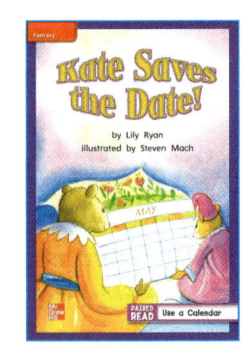

Lexile 330L

Focus on Vocabulary Use **ELL Visual Vocabulary Cards** to preteach the words *celebrate* and *time*. As you read, use gestures or visuals to teach important story words, such as *calendar, day, date, next,* and *far away*.

Read the Text

Use the Interactive Question-Response routine to help children understand the story.

Pages 2–5

Events: Beginning, Middle, End Read pages aloud and help children identify the characters, setting, and events at the beginning of the story. Point to the characters in the illustration and have children identify them. *Who is this?* (Kate, Mommy) *Where are Kate and Mommy?* (in the kitchen) *When is the party?* (next Monday) *Mommy says the party is next Monday. When Mommy says* next *Monday, she means the Monday after.* Have children repeat *next*.

Beginning *What does Kate ask?* Kate asks when the party with Amy will be. *Do you think Kate is excited?* Yes, I think Kate is excited.

Advanced/Advanced High *How do the details in the story tell you Kate is excited about the party?* I think Kate is excited about the party because she asks Mommy when the party with Amy is/will be.

Pages 6–8

Make Predictions Point to the calendar. Help children make a prediction. *Mommy gives Kate a calendar. What do you think Kate will do?* (Possible answer: use it to look at the days)

Beginning *What do Kate and Mommy see on the calendar?* Kate and Mommy see the month and days.

Intermediate *Do you predict the calendar will help Kate?* Yes, I predict the calendar will help Kate know which day Amy will come.

112 UNIT 3 WEEK 1

WEEK 1

Pages 9–11

Confirm Predictions Read pages as children follow along. *Kate saves the date.* Here, *save* has a similar meaning to *writes* or *marks*. *What does Kate do?* She marks the date on the calendar. *What was your prediction? Were you correct?* I was correct/not correct.

Intermediate Have partners discuss: *What do you think about how Kate saves the date?* I think marking a calendar is a good way to save the date. *What else can she do to remember it?* (Possible response: She can write herself a note.)

Respond to Reading Have partners work together and retell the story and respond to the questions on page 12.

Focus on Fluency

Read page 5 to model accuracy. Read the passage again and have children repeat after you. For more practice, record children reading the passage and have them select the best recording for you.

Paired Read: "Use a Calendar"

Analytical Writing **Make Connections: Write About It**

Echo-read each page with children. *What do calendars show?* Calendars show days, weeks, and months. Help children make connections between texts using the question on page 15. Calendars help us understand when things happen.

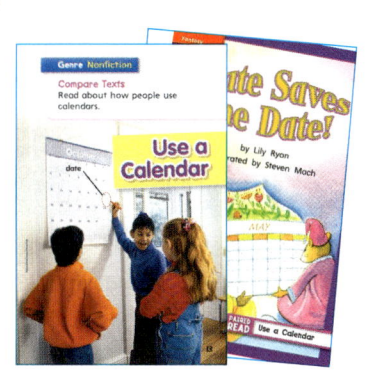

Leveled Reader

Build Knowledge: Make Connections

Talk About the Text Have partners discuss the different ways time is measured in these texts.

Write About the Text Have students add their ideas to their Build Knowledge pages of their reader's notebooks.

Self-Selected Reading

Help children choose a fiction selection from the online **Leveled Reader Library** or read the **Differentiated Text,** "Turtle Is Late."

LITERATURE CIRCLES

Lead children in conducting a literature circle, using the Thinkmark questions to guide the discussion. You may wish to discuss what children have learned about calendars from both selections in the Leveled Reader.

FORMATIVE ASSESSMENT

▶ STUDENT CHECK IN

Have partners share their Respond to Reading. Then have children reflect, using the Check-In routine.

LEVEL UP

IF children can read *Kate Saves the Date!* **ELL Level** with fluency and correctly answer the Respond to Reading questions,

THEN tell children that they will read another selection about using a calendar.

- Use pages 2–3 of *Kate Saves the Date!* **On Level** to model using Teaching Poster 30 to list the beginning of the story.

- Have children read the selection, checking their comprehension by using the graphic organizer.

ENGLISH LANGUAGE LEARNERS **113**

LESSONS 1-5

WRITING

MODELED WRITING

LESSON 1

LEARNING GOALS
We can learn how to write a sentence with strong verbs.

OBJECTIVES
Write narratives in which they include some details.

LANGUAGE OBJECTIVES
Children will narrate by writing sentences using strong verbs.

ELA ACADEMIC LANGUAGE
- verb
- Cognate: *verbo*

Writing Practice Review the sample sentences on p. 24 of the **Reading/Writing Companion**. Have children analyze each sentence using the Actor/Action Routine: *Who is the actor?* (my dog) *What is the action?* (gobbled up) *What did the dog eat?* (my homework) Then read the prompt on p. 25, and ask a volunteer to answer it. Write the sentences on the board for children to choral read. Then help children write their own sentences.

Beginning Guide partners by asking: *What happened? Why were you late?* Provide vocabulary as needed. I missed the bus. Then I was late for school!

Intermediate Have partners ask and answer questions to create sentences. Brainstorm other verbs they could use: *What is another word for* walked?

Advanced/Advanced High Have partners exchange sentences, identify any action verbs, and try to think of stronger verbs to replace them.

FORMATIVE ASSESSMENT ▸ **STUDENT CHECK IN** Partners share their sentences. Ask children to reflect, using the Check-In routine.

INTERACTIVE WRITING

LESSON 2

LEARNING GOALS
We can read and write about a Student Model.

OBJECTIVES
With guidance and support, respond to questions and suggestions from peers.

LANGUAGE OBJECTIVES
Children will discuss the Student Model and write sentences identifying strong verbs.

ELA ACADEMIC LANGUAGE
- verb
- Cognate: *verbo*

Analyze the Student Model Have children finger point as they choral read the Student Model on p. 30 of the **Reading/Writing Companion**. Use the Actor/Action Routine to review the second and third sentences. Then guide children to identify action verbs. *Raise your hand when you hear a verb.* Reread the last sentence. Say, To holler *means "to yell." Is* hollers *a strong verb?* (yes) *How do you know?* (It helps us understand Mrs. Tate's actions.) Then help children complete p. 31. Provide sentence frames as needed.

Beginning Guide partners to point to and identify the verbs in the sentences. Provide a sentence frame as needed.

Intermediate Provide sentence frames to help children identify and evaluate the action verbs: Luke used the verb follows. It is a strong verb.

Advanced/Advanced High Have partners discuss which verbs are strong verbs. Tell them to write their own sentence about what they noticed.

FORMATIVE ASSESSMENT ▸ **STUDENT CHECK IN** Have partners share their responses. Ask children to reflect, using the Check-In routine.

WEEK 1

INDEPENDENT WRITING
LESSONS 3-4

LEARNING GOALS
We can respond to a fantasy story by extending the story.

OBJECTIVES
Write narratives in which they provide some closure.

LANGUAGE OBJECTIVES
Children will narrate by writing sentences using strong verbs.

ELA ACADEMIC LANGUAGE
- *prompt*

Find Text Evidence Use the Independent Writing Routine. Help children orally retell the anchor text. Ask questions, such as: *How does the pig make the boy late?* (He asks the boy to play.) *Why is the boy telling the story to his teacher?* (to explain why he is late) Then read the prompt on p. 36 of the **Reading/Writing Companion**: *Write four more pages of the story. Tell the excuses the boy might give his mom for getting home late. An excuse is a reason you give to explain something you did wrong.*

Write a Response Work with children to fill out My Writing Outline 11. Then have them use the sentences from their outline to complete p. 36.

Writing Checklist Read the checklist with students and have them check for these items in their writing.

Beginning Have partners take turns reading their sentences aloud and raising their hand when they hear a verb.

Intermediate Have partners work to replace the verbs in sentences 1 and 2 with stronger ones.

Advanced/Advanced High Challenge partners to create their own new sentences.

FORMATIVE ASSESSMENT ▶ **STUDENT CHECK IN** Partners share their sentences from My Writing Outline. Ask children to reflect, using the Check-in routine.

SELF-SELECTED WRITING
LESSON 5

LEARNING GOALS
We can revise our writing.

OBJECTIVES
Use verbs to convey a sense of past, present, and future.

LANGUAGE OBJECTIVES
Children will inquire about their writing by checking their verbs.

ELA ACADEMIC LANGUAGE
- *verb*
- Cognate: *verbo*

Work with children to revise the group writing activity. Point to each word as you read the sentences. Stop to ask questions, such as, *Is this word a verb? Is it the correct verb for this sentence?* Then have partners work together to correct each other's sentences. Tell partners to check that they have used verbs correctly.

For support with grammar and verbs, refer to the **Language Transfers Handbook** and **Language Development Card** 4A.

FORMATIVE ASSESSMENT ▶ **STUDENT CHECK IN** Partners tell what revisions they made. Ask children to reflect, using the Check-in routine.

ENGLISH LANGUAGE LEARNERS

LESSONS 1-2

READING • LITERATURE BIG BOOK • ACCESS THE TEXT

LEARNING GOALS

We can understand things that grow in a garden as we listen to a story.

OBJECTIVES

Ask and answer questions about key details in a text.

Use illustrations and details in a story to describe its characters, setting, or events.

Compare and contrast the adventures and experiences of characters in stories.

Ask and answer questions about key details in a text read aloud or information presented orally or through other media.

LANGUAGE OBJECTIVES

Children will narrate how the family grows food in a garden, using nouns and simple sentences.

ELA ACADEMIC LANGUAGE

- noun, verb, predict
- Cognates: *verbo, predecir*

MATERIALS

Literature Big Book, *Mystery Vine*, pp. 4–32

Visual Vocabulary Cards

DIGITAL TOOLS

Have children listen to the selection as they follow along to develop comprehension and practice fluency and pronunciation.

Use the online High-Frequency Words Activity for additional support.

Mystery Vine

Prepare to Read

Build Background Display the illustration on the cover and say: *We are going to read a story about a family's garden. A garden is a place where people grow vegetables. What vegetable do you like to eat?* Draw a tomato and model for children: *I like tomatoes.* Have children repeat. Then have children draw their favorite vegetable and tell what it is. Supply vocabulary as needed and provide a sentence frame: I like ____. Then ask: *Does your family have a garden at home? What do you grow there?*

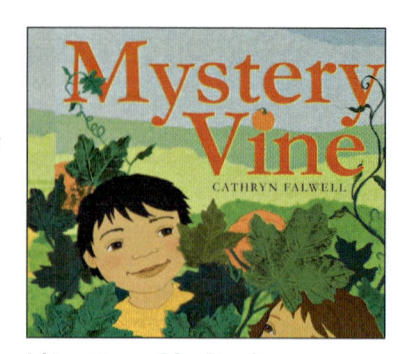

Literature Big Book

Focus on Vocabulary Use the **Visual Vocabulary Cards** to review the oral vocabulary words *bloom* and *sprout*. Use each word as a noun and as a verb and have children repeat: *A bloom is like a flower. The plants bloom. This young plant is a sprout. It sprouted out of the ground.* As you read, use gestures and visual support to clarify important words from the story, such as *seeds, vine,* and *blossoms*. Point out that *plant* can be both a noun (a thing) and a verb (an action). Say these sentences for children to repeat: *I have a green plant. I'm planting seeds.*

Summarize the Text Before reading, say this summary while pointing to the illustrations: *This story tells about a family who has a garden. They find a plant that they call a mystery vine. They want to know what kind of vegetable it will be.*

Read the Text

Use the Interactive Question-Response routine to help children understand the story.

Pages 4–9

Pages 4–5 Read the text aloud. *What season is it?* (spring) *Tell what the boy is doing.* (digging in the dirt) *Who else is digging in the dirt?* (the children's mother) Point to the girl. *What is the girl putting in the ground?* She is putting seeds in the ground. Guide children to infer the purpose of planting. *What do seeds become when they grow?* Seeds become plants. *The family watches the plants grow. They pull weeds, too. A weed is a plant that grows where people do not want it. Do people like weeds?* (no)

What does this family need to plant seeds? Discuss with a partner.

Beginning Say the words *seeds, shovel, dirt,* and *watering can* for children to point to in the picture. Have pairs point to and identify those items: *What do you see? I see* seeds/a shovel/dirt/a watering can.

116 UNIT 3 WEEK 2

WEEK 2

Intermediate Have partners take turns describing items the family needs and asking who in the picture has them. Provide these sentence frames: They need shovels. Who has a shovel? (the boy and his mother)

Advanced/Advanced High Provide a sentence frame for pairs to tell why the family needs each item in the picture: They need [shovels] to [dig in the dirt].

Pages 10–17

Pages 10–11 Read the text aloud. *What season is it?* (summer) Point to and say *tomato plants* for children to repeat. Repeat the routine for *tiny flowers, beans, poles,* and *twine.* Point to the word *showers.* Showers means "rain." *How does the rain help the plants?* Rain gives the plants water. Point to *creeping. A vine that is creeping is spreading, or covering more of the ground.*

What does the family do in the garden in summer? Discuss with a partner.

Beginning Say the verb *tie* for children to repeat. Say and model for children: *Show me how you tie your shoes.* Have pairs use these sentence frames to answer the question: The boy and his mother tie the beans to poles. The girl and the dog sit.

Intermediate Have pairs use *wh-* questions to ask and answer: Who ties the beans to poles? The boy and his mother tie beans to poles. Who sits on the ground? The girl and the dog sit there.

Advanced/Advanced High Have pairs use these sentence frames to ask and answer about each character: What do the boy and his mother/the girl/the dog do in the garden in summer? The boy and his mother tie beans to poles./The girl sits on the ground./The dog plays with the ball of twine.

Pages 18–27

Pages 18–19 Read the text aloud. *What season is it now?* (fall) *How can you tell it's fall in the picture?* The tree has red leaves. The family is wearing warm clothes. *What do you predict will happen next?* They will see/find out what is growing on the mystery vine.

Pages 24–25 Read the text aloud. *The children are using some of the pumpkins to celebrate Halloween. Say* Halloween. *They wear costumes. Say* costume. *What happens when you say "trick or treat"?* (You get candy.) Point to the jack-o'-lantern. *What does a jack-o'-lantern look like?* It looks like a face. *What is it made from?* (a pumpkin)

How are the children celebrating Halloween? Discuss with a partner.

Beginning *Do children see jack-o-lanterns on Halloween?* Yes, they see jack-o'-lanterns. Have children point to and identify parts of the jack-o'-lanterns' faces: That's a nose/mouth. Those are eyes.

Intermediate Point to and say these clothing items: *hat, shirt, pants, shoes, gloves.* Have pairs describe the children's Halloween costumes as best they can: [He is] wearing a [green hat and blue shoes].

Advanced/Advanced High Challenge children to describe what the children do on Halloween: They wear costumes. They walk to the door. They say, "Trick or treat!" They get candy. Have children act out the scenario in pairs.

FORMATIVE ASSESSMENT

❱ STUDENT CHECK IN

Have partners retell one thing that the family does in spring, summer, and fall. Then have students reflect using the Check-In routine.

Independent Time

Make a Picture Glossary Have children work together to make a picture glossary of the plant words from the story. You may wish to flip through the story and assign words before children begin. Then have them draw a picture of the plant and write about it, using these sentence frames: This is a tomato. I like/don't like tomatoes. Allow children to write what they can, help translate or elaborate, and provide correction as needed. Have children present their picture glossary to the class in alphabetical order.

ENGLISH LANGUAGE LEARNERS **117**

LESSONS 1-2

READING • SHARED READ • ACCESS THE TEXT

LEARNING GOALS

We can read and understand a play.

OBJECTIVES

Describe characters, settings, and major events in a story, using key details.

Use illustrations and details in a story to describe its characters, setting, or events.

Compare and contrast the adventures and experiences of characters in stories.

Ask questions to clear up any confusion about the topics and texts under discussion.

LANGUAGE OBJECTIVES

Children will narrate a family's teamwork in planting a garden in simple sentences.

ELA ACADEMIC LANGUAGE

- characters, play

MATERIALS

Reading/Writing Companion, pp. 48–57

Visual Vocabulary Cards

DIGITAL TOOLS

Have children listen to the selection as they follow along to develop comprehension and practice fluency and pronunciation.

Use the additional grammar video.

Grammar Video

"Time to Plant!"

Prepare to Read

Build Background Read the Essential Question aloud for children to repeat: *How do plants change as they grow?* Have children draw lines to divide a piece of paper into three parts. Say: *Plants start out as seeds. People plant the seeds. How do people help seeds grow?* They ____ the seeds. Have children draw a seed in the ground and a watering can watering it. *What happens next?* The seed becomes a ____. Have children draw the sprout. *As plants grow, they get bigger. They get more parts. What parts do they get?* They get leaves and ____. Have children draw the full-size plant with flowers.

Reading/Writing Companion, Lexile NP

Focus on Vocabulary Use the **Visual Vocabulary Cards** to review the high-frequency words *green, grow, pretty, should, together,* and *water* and the oral vocabulary words *assist, grasped, spied, bloom,* and *sprout.* Help children use some of these words to talk about their drawings. *How does the seed become a sprout?* (It grows.) *Point to your plant. What part is pretty?* The flowers are pretty. As you read, use gestures and visual support to teach important words from the play, such as: *spot* and *buds. When you spot something, you see it. Say* spot. *Say* buds. *A bud is a small new part growing on a plant. What can the girl spot?* She can spot buds.

Summarize the Text Before reading, say the summary and point to the illustrations. *This play tells about how a family plants a garden. The people in the family grow vegetables. Then they pick them.*

Read the Text

Use the Interactive Question-Response Routine to help children understand the play.

Pages 50–53

Page 50 Display the page. *This story is a play. This page tells us the names of the characters.* Read the names and ask children to repeat. Reread Beth's question for children to repeat. Explain that we use *can* to ask for permission to do something we want to do. *Who is Beth asking for permission from?* (Dad) *What does she want to do?* She wants to plant a garden. *Does Dad give her permission?* (yes)

Pages 51–53 Read the text aloud as children follow. Point to, say, and mime *drop in seeds* for children to repeat and mime. Repeat the routine for *set in plants*. Point to *Days pass* on page 53. *Days pass* means "several days later." Point to *shines. When the sun shines, it's bright. You need sunglasses!* Then point to *plinks and plunks. What sound does rain make?* (plink, plunk)

118 UNIT 3 WEEK 2

WEEK 2

How does the family work together to plant a garden? Discuss with a partner.

Beginning Have partners take turns asking and answering questions, pointing to characters as they answer. Who digs? Mom and Dad dig. Who drops in seeds? Mike drops seeds. Who sets in plants? Gramps sets in plants. Who gets water? Beth gets water.

Intermediate Provide these sentence frames for pairs to complete as they point to the characters in the illustration: Mom and Dad dig. Mike drops in seeds. Gramps sets in plants. Beth gets water.

Advanced/Advanced High Have partners cover the text on page 52 with a piece of paper so they can only see the picture and describe what each character does: Mom and Dad dig. Mike drops in five seeds. Gramps sets in green plants. Beth gets water.

Pages 54–55

Page 54 Read the text aloud. Remind children that *Days pass* means it is now several days later. *Is the sun still shining?* (yes) *What else is there?* (rain) *What does the rain do?* It drips and drops. Explain that *drip* and *drop* tell how rain sounds, like *plink* and *plunk*.

Page 55 Read the text aloud as children follow along. Point to and say *ripe* for children to repeat. When a fruit or vegetable is *ripe*, it is ready to eat. Say and mime: *I'm picking a ripe apple. I'm taking a bite.* Have children repeat and mime. Say and mime: *I'm munching on my apple.* Have children repeat. Say: *Mike has tomatoes. Do you like tomatoes?* (yes/no)

What does Mike like? Discuss with a partner.

Beginning Have partners take turns acting like Mike munching on a tomato. To munch *means "to eat."* Provide sentence frames for guessing the action: Mike likes to munch on a tomato. Yum!

Intermediate Have partners take turns asking and answering questions about what Mike likes. What does Mike like to do? He likes to take a bite and munch on the tomatoes.

Advanced/Advanced High Have children describe what Mike likes to do based on the picture. (Possible response: Mike picked these tomatoes. He is taking a bite of one. He likes to munch on the tomatoes.)

Pages 56–57

Pages 56–57 Read the text aloud as children follow along. Point to *Yikes!* on page 56. *We say* Yikes! *when we are surprised.* What surprises Beth? (lots of vegetables) Point to page 57. *Is Miss White in Beth and Mike's family?* (no) She is a neighbor or friend. What are Beth and Mike doing in the picture? They are giving Miss White vegetables from their garden.

Why do Beth and Mike give Miss White some vegetables? Discuss with a partner.

Beginning *What does the family have?* They have a lot of vegetables. *Can they eat all of the vegetables?* No, they can't eat them all.

Intermediate Help partners explain: The family picks piles/a lot of vegetables. They can't eat them all. They give a bag of vegetables to Miss White. She is happy.

Advanced/Advanced High Have pairs ask and answer these questions: What is their problem? (They pick piles of vegetables. They can't eat them all.) What is their solution? (They share their vegetables.)

FORMATIVE ASSESSMENT

▶ STUDENT CHECK IN

Have partners retell the jobs of two of the family members. Then, have children reflect using the Check-In routine.

Independent Time

Role Play Have children imagine their family is planting a garden and picking vegetables. Pair children of mixed proficiencies. Have partners role-play telling which plants their family plants, how they plant, and when they pick the vegetables. Provide sentence frames and questions if children need help: We plant___. What do you plant? ___dig(s). ___drop(s) in seeds. ___set(s) in plants. ___ water(s) them. Who does those things in your family? ___ pick(s)___ when they ___. Who picks___in your family? What do you do if you have too many___? We___. Have children present their role-plays to others in class.

ENGLISH LANGUAGE LEARNERS 119

LESSON 3

READING • ANCHOR TEXT • ACCESS THE TEXT

LEARNING GOALS

We can read and understand a play.

OBJECTIVES

Identify words and phrases in stories or poems that suggest feelings or appeal to the senses.

Identify who is telling the story at various points in a text.

Produce complete sentences when appropriate to task and situation.

LANGUAGE OBJECTIVES

Children will explain how the characters in the play solve a problem in complete sentences.

ELA ACADEMIC LANGUAGE

- exclamation, punctuation, dialogue
- Cognates: *exclamación, puntuación, diálogo*

MATERIALS

Literature Anthology, pp. 28–45

Visual Vocabulary Cards

DIGITAL TOOLS

Have children listen to the selection as they follow along to develop comprehension and practice fluency and pronunciation.

Use the online High-Frequency Words Activity for additional support.

The Big Yuca Plant

Prepare to Read

Build Background Display an image of a pumpkin: *Where does a pumpkin grow?* A pumpkin grows on a ____. Then display an image of a carrot growing underground: *Some vegetables grow underground. Can you name any?* Tell children that a *yuca* is another vegetable that grows underground. *Does anyone in your family eat this vegetable? How can you pick a root vegetable?* You can pull it out of the ____.

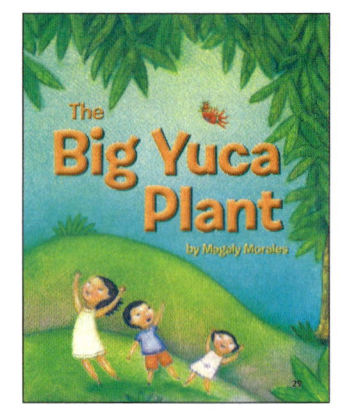

Focus on Vocabulary Use the **Visual Vocabulary Cards** to review the high-frequency words *water, grow, green, pretty, should,* and *together* and the oral vocabulary words *assist, grasped, spied, bloom,* and *sprout.* As you read, teach important words from the play, such as *root, plan,* and *tug,* using gestures and pantomime.

Literature Anthology, Lexile NP

Summarize the Text Before reading, say this summary while pointing to the illustrations: *The story is also a play. It tells about a girl who plants a yuca. The yuca grows and grows. Finally, it is too big to pick!*

Read the Text

Use the Interactive Question-Response routine to help children understand the play.

Pages 30–35

Pages 30–31 Write a period on the board and have children repeat: *This is a period.* Have children draw it in the air with a finger. Repeat with a question mark and an exclamation mark. Ask children to identify each punctuation mark as you read page 31. *Why are there question marks after Paco's words?* He asks about a plant. Then he asks if he can help. Exclamation marks show strong feeling. *Why is there an exclamation mark after "Yum!"?* Paco is excited about yucas.

Page 32–35 Read the text aloud. Say the exclamation on page 32 for children to repeat. *Why is there an exclamation mark?* Ana is cheering for the plant to grow.

How does the author help you know the characters' feelings? Discuss with a partner.

Beginning Draw a period, a question mark, and an exclamation mark. *Which mark shows strong feeling?* (the exclamation mark) Have partners find exclamation marks on pages 32–33 and help them reread the exclamations. *Is Ana excited?* Yes, Ana is excited. *Is Mom surprised?* Yes, Mom is surprised.

120 UNIT 3 WEEK 2

WEEK 2

Intermediate Have partners find the exclamation marks on pages 32 and 33 and reread the exclamations. *How does Ana feel about the plant?* She is excited for it to grow. *How does Mom feel about the plant?* She is surprised about how big it is.

Advanced/Advanced High Have partners reread pages 32–33 aloud with expression and then discuss. How is Ana feeling? (excited for the plant to grow) How is Mom feeling? (surprised about the plant's size) How does the author help you know their feelings? The author uses exclamation marks.

Pages 36–39

Pages 36–37 Read the text. *What is the problem?* The yuca is still stuck. *When something is stuck, can it move?* (no) *Which characters will tug on the yuca?* (Lola, Paco, Ana, Dad, Mom, and Pig) *Do you predict it will work?* (yes/no)

Pages 38–39 Read the text. *Do they pick the yuca?* (no) *Was your prediction correct?* (yes/no) *Who says they can't pick the yuca?* (Ana) *Who thinks they can?* (Lola) *How does she think they can do it?* (together) *When you work together, you work with others.*

How can you tell what Lola is like as a character? Discuss with a partner.

Beginning *Look at the pictures. Is Lola alone or with others?* She is with others. Have children complete this sentence based on their observations: Lola likes/doesn't like to work with others.

Intermediate Have partners answer questions: *Does Lola ask others for help?* (yes) *Who does she ask for help?* She asks Pig and Cat. Have children complete the sentence frame based on their observations: Lola likes/doesn't like to work with others.

Advanced/Advanced High Have partners complete this sentence frame: Lola likes/doesn't like to work with others. Then have them find the sentence that shows how Lola feels about working with others. (Together, we can get the yuca out.)

Pages 41–42 *Who wants to ask Rat for help?* (Lola) *Who doesn't want Rat to help?* (Paco) *What is Rat's idea?* Tie a vine to the plant and pull the vine. Have children point to the yuca and the vine in the picture.

Pages 42–43 Have children point to the yuca in the picture. Remind them that it is the root of the plant. Read the text. *Why can we see the yuca?* (They picked it.) Read the text. *Does Rat's idea work?* (yes) Explain that when someone is *wise*, he or she has smart, helpful ideas. *Who is a wise person you know?*

What do you learn from the dialogue? What do the characters think? Discuss with a partner.

Beginning *Dialogue is the characters' words. It can tell you how they feel.* Have children complete these sentences with the characters' dialogue: Paco says, "A rat is little. He can't help." Lola tells the rat, "You are little, but you are wise."

Intermediate Help children explain dialogue: *Dialogue is the characters' words. What can it tell you about the characters?* (their opinion, or how they feel) Ask children what Paco and Lola say about the rat.

Advanced/Advanced High Have children use the dialogue to retell Paco's, Lola's, and Mom's opinions of Rat: Paco says Rat is too little to help. Lola says Rat can help because he is wise. When Rat helps them get the yuca out, Mom says they must thank him.

FORMATIVE ASSESSMENT

STUDENT CHECK IN

Have partners retell how the characters feel at the end of the play. Then have children reflect using the Check-In routine.

Independent Time

Listening for Exclamations Have children take turns reading a sentence from the text for classmates to guess whether or not it is an exclamation. Encourage children to monitor each others' intonation for statements, questions, and exclamations and to repeat one another's sentences for practice.

ENGLISH LANGUAGE LEARNERS 121

LESSONS 4-5

READING • LEVELED READER • ACCESS THE TEXT

LEARNING GOALS

We can make and confirm predictions as we read a play.

OBJECTIVES

Retell stories, including key details, and demonstrate understanding of their central message or lesson.

Describe characters, settings, and major events in a story, using key details.

Identify basic similarities in and differences between two texts on the same topic (e.g., in illustrations, descriptions, or procedures).

Produce complete sentences when appropriate to task and situation.

LANGUAGE OBJECTIVES

Children will narrate the preparation for a picnic, using verbs and other key vocabulary.

ELA ACADEMIC LANGUAGE

- confirm, predict, sequence
- Cognates: *confirmar, predecir, secuencia*

MATERIALS

ELL Leveled Reader:
Yum, Strawberries!

Online Differentiated Texts,
"Our Plants"

Online ELL Visual Vocabulary Cards

DIGITAL TOOLS

Have children listen to the selection as they follow along to develop comprehension and practice fluency and pronunciation. Use Graphic Organizer 6: Sequence of Events, Time Order to enhance the lesson.

Yum, Strawberries!

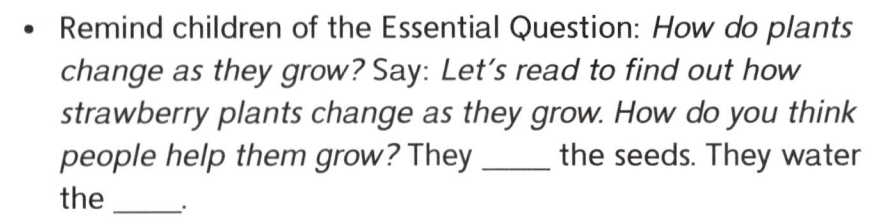

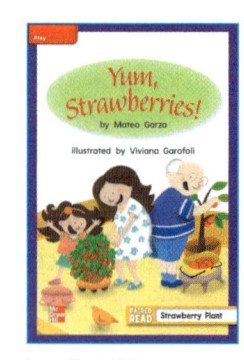

Prepare to Read

Build Background

- Remind children of the Essential Question: *How do plants change as they grow?* Say: *Let's read to find out how strawberry plants change as they grow. How do you think people help them grow?* They ____ the seeds. They water the ____.

- Point to the title and read it for children to repeat. Point to the strawberries. *These are strawberries. What color are they?* Strawberries are ____. Ask for a show of hands: *Who likes/doesn't like strawberries?*

Focus on Vocabulary Use **ELL Visual Vocabulary Cards** to preteach the words *gardening* and *ripe*. As you read, use gestures or visuals to teach important story words, such as *pot, cucumber,* and *taste*. Then say the word *ready* and have children repeat. Say: *If you are* ready, *you can start to do something right now. Are you ready to read?* Yes, I am ready to read.

Lexile NP

Read the Text

Use the Interactive Question-Response routine to help children understand the play.

Pages 2–4

Read the pages aloud as children follow along. Discuss the characters, setting, and events. *Who is in this play?* (Lily, Mom, Mike, Ivy) *The setting is a rooftop garden. That is a garden on top of a building's roof. What do Lily and Mom do?* (Mom and Lily plant strawberries.) *What do the plants need?* (The plants need water.)

Beginning Have partners work together to identify things and people in the pictures: She's Lily/Mom. That is a pot. There are flowers.

Advanced/Advanced High Have partners describe the strawberry plants in each picture: There aren't any leaves or flowers. There are leaves on the plant. Now there are flowers. Review vocabulary for parts of a plant as needed.

Pages 5–7

Make and Confirm Predictions Read as children follow along. Have children complete this sentence: Mike/Ivy has tomatoes/cucumbers. *What do Mike and Ivy do?* (share with Lily) *Can Lily share her strawberries?* (no) *Why?* (They're not ready.) Have children predict what kinds of foods the characters will have at the picnic and confirm their predictions as they read the next part of the story.

122 UNIT 3 WEEK 2

WEEK 2

Pages 8–11

Main Story Elements: Sequence of Events Help children discuss the sequence of events. *What happens after Mom and Lily pick the strawberries?* (Everyone eats the strawberries at the picnic.)

Beginning Have pairs point to the cake on page 11. *What do they taste?* They taste the cake. *Do they like the strawberries?* Yes, they like the strawberries.

Intermediate Have pairs take turns saying what the characters do at the picnic: They eat cake/vegetables/burgers. They sit outside/on the ground. They have fun.

Respond to Reading Have partners work together to retell the story and respond to the questions on page 12.

Focus on Fluency

Read pages 4–5 to model accuracy and rate. Read the passage again and have children repeat after you. For more practice, record children reading the passage and select the best recording.

Paired Read: "Strawberry Plant"

Analytical Writing — Make Connections: Write About It

Echo-read each page with children. Discuss the life cycle of a strawberry plant using the photos. Help children make connections between texts using the question on page 15: I have learned that strawberry plants first grow leaves and then flowers. The strawberries grow last.

Leveled Reader

Build Knowledge: Make Connections

Talk About the Text Have partners discuss how the plants in the texts change as they grow.

Write About the Text Have students add their ideas to the Build Knowledge pages of their reader's notebooks.

Self-Selected Reading

Help children choose a drama selection from the online **Leveled Reader Library,** or read the **Differentiated Text,** "Our Plants."

🧪 FOCUS ON SCIENCE

Children can extend their knowledge of foods we grow by completing the science activity on page 16.

LITERATURE CIRCLES

Lead children in conducting a literature circle using the Thinkmark questions to guide the discussion. You may wish to point out to children that in a play, unlike a story, the setting and characters are listed at the beginning.

FORMATIVE ASSESSMENT

❯ STUDENT CHECK IN

Have partners share their Respond to Reading. Then have children reflect, using the Check-In routine.

LEVEL UP

IF children can read *Yum, Strawberries!* **ELL Level** with fluency and correctly answer the Respond to Reading questions,

THEN tell children that they will read a more detailed version of the play.

- Use pages 2–3 of *Yum, Strawberries!* **On Level** to model, using Teaching Poster 31 to list the first event of the plot.
- Have children read the selection, checking their comprehension by using the graphic organizer.

ENGLISH LANGUAGE LEARNERS 123

LESSONS 1-5

WRITING

MODELED WRITING

LESSON 1

LEARNING GOALS

We can learn to write sentences with sensory details.

OBJECTIVES

Write narratives in which they include some details.

LANGUAGE OBJECTIVES

Children will narrate by writing sentences using the verb *would*.

ELA ACADEMIC LANGUAGE

- sensory details
- Cognates: *detalles sensoriales*

Writing Practice Review the sample sentences on p. 58 of the **Reading/Writing Companion**. Have children analyze the sentences. *Who is the actor?* (I) *What would I grow if I had a garden?* (would grow spinach) Then read the prompt on p. 59 and ask a volunteer to answer it. Write the sentences on the board for children to choral read. Then help children write their own sentences.

Beginning Provide a sentence frame to help partners create a sentence: I would grow orange pumpkins. Have them write the name of a fruit or vegetable in the second blank and a sensory detail in the first blank.

Intermediate Have partners ask and answer questions to create their sentence: *What would you grow? What would it look like?* Tell children to describe both size and color.

Advanced/Advanced High Challenge children to write another sentence with a sensory detail relating to a different sense.

FORMATIVE ASSESSMENT   ▶ **STUDENT CHECK IN** Partners share their sentences. Ask children to reflect, using the Check-In routine.

INTERACTIVE WRITING

LESSON 2

LEARNING GOALS

We can read and write about a Student Model.

OBJECTIVES

With guidance and support from adults, focus on a topic.

LANGUAGE OBJECTIVES

Children will discuss the Student Model and write sentences, identifying present-tense verbs.

ELA ACADEMIC LANGUAGE

- prompt

Analyze the Student Model Have children finger point as they choral read the Student Model on p. 64 of the **Reading/Writing Companion**. Guide children to identify the verbs. *These are present-tense verbs. What does that tell us about the action?* (It is happening now.) Guide children to notice sensory details. *What does Mike say about the tomatoes? How does he describe them?* (He says they look red and juicy.) *How will the tomato sauce taste?* (yummy) Then help children complete p. 65.

Beginning Ask partners to point to and identify sensory details and present-tense verbs. Provide sentence frames: *Look* is a present-tense verb.

Intermediate Write the words *looks, smells,* and *tastes* on the board and have partners identify at least one sensory detail for each.

Advanced/Advanced High Challenge children to explain what they noticed about the Student Model: I noticed that *look* is a present-tense verb. Elizabeth used the word *red*. It tells how the tomatoes look.

FORMATIVE ASSESSMENT   ▶ **STUDENT CHECK IN** Partners share their responses. Ask children to reflect, using the Check-In routine.

WEEK 2

INDEPENDENT WRITING
LESSONS 3-4

LEARNING GOALS
We can respond to a play by extending the play.

OBJECTIVES
Write narratives in which they include some details.

LANGUAGE OBJECTIVES
Children will narrate by writing lines for a character in a drama, using present-tense verbs.

ELA ACADEMIC LANGUAGE
- present-tense verbs, capitalize
- Cognate: *verbos*

Find Text Evidence Use the Independent Writing Routine. Help children orally retell the anchor text. Ask questions, such as: *What do the children plant?* (a yuca) *Does it grow?* (yes) Then read the prompt on p. 70 of the **Reading/Writing Companion:** *Think of a different animal that might have been able to help get the yuca plant out. Write a scene where he/she helps out. What other animal might help? How might that animal help out?*

Write a Response Work with children to fill out My Writing Outline 12. Then have them use the sentences from their outlines to complete p. 70.

Writing Checklist Read the checklist with students and have them check for these items in their writing.

Beginning Encourage partners to talk about their sentences by providing a sentence frame: *I used the present-tense verb cook.*

Intermediate Have partners read their sentences. *Listen to your partner. Raise your hand when you hear a present-tense verb.* Have partners verify that they used the correct form of the verbs.

Advanced/Advanced High Have partners identify where they used each item in their writing.

FORMATIVE ASSESSMENT ▶ **STUDENT CHECK IN** Partners share their sentences from My Writing Outline. Ask children to reflect, using the Check-in routine.

SELF-SELECTED WRITING
LESSON 5

LEARNING GOALS
We can revise our writing.

OBJECTIVES
Use verbs to convey a sense of past, present, and future.

LANGUAGE OBJECTIVES
Children will inquire about their writing by checking they are using the present tense.

ELA ACADEMIC LANGUAGE
- verb
- Cognate: *verbo*

Work with children to correct the group writing activity. Point to each word as you read the sentences. Stop to ask questions, such as, *Is this a verb? Is it in the present tense?* Then have partners work together to correct each other's sentences. Tell partners to check that they have used verbs correctly.

For support with grammar and present-tense verbs, refer to the **Language Transfers Handbook** and **Language Development Card** 4A.

FORMATIVE ASSESSMENT ▶ **STUDENT CHECK IN** Partners tell what revisions they made. Ask children to reflect, using the Check-in routine.

ENGLISH LANGUAGE LEARNERS **125**

LESSONS 1-2

READING • LITERATURE BIG BOOK • ACCESS THE TEXT

LEARNING GOALS

We can understand the events of different bedtime stories as we listen to a story.

OBJECTIVES

Describe characters and major events in a story, using key details.

Identify words and phrases in stories or poems that suggest feelings or appeal to the senses.

Compare and contrast the adventures and experiences of characters in stories.

Produce complete sentences when appropriate to task and situation.

LANGUAGE OBJECTIVES

Children will narrate how Chicken reacts to different bedtime stories, using verbs and simple sentences.

ELA ACADEMIC LANGUAGE

- *infer, title*
- Cognates: *inferir, título*

MATERIALS

Literature Big Book,
Interrupting Chicken, pp. 5–38

Visual Vocabulary Cards

DIGITAL TOOLS

Have children listen to the selection as they follow along to develop comprehension and practice fluency and pronunciation.

Use the additional grammar song.

Grammar Song

Interrupting Chicken

Prepare to Read

Build Background *We are going to read a story about a chicken who interrupts her dad as he tells her bedtime stories.* Bedtime stories *are stories people read to other people who are ready to go to bed.* Show the picture on the cover. *What do you do when someone reads you a bedtime story?* Model for children: *I listen to the bedtime story.* Have children repeat. Encourage partners to share what they do when someone reads them a story. Provide sentence frames: I ____ to the story. I ask ____ about the story.

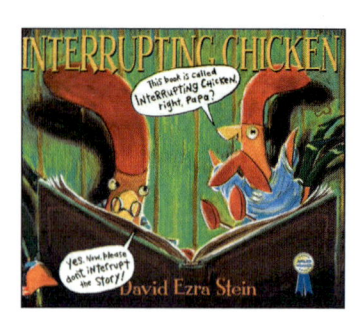

Literature Big Book

Focus on Vocabulary Use the **Visual Vocabulary Cards** to review the oral vocabulary words *hero* and *tale*. As you read, use gestures and visual support to clarify important words from the story, such as *interrupt, warn, panic, yawning, tired,* and the letters *zzzzzzz* indicating that someone is sleeping. For *interrupt,* say: *When you interrupt, you talk while someone else is speaking.* Have children repeat the word. *If someone interrupts me, I feel frustrated.* Frustrated *means "angry when you can not do something." How do you feel if someone interrupts you?* I feel frustrated/angry.

Summarize the Text Before reading, say the summary while pointing to the illustrations. *The story tells about a chicken who asks her father to read her bedtime stories. Instead of listening, she interrupts the stories. Eventually, she tells her father a story, and they both go to sleep.*

Read the Text

Use the Interactive Question-Response routine to help children understand the story.

Pages 5–15

Page 12 Read the text aloud. Point to the text. *These words look different from the other words in the story. This tells me someone new is talking. Who is talking here?* Chicken *is talking to the story characters. Chicken tells Hansel and Gretel that the woman is a witch. In stories, a* witch *is often a scary, bad character. Does Chicken want to help Hansel and Gretel?* (yes)

COLLABORATE *Why does Chicken interrupt the story? Discuss with a partner.*

Beginning Point to Chicken on page 12. Point to the people around Chicken. *What is Chicken doing?* Chicken is shouting/yelling. *How do the characters in the story look?* They look surprised.

126 UNIT 3 WEEK 3

WEEK 3

Intermediate Have partners point to the picture as they respond. *What does Chicken tell the characters?* She tells them not to go into the house. *Why does she say this?* The other character is a witch.

Advanced/Advanced High Have partners elaborate on their responses. *What can you infer about Chicken when she warns the characters?* I can infer that Chicken worries about other people.

Pages 16–27

Page 26 Read the text aloud. *Papa tells Chicken that she interrupted the story again.* Point to AGAIN in the text. *The author used all capital letters to show Papa says* again *more loudly than the other words.* Point to Papa in the picture. *Are Papa's eyes open or closed?* (open) *Maybe he is surprised Chicken interrupted a story again. Where is Papa?* He is lying on a book.

COLLABORATE *How does Papa feel when Chicken interrupts the stories? Discuss with a partner.*

Beginning Point to Papa on page 26. *Look at Papa's eyes. When I feel surprised, my eyes open wide. How do you think Papa feels?* I think Papa feels surprised. *Does Papa look tired?* Yes, Papa looks tired.

Intermediate Have partners use the text and pictures to ask and answer questions: *What do Papa's eyes look like?* Papa's eyes are open wide. *What is Papa doing?* He is lying on the book. *What does this tell you about how Papa feels?* This tells me Papa feels tired and frustrated.

Advanced/Advanced High Have partners add details to their responses. *Why might Chicken's actions make Papa feel frustrated?* Papa might feel frustrated that Chicken will not go to sleep. I can see in the picture that Chicken is awake and excited.

Pages 28–39

Page 28 Read the text aloud. *Papa asks Chicken to tell him a story. Chicken says* Um. *We say* Um *when we are thinking of what to say. What is Papa doing in the picture?* Papa is yawning and getting into bed. *Does Chicken look ready to fall asleep?* (no)

Pages 30–31 Point to page 30. *This is the title page of a story. Who wrote this story?* (Chicken) Read the story aloud. *Is the papa in the story like Chicken's real papa?* (no) *Who does he act like?* (Chicken)

COLLABORATE *What is Chicken's story about? Discuss with a partner.*

Beginning Display page 31. *Who is in bed in this story: Chicken or Papa?* Papa is in bed. *What is Chicken doing?* Chicken is reading a story to Papa.

Intermediate Have children look at the pictures and text to help them respond. *What is the title of Chicken's story?* Chicken's story is called Bedtime for Papa. *What do you see in the picture?* Chicken is reading Papa a bedtime story.

Advanced/Advanced High Ask children to elaborate on their response. *Why would Chicken include details like reading a hundred stories?* Chicken wants Papa to know what she would like to happen to her.

FORMATIVE ASSESSMENT

> STUDENT CHECK IN

Have partners retell how Chicken interrupts one of the bedtime stories. Then have children reflect, using the Check-In routine.

Independent Time

Role Play Pair children of mixed proficiencies and have them prepare a role play of a scene from *Interrupting Chicken*. Explain to children that one person should be Chicken, and one person should be Papa. Have them prepare a role play in which Papa reads a story and Chicken interrupts by telling characters what to do. Partners may use dialogue from *Interrupting Chicken* or create a similar dialogue using their own words. Give children time to plan and practice. Then have partners perform their role plays for a small group or for the class.

LESSONS 1-2

READING • SHARED READ • ACCESS THE TEXT

"The Nice Mitten"

LEARNING GOALS

We can read and understand a folktale.

OBJECTIVES

Retell stories, including key details, and demonstrate understanding of their central message or lesson.

Describe characters, settings, and major events in a story, using key details.

Use illustrations and details in a story to describe its characters, setting, or events.

Build on others' talk in conversations by responding to the comments of others through multiple exchanges.

LANGUAGE OBJECTIVES

Children will narrate what happens to the character's mitten, using verbs in the present tense.

ELA ACADEMIC LANGUAGE

- folktale, predict
- Cognate: *predecir*

MATERIALS

Reading/Writing Companion, pp. 82–91

Visual Vocabulary Cards

DIGITAL TOOLS

Have children listen to the selection as they follow along to develop comprehension and practice fluency and pronunciation.

Use the online High-Frequency Words Activity for additional support.

Prepare to Read

Build Background Read aloud the Essential Question on page 68. *This question is about a kind of story called a folktale. A folktale is a story that has been told for many, many years. It usually begins with the words "Once upon a time."* Encourage children to talk about folktales they know.

Focus on Vocabulary Use the **Visual Vocabulary Cards** to review the high-frequency words *any, from, happy, once, so,* and *upon* and the oral vocabulary words *eventually, foolish, timid, hero,* and *tale.* As you read, use gestures and visual support to teach the important story words *mittens, edge, forest, mice, hiding, hedgehog,* and *cricket.*

Reading/Writing Companion, Lexile 460L

Summarize the Text Before reading, say the summary, and point to the illustrations. *This story tells what happens when Lance loses his red mitten.*

Read the Text

Use the Interactive Question-Response routine to help children understand the story.

Pages 84–85

Page 84 Read the text aloud, and have children follow along. Point to and say the name *Lance* for children to repeat. Point to the word *went. Went means go in the past tense. Where does Lance go in this part of the story?* He goes to pick up sticks. Point to the red mittens. *Why does Lance's mom give him mittens?* She gives him mittens so his hands will not be cold.

Page 85 Read the text aloud as children follow along. Point to the phrase *keep them safe.* Say it aloud for children to repeat. *To keep something safe means to make sure nothing bad happens to it. How can you keep important things safe?* Provide an example: *You can keep important things safe by watching them.* Have children share other ways they can keep things safe. Then point to the mitten in the illustration. *Does Lance keep his mittens safe?* No, Lance does not keep one of his mittens safe. He loses a mitten. *Why does he lose a mitten?* (because he runs fast)

COLLABORATE *What do you predict will happen to Lance's mitten? Discuss with a partner.*

Beginning Use the pictures to help children discuss Lance's mitten. Point to the mitten. *Does Lance have his mitten?* No, Lance does not have his mitten. Point to the area around the mitten. *Where is Lance's mitten?* Lance's mitten is in the snow. *Does Lance see his mitten?* No, Lance does not see his mitten.

128 UNIT 3 WEEK 3

WEEK 3

Intermediate Help partners give a more specific answer. Point to Lance's mitten. *What happens to Lance's mitten?* Lance loses his mitten in the snow. *Do you think he will find his mitten?* No, I don't think Lance will find his mitten. There is a lot of snow.

Advanced/Advanced High Encourage partners to add details to their responses. *What details help you know what might happen to Lance's mitten?* The picture shows a lot of snow and a forest. I predict Lance will lose his mitten in the snow.

Pages 86–89

Page 86 Read the text aloud, and have children follow along. Point to the phrase *puffed up,* and say it aloud for children to repeat. *The phrase* puffed up *means that something has gotten bigger.* Provide an example by puffing out your cheeks: *My cheeks are puffed up.* Have children puff their cheeks.

COLLABORATE *What is happening to the mitten? Discuss with a partner.*

Beginning Display the picture of the mitten on page 86. Then display the picture on page 87. *Are more animals in the mitten?* Yes, more animals are in the mitten. *Is the mitten getting bigger or smaller?* The mitten is getting bigger.

Intermediate Help partners give a more specific answer. *What is causing the mitten to get bigger?* The mitten is getting bigger because more animals are inside it.

Advanced/Advanced High Help children elaborate on their response. Have pairs predict what will happen if more animals come into the mitten. Help partners respond, using: If more animals try to come into the mitten, they will not fit.

Pages 90–91

Page 90 Read the text aloud, and have children follow along. Point to the words *Rip! Snap! POP!* Read them aloud with intonation, and have children repeat. *Rip, snap, and pop are noises that happen when something rips or breaks. What rips?* Lance's mitten rips. Point to the phrase *not a trace. Not a trace is a phrase that means something is gone, and you can't find any of it.* Have children check their predictions.

COLLABORATE *What happens to Lance's mitten? Discuss with a partner.*

Beginning Point to Lance. *How many mittens does Lance have now?* Lance has one mitten. *Does Lance see the other mitten?* No, Lance does not see the other mitten. *Does the mitten rip?* Yes, the mitten rips.

Intermediate Help partners give a more specific answer. *What happens when more and more animals get into the mitten?* The mitten puffs up more and more. *What do the words* rip, snap, *and* pop *tell you?* The words tell me that the mitten rips open.

Advanced/Advanced High Have children revisit their predictions about what might happen to Lance's mitten. Have partners tell each other whether their prediction was correct. Help children discuss, using: My prediction was incorrect. I thought the animals would not fit in the mitten. Instead, Lance's mitten breaks.

FORMATIVE ASSESSMENT

⟩ STUDENT CHECK IN

Have partners retell what animals move into Lance's mitten. Then have children reflect, using the Check-In routine.

Independent Time

Write Dialogues Have children imagine that Lance finds his lost mitten with the animals inside it. Pair children of mixed proficiencies. Have pairs discuss this question: *What do you think Lance will say to the animals in his mitten?* Have pairs use their ideas to write a dialogue between Lance and the animals in his mitten. Provide sentence frames to help children write dialogues: Lance: I need my mitten back because ____. Animals: We need to keep the mitten because ____. When pairs have finished their dialogues, have them rehearse saying the dialogue. Have pairs perform their dialogues for another pair, a small group, or the whole class.

ENGLISH LANGUAGE LEARNERS 129

LESSON 3

READING • ANCHOR TEXT • ACCESS THE TEXT

LEARNING GOALS

We can read and understand a folktale.

OBJECTIVES

Ask and answer questions about key details in a text.

Use illustrations and details in a story to describe its characters, setting, or events.

Compare and contrast the adventures and experiences of characters in stories.

Ask questions to clear up any confusion about the topics and texts under discussion.

LANGUAGE OBJECTIVES

Children will narrate the character's journey, using verbs in the future tense and key vocabulary.

ELA ACADEMIC LANGUAGE

- past tense, repetition, pattern
- Cognate: *repetición*

MATERIALS

Literature Anthology, pp. 50–67

Visual Vocabulary Cards

DIGITAL TOOLS

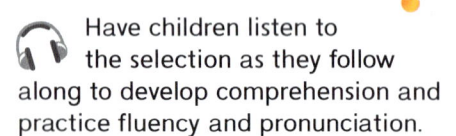

Have children listen to the selection as they follow along to develop comprehension and practice fluency and pronunciation.

Use the additional grammar video.

Grammar Video

The Gingerbread Man

Prepare to Read

Build Background *We are going to read a story about the adventures of a Gingerbread Man.* Show the picture on the title page. Ask: *What is a Gingerbread Man? A Gingerbread Man is a ____ that is shaped like a ____. What else do you see in the picture?* I see people, a cow, a ____, a ____, a ____, and ____. *We will read about what happens when the Gingerbread Man meets the people, a cow, and a duck. What do you think will happen when animals meet the cookie?* They will try to ____.

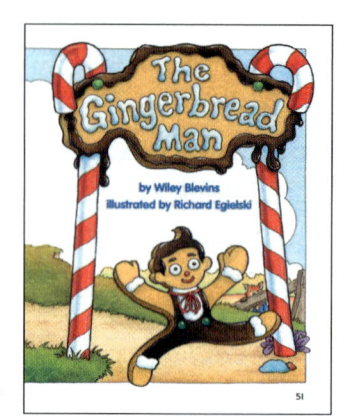

Literature Anthology, Lexile 320L

Focus on Vocabulary Use the **Visual Vocabulary Cards** to review the high-frequency words *any, from, happy, once, so,* and *upon* and the oral vocabulary words *eventually, foolish, timid, hero,* and *tale*. As you read, teach important story words, such as *ran away*, using gestures and pantomime. Run in place, and say *I am running*. Jog a few steps away from children. Say: *I am running away.* Have children repeat the action and phrase. Say: Running away *means* running from someone. *We use the past tense verb* ran *to tell about running in the past. For example: I ran yesterday.*

Summarize the Text Before reading, say the summary while pointing to the illustrations. *The story tells about two people who make a grandson out of gingerbread. Many animals try to chase the Gingerbread Man and eat him, but he is too fast. Finally, he meets a fox who is smarter than he is.*

Read the Text

Use the Interactive Question-Response routine to help children understand the story.

Pages 52–57

Pages 56–57 Read the text. Point to the repeated text on page 56, and read it aloud: *Run, run, run as fast as you can.* Say: *The author repeats the word* run *on this page.* Ask: *How many times do you see the word* run *in one sentence?* (three times) *Another word for* repeating *is* repetition. *Who is the Gingerbread Man running away from?* The Gingerbread Man is running away from Gram and Gramps. Point to page 57. *What does the Gingerbread Man repeat here?* (can, can, can) *Who is the Gingerbread Man running away from on this page?* He is running away from the black cow.

What is it like to read aloud the sentence with repeating words? Discuss with a partner.

130 UNIT 3 WEEK 3

Beginning Point to page 56. *Which word repeats on this page?* (run) Help children read the sentence with *run* aloud. *Does this word sound important when you say it three times?* Yes, it sounds important. *Do the words* run, run, run *tell you the Gingerbread Man is running fast?* (yes)

Intermediate Ask: *When you repeat something, is it important or not important?* (important) *Which word repeats on page 56?* The word run repeats. *What is the important idea in this sentence?* The Gingerbread Man wants to run away so no one can catch him.

Advanced/Advanced High Extend the discussion by having partners talk about how the story might be different if it had no repetition. If the story had no repetition, we would not know how important running away is to the Gingerbread Man.

Pages 57–59

Pages 58–59 Read the text. *Does the cow catch the Gingerbread Man?* No, the cow does not catch him. *Next, the Gingerbread Man meets a duck. What does the duck say?* The duck says, "Do not run so fast." *Does the duck want to eat the Gingerbread Man too?* Yes, the duck wants to eat him too.

How does the pattern in the story help you predict what might happen next?

Beginning Review what happens on page 57. *Does the cow want to eat the Gingerbread Man?* (yes) *What does the Gingerbread Man do?* He runs away. Point to page 58. *Does the duck want to eat the Gingerbread Man?* (yes) *What does the Gingerbread Man do?* He runs away. *Do you think the Gingerbread Man will meet more animals?* (yes)

Intermediate Point to the picture on page 58. *What does the duck want to do?* (eat the Gingerbread Man) *Is this the same as or different from what the cow wants?* It is the same. *What do you think will happen next?* The Gingerbread Man will meet another animal.

Advanced/Advanced High Extend the discussion. *Based on this pattern, what do you think will happen next?* Based on the pattern, I think the Gingerbread Man will run away from another animal.

Pages 60–65

Pages 60–61 Read the text. Point to page 61. *Does the Gingerbread Man repeat* run, run, run *when he sees the fox?* (yes) *Does the fox say he wants to catch the Gingerbread Man?* (no) *Does the fox say he wants to eat the Gingerbread Man?* (no) *What does the fox say to the Gingerbread Man?* The fox says he wants to be friends with the Gingerbread Man.

What do you notice about the pattern in the story? Discuss with a partner.

Beginning Point to the pictures of the characters. *Does the fox want to eat the Gingerbread Man?* No, the fox does not want to eat him. *Is this the same as the other animals or different?* It is different.

Intermediate Have partners ask and answer about the story's pattern. *Does the cow want to catch the Gingerbread Man?* (yes) *Does the duck want to catch him?* (yes) *Did the story's pattern change?* Yes, the fox says he does not want to catch the Gingerbread Man.

Advanced/Advanced High Have partners discuss: *What do you think when you see the pattern change?* I wonder why the fox wants to be friends.

FORMATIVE ASSESSMENT

STUDENT CHECK IN

Have partners retell who the Gingerbread Man meets when he runs away. Then have children reflect, using the Check-In routine.

Independent Time

Role Play Pair children of mixed proficiencies. Have partners select a scene from *The Gingerbread Man* to role play. Help partners decide what they will say and do in. If children would like a challenge, ask them to invent new characters for the Gingerbread Man to meet. Have children rehearse their roles and perform them for rest of the group.

READING • LEVELED READER • ACCESS THE TEXT

LESSONS 4-5

LEARNING GOALS

We can make and confirm predictions as we read a folktale.

OBJECTIVES

Ask and answer questions about key details in a text.

Use illustrations and details in a story to describe its characters, setting, or events.

Identify basic similarities in and differences between two texts on the same topic (e.g., in illustrations, descriptions, or procedures).

Ask questions to clear up any confusion about the topics and texts under discussion.

LANGUAGE OBJECTIVES

Children will narrate how two characters use a tool differently, using verbs.

ELA ACADEMIC LANGUAGE

- confirm, predict
- Cognates: *confirmar, predecir*

MATERIALS

ELL Leveled Reader:
The Magic Paintbrush

Online Differentiated Texts,
"The Sad Moon"

Online ELL Visual Vocabulary Cards

DIGITAL TOOLS

Have children listen to the selection as they follow along to develop comprehension and practice fluency and pronunciation.

Use Graphic Organizer 7: Moral to enhance the lesson.

The Magic Paintbrush

Prepare to Read

Build Background

- Remind children of the Essential Question: *What is a folktale? Let's read to find out what a special paintbrush can do.* Encourage children to ask for help when they do not understand a word or phrase.

- Point to and read aloud the title, and have children repeat it. Ask: *What is the title?* Have children point to it. Repeat the routine for the author's name. Point to the illustrations in the **Leveled Reader** to name things and actions. For example: *This is a [paintbrush]. What can you do with a [paintbrush]?*

Focus on Vocabulary Use **ELL Visual Vocabulary Cards** to preteach the words *generous* and *greedy*. As you read, use gestures or visuals to teach important story words, such as *magic, paintbrush, robe,* and *gold*. Display the cover. Have children repeat the word *magic*. *The paintbrush is magic. What do you think a magic paintbrush can do?* A magic paintbrush can paint pretty pictures.

Lexile 240L

Read the Text

Use the Interactive Question-Response routine to help children understand the story.

Pages 2–4

Make and Confirm Predictions Read pages 2–4 as children follow along. Ask questions that help children predict what the magic paintbrush will do.

Beginning *What do you do with a paintbrush?* You paint pictures. *How will this paintbrush be magic?* It will paint pictures that become real things.

Intermediate *What do you predict the magic paintbrush will do?* I predict the magic paintbrush will paint pictures of things people can use.

Pages 5–7

Read as children follow along. Help children identify cause and effect in the plot. Point to Chang. *Who is this?* (Chang) *Why does he paint the robe and the gold?* Chang takes the paintbrush from Lin-Lin.

Intermediate Have partners ask and answer: *What does Chang do with the paintbrush?* He paints a robe and gold.

Advanced/Advanced High Have partners discuss how Chang's way of using the paintbrush is different from Lin-Lin's way. Chang paints to make himself rich. Lin-Lin paints to help others.

132 UNIT 3 WEEK 3

WEEK 3

Pages 8–11

Read pages 8–11 as children follow along. Point to the pictures, and say *swim*, *heavy*, and *boat*. Have children repeat.

Beginning Help partners work together to respond and point to the pictures. *Who helps Chang?* Lin-Lin and the man in the boat help Chang.

Advanced/Advanced High Have children discuss: *How does Chang learn that friendship is more important than riches?* A friend saved his life, but his riches/gold could not help him.

Moral Remind children that folktales teach a moral, or lesson. *What is the moral of this folktale?* The moral is to be a good friend.

Respond to Reading Have partners work together to retell the story and respond to the questions on page 12.

Focus on Fluency

Read pages 10–11 to model accuracy and rate. Read the passage again and have children repeat after you. For more practice, record children reading the passage and select the best recording for you.

Paired Read: "Wanted: A Friend"

Make Connections: Write About It

Echo-read each page with children. Discuss the advice the child gets: *The child wants a friend. What is one way to make a friend?* Be a friend/himself. Help children make connections between texts using the questions on page 15. Chang and the child learned it is important to make friends.

Leveled Reader

Build Knowledge: Make Connections

Talk About the Text Have partners discuss the lessons in the texts.

Write About the Text Have students add their ideas to their Build Knowledge pages of their reader's notebooks.

Self-Selected Reading

Help children choose a folktale selection from the online **Leveled Reader Library,** or read the **Differentiated Text,** "The Sad Moon."

FOCUS ON GENRE

Children can extend their knowledge of the characteristics of a folktale by completing the genre activity on page 16.

LITERATURE CIRCLES

Lead children in conducting a literature circle using the Thinkmark questions to guide the discussion. You may wish to discuss what children have learned about friendship from both selections in the **Leveled Reader**.

FORMATIVE ASSESSMENT

STUDENT CHECK IN

Have partners share their Respond to Reading. Have children reflect, using the Check-In routine.

LEVEL UP

IF children can read *The Magic Paintbrush* **ELL Level** with fluency and correctly answer the Respond to Reading questions,

THEN tell children they will read a more detailed version of the folktale.

- Use pages 3–5 of *The Magic Paintbrush* **On Level** to model using Teaching Poster 32 to list a cause and an effect in the plot.

- Have children read the selection, checking their comprehension by using the graphic organizer.

ENGLISH LANGUAGE LEARNERS **133**

LESSONS 1-5

WRITING

MODELED WRITING

LESSON 1

LEARNING GOALS

We can write a sentence using specific words.

OBJECTIVES

Write narratives in which they recount events in sequence.

LANGUAGE OBJECTIVES

Children will narrate by writing sentences using past-tense verbs.

ELA ACADEMIC LANGUAGE

- verb
- Cognate: *verbo*

Writing Practice Review the sample sentences on p. 92 of the **Reading/Writing Companion**. Guide children to use the Actor/Action routine to analyze the first sentence: *Who is the actor?* (I) *What is the action?* (looked for my lost hamster) Then read the prompt on p. 93, and ask a volunteer to answer it. Write the sentences on the board for children to chorally read. Then have children write their own sentences. Guide children in writing their verbs in the past-tense form.

Beginning Provide sentence frames: I lost my *baseball*. I looked for it everywhere. It was *in the yard*. Supply specific vocabulary as needed.

Intermediate Have partners take turns asking and answering *what/where* questions to develop their sentences.

Advanced/Advanced High Challenge partners to include specific words in their sentences. Encourage them to share their sentences with the group.

FORMATIVE ASSESSMENT ▸ **STUDENT CHECK IN** Partners share their sentences. Ask children to reflect, using the Check-In routine.

INTERACTIVE WRITING

LESSON 2

LEARNING GOALS

We can read and write about a Student Model.

OBJECTIVES

With guidance and support, add details to strengthen writing as needed.

LANGUAGE OBJECTIVES

Children will discuss the Student Model and write sentences, identifying specific words.

ELA ACADEMIC LANGUAGE

- verbs
- Cognate: *verbos*

Analyze the Student Model Have children finger point as they chorally read the Student Model on p. 98 of the **Reading/Writing Companion**. Point out that many stories begin with the phrase "once upon a time." Then have children compare a more general sentence to the one in the Student Model to help them identify specific words. *A child lost his shoe. Is the child a boy or a girl?* (a boy) *What kind of shoe did he lose?* (a boot) Continue for the remaining sentences. Then help children complete page 99.

Beginning Ask partners to point to past-tense verbs. Provide a sentence frame: I noticed the past-tense verb *walked*. It ends in *ed*.

Intermediate Have partners describe the specific words in the Student Model: Anna used *boot* instead of *shoe*.

Advanced/Advanced High Challenge children to tell how they know a verb is past tense or future tense.

FORMATIVE ASSESSMENT ▸ **STUDENT CHECK IN** Partners share their sentences. Ask children to reflect, using the Check-In routine.

WEEK 3

INDEPENDENT WRITING

LESSONS 3-4

LEARNING GOALS

We can respond to a folktale by writing a new ending.

OBJECTIVES
Write narratives in which they provide some closure.

LANGUAGE OBJECTIVES
Children will narrate by writing sentences, using past- and future-tense verbs.

ELA ACADEMIC LANGUAGE
- verbs, past tense, future tense
- Cognate: *verbos*

Find Text Evidence Use the Independent Writing routine. Help children use text evidence to orally retell the anchor text. Ask questions, such as: *Who makes the Gingerbread Man?* (Gram) *What does he do after Gram makes him?* (runs away) Then read the prompt on p. 104 of the **Reading/Writing Companion:** *Imagine that the Gingerbread Man had chosen to go around the lake. Then write a new ending to the story. Let's pretend that the Gingerbread Man did not ride across the lake on the fox's back. We need to think about what else could happen and write a new ending.*

Work with children to fill out My Writing Outline 13. Then have them use the sentences from their outlines to complete p. 104.

Writing Checklist Read the checklist with students, and have them check for these items in their writing.

Beginning Have partners check that they used past-tense verbs: I used the past-tense verb ran.

Intermediate Encourage children to add a specific word.

Advanced/Advanced High Have partners identify where they used each item in their writing.

FORMATIVE ASSESSMENT ▸ **STUDENT CHECK IN** Partners share their sentences from My Writing Outline. Ask children to reflect, using the Check-in routine.

SELF-SELECTED WRITING

LESSON 5

LEARNING GOALS

We can revise our writing.

OBJECTIVES
Use verbs to convey a sense of past, present, and future.

LANGUAGE OBJECTIVES
Children will inquire about their writing by checking verb tenses.

ELA ACADEMIC LANGUAGE
- verbs, past tense, future tense
- Cognate: *verbos*

Work with children to revise the group writing activity. Point to each word as you read the sentences. Stop to ask questions, such as, *Is this a verb? Is it in the correct tense?* Then have partners work together to correct each other's sentences. Tell partners to check that they have used verbs correctly.

For support with grammar and past- and future-tense verbs, refer to the **Language Transfers Handbook** and **Language Development Card** 4B.

FORMATIVE ASSESSMENT ▸ **STUDENT CHECK IN** Partners tell what revisions they made. Ask children to reflect, using the Check-in routine.

LESSONS 1-2

READING • LITERATURE BIG BOOK • ACCESS THE TEXT

LEARNING GOALS

We can understand what happens long ago as we listen to a nonfiction text.

OBJECTIVES

Identify the main topic and retell key details of a text.

Distinguish between information provided by pictures or other illustrations and information provided by the words in a text.

Use the illustrations and details in a text to describe its key ideas.

Ask and answer questions about key details in a text read aloud or information presented orally or through other media.

LANGUAGE OBJECTIVES

Children will inform about how the town changed, using verbs.

ELA ACADEMIC LANGUAGE

- *past, present, compare, contrast*
- Cognates: *pasado, presente, comparar, contrastar*

MATERIALS

Literature Big Book, *The Last Train,* pp. 4–31

Visual Vocabulary Cards

DIGITAL TOOLS

Have children listen to the selection as they follow along to develop comprehension and practice fluency and pronunciation.

Use the additional grammar song.

Grammar Song

The Last Train

Prepare to Read

Build Background *We are going to read a nonfiction text about a train. The author wrote the text in the form of a song. A song is music with words that people can sing.* Then say: *Imagine you are traveling to another town. How do you travel?* Have children draw their answer and share it with a classmate: *I ride in/on a ____. Do you think people a long time ago traveled in trains? Do many people travel that way now? How do people travel now?*

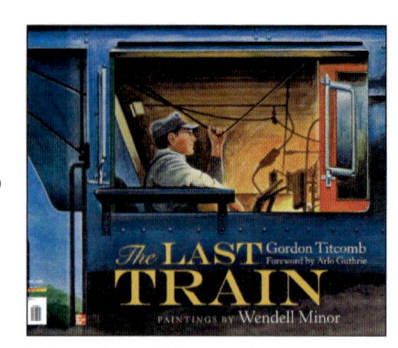

Literature Big Book

Focus on Vocabulary Use the **Visual Vocabulary Cards** to review the oral vocabulary words *century* and *past*. As you read, use gestures and visual support to clarify important words from the selection, such as: *railroad, station, tracks,* and *ticket*. Ask: *What do you need to buy to ride a train?* (a ticket) *Who works for the railroad?* Review *engineer, brakeman, porter,* and *fireman,* using pictures from the book. Then say the word *memories* for children to repeat. *A memory is something you remember from the past.* Model telling a memory you have from your childhood. Then ask: *What is your favorite memory? My favorite memory is ___.*

Summarize the Text Before reading, say this summary while pointing to the illustrations: *This song tells about the author's memories of the railroad and its workers. We'll read about what he remembers and how the memories make him feel.*

Read the Text

Use the Interactive Question-Response routine to help children understand the text.

Pages 4–15

Pages 4–5 Read the text aloud. Have children point to the *station, windows,* and *roof*. Write the term *boarded up* on the board, and underline the word *board*. Guide children to point to a *board* in the illustration to help them understand the phrase. Ask: *Do you think people use this station now?* (no) *How do you think the boy in the picture feels about that?* (sad)

Pages 10–11 Read the text aloud. On the board, draw a two-column chart with titles *Present* and *Past*. Have children help you fill it out with details from the song. (Present: now, rusty brown tracks, no trains for thirty years; Past: thirty years ago, tracks that shone like silver, trains rolling through town)

COLLABORATE *What is the railroad in this picture like now? What was it like in the past? Discuss with a partner.*

136 UNIT 3 WEEK 4

WEEK 4

Beginning Provide sentence frames to help pairs talk about the chart on the board: Now, the train tracks are brown. Thirty years ago, they were silver. Now, no trains go through the town. Thirty years ago, many trains went through the town.

Intermediate Have children contrast the railroad now and then. Help children use past-tense verbs when they tell about the past. Now, the train tracks are brown. There are no trains rolling through the town. Thirty years ago, the train tracks were silver. Many trains rolled/went through the town.

Advanced/Advanced High Have pairs take turns saying a sentence about the railroad for a partner to say whether it describes the past or the present. For example: The tracks are rusty brown. (present) Remind children to use the correct verb tenses.

Pages 16–23

Pages 16–17 Read the text aloud. Say the word *souvenir* for children to repeat. *A souvenir is an object you keep to remind you of something you did.* Show an example of one. Ask: *Do you have any souvenirs?* (yes/no) Explain that *put in twenty years* means the boy's father worked for the train company for twenty years. *The company gave him that watch as a gift.*

What souvenirs does the singer keep in his box? Discuss with a partner.

Beginning Help partners take turns pointing to items for their partners to name, using this sentence starter: I see a/an watch/family photo/hole punch/toy train/ticket/ad.

Intermediate Have pairs describe the locations of the trains they see in the illustration: There's a train on the watch/in the photo/in the box/on the ad. There are two trains in the picture at the top of the box.

Advanced/Advanced High Have partners take turns describing a souvenir in detail. (Two possible responses: A boy, father, and grandfather are in the photo. The gold watch has a picture of a train on it.)

Pages 24–30

Pages 28-29 Read the text aloud. Say: *Point to the trains. Point to the airplane.* Explain that *steam, diesel,* and *electricity* give the train power so it can move. Tell children that *rails* is another word for *tracks*. Write *railroad,* and define it as a "road made of rails." Say and point to the *contrails* for children to repeat. Ask: *Which moves faster: a train or a plane?* (a plane)

How is transportation today similar to transportation in the past? How is it different?

Beginning Have pairs agree on one item in the illustration that we did not have in the past. (airplane)

Intermediate Provide sentence starters for pairs to compare and contrast: In the past, there were no airplanes. Now, there are airplanes.

Advanced/Advanced High Have pairs compare and contrast the newer train on page 29 and the older train on page 20: Both the new train and the old train are black/have a light. The old train has steam power, but the new train has electric power.

FORMATIVE ASSESSMENT

⏵ STUDENT CHECK IN

Have partners retell how the town changed over time. Then have children reflect, using the Check-In routine.

Independent Time

Share a Memory Have children draw a special memory and a souvenir that can help them remember it. Then have them ask a partner *wh-* questions to learn about his or her memory and souvenir: Where were you? Who was there? What did you do/see? When was it? What souvenir did you keep? Have partners present their drawings to the group. Provide sentence frames if necessary: This shows my memory of ___. This souvenir is ___.

LESSONS 1-2

READING • SHARED READ • ACCESS THE TEXT

LEARNING GOALS

We can read and understand a nonfiction text.

OBJECTIVES

Ask and answer questions about key details in a text.

Describe the connection between two individuals, events, ideas, or pieces of information in a text.

With prompting and support, read informational texts appropriately complex for grade 1.

Ask and answer questions about key details in a text read aloud or information presented orally or through other media.

LANGUAGE OBJECTIVES

Children will inform about homes in the past and present using verbs.

ELA ACADEMIC LANGUAGE

- nonfiction, compare
- Cognates: *no ficción, comparar*

MATERIALS

Reading/Writing Companion, pp. 116–125

Visual Vocabulary Cards

DIGITAL TOOLS

Have children listen to the selection as they follow along to develop comprehension and practice fluency and pronunciation.

Use the additional grammar song.

Grammar Song

"Life at Home"

Prepare to Read

Build Background Read aloud the Essential Question on page 118. Say: *Think about how we do things in our homes today.* Refer to the photos on pages 121, 123, and 127: *We play games on a _____, we make _____ on a stove, and we wash dishes in a _____.* Ask: *Do you think people had these things a long time ago? We are going to read a nonfiction text about what people did at home long ago.* Explain that we use past-tense verbs like *had* and *did* to talk about the past.

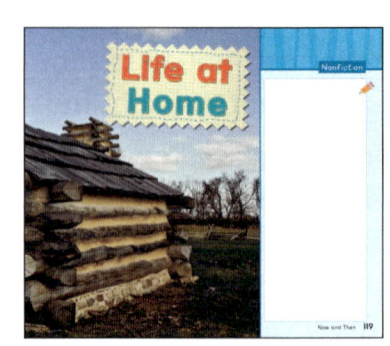

Reading/Writing Companion, Lexile 490L

Focus on Vocabulary Use the **Visual Vocabulary Cards** to review the high-frequency words *ago, boy, girl, how, people,* and *old* and the oral vocabulary words *entertainment, future, present, century,* and *past.* Display the illustrations in the text, and name the rooms. Help children make connections to their homes: *What are some rooms in your house?* (bedroom, bathroom, living/dining room, kitchen) As you read, use visual support to teach the important selection words *pot, tub,* and *sink.* Point to and say each word for children to repeat.

Summarize the Text Before reading, say this summary and point to the pictures: *This text tells about life at home in the past and today. We'll read about where people slept, how they cooked food, and how they washed dishes.*

Read the Text

Use the Interactive Question-Response routine to help children understand the text.

Pages 118–121

Pages 118–119 Read the text aloud as children follow along. Ask: *How many rooms did homes have a long time ago?* (one) *Do most homes have only one room today?* (no) *Point to the picture of a room from long ago. I see a rocking chair next to a fireplace. Are there pots in the fireplace?* (yes) *Look at the picture on page 111. What is the family doing?* They are playing a game.

Pages 120–121 Read the text aloud. Ask children to repeat the verbs *cook* and *bake. What do you make when you* cook? (food) Baking *is a kind of* cooking. *What is a food that people bake?* (bread) Discuss *fireplace, oven,* and *stove.* Explain that ovens are part of stoves now. Ask: *Do you like to help cook?* (yes/no)

How are kitchens today different from kitchens in the past? How are they the same? Discuss with a partner.

Beginning *How did people cook long ago?* They used a fireplace/a big pot on a pole/an oven. *How do people cook today?* They use a stove and small pots.

138 UNIT 3 WEEK 4

WEEK 4

Intermediate Have pairs retell details about kitchens in the past and today. Provide these sentence frames: Long ago, there was a <u>fireplace</u> in the kitchen. People cooked in <u>a pot on a pole</u>. Now, there is a <u>stove</u> in the kitchen. People cook with <u>small pots</u>.

Advanced/Advanced High Have children use both affirmative and negative statements to describe how kitchens in the past were different from today: There wasn't <u>a stove</u>. There was <u>a fireplace</u>. People used <u>one big pot</u>. They didn't use <u>many small pots</u>.

Pages 122–123

Pages 122–123 Read the text aloud, and have children follow along. Ask: *What are some crops you know?* Elicit the names of familiar fruits and vegetables. Remind children that when you *plant* something, you put a seed or young plant in the ground so it can grow. Ask: *How do you get food?* (a store/supermarket) Have children point to their own or a classmate's socks or hat. Ask: *Did your parents make this?* (no) *Where did you get it?* (at a store)

COLLABORATE *How did children help at home in the past? How do you help now? Discuss with a partner.*

Beginning Have pairs use these sentence frames to describe chores in the past and today: In the past, boys helped <u>plant crops</u>. I help <u>plant crops</u> too./I don't help <u>plant crops</u>. Girls helped <u>make socks and caps</u>. Today, I help <u>wash the dishes</u>.

Intermediate Help children name chores to list, such as: *clean my room, make my bed, make socks and caps, plant crops, wash clothes, wash the dishes.* Use gestures to clarify the meanings of any unfamiliar words. Provide these sentence frames for pairs to compare: In the past, boys/girls helped <u>plant crops/make socks and caps</u>. Today, I help <u>wash the dishes</u>.

Advanced/Advanced High Have children name chores. Provide words for more chores. Have partners ask these questions: *How did boys/girls help in the past?* (They planted crops/made socks and caps.) *How do you help at home today?* (I clean my room.)

Pages 124–125

Pages 124–125 Read the text aloud as children follow. Have children look at both pictures. Ask: *Where is/are the spoon/dishes?* (a big tub) *Where is the tub?* (outside) *Where are the father and son?* (in the kitchen) Write *dishwasher* on the board, and help children use the smaller words to determine the meaning.

COLLABORATE *How do you wash dishes today? Is it different from the past? Discuss with a partner.*

Beginning Write *dishwasher, sink,* and *tub* on the board. Provide these sentence frames for pairs to discuss: Today, we wash dishes in <u>the sink/the dishwasher</u>. In the past, people used <u>a tub</u>.

Intermediate Have children use these sentence frames to compare washing dishes today with washing dishes long ago: Today, we get water from <u>the sink</u>. We don't get water from <u>a well</u>. Now, we wash dishes in <u>the sink/the dishwasher</u>. We don't use <u>a tub</u>.

Advanced/Advanced High Have pairs ask and answer: *Where do you wash dishes?* (We wash dishes in the sink/the dishwasher.) *Where did people wash dishes in the past?* (They washed dishes outside/in a tub.) Remind children to use the correct verb tense.

FORMATIVE ASSESSMENT

▶ STUDENT CHECK IN

Have partners retell three ways that home living was different in the past. Then have children reflect, using the Check-In routine.

Independent Time

Write and Share Guide children to find two items in the text that people did not have in the past that make life easier today, such as a stove or dishwasher. Pair children of mixed proficiencies, and have them discuss ways the things make life easier for people. Encourage pairs to include drawings. Then invite pairs to share their ideas with the rest of the group. Use **Oral Language Sentence Frames,** page 5, to support children as they discuss technology they use today.

ENGLISH LANGUAGE LEARNERS 139

LESSON 3

READING • ANCHOR TEXT • ACCESS THE TEXT

Long Ago and Now

Prepare to Read

Build Background Display the title page, and read the title aloud for children to repeat. Say: *Point to the part of the picture that shows now/long ago. How do you know?* Point out that the boy is in color, but the other children are not. *Long ago, there weren't any color photos.* Then ask: *What is the boy doing? He is listening to ____. What is he using?* Help children name the *headphones*. *What are the other children doing?* Elicit guesses, and then explain that they are listening to music on a radio. *Point to the radio in the picture.* Have children draw a picture of a radio they own or have seen. Invite volunteers to share, and discuss the idea that now radios are small, but long ago they were too big to carry.

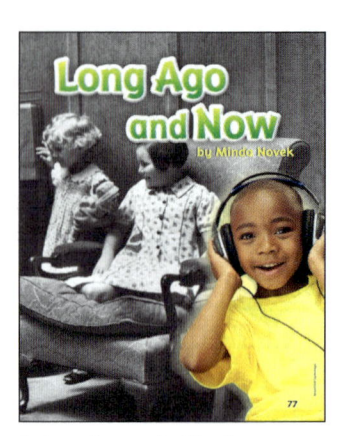

Literature Anthology, Lexile 480L

Focus on Vocabulary Use the **Visual Vocabulary Cards** to review the high-frequency words *ago, boy, girl, how, people,* and *old* and the oral vocabulary words *entertainment, future, present, century,* and *past.* As you read, use gestures to teach important selection words, such as *wagon, pump,* and *fresh.*

Summarize the Text Before reading, say this summary while pointing to the illustrations: *This text tells about life at home, at school, and in the community now and long ago. Let's find out how life was different or the same in the past.*

Read the Text

Use the Interactive Question-Response routine to help children understand the nonfiction text.

Pages 76–77

Pages 76–77 Read the text aloud. Ask: *Which photo shows the past? What did people ride in then?* (wagons) *What do people ride in now?* (cars) *Which is fast and fun: a wagon or a car?* (a car) *What took a long time to do in a wagon?* (travel to places) Tell children that when you *take a trip*, you travel to another place and stay there. Ask: *Have you taken a trip with your family? Where did you go?* Invite volunteers to share, or have children tell a classmate.

What information does the author tell about first? Next? Discuss with a partner.

Beginning Explain that *organize* means "to put things in a certain order." Reread the second paragraph on page 76 and then the paragraph on page 77. The author wrote about traveling on these pages. *Which does the author tell about first: long ago or today?* The author tells about today first.

LEARNING GOALS

We can read and understand a nonfiction text.

OBJECTIVES

Describe the connection between two individuals, events, ideas, or pieces of information in a text.

Distinguish between information provided by pictures or other illustrations and information provided by the words in a text.

Identify the reasons an author gives to support points in a text.

Describe people, places, things, and events with relevant details, expressing ideas and feelings clearly.

LANGUAGE OBJECTIVES

Children will inform about living long ago and now, using verbs.

ELA ACADEMIC LANGUAGE

- organize, compare, contrast
- Cognates: *organizar, comparar, contrastar*

MATERIALS

Literature Anthology, pp. 74–89

Visual Vocabulary Cards

DIGITAL TOOLS

Have children listen to the selection as they follow along to develop comprehension.

Use the online High-Frequency Words Activity for additional support.

140 UNIT 3 WEEK 4

WEEK 4

Intermediate *What kind of information is in each photo?* The first photo shows a car today. The second photo shows a wagon long ago. *What is the order of the texts about traveling?* The text about traveling today is first. The text about traveling long ago is next.

Advanced/Advanced High Have pairs answer with details: The author tells about life today first and then about life long ago. This shows how life long ago was different from now/today.

Pages 78–79

Pages 78–79 Read the text aloud. Point to the refrigerator, and say the word for children to repeat. *What keeps food fresh today?* (a refrigerator) *What is the boy doing?* (getting a snack) *How did people keep things cold long ago?* (a box with ice) *How did they get ice?* Trucks took ice to their homes. *Do you think it is easier or harder to keep things cool today?* (easier)

Use the photographs to talk about the information in the text with a partner.

Beginning Point to words in the text and then the photos: *food, boy, truck, man, lift, tongs, block of ice. Can the boy get a snack at home?* (yes) *What does the man in the photo use to lift the ice?* (tongs)

Intermediate Have pairs select a photo to talk about the text. (This boy can get a snack at any time. Men drove trucks filled with ice to people's homes. This man uses tongs to lift a block of ice.)

Advanced/Advanced High Have pairs describe the photos as they talk about the text: The boy is getting a snack from the refrigerator. His food is fresh. The truck has ice inside. The truck brings ice to people. The man is lifting some ice.

Pages 80–81

Pages 80–81 Read the text aloud. Have children point to the sink and the pump in the pictures. Ask: *Which one do you use to get water at home?* (the sink) *How do you get water from a sink? Show me.* Have children mime turning on a faucet. Then say and demonstrate for children to imitate your motions: *This is how you get water from a pump. You walk to the pump. You put your bucket under the pump. You pump the water. You carry the water home.* Ask: *Do you think it is easier or harder to get water today?* (easier)

The author of this story organizes information and details by what happens today and long ago. What does this help you understand?

Beginning *Are both pages about getting water or using water?* (getting water) *What do you learn about getting water today and long ago?* Today people get water from sinks. Long ago people used pumps.

Intermediate Have pairs read a sentence on each page that tells what the page is about. (Today we can get water at home. Long ago, people used to get water at a pump.) Ask: *Did people long ago get water the same way we do or in a different way?* (different)

Advanced/Advanced High Explain comparing and contrasting: Comparing *is showing how things are the same.* Contrasting *is showing how things are different. What does the author compare and contrast on these pages?* (how people get water today and how they got it long ago) *What does the author's way of contrasting help you understand?* (how different it was to get water long ago)

FORMATIVE ASSESSMENT

STUDENT CHECK IN

Have partners retell ways that life in the past and life in the present are different. Then have children reflect, using the Check-In routine.

Independent Time

Describing Pictures Assign partners a pair of "then and now" photos from pages 82–83, 84–85, or 86–87. Have one partner look at the photo of the present and the other look at the photo of the past. Provide sentence frames for children to describe their photo and ask about their partner's: *I see a ___ in my picture. Do you see a ___ in your picture? Yes, I do. / No, I see ___.* If time allows, have pairs share some of their comparisons with the class.

ENGLISH LANGUAGE LEARNERS 141

LESSONS 4-5

READING • LEVELED READER • ACCESS THE TEXT

LEARNING GOALS

We can reread to understand a nonfiction text.

OBJECTIVES

Retell key details of a text.

Use the illustrations and details in a text to describe its key ideas.

Identify basic similarities in and differences between two texts on the same topic (e.g., in illustrations, descriptions, or procedures).

Build on others' talk in conversations by responding to the comments of others through multiple exchanges.

LANGUAGE OBJECTIVES

Children will inform about differences between schools of the past and present, using verbs in the past and present tenses to make comparisons.

ELA ACADEMIC LANGUAGE

- compare, contrast, reread
- Cognates: *comparar, contrastar*

MATERIALS

ELL Leveled Reader:
Schools Then and Now

Online Differentiated Texts,
"Bath Time"

Online ELL Visual Vocabulary Cards

DIGITAL TOOLS

Have children listen to the selection as they follow along to develop comprehension and practice fluency and pronunciation. Use Graphic Organizer 8: Compare and Contrast to enhance the lesson.

Schools Then and Now

Prepare to Read

Build Background

- Remind children of the Essential Question. Say: *Let's read to find out how schools today are different than they were long ago.* Encourage children to ask for help when they do not understand a word or phrase.

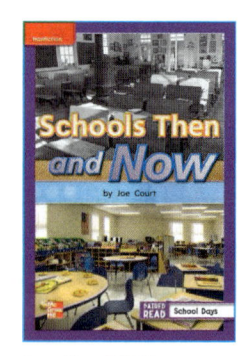

- Display the cover, and read the title aloud for children to repeat. Ask: *What place do these pictures show?* They show a ____. Have children name any items they can. Ask and have children point: *Which picture shows a classroom long ago/now?* Have children compare each picture to their classroom. Provide sentence frames with the connecting words *and/but*: This classroom has ____, but our classroom has ____. This classroom and our classroom have ____.

Focus on Vocabulary Use **ELL Visual Vocabulary Cards** to preteach the words *education* and *history*. As you read, use gestures or visuals to teach important selection words, such as *backpack, window, light, desk, chalk,* and *computer*.

Lexile 270L

Read the Text

Use the Interactive Question-Response routine to help children understand the text.

Pages 2–5

Compare and Contrast Read pages 2–5 as children follow along. Ask: *Does our school have one teacher/room, or many teachers/rooms? Is it like schools long ago?* Then guide children to compare and contrast how children get to school now and how they got to school in the past.

Beginning Have pairs find the same verb on pages 2 and 3. (walked/walk) Ask: *How are children long ago like children now?* They walked to school.

Intermediate Help partners compare going to school today and long ago: Today and long ago, children walked to school. In the past, they used horses and wagons, but now they ride in buses or cars.

Pages 6–7

Reread Read pages 6–7 as children follow along. Have children point to the *stove. How was this stove used?* Guide children to reread the text to make sure they undestand it: The stove made the school warm.

Beginning Help partners ask and answer: What makes our school warm? Hot pipes make our school warm.

142 UNIT 3 WEEK 4

WEEK 4

Advanced/Advanced High Have pairs compare and contrast: Now, <u>bulbs</u> give us light. Long ago, schools didn't have <u>bulbs</u>. Schools now have <u>windows</u> for light. Schools then had <u>windows too</u>.

Pages 8–11

Read pages 8–11 aloud. Have children summarize page 10: In the past, children used <u>chalk</u> to write on a <u>slate</u>.

Beginning Have children respond to the question in the text: *How do you write?* I use a <u>computer</u> to write.

Intermediate Have pairs brainstorm different ways they write: We use a <u>computer/crayon/pencil/pen</u> to write.

Respond to Reading Have partners work together to retell the story and respond to the questions on page 12.

Focus on Fluency

Read pages 2–3 to model accuracy and rate. Read the passage again, and have children repeat after you. For more practice, record children reading the passage and select the best recording for you.

Paired Read: "School Days"

Analytical Writing — Make Connections: Write About It

Echo-read the nonfiction text with children. Discuss similarities and differences in the charts on pages 14–15: Children long ago used <u>chalk</u>. Children today use <u>pencils</u>. Help children make connections between texts, using the question on page 15: Schools long ago had <u>one room</u>.

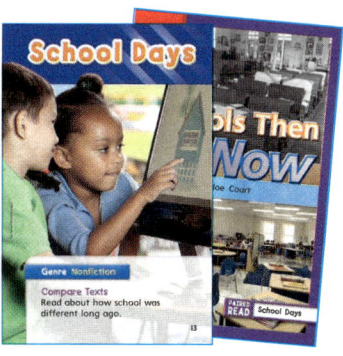

Leveled Reader

Build Knowledge: Make Connections

Talk About the Text Have partners discuss how the texts tell about life long ago and today.

Write About the Text Have students add their ideas to the Build Knowledge pages of their reader's notebooks.

Self-Selected Reading

Help children choose a nonfiction selection from the online **Leveled Reader Library,** or read the **Differentiated Text,** "Bath Time."

🌐 FOCUS ON SOCIAL STUDIES

Children can extend their knowledge of getting to school by completing the social studies activity on page 16.

LITERATURE CIRCLES

Lead children in conducting a literature circle using the Thinkmark questions to guide the discussion. You may wish to discuss what children have learned about schools long ago from both selections in the **Leveled Reader**.

FORMATIVE ASSESSMENT

❯ STUDENT CHECK IN

Have partners share their Respond to Reading. Have children reflect, using the Check-In routine.

LEVEL UP

IF children can read *Schools Then and Now* **ELL Level** with fluency and correctly answer the Respond to Reading questions,

THEN tell children they will read a more detailed version of the selection.

- Use pages 2–3 of *Schools Then and Now* **On Level** to model using Teaching Poster 39 to list details that are the same or different.
- Have children read the selection, checking their comprehension by using the graphic organizer.

ENGLISH LANGUAGE LEARNERS **143**

LESSONS 1-5

WRITING

MODELED WRITING

LESSON 1

LEARNING GOALS

We can focus on one idea when we write.

OBJECTIVES

Write informative texts in which they supply some facts about the topic.

LANGUAGE OBJECTIVES

Children will argue by writing sentences that give an opinion and a reason.

ELA ACADEMIC LANGUAGE

- idea
- Cognate: *idea*

Writing Practice Review the sample sentences on p. 128 of the **Reading/Writing Companion**. Help children use the Actor/Action routine to analyze the first sentence: *Who is the actor?* (we) *What is the action?* (have things) *What do the things do?* (help us) *When?* (today) Then read the prompt on p. 129, and ask a volunteer to answer it. Write the sentences on the board for children to chorally read. Then have children write their own sentences. Remind them to write about only one idea.

Beginning Provide sentence frames to help partners focus on one idea: Long ago, life was hard. People didn't have stoves or sinks. Help children check that their second sentence explains the idea in their first sentence.

Intermediate Have partners ask and answer questions to create their sentences: *How was life like long ago? Why?*

Advanced/Advanced High Challenge children to focus on one idea in their sentences. Encourage them to use *I think* and *because* in their sentences.

FORMATIVE ASSESSMENT ▶ **STUDENT CHECK IN** Partners share their sentences. Ask children to reflect, using the Check-In routine.

LESSON 2

LEARNING GOALS

We can read and write about a Student Model.

OBJECTIVES

With guidance and support, respond to questions and suggestions from peers.

LANGUAGE OBJECTIVES

Children will discuss and write sentences about the Student Model, using the verb *is*.

ELA ACADEMIC LANGUAGE

- *focus*
- Cognate: *foco*

Analyze the Student Model Have children finger point as they chorally read the Student Model on p. 134 of the **Reading/Writing Companion**. Read the first and last sentences. Have children raise their hands when they hear *is* or *are*. *What do these verbs tell us about the action?* (It is happening now.) *What idea did Mateo focus on?* (whether life is better now or was better in the past) Then help children complete p. 135.

Beginning Have partners take turns pointing to and identifying the words *is* and *are*: The word is tells about home life. It tells about one thing.

Intermediate Have partners work together to identify the idea Mateo focuses on. Provide a sentence frame: Mateo wrote that life is better now.

Advanced/Advanced High Have children ask and answer questions about Mateo's one idea: *Which sentence gives Mateo's opinion? Which sentences give reasons?* Then have children write original sentences.

FORMATIVE ASSESSMENT ▶ **STUDENT CHECK IN** Partners share their responses. Ask children to reflect, using the Check-In routine.

144 UNIT 3 WEEK 4

WEEK 4

INDEPENDENT WRITING

LESSONS 3-4

LEARNING GOALS

We can write an opinion about a nonfiction text.

OBJECTIVES

Write opinion pieces in which they name the book they are writing about and state an opinion.

LANGUAGE OBJECTIVES

Children will argue by writing sentences stating their opinion and giving reasons.

ELA ACADEMIC LANGUAGE

- opinion
- Cognate: *opinión*

Find Text Evidence Use the Independent Writing routine. Help children orally retell the anchor text. Ask questions, such as: *How do we travel?* (in cars) *How did people travel in the past?* (in wagons) Then read the prompt on **Reading/Writing Companion** p. 140: *Based on* Long Ago and Now, *do you think being a kid is better now, or was it better in the past? Why? Think about what you read. Would you prefer to be a kid now or in the past? We will write an opinion and give reasons, using details from the text.*

Work with children to fill out My Writing Outline 14. Then have them use the sentences from their outlines to complete p. 140.

Writing Checklist Read the checklist with students, and have them check for these items in their writing.

Beginning Have children take turns reading one sentence at a time and checking the spellings of words in their Word Banks.

Intermediate Have partners ask and answer questions to share their ideas: *What is your opinion? Why do you think so?*

Advanced/Advanced High Challenge children to add one more reason, using a detail from the text.

FORMATIVE ASSESSMENT **STUDENT CHECK IN** Partners share their sentences from My Writing Outline. Ask children to reflect, using the Check-in routine.

SELF-SELECTED WRITING

LESSON 5

LEARNING GOALS

We can revise our writing.

OBJECTIVES

Use singular and plural nouns with matching verbs in basic sentences.

LANGUAGE OBJECTIVES

Children will inquire about their writing by checking how they use *is/are*.

ELA ACADEMIC LANGUAGE

- verb
- Cognate: *verbo*

Work with children to revise the group writing activity. Point to each word as you read the sentences. Stop to ask questions, such as, *Is the verb is/are used correctly?* Then have partners work together to correct each other's sentences. Tell partners to check that they have used *is/are* correctly.

For support with grammar and the present tense of the verb *to be*, refer to the **Language Transfers Handbook** and **Language Development Card** 5A.

FORMATIVE ASSESSMENT **STUDENT CHECK IN** Partners tell what revisions they made. Ask children to reflect, using the Check-in routine.

ENGLISH LANGUAGE LEARNERS 145

READING • LITERATURE BIG BOOK • ACCESS THE TEXT

LESSONS 1-2

LEARNING GOALS

We can understand where food comes from as we listen to a nonfiction text.

OBJECTIVES

Identify the main topic and retell key details of a text.

Ask and answer questions to help determine or clarify the meaning of words and phrases in a text.

Use the illustrations and details in a text to describe its key ideas.

Describe people, places, things, and events with relevant details, expressing ideas and feelings clearly.

LANGUAGE OBJECTIVES

Children will inform about different kinds of foods, using nouns and verbs.

ELA ACADEMIC LANGUAGE

- author, steps, reread
- Cognate: *autor*

MATERIALS

Literature Big Book, *Where Does Food Come From?*, pp. 4–32

Visual Vocabulary Cards

DIGITAL TOOLS

Have children listen to the selection as they follow along to develop comprehension and practice fluency and pronunciation.

Use the online High-Frequency Words Activity for additional support.

Where Does Food Come From?

Prepare to Read

Build Background *We are going to read a nonfiction text about where different foods come from. Nonfiction text gives you facts about a topic.* Display the picture on the cover and then ask children to share ideas about where different foods come from. Say: *The boy on the cover is eating broccoli on his pizza. Where does broccoli come from?* Model for children: *Broccoli grows on plants.* Have children repeat. Then have children discuss other sources of foods. Provide sentence frames: *Food can grow on _____. Food can come from _____.*

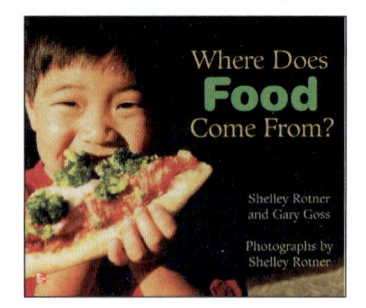

Literature Big Book

Focus on Vocabulary Use the **Visual Vocabulary Cards** to review the oral vocabulary words *delicious* and *nutritious*. Display the photographs in the text and invite children to name things that they know. As you read, use gestures and visual support to clarify important words from the selection, such as *grinding, pressing, cutting, fields, kernels,* and *popped*. Say the word *grinding with me.* Point to it in the text. Provide an example: *You can make coffee by grinding coffee beans together. What else can you grind together?* You can grind salt.

Summarize the Text Before reading, say the summary while pointing to the photographs. *The text tells where many different foods come from and how they are made.*

Read the Text

Use the Interactive Question-Response routine to help children understand the text.

Pages 4–13

Pages 4–5 Read the text aloud. Point to the boy. *The boy has a cup of hot cocoa.* Have children repeat *hot cocoa. Is he going to drink the hot cocoa?* (yes) Point to the word *chocolate* and say it for children to repeat. *What is hot cocoa made from?* Hot cocoa is made from chocolate. Point to the cocoa beans and say: *These are cocoa beans.* Have children repeat. Then ask: *How is chocolate made?* (by grinding and cooking cocoa beans) *Where do cocoa beans come from?* Cocoa beans grow on cocoa trees. Then ask: *Do you like to drink hot cocoa?* (yes/no)

How does the author help you understand where hot cocoa comes from? Discuss with a partner.

Beginning *Point to this large text:* cocoa beans. *What does the big text tell you?* It tells *you what the food is.* Point to the photo of the cocoa bean. *What does this show you?* It shows *a picture of the food.*

146 UNIT 3 WEEK 5

Intermediate Have partners point to the pictures as they respond. *What does the author show pictures of?* (cocoa beans, hot cocoa) *Why does the author show these pictures?* The author shows two of the steps the author tells about in the text.

Advanced/Advanced High Have partners think more deeply about the text. *What other ways could the author use to communicate where the food comes from?* The author could number the steps. The author could show pictures of all of the steps with arrows.

Pages 14–23

Page 16 Read the text aloud. Point to the *Did you know?* text bubble. *Authors use bubbles and boxes to give extra information. What do we learn here?* We learn what cows drink. *The text compares cows to humans. Do you drink that much?* (no)

Reread the Did you know? *bubble. Why does the author have this information in this section of the page? Discuss with a partner.*

Beginning Point to the cow. Point to the *Did you know?* box. *What do cows drink?* Cows drink water. *Do cows drink a little or a lot?* Cows drink a lot. *Are these fun facts to know?* (yes)

Intermediate Help children respond: The author wants us to read fun facts about cows. *What do cows drink?* (water) *How much do they drink compared to a human?* (500 glasses a day)

Advanced/Advanced High Help children elaborate on their response. *Why does the author compare what cows drink to what humans drink?* (to help us understand how much the cow drinks)

Pages 24–32

Page 28 Read the text aloud. Explain that *delivering* means "taking." Point to the bee and then the honey. *Honey is made in a special way. What animal makes honey?* Bees make honey. Point to and say *nectar* for children to repeat. *What do bees take to their hives?* Bees take the nectar of flowers to their hives.

What two things are needed to produce, or make, honey? Discuss with a partner.

Beginning Help children reread the text. Point to the bee. *What is this animal?* It is a bee. Point to the flower. *What is the bee on?* The bee is on the flower. *What makes honey?* Bees and flowers make honey.

Intermediate Point to the photograph of the bee on the flower. *How do bees use flowers?* Bees take nectar from flowers back to their hives. *Can bees make honey without flowers?* No, bees need flowers to make honey.

Advanced/Advanced High Help children extend their thinking. Have them think about what they know about how honey is made and discuss with a partner: *What could someone do to produce more honey?* To produce more honey, someone could plant more flowers so that the bees have more nectar.

FORMATIVE ASSESSMENT

> **STUDENT CHECK IN**

Have partners name three foods that are grown and three foods that can be made from something that is grown. Then have children reflect using the Check-In routine.

Independent Time

Write and Present Have children talk with a partner about a special food they eat at home. Encourage pairs to think about foods that are unique to their family or to their culture. Have children select one food and create a page titled *Where Does Food Come From?* Children should trace where their selected food comes from. Have them create a list of steps the food goes through from start to finish. Provide sentence frames to help children write the steps: First, the ___ starts as ___. Then, someone ___ to make it ___. After that, someone ___. Finally, you can eat ___. Encourage children to add illustrations that show the steps through which the food goes. When children are finished, have each pair present their new pages to the group.

READING • SHARED READ • ACCESS THE TEXT

LESSONS 1-2

LEARNING GOALS

We can read and understand a nonfiction text.

OBJECTIVES

Know and use various text features (e.g., headings, tables of contents, glossaries, electronic menus, icons) to locate key facts or information in a text.

Use the illustrations and details in a text to describe its key ideas.

With prompting and support, read informational texts appropriately complex for grade 1.

Produce complete sentences when appropriate to task and situation.

LANGUAGE OBJECTIVES

Children will inform about where breakfast foods come from, using time words.

ELA ACADEMIC LANGUAGE

- photographs, chart, diagram
- Cognates: *fotografías, diagrama*

MATERIALS

Reading/Writing Companion, pp. 152–161

Visual Vocabulary Cards

DIGITAL TOOLS

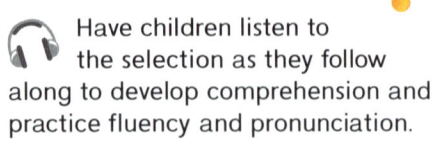

MULTIMODAL

Have children listen to the selection as they follow along to develop comprehension and practice fluency and pronunciation.

Use the online High-Frequency Words Activity for additional support.

"A Look at Breakfast"

Prepare to Read

Build Background Read the Essential Question on page 152. Have children share what they know about how we get some of our food. Use the illustrations on pages 152 and 153 to generate ideas. Point to and read aloud the title. Breakfast *is a meal people eat in the morning. Do you like to eat breakfast? We are going to read about where we get foods that many people have for breakfast.* Point to the orange juice. *This is orange juice.* Point to the bread. *This is bread. Say* bread *with me. This is jam. Say* jam *with me. What is on the bread? _____ is on the bread.*

Reading/Writing Companion, Lexile 340L

Focus on Vocabulary Use the **Visual Vocabulary Cards** to review the high-frequency words *after, buy, done, every, soon,* and *work* and the oral vocabulary words *delighted, enormous, responsibility, delicious,* and *nutritious.* As you read, use visual support to teach the important selection words *wheat, crushed, dough, plant, pulled,* and *shipped.*

Summarize the Text Before reading, say the summary and point to the illustrations. *This text tells where some breakfast foods come from. The text follows the steps the foods take from the ground to your breakfast table.*

Read the Text

Use the Interactive Question-Response Routine to help children understand the text.

Pages 154–155

Pages 154–155 Read the text, including the caption, and have children follow along. Point to the picture of the bag of flour. Say *flour* and have children repeat. *The author tells how we get bread. Do you like to eat bread?* (yes/no) Have children reread the text on page 154. Ask: *What is bread made from?* Bread is made from flour. *What is flour made from?* Flour is made from wheat. Point to the words *First, Next, Then,* and *Last* on page 155. Explain that these words help us understand the order of steps in making something. *What is the first step in making bread?* (make the dough) *What is the last step?* (put the bread in bags)

COLLABORATE

How do the illustrations help you understand where bread comes from? Discuss with a partner.

Beginning Use the pictures to review the words *wheat, bread,* and *flour.* Point to the wheat and ask: *What is flour made from?* Flour is made from wheat. *What can you make with flour?* You can make bread with flour.

148 UNIT 3 WEEK 5

WEEK 5

Intermediate Have partners give a more specific answer. *What do the photographs show?* The photos show wheat, a bag of flour, and bread. *Why does the author use these photographs?* The author wants us to know/understand where bread comes from.

Advanced/Advanced High Help partners add details to their responses. Display page 154. *What else does the author include to help you know where bread comes from?* Guide children to the answer. (the caption) Have them explain the caption: The caption tells us how wheat is made into flour.

Pages 156–157

Page 157 Read the text aloud and have children follow along. Point to the word *plant* and say it for children to repeat. *Do you see a plant on this page?* Allow children to consider the question. *Plant* has multiple meanings. It can be a living thing that grows from the ground, but here it means a place where people make things. *Point to the plant on this page.*

Where does grape jam come from? Discuss with a partner.

Beginning Help children reread the text. Guide partners to answer the question. *What do trucks bring to the plant?* Trucks bring grapes. Point to the larger photo. *What happens to the grapes at the plant?* The grapes are crushed.

Intermediate Have partners reread the text and add details to their answer. *What happens to the grapes after they arrive at the plant?* After they arrive at the plant, the grapes are crushed and cooked.

Advanced/Advanced High Help partners elaborate on their answers. *What information about where grapes come from is not explained on this page?* Where grapes are grown is not explained here.

Page 160–161

Page 158 Read the text aloud and have children follow along. Point to the truck. *The truck brings the food. Where does the truck bring the food?* The truck brings food to the store. *Point to the store.*

Page 161 Display the chart. Point to the column headings and read them aloud. Then point to the different foods. Say each one aloud and have children repeat. *This chart shows the same information as the text, but in a different form.*

What is the same about all of the foods in the chart? Discuss with a partner.

Beginning Point to the *How It Is Made* column. *What word is in every box?* (crushed) *Show me how to crush something.* Have children pantomime crushing.

Intermediate Have children identify a word that appears in each *How It Is Made* box. (crushed) Help partners give a more specific answer. *What types of things are crushed?* The things that come from trees and plants are crushed.

Advanced/Advanced High Have children extend their thinking. *How are the ways the foods are made different?* Making bread has three steps, but making orange juice has only one.

FORMATIVE ASSESSMENT

❯ STUDENT CHECK IN

Have partners retell the steps of how one of the breakfast foods is made. Then, have children reflect using the Check-In routine.

Independent Time

Art Project Have children ask and answer: *Where does our food come from?* Pair children of mixed proficiencies. Have partners create diagrams showing where different foods come from and then present their diagrams to the group. Provide sentence frames such as: ___ is/are picked. ___ is/are crushed into ___. ___ is/are ___ into ___. Have pairs add captions and labels to their illustrations to explain the steps. Provide vocabulary support as needed.

ENGLISH LANGUAGE LEARNERS **149**

LESSON 3

READING • ANCHOR TEXT • ACCESS THE TEXT

LEARNING GOALS

We can read and understand a nonfiction text.

OBJECTIVES

Ask and answer questions about key details in a text.

Use the illustrations and details in a text to describe its key ideas.

With prompting and support, read informational texts appropriately complex for grade 1.

Ask questions to clear up any confusion about the topics and texts under discussion.

LANGUAGE OBJECTIVES

Children will explain the process of producing milk, using time words and key vocabulary.

ELA ACADEMIC LANGUAGE

- *photographs*
- Cognate: *fotografías*

MATERIALS

Literature Anthology, pp. 96–103

Visual Vocabulary Cards

DIGITAL TOOLS

MULTIMODAL

Have children listen to the selection as they follow along to develop comprehension and practice fluency and pronunciation.

Use the additional grammar song.

🎵 Grammar Song

From Cows to You

Prepare to Read

Build Background *We are going to read a nonfiction text about how milk goes from a cow to you.* Show the picture on the title page and invite children to tell what they see. Point to the field and the farm. Say the words and have children repeat. Then point to the cows. *These are cows. Cows are essential to making milk.* Explain that something that is essential is something you can't do without. *Many people drink milk. Do you drink milk? Cows are essential to making milk, but many people are also important. Let's read to see how those people help us to get milk.*

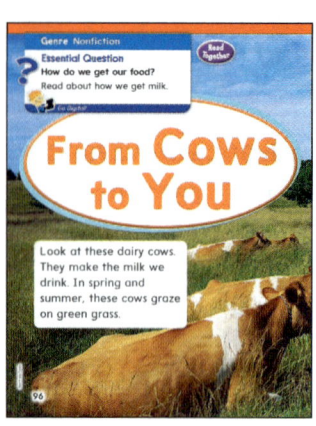

Literature Anthology, Lexile 500L

Focus on Vocabulary Use the **Visual Vocabulary Cards** to review the high-frequency words *after, buy, done, every, soon,* and *work,* and the oral vocabulary words *delighted, enormous, responsibility, delicious,* and *nutritious.* As you read, teach important selection words, such as *milk,* using gestures and pantomime. Explain that *milk* has multiple meanings. *Milk* names the white liquid many people drink, and *milk* is also an action word that talks about getting the milk out of the cow. Have children point to the picture of someone milking a cow.

Summarize the Text Before reading, say the summary and point to the illustrations. *This text explains how milk is produced. It follows the process from the farm to the grocery store.*

Read the Text

Use the Interactive Question-Response routine to help children understand the text.

Pages 96–99

Pages 96–97 Read the text aloud. Point to the cows. *What do cows make?* Cows make milk. Point to the grass. *What do cows eat in the summer?* In the summer, cows eat grass. Point to and say the word *barn* for children to repeat. *A barn is a building where animals can stay at night and in winter.* Ask: *Do you see a barn in this photo? Farmers keep hay in a barn.* Show a picture or drawing of hay and have children repeat the word. *What do cows eat in the winter?* In the winter cows eat hay. *Why is the food that the cows eat important?* Cows need good food to make good milk.

Pages 98–99 Read the text. Point to the farmer milking the cow. *This is a dairy farmer. A dairy farmer has cows that produce milk. The cows must be milked two times a day. When must the cows be milked?* They must be milked in the morning and in the evening. *There are two different ways to milk a cow.* Point to the two

150   UNIT 3 WEEK 5

WEEK 5

different ways and have children repeat *by hand* and *by machine*. Point to the tank on the truck on page 99. *This is a tank on a truck. Say* tank. *Does the tank keep the milk warm or cold?* (cold) *Warm milk can spoil. Say* spoil. *Milk that is spoiled is not good to drink. Where does the milk go next?* The milk goes in the tank truck to the <u>dairy</u>.

How do the photos help you understand how cows can be milked? Discuss with a partner.

Beginning Point to the first photograph on page 96. *How does the farmer milk the cow in this photo?* The farmer milks the cow <u>by hand</u>. Point to the second photograph. *Does this photo show another way to milk a cow?* (yes) *What is milking the cow here?* A <u>machine</u> is milking the cow.

Intermediate Have partners ask and answer about the pictures on page 98. *What does each photograph show?* The first one shows <u>a person</u>. The second one shows <u>a machine</u>. *What do the <u>photographs</u> help you understand?* They help me understand <u>different ways</u> of <u>milking</u> a cow.

Advanced/Advanced High Extend the discussion. *What are other ways photographs could help us understand the text better?* Photographs that show how cows <u>live</u> in the <u>summer</u> compared to the <u>winter</u> could help us understand that text better.

Pages 100–103

Pages 100–101 Read the text. Point to the photograph of the man working in the dairy. *At the dairy, they cook the milk to kill germs. Say* germs. *Germs can make us sick. After the milk cools, what happens to it?* The milk is put into cartons or <u>jugs</u>. *Point to where you see cartons and jugs on the next page. Where are these people?* They are at a <u>store</u>. *A store that sells milk and food is often called a* grocery store.

Pages 102–103 Read the text. Point to the photographs of the foods and help children identify them. *What are these foods made from?* These foods are made from <u>milk</u>. *How do dairy foods help us?* They make our bodies <u>strong/healthy</u>. Point to the bullet points on page 103. *These dots list surprising facts about cows. Can you imagine having 90 glasses of milk a day?* (no)

What does the author want you to understand about milk? Discuss with a partner.

Beginning Point to the pictures of the cows at the beginning of the text. *Where does milk start?* Milk starts with <u>cows</u>. Point to the picture of the girl in the grocery store toward the end of the text. *Where does milk end?* Milk ends at the <u>grocery store</u>.

Intermediate Help partners review to respond. *What's the first step in making milk?* First, the cows need to <u>eat</u> good <u>food</u>. *What comes next?* Next, the <u>farmer milks</u> the cows. Continue to prompt children with questions and sentence frames about the steps in making milk. *Does the author want you to know about all of the steps?* (yes)

Advanced/Advanced High Encourage children to elaborate on their responses. *Why does the author include all of the steps in producing milk?* The author wants us to <u>know</u> that it is a <u>difficult</u> process and <u>a lot of</u> work.

FORMATIVE ASSESSMENT

▶ STUDENT CHECK IN

Have partners retell three steps before milk arrives at the grocery store. Then have children reflect using the Check-In routine.

Independent Time

Art Project Ask children to consider all of the people and animals involved in producing milk. Have children create a visual that shows all of the people involved in producing milk. Children should add labels and captions to help explain who each person or animal is and what they do. Provide sentence frames to help children write captions for their visuals. This is a ___. The ___'s job is to ___. If needed, provide children an example to help them get started: This is a <u>dairy farmer</u>. The <u>dairy farmer</u>'s job is to <u>milk the cows</u>.

ENGLISH LANGUAGE LEARNERS 151

LESSONS 4-5

READING • LEVELED READER • ACCESS THE TEXT

LEARNING GOALS

We can reread to understand a nonfiction text.

OBJECTIVES

Retell key details of a text.

Describe the connection between two individuals, events, ideas, or pieces of information in a text.

Identify basic similarities in and differences between two texts on the same topic (e.g., in illustrations, descriptions, or procedures).

Produce complete sentences when appropriate to task and situation.

LANGUAGE OBJECTIVES

Children will inform about the process of growing and selling apples, using sequence words.

ELA ACADEMIC LANGUAGE

- nonfiction, order, reread
- Cognates: *no ficción, orden*

MATERIALS

ELL Leveled Reader:
Apples from Farm to Table

Online Differentiated Texts,
"Can It!"

Online ELL Visual Vocabulary Cards

DIGITAL TOOLS

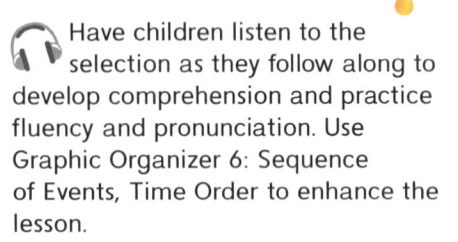

Have children listen to the selection as they follow along to develop comprehension and practice fluency and pronunciation. Use Graphic Organizer 6: Sequence of Events, Time Order to enhance the lesson.

Apples from Farm to Table

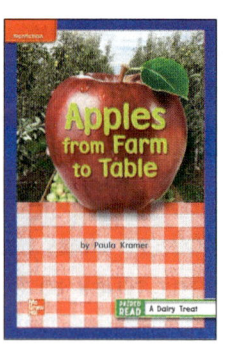

Prepare to Read

Build Background

- Remind children of the Essential Question. *Let's read to see how we get our food.* Encourage children to ask for help when they do not understand a word or phrase.

- Point to and read the title aloud. Have children repeat. Ask: *What is the title?* Have children point to and read it. Repeat the routine for the author's name. Point to the photographs in the Leveled Reader to name things and actions, for example: *What is the girl eating? She is eating an apple.*

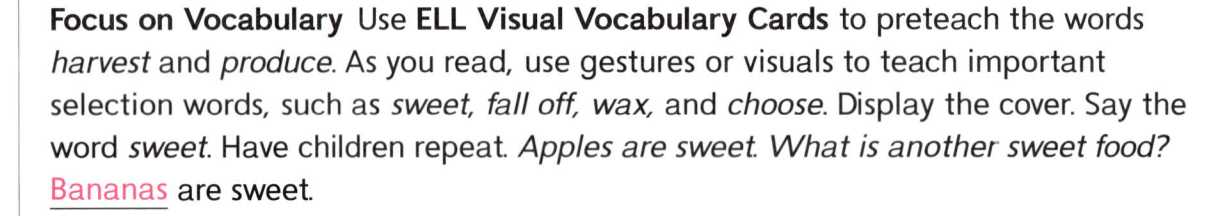

Lexile 430L

Focus on Vocabulary Use **ELL Visual Vocabulary Cards** to preteach the words *harvest* and *produce*. As you read, use gestures or visuals to teach important selection words, such as *sweet, fall off, wax,* and *choose*. Display the cover. Say the word *sweet*. Have children repeat. *Apples are sweet. What is another sweet food?* Bananas *are sweet*.

Read the Text

Use the Interactive Question-Response routine to help children understand the text.

Pages 2–4

Details: Time Order Read as children follow along. Help children describe the order of how apples grow. *What do growers do first?* First, growers take *the seeds.* What do growers do next? *Next, growers* plant *the seeds.*

Beginning Help partners point to the picture as they respond. *Where do the seeds come from?* The seeds come from inside *the apple.*

Advanced/Advanced High Have partners review the text and discuss. *Why does growing apples take a long time?* It takes a long time *because you have to wait for the* seeds *to grow into* trees.

Pages 5–7

Reread Read pages 5–7 as children follow along. Guide children to reread the passage, including the boxed texts and the caption, to understand how trees produce apples. *How do flowers turn into apples?* The blossoms fade. *Then the flowers* fall off *and apples start to* grow.

Intermediate Help children discuss. *Do the trees on page 5 have apples yet? How can you tell?* The trees don't *have apples yet. They will have* apples *after the blossoms* fall off.

152 UNIT 3 WEEK 5

Advanced/Advanced High Help children extend their thinking. *How might flowers be important to growing apples?* Flowers might help grow apples by attracting bees.

Pages 8–11

Read pages 8–11 as children follow along. Point to the pictures and say *wash, wax, trays, boxes,* and *stack*. Have children repeat.

Beginning Help partners work together to respond. *Where do you buy apples?* You buy apples at the store.

Intermediate *What is the last step before you get the apples?* Workers stack the apples at the store.

Respond to Reading Have partners work together to retell the story and respond to the questions on page 12.

Focus on Fluency

Read pages 10–11 to model accuracy and rate. Read the passage again and have children repeat after you. For more practice, record children reading and have them select the best recording.

Paired Read: "A Dairy Treat"

Analytical Writing **Make Connections: Write About It**

Echo-read each page with children. Discuss the steps of making yogurt. *What comes first?* First, milk is heated to kill germs. Help children make connections between texts using the questions on page 15: Apples and yogurt get to stores in trucks.

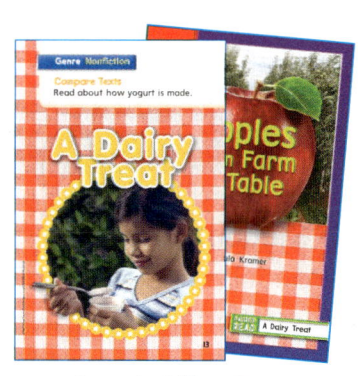

Leveled Reader

Build Knowledge: Make Connections

Talk About the Text Have partners discuss how we get apples.

Write About the Text Have students add their ideas to the Build Knowledge pages of their reader's notebooks.

Self-Selected Reading

Help children choose a nonfiction selection from the online **Leveled Reader Library** or read the **Differentiated Text,** "Can It!"

WEEK 5

🌐 FOCUS ON SOCIAL STUDIES

Children can extend their knowledge of goods and services by completing the social studies activity on page 16.

LITERATURE CIRCLES

Lead children in conducting a literature circle, using the Thinkmark questions to guide the discussion. You may wish to discuss what children have learned about how we get our food from both selections in the Leveled Reader.

FORMATIVE ASSESSMENT

⊙ STUDENT CHECK IN

Have partners share their Respond to Reading. Have children reflect using the Check-In routine.

LEVEL UP

IF children can read *Apples from Farm to Table* **ELL Level** with fluency and correctly answer the Respond to Reading questions,

THEN tell children that they will read a more detailed version of the selection.

- Use pages 5–6 of *Apples from Farm to Table* **On Level** to model, using Teaching Poster 31 to list the events in sequence.

- Have children read the selection, checking their comprehension by using the graphic organizer.

ENGLISH LANGUAGE LEARNERS **153**

LESSONS 1-5

WRITING

MODELED WRITING

LESSON 1

LEARNING GOALS

We can learn how to give reasons for an opinion.

OBJECTIVES

Write opinion pieces in which they supply a reason for the opinion.

LANGUAGE OBJECTIVES

Children will argue by writing sentences stating their opinion and a reason.

ELA ACADEMIC LANGUAGE

- opinion
- Cognate: *opinión*

Writing Practice Review the sample sentences on p. 162 of the **Reading/Writing Companion**. Have children analyze the first sentence. *What is the subject of the sentence? What is the writer talking about?* (apples) *What can we tell about them?* (They are the writer's favorite fruit.) Read the prompt on p. 163 and ask a volunteer to answer it. Write the sentences for children to choral read. Then help children write their own sentences.

Beginning Provide sentence frames to help children give their opinion and a reason: Carrots are my favorite food. They are crunchy!

Intermediate Encourage partners to give two reasons. If needed, provide questions to prompt reasons: *What are they like? How do they taste?*

Advanced/Advanced High Have children write sentences, including their opinion and two reasons. Have them share their sentences in pairs.

FORMATIVE ASSESSMENT ❯ **STUDENT CHECK IN** Partners share their sentences. Ask children to reflect, using the Check-In routine.

INTERACTIVE WRITING

LESSON 2

LEARNING GOALS

We can read and write about a Student Model.

OBJECTIVES

Respond to questions and suggestions from peers.

LANGUAGE OBJECTIVES

Children will discuss and write about the Student Model, identifying an opinion and reasons.

ELA ACADEMIC LANGUAGE

- opinion
- Cognate: *opinión*

Analyze the Student Model Have children finger point as they choral read the Student Model on page 168 of the **Reading/Writing Companion**. Then guide children to find the contraction in the last sentence. (isn't) Prompt children to identify the reasons Lisa gives to support her opinion. *What is one reason Lisa gives to tell why she thinks bread is the hardest breakfast food to make?* (Big machines have to crush the wheat.) Then help children complete p. 169. Provide sentence frames as needed.

Beginning Have partners identify the contraction in the text. Provide a sentence frame: I noticed the contraction *isn't*.

Intermediate Have partners ask and answer questions about Lisa's opinion: *Which sentence gives Lisa's opinion? Which sentences give reasons?*

Advanced/Advanced High Challenge children to write about Lisa's text using their own sentences. Have them share their sentences.

FORMATIVE ASSESSMENT ❯ **STUDENT CHECK IN** Partners share their sentences. Ask children to reflect, using the Check-In Routine.

WEEK 5

INDEPENDENT WRITING

LESSONS 3-4

LEARNING GOALS

We can write an opinion about a nonfiction text.

OBJECTIVES

Write opinion pieces in which they name the book they are writing about, state an opinion, and supply reasons for the opinion.

LANGUAGE OBJECTIVES

Children will argue by writing sentences that state their opinion and reasons.

ELA ACADEMIC LANGUAGE

- opinion, reason
- Cognates: *opinión, razón*

Find Text Evidence Use the Independent Writing routine. Help children orally retell the anchor text using text evidence. Ask questions, such as *Where do we get milk?* (from dairy cows) *What do cows eat?* (grass and hay) Then read the prompt on p. 173 of the **Reading/Writing Companion:** *Based on* From Cows to You, *which job in the milk process would you rather have? Why? Farmers, dairy workers, and truck drivers work hard so you can have milk to drink. Which job would you most like to do? We need to write an opinion and give reasons.*

Work with children to fill out My Writing Outline 15. Then have them use the sentences from their outlines to complete p. 173.

Writing Checklist Read the checklist with students and have them check for these items in their writing.

Beginning Provide a sentence frame to help partners talk about their sentences: *I wrote an opinion.*

Intermediate Have partners share their opinions and reasons.

Advanced/Advanced High Challenge children to write one more reason to support their opinion.

FORMATIVE ASSESSMENT ❯ **STUDENT CHECK IN** Partners share their sentences from My Writing Outline. Ask children to reflect, using the Check-in routine.

SELF-SELECTED WRITING

LESSON 5

LEARNING GOALS

We can revise our writing.

OBJECTIVES

Demonstrate command of the conventions of standard English grammar and usage.

LANGUAGE OBJECTIVES

Children will inquire about their writing by checking contractions.

ELA ACADEMIC LANGUAGE

- publish
- Cognate: *publicar*

Work with children to revise the group writing activity. Point to each word as you read the sentences. Stop to ask questions, such as *Is this a contraction? Should it have an apostrophe?* Then have partners work together to correct each other's sentences before they publish them. Tell partners to check that they have written their contractions correctly.

For support with grammar and contractions, refer to the **Language Transfers Handbook** and **Language Development Cards** 35A and 35B.

FORMATIVE ASSESSMENT ❯ **STUDENT CHECK IN** Partners tell what revisions they made. Ask children to reflect, using the Check-in routine.

ENGLISH LANGUAGE LEARNERS 155

UNIT 3

Summative Assessment
Get Ready for Unit Assessment

Unit 3 Tested Skills

LISTENING AND READING COMPREHENSION	VOCABULARY	GRAMMAR	SPEAKING AND WRITING
• Listening Actively • Details	• Words and Categories	• Verbs • Contractions	• Presenting • Composing/Writing • Supporting Opinions • Retelling/Recounting

Create a Student Profile

Record data from the following resources in the Student Profile charts on pages 356–357 of the Assessment book.

COLLABORATIVE	INTERPRETIVE	PRODUCTIVE

• Collaborative Conversations Rubrics
  • Listening
  • Speaking
	• Leveled Unit Assessment
	  • Listening Comprehension
	  • Reading Comprehension
	  • Vocabulary
	  • Grammar
	• Presentation Rubric
	  • Listening
	• *Wonders* Unit Assessment
		• Weekly Progress Monitoring
		• Leveled Unit Assessment
		  • Speaking
		  • Writing
		• Presentation Rubric
		  • Speaking
		• Write to Sources Rubric
		• *Wonders* Unit Assessment

The Foundational Skills Kit, Language Development Kit, and Adaptive Learning provide additional student data for progress monitoring.

Level Up

Use the following chart, along with your Student Profiles, to guide your Level Up decisions.

LEVEL UP	If **BEGINNING** level students are able to do the following, they may be ready to move to the **INTERMEDIATE** level:	If **INTERMEDIATE** level students are able to do the following, they may be ready to move to the **ADVANCED** level:	If **ADVANCED** level students are able to do the following, they may be ready to move to **ON** level:
COLLABORATIVE	• participate in collaborative conversations using basic vocabulary and grammar and simple phrases or sentences • discuss simple pictorial or text prompts	• participate in collaborative conversations using appropriate words and phrases and complete sentences • use limited academic vocabulary across and within disciplines	• participate in collaborative conversations using more sophisticated vocabulary and correct grammar • communicate effectively across a wide range of language demands in social and academic contexts
INTERPRETIVE	• identify details in simple read alouds • understand common vocabulary and idioms and interpret language related to familiar social, school, and academic topics • make simple inferences and make simple comparisons • exhibit an emerging receptive control of lexical, syntactic, phonological, and discourse features	• identify main ideas and/or make some inferences from simple read alouds • use context clues to identify word meanings and interpret basic vocabulary and idioms • compare, contrast, summarize, and relate text to graphic organizers • exhibit a limited range of receptive control of lexical, syntactic, phonological, and discourse features when addressing new or familiar topics	• determine main ideas in read alouds that have advanced vocabulary • use context clues to determine meaning, understand multiple-meaning words, and recognize synonyms of social and academic vocabulary • analyze information, make sophisticated inferences, and explain their reasoning • command a high degree of receptive control of lexical, syntactic, phonological, and discourse features
PRODUCTIVE	• express ideas and opinions with basic vocabulary and grammar and simple phrases or sentences • restate information or retell a story using basic vocabulary • exhibit an emerging productive control of lexical, syntactic, phonological, and discourse features	• produce coherent language with limited elaboration or detail • restate information or retell a story using mostly accurate, although limited, vocabulary • exhibit a limited range of productive control of lexical, syntactic, phonological, and discourse features when addressing new or familiar topics	• produce sentences with more sophisticated vocabulary and correct grammar • restate information or retell a story using extensive and accurate vocabulary and grammar • tailor language to a particular purpose and audience • command a high degree of productive control of lexical, syntactic, phonological, and discourse features

READING • SHARED READ • ACCESS THE TEXT

LESSONS 1–2

LEARNING GOALS

We can read and understand a folktale.

OBJECTIVES

Describe characters, settings, and major events in a story, using key details.

Identify words and phrases in stories or poems that suggest feelings or appeal to the senses.

Compare and contrast the adventures and experiences of characters in stories.

Build on others' talk in conversations by responding to the comments of others through multiple exchanges.

LANGUAGE OBJECTIVES

Children will narrate how the two characters compete in a race, using verbs.

ELA ACADEMIC LANGUAGE

- folktale, predict, dialogue
- Cognates: *predecir, diálogo*

MATERIALS

Reading/Writing Companion, pp. 14–23

Visual Vocabulary Cards

DIGITAL TOOLS

Have children listen to the selection as they follow along to develop comprehension and practice fluency and pronunciation.

Use the online ELL Vocabulary Practice for additional support.

"Snail and Frog Race"

Prepare to Read

Build Background Read aloud the Essential Question on page 14. Have children share something they know about the bodies of familiar animals, such as dogs or cats. For example: *A cat has four legs and a tail.* Point to and read aloud the title. *We are going to read about a race that happens between a snail and a frog.* Point to the snail. *This is Snail. Say* snail *with me.* Point to the frog. *This is Frog. Say* frog *with me. Snail and Frog play together.*

Reading/Writing Companion, Lexile 270L

Focus on Vocabulary Use the **Visual Vocabulary Cards** to review the high-frequency words *about, animal, carry, eight, give,* and *our* and the oral vocabulary words *appearance, determined, feature, predicament,* and *relief.* As you read, use gestures and visual support to teach important story words, such as *splendid, special, hopped, past, gate, inched, trail, long,* and *slide.* Use the following routine for each new word: Point to the frog hopping. Say the word *hopped*. Have children repeat. Ask: *What did the frog do? The frog* hopped.

Summarize the Text Before reading, say the summary and point to the illustrations. *This story tells about a race that happens between Snail and Frog. They move in different ways as they each try to win the race.*

Read the Text

Use the Interactive Question-Response routine to help children understand the story.

Pages 16–17

Page 16 Read the text aloud, and have children follow along. *The text says this is a tale.* Review that a tale is a story. Review the meaning of *splendid*. Say: *Look at the picture. Is a* splendid *day a good day or a bad day? A splendid day is a* good day. *How do you know? The sun is* shining. *Snail and Frog are* smiling. *What is Frog doing? Frog is* hopping past *Snail.*

Page 17 Read the text aloud. Point to and say *race*, and have children repeat it. *To* race *is to try to win by doing an action the fastest.* Provide an example: *Children race to see who runs the fastest.* Point to Snail. *Snail wants to play with Frog. What does Frog want to do? Frog wants to* race *Snail to their school.*

COLLABORATE *What do Snail and Frog decide to do? Discuss with a partner.*

Beginning Guide partners to answer the question. Point to the illustration of Snail and Frog talking. *This is Snail. Snail and Frog are talking. What does Snail want to*

158 UNIT 4 WEEK 1

WEEK 1

do? Snail wants to play. *What does Frog want to do?* Frog wants to race.

Intermediate Have partners give details about their answers. *Where does Frog want to race?* Frog wants to race to the school.

Advanced/Advanced High Help children elaborate on their responses as they discuss with a partner: *What do you predict will happen after Snail and Frog agree to race?* Encourage children to use *I predict* and *because* in their responses. I predict Frog will win because frogs are faster than snails.

Pages 18–21

Page 19 Read aloud the text as children follow along. Point to and say the word *tip* for children to repeat. *When people give a* tip, *they share an idea of what to do. What tip does Frog give?* Frog tells Snail to hop and not carry a shell. Point to Snail's shell on page 18. *Is a* shell *hard or soft?* (hard) *Snail says he cannot hop. Why?* He does not have long legs.

How are Snail's body and Frog's body different? Discuss with a partner.

Beginning Help children use the pictures on pages 18 and 19 to respond. *Does Snail have legs?* (no) *Can Snail move fast?* No, Snail cannot move fast. *Does Frog have legs?* Yes, Frog has legs. *What are Frog's leg's like?* Frog's legs are long. Frog's legs help her hop.

Intermediate Help partners give details about their answers. *Do Snail and Frog move the same way?* No, Snail inches along, and Frog hops.

Advanced/Advanced High *How can Frog's body help her in the race?* Frog's legs can help her move fast. *How can Snail's body affect him in the race?* Snail has no legs, so he cannot move very fast.

Pages 22–23

Page 23 Read the text aloud as children follow along. Point to Snail. *Snail is inside the gate! Snail used his body to get through the gate. What is Snail's body like?* Snail's body is sticky. *Who wins the race?* (Snail)

How does Snail's body help him win? Discuss with a partner.

Beginning Point to Frog on the previous page. *Can Frog get through the gate?* (no) Point to Snail on page 23. *Can Snail get through the gate?* Yes, Snail can get through the gate.

Intermediate Have partners add details to their answers. *What helps Snail get through the gate?* His sticky body helps him get through the gate.

Advanced/Advanced High Help children review what they predicted would happen after Snail and Frog agreed to race. *Was your prediction correct?* It was not correct/correct because I thought Frog would/Snail would win.

FORMATIVE ASSESSMENT

> **STUDENT CHECK IN**

Have partners retell how the two characters in the folktale are different. Then have children reflect, using the Check-In routine.

Independent Time

Dialogue Have children ask and answer: *How do animals' bodies help them?* Pair children of mixed proficiencies. Have them discuss what Snail and Frog might say to each other after Snail wins the race. Ask children to consider what questions Snail and Frog might have for each other. Provide examples: *How do you move so fast? How did you get through the gate?* Then have partners work together to write a dialogue, imagining the conversation between Snail and Frog after Snail wins the race. Encourage children to include in their dialogues details about how each animal's body helps it in the race. Provide sentence frames if children need help crafting their dialogues: I used my ___ to go fast. I used my ___ to go through the gate. When children are finished, encourage them to rehearse and present their dialogues to another pair, a small group, or the class.

ENGLISH LANGUAGE LEARNERS **159**

LESSON 3

READING • ANCHOR TEXT • ACCESS THE TEXT

LEARNING GOALS

We can read and understand a folktale.

OBJECTIVES

Retell stories, including key details, and demonstrate understanding of their central message or lesson.

Describe characters, settings, and major events in a story, using key details.

Use illustrations and details in a story to describe its characters, setting, or events.

Produce complete sentences when appropriate to task and situation.

LANGUAGE OBJECTIVES

Children will narrate the characters' feelings in complete sentences.

ELA ACADEMIC LANGUAGE

- illustration, author, folktale
- Cognates: *ilustración, autor*

MATERIALS

Literature Anthology, pp. 10–29

Visual Vocabulary Cards

DIGITAL TOOLS

Have children listen to the selection to develop comprehension as they follow along.

Use the additional grammar video.

Grammar Video

Little Rabbit

Prepare to Read

Build Background *We are going to read a folktale about a rabbit who is very worried that something bad is happening.* Show the picture on the title page, and invite children to tell what they see. Point to the rabbit, flowers, and grass as you say the words *rabbit, flowers,* and *grass.* Have children repeat. Then point again to the rabbit. *This is Little Rabbit. Little Rabbit is running because he is scared.* Review that *scared* is another word for *afraid. Have you ever been scared? What did you do? I was scared during _____, so I _____.*

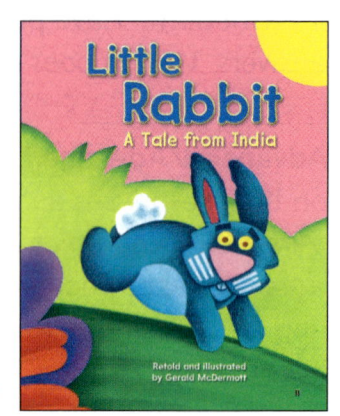

Literature Anthology, Lexile 180L

Focus on Vocabulary Use the **Visual Vocabulary Cards** to review the high-frequency words *about, animal, carry, eight, give,* and *our* and the oral vocabulary words *appearance, determined, feature, predicament,* and *relief.* Before reading the story, clarify vocabulary children will need for understanding. As you read, use gestures and pantomime to teach important story words, such as *falling.*

Summarize the Text Before reading, say the summary while pointing to the illustrations. *The story tells about Little Rabbit, who thinks the forest is falling. He runs through the forest and tells the other animals the forest is falling. Finally, Lion stops them and shows them the forest isn't falling.*

Read the Text

Use the Interactive Question-Response routine to help children understand the story.

Pages 12–15

Page 13 Read the text. Point to Little Rabbit. *What does Little Rabbit think could happen?* Little Rabbit thinks the forest could fall. *Little Rabbit starts to think the forest could fall. He is worried.* Say *worried. When you are* worried, *you think about a problem that might happen. What does Little Rabbit worry about?* Little Rabbit worries about what will happen to him if the forest falls. *What does the picture show is falling?* (a banana) *Do you think the forest is falling?* (no)

Page 15 Read the text. Point to Little Rabbit. *What is Little Rabbit doing?* Little Rabbit is hopping/running. *What does Little Rabbit yell to Fox?* "The forest is falling!" *Do you think Fox will feel scared?* (yes/no) *What does Little Rabbit want Fox to do?* Little Rabbit wants Fox to leave and run with him.

COLLABORATE *How do the illustrations help you know how Little Rabbit is feeling? Discuss with a partner.*

160 UNIT 4 WEEK 1

WEEK 1

Beginning Point to page 15. Say: *People and animals run when they are scared. Does Little Rabbit look scared?* Yes, Little Rabbit looks scared. *What is he doing in the illustration?* He is running/hopping.

Intermediate Have partners discuss the pictures on pages 13 and 15. *What is Little Rabbit doing in this illustration?* Little Rabbit is thinking/running. *How does Little Rabbit look?* He looks worried/scared.

Advanced/Advanced High Guide children to extend their thinking. *What other details in the illustrations tell you more about Little Rabbit?* Little Rabbit's eyes look very big. When someone is scared, his or her eyes are often very big.

Pages 16–21

Page 17 Read the text. *Deer asks a question like Fox's question. What does Deer ask?* Why are you running so fast? *Does Deer join Little Rabbit and Fox?* (yes)

Page 18 Read the text. *Three animals are running now. They stop for Ox. What does Ox think they are doing?* Ox thinks they are playing a game.

Page 19 Read the text. *What wakes up Tiger?* (the running animals) *How do you know Tiger will join them?* Tiger says, "Wait for me."

COLLABORATE *How does the author show how news about the forest spreads? Discuss with a partner.*

Beginning Point to page 17: *Who tells Deer the forest is falling?* Fox tells Deer. Point to page 18: *Who tells Ox the forest is falling?* Deer tells Ox. Point to page 19. *Who tells Tiger the forest is falling?* (Ox)

Intermediate Point to page 19. *Does the author have the first animal or the last animal tell Tiger the forest is falling?* The author has the last animal tell Tiger.

Advanced/Advanced High Help children extend their thinking. *Why does the author have other animals say the forest is falling?* The author wants to show they think the forest is falling too.

Pages 22–27

Pages 24–25 Read the text. Point to page 24. *Who is talking?* (Lion) *What does Lion want to know?* (who said the forest is falling) Point to the word *thump* on page 25. *A thump is a sound made when something falls. What does Lion want to do?* Lion wants to visit the place where Little Rabbit heard a big thump.

COLLABORATE *How does the story change when Lion appears? Discuss with a partner.*

Beginning Point to the picture on page 24. *Are the animals running?* No, the animals are not running. *What are the animals doing?* The animals are listening. *Whom are the animals listening to?* The animals are listening to Lion.

Intermediate Help partners review to respond. *What are the animals doing on the other pages?* On the other pages, the animals are running. *Are the animals running now?* No, the animals are not running. *Why do the animals stop running?* The animals stop to listen to Lion.

Advanced/Advanced High Help children extend their thinking. *How do the other animals respond when they hear the forest is falling?* They are scared, and they run. *How does Lion respond?* Lion asks to see where the forest is falling. *How does Little Rabbit respond to Lion?* He lets Lion carry him.

FORMATIVE ASSESSMENT

STUDENT CHECK IN

Have partners retell how the other characters react to Little Rabbit's news. Have partners discuss how the characters' feelings change. Then have children reflect, using the Check-In routine.

Independent Time

Role Play Select a spread from *Little Rabbit*. Pair or group children of mixed proficiencies. Have them prepare a role play of the spread. Encourage children to reread the spread as they prepare and to think about performing the role play with appropriate intonation. Then have children rehearse their role play. After they have rehearsed, encourage them to share their role play with another pair or small group or with the whole class.

ENGLISH LANGUAGE LEARNERS 161

LESSONS 4–5

READING • LEVELED READER • ACCESS THE TEXT

LEARNING GOALS

We can ask and answer questions to understand a folktale.

OBJECTIVES

Ask and answer questions about key details in a text.

Describe major events in a story, using key details.

Compare and contrast the adventures and experiences of characters in stories.

Ask questions to clear up any confusion about the topics and texts under discussion.

LANGUAGE OBJECTIVES

Children will narrate how the characters compete in a race, using adjectives.

ELA ACADEMIC LANGUAGE

- sequence, folktale
- Cognate: *secuencia*

MATERIALS

ELL Leveled Reader:
Snail's Clever Idea

Online Differentiated Text,
"Giraffe's Neck"

Online ELL Visual Vocabulary Cards

DIGITAL TOOLS

Have children listen to the selection as they follow along to develop comprehension and practice fluency and pronunciation. Use Graphic Organizer 6: Sequence of Events, Time Order to enhance the lesson.

Snail's Clever Idea

Prepare to Read

Build Background

- Remind children of the Essential Question. *Let's read to see how one animal's body helps it.* Encourage children to ask for help when they do not understand a word or phrase.

- Point to and read aloud the title, and have children repeat. Ask: *What is the title?* Have children point to it. Explain that *clever* means "quick to learn." Point to the illustrations in the **Leveled Reader** to name things and actions. For example: *The fox is laughing. When do you laugh?*

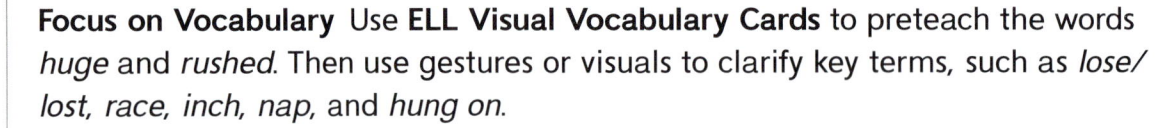

Lexile 400L

Focus on Vocabulary Use **ELL Visual Vocabulary Cards** to preteach the words *huge* and *rushed*. Then use gestures or visuals to clarify key terms, such as *lose/lost, race, inch, nap,* and *hung on*.

Read the Text

Use the Interactive Question-Response routine to help children understand the story.

Pages 2–5

Ask and Answer Questions Read pages 2–5 as children follow along. Guide children to ask and answer questions to understand the text. Model for children: *What will Fox and Snail do?* Fox and Snail will race. *Why does Fox laugh?* Fox laughs because Snail is so small.

Beginning Help partners point to the pictures as they respond. *Which animal is big?* Fox is big. *Which animal is small?* Snail is small.

Intermediate Help partners respond. *Why does Fox think he will win the race?* Fox thinks he will win because he is bigger than Snail.

Pages 6–7

Read pages 6–7 as children follow along. Ask questions to help children ask and answer questions about the story. *Why does Fox take a nap?* Fox takes a nap to give Snail a head start. This means Snail will start first. *What does Snail do while Fox is asleep?* Snail walks onto Fox's tail. Fox will carry Snail to the gate.

Intermediate *What is Snail's idea to help him win the race?* Snail's idea is to hide in Fox's tail. Fox will carry Snail in the race.

Advanced/Advanced High Have partners discuss Snail's idea. Ask: *Can Snail win the race with this idea? Why?*

162 UNIT 4 WEEK 1

WEEK 1

Pages 8–12

Main Story Elements: Sequence of Events Read pages 8–11 as children follow. Ask questions to help them describe sequence. *What happens after Fox stops?* Snail walks to the gate. Snail wins the race.

Beginning Help partners work together to respond. *What happens after Fox goes to the gate?* He sees Snail. *What happens when he sees Snail?* Fox knows he has lost the race.

Advanced/Advanced High Have partners look at each spread. *Explain how Fox realizes he has lost the race.* He realizes he has lost when he sees Snail at the gate in front of him.

Respond to Reading Have partners work together to retell the story and respond to the questions on page 12.

Focus on Fluency

Read pages 10–11 to model reading with accuracy. Read the passage again, and have children repeat after you. For more practice, record children reading the passage. Have them select the best recording.

Paired Read: "Snails: Small, Slow, and Slimy"

Analytical Writing **Make Connections: Write About It**

Echo-read each page with children. Discuss what the chart shows: *The chart shows where snails live. Where do snails live?* Snails live under rocks and logs. Help children make connections between texts, using the prompt on page 15. Snails can hang on to things because they are slimy.

Leveled Reader

Build Knowledge: Make Connections

Talk About the Text Have partners discuss how the animals' bodies in the texts help them.

Write About the Text Have students add their ideas to the Build Knowledge pages of their reader's notebooks.

Self-Selected Reading

Help children choose a nonfiction selection from the online **Leveled Reader Library**, or read the **Differentiated Text**, "Giraffe's Neck."

FOCUS ON GENRE

Children can extend their knowledge of characteristics of folktales by completing the genre activity on page 16.

LITERATURE CIRCLES

Lead children in conducting a literature circle using the Thinkmark questions to guide the discussion. You may wish to discuss what children have learned about how different animals use their bodies from both selections in the **Leveled Reader**.

FORMATIVE ASSESSMENT

❯ STUDENT CHECK IN

Have partners share their Respond to Reading. Have children reflect using the Check-In Routine.

LEVEL UP

IF children can read *Snail's Clever Idea* **ELL Level** with fluency and correctly answer the Respond to Reading questions,

THEN tell children they will read a more detailed version of the story.

- Use pages 2–3 of *Snail's Clever Idea* **On Level** to model using Teaching Poster 31 to list events for the *First* box.

- Have children read the selection, checking their comprehension by using the graphic organizer.

ENGLISH LANGUAGE LEARNERS 163

LESSONS 4–5

READING • GENRE PASSAGE • ACCESS THE TEXT

LEARNING GOALS

We can apply skills and strategies to a folktale.

OBJECTIVES

Ask and answer questions about key details in a text.

Describe characters and major events in a story, using key details.

Use illustrations and details in a story to describe its characters, setting, or events.

Ask questions to clear up any confusion about the topics and texts under discussion.

LANGUAGE OBJECTIVES

Children will narrate the sequence of the story, using words *first* and *next*.

Children will inquire about the story by ask and answer questions.

ELA ACADEMIC LANGUAGE

- questions, sequence, folktale
- Cognate: *secuencia*

MATERIALS

Online ELL Genre Passage, "The Magpie's Nest"

"The Magpie's Nest"

Prepare to Read

Build Background Review what children have learned about how animals' bodies help them. *What are some ways that animals use their bodies?* Animals use their bodies to ____. Allow children to share ideas about ways animals use their bodies. Tell children they will be reading about how a bird uses its beak to make a nest.

Lexile 300L

Focus on Vocabulary Use the **Define, Example, Ask** routine to preteach difficult or unfamiliar story words, such as *nest, teach, mud,* and *twigs.* As you read, use gestures or visuals to clarify other story words as needed.

Read the Text

Use the Interactive Question-Response routine to help children understand the story.

Page E1

Paragraphs 1–2 Read the text aloud as children follow along. Point to the illustration. *There are many birds in the picture.* Point to the bird in the nest. *This bird is called a* magpie. Remind children that they can **use a dictionary** to find meanings of unfamiliar words. *Its name in the story is also Magpie. Say* magpie *with me. Which bird has a nest?* Magpie has a nest.

Beginning Point to the birds outside the nest in the illustration. *Do these birds have nests?* No, they do not have nests. *Does Magpie have a nest?* (yes) *What do the other birds want?* The other birds want to make nests like Magpie's nest.

Paragraphs 3–5 Read the text aloud as children follow along. Point to and say the phrase *hard work,* and have children repeat it. *Hard work is difficult work that takes a long time to do.* Model **asking and answering** questions: *What does Magpie say is hard work?* Magpie says it is hard work to make a nest.

Advanced/Advanced High Have partners *ask and answer:* Why do you think Owl says "Uh oh" after Magpie says making a nest is hard work? Owl might know that the other birds do not like to work hard. Do you think the other birds will learn to build nests? No, the birds will not learn because they do not like to work hard.

Page E2

Paragraphs 1–2 Read the text aloud. Help children talk about *sequence.* Ask: *What is the first thing Magpie gets?* First, Magpie gets mud. *What does Thrush do when Magpie gets mud?* Thrush says he will make a mud nest. Then he flies away.

164 UNIT 4 WEEK 1

WEEK 1

Intermediate Have partners *ask and answer questions:* What is the first thing Magpie gets? The first thing Magpie gets is mud. Is Magpie done telling how to make a nest? No, Magpie is not done. Why does Thrush fly off? He wants to make his nest out of only mud.

Paragraphs 3–4 Read the text aloud as children follow along. *What is the next thing Magpie gets?* Magpie gets twigs. *What does Blackbird do after Magpie gets twigs?* Blackbird flies away. She makes a nest of twigs.

Beginning Have children work with a partner to describe the *sequence* of events. Provide sentence frames to help children respond: First, Magpie gets mud. Next, Magpie gets twigs.

Paragraphs 5–7 Read the text aloud. Say the word *silly,* and make a silly face. Have children repeat. *Something that is silly is not serious. Why does Magpie say the birds are silly?* They do not learn what Magpie can teach them.

Advanced Ask: *What does Magpie do?* Have partners explain: Magpie works hard on the nest. *What does Magpie think of the other birds?* She thinks the other birds don't want to work hard.

Advanced High Have children discuss with a partner: *Why do the birds make different nests?* Encourage children to include details from the folktale in their response: The birds make different nests because they pick different materials to use.

Respond to Reading

Use the following instructions to help children answer the questions on page E3.

1. **Folktale** Have children describe the illustrations. Ask questions to help them complete the sentence: *Do all the birds look the same?* (No, they have different colors.) *Why do all the birds' nests look different?* (They use different things to make their nests.) *How can you tell this story is a folktale?* (Possible answer: It has animal characters.)

2. **Main Story Elements: Sequence** Discuss the order of events in the story with children. Ask: *What do the other birds do after Magpie tries to teach them?* (They leave to make their nests.) *What does Magpie think about the other birds?* (She thinks they are silly. She can't teach them.)

3. **Fluency** Have children take turns reading the passage to a partner. As they read, have them fill in the chart on page E3.

Build Knowledge: Make Connections

Talk About the Text Have partners discuss how the birds' bodies help them build nests.

Write About the Text Have students add their ideas to the Build Knowledge pages of their reader's notebooks.

FORMATIVE ASSESSMENT

⊘ STUDENT CHECK IN

Have partners share their Respond to Reading. Then have children reflect, using the Check-In routine.

LEVEL UP

IF children read the **ELL Level** fluently and answered the questions,

THEN pair them with children who have proficiently read the **On Level.** Have them

- partner read the **On Level** passage.
- describe the sequence of events in the story.

ENGLISH LANGUAGE LEARNERS **165**

LESSONS 1–5

WRITING

MODELED WRITING

LESSON 1

LEARNING GOALS
We can learn how to write using descriptive words.

OBJECTIVES
Write narratives in which they include some details.

LANGUAGE OBJECTIVES
Children will inform by writing a sentence with a descriptive word.

ELA ACADEMIC LANGUAGE
- analyze, descriptive
- Cognates: *analizar, descriptivo*

Writing Practice Review the sample on p. 24 of the **Reading/Writing Companion**. Help children use the Actor/Action routine to analyze each sentence: The actors in this sentence are John and I. The action is (we) did it. Then read the prompt on p. 25, and guide a volunteer to answer it. *What did you do?* (I finished a puzzle.) *How can you describe the puzzle?* It was a tough puzzle. Rewrite the sentence on the board for children to chorally read. Then have partners work on their own sentences together.

Beginning Help partners create their sentence: *Who is the actor?* (I) *What did you do?* (built) *What did you build?* (a model airplane) Provide a sentence frame if needed.

Intermediate Have partners ask and answer *who/what* questions to create their sentences. Help children add a descriptive word.

Advanced/Advanced High Challenge children to include at least one descriptive word in their sentences.

FORMATIVE ASSESSMENT ▶ **STUDENT CHECK IN** Partners share their sentences. Ask children to reflect, using the Check-In routine.

INTERACTIVE WRITING

LESSON 2

LEARNING GOALS
We can read and write about a Student Model.

OBJECTIVES
With guidance and support from adults, focus on a topic.

LANGUAGE OBJECTIVES
Children will discuss and write sentences about the Student Model, identifying the verb *was*.

ELA ACADEMIC LANGUAGE
- descriptive, prompt
- Cognate: *descriptivo*

Analyze the Student Model Have children finger point as they chorally read the Student Model on p. 32 of the **Reading/Writing Companion**. Use the Actor/Action routine to review each sentence: *Who are the actors?* (Frog and Snail) *What do we know about them?* (They were off.) Check that children understand the meaning of this idiom. (They had started the race.) Then point out the verb *was*. Ask whether it tells about one thing or more than one thing. Then help children complete p. 33.

Beginning Have partners point to examples of descriptive words from the text. Then provide a sentence frame: I notice the descriptive word *sticky*.

Intermediate Have partners ask and answer questions: What do you notice about Ana's writing? Ana uses the verb *was*.

Advanced/Advanced High Challenge children to use their own sentences to write about the text. Encourage children to share their ideas.

FORMATIVE ASSESSMENT ▶ **STUDENT CHECK IN** Partners share their responses. Ask children to reflect, using the Check-In routine.

WEEK 1

INDEPENDENT WRITING
LESSONS 3-4

LEARNING GOALS
We can use text evidence to respond to a folktale.

OBJECTIVES
Write informative texts in which they supply some facts about the topic.

LANGUAGE OBJECTIVES
Children will inform by writing sentences, using the verb *was* or *were*.

ELA ACADEMIC LANGUAGE
- *evidence*
- Cognate: *evidencia*

Find Text Evidence Use the **Independent Writing** routine. Help children use text evidence to orally retell the anchor text. Ask questions, such as: *What does Little Rabbit think?* (He thinks the forest is falling.) *What does he do?* (He runs; he tells the other animals.) Then read the prompt on p. 38 of the **Reading/Writing Companion**: *Based on the story, what is something Rabbit might be thinking about at the end? Use evidence from the text in your answer. We need to pay attention to how Rabbit looks at the end of the story. It is a clue to what he is thinking.*

Write a Response Work with children to fill out My Writing Outline 16. Then have them use the sentences from their outlines to complete p. 38.

Writing Checklist Read the checklist with students, and have them check for these items in their writing.

Beginning Have partners take turns reading their sentences to each other.

Intermediate Encourage partners to identify descriptive words.

Advanced/Advanced High Have partners identify where they used each item in their writing.

FORMATIVE ASSESSMENT ▶ **STUDENT CHECK IN** Partners share their sentences from My Writing Outline. Ask children to reflect, using the Check-in routine.

SELF-SELECTED WRITING
LESSON 5

LEARNING GOALS
We can revise our writing.

OBJECTIVES
Use singular and plural nouns with matching verbs in basic sentences.

LANGUAGE OBJECTIVES
Children will inquire about their writing by checking that *was* and *were* are used correctly.

ELA ACADEMIC LANGUAGE
- *publish*
- Cognate: *publicar*

Work with children to revise the group writing activity. Point to each word as you read the sentences. Stop to ask questions, such as, *Is was/were used correctly here?* If needed, write a sentence using *was/were* incorrectly, and work together to revise the sentence. Then have partners revise each other's sentences before publishing their writing.

For support with grammar and *was* and *were*, refer to the **Language Transfers Handbook** and **Language Development Card** 5B.

FORMATIVE ASSESSMENT ▶ **STUDENT CHECK IN** Partners tell what revisions they made. Ask children to reflect, using the Check-in routine.

ENGLISH LANGUAGE LEARNERS **167**

READING • SHARED READ • ACCESS THE TEXT

LESSONS 1–2

LEARNING GOALS
We can read and understand a nonfiction text.

OBJECTIVES
Describe the connection between two pieces of information in a text.

Use the illustrations and details in a text to describe its key ideas.

With prompting and support, read informational texts appropriately complex for grade 1.

Produce complete sentences when appropriate to task and situation.

LANGUAGE OBJECTIVES
Children will inform about how fish work as a team, using key vocabulary and simple sentences.

ELA ACADEMIC LANGUAGE
- nonfiction, image
- Cognates: *no ficción, imagen*

MATERIALS
Reading/Writing Companion, pp. 50–59

Visual Vocabulary Cards

DIGITAL TOOLS
Have children listen to the selection as they follow along to develop comprehension and practice fluency and pronunciation.

Use the online ELL Vocabulary Practice for additional support.

"A Team of Fish"

Prepare to Read

Build Background Read aloud the Essential Question on page 50. Have children share what they know about how animals help each other. Use the images on pages 56 and 57 to generate ideas. Point to and read the title aloud. *We are going to read a nonfiction text about fish and how they work together as a team. A team is usually a group of people who play or work together. Do you play on a team?* Point to the picture of one of the fish. *This is a fish. Say* fish *with me.* Point to the group of fish. *The fish swim together in a big group. Fish can help each other when they swim in a big group.*

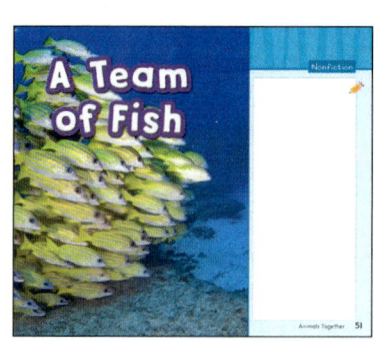

Reading/Writing Companion, Lexile 340L

Focus on Vocabulary Use the **Visual Vocabulary Cards** to review the high-frequency words *because, blue, into, or, other,* and *small* and the oral vocabulary words *behavior, beneficial, dominant, endangered,* and *instinct.* As you read, use gestures and visual support to teach important selection words, such as *danger, partner, alone, bunch,* and *school.*

Summarize the Text Before reading, say the summary while pointing to the photographs. *The text tells about why fish swim together. Fish swim together in schools to help each other look for food and stay safe.*

Read the Text

Use the Interactive Question-Response routine to help children understand the text.

Pages 52–55

Page 53 Read the text aloud as children follow along. *Fish can swim alone. Can you show me a fish that is alone?* Guide children to point to a single fish. Point to two fish near each other. *What do we call two fish who swim together?* Fish who swim together are partners. Have children give examples of activities they might do with a partner: I play catch with a partner. Point to the word *school. A school is a big group of fish. Can you point to the school of fish in this image? How many fish are in this school?* There are about ten fish in this school.

What are the different ways fish swim? Discuss with a partner.

Beginning Point to the fish swimming alone near the bottom of the page. *Can fish swim alone?* Yes, fish can swim alone. Point to the group of fish in the center of the page. *Can fish swim in a bunch?* Yes, fish can swim in a bunch. *What is another name for a bunch of fish?* Another name for a bunch of fish is a school.

168 UNIT 4 WEEK 2

WEEK 2

Intermediate Guide partners to point to the pictures as they respond. *Can fish swim alone?* Yes, fish can swim alone. Have children point to a fish swimming alone. Repeat for fish swimming in pairs and in a school.

Advanced/Advanced High Help partners extend their thinking. *Why might fish swim in different ways?* Have partners consider why fish might swim alone or in a school. Help children respond with a sentence frame: Fish might swim alone to get more food.

Pages 56–57

Page 56 Read the page aloud, and have children follow along. Point to the word *chief,* and say it aloud for children to repeat. Chief *is another word for* main or most important. *What is the chief reason you come to school?* The chief reason I come to school is to learn. *What is the chief reason it is not safe for fish to swim alone?* The chief reason it is not safe is danger. Then help children infer what the sentence with *snapped up* means. A fish can get caught and eaten.

Why do fish swim together? Discuss with a partner.

Beginning Point to the large, single fish on the page. *Can a fish hide when it's swimming alone?* (no) Point to the school of fish. *Can a fish hide in a school?* Yes, a fish can hide in a school.

Intermediate Help partners give details in their answers. *What can happen to a fish swimming alone?* A fish alone can get snapped up. *What can fish do in a school?* Fish can hide in a school.

Advanced/Advanced High Help partners extend their thinking. *How does the school benefit small fish?* Small fish can hide from bigger fish.

Pages 58–59

Page 58 Read the text aloud, and have children follow along. *Where is the big fish?* Have children point to the big fish. *Does the big fish go near the school?* No, the big fish stays away. *What does the school look like?* The school looks like a huge fish!

How does swimming in a school help keep fish safe? Discuss with a partner.

Beginning Point to a fish in the school of fish. *Is this fish big or small?* That fish is small. Point to the school of fish. *Is the school big or small?* The school is big. *Is the big fish scared of a small fish?* (no) *Is the big fish scared of a school of fish?* (yes)

Intermediate Help partners add details to their answers. *Is the school of fish big or small?* The school of fish is big. *What does the school look like to the big fish?* The school looks like a huge fish.

Advanced/Advanced High Help partners elaborate on their answers. *What does the school of fish do that a fish swimming alone can't?* The school of fish looks big. The school of fish scares away the big fish.

FORMATIVE ASSESSMENT

❯ STUDENT CHECK IN

Have partners retell how swimming in a group can help fish of all sizes. Then, have children reflect using the Check-In Routine.

Independent Time

Write a Chant Put children into groups of mixed proficiencies. Have groups write a chant about how fish work as a team and help each other. If children need support getting started, have them complete sentence frames to gather ideas about how fish help each other: Fish can hide in a school. Schools make fish look huge. Schools make big fish stay away. Schools keep fish safe. Then help groups put their words into a rhyme. Encourage groups to use clapping, snapping, or stomping. Have them practice and present them to another group or the whole class.

ENGLISH LANGUAGE LEARNERS **169**

LESSON 3

READING • ANCHOR TEXT • ACCESS THE TEXT

LEARNING GOALS

We can read and understand a nonfiction text.

OBJECTIVES

Distinguish between information provided by pictures or other illustrations and information provided by the words in a text.

Use the illustrations and details in a text to describe its key ideas.

Identify the reasons an author gives to support points in a text.

Build on others' talk in conversations by responding to the comments of others through multiple exchanges.

LANGUAGE OBJECTIVES

Children will inform about how animal teams work together, using singular and plural nouns.

ELA ACADEMIC LANGUAGE

- photographs, author, label
- Cognates: *fotografías, autor*

MATERIALS

Literature Anthology, pp. 36–55

Visual Vocabulary Cards

DIGITAL TOOLS

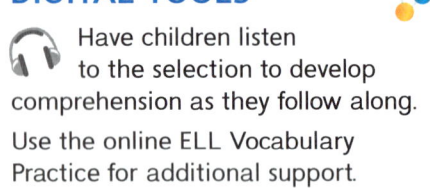

Have children listen to the selection to develop comprehension as they follow along.

Use the online ELL Vocabulary Practice for additional support.

Animal Teams

Prepare to Read

Build Background *We are going to read a nonfiction text about how different animals help one another. Nonfiction texts give true information.* Display the title page, and invite children to tell what they see. Point to the two fish. *These two fish can help each other.* Then display pages 38–39. Point to the *giraffe* and the *bird*, then the *shrimp* and the *fish*. Say the words, and have children repeat. *The animals in each pair are different, but they can help each another. Does someone at school help you? My _____ helps me when _____.*

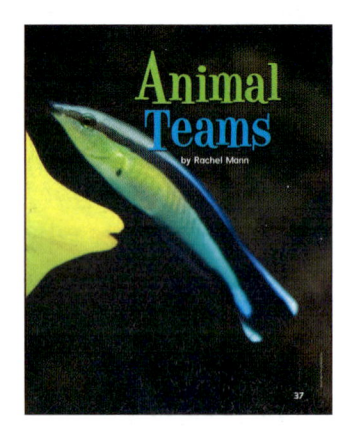

Literature Anthology, Lexile 480L

Focus on Vocabulary Use the **Visual Vocabulary Cards** to review the high-frequency words *because, blue, into, or,* and *other* and the oral vocabulary words *behavior, beneficial, dominant, endangered,* and *instinct*. Before reading the text, clarify any vocabulary words children will need for understanding. As you read, use gestures and pantomime to teach important story words or phrases, such as *odd friends*.

Summarize the Text Before reading, say the summary while pointing to the illustrations. *The text tells about unexpected animal teams. These teams are very different, but the animals help each other in important ways.*

Read the Text

Use the Interactive Question-Response routine to help children understand the text.

Pages 38–43

Pages 40–41 Read the text. Point to the giraffe, and say: *This is a giraffe.* Have children repeat. *Where are the birds?* One bird is on the giraffe's back. The other bird is on the giraffe's head. *What is that bird doing?* It is eating bugs off the giraffe's head. *Does this help the giraffe?* (yes) *How does this help the bird?* It gives the bird food to eat and keeps the bird safe.

Pages 42–43 Read the text. Point to the goby fish and the blind shrimp on page 42. *This fish and shrimp are an animal team. They help each other.* Point to the goby fish. *This fish can see. Can the blind shrimp see?* No, the blind shrimp cannot see. *How does the goby help the shrimp?* The goby looks for danger. *How does the shrimp know when it's time to hide?* It's time to hide when the goby flicks its tail. Point to the shrimp on page 43. *The shrimp helps the goby too. How does the shrimp help the goby?* The shrimp lets the goby hide.

How do the text and photographs help you understand how the animals work as a team? Discuss with a partner.

170 UNIT 4 WEEK 2

WEEK 2

Beginning Point to the picture of the shrimp and goby fish on page 43. *What do you see in the photograph?* I see the shrimp and goby fish. *Does the text say they hide or swim?* The text says they hide. *Where do they hide?* They hide in a hole. Guide children to point to the hole around the animals in the photo.

Intermediate Point to the picture on page 43. *What does the photograph show?* The photograph shows the shrimp and goby fish. *What do both the text and the photograph help you understand?* The text and photo help me understand that the shrimp and fish hide together.

Advanced/Advanced High Extend the discussion by having partners tell more information they learned from both the text and the photograph. I learned that the shrimp and goby fish hide together. I learned that they hide in a hole until it seems safe to leave/go out.

Pages 44–47

Page 46–47 Read the text. *What does the clown fish need?* The clown fish needs a safe home. *Where does the clown fish live?* It lives in the sea anemone. *The sea anemone helps the clown fish by stinging other fish. The word* stinging *means "hurting with a sharp pointed part." Bees can sting too.* Ask: *Does the clown fish help the sea anemone?* (yes) *How?* It chases away big fish from the sea anemone.

How does the author help you understand the information about this animal team? Discuss with a partner.

Beginning Help partners point to the pictures as they respond. *The clown fish lives in the sea anemone. Point to the sea anemone. Is the clown fish safe here?* (yes) *Point to where the author tells why.* Have children point to the question and answer on page 46.

Intermediate Help partners review to respond. *Point to where the author asks a question. What does the author ask?* The author asks why the clown fish is safe.

Advanced/Advanced High Have partners extend their thinking by discussing other questions the author could ask to help readers understand. For example: *Does the sea anemone's sting hurt the clown fish?*

Pages 48–51

Page 50 Read the text. *The author shares another example of an animal team.* Point to the cleaner fish. *How does the cleaner fish help other fish?* It cleans the other fish. *How does this help the cleaner fish?* The cleaner fish gets food.

Why does the author show so many different animal teams? Discuss with a partner.

Beginning Display the photos of different animal teams. *Do the animals on each team help each other?* Yes, the animals on each team help each other.

Intermediate Help partners review to respond. *Are the animals in a team often similar or different?* The animals in a team are often different.

Advanced/Advanced High Extend the discussion. Have partners ask and answer: How have the different examples changed how you think about animal teams? I understand that many different animals help each other.

FORMATIVE ASSESSMENT

> STUDENT CHECK IN

Have partners retell different ways animals help each other. Then have children reflect, using the Check-In routine.

Independent Time

Draw and Share Help children make connections between the ideas in the text and their own lives. Pair children of mixed proficiencies. Have partners discuss: *How do people in your family help each other?* Have pairs take turns asking and answering questions. Provide sentence frames to help children respond: How does your mother help you? My mother helps me by making dinner. How do you help your mother? I help my mother by setting the table. Then have children draw a picture to show how people in their families help each other. Have children label their illustrations and then share them with the group and tell how people in their families help each other.

ENGLISH LANGUAGE LEARNERS 171

LESSONS 4–5

READING • LEVELED READER • ACCESS THE TEXT

LEARNING GOALS

We can ask and answer questions to understand a nonfiction text.

OBJECTIVES

Identify the main topic and retell key details of a text.

Use the illustrations and details in a text to describe its key ideas.

Identify basic similarities in and differences between two texts on the same topic (e.g., in illustrations, descriptions, or procedures).

Ask questions to clear up any confusion about the topics and texts under discussion.

LANGUAGE OBJECTIVES

Children will inquire about penguins by asking and answering questions about the text.

ELA ACADEMIC LANGUAGE

- details
- Cognate: *detalles*

MATERIALS

ELL Leveled Reader: *Penguins All Around*

Online Differentiated Text, "Wolf Pack!"

Online ELL Visual Vocabulary Cards

DIGITAL TOOLS

Have children listen to the selection as they follow along to develop comprehension and practice fluency and pronunciation. Use Graphic Organizer 6: Topic and Relevant Details to enhance the lesson.

Penguins All Around

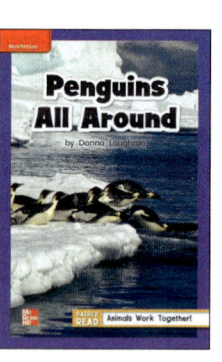

Prepare to Read

Build Background

- Remind children of the Essential Question: *Let's read to find out how animals help each other.* Encourage children to ask for help when they do not understand a word or phrase.
- Point to and read aloud the title, and have children repeat it. Ask: *What is the title?* Have children point to it. Repeat with the author's name. Point to the photos in the Leveled Reader to name things and actions. *This is a penguin's nest. What is the penguin's nest made of?*

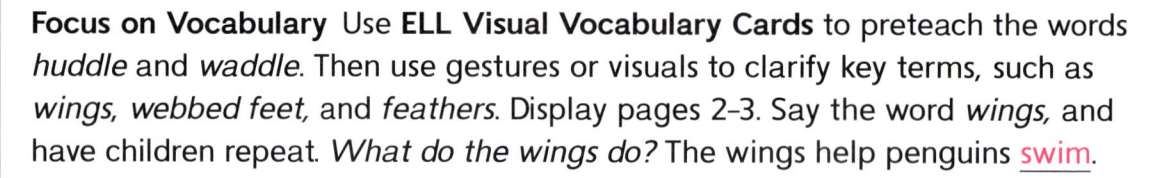

Lexile 340L

Focus on Vocabulary Use **ELL Visual Vocabulary Cards** to preteach the words *huddle* and *waddle*. Then use gestures or visuals to clarify key terms, such as *wings*, *webbed feet*, and *feathers*. Display pages 2–3. Say the word *wings,* and have children repeat. *What do the wings do?* The wings help penguins swim.

Read the Text

Use the Interactive Question-Response routine to help children understand the text.

Pages 2–5

Beginning Help partners point to the pictures as they respond. *What are the penguins doing?* They are diving into the water. *What are the penguins looking for?* Point to the picture that shows what they are looking for.

Intermediate Help partners respond: *Why are the penguins diving?* The penguins are looking for food. *What do penguins eat?* Penguins eat krill.

Advanced/Advanced High *Why do penguins dive into the sea?* Penguins dive into the sea to look for food. They eat krill.

Topic and Relevant Details Read page 5 as children follow along. Discuss the topic and relevant details with them. *The topic tells that penguins eat small fish. What are the details?* The penguins eat krill. Krill look like small shrimp.

Pages 6–9

Ask and Answer Questions Read page 8. Guide partners to ask and answer questions about penguins' nests. Point to the nest. Model asking a question: *This nest is made of grass. Some are made of stones. Why are some nests made of grass and others made of stones?*

Beginning Guide pairs to ask and answer about the caption: Did this penguin use stones or grass for its nest? This penguin used grass.

172 UNIT 4 WEEK 2

WEEK 2

Intermediate Have pairs ask and answer: Did this penguin use stones for its nest? (no) What did this penguin use? This penguin used grass.

Pages 10–12

Read page 10 as children follow along. *After the chicks hatch, Mom and Dad care for them. The picture shows Mom feeding her chick.*

Intermediate Have pairs use the picture on the left to respond. *What is the penguin doing?* The penguin is keeping the chicks warm.

Advanced/Advanced High Have partners ask and answer: How do penguins care for their chicks? They keep their chicks warm and fed.

Respond to Reading Have partners work together to retell the story and respond to the questions on page 12.

Focus on Fluency

Read pages 10–11 to model appropriate phrasing. Read the passage again, and have children repeat after you.
For more practice, record children reading the passage. Have them select the best recording for you.

Paired Read: "Animals Work Together!"

Analytical Writing **Make Connections: Write About It**

Echo-read each page with children. Discuss how animals live and work together: Dolphins live in groups. They stay safe together. Help children make connections between texts: Penguins are like ants because they build nests.

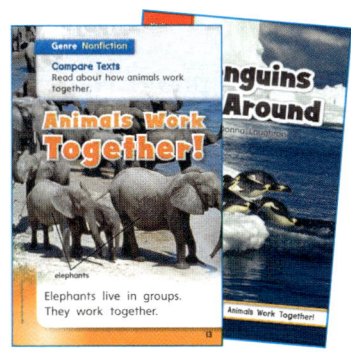

Leveled Reader

Build Knowledge: Make Connections

Talk About the Text Have partners discuss how the animals in these texts help each other.

Write About the Text Have students add their ideas to the Build Knowledge pages of their reader's notebooks.

Self-Selected Reading

Help children choose a nonfiction selection from the online **Leveled Reader Library**, or read the **Differentiated Text**, "Wolf's Pack!"

FOCUS ON SCIENCE

Children can extend their knowledge of animals by completing the science activity on page 16.
STEM

LITERATURE CIRCLES

Lead children in conducting a literature circle using the Thinkmark questions to guide the discussion. You may wish to discuss what children have learned from both selections in the **Leveled Reader** about how different groups of animals help each other.

FORMATIVE ASSESSMENT

STUDENT CHECK IN

Have partners share their Respond to Reading. Then have children reflect, using the Check-In routine.

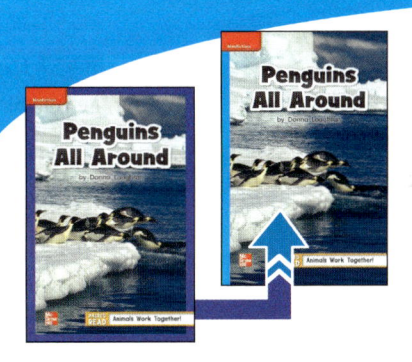

LEVEL UP

IF children can read *Penguins All Around* **ELL Level** with fluency and correctly answer the Respond to Reading questions,

THEN tell children they will read a more detailed version of the selection.

- Use pages 2–3 of *Penguins All Around* **On Level** to model using Teaching Poster 33 to list key details.

- Have children read the selection, checking their comprehension by using the graphic organizer.

ENGLISH LANGUAGE LEARNERS 173

LESSONS 4–5

READING • GENRE PASSAGE • ACCESS THE TEXT

LEARNING GOALS

We can apply skills and strategies to a nonfiction text.

OBJECTIVES

Ask and answer questions about key details in a text.

Identify the main topic and retell key details of a text.

Describe the connection between two individuals, events, ideas, or pieces of information in a text.

Produce complete sentences when appropriate to task and situation.

LANGUAGE OBJECTIVES

Children will discuss the topic and relevant details using complete sentences.

Children will inquire about the topic by asking and answering questions.

ELA ACADEMIC LANGUAGE

- relevant details, illustration, nonfiction
- Cognates: *detalles relevantes, ilustración, no ficción*

MATERIALS

Online ELL Genre Passage, "The Ocean Food Chain"

"The Ocean Food Chain"

Prepare to Read

Build Background Review what children have learned about how animals help each other. *What is one way animals help each other?* Some animals _____ each other. Allow children to share ideas about other ways animals help each other. *We are going to read about how living things in the ocean help each other.*

Lexile 300L

Focus on Vocabulary Use the **Define, Example, Ask** routine to preteach difficult or unfamiliar selection words: *energy, pass, chain, link,* and *shines.* Use gestures or visuals to clarify other selection words as needed.

Read the Text

Use the Interactive Question-Response routine to help children understand the text.

Page E1

Paragraph 1 Read the text aloud. Remind children they can look at **sentence clues,** or how a word is used in the sentence, to figure out a word's meaning. Point to the word *energy.* Ask: *What does* energy *mean in this selection?* (something people and animals need to survive) *People and animals get energy from the food they eat. What is a food you eat that gives you energy?* [Apples] give(s) me energy.

Beginning Point to the photo. Have children identify the **topic and relevant details:** *In the photo, I see* fish *and* plants *in the ocean. What do all the plants and animals in the photo need?* The plants and animals need energy.

Paragraph 2 Read the text aloud. Point to the term *pass,* and pantomime passing an object to someone. Have children repeat. *To pass something is to give it to another. When living things pass energy, they give energy to another living thing.*

Advanced/Advanced High Point to the phrase *food chain.* Have children **ask and answer questions** with a partner: *Why is passing energy called a food chain?* Help children respond: *It's called a* food chain *because all the* parts *are* connected, *like a* chain.

Paragraph 3 Read the text aloud, and have children follow along. Point to the phrase *soak up,* and have children repeat. *The phrase* soak up *means "to take in and use." What do plants soak up?* Plants soak up the sun.

Intermediate Ask: *How do these* **relevant details** *tell the topic of the text?* Have partners discuss, using a sentence frame: These details tell how plants get energy.

174 UNIT 4 WEEK 2

WEEK 2

Page E2

Paragraph 1 Read the text aloud. Then say: *This illustration shows how living things pass energy to each other. Where do the plants get energy?* The plants gets energy from the sun.

Beginning Have partners *ask and answer questions* about how plants, small fish, and big fish get energy. Provide a model: Where do plants get energy? Plants get energy from the sun. Repeat with *small fish* and *big fish*.

Paragraphs 2–3 Read the text aloud. Remind children that *linked* means "connected." Ask: *How are the big fish and the biggest fish linked?* Big fish pass energy to the biggest fish.

Advanced Have partners point to parts of the illustration as they explain the entire food chain using sequence words: First, plants get energy from the sun. Next, small fish get energy from eating plants. Then, big fish get energy from eating small fish. Finally, the biggest fish get energy from eating big fish.

Advanced High Have partners *ask and answer:* What is this text mostly about? It is mostly about the food chain. Which details does the author include to explain the topic? The author tells how living things in the ocean get their energy.

Respond to Reading

Use the following instructions to help children answer the questions on page E3.

1. **Nonfiction** Remind children that a *fact* is what is known to be true. Ask questions, such as: *What is a fact on page E1? What is a fact on page E2?* (Possible answers: Plants get energy from the sun; small fish eat plants.) *What are the facts mostly about?* (a food chain in the ocean)

2. **Topic and Relevant Details** Guide children to understand the illustration. Ask: *What relevant or important details do the arrows show?* (how energy passes between living things) *What do the details in the illustration help you understand?* (which living things are part of the food chain)

3. **Fluency** Have children take turns reading the first paragraph to a partner. As they read, have them fill in the chart on page E3.

Build Knowledge: Make Connections

Talk About the Text Have partners discuss how the animals in this text help each other.

Write About the Text Have students add their ideas to the Build Knowledge pages of their reader's notebooks.

FORMATIVE ASSESSMENT

❯ STUDENT CHECK IN

Have partners share their Respond to Reading. Then have children reflect, using the Check-In routine.

LEVEL UP

IF children read the ELL Level fluently and answered the questions,

THEN pair them with children who have proficiently read the On Level. Have them

- partner read the On Level passage.
- identify the main idea of the text and explain key details that support the main idea.

ENGLISH LANGUAGE LEARNERS

LESSONS 1–5

WRITING

MODELED WRITING
LESSON 1

LEARNING GOALS

We can introduce a topic when we write.

OBJECTIVES

Write opinion pieces in which they state an opinion and supply reasons for the opinion.

LANGUAGE OBJECTIVES

Children will argue by writing a topic sentence using the verb *prefer*.

ELA ACADEMIC LANGUAGE

- opinion
- Cognate: *opinión*

Writing Practice Review the sample on p. 60 of the **Reading/Writing Companion**. Use the Actor/Action routine to guide children to analyze each sentence: *Who is the actor?* (I) *What is the action?* (like to cook with my family) Then read the prompt on p. 61, and ask children to answer it. Guide them to give a topic sentence and then a reason for the opinion. Write the sentences on the board for children to chorally read. Then ask partners to write their own sentences.

Beginning Help partners create their sentences: *Who is the actor?* (I) *What do you like to do?* (play baseball) *Do you like to play alone or with others?* (with my team) *Why?* (It is fun.) Provide sentence frames.

Intermediate Have partners ask and answer *who/what* questions to create their opinion sentences. Provide a sentence frame for the reason: It is fun to work together.

Advanced/Advanced High Challenge children to include a topic sentence and a reason for their opinions. Encourage children to share their ideas.

FORMATIVE ASSESSMENT ▶ **STUDENT CHECK IN** Partners share their sentences. Ask children to reflect, using the Check-In routine.

INTERACTIVE WRITING
LESSON 2

LEARNING GOALS

We can read and write about a Student Model.

OBJECTIVES

With guidance and support from adults, focus on a topic.

LANGUAGE OBJECTIVES

Children will discuss and write about the Student Model.

ELA ACADEMIC LANGUAGE

- opinion, evidence
- Cognates: *opinión, evidencia*

Analyze the Student Model Have children finger point as they chorally read the Student Model on p. 68 of the **Reading/Writing Companion**. Use the Actor/Action routine to review the first two sentences. Then guide children to think about the Writing Trait: *Which sentence introduces the topic?* (the first) *Which part of the second sentence is the opinion?* (It's good) *Which part is the reason?* (Little fish look for food together.) Then help children complete p. 69.

Beginning Have partners point to opinions and reasons in the text. Then provide a sentence frame: I notice the verb has. It tells about one fish.

Intermediate Have partners ask and answer questions: *What did you notice about Andrew's writing?* He uses reasons to support his opinions.

Advanced/Advanced High Challenge children to write their own sentences about the text. Encourage children to share their ideas.

FORMATIVE ASSESSMENT ▶ **STUDENT CHECK IN** Partners share their responses. Ask children to reflect, using the Check-In routine.

WEEK 2

INDEPENDENT WRITING

LESSONS 3-4

LEARNING GOALS

We can write an opinion about a nonfiction text.

OBJECTIVES

Write opinion pieces in which they state an opinion and supply reasons for the opinion.

LANGUAGE OBJECTIVES

Children will argue by writing a sentence that includes a topic.

ELA ACADEMIC LANGUAGE

- *opinion, reasons*
- Cognates: *opinión, razones*

Find Text Evidence Follow the Independent Writing routine. Help children use text evidence to orally retell the anchor text. Ask questions, such as: *How do some birds help big animals?* (They eat bugs off their skin.) *How do the goby fish and blind shrimp stay safe?* (The goby looks for danger; the shrimp shares its hiding place.) Then read the prompt on p. 74 of the **Reading/Writing Companion:** *Which animal team do you think is most interesting? Why? We need to give an opinion about the most interesting animal team. Then we need to give reasons for having this opinion.*

Write a Response Work with children to fill out My Writing Outline 17. Then have them use the sentences from their outlines to complete p. 74.

Writing Checklist Read the checklist with students, and have them check for these items in their writing.

Beginning Provide sentence frames to help partners talk about their sentences: I use the verb *have* in the *last* sentence.

Intermediate Encourage partners to identify their opinions and reasons.

Advanced/Advanced High Have partners identify where they used each item in their writing.

FORMATIVE ASSESSMENT > **STUDENT CHECK IN** Partners share their sentences from My Writing Outline. Ask children to reflect, using the Check-in routine.

SELF-SELECTED WRITING

LESSON 5

LEARNING GOALS

We can revise our writing.

OBJECTIVES

Use singular and plural nouns with matching verbs in basic sentences.

LANGUAGE OBJECTIVES

Children will inquire about their writing by identifying errors in using *has* or *have*.

ELA ACADEMIC LANGUAGE

- *analyze, descriptive*
- Cognates: *analizar, descriptivo*

Work with children to revise the group writing activity. Point to each word as you read the sentences. Stop to ask questions, such as: Is *has/have* used correctly here? If needed, write a sentence using *has/have* incorrectly, and work together to revise the sentence. Then have partners revise each other's sentences before publishing their writing.

For support with grammar and using *has* and *have,* refer to the **Language Transfers Handbook** and **Language Development Card** 6A.

FORMATIVE ASSESSMENT > **STUDENT CHECK IN** Partners tell what revisions they made. Ask children to reflect, using the Check-in routine.

ENGLISH LANGUAGE LEARNERS

LESSONS 1–2

READING • SHARED READ • ACCESS THE TEXT

LEARNING GOALS
We can read and understand a nonfiction text.

OBJECTIVES

Retell key details of a text.

Describe the connection between two individuals, events, ideas, or pieces of information in a text.

Know and use various text features (e.g., headings, tables of contents, glossaries, electronic menus, icons) to locate key facts or information in a text.

Build on others' talk in conversations by responding to the comments of others through multiple exchanges.

LANGUAGE OBJECTIVES

Children will inform about what wild animals eat, using key vocabulary.

ELA ACADEMIC LANGUAGE

- nonfiction, chart
- Cognate: *no ficción*

MATERIALS

Reading/Writing Companion, pp. 86–95

Visual Vocabulary Cards

DIGITAL TOOLS

Have children listen to the selection as they follow along to develop comprehension and practice fluency and pronunciation.

Use the additional grammar video.

Grammar Video

"Go Wild!"

Prepare to Read

Build Background Read aloud the Essential Question on page 86. Have children share what they know about animals living in nature. Use the image on pages 86 and 87 to generate ideas. Point to and read aloud the title. *We are going to read a nonfiction text about how animals survive in the wild. In the wild is another way to say in nature. Survive means "continue to live."* Point to the picture. *This is a tiger. Say tiger with me. Tigers live in the wild.*

Reading/Writing Companion, Lexile 530L

Focus on Vocabulary Use the **Visual Vocabulary Cards** to review the high-frequency words *find, food, more, over, start,* and *warm* and the oral vocabulary words *communicate, provide, superior, survive,* and *wilderness*. As you read, use gestures and visual support to teach important selection words, such as *search, seek, snow, catch, gulp, hunt,* and *sense*.

Summarize the Text Before reading, say the summary and point to the images. *This text tells how different animals survive in the wild. It tells what the animals eat and how they find their food.*

Read the Text

Use the Interactive Question-Response routine to help children understand the text.

Pages 88–89

Page 88 Read the text aloud, and ask children to point to the hippos. Point to the word *need*, and say it for children to repeat. *A need is something you must have.* Provide an example: *I'm thirsty. I need water.* Have children give examples of things they need. Point to the words *live* and *grow*. Say the words aloud, and have children repeat them. Ask: *What helps the hippos live and grow?* Plants help hippos live and grow. Point to and say the word *don't* for children to repeat. Explain that *don't* is a contraction of *do not*. Ask: *Do you and your friends eat the same things?* No, we don't. Point to *130 pounds*. *A pound is a measure of weight. It tells how heavy something is. Is 130 pounds of grass heavy or light?* (heavy)

What do all animals need to survive in nature? Discuss with a partner.

Beginning Use the pictures as visual support to help children answer the question. Point to the big hippo. *This is a hippo. What is the hippo doing?* The hippo is eating. *What is the hippo eating?* The hippo is eating plants. *Do all animals eat plants?* No, not all animals eat plants.

178 UNIT 4 WEEK 3

WEEK 3

Intermediate Help partners give a more specific answer. *Do all animals need food?* Yes, all animals need food. *Do all animals, like hippos, eat plants?* No, not all animals eat plants. Have children share examples of other foods animals eat.

Advanced/Advanced High Help partners elaborate on their answers. *How is what animals need to survive the same but different?* All animals need food, but they need different kinds of food.

Pages 90–91

Page 90 Read the text aloud, and have children follow along. Point to the phrase *goes after*. Goes after means the same as chases. *What does the big frog go after?* The big frog goes after mice.

How does the image help you understand what the text says? Discuss with a partner.

Beginning Point to the frog. *This frog is using its tongue to catch food. What is the frog trying to catch? Point to it.* The frog is trying to catch an insect. *What does the picture help you know?* It helps me know how the frog catches its food.

Intermediate Help partners give details about their answers. *What do you see in the picture?* I see the frog catching an insect. *What does the picture help you understand?* It helps me understand how frogs get food.

Advanced/Advanced High Help partners elaborate on how visual support helps them understand the text. Have children use details from the text to answer: *Why does the frog need a long tongue?* The frog needs a long tongue because it does not have teeth.

Pages 92–95

Page 94 Read the text aloud, and have children follow along. Point to the phrase *sense of smell*. Say it aloud, and have children repeat. *A strong sense of smell helps the bear find food.* Point to the bear. *What helps the bear catch food?* Sharp teeth and claws help the bear catch food.

How much food does the bear eat each day compared to other animals? Use the chart on page 95, and discuss with a partner.

Beginning Help children understand the chart to respond to the question. Point to the green bar. *The green bar shows how much food a hippo eats in a day. How much food does the hippo eat in a day?* The hippo eats 130 pounds of food each day. Help children use the chart to say how much other animals eat.

Intermediate Help children understand the chart to respond to the question. *Which animal in the text eats the most food in a day?* The hippo eats the most food in a day. *Which animal eats the least?* The chart says the squirrel eats the least.

Advanced/Advanced High Help partners add details to their responses. *Why might bears and hippos eat the most food in a day?* They eat the most food because they are the biggest animals. *Which animals eat both plants and animals?* The ostrich and bear eat both plants and animals.

FORMATIVE ASSESSMENT

▶ STUDENT CHECK IN

Have partners retell what the wild animals from the text eat. Then have children reflect, using the Check-In routine.

Independent Time

Writing Activity Create a two-column chart on the board. Label one side *Animals* and the other side *What They Need to Survive*. Have children copy the chart. Have them work independently or with a partner to complete the chart, using examples from the text. Under *Animals*, children should write the names of the animals discussed in the text. Under *What They Need to Survive*, children should record details from the text about what each animal eats and how it hunts. After children have recorded information from the text, encourage them to add their own examples and share them with a partner.

ENGLISH LANGUAGE LEARNERS 179

LESSON 3

READING • ANCHOR TEXT • ACCESS THE TEXT

LEARNING GOALS

We can read and understand a nonfiction text.

OBJECTIVES

Use the illustrations and details in a text to describe its key ideas.

Identify the reasons an author gives to support points in a text.

With prompting and support, read informational texts appropriately complex for grade 1.

Build on others' talk in conversations by responding to the comments of others through multiple exchanges.

LANGUAGE OBJECTIVES

Children will inform about how vultures get their food, using key vocabulary.

ELA ACADEMIC LANGUAGE

- illustration, repetition
- Cognates: *ilustración, repetición*

MATERIALS

Literature Anthology, pp. 60–89

Visual Vocabulary Cards

DIGITAL TOOLS

🎧 Have children listen to the selection to develop comprehension as they follow along.

Use the additional grammar song.

🎵 Grammar Song

Vulture View

Prepare to Read

Build Background *We are going to read a nonfiction text about how a particular type of bird gets its food.* Show the picture on the title page, and invite children to tell what they see. Point to the vultures. Say the word *vultures,* and have children repeat it. Explain that a vulture is a type of large bird. Point to the picture of the vulture's head. *This is the animal we are going to read about, the vulture.* Point to the vulture's beak, and say: *This is the vulture's beak. Does its beak look sharp? What color is this vulture's head? This vulture's beak looks ____. Its head is ____. What color is its body? Its body is ____.*

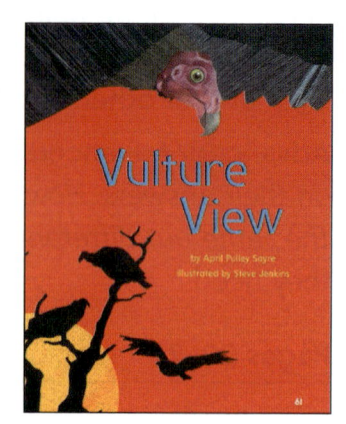

Literature Anthology, Lexile 70L

Focus on Vocabulary Use the **Visual Vocabulary Cards** to review the high-frequency words *find, food, more, over, start,* and *warm* and the oral vocabulary words *communicate, provide, superior, survive,* and *wilderness*. Before reading the story, clarify the vocabulary children will need for understanding. As you read, use gestures and pantomime to teach important selection words, such as *rising*. Pantomime gradually standing up as you slowly extend your arms. Say: *I am rising.* Have children repeat the pantomime and words. Ask: *Is the sun rising when it comes up or when it goes down?* The sun is rising when it comes up.

Summarize the Text Before reading, say the summary while pointing to the illustrations. *The text tells about what a particular bird, the vulture, eats. The text explains that vultures like to eat animals that are already dead.*

Read the Text

Use the Interactive Question-Response routine to help children understand the text.

Pages 64–67

Pages 66–67 Read the text. Point to the vulture's wings. *This vulture's wings are spread out wide. When a bird flies, it spreads out its wings like this. What is this vulture doing?* The vulture is flying. *Some of the words in the text tell you how the vulture flies.* Point to and say the word *tilt* for children to repeat. Pantomime flying and tilting your arms. Say: *Turkey vultures tilt their bodies like this when they fly. Have you seen a bird or an airplane tilt as it flies?* Point to the word *soar,* and say it for children to repeat. *Soar is a word that describes the way birds fly when they do not move their wings. Have you seen a bird soar?* Point to the word *scan*. *Scan means "to look at a place in order to find something." What are the turkey vultures looking for?* They are looking for food they can eat. *Do you think they will find food they like?* (yes/no)

180 UNIT 4 WEEK 3

How does the author help you picture what is happening? Discuss with a partner.

Beginning Have children imitate your acting out the words *tilt* and *soar* as they say these sentences with you: *I am tilting. I am soaring.* Say: *What do the words* tilt *and* soar *tell you?* The words *tilt* and *soar* tell me how vultures fly.

Intermediate Say the words *tilt* and *soar,* and have children repeat. Explain that *tilting* and *soaring* are two things vultures do as they fly. Have partners ask and answer: When you read *tilt* and *soar,* what do you picture? I picture the way vultures move when they fly.

Advanced/Advanced High Extend the discussion by having partners talk about what other words the author might have used to help readers picture what the vultures are doing. Provide this sentence frame: The author might have used the word swooped.

Pages 68–79

Pages 76–77 Read the text. *The vultures land near the dead deer.* Point to the word *dine. Dine is another word for* eat. *What are the vultures going to eat?* They are going to eat the dead deer.

Pages 78–79 Read the text. Point to the word *preen. When birds* preen, *they make sure their feathers are clean. When do the vultures* preen? The vultures preen after they eat.

How do the illustrations help you understand how vultures eat? Discuss with a partner.

Beginning Help partners point to the pictures as they respond. Display pages 76–77. *What do the vultures do?* They land near the deer. Display page 79. *What do the vultures do now?* They clean themselves.

Intermediate Help partners review the illustrations to respond. *What do the vultures do before they eat?* They land near the deer. *What do the vultures do after they eat?* They clean and preen themselves.

Advanced/Advanced High Extend the discussion by having partners tell other details they learned from the illustrations about how vultures eat. I learned that vultures eat in large groups.

Pages 80–87

Pages 82–83 Read the text. Point to the vultures. *The sun is beginning to go down. Point to where the author uses repetition with, or repeats, the word* down. Guide children to point to the instances of *down. Where are the vultures going?* The vultures are going down. Point to the word *glide,* and explain that it means to move smoothly and easily. *Have you seen a bird glide?*

What do the author's words help you picture? Discuss with a partner.

Beginning Point to the vultures' wings. *What do the wings help vultures do?* The wings help vultures fly. *Which words does the author use to talk about the wings?* The author uses the words glide and ride.

Intermediate Say the phrases *wings glide, wings ride.* Have children repeat. *Why does the author use these words?* The author wants readers to know that the vultures' wings help them fly smoothly and easily.

Advanced/Advanced High Extend the discussion by having partners explain what they visualize, or see, when they read about the vultures flying. When I read *glide,* I picture birds with giant wings flying without flapping their wings.

FORMATIVE ASSESSMENT

▶ STUDENT CHECK IN

Have partners retell how vultures move and look for the food they eat. Then have children reflect, using the Check-In routine.

Independent Time

My Favorite Animal Pair children of mixed proficiencies. Ask pairs to describe a favorite animal and what it eats. Provide a sentence frame to help children respond: My favorite animal is the ___. It eats ___. Have pairs work together to write about what their chosen animal eats. Encourage children to add illustrations to their sentences. When pairs have finished writing and illustrating their sentences, encourage them to share their sentences with another pair, a small group, or the whole class.

LESSONS 4–5

READING • LEVELED READER • ACCESS THE TEXT

LEARNING GOALS

We can ask and answer questions to understand a nonfiction text.

OBJECTIVES

Ask and answer questions about key details in a text.

Identify the main topic and retell key details of a text.

Describe the connection between two individuals, events, ideas, or pieces of information in a text.

Ask questions to clear up any confusion about the topics and texts under discussion.

LANGUAGE OBJECTIVES

Children will inquire about the topic by asking and answering questions.

ELA ACADEMIC LANGUAGE

- details
- Cognate: *detalles*

MATERIALS

ELL Leveled Reader: *Go Gator!*

Online Differentiated Text, "Crocodiles!"

Online ELL Visual Vocabulary Cards

DIGITAL TOOLS

Have children listen to the selection as they follow along to develop comprehension and practice fluency and pronunciation. Use Graphic Organizer 3: Topic and Relevant Details to enhance the lesson.

Go, Gator!

Prepare to Read

Build Background

- Remind children of the Essential Question. *Let's read to find out how an alligator survives in nature*. Encourage children to ask for help when they do not understand a word or phrase.
- Point to and read aloud the title, and have children repeat it. Ask: *What is the title?* Have children point to it. Repeat the routine for the author's name. Point to the photographs in the **Leveled Reader** to name things and actions. For example: *The alligator is below the water. Can you see its body?*

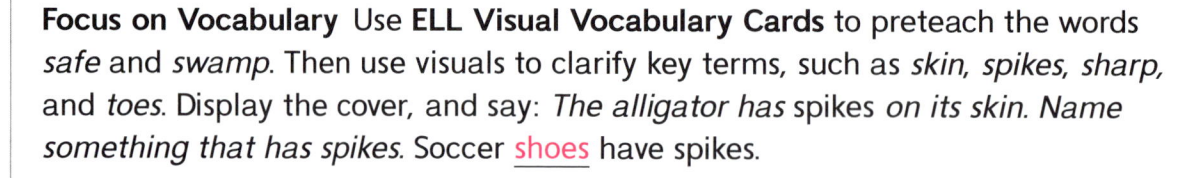

Lexile 270L

Focus on Vocabulary Use **ELL Visual Vocabulary Cards** to preteach the words *safe* and *swamp*. Then use visuals to clarify key terms, such as *skin*, *spikes*, *sharp*, and *toes*. Display the cover, and say: *The alligator has* spikes *on its skin. Name something that has spikes.* Soccer shoes *have spikes*.

Read the Text

Use the Interactive Question-Response routine to help children understand the text.

Pages 2–5

Topic and Relevant Details Read pages 2–5. Ask questions to help children identify the topic and relevant details. *What animal is this?* (alligator) *Where does it live?* (swamp)

Beginning Help partners respond to pages 2–3. *What is this text mostly about?* It is mostly about where alligators live. *Point to the green part of the map.*

Intermediate For each page, have children tell a partner the main idea. On page 2, the main idea is that the alligator lives in a swamp.

Advanced/Advanced High Help partners extend their discussion. Ask: *Why does the author include the map on page 3?* The author includes the map to show readers where in the United States the alligators live.

Pages 6–9

Ask and Answer Questions Read pages 8–9 as children follow along. Point to the alligator's front feet. *These are the front feet. Let's point to the back feet.* Guide children to ask and answer questions to understand the text.

Intermediate Have partners respond and then ask their own questions: *How do alligators run fast?* They use their toes.

182 UNIT 4 WEEK 3

WEEK 3

Advanced/Advanced High Have partners discuss each page: How does the alligator's body help it? Toes help it run.

Pages 10–12

Read pages 10–11 as children follow along. Point to pictures, and say *baby alligators, eggs*, and *nest*. Have children repeat.

Beginning Help partners point to pictures. *Where do baby alligators come from?* Baby alligators come from eggs.

Intermediate *What do baby alligators need to survive?* Baby alligators need a mom to keep them safe.

Respond to Reading Have partners work together to retell the story and respond to the questions on page 12.

Focus on Fluency

Read pages 10–11 to model appropriate expression. Read the passage again, and have children repeat after you. For more practice, record children reading the passage, and have them select the best recording.

Paired Read: "Ducklings"

Make Connections: Write About It

Echo-read each page with children. Discuss what the ducklings in the poem do: The ducklings waddle and swim. Have children use the question on page 15 to make connections between the texts: Ducklings and baby alligators need their mothers to take care of them.

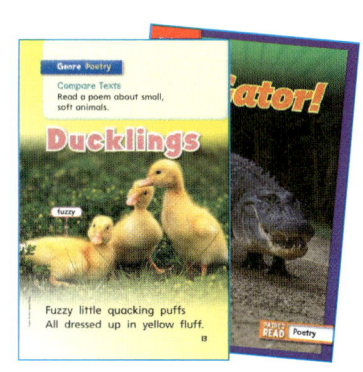

Leveled Reader

Build Knowledge: Make Connections

Talk About the Text Have partners discuss how the animals in the texts survive in nature.

Write About the Text Have students add their ideas to the Build Knowledge pages of their reader's notebooks.

Self-Selected Reading

Help children choose a nonfiction selection from the online **Leveled Reader Library,** or read the **Differentiated Text,** "Crocodiles!"

FOCUS ON SCIENCE

Children can extend their knowledge of wild animals by completing the science activity on page 16. **STEM**

LITERATURE CIRCLES

Lead children in conducting a literature circle using the Thinkmark questions to guide the discussion. You may wish to discuss what children have learned from both selections in the **Leveled Reader** about different ways in which animals live in the wild.

FORMATIVE ASSESSMENT

STUDENT CHECK IN

Have partners share their Respond to Reading. Have children reflect, using the Check-In routine.

LEVEL UP

IF children can read *Go, Gator!* **ELL Level** with fluency and correctly answer the Respond to Reading questions,

THEN tell children they will read a more detailed version of the selection.

- Use pages 2–3 of *Go, Gator!* **On Level** to model using Teaching Poster 33 to list key details.
- Have children read the selection, checking their comprehension by using the graphic organizer.

ENGLISH LANGUAGE LEARNERS 183

LESSONS 4–5

READING • GENRE PASSAGE • ACCESS THE TEXT

LEARNING GOALS

We can apply skills and strategies to a nonfiction text.

OBJECTIVES

Ask and answer questions about key details in a text.

Identify the main topic and retell key details of a text.

With prompting and support, read informational texts appropriately complex for grade 1.

Ask questions to clear up any confusion about the topics and texts under discussion.

LANGUAGE OBJECTIVES

Children will explain the topic and relevant details in complete sentences

Children will inquire about the text by asking and answering questions.

ELA ACADEMIC LANGUAGE

- photo, text, title
- Cognates: *foto, texto, título*

MATERIALS

Online ELL Genre Passage, "Amazing Octopuses"

"Amazing Octopuses"

Prepare to Read

Build Background Review what children have learned about how animals survive in nature. *What is something all animals need to survive?* All animals need ____. Allow children to share ideas about other ways in which animals survive. Tell children they will be reading about how a sea animal called an octopus survives. Point to the octopus on page E1. Say: *This is an octopus. Say octopus with me.*

Lexile 300L

Focus on Vocabulary Use the **Define, Example, Ask** routine to preteach difficult or unfamiliar selection words, such as *travel, crawl, squeeze, spaces, squirt, tricky, enemy, attacked,* and *shelter*. Use gestures or visuals to clarify other selection words as needed.

Read the Texts

Use the Interactive Question-Response routine to help children understand the text.

Page E1

Paragraph 1 Read the text aloud as children follow along. Point to the photo. *What animal do you see in the photo?* I see an octopus in the photo. Point to the octopus's arms. *What do you notice about the octopus's body?* The octopus has many arms.

Intermediate Have children talk with a partner about the **topic and relevant details.** Help children respond, using the sentence frame: The text is mostly about how the octopus uses its body in many ways. This is the topic.

Paragraph 2 Read the text aloud, and help children look for **word categories.** *The octopus can crawl. The octopus can swim.* Crawl *and* swim *are alike because they are verbs. They tell what the octopus can do.* Help children look for other verbs they can put in the same category.

Advanced/Advanced High Have children **ask and answer questions** with a partner: How does the octopus travel? The octopus can crawl slowly. The octopus can swim very fast.

Paragraph 3 Read the text aloud as children follow along. *The octopus's body can squeeze into small spaces.* Have children pantomime squeezing into a small space. *This is one way the octopus can hide to protect itself.*

Intermediate Have children **ask and answer questions:** How can squirting ink protect the octopus? The ink makes the water dark.

184 UNIT 4 WEEK 3

WEEK 3

Page E2

Paragraph 1 Read the text. Point to the word *tricky*. *If you are tricky, you make someone believe something that isn't true.* Point to *lose an arm*. *Lose an arm means an arm comes off. What happens if the octopus loses an arm?* The arm will grow back.

Beginning Help partners talk about **relevant details** using the photo. *What do the octopus's arms look like?* They look like snakes. *How does this help the octopus?* It helps the octopus scare an enemy.

Paragraph 2 Read the text. Point to the word *sleepy*. Say *sleepy*, and pantomime yawning. Have children repeat the word and action. *When the octopus gets sleepy, it makes a shelter. What does the octopus do there?* The octopus takes a nap.

Advanced Have partners review **relevant details** about what an octopus does after a long day. Encourage them to use longer sentences than in the text: The octopus builds its own shelter. Then it crawls inside and takes a nap.

Advanced High Have children review the text with a partner: *What is the main idea of the selection?* Octopuses use their bodies to survive. *What relevant details in this paragraph tell about the topic?* The octopus can use its body to build its own shelter.

Respond to Reading

Use the following instructions to help children answer the questions on page E3.

1. **Nonfiction** Have children describe the photos. *What is the octopus doing in the first photo? What does the octopus look like in the second photo? What do both photos show you about octopuses?* (swimming; sleeping; they can hide)

2. **Topic and Relevant Details** Discuss with children what they learned about octopuses in the text. Ask: *What is the text mostly about?* (what octopuses can do) *Does the title, "Amazing Octopuses," match what the text is mostly about?* (Possible answer: Yes, because the text is about all the amazing things octopuses can do.)

3. **Fluency** Have children take turns reading the first paragraph to a partner. As they read, have them fill in the chart on page E3.

Build Knowledge: Make Connections

Talk About the Text Have partners discuss how octopuses survive in nature.

Write About the Text Have students add their ideas to the Build Knowledge pages of their reader's notebooks.

FORMATIVE ASSESSMENT

STUDENT CHECK IN

Have partners share their Respond to Reading. Then have children reflect, using the Check-In routine.

LEVEL UP

IF children read the ELL Level fluently and answered the questions,

THEN pair them with children who have proficiently read the On Level. Have them

- partner-read the On Level passage.
- identify the topic of the text and explain relevant details that tell about the topic.

ENGLISH LANGUAGE LEARNERS 185

LESSONS 1–5

WRITING

MODELED WRITING

LESSON 1

LEARNING GOALS
We can learn how to write about a main topic.

OBJECTIVES
Write informative texts in which they supply some facts about the topic.

LANGUAGE OBJECTIVES
Children will explain by writing sentences, using science vocabulary.

ELA ACADEMIC LANGUAGE
- idea, details
- Cognates: *idea, detalles*

Writing Practice Review the sample on p. 96 of the **Reading/Writing Companion**. Help children analyze the sentences using the Actor/Action Routine: *Who is the actor in the first part of the sentence?* (I) *What is the action?* (think frogs are interesting) Then read the prompt on p. 97 and ask children to answer it as a group. Write the sentences on the board for children to choral read. Then ask partners to write their own sentences.

Beginning Help partners create their sentences: *What is your favorite wild animal?* (a big cat) *What is it like?* (fast) Provide sentence frames if needed.

Intermediate Have partners ask and answer *who/what* questions to create their sentences. Have them include at least one supporting detail.

Advanced/Advanced High Challenge children to include a main idea and two supporting details and to share these with the group.

FORMATIVE ASSESSMENT ⊙ **STUDENT CHECK IN** Partners share their sentences. Ask children to reflect, using the Check-In routine.

INTERACTIVE WRITING

LESSON 2

LEARNING GOALS
We can read and write about a Student Model.

OBJECTIVES
With guidance and support, add details to strengthen writing as needed.

LANGUAGE OBJECTIVES
Children will discuss and write sentences about the Student Model, using the words *idea* and *details*.

ELA ACADEMIC LANGUAGE
- idea, details
- Cognates: *idea, detalles*

Analyze the Student Model Have children finger point as they chorally read the Student Model on p. 104 of the **Reading/Writing Companion**. Use the Actor/Action Routine to review each sentence. *Who are the actors?* (the animals) *What do they do?* (use their bodies) *What do they use their bodies to do?* (to get food) Guide children to think about the Writing Trait: *Which sentence tells the main idea? Which sentences give supporting details about the main idea?* Then help children complete p. 105.

Beginning Have partners point to examples of supporting details in the text. Provide a sentence frame: I notice supporting details.

Intermediate Have partners ask and answer questions: *What did you notice about David's writing?* He uses a main idea sentence.

Advanced/Advanced High Challenge children to write their own sentences about the text. Encourage children to share their ideas.

FORMATIVE ASSESSMENT ⊙ **STUDENT CHECK IN** Partners share their responses. Ask children to reflect, using the Check-In routine.

WEEK 3

INDEPENDENT WRITING

LESSONS 3-4

LEARNING GOALS

We can use text evidence to respond to a nonfiction text.

OBJECTIVES

Write informative texts in which they name a topic and supply some facts about the topic.

LANGUAGE OBJECTIVES

Children will inform by writing sentences, using the verb *use*.

ELA ACADEMIC LANGUAGE

- text
- Cognate: *texto*

Find Text Evidence Follow the Independent Writing routine. Help children use text evidence to retell the anchor text. Ask questions, such as: *Which body part do vultures use to fly?* (wings) *How do vultures find food?* (They look; they smell/sniff.) Then read the prompt on p. 110 of the **Reading/Writing Companion:** *How do vultures use their body parts to help them find food? We read about how vultures get food. What body parts help them? Let's find text evidence to write about how vultures find food.*

Write a Response Work with children to complete My Writing Outline 18. Then have them use the sentences from their outlines to complete p. 110.

Writing Checklist Read the checklist with students, and have them check for these items in their writing.

Beginning Provide sentence frames to help partners talk about their sentences: My *first* sentence is the *main idea*.

Intermediate Encourage partners to identify the main idea and check that the supporting details give more information about it.

Advanced/Advanced High Have partners identify where they used each item in their writing.

FORMATIVE ASSESSMENT ❯ **STUDENT CHECK IN** Partners share their sentences from My Writing Outline. Ask children to reflect, using the Check-in routine.

SELF-SELECTED WRITING

LESSON 5

LEARNING GOALS

We can revise our writing.

OBJECTIVES

Use singular and plural nouns with matching verbs in basic sentences.

LANGUAGE OBJECTIVES

Children will inquire about their writing by checking the verbs *go* and *do*.

ELA ACADEMIC LANGUAGE

- verb
- Cognate: *verbo*

Work with children to revise the group writing activity. Point to each word as you read the sentences. Stop to ask questions, such as, Is *go/do* used correctly here? If needed, write *go* and *do* incorrectly in sentences, and work together to revise them. Then have partners revise each other's sentences before publishing their writing.

For support with grammar and *go* and *do*, refer to the **Language Transfers Handbook** and **Language Development Cards** 7A and 8A.

FORMATIVE ASSESSMENT ❯ **STUDENT CHECK IN** Partners tell what revisions they made. Ask children to reflect, using the Check-in routine.

ENGLISH LANGUAGE LEARNERS 187

LESSONS 1–2

READING • SHARED READ • ACCESS THE TEXT

LEARNING GOALS

We can read and understand a fantasy story.

OBJECTIVES

Ask and answer questions about key details in a text.

Use illustrations and details in a story to describe its characters, setting, or events.

Compare and contrast the adventures and experiences of characters in stories.

Ask questions to clear up any confusion about the topics and texts under discussion.

LANGUAGE OBJECTIVES

Children will narrate the story, using key vocabulary.

ELA ACADEMIC LANGUAGE

- fantasy, inference, compare, contrast
- Cognates: *fantasía, inferencia, comparar, contrastar*

MATERIALS

Reading/Writing Companion, pp. 122–131

Visual Vocabulary Cards

DIGITAL TOOLS

Have children listen to the selection as they follow along to develop comprehension and practice fluency and pronunciation.

Use the additional grammar video.

Grammar Video

"Creep Low, Fly High"

Prepare to Read

Build Background Read aloud the first part of the Essential Question: *What insects do you know?* Use the illustrations on pages 122–123 to generate ideas. Point to and say *caterpillar, bee, ladybug, grasshopper,* and *ant* for children to repeat. *Which of these insects do you see at home? On the playground? Do you like insects? Why or why not?* Children may say they find insects interesting or yucky. *In the pictures, do the insects look friendly or scary?* Point to and read aloud the title. Explain that *creep* means "to move close to the ground."

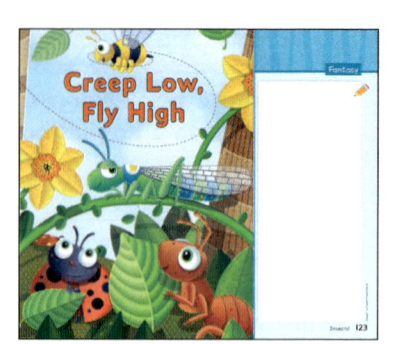

Reading/Writing Companion, Lexile 290L

Focus on Vocabulary Use the **Visual Vocabulary Cards** to review the high-frequency words *caught, flew, know, laugh, listen,* and *were* and the oral vocabulary words *different, flutter, imitate, protect,* and *resemble.* As you read, use gestures and visual support to teach important story words, such as *beautiful, fancy, boast,* and *brag.* Tell children that *boast* and *brag* have the same meaning. Give an example, such as: *I got an A on that test.* Exaggerate the intonation to convey a bragging tone. Have children repeat, copying your intonation. Then have children chorally read the word *missing* on page 127. Say: *When something is missing, you can't find it.*

Summarize the Text Before reading, say this summary and point to the illustrations: *This story tells about five insect friends. One of them goes missing! Let's read to find out what happens.*

Read the Text

Use the Interactive Question-Response routine to help children understand the story.

Pages 124–125

Pages 124–125 Read the text aloud as children follow along. Have children demonstrate the verbs *hop, dash, buzz, fly,* and *zip around* while repeating each word three times. Model gestures as needed. Ask: *How many insect friends are there?* Have children point and count. (five) *These insect friends are in a field.* Say *field* with me. *What can you see in a field?* (plants, flowers)

What can each insect do? Discuss with a partner.

Beginning Review the insects and verbs on these pages. Have partners take turns completing this sentence frame: [Grasshopper] can [hop].

Intermediate Have partners take turns asking about what each insect can do and answering in a complete sentence: *Who can hop?* (Grasshopper can hop.)

188 UNIT 4 WEEK 4

WEEK 4

Advanced/Advanced High Have children ask and answer about what the insects can do. Have partners explain any "no" answers: Can Ant hop? (No, he can't hop. He can dash fast.)

Pages 126–129

Pages 126–127 Read page 126 aloud. Demonstrate and say the word *sigh* for children to echo. Ask: *Who sighs in this story?* (Caterpillar) *How do you think he feels?* (sad) *Why is he sad?* Prompt children to make an inference: *What can Caterpillar do?* (creep) *Can he hop like Grasshopper/dash fast like Ant/fly high like Bee/zip around like Ladybug?* (no) Elicit that Caterpillar is sad because he can't do those things. Then read page 127 aloud. Ask: *Who is missing?* (Caterpillar) *Can his friends find him?* (no)

Pages 128–129 Read the text aloud. Ask: *Where does Ant think Caterpillar is?* (hiding because he is sad) *Who agrees with Ant?* (Grasshopper) *They want to cheer up Caterpillar.* To cheer up someone means to say something nice to help him or her feel better. Say *cheer up*. Write Ant and Grasshopper's idea of what happened on the board. Ask: *What did Bee see?* (a bird) *What does he think happened to Caterpillar?* (The bird caught him.) *Who agrees with Bee?* (Ladybug) *What do they want to do?* (help Caterpillar) Add Bee and Ladybug's idea to the board.

COLLABORATE *Where do you think Caterpillar is? Discuss with a partner.*

Beginning Have children share their ideas or choose one from the board: I think Caterpillar is hiding/in a bird's mouth. Have children draw what they think.

Intermediate Have children share ideas about where Caterpillar is and how he feels: I think Caterpillar is hiding/in a bird's mouth. He feels sad/nervous. Have children draw the inference they made.

Advanced/Advanced High Have children give a more detailed inference about what happened to Caterpillar: I think Caterpillar is hiding because he can't hop or fly. Have children draw what they infer.

Pages 130–131

Pages 130–131 Read the text aloud as children follow along. *Who is the "beautiful bug with gold wings"?* (Caterpillar) *What was he doing?* Say and gesture for children to imitate: *He wrapped up. He rested. He popped out as a butterfly! Now Caterpillar can flit and dip.* Gesture to show the meaning of each verb, and have children repeat each word. Have children revisit their drawings. *Was your idea correct?*

COLLABORATE *How is Caterpillar the same as before? How is he different? Discuss with a partner.*

Beginning Have pairs compare the pictures of Butterfly on page 131 and Caterpillar on page 122 and discuss: *What color is Caterpillar/Butterfly?* (green and yellow) *What does Butterfly have?* (wings)

Intermediate Have pairs use sentence frames to contrast Caterpillar's and Butterfly's abilities: Caterpillar can creep. He can't fly. Butterfly can flit and dip.

Advanced/Advanced High Have pairs compare and contrast Caterpillar and Butterfly: Both are green and yellow. Caterpillar can creep, but Butterfly can fly. Caterpillar feels sad, but Butterfly feels happy.

FORMATIVE ASSESSMENT

> STUDENT CHECK IN

Have partners retell what happened to Caterpillar. Then have children reflect, using the Check-In routine.

Independent Time

Role Play Group children of mixed proficiencies, and have them take the roles of Caterpillar or Butterfly and his friends. Children can make name tags to remember their roles. Ask each "insect" to say and act out what the insect can do. Other "insects" should copy the action and say, "I can too!" if they have the same ability. Ask: *How are you alike? What can you all do?* Invite groups to present their actions to the class: We can ___ and ___.

ENGLISH LANGUAGE LEARNERS 189

LESSON 3

READING • ANCHOR TEXT • ACCESS THE TEXT

LEARNING GOALS

We can read and understand a fantasy story.

OBJECTIVES

Ask and answer questions about key details in a text.

Identify words and phrases in stories or poems that suggest feelings or appeal to the senses.

Describe people, places, things, and events with relevant details, expressing ideas and feelings clearly.

LANGUAGE OBJECTIVES

Children will narrate what pets do in a show, using key vocabulary.

ELA ACADEMIC LANGUAGE

- author, illustrations
- Cognates: *autor, ilustraciones*

MATERIALS

Literature Anthology, pp. 92–125

Visual Vocabulary Cards

DIGITAL TOOLS — MULTIMODAL

Have children listen to the selection to develop comprehension as they follow along.

Use the online ELL Vocabulary Practice for additional support.

Hi! Fly Guy

Prepare to Read

Build Background Say: *We are going to read a fantasy story about a boy and his pet fly.* Display the picture on the title page. Point to the fly, and say: *This is a fly.* Have children repeat. Point out that *fly* can be a noun or a verb. Ask: *What does a fly do?* It _____. *A fly makes a buzzing sound. Can you say* buzz? *What do you do when you see a fly in your house?* When I see a fly in my house, I _____. Encourage children to use descriptions or nonverbal cues, such as gestures, to convey their ideas if they do not know the exact words in English.

Literature Anthology, Lexile 200L

Focus on Vocabulary Use the **Visual Vocabulary Cards** to review the high-frequency words *caught, flew, know, laugh, listen,* and *were* and the oral vocabulary words *different, flutter, imitate, protect,* and *resemble.* As you read, use gestures and pantomime to teach important story words, such as *pets* and *pests.*

Summarize the Text Before reading, say this summary while pointing to the illustrations: *The story tells about a boy who has a pet fly and takes him to a pet show. The judges don't think a fly can be a pet, so the fly decides to show them that it can be a pet.*

Read the Text

Use the Interactive Question-Response routine to help children understand the story.

Pages 94–103

Pages 100–103 Read the text aloud. Have children trace the fly's path from the top of the page to the boy's nose. Point to the word *boink. Boink is a sound word an author might include when characters bump into things. Say* boink *with me. How do the fly and the boy meet?* The fly bumps into the boy's nose. *What is the boy thinking when he says, "A pet"?* He's thinking the fly can be his pet.

Pages 102–103 Read the text aloud. Stomp your foot, and say: *I stomp my feet when I'm angry.* Point to the fly on page 102. *The fly stomps his foot. Does the fly like being in the jar?* (no) *Why does the boy say the fly is the smartest fly in the world?* He hears the fly say his name. *What do you think the boy's name is?* (Buzz) *Yes, the fly makes the sound* Buzz. Buzz *must be the boy's name.*

COLLABORATE *How does the author show you how the fly and the boy feel?*

Beginning Help children point to the fly on page 102. *Does the fly look angry or happy?* (angry) *What does it say?* (Buzz!) *What does it do?* (stomps its foot) Repeat the questions about the boy for page 103.

190 UNIT 4 WEEK 4

WEEK 4

Intermediate Have pairs point to what the fly says on page 102. (Buzz!) Then have them ask and answer: *Does the fly seem happy or angry?* (angry) Have them repeat for page 103. *Did the author show you how the fly and the boy feel?* (yes) *What did the author use to show how they feel?* (text and pictures)

Advanced/Advanced High Have pairs identify the words on pages 102–103 that tell what each character says. Have partners take turns asking and answering: How does the fly feel? The boy? Have partners share how the author shows them how the characters feel: The pictures and words show the fly is angry and the boy is happy.

Pages 104–115

Pages 112–113 Read the text aloud. *The judges are laughing. Say* laugh *with me. What do the judges say about Buzz's fly?* (Flies can't be pets.) *Why?* (Flies are pests.) Review the pronunciation of *pets* and *pests*.

Pages 114–115 Read the text aloud. *We say "Shoo!" to tell flies and other pests to go away. What does "fancy" flying look like?* Have children trace the path.

How do the illustrations help you know the judges' point of view?

Beginning Point to the picture on pages 112–113 to help children see the judges' point of view. *Whom does one judge point at?* (Buzz) *What do the judges do?* They laugh. *Do they think a fly is a pet?* (no)

Intermediate Have children look at the pictures on pages 112–115. *What are the judges doing?* (laughing, watching the fly) *How do they feel?* The judges think a fly is funny. Then they are surprised.

Advanced/Advanced High Have pairs discuss how the pictures show the judges' point of view: On page 112, the judges are laughing and pointing at Buzz. They think a fly is a funny/strange pet. On page 115, the judges look surprised to see Fly Guy's fancy flying.

Pages 116–121

Pages 116–117 Read the text aloud. Tricks *are special, surprising things animals can do. Often people teach animals to do tricks. A dog that sits when you say "sit" is doing a* trick. *What trick can Fly Guy do? Look back at page 115 if you aren't sure.* (fancy flying)

Pages 118–119 Read the text aloud. Ask: *What can Fly Guy do?* He can say the boy's name. He can fly high.

Pages 120–121 Read the text aloud. Ask: *What can Fly Guy do?* (fly into a jar) *Why does he fly into that jar?* (It's his home.)

How does the author show that Fly Guy can be a pet?

Beginning Have children say *Fly Guy, a pet,* or *both* to tell who each phrase describes: *can do tricks* (both), *can say Buzz's name* (Fly Guy), *knows its home* (both).

Intermediate Help partners review what Fly Guy does that shows he is a pet: Fly Guy can do tricks and go back to his home.

Advanced/Advanced High Have pairs elaborate by listing everything Fly Guy can do. Fly Guy can do a fancy flying trick, say his owner's name, fly high, and dive down to his home in a jar.

FORMATIVE ASSESSMENT

❯ STUDENT CHECK IN

Have partners retell how the judges' point of view changes during the story. Then have children reflect, using the Check-In routine.

Independent Time

Ask Questions Pair children of mixed proficiencies. Have partners take turns asking and answering *wh-* questions to describe the pictures in Chapter 2 on pages 104–111. Before children begin, clarify any unfamiliar words for items in the pictures, such as *fly swatter* and *hot dog*. Children can ask, for example: Who is in the picture? What is Dad doing? How does he feel about flies? What is the fly's name? What does he eat? Where does he eat? How does he feel? Then have partners present some of their questions and answers to the rest of the group.

ENGLISH LANGUAGE LEARNERS 191

READING • LEVELED READER • ACCESS THE TEXT

LESSONS 4–5

LEARNING GOALS

We can visualize what is happening as we read a story.

OBJECTIVES

Retell stories, including key details, and demonstrate understanding of their central message or lesson.

Use illustrations and details in a story to describe its characters, setting, or events.

Compare and contrast the adventures and experiences of characters in stories.

Build on others' talk in conversations by responding to the comments of others through multiple exchanges.

LANGUAGE OBJECTIVES

Children will narrate the characters' problem, using nouns.

ELA ACADEMIC LANGUAGE

- fantasy, visualize, retell
- Cognates: *fantasía, visualizar*

MATERIALS

ELL Leveled Reader: *The Hat*

Online Differentiated Text, "Bee Yourself"

Online ELL Visual Vocabulary Cards

DIGITAL TOOLS

Have children listen to the selection as they follow along to develop comprehension and practice fluency and pronunciation. Use Graphic Organizer 9: Narrator to enhance the lesson.

The Hat

Lexile 230L

Prepare to Read

Build Background

- Remind children of the Essential Question. Say: *Let's read a story about some insects we know and some insects that are new to us.* Encourage children to ask for help when they do not understand a word or phrase.

- Use the labels on the illustrations to review or preteach insects: *grasshopper, ladybug, ant, inchworm, water beetle.* An *inchworm is a worm that is an inch long. Where does a water beetle live?* It lives in the ____.

Focus on Vocabulary Use **ELL Visual Vocabulary Cards** to preteach *blocks* and *gust*. List irregular past-tense verbs from the story, and elicit base forms: *put–put, went–go, were–be, said–say, came–come, swam–swim,* and *caught–catch*.

Read the Text

Use the Interactive Question-Response routine to help children understand the story.

Pages 2–5

Read Chapter 1 as children follow along. On pages 2–3, point to and say *shop, hat,* and *love* for children to repeat. Have them trace Grasshopper's path and say *hop*.

Beginning Have pairs point to and identify the characters pictured on pages 4–5. Ask: *Who is wearing a hat?* (Grasshopper)

Advanced/Advanced High Have pairs monitor comprehension by reading quotes from pages 4–5 for each other to guess: Who said, ["Your hat is too big for me"]? (Inchworm) Have the other partner cover the text with a piece of paper.

Pages 6–7

Visualize Read the text as children follow along. Discuss the meaning of the phrase "big gust" in the first paragraph on page 6 with children to help them visualize what happens to the hat. *What did the big gust of wind do to the hat?* (The hat blew off.) Have volunteers act out the first paragraph.

Intermediate Ask: *What is the problem in this story? Act it out.* Have pairs act out the wind's blowing the grasshopper's hat off.

Advanced/Advanced High Have pairs read the last sentence, and prompt them to make a prediction: *How do you think Grasshopper will solve her problem?* (Her friends will help her.)

192 UNIT 4 WEEK 4

WEEK 4

Pages 8–12

Narrator Review with children that the narrator can be a character inside the story or a speaker outside the story. Remind children of the clue words that help identify the narrator. Point to the phrase "Ladybug said" on page 8, and ask: *Is this the narrator speaking or is it Ladybug?* (the narrator) Have children point to the sentence "I'm sorry." Ask: *Is the narrator speaking or is Ladybug?* (Ladybug) Have children point to the phrase "Inchworm said" on page 9, and ask: *Is the narrator speaking or is Inchworm?* (the narrator)

Beginning Have children point to other clue words on pages 8–11. Help children identify whether the character or narrator is speaking.

Intermediate Have pairs complete this sentence frame: The narrator of this story is a(n) [character/outside speaker]. (outside speaker)

Respond to Reading Have partners work together to retell the story and respond to the questions on page 12.

Focus on Fluency

Read pages 6–7 to model appropriate phrasing. Read the passage again, and have children repeat it. For more practice, record children reading the passage, and have them select the best recording.

Paired Read: "Let's Look at Insects!"

Make Connections: Write About It

Echo-read each page with children. Discuss insects. *What are some jumping insects?* (flea, grasshopper, crickets, froghoppers) Have children make connections between texts using the question on page 15: I saw a grasshopper in *The Hat*.

Leveled Reader

Build Knowledge: Make Connections

Talk About the Text Have partners discuss what they learned about insects from the texts.

Write About the Text Have students add their ideas to the Build Knowledge pages of their reader's notebooks.

Self-Selected Reading

Help children choose a nonfiction selection from the online **Leveled Reader Library,** or read the **Differentiated Text,** "Bee Yourself!"

FOCUS ON SCIENCE

Children can extend their knowledge of insects by completing the science activity on page 16. **STEM**

LITERATURE CIRCLES

Lead children in conducting a literature circle using the Thinkmark questions to guide the discussion. You may wish to discuss what children have learned about insects from both selections in the **Leveled Reader**.

FORMATIVE ASSESSMENT

STUDENT CHECK IN

Have partners share their Respond to Reading. Have children reflect, using the Check-In routine.

LEVEL UP

IF children can read *The Hat* **ELL Level** with fluency and correctly answer the Respond to Reading questions,

THEN tell children they will read a more detailed version of the story.

- Use pages 2–3 of *The Hat* **On Level** to model using Teaching Poster 35 to list clues about the point of view.
- Have children read the selection, checking their comprehension by using the graphic organizer.

ENGLISH LANGUAGE LEARNERS **193**

LESSONS 4–5

READING • GENRE PASSAGE • ACCESS THE TEXT

LEARNING GOALS

We can apply skills and strategies to a fantasy.

OBJECTIVES

Explain major differences between books that tell stories and books that give information, drawing on a wide reading of a range of text types.

Identify who is telling the story at various points in a text.

Use illustrations and details in a story to describe its characters, setting, or events.

Produce complete sentences when appropriate to task and situation.

LANGUAGE OBJECTIVES

Children will discuss the narrator using complete sentences.

ELA ACADEMIC LANGUAGE

- alike, different, fantasy
- Cognates: *diferente, fantasía*

MATERIALS

Online ELL Genre Passage, "The Tomato Adventure"

"The Tomato Adventure"

Prepare to Read

Build Background Have children discuss what they know about insects. *How are insects alike and different?* Prompt children to think about insects' abilities: Insects can ____. Have children draw or name an insect with each ability. Ask: *Can all insects do that?* Tell children they are going to read about two insects with different abilities. Have children look at the illustration on page E1. Ask: *Who can fly?* The ____ can fly. *Can the caterpillar fly?*

Lexile 300L

Focus on Vocabulary Use the **Define, Example, Ask** routine to preteach difficult or unfamiliar story words, such as *caterpillar*, *bee*, and *tomato*. As you read, use gestures or visuals to clarify other story words as needed. Point out that the plural of *tomato* is *tomatoes*. Lead children in saying *stretch* and *wiggle* as they stretch their arms and wiggle their fingers. Read the title aloud, and use the cognate *aventura* to help children understand the meaning of *adventure*. Invite one or two volunteers to share an adventure they have had or read about.

Read the Text

Use the Interactive Question-Response routine to help children understand the story.

Page E1

Paragraphs 1–3 Read the text. Have children complete this sentence frame: When you are hungry, you want food. Explain that the question "What's wrong?" is asking what the problem is. Then have children tell what they know about Kevin so far.

Beginning Have pairs point to Kevin in the picture and describe him: Kevin is a caterpillar. He feels sad and hungry.

Advanced/Advanced High Have pairs describe Kevin: Kevin is a caterpillar. He feels hungry. He wants to eat tomatoes in the garden.

Paragraphs 4–5 Read the text aloud. Remind students that the **narrator** can be a character inside the story or outside the story. Ask: *What does the narrator talk about?* The narrator talks about a caterpillar and a bee. *Which words tell that the narrator is outside the story?* (*he, Bumble, Kevin*)

Advanced Have pairs work together to *visualize* the text: *Let's picture what Kevin looks like when he moves. Kevin is too slow. Kevin can't go across the garden. This makes him sad.*

Advanced High Have children *visualize* the text: Kevin is too slow, so he can't go across the garden. Because he can't go across the garden, he can't get the tomatoes.

194 UNIT 4 WEEK 4

WEEK 4

Page E2

Paragraphs 1–3 Read the text aloud. Remind children that they can use *sentence clues* when they do not know what a word means. *We know* suddenly *means "all of a sudden" because the author tells us that Kevin is in the air now.* Read the text again, and have children close their eyes and *visualize* to help them create a mental image of what is happening. Ask: *Why can Bumble help Kevin?* (Bumble can fly.)

Beginning Provide sentence frames to help children retell this section: Bumble can fly. He carries Kevin through the air. Kevin feels like he is flying.

Intermediate Have partners retell: Bumble picks up Kevin and flies into the air.

Paragraphs 4–6 Read the text aloud as children follow along. To monitor comprehension, ask: *Why does Bumble put Kevin onto a tomato?* He knows Kevin likes tomatoes. *Why does Kevin need Bumble's help?* Kevin is too slow. He can't get across the garden.

Beginning *How do you think Kevin feels while "flying"?* Help children respond: He feels excited/happy.

Advanced/Advanced High Have pairs find and read aloud the most exciting part of the story for Kevin.

Respond to Reading

Use the following instructions to help children answer the questions on page E3.

1. **Fantasy** Remind children that in fantasy stories, things happen that never happen in real life. Make statements about the story for children to answer *real* or *fantasy*: Bees can fly. (real) Caterpillars can walk. (real) Caterpillars eat tomatoes. (real) Bugs help each other. (real in some cases) Bugs can talk. (fantasy)

2. **Narrator** How does Bumble help Kevin? (He helps him get tomatoes.) Reread line 7 on page E2. Ask: Which words does the narrator use to tell what Kevin told Bumble? (Kevin said)

3. **Fluency** Have partners take turns reading the first paragraph. As they read, have them fill in the chart on page E3.

Build Knowledge: Make Connections

Talk About the Text Have partners discuss how Kevin the caterpillar is similar to other characters they have read about.

Write About the Text Have students add their ideas to the Build Knowledge pages of their reader's notebooks.

FORMATIVE ASSESSMENT

▶ STUDENT CHECK IN

Have partners share their Respond to Reading. Then have children reflect, using the Check-In routine.

LEVEL UP

IF children read the **ELL Level** fluently and answered the questions,

THEN pair them with children who have proficiently read the **On Level.** Have them

- partner-read the **On Level** passage.
- identify events in the story that have a cause-and-effect relationship.

ENGLISH LANGUAGE LEARNERS

LESSONS 1–5

WRITING

MODELED WRITING

LESSON 1

LEARNING GOALS

We can learn how to write a concluding statement.

OBJECTIVES
Write informative texts in which they provide some sense of closure.

LANGUAGE OBJECTIVES
Children will inform by writing a sentence that includes a descriptive detail.

ELA ACADEMIC LANGUAGE
- detail
- Cognate: *detalle*

Writing Practice Review the sample on p. 132 of the **Reading/Writing Companion**. Help children use the Actor/Action routine to analyze the sentences: *Who is the actor?* (my favorite insect) *What do we learn about it?* (It is a caterpillar.) Then read the prompt on p. 133, and ask children to answer it as a group. Write the sentences on the board for children to chorally read. Then ask partners to write their own sentences.

Beginning *What is your favorite insect?* (a dragonfly) Have children add a descriptive detail: *What does it have?* It has long wings. Provide a sentence frame for the complete sentence.

Intermediate Have partners ask and answer *who/what* questions to create their sentences. Elicit descriptive details: *What does it look like?*

Advanced/Advanced High Challenge children to add a concluding statement that retells why they like this insect. Have them share the statement.

FORMATIVE ASSESSMENT ▶ **STUDENT CHECK IN** Partners share their sentences. Ask children to reflect, using the Check-In routine.

INTERACTIVE WRITING

LESSON 2

LEARNING GOALS

We can read and write about a Student Model.

OBJECTIVES
Add details to strengthen writing as needed.

LANGUAGE OBJECTIVES
Children will discuss and write sentences about the Student Model, identifying the concluding statement.

ELA ACADEMIC LANGUAGE
- text, concluding statement
- Cognate: *texto*

Analyze the Student Model Have children finger point as they chorally read the Student Model on p. 140 of the **Reading/Writing Companion**. Use the Actor/Action Routine to review each sentence. *Who is the actor?* (Caterpillar) *What do we learn about him?* (He is sad.) *When is he sad?* (at the beginning of the story) Then guide children to identify descriptive details in the text. *What word can we use to describe Caterpillar at the end of the story?* (happy) Finally, help children complete p. 141.

Beginning Have partners point to examples of descriptive details in the text. *What is a descriptive detail about Caterpillar?* (He can't dash fast.)

Intermediate Have partners ask and answer questions: *What did you notice about Amy's writing?* She used the word *see*.

Advanced/Advanced High Challenge children to write their own sentences about the text. Encourage children to share their ideas.

FORMATIVE ASSESSMENT ▶ **STUDENT CHECK IN** Partners share their responses. Ask children to reflect, using the Check-In routine.

---

196 UNIT 4 WEEK 4

WEEK 4

INDEPENDENT WRITING
LESSONS 3-4

LEARNING GOALS
We can use text evidence to respond to a fantasy story.

OBJECTIVES
Write narratives in which they recount events in sequence.

LANGUAGE OBJECTIVES
Children will explain by writing a sentence, using the verb *see*.

ELA ACADEMIC LANGUAGE
- *evidence*
- Cognate: *evidencia*

Find Text Evidence Follow the Independent Writing routine. Help children use text evidence to orally retell the anchor text. Ask questions, such as: *How does Buzz catch the fly?* (He puts it in a jar.) *What does the fly say?* ("Buzz!") *Why is the boy happy?* (His name is Buzz.) Then read the prompt on p. 146 of the **Reading/Writing Companion**: *Why do Buzz's parents and the judges change their minds about Fly Guy? At the beginning, do they think flies can be pets? What about at the end? We need to look for text evidence to write about what changes their opinion.*

Write a Response Work with children to complete My Writing Outline 19. After they have completed their outlines, have children complete p. 146.

Writing Checklist Read the checklist with students, and have them check for these items in their writing.

Beginning Provide sentence frames to help partners talk about their sentences: *I use a concluding statement at the end.*

Intermediate Encourage partners to identify each other's concluding statements, and challenge them to add one more descriptive detail.

Advanced/Advanced High Have partners identify where they use each checklist item in their writing.

FORMATIVE ASSESSMENT ❯ **STUDENT CHECK IN** Partners share their sentences from My Writing Outline. Ask children to reflect, using the Check-In routine.

SELF-SELECTED WRITING
LESSON 5

LEARNING GOALS
We can revise our writing.

OBJECTIVES
Use verbs to convey a sense of past, present, and future.

LANGUAGE OBJECTIVES
Children will inquire about their writing by checking *see* and *saw*.

ELA ACADEMIC LANGUAGE
- *verb*
- Cognate: *verbo*

Work with children to revise the group writing activity. Point to each word as you read the sentences. Stop to ask questions: *Is the verb see/saw used correctly here?* If needed, use *see* and *saw* incorrectly in sentences, and work together to revise them. Then have partners revise each other's sentences before publishing their writing.

For support with grammar and *see/saw,* refer to the **Language Transfers Handbook** and **Language Development Cards** 9A and 9B.

FORMATIVE ASSESSMENT ❯ **STUDENT CHECK IN** Partners tell what revisions they made. Ask children to reflect, using the Check-In routine.

ENGLISH LANGUAGE LEARNERS

READING • SHARED READ • ACCESS THE TEXT

LESSONS 1–2

LEARNING GOALS

We can read and understand a nonfiction text.

OBJECTIVES

Retell key details of a text.

Know and use various text features (e.g., headings, tables of contents, glossaries, electronic menus, icons) to locate key facts or information in a text.

With prompting and support, read informational texts appropriately complex for grade 1.

Produce complete sentences when appropriate to task and situation.

LANGUAGE OBJECTIVES

Children will inform about guide dogs, using verbs with *-ing*.

ELA ACADEMIC LANGUAGE

- visualize, setting, caption, evidence
- Cognates: *visualizar, evidencia*

MATERIALS

Reading/Writing Companion, pp. 158–167

Visual Vocabulary Cards

DIGITAL TOOLS

Have children listen to the selection as they follow along to develop comprehension and practice fluency and pronunciation.

Use the additional grammar song.

🎵 Grammar Song

"From Puppy to Guide Dog"

Prepare to Read

Build Background Read aloud the Essential Question on page 158. Have children share what they know about animals helping people. Use the photo on pages 158–159 to generate ideas. *This is a guide dog. A guide dog helps people. The woman is in a wheelchair. Say* wheelchair. *How can the dog help her? The dog can _____.* Point to and read the title. *A puppy is a baby dog. We are going to read about how a puppy becomes a guide dog.* Read the introduction aloud.

Reading/Writing Companion, Lexile 680L

Focus on Vocabulary Use the **Visual Vocabulary Cards** to review the high-frequency words *found, hard, near, woman, would,* and *write* and the oral vocabulary words *advice, career, remarkable, soothe,* and *trust.* As you read, use gestures and visual support to teach important selection words, such as *clever, signal, checkups, train* (verb), *trainer, lead, cross* (verb), and *tasks.*

Summarize the Text Before reading, say this summary and point to the photographs: *This article tells how people train puppies to be guide dogs. The dogs learn how to help people with everyday tasks in different situations.*

Read the Text

Use the Interactive Question-Response routine to help children understand the text.

Pages 160–163

Pages 160–161 Read the text aloud as children follow along. *Point to Mickey. How old will he be when he starts training to be a guide dog?* (eight weeks old) *Whom will he help?* (a person who cannot see)

Pages 162–163 Read the text aloud as children follow along. Explain that to "get used to" something is to become comfortable with it. Have children look at the photo on page 162. *Why is this puppy at the vet's?* (to stay healthy) Point to the bottom photo on page 163. *What is this puppy learning?* This puppy is learning to guide a person around objects. To help children visualize, demonstrate by guiding a child around classroom desks.

👥 *What settings must a future guide dog get used to? Discuss with a partner.*

Beginning Remind children that like the setting of a story, a *setting* is a place. Have pairs find and read aloud three places in the text. (city, homes, shops)

198 UNIT 4 WEEK 5

Intermediate Have pairs identify different settings in the text (city, homes, shops) and then describe the settings pictured on page 163: *The dog is* at/on *a* sports event/street.

Advanced/Advanced High Have pairs describe what the dog is doing in each setting pictured on page 163: *The dog is* sitting in a crowd *at a* sports event. *The dog is* walking around objects *on a* street.

Pages 164–165

Pages 164–165 Before reading the main text, point to the fact box, and read it aloud as children follow along. Ask: *What other settings do guide dogs need to get used to?* (restaurants, stores, school) Then read the text on page 164 aloud as children follow along. Clarify the word *traffic,* using the Spanish cognate *tráfico.* Have children look at the picture as you read the caption aloud. Ask: *What are the woman and the dog doing?* (crossing the street) Point to and say *crosswalk.* Then say: *Think about your own experience. What are some rules you should follow when you cross the street?* (look both ways, wait for a "walk" signal, cross only at a crosswalk) *How does a guide dog help a person who cannot see do this? It looks for* traffic *and stops at a* red signal. *It walks in the* crosswalk. Then read the main text on page 164 aloud.

How can dogs help people who cannot move or walk? Discuss with a partner.

Beginning Help children read the caption on page 165 aloud. Have pairs match tasks to pictures: *This dog* reaches/gets an object. *This dog* gets an elevator.

Intermediate Have pairs read the caption on page 165. Then have them describe the dog's task shown in the elevator picture: *The dog is* pushing a button. *This helps the person* get an elevator *to open.*

Advanced/Advanced High Have pairs read the caption on page 165. Have them describe each dog's task and how it helps the person; for example: *The dog* pushes the button. *This will make* the elevator *come and open* the door *so* the man *can get into it.*

Pages 166–167

Pages 166–167 Read the text and caption aloud as children follow along. *A sound is what you hear with your ears.* Have children point to their ears. Use realia and gestures to convey meanings of *a bell ringing, a yell,* and the verbs *tug* and *poke. Why does the dog tug or poke the person? What is it trying to say?* (There is a sound.) Read the fact box on page 166. Give examples to clarify what it means to *bother* a dog, such as calling it or petting it. *Why shouldn't you bother a guide dog? Guide dogs have important* tasks to do.

The text says, "Training a guide dog helps a lot of people." Whom do guide dogs help? Discuss with a partner.

Beginning Help pairs look back at the photos for two kinds of people that guide dogs help: *Guide dogs help people who cannot* see/hear/walk/reach.

Intermediate Have children find evidence in the text of four kinds of people who are helped: *Guide dogs help people who cannot* see, walk, move, or hear.

Advanced/Advanced High Have pairs elaborate on how guide dogs help each type of person. For example: *Guide dogs help people who* cannot see cross streets.

FORMATIVE ASSESSMENT

▶ STUDENT CHECK IN

Have partners retell three ways a guide dog can help people each day. Then have children reflect, using the Check-In routine.

Independent Time

Talk About It Pair children of mixed proficiencies. Have them pretend they are guide dog trainers. Have partners visualize and discuss this scenario: *You just got a new puppy! It will be a guide dog someday. How can you help train the dog?* Have pairs brainstorm ideas based on the text to share with the group.

READING • ANCHOR TEXT • ACCESS THE TEXT

LESSON 3

LEARNING GOALS

We can read and understand a nonfiction text.

OBJECTIVES

Retell key details of a text.

Know and use various text features (e.g., headings, tables of contents, glossaries, electronic menus, icons) to locate key facts or information in a text.

With prompting and support, read informational texts appropriately complex for grade 1.

Produce complete sentences when appropriate to task and situation.

LANGUAGE OBJECTIVES

Children will inform about how Koko learned from Penny, using sequence words.

ELA ACADEMIC LANGUAGE

- information, caption, sequence
- Cognates: *información, secuencia*

MATERIALS

Literature Anthology, pp. 130–137

Visual Vocabulary Cards

DIGITAL TOOLS

Have children listen to the selection to develop comprehension as they follow along.

Use the online ELL Vocabulary Practice for additional support.

Koko and Penny

Prepare to Read

Build Background Remind children of the Essential Question: *How do people work with animals?* Ask: *Where do people work with wild animals, like lions and tigers? They work at a _____.* Elicit children's experiences at a zoo. Ask questions such as: *What is one animal you saw? What did it look like?* Encourage children to describe interactions they had with the animal: *What did it do? Did you talk to it? Did it answer you? Why?* Animals can't _____. Then display and read the title. Say the word *gorilla* for children to repeat as they point to the gorilla in the picture. Ask children to raise their hands if they have seen a gorilla at a zoo. *The gorilla's name is Koko. The woman's name is Penny. She is Koko's teacher. We are going to read about what Penny teaches Koko to do.*

Literature Anthology, Lexile 370L

Focus on Vocabulary Use the **Visual Vocabulary Cards** to review the high-frequency words *found, hard, near, woman, would,* and *write* and the oral vocabulary words *advice, career, remarkable, soothe,* and *trust*. As you read, use gestures and pantomime to teach important story words such as *signs* and *signals*.

Summarize the Text Before reading, say this summary while pointing to the images: *This text tells about a gorilla named Koko and a special teacher named Penny. Penny teaches Koko hand signs for many different words.*

Read the Text

Use the Interactive Question-Response routine to help children understand the text.

Pages 130–133

Pages 130–131 Read the text aloud. Ask children if they have ever "jumped into the arms" of a parent or grandparent. Ask: *Why do you do that?* (to hug them, to show you love them) Explain that *pulled her near* is another way to say that Koko hugged Penny. Have children point to the pictures on page 131 as you read the caption aloud. Reread the last sentence on page 130. *What did Penny want?* (Penny wanted to see what Koko could do.) Say: *This is why Penny wants to study Koko.* To study *means "to try to learn something."* Prompt children to make a prediction: *How do you think Penny will study Koko?* (watch her, teach her)

Pages 132–133 Read page 132 aloud. *How doess Penny teach Koko words?* She shows Koko hand signs and signals. *What do you think Koko does after that?* She makes the same hand sign or signal. *Why does Koko sign* cookie*?* She wants a cookie. Have children look at the photo as you read the caption aloud. Have children repeat the word *sip* and mime sipping a drink from a cup. Follow this

200 UNIT 4 WEEK 5

routine for the photos on page 133. Then ask: *What words does Koko know?* (cookie, sip, loves, toothbrush) Read the main text on page 133. *What other words does Koko know?* Have children make the signs as they answer. (happy, sad) *How many words does Koko know?* (more than 1,000)

COLLABORATE *Why does the author present information in order? Discuss with a partner.*

Beginning Tell children we can use *first* and *next* to tell order. *What hand sign does Koko learn first: the sign for* toothbrush *or for* cookie? (the sign for *cookie*) *Does Koko learn all her signs at one time?* (no)

Intermediate Have pairs use sequence words: First, Koko asks for things she wants. Next, Koko learns more words for things and actions. Last, Koko learns words for feelings. *Does reading the information in order help you understand Koko?* (yes)

Advanced/Advanced High Have pairs tell the order in which Koko learns signs: First, Koko learns words for things she wants. Next, Koko learns more words for things and actions. Last, Koko learns words for feelings. *What does showing the words Koko learned in order tell you?* It tells me Koko learns one word at a time.

Pages 134–137

Pages 134–135 Read the text. Ask questions to help children retell: *On this page, Does Penny teach Koko to sign words?* (no) *What does she teach Koko?* (how to write) Read the caption as children look at the picture. *Can Koko write her name?* (yes) *Why does Koko sign* cat? She wants *a cat. What does Penny do?* She gives Koko a kitten. *What is a kitten?* (a baby cat) *Koko is kind to the kitten. Being* kind *means "being nice and friendly." Why is Koko remarkable?* She can write. She has a pet.

Pages 136–137 Read the text aloud. Point to the photo on page 136: *What can Koko do?* (She can paint.) Read the caption and say: *Point to a red color in Koko's painting.*

COLLABORATE *How do the captions help you understand the photos? Discuss with a partner.*

Beginning Have children look back at the photos and captions on pages 132–133. Have pairs imitate each sign Koko makes and find the corresponding word in the captions. (sip, loves, toothbrush) *Do the captions help you understand the photos?* (yes)

Intermediate Have children look back at the photos and captions on pages 132–133. Have pairs make each sign as they say each word. Then help them respond: The captions tell the word for each hand sign Koko makes.

Advanced/Advanced High Have children review the photos and captions on pages 132–133. Have pairs make the signs as they say the words. Then have partners cover the captions and look only at the photos. Ask: *What information do the captions give that you do not get from the pictures?* (the words)

FORMATIVE ASSESSMENT

❯ STUDENT CHECK IN

Have partners retell the types of things that Koko learned. Then, have children reflect using the Check-In Routine.

Independent Time

Discuss Photos Have children use photos in the selection and what they know to make inferences. Pair children of mixed proficiencies, and have them ask and answer questions about the photo of Koko on page 134, such as: *What is Koko doing? Koko is ___. Is it easy or hard for her to write? It is ___. How do you know?* Have partners follow a similar process for the photo of Koko on page 135, asking questions such as: *How does Koko feel? Is the kitten afraid of Koko? How do you know?* Finally, have partners ask and answer to compare the photos of Penny hugging Koko on page 137 and on page 131, such as: *How are the photos alike? Both show ___. How are the photos different? Koko is ___. Do you think Koko's and Penny's feelings for each other have changed?* Have partners retell their responses to the group.

LESSONS 4–5

READING • LEVELED READER • ACCESS THE TEXT

LEARNING GOALS

We can visualize to understand a nonfiction text.

OBJECTIVES

Describe the connection between two individuals, events, ideas, or pieces of information in a text.

Distinguish between information provided by pictures or other illustrations and information provided by the words in a text.

Identify basic similarities in and differences between two texts on the same topic (e.g., in illustrations, descriptions, or procedures).

Describe people, places, things, and events with relevant details, expressing ideas and feelings clearly.

LANGUAGE OBJECTIVES

Children will explain how a dog can learn, using sequence words.

ELA ACADEMIC LANGUAGE

- visualize
- Cognates: *visualizar*

MATERIALS

ELL Leveled Reader: *Teach a Dog!*

Online Differentiated Text, "Helping Horses"

Online ELL Visual Vocabulary Cards

DIGITAL TOOLS

Have children listen to the selection as they follow along to develop comprehension and practice fluency and pronunciation. Use Graphic Organizer 6: Sequence of Events, Time Order to enhance the lesson.

Teach a Dog!

Prepare to Read

Build Background

- Remind children of the Essential Question: *How do people work with animals?* Say: *Let's read to find out what people teach their dogs.* Encourage children to ask for clarification when they do not understand a word or phrase.

- Read the title for children to repeat. Ask for a show of hands: *Who has a pet dog?* Have children tell about their dogs: I have a dog. His/Her name is ____. He/She is ____. Ask: *Do you play with/feed/walk your dog?*

Focus on Vocabulary Use **ELL Visual Vocabulary Cards** to preteach the words *behave* and *rules*. Then use the pictures in the **Leveled Reader** to clarify key terms, such as *treat, leash,* and *collar*.

Lexile 220L

Read the Text

Use the Interactive Question-Response routine to help children understand the text.

Pages 2–5

Details: Time Order Read pages 2–5 as children follow along. Discuss the steps of teaching a dog with children. say: *Let's look for time order words, like* first *and* next. *What is the first step?* (show the dog how to sit) *What is the next step?* (teach the dog to stay)

Beginning Have pairs find and practice saying the three commands from the text: *sit, stay,* and *come.* Encourage pairs to perform each command.

Intermediate Provide sentence frames to help partners describe teaching the dog one command: I say, "Sit." The dog sits. I give the dog a treat.

Pages 6–7

Visualize Read pages 6–7 as children follow along. To help children visualize this section of the text, say: *Let's picture a dog with its tail down. What does this signal mean?* (The dog is sad.)

Beginning Ask: *What is the dog saying with its body?* Have children point to each picture as you say the corresponding sentence for them to repeat: *"I'm scared." "I want a treat." "I love you." "I want to play!"*

Advanced/Advanced High Have pairs take turns describing a dog's actions in a photo and guessing the corresponding feeling: This dog's tail is down. He feels scared.

202 UNIT 4 WEEK 5

WEEK 5

Pages 8–12

Read pages 8-9 as children follow along. Ask: *What are some rules for walking a dog?*

Intermediate Have pairs look at each picture and point to and name the things they need to walk a dog. (leash, collar)

Advanced/Advanced High Say: *You are walking your dog. The dog pants/pulls on the leash. What should you do?* Have pairs discuss.

Respond to Reading Have partners work together to retell the selection and respond to the questions on page 12.

Focus on Fluency

Read pages 4-5 to model appropriate intonation. Read the passage again, and have children repeat after you. For more practice, record children reading the passage. Have them select the best recording.

Paired Read: "Working with Dolphins"

Analytical Writing — Make Connections: Write About It

Echo-read each page with children. Discuss what dolphins can do: *Dolphins can jump and stand.* Help children make connections between texts, using the question on page 15: People give animals treats when they follow commands.

Leveled Reader

Build Knowledge: Make Connections

Talk About the Text Have partners discuss how people in the texts work with animals.

Write About the Text Have children add their ideas to the Build Knowledge pages of their reader's notebooks.

Self-Selected Reading

Help children choose a nonfiction selection from the online **Leveled Reader Library,** or read the **Differentiated Text,** "Helping Horses."

FOCUS ON SOCIAL STUDIES

Children can extend their knowledge of pets by completing the social studies activity on page 16.

LITERATURE CIRCLES

Lead children in conducting a literature circle using the Thinkmark questions to guide the discussion. You may wish to discuss what children have learned from both selections in the **Leveled Reader** about working with animals.

FORMATIVE ASSESSMENT

STUDENT CHECK IN

Have partners share their Respond to Reading. Have children reflect, using the Check-In routine.

LEVEL UP

IF children can read *Teach a Dog!* **ELL Level** with fluency and correctly answer the Respond to Reading questions,

THEN tell children they will read a more detailed version of this selection.

- Use page 4 of *Teach a Dog!* **On Level** to model using Teaching Poster 31 to list sequence clues.
- Have children read the selection, checking their comprehension by using the graphic organizer.

ENGLISH LANGUAGE LEARNERS

LESSONS 4–5

READING • GENRE PASSAGE • ACCESS THE TEXT

LEARNING GOALS

We can apply skills and strategies to a nonfiction text.

OBJECTIVES

Retell key details of a text.

Describe the connection between two individuals, events, ideas, or pieces of information in a text.

With prompting and support, read informational texts appropriately complex for grade 1.

Produce complete sentences when appropriate to task and situation.

LANGUAGE OBJECTIVES

Children will inform about what happens at the vet using time order words *first* and *next*.

ELA ACADEMIC LANGUAGE

- order, details
- Cognates: *orden, detalles*

MATERIALS

Online ELL Genre Passage, "Vets Help Pets"

"Vets Help Pets"

Prepare to Read

Build Background Ask: *When do you go to the doctor?* Elicit from children that they visit the doctor when they are sick or want a checkup. Say: *Your doctor helps when you are sick and can keep you healthy too.* Then ask: *Who helps pets when they are sick?* To answer, read the title chorally with children.

Lexile 300L

Focus on Vocabulary Use the **Define, Example, Ask** routine to preteach difficult words or unfamiliar concepts, such as *healthy* and *sick* as an antonym pair. Write the word *weigh* on the board and say it for children to repeat. Pick up something heavy, exaggerating the difficulty, and say: *This weighs a lot! It's heavy!* Pick up something light and say: *This doesn't weigh a lot. It's light!*

Read the Text

Use the Interactive Question-Response routine to help children understand the text.

Page E1

Paragraphs 1–2 Read the text aloud. Help children **visualize** by creating a mental picture about what a vet does. *People see how much they weigh by standing on a scale. How do you think vets weigh pets?* (put them on a scale)

Beginning Provide a sentence frame to help children define the word *vet* based on the text: A vet is a <u>doctor</u> who helps <u>pets</u> when they are <u>sick</u>.

Advanced/Advanced High Have pairs write a definition for *vet* in their own words. Have them use a dictionary or glossary to check their work.

Paragraphs 3–5 Read the text aloud as children follow along. Ask questions to help children review **time order**: *What does a vet do first?* (weighs the pet) *What does the vet do next?* (looks in the pet's mouth and ears)

Beginning Have partners look at the picture and take turns pointing and describing: I see a <u>vet</u> and a <u>dog</u>. The vet is looking at the dog's <u>ear</u>.

Intermediate Have children describe what is happening in the picture: The <u>vet</u> is looking in <u>the dog's ear</u>. He's looking for a <u>problem</u>.

Page E2

Paragraphs 1–3 Read the text aloud as children follow along. Point out the word *healthy,* and remind children that they can look for a **base word** to figure out the meaning of a word. Health *is the base word. The letter -y is added to mean "has health."* Discuss what the vet wants for all animals. *What is a healthy animal?* (It is well and not sick.)

204 UNIT 4 WEEK 5

WEEK 5

Advanced Have pairs use the text on pages E1 and E2 to answer: *What does the vet do before he or she decides what to do?* The vet weighs the pet and looks all over for the problem. Sometimes, the vet does tests. Have children find the **time-order** words *first, next,* and *finally* to understand the order.

Advanced High Ask: *How does the vet decide what to do? What questions might a vet ask?* Have pairs brainstorm questions based on the text. (What does the pet weigh? Is/Are the pet's mouth/ears/bones OK? Do I need to do tests?)

Paragraph 3 Read the text aloud as children follow along. To monitor comprehension, ask: *What do vets need to know?* They need to know a lot about many animals. *How do vets feel about animals?*

Beginning Have children use this sentence frame to answer the question: Vets want animals to be healthy.

Intermediate Provide this sentence frame to help pairs answer: Vets like animals. Vets want to help them be healthy.

Respond to Reading

Use the following instructions to help children answer the questions on page E3.

1. **Nonfiction** Remind children that nonfiction texts are about real events and topics. Have children look at the photos on pages E1 and E2. Elicit or point out that because this text is nonfiction, it includes photos of real animals, people, and jobs. Have children compare the photos to help them answer the question. Ask: *Who is the vet? What is he doing in both photos?* He is looking at/helping the pet.

2. **Details: Time Order** Have children echo-read each sentence on page E2. Help them find the detail in the second paragraph that tells what the vet does at the end. Ask: *Which word tells you what the vet does at the end? (finally)*

3. **Fluency** Have children take turns reading the first paragraph to a partner. As they read, have them fill in the chart on page E3.

Build Knowledge: Make Connections

Talk About the Text Have partners discuss how vets work with animals.

Write About the Text Have students add their ideas to the Build Knowledge pages of their reader's notebooks.

FORMATIVE ASSESSMENT

❯ STUDENT CHECK IN

Have partners share their Respond to Reading. Then have children reflect, using the Check-In routine.

LEVEL UP

IF children read the **ELL Level** fluently and answered the questions,

THEN pair them with children who have proficiently read the **On Level.** Have them

- partner-read the **On Level** passage.
- identify the order of events in the text.

ENGLISH LANGUAGE LEARNERS **205**

LESSONS 1–5

WRITING

MODELED WRITING

LESSON 1

LEARNING GOALS

We can learn how to write a sentence that introduces the topic.

OBJECTIVES

Write narratives in which they include some details and recount events in sequence.

LANGUAGE OBJECTIVES

Children will narrate by writing a sentence that introduces their topic.

ELA ACADEMIC LANGUAGE

- topic

Writing Practice Review the sample on p. 168 of the **Reading/Writing Companion**. Help children use the Actor/Action routine to analyze the sentences: The actor is my dad and I. The action is walk our dog. Every morning tells more about the action. Then read the prompt on p. 169, and ask children to answer it as a group before writing it on the board. Then ask children to write their own sentences.

Beginning Help partners think of their topic sentence: *Who is the actor?* (I) *What animal did you see?* (a raccoon) Provide a sentence frame.

Intermediate Have partners ask and answer *who/what* questions to create their sentences. For the topic sentence, they can ask: *What animal did you see? What more can you tell about the topic?*

Advanced/Advanced High Challenge children to replace one word with a more specific word. Have them share both versions of the sentence.

FORMATIVE ASSESSMENT ❯ **STUDENT CHECK IN** Partners share their sentences. Ask children to reflect, using the Check-In routine.

INTERACTIVE WRITING

LESSON 2

LEARNING GOALS

We can read and write about a Student Model.

OBJECTIVES

Respond to questions and suggestions from peers.

LANGUAGE OBJECTIVES

Children will discuss and write sentences about the Student Model, identifying specific words.

ELA ACADEMIC LANGUAGE

- adverb
- Cognate: adverbio

Analyze the Student Model Have children finger point as they chorally read the Student Model on p. 176 of the **Reading/Writing Companion**. Use the Actor/Action Routine to review each sentence. The actor is a guide dog. The action is can do many things. Next guide children to identify specific words. *Is many things specific or general?* (general) *Is inside and outside things general or specific?* (specific) Help children complete p. 177.

Beginning Have partners point to an example of an adverb from the text. I notice the adverb then. It tells when the action happened.

Intermediate Have partners ask and answer questions: *What did you notice about Hassan's writing?* Hassan uses specific words. For example, he uses inside and outside.

Advanced/Advanced High Challenge children to write their own sentences about the text. Encourage children to share their ideas.

FORMATIVE ASSESSMENT ❯ **STUDENT CHECK IN** Partners share their responses. Ask children to reflect, using the Check-In routine.

206 UNIT 4 WEEK 5

WEEK 5

INDEPENDENT WRITING

LESSONS 3–4

LEARNING GOALS
We can use text evidence to respond to a nonfiction text.

OBJECTIVES
Write informative texts in which they name a topic and supply some facts about the topic.

LANGUAGE OBJECTIVES
Children will explain by writing a sentence, using a specific word.

ELA ACADEMIC LANGUAGE
- topic

Find Text Evidence Follow the Independent Writing routine. Help children use text evidence to orally retell the anchor text. Ask questions, such as: *What kind of animal is Koko?* (a gorilla) *Where did Penny find her?* (in a zoo) *How does Penny teach Koko to make words?* (hand signs and signals) Then read the prompt on p. 181 of the **Reading/Writing Companion:** *How did learning sign language affect Koko's relationship with Penny? We need to think about what Koko could do after she learned sign language.*

Write a Response Work with children to complete My Writing Outline 20. Then have them use the sentences from their outlines to complete p. 181.

Writing Checklist Read the checklist with students, and have them check for these items in their writing.

Beginning Provide sentence frames to help partners talk about their sentences: I use the specific word *communicate*.

Intermediate Have partners identify each other's topic sentences, and challenge them to add specific words.

Advanced/Advanced High Have partners identify where they use each item in their writing.

FORMATIVE ASSESSMENT ▶ **STUDENT CHECK IN** Partners share their sentences from My Writing Outline. Ask children to reflect, using the Check-In routine.

SELF-SELECTED WRITING

LESSON 5

LEARNING GOALS
We can revise our writing.

OBJECTIVES
Use commas in dates and to separate single words in a series.

LANGUAGE OBJECTIVES
Children will inquire about their writing by checking commas in a series.

ELA ACADEMIC LANGUAGE
- publish
- Cognates: *publicar*

Work with children to revise the group writing activity. Point to each word as you read the sentences. Stop to ask questions, such as: Do we need a comma here? Work together to add a word or words in one of the sentences to create a series, and then review where commas are needed. Then have partners revise each other's sentences before publishing their writing.

For support with grammar and adverbs, refer to the **Language Transfers Handbook** and **Language Development Card** 15A.

FORMATIVE ASSESSMENT ▶ **STUDENT CHECK IN** Partners tell what revisions they made. Ask children to reflect, using the Check-In routine.

ENGLISH LANGUAGE LEARNERS 207

UNIT 4

Summative Assessment
Get Ready for Unit Assessment

Unit 4 Tested Skills

LISTENING AND READING COMPREHENSION	VOCABULARY	GRAMMAR	SPEAKING AND WRITING
• Listening Actively • Details	• Words and Categories	• Verbs • Adverbs	• Expressing Opinions • Presenting • Composing/Writing • Retelling/Recounting

Create a Student Profile

Record data from the following resources in the Student Profile charts on pages 356–357 of the Assessment book.

COLLABORATIVE	INTERPRETIVE	PRODUCTIVE

• Collaborative Conversations Rubrics
  • Listening
  • Speaking
	• Leveled Unit Assessment
	  • Listening Comprehension
	  • Reading Comprehension
	  • Vocabulary
	  • Grammar
	• Presentation Rubric
	  • Listening
	• *Wonders* Unit Assessment
		• Weekly Progress Monitoring
		• Leveled Unit Assessment
		  • Speaking
		  • Writing
		• Presentation Rubric
		  • Speaking
		• Write to Sources Rubric
		• *Wonders* Unit Assessment

The Foundational Skills Kit, Language Development Kit, and Adaptive Learning provide additional student data for progress monitoring.

Level Up

Use the following chart, along with your Student Profiles, to guide your Level Up decisions.

LEVEL UP	If **BEGINNING** level students are able to do the following, they may be ready to move to the **INTERMEDIATE** level:	If **INTERMEDIATE** level students are able to do the following, they may be ready to move to the **ADVANCED** level:	If **ADVANCED** level students are able to do the following, they may be ready to move to **ON** level:
COLLABORATIVE	• participate in collaborative conversations using basic vocabulary and grammar and simple phrases or sentences • discuss simple pictorial or text prompts	• participate in collaborative conversations using appropriate words and phrases and complete sentences • use limited academic vocabulary across and within disciplines	• participate in collaborative conversations using more sophisticated vocabulary and correct grammar • communicate effectively across a wide range of language demands in social and academic contexts
INTERPRETIVE	• identify details in simple read alouds • understand common vocabulary and idioms and interpret language related to familiar social, school, and academic topics • make simple inferences and make simple comparisons • exhibit an emerging receptive control of lexical, syntactic, phonological, and discourse features	• identify main ideas and/or make some inferences from simple read alouds • use context clues to identify word meanings and interpret basic vocabulary and idioms • compare, contrast, summarize, and relate text to graphic organizers • exhibit a limited range of receptive control of lexical, syntactic, phonological, and discourse features when addressing new or familiar topics	• determine main ideas in read alouds that have advanced vocabulary • use context clues to determine meaning, understand multiple-meaning words, and recognize synonyms of social and academic vocabulary • analyze information, make sophisticated inferences, and explain their reasoning • command a high degree of receptive control of lexical, syntactic, phonological, and discourse features
PRODUCTIVE	• express ideas and opinions with basic vocabulary and grammar and simple phrases or sentences • restate information or retell a story using basic vocabulary • exhibit an emerging productive control of lexical, syntactic, phonological, and discourse features	• produce coherent language with limited elaboration or detail • restate information or retell a story using mostly accurate, although limited, vocabulary • exhibit a limited range of productive control of lexical, syntactic, phonological, and discourse features when addressing new or familiar topics	• produce sentences with more sophisticated vocabulary and correct grammar • restate information or retell a story using extensive and accurate vocabulary and grammar • tailor language to a particular purpose and audience • command a high degree of productive control of lexical, syntactic, phonological, and discourse features

READING • SHARED READ • ACCESS THE TEXT

LESSONS 1-2

LEARNING GOALS

We can read and understand a fantasy story.

OBJECTIVES

Describe characters, settings, and major events in a story, using key details.

Compare and contrast the adventures and experiences of characters in stories.

Describe people, places, things, and events with relevant details, expressing ideas and feelings clearly.

Produce complete sentences when appropriate to task and situation.

LANGUAGE OBJECTIVES

Children will narrate the characters' points of view, using adjectives, verbs, and complete sentences.

ELA ACADEMIC LANGUAGE

- classify, category, illustration
- Cognates: *clasificar, categoría, ilustración*

MATERIALS

Reading/Writing Companion, pp. 14–23

Visual Vocabulary Cards

DIGITAL TOOLS

MULTIMODAL

Have children listen to the selection as they follow along to develop comprehension and practice fluency and pronunciation.

Use the online ELL Vocabulary Practice for additional support.

"A Barn Full of Hats"

Prepare to Read

Build Background Read aloud the Essential Question on page 14. Have children share ideas for classifying things. Use the illustration on page 18 to help generate the idea that hats can be classified by color and shape. Point to and read aloud the title. *We are going to read a story about some animals in a barn.* Point to the barn. *Say* barn *with me. The title says the barn is full of hats. Do you think the barn has a lot of hats or a few hats?* Point to the animals. *The animals are wearing hats. Say* wearing hats *with me. Did you wear a hat today? Yes/No, I _____.*

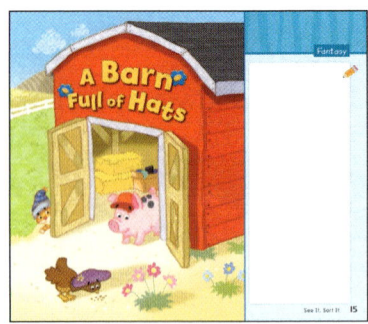

Reading/Writing Companion, Lexile 320L

Focus on Vocabulary Use the **Visual Vocabulary Cards** to review the high-frequency words *four, large, none, only, put,* and *round* and the oral vocabulary words *classify, distinguish, entire, organize,* and *startled.* Display the illustrations in the text, and point to the pictures for *box, pulled out, flat, marched away, yarn,* and *floppy.* Use the following routine for each new word or phrase: Point to the box. Say the word *box.* Have children point to the picture and repeat the word. *The animals are looking at a box in the barn. What is in the barn?* Have children respond: A box is in the barn.

Summarize the Text Before reading, say the summary while pointing to the illustrations. *The story tells about a group of animals who find a box of hats. The animals sort the hats to find the right hat for each animal.*

Read the Text

Use the Interactive Question-Response routine to help children understand the story.

Pages 14–17

Pages 16–17 Read the text aloud. Point to the box. *What do the animals find in the barn?* The animals find a box in the barn. *What is inside the box?* (hats) Point to the sentence "Hats, hats, and more hats!" *When the author repeats* hats, *I think there are a lot of hats in the box.* Point to the illustration on page 17. *Who says he wants a hat?* Horse says he wants a hat.

What is Horse's point of view? How do you know? Discuss with a partner.

Beginning Point to the animals on page 17. Point to Horse. *Does Horse look happy?* Yes, Horse looks happy. *Does Horse want a hat?* Yes, Horse wants a hat. *Point to the text that helps you know this.* Check that partners point to "'I do!' cried Horse."

210 UNIT 5 WEEK 1

WEEK 1

Intermediate Have partners point to the pictures as they respond. *Does Horse look happy?* Yes, Horse looks happy. *Does Horse want a hat?* Yes, Horse wants a hat. *What does Horse say that tells you he wants a hat?* Horse says I do! when Hen asks who wants a hat.

Advanced/Advanced High Have partners add details to their responses. *What does Horse say that tells you what he thinks about the hats?* Horse says I do! when Hen asks who wants a hat. Horse explains why hats are good.

Pages 18–21

Pages 18–19 Read the text aloud. Point to the illustration on page 18. *Hen pulls out the first hat. Does Horse like the hat?* No, Horse does not like the hat. *What does Horse think of the hat?* He thinks it is too flat. Point to the hen. *Hen clucks.* Clucking *is the sound a hen makes. Why does Hen take the flat hat?* She thinks it will make a good nest. Point to the illustration on page 19. *Pig pulls out the next hat. Does Horse like the hat?* No, Horse does not like the hat. *What does Horse think of the hat?* He thinks it is too red.

What are some categories the animals use to talk about the hats? Discuss with a partner.

Beginning Point to the images of the hats the animals pull out of the box. *What does Horse say about the first hat?* He says it is flat. *What does Horse say about the second hat?* He says it is red.

Intermediate Have partners point to the illustrations as they discuss the categories the animals use to talk about the hats. The animals talk about the shapes and colors of the hats.

Advanced/Advanced High Have partners discuss which category is most important for the animals to think about. Have children suggest other categories. The animals could sort the hats by size.

Pages 22–23

Page 22 Read the text aloud. Point to the illustration of Farmer Clark wearing the floppy hat. Then point to the illustration of Horse wearing the hat on page 23. *What is Horse wearing?* Horse is wearing Farmer Clark's hat. Point to Farmer Clark. *Does Farmer Clark look angry?* No, Farmer Clark does not look angry. Point to the animals. *Do all the animals have hats?* Yes, they all have hats.

What is the farmer's point of view? How do you know? Discuss with a partner.

Beginning Point to the image of Farmer Clark. *Does Farmer Clark have a hat?* No, Farmer Clark does not have a hat. *How does Farmer Clark look?* Farmer Clark looks happy. *Point to words that tell you he is happy.* Children should point to "Farmer Clark laughed."

Intermediate Have partners point to the pictures as they respond. *What does Farmer Clark do when Horse takes his hat?* Farmer Clark laughs when Horse takes his hat.

Advanced/Advanced High Help partners add details to their responses. *What details in the story tell you how Farmer Clark feels when Horse takes his hat?* When Farmer Clark laughs, it tells me he thinks it's funny that Horse took his hat.

FORMATIVE ASSESSMENT

▶ STUDENT CHECK-IN

Have partners retell the characters' opinions about the different kinds of hats. Then have children reflect, using the Check-In routine.

Independent Time

Role Play Group children of mixed proficiencies. Have groups select a spread from the story that they enjoy. Then have the groups assign each child a role from the story. For example, one child will be Horse, one will be Pig, one will be Hen, and one will be Cat. Have children work together to prepare a role play of their selected spread. Groups should include dialogue and movements in their role play. Encourage groups to use props if needed. After groups have finished rehearsing, have them present their role play to another group or the whole class.

LESSON 3

READING • ANCHOR TEXT • ACCESS THE TEXT

LEARNING GOALS

We can read and understand a fantasy story.

OBJECTIVES

Retell stories, including key details, and demonstrate understanding of their central message or lesson.

Identify words and phrases in stories or poems that suggest feelings or appeal to the senses.

Use illustrations and details in a story to describe its characters, setting, or events.

Produce complete sentences when appropriate to task and situation.

LANGUAGE OBJECTIVES

Children will narrate how the characters solve a problem, using words of feeling, key vocabulary, and complete sentences.

ELA ACADEMIC LANGUAGE

- fantasy, illustration, glossaries
- Cognates: *fantasía, ilustración, glosarios*

MATERIALS

Literature Anthology, pp. 140–155

Visual Vocabulary Cards

DIGITAL TOOLS

Have children listen to the selection as they follow along to develop comprehension and practice fluency and pronunciation.

Use the additional grammar video.

Grammar Video

A Lost Button

Prepare to Read

Build Background *We are going to read a fantasy story about two friends who look for a button that is missing.* Show the picture on the title page, and invite children to tell what they see. Point to *frog, toad, bird, flowers,* and *grass.* Say the words, and have children repeat them. Then point to Toad's jacket. *Toad is wearing a jacket. Say* jacket *with me. The round things on Toad's jacket are* buttons. Point to the buttons. Say buttons *with me. When we wear clothes with buttons, a button can come off. We might lose that button. When I lose a button, I look for it. What do you do when you lose something?* I ____ it.

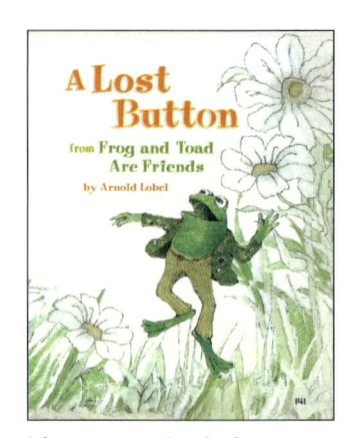

Literature Anthology, Lexile 340L

Focus on Vocabulary Use the **Visual Vocabulary Cards** to review the high-frequency words *four, large, none, only, put,* and *round,* and the oral vocabulary words *distinguish, classify, organize, entire,* and *startled.* Before reading the story, clarify vocabulary children will need for understanding. As you read, teach important story words, such as *lost* and *find,* using gestures and pantomime.

Summarize the Text Before reading, say the summary while pointing to the illustrations. *The story tells about two friends who are looking for a lost button. The friends use different categories to decide which button they are looking for.*

Read the Text

Use the Interactive Question-Response routine to help children understand the story.

Pages 142–147

Pages 146–147 Read the text aloud as children follow along. Point to the word *found,* and say it aloud for children to repeat. Found *means the same as* find, *but it talks about the past.* Point to the sparrow. *A sparrow is a type of bird. What did the sparrow find?* The sparrow found a button. *Did the sparrow find Toad's button?* No, the sparrow did not find Toad's button.

COLLABORATE *How does the author show that Frog is a good friend? Discuss with a partner.*

Beginning *What happens to Toad?* Toad loses a button. Then point to page 147. *What does the illustration show?* The illustration shows Frog talking to Toad. Point to Frog's quote. *What does Frog say?* Frog says, "Here is your button." *How is Frog a good friend?* Frog helps Toad look for his button.

Intermediate Guide partners to give more specific answers. *What problem does Toad have?* Toad lost his button. Point to the first paragraph back on page 144.

212 UNIT 5 WEEK 1

WEEK 1

What does Frog say to help Toad feel better? Frog says, "Don't worry." *Point to page 147. What do the text and picture show Frog is doing?* Frog is helping Toad look for his button. *Is the button that Frog finds Toad's button?* (no) *What do you think Frog will do next?* I think Frog will keep looking for the button.

Advanced/Advanced High Help partners add details to their responses. *Why does looking for the button make Frog a good friend?* Frog is trying to do something to make Toad happy. *What do you predict Frog will do next?* I think Frog will keep looking for Toad's button.

Pages 148–151

Pages 150–151 Read the text *He was very angry*. Point to the picture. *The picture shows that Toad is angry.* Point to the phrase *covered with buttons,* and read it aloud for children to repeat. *The phrase* covered with buttons *means a lot of buttons.* Point to the picture on page 151. *What does Toad see on the floor?* Toad sees a button. *Is it Toad's button?* Yes, it is Toad's button.

How does the author show Toad's feelings? Discuss with a partner.

Beginning Guide partners to answer the question. Point to Toad on page 150. *How does Toad look?* Toad looks angry. *Which words on the page tell you Toad is angry?* Angry and screamed tell me Toad is angry.

Intermediate Help partners give details with their answers. *Which words and phrases in the story tell you how Toad feels?* Jumped up and down, screamed, and slammed tell me Toad is angry. *Why does Toad feel this way?* Toad cannot find his button anywhere.

Advanced/Advanced High Help partners elaborate on their answers. *Which words and phrases in the story tell you how Toad feels?* Jumped up and down, screamed, and slammed tell me Toad is angry. *Why does the author choose these words?* Jumped up and down tells that Toad is so mad he can't stand still. Screamed tells that he is so mad he can't speak softly.

Pages 152–153

Pages 152–153 Read the text aloud as children follow along. Point to the illustration at the bottom of the page. *Toad sews buttons on his jacket. He uses a needle and thread from his sewing box.* Pantomime sewing and say: *I am sewing.* Have children mimic you and repeat. Point to Frog on page 152. *What does Frog think of the jacket?* Frog thinks it is beautiful.

How does the author help you understand that Toad is a good friend? Discuss with a partner.

Beginning Review what happens on page 151. *How does Toad feel?* (sad) *Is Toad sad he made trouble for Frog?* (yes) Point to the pictures on pages 152–153. *What does Toad do?* Toad sews buttons on his jacket. He gives the jacket to Frog. *How does Frog feel?* Frog feels happy.

Intermediate Have partners review page 151. *Why is Toad sad?* Frog helps him look for his button when his button is really in his home. Point to page 152. *How do the illustration and words show Toad is a good friend?* Toad sews buttons on his jacket and gives it to Frog. *How do you know Frog is happy?* The text and illustration show that Frog jumps for joy.

Advanced/Advanced High Help partners elaborate on their responses. *Why does Toad want to do something nice for Frog?* Toad wants to do something nice for Frog because Frog tried to find his button.

FORMATIVE ASSESSMENT

STUDENT CHECK IN

Have children retell how the characters solved the problem. Then have children reflect, using the Check-In routine.

Independent Time

Vocabulary Building Pair children of mixed proficiencies. Have pairs look back over the text and identify the words Toad uses to describe his button and the buttons he finds. For example, on page 145, partners might identify the words *black* and *white*. For each word, have children write the word, draw a picture to help them remember, and use the word in a sentence. Have children add the words to their visual glossaries and share their glossaries with the group.

ENGLISH LANGUAGE LEARNERS 213

LESSONS 4-5

READING • LEVELED READER • ACCESS THE TEXT

LEARNING GOALS

We can make and confirm predictions as we read a fantasy.

OBJECTIVES

Retell stories, including key details, and demonstrate understanding of their central message or lesson.

Identify who is telling the story at various points in a text.

Use illustrations and details in a story to describe its characters, setting, or events.

Identify basic similarities in and differences between two texts on the same topic (e.g., in illustrations, descriptions, or procedures).

LANGUAGE OBJECTIVES

Children will narrate how the character sorts, using verbs with -ing.

ELA ACADEMIC LANGUAGE

- narrator
- Cognate: narrador

MATERIALS

ELL Leveled Reader, *Dog Bones*

Online Differentiated Text, "Time to Eat"

Online ELL Visual Vocabulary Cards

DIGITAL TOOLS

Have children listen to the selection as they follow along to develop comprehension and practice fluency and pronunciation. Use Graphic Organizer 9: Narrator to enhance the lesson.

Dog Bones

Prepare to Read

Build Background

- Remind children of the Essential Question. *Let's read to find out how sorting helps Max.* Encourage children to ask for help when they do not understand a word or phrase.

- Point to and read aloud the title, and have children repeat it. Ask: *What is the title?* Have children point to it. Repeat the routine for the author's name. Point to the illustrations in the **Leveled Reader** to name things and actions. For example: *This is a bone. What do dogs do with bones? Dogs chew bones.*

Focus on Vocabulary Use the **ELL Visual Vocabulary Cards** to preteach the words *contest* and *proud*. As you read, use gestures or visuals to teach important story words, such as *poster, win, sniffs, digging,* and *pile*.

Lexile 260L

Read the Text

Use the Interactive Question-Response routine to help children understand the story.

Pages 2–5

Make Predictions Read pages 2–5 as children follow along. Point to Max. *Max is looking for his bones.* Ask questions to help children predict what will happen with Max's bones.

Beginning Help partners point to the pictures as they respond. *What is Max doing to find his bones?* Max is sniffing. Max is digging. *Will Max find his bones?* Yes, Max will find his bones.

Intermediate Help partners respond: *Do you predict Max will find his bones? Why?* I predict Max will find his bones because he is looking hard.

Pages 6–9

Beginning Have partners point to the pictures as they tell each other how Max sorts the bones. Max has small bones. Max has large bones.

Advanced/Advanced High Have partners discuss why Max sorts the bones the way he does. He sorts them by size to know which is biggest.

Confirm Predictions Read pages 6–9 as children follow along. Review *bunch, small, pile,* and *large*. Help children confirm their predictions: My prediction was right/wrong.

214 UNIT 5 WEEK 1

WEEK 1

Pages 10–11

Read pages 10–11 as children follow along. Ask questions to help children understand Max's point of view at the end of the story.

Intermediate Point to Bob. *Why is Bob sad?* He has no <u>bones</u>. Point to page 11. *Why is Max happy?* He <u>helped</u> his friend.

Advanced/Advanced High Have children discuss with a partner why Max is happy. <u>Helping</u> is better than <u>winning</u>.

Narrator Help children point to words that are clues to identify the narrator. Discuss with them whether the narrator is a character inside the story or an outside speaker. (outside speaker)

Respond to Reading Have partners work together to retell the story and respond to the questions on page 12.

Focus on Fluency

Read pages 10–11 to model reading with accuracy. Read the passage again, and have children repeat after you. For more practice, record children reading the passage, and select their best recordings.

Paired Read: "Sorting Balls"

Analytical Writing **Make Connections: Write About It**

Echo-read each page with children. Discuss ways things can be sorted: *These are balls. What size are these balls?* These balls are <u>small/bigger</u>. Have children make connections between texts, using the question on page 15. Things can be sorted by <u>size</u>.

Leveled Reader

Build Knowledge: Make Connections

Talk About the Text Have partners discuss how things in the texts are classified and categorized.

Write About the Text Have students add their ideas to the Build Knowledge pages of their reader's notebooks.

Self-Selected Reading

Help children choose a fantasy selection from the online **Leveled Reader Library,** or read the **Differentiated Text,** "Time to Eat."

FOCUS ON GENRE

Children can extend their knowledge of the characteristics of a fantasy by completing the genre activity on page 16.

LITERATURE CIRCLES

Lead children in conducting a literature circle using the Thinkmark questions to guide the discussion. You may wish to discuss what children have learned about sorting from the two selections in the **Leveled Reader**.

FORMATIVE ASSESSMENT

▸ STUDENT CHECK IN

Have partners share their Respond to Reading. Have children reflect, using the Check-In routine.

LEVEL UP

IF children can read *Dog Bones* **ELL Level** with fluency and correctly answer the Respond to Reading questions,

THEN tell children they will read a more detailed version of the story.

- Use page 2 of *Dog Bones* **On Level** to model using Teaching Poster 35 to list a point of view.

- Have children read the selection, checking their comprehension by using the graphic organizer.

ENGLISH LANGUAGE LEARNERS 215

LESSONS 4-5

READING • GENRE PASSAGE • ACCESS THE TEXT

LEARNING GOALS

We can apply skills and strategies to a fantasy.

OBJECTIVES

Explain major differences between books that tell stories and books that give information, drawing on a wide reading of a range of text types.

Identify words and phrases in stories or poems that suggest feelings or appeal to the senses.

Use illustrations and details in a story to describe its characters, setting, or events.

Produce complete sentences when appropriate to task and situation.

LANGUAGE OBJECTIVES

Children will inquire about the story by making and confirming predictions using key vocabulary.

ELA ACADEMIC LANGUAGE

- fantasy, predict
- Cognates: *fantasía, predecir*

MATERIALS

Online ELL Genre Passage, "Cow Has a Party"

"Cow Has a Party"

Prepare to Read

Build Background Review what children have learned about the different ways they can sort things. *What are some categories we can use to sort things?* We can sort things by size/color/shape. Allow children to share ideas about other ways objects can be classified. Tell children they will be reading about animals who prepare for a party by sorting party supplies.

Lexile 400L

Focus on Vocabulary Use the Define, Example, Ask routine to preteach difficult words or unfamiliar concepts, such as *supplies, brush, sigh, wool, forever,* and *decorations*. Invite children to add new words to their glossaries.

Read the Text

Use the Interactive Question-Response routine to help children understand the story.

Page E1

Paragraphs 1–2 Read the text aloud as children follow along. Point to the word *supplies*. Say the word aloud, and have children repeat it. *Supplies are things you need so you can do something. What supplies do you need for school?* Supplies I need for school are pencils and paper. Point to *excited* in paragaph 2. *When you are excited, you are happy and really want to do something. Why are the animals excited?* The animals are excited about Cow's party.

Remind children that they can look for clues in the text to figure out a word's meaning. *Words can have multiple meanings.* Review how *brush* is used as a verb, not as a noun, in the sentence.

Beginning Point to the illustration. Have partners ask and answer: What does Farmer Flora have? Farmer Flora has supplies for Cow's party.

Paragraphs 3–5 Read the text aloud as children follow along. Review *sigh* by demonstrating a sigh. Have children repeat the word and action. *Do you sigh when you are happy or sad?* (sad) Point to and say *forever*. Have children repeat. *We say* forever *when we are thinking about a very long time.* Help children think about the **narrator**. *The narrator tells the story. The narrator can be inside the story or outside the story. Who are the characters in the story?* (Farmer Flora and the animals) *Are they telling the story?* (no) *Who is telling the story?* (a narrator)

Intermediate Have partners take turns **predicting** how the animals will solve the problem. What will the animals do? I predict the animals will start preparing the party while Farmer Flora is gone.

WEEK 1

Advanced High Have partners identify the words/phrases for time and classify them: *Which word and phrase have a similar meaning?* (takes long, forever) *Which phrase has the opposite meaning?* (right back) Have children create their own sentences with the terms.

Page E2

Paragraphs 1–3 Read the text aloud. Help children correct or *confirm* their predictions. *What can the animals do?* They can set up the party. *To set up something is to get it ready. How do the animals set up the party?* They sort the supplies and do special jobs.

Advanced/Advanced High Have partners discuss how the animals sort the supplies. Encourage children to extend their thinking by discussing other categories the animals could use to sort. *The animals could* sort *by* weight/color/size.

Paragraphs 4–5 Read the text aloud as children follow along. Point to *get back*. *To get back is to return.* Point to the picture. *When Farmer Flora and Sheep get back, what do they see?* They see the party is ready to start/begin.

Intermediate Have pairs discuss the reasons the other animals get the party ready while Farmer Flora and Sheep are away. Help children respond: *The animals get the party ready because they are* excited *for it to* start/begin.

Respond to Reading

Use the following instructions to help children answer the questions on page E3.

1. **Fantasy** Have children describe what they see in the illustrations. Ask questions to help children complete the sentence. *Are the animals standing like people or animals?* (people) *Are the animals wearing clothes?* (yes) *Do the animals talk to Farmer Flora?* (yes)

2. **Make and Confirm Predictions** Discuss with children the problem Rooster, Goat, and Cow have. Farmer Flora leaves and does not set up things for the party. Have children discuss what they predicted the animals would do: *I predicted ___.* Then ask: *What do the animals do?* They work together to sort supplies and set up for the party.

3. **Fluency** Have children take turns reading the passage to a partner. As they read, fill in the chart on page E3.

Build Knowledge: Make Connections

Talk About the Text Have partners discuss how the animals classified and categorized the party supplies.

Write About the Text Have students add their ideas to the Build Knowledge pages of their reader's notebooks.

FORMAIVE ASSESSMENT

⟫ STUDENT CHECK IN

Partners will share their Respond to Reading. Ask children to reflect, using the Check-In routine.

LEVEL UP

IF children read the ELL Level fluently and answered the questions,

THEN pair them with children who have proficiently read the On Level. Have them

- partner-read the On Level passage.
- make and confirm predictions about events in the story.

ENGLISH LANGUAGE LEARNERS **217**

LESSONS 1-5 WRITING

MODELED WRITING

LESSON 1

LEARNING GOALS

We can learn to write sentences with different lengths.

OBJECTIVES

Write opinion pieces in which they introduce the topic.

LANGUAGE OBJECTIVES

Children will argue by writing sentences using descriptive words.

ELA ACADEMIC LANGUAGE

- opinion, sentence
- Cognate: *opinión*

Writing Practice Review the sample on p. 24 of the **Reading/Writing Companion**. Have children analyze each sentence using the Actor/Action routine: *Who is the actor?* (I) *What is the action?* (would choose) *What would the actor choose?* (a bright red hat) Then read the prompt on p. 25 and ask a volunteer to answer it. Guide children to use descriptive words: *Is your cap black or red?* Write their sentences on the board and ask them to chorally read. Then help children write their own sentences on p. 25.

Beginning Help partners create their sentences by asking guiding questions: *What do you like?* (a hat) *What color is your hat?* (yellow) *Is it soft?* (yes) Provide sentence frames and vocabulary as necessary.

Intermediate Have partners ask and answer *what* questions to create their sentences. To elicit descriptive words, encourage children to ask: *What does the hat look like?*

Advanced/Advanced High Challenge children to write one long sentence and one short sentence. Ask them to identify each one.

FORMATIVE ASSESSMENT ▶ **STUDENT CHECK IN** Partners share their sentences. Ask children to reflect, using the Check-In routine.

INTERACTIVE WRITING

LESSON 2

LEARNING GOALS

We can read and write about a Student Model.

OBJECTIVES

With guidance and support from adults, focus on a topic.

LANGUAGE OBJECTIVES

Children will discuss and write sentences about a Student Model, identifying the joining word *and*.

ELA ACADEMIC LANGUAGE

- sentences, descriptive
- Cognate: *descriptivo*

Analyze the Student Model Have children chorally read the Student Model on p. 32 of the **Reading/Writing Companion**. Use the Actor/Action routine to review the last sentence: *Who is the actor in the first part of the sentence?* (Horse) *What is the action?* (got) *Who is the actor in the second part of the sentence?* (it) *What is the action?* (helped) *Which word joins the two sentences?* (and) Then help children complete p. 33.

Beginning Have partners point to examples of descriptive words. Provide a sentence frame: I noticed the word *flat*. It describes a *hat*.

Intermediate Have partners ask and answer questions: *What do you notice about Ana's writing?* She uses the word *and* to join two sentences.

Advanced/Advanced High Challenge children to use their own sentences to write about the text. Encourage children to share their ideas.

FORMATIVE ASSESSMENT ▶ **STUDENT CHECK IN** Partners share their sentences. Ask children to reflect, using the Check-In routine.

WEEK 1

INDEPENDENT WRITING

LESSONS 3-4

LEARNING GOALS

We can write an opinion about a fantasy story.

OBJECTIVES

Write opinion pieces in which they supply a reason for the opinion.

LANGUAGE OBJECTIVES

Children will argue by writing a sentence with the joining word *and*.

ELA ACADEMIC LANGUAGE

- *opinion*
- Cognate: *opinión*

Find Text Evidence Use the Independent Writing routine. Help children use text evidence to orally retell the anchor text. Ask questions, such as: *What does Toad lose?* (a button) *Who helps him look for it?* (Frog) *Does Frog find buttons?* (yes) Then read the prompt on p. 38 of the **Reading/Writing Companion:** *In A Lost Button, do you think Frog or Toad is the better friend? Why? We need to give an opinion about who is a better friend. Then we need to describe how he is a good friend.*

Write a Response Work together to complete My Writing Outline 21. Then have children use the sentences from their outlines to complete p. 38.

Writing Checklist Read the checklist with children and have them check for these items in their writing.

Beginning Have partners take turns sharing their sentences. Provide a sentence frame: *I used the word and to join sentences.*

Intermediate Ask children to identify their longest and shortest sentence and then help them check this item off the checklist.

Advanced/Advanced High Have partners identify where they used each item in their writing.

FORMATIVE ASSESSMENT ▸ **STUDENT CHECK IN** Partners share their sentences from My Writing Outline. Ask children to reflect, using the Check-in routine.

SELF-SELECTED WRITING

LESSON 5

LEARNING GOALS

We can revise our writing.

OBJECTIVES

Use frequently occurring conjunctions.

LANGUAGE OBJECTIVES

Children will inquire about their writing by checking how they are joining sentences.

ELA ACADEMIC LANGUAGE

- *sentence*

Work with children to revise the group writing activity. Point to each word as you read the sentences. Stop to ask questions, such as: *Do we need to add a word to join these sentences?* If needed, write a compound sentence without a joining word and work together to revise the sentence. Then have partners revise each other's sentences before publishing their writing.

For support with grammar and using joining words, refer to the **Language Transfers Handbook** and **Language Development Cards** 27A and 34A.

FORMATIVE ASSESSMENT ▸ **STUDENT CHECK IN** Partners tell what revisions they made. Ask children to reflect, using the Check-in routine.

LESSONS 1-2

READING • SHARED READ • ACCESS THE TEXT

LEARNING GOALS

We can read and understand a fantasy story.

OBJECTIVES

Retell stories, including key details, and demonstrate understanding of their central message or lesson.

Use illustrations and details in a story to describe its characters, setting, or events.

Build on others' talk in conversations by responding to the comments of others through multiple exchanges.

Produce complete sentences when appropriate to task and situation.

LANGUAGE OBJECTIVES

Children will narrate what Fern learns about clouds, using verbs in the past tense, adjectives, and complete sentences.

ELA ACADEMIC LANGUAGE

- events, sequence
- Cognates: *eventos, secuencia*

MATERIALS

Reading/Writing Companion, pp. 50–59

Visual Vocabulary Cards

DIGITAL TOOLS

MULTIMODAL

Have children listen to the selection as they follow along to develop comprehension and practice fluency and pronunciation.

Use the additional grammar song.

🎵 Grammar Song

"A Bird Named Fern"

Prepare to Read

Build Background Read aloud the Essential Question on page 50. If possible, have children look out a window and observe the sky. *Do you see the sun? Is it raining? What color is the sky?* Have children describe the sky in the illustration on pages 50–51. *What color is the sky?* The sky is ____. Say the word *clouds* for children to repeat. *What color are the clouds?* The clouds are ____. Point to and read the title for children to repeat. *How many birds do you see?* I see ____ birds. *Which bird do you think is Fern? Is she a mom bird or a young bird?*

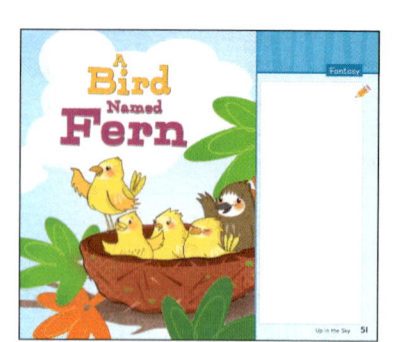

Reading/Writing Companion, Lexile 360L

Focus on Vocabulary Use the **Visual Vocabulary Cards** to review the high-frequency words *another, climb, full, great, poor,* and *through* and the oral vocabulary words *certain, observe, remained, thoughtful,* and *vast*. Display the illustrations, and point to the pictures for *boat, wings, soaked,* and *dry off.* Use the following routine for each new word: Point to the boat, or sketch one on the board, if needed for clarity. Say the word *boat*. Have children point to the picture and repeat the word. *To travel across the water, you need a boat. How do you travel on water?* You ride in a boat.

Summarize the Text Before reading, say the summary while pointing to the illustrations. *Fern is a bird who flies up to learn more about clouds. She finds out they aren't like boats or beds. Then rain falls from the clouds.*

Read the Text

Use the Interactive Question-Response routine to help children understand the story.

Pages 52–53

Pages 52–53 Read the text aloud as children follow along. *Fern asks questions to learn new things. She is curious. Say* curious. *Are you curious too?* Read Fern's question aloud. Explain that when Fern asks, "What is it doing there?" she means "Why is it there?" *Where do you usually see boats?* Boats are in the water, not in the sky. Point to the picture of the "boat." *What is it really?* It looks like a boat, but it's really a cloud. *How do you know?* Clouds are white shapes in the sky.

COLLABORATE *What do you know about Fern? Discuss with a partner.*

Beginning Help children reread page 53. *Does Fern ask a lot of questions?* Yes, she asks a lot of questions. *Why does Fern ask questions?* She wants to know about everything. *Is Fern curious?* Yes, she is curious.

220 UNIT 5 WEEK 2

WEEK 2

Intermediate Have pairs complete this sentence frame: Fern is curious. Then have them find and read aloud two sentences from the story that show that Fern is curious.

Advanced/Advanced High Have partners add details to their responses: Fern is curious. She asks a lot of questions. She wants to find out the answers.

Pages 54–57

Pages 54–55 Read the text aloud as children follow along. Explain that Fern says "It would be great" to show she wants to do something. *What does she want to do?* She wants to ride on the boat in the sky. Lead children in gesturing to demonstrate *stretched* and *took off*. Point to the cloud on page 55. *This is a fluffy cloud. Fluffy means "soft and light, not heavy." What does the "boat" look like now?* It looks like a fluffy bed.

Pages 56–57 Read the text aloud, and have children follow along. Help children relate the verb *sleep* to the adjective *sleepy*. Explain that *rest* can mean the same as *sleep*. *What do you do when you feel sleepy?* I go to bed. *What happened when Fern tried to go to bed?* She fell through. Have children look at Fern's expression in the pictures. *How do you think Fern felt?* (surprised, unhappy)

What happens to Fern on page 57? Talk about the cause and effect. Discuss with a partner.

Beginning Help partners use the pictures and these sentence frames to tell the cause of why Fern fell: Fern flew to the cloud. She fell through the cloud. She fell through another cloud. She decided to go home.

Intermediate Have pairs complete these sentence frames with the correct cause and effect from the story: Fern leaped on the cloud and fell through it. She fell through a second cloud. She decided to ask her mom and dad to explain.

Advanced/Advanced High Have pairs retell the main events with details: Fern flew up to the cloud she saw. She jumped/leaped on the cloud and fell through it. Then she tried to land on another cloud but fell through it too. She decided to go home to ask her mom and dad to explain.

Pages 58–59

Pages 58–59 Read the text aloud, and have children follow along. Ask questions to help them demonstrate comprehension. Reread the second sentence. *What are the "beds"?* They are clouds. Have children turn back to pages 58–59 if they are unsure. *Why are they dark gray?* They are rain/storm clouds. *How did Fern get wet?* She flew home through the rain.

What did Fern's mom and dad do when she got home? Discuss with a partner.

Beginning Have pairs identify two things Mom and Dad did when Fran got home. Have children point to and read the sentences aloud.

Intermediate Have pairs complete these sentence frames: Mom and Dad dried Fern off. Then they taught Fern about clouds.

Advanced/Advanced High Help partners extend their thinking. *What do you think Mom and Dad taught Fern about clouds?* Clouds are not like beds or boats. You can't sit or ride on them. Clouds cause rain.

FORMATIVE ASSESSMENT

STUDENT CHECK-IN

Have partners retell why Fern is curious and confused about the clouds. Then have children reflect, using the Check-In routine.

Independent Time

Connect Text to Self Group children of mixed proficiency levels. Have them draw and describe themselves in a rainstorm. Encourage children to tell what they see in the sky (clouds, rain, lightning) and the colors they see. You may also wish to have children make sound effects for thunder and rain. Discuss: *How do you stay dry when it rains and not get soaked like Fern?* I wear a raincoat/rain boots. I use an umbrella.

ENGLISH LANGUAGE LEARNERS **221**

LESSON 3

READING • ANCHOR TEXT • ACCESS THE TEXT

LEARNING GOALS

We can read and understand a fantasy story.

OBJECTIVES

Retell stories, including key details, and demonstrate understanding of their central message or lesson.

Describe characters, settings, and major events in a story, using key details.

Use illustrations and details in a story to describe its characters, setting, or events.

Build on others' talk in conversations by responding to the comments of others through multiple exchanges.

LANGUAGE OBJECTIVES

Children will narrate what Kitten thinks about the moon, using descriptive words, verbs, and complete sentences.

ELA ACADEMIC LANGUAGE

- illustration, repeated, retell
- Cognates: *ilustración, repetido*

MATERIALS

Literature Anthology, pp. 162–195

Visual Vocabulary Cards

DIGITAL TOOLS

Have children listen to the selection as they follow along to develop comprehension.

Use the additional grammar song.

Grammar Song

Kitten's First Full Moon

Prepare to Read

Build Background *We are going to read a story about a kitten who sees the moon.* Point to the moon in the picture on the title page. Say the word *moon,* and have children repeat it. *When can we see the moon? We can see the moon at _____. Is the moon always the same shape?* Invite volunteers to draw shapes of the moon, including a crescent, half circle, and circle. Point to the circle. *This is a full moon.* Have children repeat. *Here,* full means "complete."

Literature Anthology, Lexile 550L

Focus on Vocabulary Use the **Visual Vocabulary Cards** to review the high-frequency words *another, climb, full, great, poor,* and *through* and the oral vocabulary words *certain, observe, remained, thoughtful,* and *vast.* Before reading the story, clarify vocabulary children will need for understanding. As you read, use gestures and pantomime to teach important story words, such as *through, past, from, to, in,* and *by*.

Summarize the Text Before reading, say the summary while pointing to the illustrations. *The story tells about a kitten who thinks a full moon is a bowl of milk.*

Read the Text

Use the Interactive Question-Response routine to help children understand the story.

Pages 164–173

Pages 164–165 Read the text. Say the word *bowl* for children to repeat. *What can you eat in a bowl?* (soup, cereal) *Picture a bowl you have at home. What shape is it? The top of the bowl is a* circle. Have children look at the picture. *Point to the full moon. What shape is it?* (a circle) *What color is it?* (white) *What does Kitten think the full moon is? She thinks it is a* bowl of milk. *Do cats like milk?* (yes)

Pages 166–169 Read the text. Lead children to act out what Kitten does on page 166. Point to Kitten's tongue. Say *tongue,* and have children repeat it. *How do cats drink? They lick with their* tongues. *Do you lick with your tongue when you drink?* (no) *What do you think Kitten tries to do?* (drink milk) *What happens? She licks a* bug *with her* tongue!

Pages 170–173 Read the text. Use the pictures to help children understand *sprang* and *tumbled.* Point to page 170. *What does Kitten try to do? She tries to* jump up *to the* moon. Point to page 171. *What happens? She* falls down. Point to *Poor Kitten! We say poor when a bad event happens to someone.*

What is the author's purpose for repeating some parts of the story? Discuss with a partner.

222 UNIT 5 WEEK 2

WEEK 2

Beginning Help pairs tell what happens to Kitten. *What happens when she tries to lick the bowl?* Kitten gets a bug on her tongue. *What happens when she tries to jump from the porch?* Kitten tumbles off the porch. *Is this text fun to read?* (yes)

Intermediate Help partners think about Kitten's actions. *Is Kitten able to drink the milk?* (no) *What keeps happening to Kitten?* Kitten keeps missing the bowl of milk.

Advanced/Advanced High Help pairs infer. *Why does Kitten keep trying to drink the milk?* She drinks milk from a bowl. *What do you think will happen next?* Kitten will try to drink the milk again.

COLLABORATE *Why does the author repeat the sentence? Discuss with a partner.*

Beginning Have children scan pages 167–173 to find a repeated sentence. (Still, there was the little bowl of milk, just waiting.) Help pairs read it aloud together, with one partner looking at pages 168–169 and the other one looking at pages 172–173.

Intermediate Have pairs find and read the repeated sentence. Then have them respond to the question: Kitten still thinks the moon is a bowl of milk.

Advanced/Advanced High Have pairs reread the repeated sentence and decide whether it shows what Kitten thinks or what is real.

Pages 174–181

Pages 174–175 Read the text. Have children trace Kitten's path in the illustrations. *Does Kitten get closer to the moon?* (no) *Why can't Kitten get to the moon?* It is far away in the sky. *Does Kitten know that?* (no)

Pages 176–177 Have children read the repeated sentence with you chorally, and remind them that they have seen this sentence before. Have children make a prediction based on the repetition. *What do you think Kitten will do next?* She will try again.

Pages 178–179 Read the text. *Why does Kitten climb the tree?* She wants to reach the bowl of milk in the sky. *Why is she scared?* She is at the top of a tall tree!

Pages 180–181 Read the text. *Do you think Kitten is still scared?* (no) *We say "What a [night]!" to show excitement about something. Why is Kitten excited?* She sees a bigger bowl of milk. *Where is it?* (in the pond) *Can a bowl of milk be in a pond?* (no) Teach children the word *reflection*. *When you look in a mirror, you can see yourself. That is a* reflection.

COLLABORATE *How does the illustration on pages 180 and 181 help you understand what is happening in the story? Discuss with a partner.*

Beginning Have pairs point to the moon and its reflection in the illustration. *Which is bigger, the moon or its reflection?* The moon's reflection is bigger. Help children reread the text. *What does Kitten think is a bigger bowl of milk?* (the moon's reflection)

Intermediate Have pairs describe the illustration: The moon is in the sky. The moon's reflection is in the pond. Kitten thinks it is a bigger bowl of milk.

Advanced/Advanced High Have pairs describe the illustration in detail: The moon is in the sky. Kitten is at the top of the tree. Kitten sees the moon's reflection in the pond. It looks like a bigger bowl of milk.

FORMATIVE ASSESSMENT

STUDENT CHECK IN

Have partners retell how Kitten interacts with the moon and why. Then have children reflect, using the Check-In routine.

Independent Time

Retell the Ending Pair children of mixed proficiency levels, and have them retell the end of the story on pages 182–193. Encourage children to use the illustrations to help them understand the text. Provide sentence frames to help children write their retelling: Kitten climbed down the ___. Kitten jumped into the ___. Kitten was ___. Kitten went ___. There was a ___. She ___. Have volunteer pairs present their retelling to the rest of the group.

ENGLISH LANGUAGE LEARNERS 223

LESSONS 4-5

READING • LEVELED READER • ACCESS THE TEXT

LEARNING GOALS

We can make and confirm predictions as we read a fantasy.

OBJECTIVES

Ask and answer questions about key details in a text.

Describe characters, settings, and major events in a story, using key details.

Build on others' talk in conversations by responding to the comments of others through multiple exchanges.

Ask questions to clear up any confusion about the topics and texts under discussion.

LANGUAGE OBJECTIVES

Children will narrate what happened to the caterpillar in the story, using complete sentences.

ELA ACADEMIC LANGUAGE

- confirm
- Cognate: *confirmar*

MATERIALS

ELL Leveled Reader, *Hide and Seek*

Online Differentiated Text, "Cora"

Online ELL Visual Vocabulary Cards

DIGITAL TOOLS

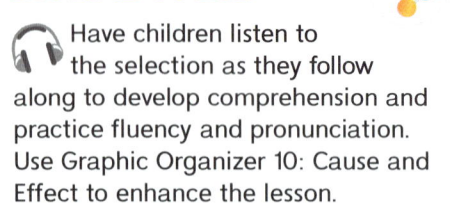

Have children listen to the selection as they follow along to develop comprehension and practice fluency and pronunciation. Use Graphic Organizer 10: Cause and Effect to enhance the lesson.

Hide and Seek

Prepare to Read

Build Background

- Remind children of the Essential Question: *What can you see in the sky?* Encourage children to ask for help when they do not understand the text.

- Point to the title, and read it aloud for children to repeat. *What are the rules of hide and seek?* One player closes his or her ____ and then ____. The others ____ so the first player can't ____ them. The first player looks for them and tries to ____ them. *Have you ever played?*

Lexile 310L

Focus on Vocabulary Use the **ELL Visual Vocabulary Cards** to preteach the words *become* and *playing*. As you read, use gestures or visuals to teach important selection words, such as *rabbit, caterpillar, leaped, hill,* and *butterfly*.

Read the Text

Use the Interactive Question-Response routine to help children understand the story.

Pages 2–5

Make Predictions Read pages 2–3 aloud. Explain that *flutter* has a similar meaning as *fly*. Help children make a prediction about Flutter: I think Flutter will fly to the sun.

Beginning Have pairs point to Flutter and complete these sentence frames to make a prediction: *Flutter* means "fly." I think Flutter will fly.

Intermediate Help pairs respond: *What does Flutter say?* (I hope to fly to the sun one day.) *What do you think will happen?* I think Flutter will fly to the sun.

Advanced/Advanced High Help children add more detail: *Flutter* means "fly." The caterpillar hopes to fly one day, but she can't fly now.

Pages 6–9

Events: Cause and Effect Read pages 6–7 as children follow along. Support children by helping them use cause and effect to understand the main events in this part of the story.

Beginning Help pairs identify a cause on page 6: *Why does Harry think Flutter is playing hide and seek?* He cannot find Flutter.

Intermediate Have pairs identify an effect: *Harry thinks Flutter is playing hide and seek. What is the effect?* He looks for Flutter.

224 UNIT 5 WEEK 2

WEEK 2

Advanced/Advanced High Have pairs reread page 6 and decide which sentence is the cause and which is the effect.

Pages 10–12

Read pages 10–11 aloud as children follow along. To support understanding, guide them to explain why Flutter is hiding. Help students correct or **confirm predictions** from the previous pages.

Beginning Help children use pictures to identify Flutter. *Point to Flutter on pages 2–3 and 10–11.* Flutter is a caterpillar/butterfly.

Intermediate Help partners explain what happens to Flutter: *Now Flutter is a* butterfly. *She can* fly to the sun.

Advanced/Advanced High Have pairs discuss: *Was Flutter playing hide and seek?* No, she wasn't. *She was* becoming a butterfly.

Respond to Reading Have partners work together to retell the story and respond to the questions on page 12.

Focus on Fluency

Read pages 10–11 to model appropriate intonation. Read the passage again, and have children repeat after you.

Paired Read: "Our Sun Is a Star!"

Make Connections: Write About It

Echo-read with children. Discuss: *What goes around the sun?* Earth and the moon go around the sun. Help children make connections, using the questions on page 15. The sun feels warm to Harry. The sun feels warm to people, but it can burn them.

Leveled Reader

Build Knowledge: Make Connections

Talk About the Text As they read these texts, have partners discuss what they can see in the sky.

Write About the Text Have students add their ideas to the Build Knowledge pages of their reader's notebooks.

Self-Selected Reading

Help children choose a fiction selection from the online **Leveled Reader Library,** or read the **Differentiated Text,** "Cora."

FOCUS ON SCIENCE

Children can extend their knowledge of things we see in the sky by completing the science activity on page 16. **STEM**

LITERATURE CIRCLES

Lead children in conducting a literature circle using the Thinkmark questions to guide the discussion. You may wish to discuss what children have learned about the characters Harry and Flutter in *Hide and Seek* in the **Leveled Reader.**

FORMATIVE ASSESSMENT

STUDENT CHECK IN

Have partners share their Respond to Reading. Have children reflect, using the Check-In routine.

LEVEL UP

IF children can read *Hide and Seek* **ELL Level** with fluency and correctly answer the Respond to Reading questions,

THEN tell children they will read a more detailed version of the story.

- Use page 3 of *Hide and Seek* **On Level** to model using Teaching Poster 32 to list a cause and an effect in the selection.
- Have children read the selection, checking their comprehension by using the graphic organizer.

ENGLISH LANGUAGE LEARNERS **225**

LESSONS 4-5

READING • GENRE PASSAGE • ACCESS THE TEXT

LEARNING GOALS

We can apply skills and strategies to a fantasy.

OBJECTIVES

Describe characters, settings, and major events in a story, using key details.

Explain major differences between books that tell stories and books that give information, drawing on a wide reading of a range of text types.

Build on others' talk in conversations by responding to the comments of others through multiple exchanges.

Produce complete sentences when appropriate to task and situation.

LANGUAGE OBJECTIVES

Children will use complete sentences to discuss cause and effect in events.

ELA ACADEMIC LANGUAGE

- cause, effect, sequence
- Cognates: *causa, efecto, secuencia*

MATERIALS

Online ELL Genre Passage, "Little Turtle's Dream," pp. E1–E3

"Little Turtle's Dream"

Prepare to Read

Build Background Have volunteers come to the board to draw things they can see in the sky, such as the sun, clouds, the moon, and stars. Point to each drawing, and say the word for it chorally with children. *Which ones can you see at night?* We can see the _____ and _____ at night. Help children connect the words to their own experiences. *Do you ever look up at the moon and stars? How does it make you feel? Would you like to fly into space to see them better?*

Lexile 400L

Focus on Vocabulary Use the Define, Example, Ask routine to preteach difficult words or unfamiliar concepts, such as *log, dizzy, rocket, got ready for bed, kiss,* and *dream*. Ask questions such as: *How do you get ready for bed?* (brush my teeth, change into pajamas, kiss a parent goodnight) *Did you have a dream last night? What did you dream about?* Invite children to add new vocabulary to their glossaries.

Read the Text

Use the Interactive Question-Response routine to help children understand the story.

Page E1

Paragraph 1 Read the text aloud, and have children follow along. Tell them *gaze* means "look at." Say the word *bright* for children to repeat, and explain that something *bright* has a lot of light and is easy to see.

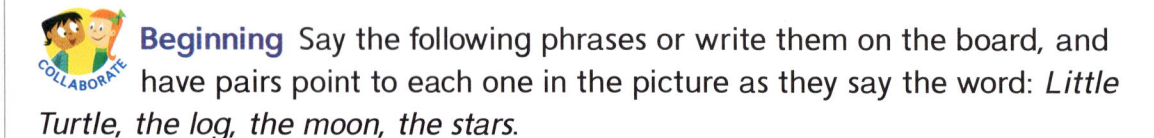

Beginning Say the following phrases or write them on the board, and have pairs point to each one in the picture as they say the word: *Little Turtle, the log, the moon, the stars*.

Paragraphs 2–4 Read the text aloud as children follow along. Help them understand the expressions in the dialogue. *We say* Oops! *when we fall or make a mistake. We ask* Are you all right? *to make sure someone is okay or not hurt.*

Intermediate Have children use **cause and effect** to help them understand events in the story. *What causes Little Turtle to get dizzy?* He is looking at the sky. *What is the effect?* He falls off the log.

Paragraph 5 Read the text aloud, and help children **make a prediction.** Explain that *one day* means "sometime in the future."

Advanced Have partners discuss what they think will happen to Little Turtle: Little Turtle will fly on a rocket to the stars.

226 UNIT 5 WEEK 2

WEEK 2

Advanced High Have partners discuss their predictions about Little Turtle. They might consider if he will fly or will write about or draw stars.

Page E2

Paragraph 1 Read the text aloud. *What is Little Turtle doing now?* He is getting ready for bed. *What do you think he will do next?* (sleep)

Intermediate Provide sentences to help children **make a prediction:** Little Turtle gets ready for bed. I think he will sleep/dream about the stars.

Paragraphs 2–3 Read the text aloud as children follow along. *What is Little Turtle thinking about as he goes to sleep?* He is thinking about flying to the stars.

Advanced/Advanced High Help pairs find text evidence to answer: *Who gives Little Turtle the idea to fly to the stars?* (Mama Turtle says, "Maybe one day you'll fly on a rocket to the stars.")

Paragraph 4 Read the text aloud, and have children *confirm* their predictions. My prediction was right/wrong. *What is Little Turtle's dream?* He flies on a rocket to the stars with Mama.

Beginning Have pairs take turns pointing to and telling what they see in the illustration: My prediction was right/wrong. I see Little Turtle/Mama Turtle/stars/a bed/a rocket.

Intermediate Have children tell why their prediction was right or wrong. I predicted Little Turtle would fly to the stars. I was right/wrong because he had a dream about flying to the stars.

Respond to Reading

Use the following instructions to help children answer the questions on page E3.

1. **Fantasy** Have children describe the characters in the story. Ask questions to help children complete the sentence: *Can turtles look at the sky?* (yes) *Can turtles fall off a log?* (yes) *Can turtles talk?* (no)

2. **Events: Cause and Effect** Tell children they can think about events in a story and why the events happen. *What does Mama Turtle say to Little Turtle?* ("Are you all right, dear?") This is an event. *Why does this happen?* (because Little Turtle falls of the log) This is the cause, or why the event happened. *What else does Mama Turtle do?* She gives him a kiss.

3. **Fluency** Have children take turns reading the first paragraph to a partner. As they read, fill in the chart on page E3.

Build Knowledge: Make Connections

Talk About the Text Have partners discuss what Little Turtle sees in the sky.

Write About the Text Have students add their ideas to the Build Knowledge pages of their reader's notebooks.

FORMATIVE ASSESSMENT

❯ STUDENT CHECK IN

Have partners share their Respond to Reading. Ask children to reflect, using the Check-In routine.

LEVEL UP

IF children read the ELL Level fluently and answered the questions,

THEN pair them with children who have proficiently read the On Level. Have them

- partner-read the On Level passage.
- identify one cause and one effect in the passage.

ENGLISH LANGUAGE LEARNERS 227

LESSONS 1-5

WRITING

MODELED WRITING

LESSON 1

LEARNING GOALS
We can learn to write using strong verbs.

OBJECTIVES
Write informative texts in which they supply some facts about the topic.

LANGUAGE OBJECTIVES
Children will inform by writing a sentence with a strong verb.

ELA ACADEMIC LANGUAGE
- verb
- Cognate: *verbo*

Writing Practice Review the sample on p. 60 of the **Reading/Writing Companion** by pointing to each word as children chorally read. Guide children to use the Actor/Action routine to analyze the sentences: *Who are the actors?* (Tom and I) *What is the action?* (spotted the North Star) *When?* (last night) Then read the prompt on p. 61 and ask children to answer it as a group. Write their sentences on the board and have children chorally read them. Then help children write their own sentences.

Beginning *What did you see in the sky?* (a shooting star) *What did you do when you saw it?* (smiled) Provide sentence frames if needed.

Intermediate Have partners ask and answer *who/what* questions to create their sentences. They can use the sample as a model for using strong verbs.

Advanced/Advanced High Challenge children to include at least two strong verbs and to share these with the group.

FORMATIVE ASSESSMENT ▶ **STUDENT CHECK IN** Partners share their sentences. Ask children to reflect, using the Check-In routine.

INTERACTIVE WRITING

LESSON 2

LEARNING GOALS
We can read and write about a Student Model.

OBJECTIVES
With guidance and support from adults, focus on a topic.

LANGUAGE OBJECTIVES
Children will discuss and write sentences about a Student Model, identifying an adjective.

ELA ACADEMIC LANGUAGE
- prompt, adjective
- Cognate: *adjetivo*

Analyze the Student Model Have children finger point as they chorally read the Student Model on p. 68 of the **Reading/Writing Companion.** Use the Actor/Action routine to review each sentence. Point out the adjectives in the sentences. *(new, many)* These are words that help describe other words. Which strong verb does the author use to tell us how Fern sees a new thing in the sky? *(wonders)* Help children complete p. 69.

Beginning Have partners point to and identify adjectives and strong verbs. Provide sentence frames: I notice Carla uses the adjective *new*.

Intermediate Have partners ask and answer questions: *What did you notice about Carla's writing?* She uses *strong verbs*, like *spots* and *needs*.

Advanced/Advanced High Challenge children to explain what they notice in the Student Model: Carla writes *spots* instead of *sees*.

FORMATIVE ASSESSMENT ▶ **STUDENT CHECK IN** Partners share their responses. Ask children to reflect, using the Check-In routine.

228 UNIT 5 WEEK 2

WEEK 2

INDEPENDENT WRITING

LESSONS 3-4

LEARNING GOALS

We can use text evidence to respond to a fantasy story.

OBJECTIVES

Write informative texts in which they provide some sense of closure.

LANGUAGE OBJECTIVES

Children will inform by writing a sentence using an adjective.

ELA ACADEMIC LANGUAGE

- *respond, evidence*
- Cognates: *responder, evidencia*

Find Text Evidence Follow the Independent Writing routine. Help children use text evidence to orally retell the anchor text. Ask questions, such as: *What does Kitten think she sees in the sky?* (a bowl of milk) *How does she try to reach it?* (licks, jumps, chases it, climbs a tree) Then read the prompt on p. 74 of the **Reading/Writing Companion:** *How does the author show that Kitten is curious? What are the different ways that Kitten tries to reach the moon in the sky?*

Write a Response Work together to complete My Writing Outline 22. Then have children use the sentences from their outlines to complete p. 74.

Writing Checklist Read the checklist with children and have them check for these items in their writing.

Beginning Have partners take turns reading their sentences to each other. Then provide sentence frames to help them talk about their sentences: *I used the adjective many*.

Intermediate Encourage partners to read each other's sentences and add an adjective to one of their sentences.

Advanced/Advanced High Have partners identify where they used each item in their writing.

FORMATIVE ASSESSMENT ❯ **STUDENT CHECK IN** Partners share their sentences from My Writing Outline. Ask children to reflect, using the Check-in routine.

SELF-SELECTED WRITING

LESSON 5

LEARNING GOALS

We can revise our writing.

OBJECTIVES

Use frequently occurring adjectives.

LANGUAGE OBJECTIVES

Children will inquire about their writing by adding an adjective to a sentence.

ELA ACADEMIC LANGUAGE

- *adjective*
- Cognate: *adjetivo*

Work with children to revise the group writing activity. Point to each word as you read the sentences. Stop to ask questions, such as: *Can we add an adjective to tell more about this noun?* If needed, write a simple sentence and work together to add an adjective to the sentence. Then have partners revise each other's sentences before publishing their writing.

For support with grammar and using adjectives, refer to the **Language Transfers Handbook** and **Language Development Cards** 10A–12B.

FORMATIVE ASSESSMENT ❯ **STUDENT CHECK IN** Partners tell what revisions they made. Ask children to reflect, using the Check-in routine.

ENGLISH LANGUAGE LEARNERS

LESSONS 1-2

READING • SHARED READ • ACCESS THE TEXT

LEARNING GOALS

We can read and understand a nonfiction text.

OBJECTIVES

Use the photographs and details in a text to describe its key ideas.

With prompting and support, read informational texts appropriately complex for grade 1.

Build on others' talk in conversations by responding to the comments of others through multiple exchanges.

Produce complete sentences when appropriate to task and situation.

LANGUAGE OBJECTIVES

Children will inform about Tomotaka Takahashi's path to invent robots, using verbs in the past tense.

ELA ACADEMIC LANGUAGE

• problem, solve, solution
• Cognates: problema, solución

MATERIALS

Reading/Writing Companion, pp. 86–95

Visual Vocabulary Cards

DIGITAL TOOLS

Have children listen to the selection as they follow along to develop comprehension and practice fluency and pronunciation.

Use the additional grammar video.

Grammar Video

"The Story of a Robot Inventor"

Prepare to Read

Build Background Read aloud the Essential Question on page 86. Have children share what they know about inventions. Use the photos on pages 86–89 to generate ideas. Point to and read the title aloud. *We are going to read about Mr. Takahashi.* Point to Mr. Takahashi. *This is Mr. Takahashi. Say* Mr. Takahashi *with me.* Point to the robots. *Mr. Takahashi invents robots. Say* robots *with me.*

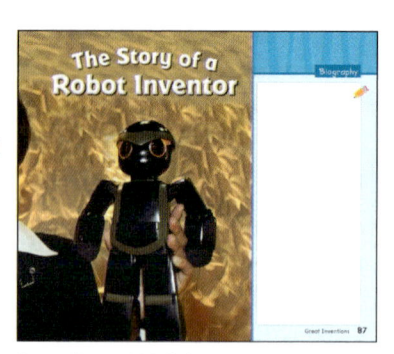

Reading/Writing Companion, Lexile 420L

Focus on Vocabulary Use the **Visual Vocabulary Cards** to review the high-frequency words *began, better, guess, learn, right,* and *sure* and the oral vocabulary words *complicated, curious, device, imagine,* and *improve.* Display the illustrations in the text, and invite children to name things they know. Preteach new vocabulary, such as *blocks, forms, comic books, idea, person, bend,* and *contests.* Point to the picture of blocks on page 88. Say: *Blocks are toys children play with. Say* blocks *with me. You can use blocks to build things. What can you build with blocks?* You can build a house/tower/building *with blocks.*

Summarize the Text Before reading, say the summary, and point to the illustrations. *This text tells about Tomotaka Takahashi, a man who invents robots. Mr. Takahashi was not happy with the robots he was seeing because they did not move like real people. He decided to invent a better robot.*

Read the Text

Use the Interactive Question-Response routine to help children understand the text.

Pages 88–89

Pages 88–89 Read the text aloud. Point to the map. *The circle shows the country of Japan. Say* Japan *with me. Where was Mr. Takahashi born?* (Japan) Invite children to tell what they know about Japan. *What did Mr. Takahashi like to do as a child?* Mr. Takahashi liked to build/play *with blocks. What did Mr. Takahashi like to do as he got older?* He liked to read *comic books. What did he see in his comic books?* He saw a robot *that looked like a* person/child.

COLLABORATE *What big ideas did Mr. Takahashi have as a boy? Discuss with a partner.*

Beginning Point to the image of Mr. Takahashi and his robots. *Do the robots look like people?* Yes, the robots look like people. *Where did Mr. Takahashi get his idea?* He got his idea from a comic book.

Intermediate Have partners point to the robots in the picture as they respond. *What is Mr. Takahashi holding?* He is holding a robot *he made. What do his*

230 UNIT 5 WEEK 3

WEEK 3

robots look like? His robots *look like* people. *Where did Mr. Takahashi get his idea?* Mr. Takahashi got his idea from a comic book.

Advanced/Advanced High Have partners elaborate on their responses. *What did Mr. Takahasi do as a young person that prepared him for inventing robots?* As a child, he made things with blocks. Then he read comic books. *How did Mr. Takahashi get his idea to make robots that look like people?* Mr. Takahashi read a comic book *about a* robot *that* looked like *a* person.

Pages 90–93

Pages 90–91 Read the text aloud. Point to Mr. Takahashi. *Mr. Takahashi started to study robots. What did he want to learn?* (how robots move) Point to the robot. *This is one of his robots.* Encourage children to tell how this robot is different from other robots. *What can this robot do?* It can bend its knees *and move like a* person.

What problem did Mr. Takahashi have with the robots he was studying? Discuss with a partner.

Beginning Use the pictures to review the parts of the body, especially *arms, legs,* and *knees*. *When Mr. Takahashi was studying robots, did they walk like people?* No, *they did* not walk *like people. Do Mr. Takahashi's robots move like people?* (yes)

Intermediate Help partners give details for their answers. *What did Mr. Takahashi see when he studied robots?* Mr. Takahashi saw that the robots *did not move their* bodies *like people do.*

Advanced/Advanced High Help partners elaborate. *What problem did Mr. Takahasi want to solve?* He wanted the robots *to* move *more like* real people.

Pages 94–95

Page 94 Read the text aloud, and have children follow along. *Mr. Takahashi had problems to solve for the robot races.* Point to and say the word *waterproof* for children to repeat. *Things that are* waterproof *are safe from water.* Point to the word *fins,* and draw a fish with a fin. *Fins help fish swim. What was Mr. Takahashi's solution for his swimming robot?* He made it waterproof. *He gave it short arms like* fins. *How did short arms help?* The robot could swim *faster.*

What steps did Mr. Takahashi take to get his robots ready for races? Discuss with a partner.

Beginning Guide partners to answer questions. *What is this robot doing?* It is running. *What else can Mr. Takahashi's robots do?* They can swim *and* ride *bikes. How did Mr. Takahashi help his swimming robot?* He made it waterproof. *He gave it* arms *like fins.*

Intermediate Help partners give details with their responses. *What did Mr. Takahashi do to improve one of his robots?* He gave his swimming *robot arms like* fins *so it could* swim *faster.*

Advanced/Advanced High Help partners elaborate on their responses. *What did Mr. Takahashi help his robots be able to do?* He helped them be able to swim, ride bikes long distances, *and* run.

FORMATIVE ASSESSMENT

▶ STUDENT CHECK IN

Have partners retell what kinds of robots Mr. Takahashi invented. Then have children reflect, using the Check-In routine.

Independent Time

Text-to-Community Connections Pair children of mixed proficiencies, and have them discuss inventions they use at home or in their communities. Examples could include items like street lights or recycling bins. Then have children discuss ways these inventions might be made better, like Mr. Takahashi did with the robots. Provide a sentence frame: One invention I use in the community is [street lights]. The invention would be better if [they only came on when it is dark]. Allow pairs to write what they can, help translate or elaborate, and then provide corrections as needed. Have partners present their ideas to another pair, a small group, or the whole class.

ENGLISH LANGUAGE LEARNERS

LESSON 3

READING • ANCHOR TEXT • ACCESS THE TEXT

LEARNING GOALS

We can read and understand a nonfiction text.

OBJECTIVES

Use the illustrations and details in a text to describe its key ideas.

Identify the reasons an author gives to support points in a text.

With prompting and support, read informational texts appropriately complex for grade 1.

Produce complete sentences when appropriate to task and situation.

LANGUAGE OBJECTIVES

Children will inform about Thomas Edison's life and experiences, using key vocabulary and complete sentences.

ELA ACADEMIC LANGUAGE

- problem, solve, retell
- Cognate: *problema*

MATERIALS

Literature Anthology, pp. 202–221

Visual Vocabulary Cards

DIGITAL TOOLS

Have children listen to the selection as they follow along to develop comprehension and practice fluency and pronunciation.

Use the online ELL Vocabulary Practice for additional support.

Thomas Edison, Inventor

Prepare to Read

Build Background *We are going to read a story about one of history's most famous inventors.* Show the picture on the title page and invite childen to tell what they see. Point to the *bottles, birdcage, newspaper,* and *printing press.* Say the words and have children repeat. Then point to the boy on the page. *This is Thomas Edison. Even when he was young, he liked to try to solve problems and understand how things work. Have you ever tried to find out how something works? What happened? I tried to find out how a ____ works.*

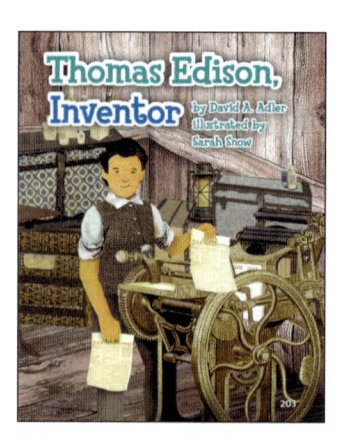

Literature Anthology, Lexile 510L

Focus on Vocabulary Use the **Visual Vocabulary Cards** to review the high-frequency words *began, better, guess, learn, right,* and *sure* and the oral vocabulary words *complicated, curious, device,* and *improve.* As you read, teach important selection words, such as *experiments,* using gestures and pantomime.

Summarize the Text Before reading, say the summary while pointing to the illustrations. *The story tells about the inventor Thomas Edison. When he was young, he liked to try to solve problems. As he got older, he invented many important things, including the light bulb.*

Read the Text

Use the Interactive Question-Response Routine to help children understand the text.

Pages 204–209

Pages 205–206 Read the text. Point to the boy on the page. *Young Tom wanted to know what would happen if he sat on an egg. What did Tom do?* Tom made a nest and sat on an egg. Point to the word *Splat!* Splat! *tells a sound something squishy makes when it breaks. Say* splat *with me. What happened to the egg when Tom sat on it?* It broke and made a mess. Point to the children on page 206. *Young Tom saw that birds ate worms. He knew that birds could fly. He wondered if people could fly if they ate worms. Say* worms *with me. What did the girl do?* She drank chopped worms in water. *Things that are* chopped *are cut up in little pieces. Did she fly?* No, she did not fly. She got sick.

Why does the author include stories about Tom Edison when he was young? Discuss with a partner.

Beginning Have partners point to the pictures as they respond, starting with page 205: *What did Tom do?* He sat on an egg. *Why?* He wanted to see what would happen. Point to page 206. *What did Tom do?* He gave the girl worms in water to

232 UNIT 5 WEEK 3

WEEK 3

drink. *Why?* He wanted to see if she would fly like a bird. *Did young Tom like to find answers to his questions?* (yes)

Intermediate Point to page 205. *Why did Tom sit on an egg?* He wanted to see what would happen if he took the place of a goose. Point to page 206. *Why did Tom have the girl drink water with worms?* He wanted to see if she would fly. *What did young Tom want to do in these stories?* He wanted to answer his questions.

Advanced/Advanced High Have children extend the discussion by asking and answering: What do these stories tell you about young Tom? They tell you that he is a person who likes to solve problems.

Pages 210–213

Pages 212–213 Read the text aloud. Point to Tom on page 213. *Tom needed a job to pay for his experiments. What job did Tom get?* Tom sold candies and newspapers. *What work did Tom do later?* Tom printed his own newspaper. *Did Tom do experiments while he worked?* Yes, he set up a lab on the train.

COLLABORATE *Why does the author include stories about Tom as he got older? Discuss with a partner.*

Beginning Point to the picture of Tom. *What is Tom doing?* Tom is selling newspapers. *Why is Tom selling newspapers?* He needs money for experiments. *Does this tell about another problem Tom solves?* (yes)

Intermediate Have partners review to respond. *Why did Tom get a job?* (to pay for his experiments) *What was his job?* He sold newspapers on the train. *What does this tell you about Tom?* He solved problems.

Advanced/Advanced High Extend the discussion by having partners tell what kind of person Tom was. Tom got a job to pay for his experiments. He even did experiments at work. This tells me he was good at solving problems and loved doing experiments.

Page 214

Page 214 Read the text. *Were there phones at this time?* (no) People used a telegraph to send messages. Point to the telegraph. *This is a telegraph.* Have children repeat. *The messages were in code. Code is a way to write without letters. What was Tom's job?* Tom's job was to send and receive messages in code.

COLLABORATE *How does the author show that Tom kept trying new things? Discuss with a partner.*

Beginning Point to the beginning of the second paragraph. *What does the author say Tom learned?* He learned the code for the telegraph. Point to the third sentence of the second paragraph. *What new thing did Tom try?* He used the telegraph in new ways.

Intermediate *What does the author tell you first?* The author says that Tom learned a telegraph code. *What does the author tell you at the end?* Tom invented new and improved ways to use the telegraph.

Advanced/Advanced High Extend the discussion by having partners tell what they understand when they read how Tom kept trying new things. This helps me understand that Thomas Edison spent his life trying to solve problems in new and improved ways.

FORMATIVE ASSESSMENT

⮞ STUDENT CHECK IN

Have partners retell different moments of Thomas Edison's life. Then have children reflect using the Check-In routine.

Independent Time

Revisit Retelling After reading the selection, have children revisit Respond to the Text, Retell from the Whole Group lesson. Pair students of mixed proficiencies. Have pairs add details to their retellings. Encourage them to focus on elaborating on why Thomas Edison did experiments, what kind of experiments he did, and what the results were. Provide sentence frames to help pairs add details: Thomas Edison wanted to know if worms made people fly. He made a girl drink a cup of water with worms. He wanted to see if she would fly. She got sick. She did not fly. Encourage pairs to share their retellings with another pair, a small group, or the whole class.

ENGLISH LANGUAGE LEARNERS **233**

LESSONS 4-5

READING • LEVELED READER • ACCESS THE TEXT

LEARNING GOALS

We can ask and answer questions about a nonfiction text.

OBJECTIVES

Ask and answer questions about key details in a text.

Identify basic similarities in and differences between two texts on the same topic (e.g., in illustrations, descriptions, or procedures).

With prompting and support, read informational texts appropriately complex for grade 1.

Ask and answer questions about key details in a text read aloud or information presented orally or through other media.

LANGUAGE OBJECTIVES

Children will explain how the Wright brothers solved problems, using descriptive words.

ELA ACADEMIC LANGUAGE

- biography, problem, solution
- Cognates: *biografía, problema, solución*

MATERIALS

ELL Leveled Reader,
The Wright Brothers

Online Differentiated Text,
"James Naismith"

Online ELL Visual Vocabulary Cards

DIGITAL TOOLS

Have children listen to the selection as they follow along to develop comprehension and practice fluency and pronunciation. Use Graphic Organizer 11: Problem and Solution to enhance the lesson.

The Wright Brothers

Prepare to Read

Build Background

- Remind children of the Essential Question. *Let's read to find out what the Wright Brothers invented.* Encourage children to ask for help when they do not understand a word or phrase.

- Point to and read aloud the title and have children repeat. Ask: *What is the title?* Have children point to it. Repeat the routine with the author's name. Point to the photographs to name things and actions; for example: *These are wheels. What can wheels help you do?*

Lexile 430L

Focus on Vocabulary Use the **ELL Visual Vocabulary Cards** to preteach the words *flight* and *tested*. As you read, use gestures or visuals to teach important selection words, such as *airplane, hockey, print shop, beach,* and *seconds*.

Read the Text

Use the Interactive Question-Response Routine to help children understand the text.

Pages 2–5

Ask and Answer Questions Read pages 4–5 as children follow along. Guide children to ask and answer questions about the Wright brothers' lives. Point to the phrases *got hurt* and *spent the time*. Read them aloud and have children repeat.

Beginning *How did Wilbur get hurt?* He got hurt playing hockey. *Where did the brothers work?* They worked in a print shop.

Intermediate Help partners retell the text: *How did the Wright brothers spend their early lives?* The brothers played and worked. Wilbur got hurt.

Pages 6–7

Details: Problem and Solution Read pages 6–7 as children follow along. Ask questions to help them describe the problem and solution. Point to the first bike. *How is this bike different from bikes today?* Its wheels are different sizes. *Which bike is safer?* (the second bike)

Intermediate *What problem did the Wright brothers solve?* They made bikes safer. *How?* They made the two wheels the same size.

Advanced/Advanced High Have partners ask and answer: *What was the problem?* The bike was dangerous. *How did the Wright brothers solve the problem?* They made a safer bike.

234 UNIT 5 WEEK 3

WEEK 3

Pages 8–11

Read pages 10–11 as children follow along. Point to the pictures and say *plane, flew, flight,* and *statue*. Have children repeat. Explain that *to honor* means "to show special thoughts for a person." Have children repeat *honor*.

Beginning Have partners point to the pictures: *Why are the Wright brothers honored?* They started airplane flight.

Advanced/Advanced High Have partners discuss: *What problem did the Wright brothers solve?* They solved the problem of how people can fly.

Respond to Reading Have partners work together to retell the story and respond to the questions on page 12.

Focus on Fluency

Read pages 10–11 to model reading at an appropriate rate. Read the passage again and have children repeat after you. For more practice, record children reading the passage and select their best recording.

Paired Read: "Fly Away, Butterfly"

Make Connections: Write About It

Echo-read each page with children. Discuss butterflies: *Where do butterflies fly?* Butterflies fly to daisies. Help children make connections between texts, using the question on page 15. Both butterflies and planes fly.

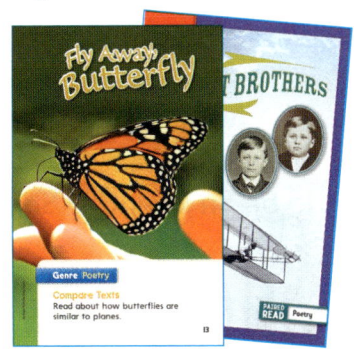

Leveled Reader

Build Knowledge: Make Connections

Talk About the Text Have partners discuss how the topics of the texts are similar to or different from other things that fly.

Write About the Text Have students add their ideas to their Build Knowledge pages of their reader's notebooks.

Self-Selected Reading

Help children choose a biography selection from the online **Leveled Reader Library,** or read the **Differentiated Text,** "James Naismith."

FOCUS ON SCIENCE

Children can extend their knowledge of things that fly by completing the science activity on page 16. **STEM**

LITERATURE CIRCLES

Lead children in conducting a literature circle, using the Thinkmark questions to guide the discussion. You may wish to discuss what children have learned about flying from the two selections in the Leveled Reader.

FORMATIVE ASSESSMENT

STUDENT CHECK IN

Have partners share their Respond to Reading. Have children reflect using the Check-In routine.

LEVEL UP

IF children can read *The Wright Brothers* **ELL Level** with fluency and correctly answer the Respond to Reading questions,

THEN tell children that they will read a more detailed version of the selection.

- Use page 8 of *The Wright Brothers* **On Level** to model using Teaching Poster 36 to list the story problem.

- Have children read the selection, checking their comprehension by using the graphic organizer.

ENGLISH LANGUAGE LEARNERS 235

LESSONS 4-5

READING • GENRE PASSAGE • ACCESS THE TEXT

LEARNING GOALS

We can apply skills and strategies to a biography.

OBJECTIVES

Explain major differences between books that tell stories and books that give information, drawing on a wide reading of a range of text types.

Ask and answer questions to help determine or clarify the meaning of words and phrases in a text.

Ask questions to clear up any confusion about the topics and texts under discussion.

Ask and answer questions about key details in a text read aloud or information presented orally or through other media.

LANGUAGE OBJECTIVES

Children will discuss details that tell about problems and solutions using complete sentences.

ELA ACADEMIC LANGUAGE

- solve, problem, photograph, solution
- Cognates: *problema, fotografía, solución*

MATERIALS

Online ELL Genre Passage, "The Sun Queen," pp. E1–E3

"The Sun Queen"

Prepare to Read

Build Background Review what children have learned about inventions. *What are some of the reasons people create inventions?* People create inventions to solve _____. Allow children to share ideas about inventions. Tell them they will be reading about two women who invented something very important.

Lexile 400L

Focus on Vocabulary Use the **Define, Example, Ask** routine to preteach difficult words or unfamiliar concepts, such as *power, heated, shined, windows,* and *oven.* Invite children to add new vocabulary to their glossaries.

Read the Text

Use the Interactive Question-Response routine to help children understand the text.

Page E1

Paragraphs 1–2 Read the text aloud as children follow along. Point to the photo. *Who is shown in the photograph?* (Maria Telkes) *Maria Telkes was an inventor. What do you think an inventor does?* An inventor invents new things. *What was Maria's job?* She was a teacher and a scientist.

Advanced/Advanced High Have children ask and answer questions with a partner to deepen their understanding of the text. *How did Maria Telkes's life prepare her to be an inventor?* She was a teacher and a scientist. She knew a lot about science.

Paragraph 3 Read the text aloud as children follow along. Point to the word *power* and say it aloud for children to repeat. *Power is the electricity used to run things. Name something in the classroom that uses power.* The lights use power.

Beginning Help partners talk about the problem and solution: People use a lot of power. Maria Telkes wanted to find a new way to get power.

Intermediate Guide children to describe the problem and solution in the text. *What problem did Maria Telkes see?* People used a lot of power. *How did she want to solve the problem?* She wanted to find a new way to get power.

Page E2

Paragraphs 1–2 Read the text aloud while children follow along. Point to the sun. *Maria Telkes and Eleanor Raymond's invention used the sun. Point to the house. What did the invention use the sun to do?* It used the sun to heat a house. *Point to the windows. How did the sun heat the house?* The sun heated the house by shining into big windows.

236 UNIT 5 WEEK 3

WEEK 3

Details: Problem and Solution Remind children that a problem is something a person wants to solve. The solution is how a person solves the problem. Point to the house in the picture. *What did Maria and Eleanor want to do? They wanted to* heat the house. *How did they do it? They* used the sun .

Beginning Help partners tell how Maria Telkes's invention was the solution to an important problem. *Look back at paragraph 3. What problem did Maria Telkes see?* People used a lot of power. *What did Maria Telkes want to do?* She wanted to find a different way to get power. Point to the illustration on page E2. *How did Maria Telkes's invention get power?* It got power from the sun. *Point to how you know.* Guide children to point to the sun in the illustration.

Paragraph 3 Read the text aloud while children follow along. Point to the word *awards*. Say it aloud and have children repeat. *An award is a way for someone to say "good job" for doing something important. What did Maria Telkes win awards for?* She won awards for her work with the sun's power.

Advanced Have partners use this paragraph and the text on page E1 to ask and answer questions: *How old was Maria when she died?* (She was 95 years old.) *Why was her work important?* She invented a way to get power from the sun.

Advanced High Have partners discuss why people might have used the word Queen as part of Maria Telkes's nickname. (They might have used *queen* because she was known as a leader in using the sun.)

Respond to Reading

Use the following instructions to help children answer the questions on page E3.

1. **Biography** Have children describe the genre they read. Ask questions to help them complete the sentence. For example: *Who is in the photo? Was she a real person? Does the text tell when she was born?*

2. **Ask and Answer Questions** Discuss with children what they learned about Maria Telkes's invention. Ask: *What does Maria Telkes's invention do? What does her invention use to make power?*

3. **Fluency** Have children take turns reading the first paragraph to a partner. As they read, fill in the chart on page E3.

Build Knowledge: Make Connections

Talk About the Text Have partners discuss the inventions Maria Telkes created.

Write About the Text Have students add their ideas to the Build Knowledge pages of their reader's notebooks.

FORMATIVE ASSESSMENT

▶ STUDENT CHECK IN

Partners will share their Respond to Reading. Ask children to reflect using the Check-In routine.

LEVEL UP

IF students read the ELL Level fluently and answered the questions,

THEN pair them with students who have proficiently read the On Level. Have them

- partner read the On Level passage.
- ask and answer questions to deepen understanding.

ENGLISH LANGUAGE LEARNERS

LESSONS 1-5

WRITING

MODELED WRITING

LESSON 1

LEARNING GOALS
We can learn to write events in order.

OBJECTIVES
Write narratives in which they recount events in sequence.

LANGUAGE OBJECTIVES
Children will inform by writing a sentence using a time-order word.

ELA ACADEMIC LANGUAGE
- events
- Cognate: *eventos*

Writing Practice Have children choral read the sample sentences on p. 96 of the **Reading/Writing Companion**. Help them analyze the sentences, using the Actor/Action routine: *Who is the actor in the first part?* (I) *What is the action?* (if had a robot) *Who is the actor in the second part?* (it) *What is the action?* (would help me a lot) Then read the prompt on p. 97 and ask children to answer it as a group. Write their sentences on the board and ask them to choral read. Then help them write their own sentences.

Beginning Provide sentence frames to help children create their sentences: *My robot would help me. First, it would make me a snack.*

Intermediate Have partners ask and answer questions to create their sentences: *What would your robot do? What would it do first/next/last?*

Advanced/Advanced High Encourage children to reread their sentences and to check that the order of events makes sense before sharing them with the group.

FORMATIVE ASSESSMENT ▶ **STUDENT CHECK IN** Partners share their sentences. Ask children to reflect, using the Check-In routine.

INTERACTIVE WRITING

LESSON 2

LEARNING GOALS
We can read and write about a Student Model.

OBJECTIVES
Respond to questions and suggestions from peers.

LANGUAGE OBJECTIVES
Children will discuss and write sentences about a Student Model, identifying time-order words.

ELA ACADEMIC LANGUAGE
- events
- Cognate: *eventos*

Analyze the Student Model Have children choral read the Student Model on p. 104 of the **Reading/Writing Companion**. Use the Actor/Action routine to review the second sentence: *Who is the actor?* (Mr. Takahashi) *What is the action?* (made shapes) *How?* (with blocks) Have children identify the word that tells order in the sentence. (first) *Emily wrote the steps that Mr. Takahashi took to become a good inventor.* Then help children complete p. 105.

Beginning Have partners point to words that tell order. Then provide a sentence frame: *Emily used first to tell the order of events.*

Intermediate Have partners ask and answer questions: *What did you notice about Emily's writing?* She used words that tell order.

Advanced/Advanced High Challenge children to write about the text, using their own sentences. Encourage them to share their ideas.

FORMATIVE ASSESSMENT ▶ **STUDENT CHECK IN** Partners share their responses. Ask children to reflect, using the Check-In routine.

WEEK 3

INDEPENDENT WRITING

LESSONS 3-4

LEARNING GOALS

We can use text evidence to respond to a nonfiction text.

OBJECTIVES

Write informative texts in which they provide some sense of closure.

LANGUAGE OBJECTIVES

Children will write sentences with words that tell the order of events.

ELA ACADEMIC LANGUAGE

- text
- Cognate: *texto*

Find Text Evidence Follow the Independent Writing routine. Help children orally retell the anchor text. Ask questions, such as: *What are some experiments young Tom did?* (sat on a nest, fed worms to a girl) *What is one job that he had?* (he wrote and sold his own newspaper) Then read the prompt in the **Reading/Writing Companion,** p. 110: *What made Thomas Edison a good inventor? What qualities did Thomas Edison have? How did they help him become a good inventor?*

Write a Response Work together to complete My Writing Outline 23. Then have children use the sentences from their outline to complete p. 110.

Writing Checklist Read the checklist with children and have them check for these items in their writing.

Beginning Provide sentence frames to help children talk about their sentences: I used the word *first* to tell the order of *events*.

Intermediate Encourage partners to read each other's writing and check for complete sentences.

Advanced/Advanced High Have partners identify where they used each item in their writing.

FORMATIVE ASSESSMENT ▶ **STUDENT CHECK IN** Partners share their sentences from My Writing Outline. Ask children to reflect, using the Check-in routine.

SELF-SELECTED WRITING

LESSON 5

LEARNING GOALS

We can revise our writing.

OBJECTIVES

Use frequently occurring adjectives.

LANGUAGE OBJECTIVES

Children will inquire about their writing by checking adjectives that compare.

ELA ACADEMIC LANGUAGE

- compare
- Cognate: *comparar*

Work with children to revise the group writing activity. Point to each word as you read the sentences. Stop to ask questions, such as: *Is this adjective comparing a noun to another noun?* If needed, write a sentence using a comparative adjective incorrectly and work together to revise it. Then have partners revise each other's sentences.

For support with grammar and *adjectives that compare*, refer to the **Language Transfers Handbook** and **Language Development Card** 13A.

FORMATIVE ASSESSMENT ▶ **STUDENT CHECK IN** Partners tell what revisions they made. Ask children to reflect, using the Check-in routine.

ENGLISH LANGUAGE LEARNERS 239

READING • SHARED READ • ACCESS THE TEXT

LESSONS 1-2

LEARNING GOALS

We can read and understand a realistic fiction.

OBJECTIVES

Describe characters, settings, and major events in a story, using key details.

Identify words and phrases in stories or poems that suggest feelings or appeal to the senses.

Use illustrations and details in a story to describe its characters, setting, or events.

Produce complete sentences when appropriate to task and situation.

LANGUAGE OBJECTIVES

Children will describe different sounds that the characters hear, using verbs with -ing and key vocabulary.

ELA ACADEMIC LANGUAGE

- problem, solution, realistic
- Cognates: *problema, solución, realista*

MATERIALS

Reading/Writing Companion, pp. 122–131

Visual Vocabulary Cards

DIGITAL TOOLS

Have children listen to the selection as they follow along to develop comprehension and practice fluency and pronunciation.

Use the additional grammar video.

Grammar Video

"Now, What's That Sound?"

Prepare to Read

Build Background Read aloud the Essential Question on page 122. Have children repeat the word *sound*. *What is a sound?* A sound is something you ____ with your ears. Have children close their eyes. *Listen. Do you know what makes this sound?* Make a few simple sounds for them to identify, such as stapling papers or sharpening a pencil. Have children point to and read the selection title. Point to the two main characters. *They hear a sound, but they don't know what makes it.*

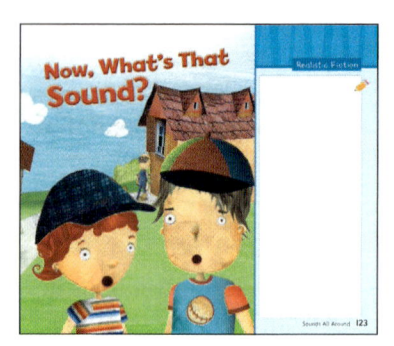

Reading/Writing Companion, Lexile 240L

Focus on Vocabulary Use the **Visual Vocabulary Cards** to review the high-frequency words *color, early, instead, nothing, oh,* and *thought* and the oral vocabulary words *distract, nervous, senses, squeaky,* and *volume*. Display the illustrations for *board, saw, broom, deck,* and *driveway*. Use the following routine: Point to the saw. Say the word *saw*. Have children point to the picture and repeat the word. *He is cutting a board. What is he cutting?* He is cutting a board.

Summarize the Text Before reading, say the summary and point to the illustrations. *This story tells about two children who look for what makes a sound.*

Read the Text

Use the Interactive Question-Response Routine to help children understand the story.

Pages 124–125

Pages 124–125 Read the text aloud. *Point to Gilbert and Marta on page 124. What sound do they hear?* Help children find the words in the illustration and the corresponding italicized words in the text. Explain that the words in italics are sound words. Follow the same routine for the sound words on page 125.

What makes the sound Gilbert and Marta hear in the garage? Discuss with a partner.

Beginning List people and objects for children to point to and identify in the illustration: *Gilbert, Marta, Dad, board, saw*. Then have them read the sound words aloud. *What makes that sound?* Dad is cutting a board with his saw.

Intermediate Have pairs respond by answering *wh-* questions: *Who do Gilbert and Marta see?* They see Dad. *What is he doing?* He is cutting a board. *What is he using?* He is using a saw. *What sound does it make?* (Zing, zing, zing.)

Advanced/Advanced High Help partners elaborate on their answers: Dad is cutting a board with his saw in the garage. The saw makes a smooth sound: zing, zing, zing. It isn't the same as the first sound.

240 UNIT 5 WEEK 4

WEEK 4

Pages 126–129

Pages 126–127 Read the text aloud as children follow along. Point to the deck. *What is this?* Help children recall the word *deck*. *Where are Marta, Gilbert, and Gramps?* They are on the deck. Say *sweep* as you do the motion and have children mimic you. *What does Gramps use to sweep?* He sweeps with a broom. *What sound does it make?* Help children read the italicized words in the text and illustration. *Is this the sound Marta and Gilbert heard?* (no) *How is it different?* It's softer. To reinforce meaning, have children say the original sound *Tap-tap-tap. Rat-a-tat-tat* at normal volume and then whisper *Swish, swish, swish*.

Pages 128–129 Read the text aloud as children follow along. Point to the word *sighed* and sigh for children to imitate. Then say *hopeless* for children to repeat. Use problem and solution to clarify meaning. *What is Gilbert and Marta's problem in the story?* They don't know what makes the sound. *Does Marta think they can solve the problem?* No. She thinks it's hopeless.

What makes the sounds Gilbert and Marta hear? Discuss with a partner.

Beginning Have pairs find the italicized words in the text and the words in the picture on page 128 and read them aloud as they imitate Ana's motion.

Intermediate Have pairs chorally read the sound words in the text and the picture on page 128 aloud and then describe the action that causes that sound: Ana is bouncing a ball.

Advanced/Advanced High Help children make an inference about the sound words in the picture on page 129 Have pairs read the sound words aloud together and then look at the illustration on page 128 to figure out what might make those noises. Help children describe what happens; for example: Ana bounces the ball and throws it. The ball makes this sound when it goes through the hoop.

Pages 130–131

Pages 130–131 Read the text aloud as children follow along. Have children raise a hand each time they hear the sound words. *What do Gilbert and Marta see?* (a bird) *Where is it?* It's in a tree. *What is it doing?* It's pecking for bugs. Have children repeat the word *peck* as they imitate a bird pecking for food.

What makes the sound Gilbert and Marta heard at the beginning of the story? Why? Discuss with a partner.

Beginning Have children read the italicized words in the text and the words in the picture while tapping their desks to imitate the sound. Have pairs complete this sentence frame: The woodpecker is tapping on the tree.

Intermediate Help pairs add details to their answer: The woodpecker is tapping on the tree. It is looking for bugs. It wants to eat them.

Advanced/Advanced High Help pairs extend their thinking: *Why is the woodpecker tapping on the tree?* It is tapping on the tree because bugs live there. It wants to eat the bugs.

FORMATIVE ASSESSMENT

❯ STUDENT CHECK IN

Have partners say what sounds the characters heard. Then, have children reflect using the Check-In routine.

Independent Time

Describing Sounds Pair children of mixed proficiency levels. Have them take turns saying a sound from the story for their partner to guess what makes it. Remind them to speak clearly. Provide sentence frames for guesses: [Gramps] is [sweeping] the [deck] with a [broom]. If children have trouble guessing from the sound alone, allow partners to use gestures or display the illustrations from the story. Have each pair choose one sound to demonstrate and describe for the class.

LESSON 3

READING • ANCHOR TEXT • ACCESS THE TEXT

LEARNING GOALS

We can read and understand realistic fiction.

OBJECTIVES

Retell stories, including key details, and demonstrate understanding of their central message or lesson.

Identify words and phrases in stories or poems that suggest feelings or appeal to the senses.

Distinguish between information provided by pictures or other illustrations and information provided by the words in a text.

Ask and answer questions about what a speaker says in order to gather additional information or clarify something that is not understood.

LANGUAGE OBJECTIVES

Children will narrate how the character learns a new skill, using present-tense verbs and complete sentences.

ELA ACADEMIC LANGUAGE

- illustrations
- Cognate: *ilustraciones*

MATERIALS

Literature Anthology, pp. 226–255
Visual Vocabulary Cards

DIGITAL TOOLS

Have children listen to the selection as they follow along to develop comprehension and practice fluency and pronunciation.

Use the online ELL Vocabulary Practice for additional support.

Whistle for Willie

Prepare to Read

Build Background *We are going to read a story about a boy who wants to whistle to call his dog.* Display the picture on the title page and read the title aloud. *Point to the boy/dog. Which one do you think is Willie?* Willie is the ____. *The boy is whistling.* Say the word *whistle* and have children repeat. Demonstrate whistling and invite children who can whistle to do so. *Is it difficult to whistle?*

Focus on Vocabulary Use the **Visual Vocabulary Cards** to review the high-frequency words *color, early, instead, nothing, oh,* and *thought* and the oral vocabulary words *distract, nervous, senses, squeaky,* and *volume*. Before reading the story, clarify vocabulary children will need for understanding. As you read, teach important story words, such as *blow* and *cheeks,* using gestures and pantomime.

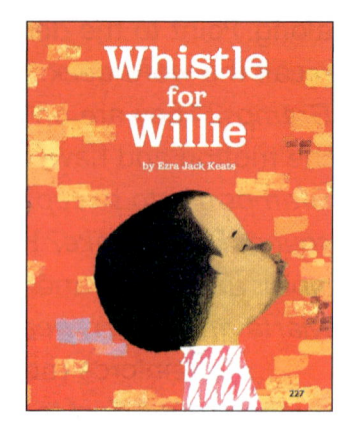

Literature Anthology, Lexile 520L

Summarize the Text Before reading, say the summary while pointing to the illustrations. *The story tells about a boy named Peter. He tries to whistle to call his dog, Willie. Peter can't whistle at first, but he keeps practicing!*

Read the Text

Use the Interactive Question-Response Routine to help children understand the story.

Pages 228–233

Pages 228–230 Read the text aloud. *What does Peter see?* A boy is playing with his dog. The boy whistles. The dog runs to him. *Can Peter do the same thing with Willie?* (no) *Why?* He can't whistle.

Pages 231–233 Read the text aloud. Remind children that we use *instead* to say we're doing something different. *What does Peter do instead of trying to whistle?* He turns around faster and faster. *When I turn around fast, I feel dizzy. Say* dizzy.

COLLABORATE *How does Peter feel? How does the author let you know how Peter feels? Discuss with a partner.*

Beginning To help pairs understand how Peter feels, have them imitate Peter on page 231 by spinning around twice. Then have them lean like Peter does. *Can Peter stand up straight now?* (no) *Does Peter feel dizzy?* Yes, he feels dizzy.

Intermediate Have pairs review pages 232–233. Have partners answer: *What does the text say happens?* Everything turns. *Why does the picture show lights moving?* It shows how Peter feels. He feels dizzy.

242 UNIT 5 WEEK 4

WEEK 4

Advanced/Advanced High Have children point to the line between the ground and walls on pages 232–233. *What do the picture and text show Peter thinks?* Peter thinks the ground is moving. He feels dizzy. *Why does he feel dizzy?* He turned around a lot.

Pages 234–247

Pages 236–237 Read the text aloud. *What does the boy try to do again?* (whistle) *Why are his cheeks tired?* He keeps trying to whistle.

How does the author let you know that Peter won't give up trying to whistle? Discuss.

Beginning Have one partner reread page 237 while the other does the motions of blowing and whistling. *Why is Peter blowing?* He is trying to whistle. *Does he try one time or many times?* He tries many times.

Intermediate Have pairs look back and find each time Peter tries to whistle. Suggest using the pictures to help them recall. Examples: Peter tries to whistle when he hides in a carton. He tries again by a door.

Advanced/Advanced High Have pairs describe parts of the story where Peter tries to whistle, what he does, and whether he gives up; for example: Peter hides in a carton and tries to whistle to Willie, but he can't. He doesn't give up. He tries to whistle again by his door.

Pages 238–239 Read the text aloud. *Whose hat is Peter wearing?* He is wearing his father's hat. *Why?* He wants to feel grown up. *Why? What can most grown-ups do that Peter can't?* They can whistle.

Pages 240–241 Read the text aloud. *Who is Peter pretending to be?* (his father) Reread the second paragraph on page 240. *Is Peter saying what a father might say?* (yes)

Pages 242–247 Read the text aloud. *When can Peter whistle for the first time? Point to the picture.* (pages 246–247) *Where is Peter?* He is under the carton. *Why is he whistling?* He wants to call Willie. Turn back to pages 234–235 and compare. *Does Peter hide there, too?* (yes) *Can he whistle?* (no)

Pages 248–253

Pages 248–249 Read the text aloud. Explain that *raced* means "ran."

How does the author help you know how Peter feels when he finally whistles? Discuss.

Beginning Help partners respond. Peter whistles for his parents/dog. He whistles on an errand. *Why does he whistle all the time?* He likes whistling.

Intermediate Have children describe Peter's whistling in more detail and draw a conclusion. Peter whistles for his parents/dog. He whistles on the way to the grocery store. He whistles a lot! He loves whistling.

Advanced/Advanced High Help pairs make an inference based on their own experience: *What do you run home to show your parents?* (a good grade, a new skill) *How do you feel?* I feel happy/proud. Peter feels happy/proud because he can whistle.

Pages 250–251 Read the text aloud. *What can Peter do now?* He can whistle. *Why does he run home?* He wants to whistle for his parents. *How do his parents feel about his whistling?* They love it. *How does his dog feel about it?* Willie loves it, too.

Pages 252–253 Read the text aloud. Explain that when you *go on an errand*, you go somewhere to buy or do something necessary. *What errand is Peter doing?* He is going to the grocery store.

FORMATIVE ASSESSMENT

STUDENT CHECK IN

Children retell what Peter accomplishes in the end. Then have children reflect, using the Check-In routine.

Independent Time

Connect Text to Self Have children think of a skill they have learned, such as tying their shoes or riding a bike. Have partners describe the skill and answer questions: *Did you keep trying or did you give up? Was it difficult or easy to learn? Are you proud of what you learned?* Have pairs share with the group.

LESSONS 4-5

READING • LEVELED READER • ACCESS THE TEXT

LEARNING GOALS

We can ask and answer questions about a realistic fiction story.

OBJECTIVES

Identify words and phrases in stories or poems that suggest feelings or appeal to the senses.

Use illustrations and details in a story to describe its characters, setting, or events.

Ask and answer questions about key details in a text read aloud or information presented orally or through other media.

Ask and answer questions about what a speaker says in order to gather additional information or clarify something that is not understood.

LANGUAGE OBJECTIVES

Children will narrate how the characters solve a problem, using key vocabulary and complete sentences.

ELA ACADEMIC LANGUAGE

- problem, solution
- Cognates: *problema, solución*

MATERIALS

ELL Leveled Reader, *Down on the Farm*

Online Differentiated Text, "Music to My Ears"

Online ELL Visual Vocabulary Cards

DIGITAL TOOLS

Have children listen to the selection as they follow along to develop comprehension and practice fluency and pronunciation. Use Graphic Organizer 11: Problem and Solution to enhance the lesson.

Down on the Farm

Prepare to Read

Build Background

- Remind children of the Essential Question: *What sounds can you hear? How are they made?* Encourage children to ask for help when they do not understand a word or phrase.
- Point to the title. *What can you see on a farm?* Elicit names of familiar farm animals, vegetables, and items, such as a red barn or tractor, and list them on the board. Read each word for children to repeat.

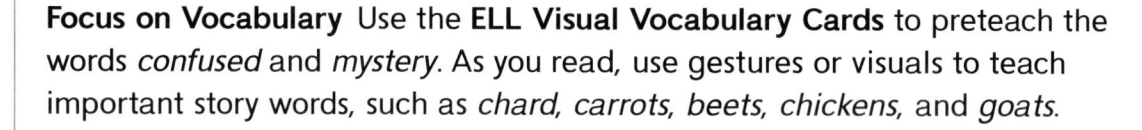

Lexile 170L

Focus on Vocabulary Use the **ELL Visual Vocabulary Cards** to preteach the words *confused* and *mystery*. As you read, use gestures or visuals to teach important story words, such as *chard, carrots, beets, chickens,* and *goats*.

Read the Text

Use the Interactive Question-Response Routine to help children understand the story.

Pages 2–3

Ask and Answer Questions Read pages 2–3. Have children point to Jacy and Mom. Help children ask and answer questions: What sounds does Jacy hear? Jacy hears sounds in the city.

Beginning Guide children to read the speech bubbles aloud and name who or what makes each sound: "[Toot!]" That's a [bus].

Intermediate Help partners take turns asking and answering questions about the sounds: What sound does the [bicycle] make? "[Ring]!" goes the [bicycle].

Advanced/Advanced High Have partners take turns describing the sounds. (The woman is talking on her phone. She says, "Hello!")

Pages 4–7

Read pages 4–7. *Why isn't this place like a farm?* It doesn't have a red barn or cows. *How is it like a farm?* It has chickens and rows of plants.

Beginning Help children identify Jacy's problem. *What does Jacy hear?* (a sound) *Does she know what it is?* (no)

Intermediate Have pairs talk about the problem: Jacy hears a sound. She does not know what is making the sound. We will read to find the solution.

Pages 8–11

Details: Problem and Solution Read pages 8–11 as children follow along. *Did Jacy solve her problem?* (yes) *What makes the sound?* (goats) Point to and say *milk*

244 UNIT 5 WEEK 4

WEEK 4

and *cheese* for children to repeat. *Why are there goats at Stella's farm?*

Beginning Help partners answer the question: Stella gets milk from the goats.

Advanced/Advanced High Point to the picture on page 11. *Why is Stella milking the goat?* She needs the goat's milk to make cheese.

Respond to Reading Have partners work together to retell the story and respond to the questions on page 12.

Focus on Fluency

Read pages 8–9 to model reading with expression. Read the passage again and have children repeat after you. For more practice, record children reading the passage and select the best recording.

Paired Read: "How to Make a Rain Stick"

Make Connections: Write About It

Echo-read each page with children. Have children mime each step after you read it and imitate the rain sound at the end. Help them make connections between texts, using the question on page 15. On the farm, the goats make the Maaa. Maa sound. In the rain stick, the dry rice makes the rain sound.

Leveled Reader

Build Knowledge: Make Connections

Talk About the Text Have partners discuss the sounds described in the texts.

Write About the Text Have students add their ideas to the Build Knowledge pages of their reader's notebooks.

Self-Selected Reading

Help children choose a fiction selection from the online **Leveled Reader Library,** or read the **Differentiated Text,** "Music to My Ears."

FOCUS ON SCIENCE

Children can extend their knowledge of sounds by completing the science activity on page 16. **STEM**

LITERATURE CIRCLES

Lead children in conducting a literature circle, using the Thinkmark questions to guide the discussion. You may wish to discuss what children have learned about sounds from the two selections in the Leveled Reader.

FORMATIVE ASSESSMENT

STUDENT CHECK IN

Have partners share their Respond to Reading. Have children reflect, using the Check-In routine.

LEVEL UP

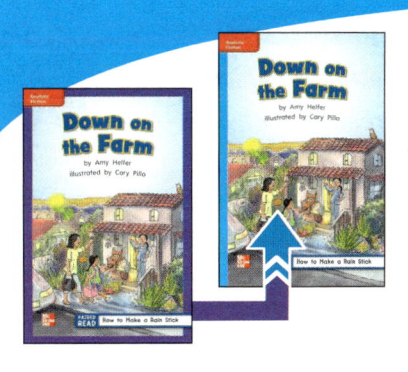

IF children can read *Down on the Farm* **ELL Level** with fluency and correctly answer the Respond to Reading questions,

THEN tell children that they will read a more detailed version of the story.

- Use pages 2–3 of *Down on the Farm* **On Level** to model using Teaching Poster 36 to list the story problem.
- Have children read the selection, checking their comprehension by using the graphic organizer.

ENGLISH LANGUAGE LEARNERS **245**

LESSONS 4-5

READING • GENRE PASSAGE • ACCESS THE TEXT

LEARNING GOALS

We can apply skills and strategies to a realistic fiction story.

OBJECTIVES

Describe characters, settings, and major events in a story, using key details.

Identify words and phrases in stories or poems that suggest feelings or appeal to the senses.

Explain major differences between books that tell stories and books that give information, drawing on a wide reading of a range of text types.

Describe the connection between two individuals, events, ideas, or pieces of information in a text.

LANGUAGE OBJECTIVES

Children will discuss details that tell problem and solution using complete sentences.

ELA ACADEMIC LANGUAGE

- realistic fiction, setting, characters
- Cognate: *ficción realista*

MATERIALS

Online ELL Genre Passage, "The Class Trip," pp. E1–E3

"The Class Trip"

Lexile 400L

Prepare to Read

Build Background Have children close their eyes and visualize themselves in their yard or in a park. Encourage them to picture the plants and animals there. *What sounds do you hear? Who or what makes them?* Elicit sounds such as birds singing. *We are going to read about the sounds one girl hears on a class trip.*

Focus on Vocabulary Use the Define/Example/Ask routine to preteach difficult words or unfamiliar concepts, such as *field trip, woods, leaves,* and *branches*. To provide further prereading support, follow the same routine for these adjectives from the story: *boring, surprised, quiet,* and *interesting*. Invite children to add new vocabulary to their glossaries.

Read the Text

Use the Interactive Question-Response routine to help children understand the story.

Page E1

Paragraph 1 Read the text aloud and have children follow along. Guide children to describe the setting: *Where does Kate live?* She lives in the city. *Where is she now?* She is in the woods. *Who else is there?* Kate's science class is there.

Beginning Help children use the illustration on page E1 to clarify the characters and setting of the story. *Point to Kate/her science class. What do you see in the woods?* (trees) *Point to the leaves. Point to the branches.*

Paragraphs 2–3 Read the text aloud as children follow along. *What will the class do on the field trip?* They will look at leaves and draw them. *What is Kate's problem in the story?* She thinks the field trip will be boring.

Advanced/Advanced High Ask questions to help children understand the *problem. What does Kate think?* (the field trip will be boring) *What does the teacher want the class to do?* (look at leaves and draw them)

Paragraph 4 Model being quiet. Then say the word. Repeat for *loud*. Read the text aloud and help children figure out the meaning of *louder*. Have children look for the word and help them identify the **suffix**. *What word part or suffix was added to the word loud?* (-er) *We add the suffix -er to compare. Think about the woods and the city. Where is it louder?* It is louder in the city.

Intermediate Have children extend their answer. *What do you think Kate hears in the city?* (car horns, traffic)

Advanced/Advanced High Have partners compare the woods with the city. It is quiet in the woods, but it is loud in the city. You hear birds and the

246 UNIT 5 WEEK 4

wind in the woods, but you hear car horns and traffic in the city.

Page E2

Paragraph 1 Read the text aloud as children follow along. Say the words *oak* and *maple* for children to repeat. Explain that these are different kinds of trees.

Intermediate Have children find a sentence in the text to answer this question: *Why is Kate drawing maple and oak leaves?* (Her teacher said, "Today we will look at leaves and draw them.")

Paragraph 2 Read the text aloud as children follow along. Tell children that when something happens *suddenly*, it happens very quickly. Explain that the author uses the expression *just in time* to show that Kate turns when the deer runs by. Say *crack* for children to repeat. *This word imitates a sound.* Clap your hands sharply to make a cracking sound and have children mimic you.

Intermediate Guide children to infer: *What caused the branch to crack?* The deer ran over the branch. This caused the branch to crack/break.

Paragraph 3 Read the text aloud as children follow along. *What does Kate think about the woods now?* It has interesting leaves and sounds. *What interesting sounds did Kate hear in the woods?* (birds, wind, the crack of a branch) *Did this solve Kate's problem?* (yes)

Beginning Have children point to the items in the pictures as they answer. Guide them to notice the words next to the bird in the picture on page E1. *What sound do the birds make?* (chirp, chirp)

Events: Problem and Solution Have children talk about how Kate felt at the beginning of the story. *Kate didn't want to go to the woods. Did Kate have the same problem at the end?* (no) *What changed?* Kate thinks the field trip is fun. The woods have interesting leaves and sounds.

Respond to Reading

Use the following instructions to help children answer the questions on page E3.

1. **Realistic Fiction** Remind children that realistic fiction has made-up characters and events, but it could happen in real life. Ask about the setting: *Where does this story take place?* (in the woods) *What do the characters see?* (trees, leaves, branches, a deer) *Can people see those things in real life?* (yes)

2. Tell children that to find out how characters change, they can compare the beginning and end of the story. *What does Kate think at the beginning?* She thinks the field trip is boring. *What does she think at the end?* She thinks the field trip is fun and interesting.

3. **Fluency** Have partners take turns reading the first paragraph. As they read, fill in the chart on page E3.

Build Knowledge: Make Connections

Talk About the Text Have partners discuss the sounds described in the text.

Write About the Text Have students add their ideas to the Build Knowledge pages of their reader's notebooks.

FORMATIVE ASSESSMENT

▶ STUDENT CHECK IN

Partners will share their Respond to Reading. Ask children to reflect using the Check-In routine.

LEVEL UP

IF students read the ELL Level fluently and answered the questions,

THEN pair them with students who have proficiently read the On Level. Have them

- partner read the On Level passage.
- describe a character's feelings and the setting in a story.

LESSONS 1-5

WRITING

MODELED WRITING

LESSON 1

LEARNING GOALS
We can learn to vary the beginnings of our sentences.

OBJECTIVES
Write narratives in which they include some details.

LANGUAGE OBJECTIVES
Children will narrate by writing sentences, using different words for the beginning of each sentence.

ELA ACADEMIC LANGUAGE
- sentence

Writing Practice Have children echo read the sample sentences on p. 132 of the **Reading/Writing Companion**. Help them analyze the sentences: *Who is the actor?* (Nat and I) *What is the description?* (hear a lot of sounds at school) Then read the prompt on p. 133 and ask children to answer it as a group. Write their sentences on the board and ask them to choral read. Then help them write their own sentences.

Beginning Have partners use the sample as a model for their first sentence. Then for each sound, prompt them to name the actor (the sound) and the action. (the noise it makes) *What do you hear? What does it do?*

Intermediate Have partners ask and answer *who/what* questions to create their sentences. Remind them to focus on one event. *What do you hear at home?*

Advanced/Advanced High Have children exchange sentences and suggest ways to vary the beginnings. Have them share their ideas with the group.

FORMATIVE ASSESSMENT ▸ **STUDENT CHECK IN** Partners share their sentences. Ask children to reflect, using the Check-In routine.

INTERACTIVE WRITING

LESSON 2

LEARNING GOALS
We can read and write about a Student Model.

OBJECTIVES
Respond to questions and suggestions from peers.

LANGUAGE OBJECTIVES
Children will discuss and write sentences about the Student Model, identifying the words *an, this,* or *that*.

ELA ACADEMIC LANGUAGE
- sentence

Analyze the Student Model Have children choral read the Student Model on **Reading/Writing Companion** p. 140. Use the Actor/Description routine to review the first sentence: *Who are the actors?* (Tom and I) *What is the description?* (heard an interesting sound at school) Have children raise their hand when they hear *an, this,* or *that*. Then help them complete p. 141.

Beginning Have partners point to examples of special adjectives. Provide a sentence frame: I noticed the word *an* before a noun that starts with a vowel.

Intermediate Have partners ask and answer questions: *What did you notice about Jacob's writing?* He used different words to begin each sentence.

Advanced/Advanced High Challenge children to write about the text, using their own sentences. Encourage them to share their ideas.

FORMATIVE ASSESSMENT ▸ **STUDENT CHECK IN** Partners share their responses. Ask children to reflect, using the Check-In routine.

WEEK 4

INDEPENDENT WRITING

LESSONS 3-4

LEARNING GOALS
We can respond to realistic fiction by writing a new story.

OBJECTIVES
Write narratives in which they recount events in sequence.

LANGUAGE OBJECTIVES
Children will narrate by writing sentences using the adjective *a*.

ELA ACADEMIC LANGUAGE
- *prompt, adjective*
- Cognate: *adjetivo*

Find Text Evidence Follow the Independent Writing routine. Help children use text evidence to orally retell the anchor text. Ask questions, such as: *What does Peter want to do?* (whistle) *What does he do instead?* (spins around) *Why does he hide in a carton?* (to fool Willie) Then read the prompt on p. 146 of the **Reading/Writing Companion:** *Use what you know about Peter to write a new story about a time he learned to play a musical instrument or to sing a special song. We need to write another story about Peter. We need to tell how he learned to do something new.*

Write a Response Work together to complete My Writing Outline 24. Then have children use the sentences from their outline to complete p. 146.

Writing Checklist Read the checklist with children and have them check for these items in their writing.

Beginning Provide sentence frames to help partners talk about their sentences: *I used the word* a *before the noun* song.

Intermediate Have partners read each other's writing and check that each sentence begins in a different way.

Advanced/Advanced High Have partners use the sentence starters on p. T324 of the **Teacher's Edition** to create new sentences.

FORMATIVE ASSESSMENT ❯ **STUDENT CHECK IN** Partners share their sentences from My Writing Outline. Ask children to reflect, using the Check-in routine.

SELF-SELECTED WRITING

LESSON 5

LEARNING GOALS
We can revise our writing.

OBJECTIVES
Use frequently occurring adjectives.

LANGUAGE OBJECTIVES
Children will inquire about their writing by checking adjectives *a, an, this,* or *that*.

ELA ACADEMIC LANGUAGE
- *adjective*
- Cognate: *adjetivo*

Work with children to revise the group writing activity. Point to each word as you read the sentences. Stop to ask questions, such as: *Can we use the adjective* this *here?* If needed, write a sentence using *a, an, this,* or *that* incorrectly and work together to revise it. Then have partners revise each other's sentences before publishing them.

For support with grammar and *a, an, this,* and *that,* refer to the **Language Transfers Handbook** and **Language Development Cards** 14A and 14B.

FORMATIVE ASSESSMENT ❯ **STUDENT CHECK IN** Partners tell what revisions they made. Ask children to reflect, using the Check-in routine.

READING • SHARED READ • ACCESS THE TEXT

LESSONS 1-2

LEARNING GOALS

We can read and understand a nonfiction text.

OBJECTIVES

Describe the connection between two individuals, events, ideas, or pieces of information in a text.

Use the photographs and details in a text to describe its key ideas.

With prompting and support, read informational texts appropriately complex for grade 1.

Build on others' talk in conversations by responding to the comments of others through multiple exchanges.

LANGUAGE OBJECTIVES

Children will inform about the process of building ships, using sequence words, key vocabulary, and complete sentences.

ELA ACADEMIC LANGUAGE

- nonfiction
- Cognate: *no ficción*

MATERIALS

Reading/Writing Companion, pp. 158–167

Visual Vocabulary Cards

DIGITAL TOOLS

Have children listen to the selection as they follow along to develop comprehension and practice fluency and pronunciation.

Use the online ELL Vocabulary Practice for additional support.

"The Joy of a Ship"

Prepare to Read

Build Background Read aloud the Essential Question on page 158. Have children share what they know about how to build things. Use the images on pages 158–159 to generate ideas. Point to and read aloud the title. *We are going to read a nonfiction story about ships.* Point to the ship. *This is a ship. Say* ship *with me. A ship is a really big boat. We are going to learn how ships are built.*

Reading/Writing Companion, Lexile 560L

Focus on Vocabulary Use the **Visual Vocabulary Cards** to review the high-frequency words *above, build, fall, knew, money,* and *toward* and the oral vocabulary words *contented, intend, marvelous, project,* and *structure*. Display the images in the text for *workers, frame, dock, melted, joints, helmet,* and *leaks*. Use the following routine: Point to the workers in the photos on page 160. Say the word *workers*. Have children point to the picture and repeat the word. *Many workers build a ship. Who builds a ship?* Help children respond: Many workers build a ship.

Summarize the Text Before reading, say the summary and point to the illustrations. *This text tells about the steps it takes to build a ship.*

Read the Text

Use the Interactive Question-Response Routine to help children understand the story.

Pages 160–163

Pages 160–161 Read the text aloud. Point to the ship frame. *Workers build the ship frame first.* Point to a crane. *Cranes hoist big pieces of steel. Here,* hoist *means "lift something with a machine." What do the workers build first?* (the frame)

Pages 162–163 Read the text aloud. Point to the word *melt*. *To* melt *something is to make it so hot that it turns into a liquid. What do the workers melt?* The workers melt metal. *What do the workers make with the melted metal?* They make steel. Point to page 163. *A worker heats the edges of sheets, or sections, of steel.* Point to the word *join*. *To* join *things is to connect them. What does the worker join?* The worker joins the steel sheets/sections.

How do people work together to build a ship? Discuss with a partner.

Beginning Use the pictures to review the words *melt* and *join*. Say: *Some workers melt metal to make steel. Other workers join steel sections.* Point to page 162.

250 UNIT 5 WEEK 5

WEEK 5

What do the workers do? The workers melt metal. Point to page 163. *What does this worker do?* This worker joins the steel sections.

Intermediate Help partners give a more specific answer. *What do the workers do first?* They melt two kinds of metal. Point to the melted metal. *What do the workers do next?* The workers join sheets of steel. Point to where the workers join the steel.

Advanced/Advanced High Help partners elaborate. *What happens to steel when it gets cold?* It gets hard. *Why do the workers wear gloves and helmets?* The workers put on gloves and helmets to protect their hands and heads.

Pages 164–165

Page 164 Read the text aloud as children follow along. Point to the word *check*. To *check* something is to make sure it is good or correct. *What do the workers check?* The workers check the joints. Point to the word *leak*. If something *leaks*, water gets through it.

What might happen if water gets into the boat? Discuss with a partner.

Beginning Guide partners to answer the question. Point to the boat. *The boat is on land, but the boat will go in the water. If the joints leak, what will get inside the boat?* Water will get inside the boat.

Intermediate Help partners give details about their answers. *If the joints leak, what will get inside the boat?* Water will get inside the boat. *What can happen if there is too much water?* The boat can sink.

Advanced/Advanced High Help partners elaborate on their answers. *How can the workers prevent the boat from leaking?* The workers can do a good job joining the steel. Then the workers can check for leaks.

Pages 166–167

Page 167 Read the text aloud and have children follow. Point to each ship. Read the name aloud and have children repeat. Have children tell what they see in each photograph. *What does the ice breaker ship do?* It breaks ice. *What do you see on the cargo ship?* (lots of boxes) Cargo ships carry goods. *Goods are things to sell.* Point to the runway. *This is a* runway. Have children repeat. *What uses a runway?* (a plane)

How do people use the different types of ships shown? Discuss with a partner.

Beginning Point to each ship. Ask questions to guide children to think about what each ship does. *What does the ice breaker ship go through?* It goes through the ice. *Look at the runway. What does an aircraft carrier do?* It carries airplanes.

Intermediate Help partners give details in their responses; for example: *What is the aircraft carrier used for?* It is used to carry airplanes. *What details tell you that?* I see a runway and planes on the ship. Have children point to the details in the photograph.

Advanced/Advanced High Help partners elaborate on their answers. *How are these ships similar?* They are all very large and do an important job. *How are these ships different?* Some move things, like goods and airplanes. Others help do a job, like break ice.

FORMATIVE ASSESSMENT

▶ STUDENT CHECK IN

Have partners retell how the workers build a ship. Then, have children reflect, using the Check-in routine.

Independent Time

Listen and Summarize Pair children of mixed proficiency levels. Have pairs listen actively to pages 160–164 multiple times. Then have them summarize the text. Children should focus on telling the steps needed to build a ship. Provide sentence frames as needed: To build a ship, first you build a frame. Next, you melt metal to create steel. Then, you join the steel sections together. After that, you check the joints. Finally, you paint the ship. After children have summarized with their partners, encourage them to share their summaries with another pair, a small group, or the whole class.

ENGLISH LANGUAGE LEARNERS **251**

LESSON 3

READING • ANCHOR TEXT • ACCESS THE TEXT

Building Bridges

Prepare to Read

Build Background *We are going to read a text about bridges.* Show the picture on the title page and invite children to tell what they see. Point to the *bridge, towers, wires,* and *road.* Say the words and have children repeat. *This bridge goes over land. What do most bridges go over? They go over ____. This is a unique, or special, bridge. It is the tallest bridge in the world.* Point to the number above the bridge. *This bridge is 1,125 feet tall.* Point to and say *1,125* for children to repeat.

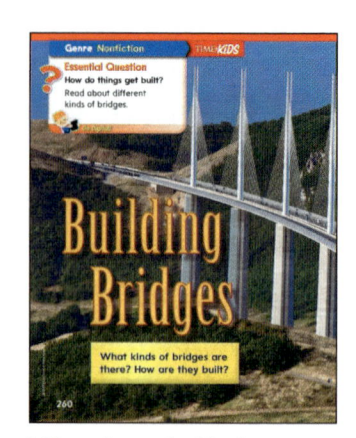

Focus on Vocabulary Use the **Visual Vocabulary Cards** to review the high-frequency words *above, build, fall, knew, money,* and *toward* and the oral vocabulary words *contented, intend, marvelous, project,* and *structure.* As you read, teach important story words, such as *stretches,* using gestures and pantomime.

Summarize the Text Before reading, say the summary while pointing to the illustrations. *The text tells about some of the world's most interesting bridges. It tells facts about each bridge and how it is unique.*

Literature Anthology, Lexile 550L

Read the Text

Use the Interactive Question-Response routine to help children understand the text.

Pages 260–263

Page 261 Read the text, including the caption. Point to the bridge on pages 260–261. *This bridge goes across a wide valley. A valley is the low land between hills.* Point to the vertical line on page 261. *How high is this bridge? This bridge is 1,125 feet high. What goes on this bridge? Cars go on this bridge.*

Page 262 Read the text. Point to the bridge. *This bridge is in Florida. Say Florida with me. How many miles long is this bridge? This bridge is four miles long. Sturdy wires help to hold up the bridge. Sturdy means "strong." Say sturdy with me.* Read the caption. *What is this bridge made of?* (steel and concrete) *Do you think this bridge will fall?* No, *it is* sturdy/strong.

Page 263 Read the text. Point to the arches on the bridge. *This is an arch bridge. What goes through the arches?* (boats) *What is this bridge made of?* (brick)

How does the author's use of captions help you understand the text? Discuss with a partner.

Beginning Help partners point to the caption on page 263 as they respond. Point to 2,000. *This number is two thousand. Say two thousand with me. How old is this*

LEARNING GOALS

We can read and understand a nonfiction text.

OBJECTIVES

Describe the connection between two individuals, events, ideas, or pieces of information in a text.

Know and use various text features to locate key facts or information in a text.

Identify the reasons an author gives to support points in a text.

Build on others' talk in conversations by responding to the comments of others through multiple exchanges.

LANGUAGE OBJECTIVES

Children will inform about different bridges around the world, using descriptive words, numbers, and complete sentences.

ELA ACADEMIC LANGUAGE

• caption, fact, key words

MATERIALS

Literature Anthology, pp. 260–267

Visual Vocabulary Cards

DIGITAL TOOLS MULTIMODAL

Have children listen to the selection as they follow along to develop comprehension and practice fluency and pronunciation.

Use the additional grammar video.

Grammar Video

252 UNIT 5 WEEK 5

bridge? It is more than 2,000 *years old. What does this fact tell you about the bridge?* It tells me that the bridge is very old.

Intermediate Have children point to the caption on page 263. *How old is this bridge?* It is more than 2,000 *years old. Does the author give a fact or an opinion?* The author gives a fact. *What does this help you know about the bridge?* It helps me know how old the bridge is. Point to the caption on page 262. *What does this caption help you know about the bridge in the text?* (what the bridge is made of)

Advanced/Advanced High Extend the discussion by having pairs tell what would be different if the text didn't have the information in the captions. The captions tell facts about the bridges. If the text didn't have captions, I wouldn't know those facts.

Pages 264–267

Page 264 Read the text and caption. *What does this bridge go over?* This bridge goes over a river. Point to the triangles. *What are these triangles made of?* The triangles are made of steel. *What do the triangles support?* The triangles support the road.

Page 265 Read the text. *Where is this bridge located?* This bridge is in California. Point to the *cables* and *towers.* Have children say the words with you. *What are important parts of this bridge?* Cables and towers are important parts. *What do the towers do?* The towers support the cables. *What color is this bridge painted?* It is painted orange. *Why is the bridge orange?* The bridge is orange to stand out in the fog.

Pages 266–267 Read the text. Point to the flat bridge on page 266. *This bridge is flat. What happens when a boat wants to go past the bridge?* Point to page 267. *The bridge moves. It curls into a circle.* Help children with their pronunciation of *curls* and *circle.*

Why does the author ask and answer questions in the text? Discuss with a partner.

Beginning Point to the third sentence on page 266: *What happens when a boat comes toward the bridge?* Ask: *Is this a question or an answer?* It is a question. *What does the author's question help you think about?* It helps me think about what the bridge does for boats. Point to the answer after the question. *What does the answer tell you?* It tells me this bridge is different/special.

Intermediate Have partners point to the question on page 266. *What does this question make you think about?* This question makes me think about what happens to the bridge when there is a boat. *What comes after the question?* The author gives the answer. *What does that answer help you to understand?* The answer helps me understand something special about the bridge.

Advanced/Advanced High Extend the discussion by having partners talk about why the author asks and answers questions in the text. The questions the author asks tell something special about the bridge. The author's answers give more special information about the bridge.

FORMATIVE ASSESSMENT

▸ STUDENT CHECK IN

Children retell about different bridges around the world. Then have children reflect, using the Check-In routine.

Independent Time

Interactive Word Wall Pair children of mixed proficiencies. Have partners review the text and identify key words used to talk about the unique bridges and how they were built. Words might include *high, wide, valley, stretches, cable, wires, towers, sturdy, arch, brick, truss, tubes,* and *joyful.* Have children write the words on slips of paper and add them to a Word Wall. Once the words are on the wall, have children complete an open sort by grouping words that go together. For example, children might group adjectives or building materials together. Encourage partners to discuss why they put the words together. Provide sentence frames to help children respond: Cable and wires are together. They are both used to build bridges.

LESSONS 4-5

READING • LEVELED READER • ACCESS THE TEXT

LEARNING GOALS

We can ask and answer questions about a nonfiction text.

OBJECTIVES

Ask and answer questions to help determine or clarify the meaning of words and phrases in a text.

Distinguish between information provided by pictures or other illustrations and information provided by the words in a text.

Identify basic similarities in and differences between two texts on the same topic (e.g., in illustrations, descriptions, or procedures).

Ask and answer questions about key details in a text read aloud or information presented orally or through other media.

LANGUAGE OBJECTIVES

Children will inform about a type of home called a yurt, using key vocabulary and complete sentences.

ELA ACADEMIC LANGUAGE

- *causes, effects, retell*
- Cognates: *causas, efectos*

MATERIALS

ELL Leveled Reader,
What Is a Yurt?

Online Differentiated Text, "Tree Houses"

Online ELL Visual Vocabulary Cards

DIGITAL TOOLS

Have children listen to the selection as they follow along to develop comprehension and practice fluency and pronunciation. Use Graphic Organizer 10: Cause and Effect to enhance the lesson.

What Is a Yurt?

Prepare to Read

Build Background

- Remind children of the Essential Question. *A yurt is a strong tent that some people use as a home. Let's read to see how a yurt gets built.* Encourage children to ask for help when they do not understand a word or phrase.

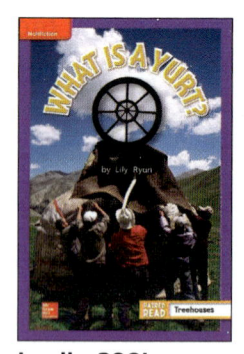

- Point to and read aloud the title and have children repeat. Ask: *What is the title?* Have children point to it. Repeat the routine for the author's name. Point to the illustrations to name things and actions. For example: *This is a tent. When might you use a tent?*

Lexile 390L

Focus on Vocabulary Use the **ELL Visual Vocabulary Cards** to preteach the words *camp* and *canvas*. As you read, use gestures or visuals to teach important selection words, such as *roof, wool mat, round,* and *balance*.

Read the Text

Use the Interactive Question-Response routine to help children understand the text.

Pages 2–5

Details: Cause and Effect Read pages 4–5 as children follow along. Point to and say *yurt, nomads,* and *camels.* Have children repeat the words. Help partners explain causes and effects.

Beginning Have partners respond: *Did the nomads move a lot?* (yes) *Why did nomads live in yurts?* They could take the yurts with them.

Advanced/Advanced High Have partners explain why a yurt was a good home for nomads. A yurt was a good home for nomads because they could carry it easily on a camel's back.

Pages 6–9

Ask and Answer Questions Read pages 6–8. Point to and say *frame* and *covered.* Have children repeat the words. Then have them ask and answer questions.

Beginning Help partners ask and answer questions to deepen understanding of how a yurt is made: *What do they make first?* They make a round frame. *What happens next?* They cover the frame with canvas.

Intermediate Have partners point to the photos as they retell how a yurt is built. First, they make a round frame. Next, they put canvas on the frame. Then they cover the roof.

WEEK 5

Pages 10–11

Read pages 10–11 as children follow along. Point to pictures and say *homes*, *kit*, and *cost*. Have children point to and repeat the words.

Intermediate Partners ask and answer: Do some people live in yurts year round? Yes, they live in yurts, like in other homes. How can you make a yurt? You can make a yurt with a yurt kit.

Advanced/Advanced High Have children ask their partner why people might like living in yurts. People might like living in yurts because they want to be closer to nature.

Respond to Reading Have partners work together to retell the story and respond to the questions on page 12.

Focus on Fluency

Read pages 2–3 to model appropriate intonation and phrasing. Read the passage again and have children repeat. For more practice, record children reading the passage and select the best recording.

Paired Read: "Treehouses"

Analytical Writing — Make Connections: Write About It

Echo-read each page with children. Discuss what the treehouses are like: *What does this treehouse have?* It has stairs and a bed. Help children make connections between texts using the question on page 15. People can live in both treehouses and yurts.

Leveled Reader

Build Knowledge: Make Connections

Talk About the Text Have partners discuss how the things in the texts are built.

Write About the Text Have students add their ideas to the Build Knowledge pages of their reader's notebooks.

Self-Selected Reading

Help children choose a nonfiction selection from the online **Leveled Reader Library** or read the **Differentiated Text**, "Tree Houses."

FOCUS ON SCIENCE

Children can extend their knowledge of camping by completing the science activity on page 16.

STEM

LITERATURE CIRCLES

Lead children in conducting a literature circle, using the Thinkmark questions to guide the discussion. You may wish to discuss what children have learned about building different shelters from reading the two selections in the Leveled Reader.

FORMATIVE ASSESSMENT

STUDENT CHECK IN

Have partners share their Respond to Reading. Have children reflect, using the Check-In routine.

LEVEL UP

IF children can read *What Is a Yurt?* **ELL Level** with fluency and correctly answer the Respond to Reading questions,

THEN tell children that they will read a more detailed version of the selection.

- Use page 5 of *What Is a Yurt?* **On Level** to model using Teaching Poster 32 to list a cause and its effect.

- Have children read the selection, checking their comprehension by using the graphic organizer.

ENGLISH LANGUAGE LEARNERS 255

READING • GENRE PASSAGE • ACCESS THE TEXT

LESSONS 4-5

LEARNING GOALS

We can apply skills and strategies to nonfiction.

OBJECTIVES

Explain major differences between books that tell stories and books that give information, drawing on a wide reading of a range of text types.

Distinguish between information provided by pictures or other illustrations and information provided by the words in a text.

With prompting and support, read informational texts appropriately complex for grade 1.

Ask questions to clear up any confusion about the topics and texts under discussion.

LANGUAGE OBJECTIVES

Children will explain details that tell about cause and effect using complete sentences.

ELA ACADEMIC LANGUAGE

- cause, effect, paragraph
- Cognates: *causa, efecto, párrafo*

MATERIALS

Online ELL Genre Passage, "Baya Weavers," pp. E1–E3

"Baya Weavers"

Prepare to Read

Build Background Review what children have learned about how different structures are built. *What do you need to build something?* You need the right ____. Allow children to share ideas about what else is needed. Tell them they will be reading about how a bird called the baya weaver builds a nest.

Lexile 400L

Focus on Vocabulary Use the Define/Example/Ask routine to preteach difficult words or unfamiliar concepts, such as *weave, loop, a thousand, blades of grass, male,* and *female.* Invite children to add new vocabulary to their glossaries.

Read the Text

Use the Interactive Question-Response routine to help children understand the text.

Page E1

Paragraph 1 Read the text aloud as children follow along. Point to the photo. *What animal is in the photo?* A baya weaver *is in the photo. Point to the word* weave. *To* weave *is to put materials together in a way that makes them very strong. What do the birds weave?* The birds weave their nests.

Intermediate Have partners take turns asking and answering questions to deepen their understanding: *Where is the baya weaver from?* Provide a sentence frame if needed to help children respond: The baya weaver is from Asia.

Paragraph 2 Read the text aloud. Model asking and answering questions: *What does the bird use to make a nest?* The bird uses grass. *Where does the bird put the grass?* It puts the grass on the tree branch. *What does the bird add next?* The bird adds more grass and a grass roof.

Beginning Point to the photo. *What does the bird have in its beak?* The bird has grass. *Where does the bird put the grass?* It puts the grass on a tree branch.

Page E2

Paragraph 1 Read the text aloud as children follow along. Point to the photo. *Does the bird use many blades of grass or just a few?* (many) Help children review cause and effect: *The bird uses many blades of grass. This is the cause. This helps make the nest* strong. *This is the effect.*

Intermediate Help children discuss with a partner: *Why does the baya weaver use more than a thousand blades of grass?* He uses more than a thousand blades of grass to make sure his nest is strong.

256 UNIT 5 WEEK 5

WEEK 5

Paragraph 2 Read the text aloud as children follow along. Review cause and effect. *Why does the bird flap his wings?* (to get a female to look at the nest) *What is the cause?* (bird flapping his wings) *What is the effect?* (female looking at the nest) *What does the female do next?* She tests the nest.

Advanced Help partners discuss when a female will look at a nest and when she will move in. She will look when a male flaps his wings, and she will move in when the nest is strong.

Advanced High Help partners elaborate on cause and effect relationships in the text; for example: What is the effect of the male bird making a strong nest? A female moves in, and then they can start a family.

Paragraph 3 Read the text aloud as children follow along. *What can keep eggs safe?* (a strong nest) *What does the male do after the female moves in?* He adds more grass to the nest. *What can happen after the female moves in?* They can start a family.

Advanced/Advanced High Help partners talk about cause and effect relationships in the text; for example: What could the effect be if the bird's nest is not strong? If the nest is not strong, the eggs could fall and break.

Respond to Reading

Use the following instructions to help children answer the questions on page E3.

1. **Nonfiction** Have children describe what they see in the photos. Ask questions to help them complete the sentence. For example: *What does the bird have in its beak in the first photo? What do you see in the second photo? What does the nest look like?*

2. **Details: Cause and Effect** Discuss with children what they learned about the baya weavers' nests. Ask: *What do the birds keep in the nest?* (eggs) *What will happen if the nest is strong?* (They will start a family.)

3. **Fluency** *Have children take turns reading the first paragraph to a partner. As they read, fill in the chart on page E3.*

Build Knowledge: Make Connections

Talk About the Text Have partners discuss how nests are built.

Write About the Text Have students add their ideas to their Build Knowledge pages of their reader's notebooks.

FORMATIVE ASSESSMENT

❯ STUDENT CHECK IN

Partners will share their Respond to Reading. Ask children to reflect, using the Check-In routine.

LEVEL UP

IF students read the ELL Level fluently and answered the questions,

THEN pair them with students who have proficiently read the On Level. Have them

- partner read the On Level passage.
- explain cause and effect relationships in nonfiction text.

ENGLISH LANGUAGE LEARNERS **257**

LESSONS 1-5

WRITING

MODELED WRITING
LESSON 1

LEARNING GOALS
We can learn how to write a concluding statement.

OBJECTIVES
Write opinion pieces in which they provide some sense of closure.

LANGUAGE OBJECTIVES
Children will argue by writing a sentence that gives their opinion.

ELA ACADEMIC LANGUAGE
- opinion
- Cognate: *opinión*

Writing Practice Have children choral read the sample on p. 168 of the **Reading/Writing Companion**. Define the word *leaks* in the first sentence: *Leaks are places where water gets in.* Help children analyze the remaining sentences using the Actor/Action routine: *Who is the actor?* (I) *What is the action?* (would like to ride the ferry) Then read the prompt on p. 169 and ask children to answer it as a group. Write the sentences on the board for children to choral read. Then help them write their own sentences.

Beginning Provide sentence frames to help partners create their sentences: *I would like to go on a cruise ship. I could visit many places!* Supply vocabulary as needed.

Intermediate Have pairs ask and answer *who/what* questions to name the ship, and *why* questions to give reasons. Provide sentence frames as needed.

Advanced/Advanced High Encourage children to share their sentences with the group and identify their opinion, reasons, and concluding statement.

FORMATIVE ASSESSMENT ▸ **STUDENT CHECK IN** Partners share their sentences. Ask children to reflect, using the Check-In routine.

INTERACTIVE WRITING
LESSON 2

LEARNING GOALS
We can read and write about a Student Model.

OBJECTIVES
Respond to questions and suggestions from peers.

LANGUAGE OBJECTIVES
Children will discuss and write sentences about a Student Model, identifying a prepositional phrase.

ELA ACADEMIC LANGUAGE
- prepositional phrase

Analyze the Student Model Have children finger point as they choral read the Student Model on p. 176 of the **Reading/Writing Companion**. Use the Actor/Description routine to review the sentences: *Who is the actor?* (I) *What is the description?* (think painting on a ship would be the most fun) Have children raise their hand to identify prepositions. Then help them complete p. 177.

Beginning Have partners point to prepositions. Provide sentence frames: *I noticed the preposition on*.

Intermediate Have partners ask and answer questions: *What did you notice about Michael's writing?* He used the prepositional phrase *on the ship*.

Advanced/Advanced High Challenge children to write about the text using their own sentences. Encourage them to share their ideas.

FORMATIVE ASSESSMENT ▸ **STUDENT CHECK IN** Partners share their responses. Ask children to reflect, using the Check-In routine.

---

258 UNIT 5 WEEK 5

WEEK 5

INDEPENDENT WRITING
LESSONS 3-4

LEARNING GOALS

We can write an opinion about a nonfiction text.

OBJECTIVES

Write opinion pieces in which they provide some sense of closure.

LANGUAGE OBJECTIVES

Children will argue by writing a sentence using a preposition.

ELA ACADEMIC LANGUAGE

- *opinion, reasons*
- Cognates: *opinión, razones*

Find Text Evidence Use the Independent Writing routine. Help children orally retell the anchor text. Ask questions, such as: *Why is the bridge in France interesting?* (It is the highest car bridge in the world.) *How long is the Sunshine Skyway Bridge in Florida?* (four miles) Then read the prompt on p. 181 of the **Reading/Writing Companion**: *Which bridge do you think is the most interesting? Why? Think about the different bridges you read about. Decide which one is the most interesting in your opinion.*

Write a Response Work together to complete My Writing Outline 25. Then have children use the sentences from their outline to complete p. 181.

Writing Checklist Read the checklist with children and have them check for these items in their writing.

Beginning Provide sentence frames to help partners talk about their sentences: I used the preposition *in*.

Intermediate Encourage partners to read each other's writing and check for an opinion, at least one reason, and a concluding statement.

Advanced/Advanced High Have children use the sentence starters on p. T406 of the **Teacher's Edition** to create new sentences.

FORMATIVE ASSESSMENT ▶ **STUDENT CHECK IN** Partners share their sentences from My Writing Outline. Ask children to reflect, using the Check-in routine.

SELF-SELECTED WRITING
LESSON 5

LEARNING GOALS

We can revising our writing.

OBJECTIVES

Use frequently occurring prepositions.

LANGUAGE OBJECTIVES

Children will inquire about their writing by checking their prepositions.

ELA ACADEMIC LANGUAGE

- *preposition*
- Cognate: *preposición*

Work with children to revise the group writing activity. Point to each word as you read the sentences. Stop to ask questions, such as: *Can we use the preposition* of *here?* If needed, write a sentence using a preposition incorrectly and work together to revise the sentence. Then have partners revise each other's sentences before publishing them.

For support with grammar and prepositions, refer to the **Language Transfers Handbook** and **Language Development Cards** 18A, 18B, and 20A.

FORMATIVE ASSESSMENT ▶ **STUDENT CHECK IN** Partners tell what revisions they made. Ask children to reflect, using the Check-in routine.

ENGLISH LANGUAGE LEARNERS **259**

UNIT 5

Summative Assessment
Get Ready for Unit Assessment

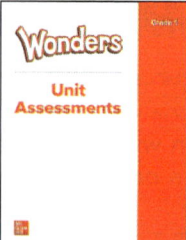

Unit 5 Tested Skills

LISTENING AND READING COMPREHENSION	VOCABULARY	GRAMMAR	SPEAKING AND WRITING
• Listening Actively • Details	• Words and Categories	• Conjunctions • Adjectives • Articles • Prepositions	• Expressing Opinions • Presenting • Composing/Writing • Retelling/Recounting

Create a Student Profile

Record data from the following resources in the Student Profile charts on pages 356–357 of the Assessment book.

COLLABORATIVE	INTERPRETIVE	PRODUCTIVE

• Collaborative Conversations Rubrics
  • Listening
  • Speaking
	• Leveled Unit Assessment
	  • Listening Comprehension
	  • Reading Comprehension
	  • Vocabulary
	  • Grammar
	• Presentation Rubric
	  • Listening
	• *Wonders* Unit Assessment
		• Weekly Progress Monitoring
		• Leveled Unit Assessment
		  • Speaking
		  • Writing
		• Presentation Rubric
		  • Speaking
		• Write to Sources Rubric
		• *Wonders* Unit Assessment

The Foundational Skills Kit, Language Development Kit, and Adaptive Learning provide additional student data for progress monitoring.

Level Up

Use the following chart, along with your Student Profiles, to guide your Level Up decisions.

LEVEL UP	If **BEGINNING** level students are able to do the following, they may be ready to move to the **INTERMEDIATE** level:	If **INTERMEDIATE** level students are able to do the following, they may be ready to move to the **ADVANCED** level:	If **ADVANCED** level students are able to do the following, they may be ready to move to **ON** level:
COLLABORATIVE	• participate in collaborative conversations using basic vocabulary and grammar and simple phrases or sentences • discuss simple pictorial or text prompts	• participate in collaborative conversations using appropriate words and phrases and complete sentences • use limited academic vocabulary across and within disciplines	• participate in collaborative conversations using more sophisticated vocabulary and correct grammar • communicate effectively across a wide range of language demands in social and academic contexts
INTERPRETIVE	• identify details in simple read alouds • understand common vocabulary and idioms and interpret language related to familiar social, school, and academic topics • make simple inferences and make simple comparisons • exhibit an emerging receptive control of lexical, syntactic, phonological, and discourse features	• identify main ideas and/or make some inferences from simple read alouds • use context clues to identify word meanings and interpret basic vocabulary and idioms • compare, contrast, summarize, and relate text to graphic organizers • exhibit a limited range of receptive control of lexical, syntactic, phonological, and discourse features when addressing new or familiar topics	• determine main ideas in read alouds that have advanced vocabulary • use context clues to determine meaning, understand multiple-meaning words, and recognize synonyms of social and academic vocabulary • analyze information, make sophisticated inferences, and explain their reasoning • command a high degree of receptive control of lexical, syntactic, phonological, and discourse features
PRODUCTIVE	• express ideas and opinions with basic vocabulary and grammar and simple phrases or sentences • restate information or retell a story using basic vocabulary • exhibit an emerging productive control of lexical, syntactic, phonological, and discourse features	• produce coherent language with limited elaboration or detail • restate information or retell a story using mostly accurate, although limited, vocabulary • exhibit a limited range of productive control of lexical, syntactic, phonological, and discourse features when addressing new or familiar topics	• produce sentences with more sophisticated vocabulary and correct grammar • restate information or retell a story using extensive and accurate vocabulary and grammar • tailor language to a particular purpose and audience • command a high degree of productive control of lexical, syntactic, phonological, and discourse features

LESSONS 1-2

READING • SHARED READ • ACCESS THE TEXT

"Super Tools"

Prepare to Read

Build Background Read aloud the Essential Question on page 14. Have children share ideas about things that make people's lives better. Use the illustrations on pages 14–15 to generate ideas. Point to and read aloud the title. *We are going to read about a girl named Lucy.* Point to Lucy. *This is Lucy. Say the name* Lucy *with me.* Point to the markers, pencils, and computer on the desk. *These are tools. These are tools Lucy uses. Say* tools *with me.*

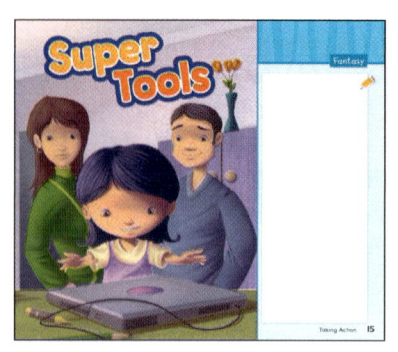

Reading/Writing Companion, Lexile 430L

Focus on Vocabulary Use the **Visual Vocabulary Cards** to review the high-frequency words *answer, brought, busy, door, enough,* and *eyes,* and the oral vocabulary words *argument, conflict, fair, risk,* and *theft.* As you read, use gestures and visual support to teach important story words, such as *pencils, pens, markers,* and *crayons.* Use the following routine: Point to the pencil. Say the word *pencil.* Have children point to the picture on page 14 and repeat the word. Say: *Lucy has a pencil on her desk. What does Lucy have?* Help children respond with a sentence frame: Lucy has a pencil.

Summarize the Text Before reading, say the summary and point to the illustrations. *This story tells about what happens when Lucy gets a new tool, a computer. Her other tools want to remind her about the great things they can do.*

Read the Text

Use the Interactive Question-Response routine to help children understand the story.

Pages 16–17

Pages 16–17 Read the text aloud. Point to the illustration on page 16. *What is Lucy typing on?* (a computer) Point to the picture on page 17. *These writing tools have faces, and they can talk! Now we know that this story is a fantasy. It couldn't really happen. Listen as I read what they say:* "Lucy hasn't used us in weeks!" cried the markers. "Can we demand to be used?" asked the crayons. Point to the word *useless* in the first paragraph. Useless *means "not able to do what is needed." How do the writing tools feel?* The writing tools feel sad and useless.

Why are the writing tools upset? Discuss with a partner.

Beginning Use the pictures to review the words *computer, typing, pencils, markers,* and *crayons.* Point to the writing tools. *How do the writing tools feel?* The writing tools feel sad. *Why are the writing tools sad?* Point to Lucy. Lucy is typing on her computer. She is not using the writing tools.

LEARNING GOALS

We can read and understand a fantasy story.

OBJECTIVES

Retell stories, including key details, and demonstrate understanding of their central message or lesson.

Describe characters, settings, and major events in a story, using key details.

Use illustrations and details in a story to describe its characters, setting, or events.

Describe people, places, things, and events with relevant details, expressing ideas and feelings clearly.

LANGUAGE OBJECTIVES

Children will narrate how the character creates a report, using pronouns and key vocabulary.

ELA ACADEMIC LANGUAGE

- fantasy, details, reread
- Cognates: *fantasía, detalles*

MATERIALS

Reading/Writing Companion, pp. 14–23

Visual Vocabulary Cards

DIGITAL TOOLS

Have children listen to the selection as they follow along to develop comprehension and practice fluency and pronunciation.

Use the ELL Vocabulary Practice for additional support.

262 UNIT 6 WEEK 1

Intermediate Help partners give a more specific answer. *What is Lucy doing?* She is typing on her computer. Point to the writing tools. *Does Lucy write with her writing tools?* No, Lucy does not write with her writing tools.

Advanced/Advanced High Help partners add details to their responses. Point to the writing tools in the cup on page 16. *Why are the writing tools looking at Lucy and the computer?* They want to see what Lucy is doing with the computer.

Pages 18–19

Pages 18–19 Read the text aloud as children follow. *Lucy is using her computer to write a report. Say* report *with me. What is her report about?* Her report is about birds. Point to the writing tools on page 19. *What are the tools doing?* The tools are making a picture of a bird. *The text says the picture is good enough to frame. Did the tools do a good job?* (yes)

What plan do the tools have? Discuss with a partner.

Beginning Point to the pencils on page 19. *What are the pencils doing?* The pencils are drawing. *What are they drawing?* They are drawing a bird. *What is the drawing for?* The drawing is for Lucy's report.

Intermediate Help partners give details with their answers. *What are the writing tools drawing?* They are drawing a bird with a sun and a blue sky. *Why are they drawing a bird?* They are drawing a bird for Lucy's report.

Advanced/Advanced High Have partners elaborate on their answers. *Why do the writing tools want to draw a bird for Lucy's report?* The writing tools want to show Lucy the great things they can do.

Pages 20–23

Page 21 *Mom and Dad think Lucy drew the picture. What does Lucy say about drawing?* Lucy says it's fun to draw. *Lucy is reminded that she likes to use markers, crayons, and pencils. What do you think Lucy will do next?* I think she will draw.

Page 22–23 Read the text aloud as children follow along. Point to Lucy drawing. *Lucy decides to draw her own picture. What is the picture for?* The picture is for Lucy's report.

What does Lucy decide to do with her writing tools? Discuss with a partner.

Beginning Guide children to answer the question. Point to Lucy's drawing on page 22. *What is Lucy drawing?* Lucy is drawing a bird. *What is Lucy using to draw?* Lucy is using a pencil to draw.

Intermediate Help partners give details with their answers. Point to Lucy's drawing. *What is Lucy doing?* Lucy is drawing a picture for her report. *What is Lucy using to draw her picture?* Lucy is using pencils, markers, and crayons.

Advanced/Advanced High Help partners elaborate on their answers. *How did Lucy's view toward her writing tools change?* When she got her computer, she didn't use them. But then she remembered that drawing is fun.

FORMATIVE ASSESSMENT

▶ STUDENT CHECK IN

Have partners retell what Lucy does to create a report. Then, have children reflect using the Check-In routine.

Independent Time

Role Play Pair children of mixed proficiencies. Have pairs select their favorite page spread from the text. Ask them to reread the text to reinforce comprehension. Then have children prepare a role play of their pages. Encourage children to think about and gather any props they will need for their role play. Then have pairs rehearse their role plays. Once children feel comfortable with their role plays, have them present their role plays to another pair, a small group, or the whole class.

LESSON 3

READING • ANCHOR TEXT • ACCESS THE TEXT

Click, Clack, Moo: Cows That Type

LEARNING GOALS

We can read and understand a fantasy story.

OBJECTIVES

Retell stories, including key details, and demonstrate understanding of their central message or lesson.

Use illustrations and details in a story to describe its characters, setting, or events.

Compare and contrast the adventures and experiences of characters in stories.

Describe people, places, things, and events with relevant details, expressing ideas and feelings clearly.

LANGUAGE OBJECTIVES

Children will narrate the characters' notes and reactions, using adjectives and complete sentences.

ELA ACADEMIC LANGUAGE

- fantasy, dialogue, point of view
- Cognates: *fantasía, diálogo, punto de vista*

MATERIALS

Literature Anthology, pp. 270-295

Visual Vocabulary Cards

DIGITAL TOOLS

Have children listen to the selection as they follow along to develop comprehension and practice fluency and pronunciation.

Use the additional grammar video.

Grammar Video

Prepare to Read

Build Background *We are going to read a fantasy story about cows that can type.* Show the picture on the title page, and invite children to tell what they see. Point to the *cows, chickens, duck, typewriter,* and *paper.* Say the words, and have children repeat. Explain that people used typewriters before they had computers. Then point to the cow typing. *This is a special cow. This cow can type. This cow writes letters to ask the farmer for things. Have you ever asked someone for something? What happened?*

Literature Anthology, Lexile 380L

Focus on Vocabulary Use the **Visual Vocabulary Cards** to review the high-frequency words *answer, brought, busy, door, enough,* and *eyes,* and the oral vocabulary words *argument, conflict, fair, risk,* and *shift.* As you read, use gestures and pantomime to teach important story words, such as *impossible, strike, impatient,* and *deal.*

Summarize the Text Before reading, say the summary while pointing to the illustrations. *The story tells about animals who ask Farmer Brown for things by writing him letters. When Farmer Brown says no, the animals refuse to work!*

Read the Text

Use the Interactive Question-Response routine to help children understand the story.

Pages 272–275

Pages 272–275 Read the text. Point to Farmer Brown on page 273. *This is Farmer Brown. Does Farmer Brown look happy?* No, Farmer Brown does not look happy. Point to the first line of text on page 272. *Farmer Brown has a problem. What is Farmer Brown's problem?* His cows like to type. *What does Farmer Brown hear all day long?* Farmer Brown hears "click, clack, moo". He can't believe his ears. *When I use the expression "I can't believe my ears," I mean that I am so surprised that I think I imagined what I heard.* Point to pages 274–275. *Now Farmer Brown can't believe his eyes. What is he surprised to see?* (a letter from the cows) *Farmer Brown is frustrated. When you are frustrated, you are angry that you cannot do something.*

COLLABORATE *How does the author show that Farmer Brown is frustrated? Discuss with a partner.*

Beginning Say the word *frustrated,* and act it out. Have children imitate you and say the word. Say: *Point to Farmer Brown. Does Farmer Brown show he is frustrated on his body or on his face? Point to it.* He looks frustrated on his face.

264 UNIT 6 WEEK 1

WEEK 1

Intermediate Say the word *frustrated*. Have children repeat. Correct pronunciations as needed. Have children point to the text and images as they respond: *How do you know Farmer Brown is frustrated?* His face and his words tell me he is frustrated.

Advanced/Advanced High Extend the discussion by having partners elaborate on their responses: *Why does Farmer Brown feel frustrated?* He is frustrated because he hears typing all day.

Pages 280–283

Pages 280–283 Read the text. Point to page 280. *The cows are impatient. When you are impatient, you are tired of waiting. Whom are the cows impatient with?* They are impatient with Farmer Brown. Point to the letter. *What do the cows and hens do in response?* They tell Farmer Brown they are closed. Point to the word *furious* on page 283. *Farmer Brown is furious. Furious means "very angry." Do you ever feel furious?*

Look at pages 280–283. How does the author show that Farmer Brown is furious? Discuss.

Beginning Help partners point to the pictures as they respond. Point to the letter on page 280. *Can Farmer Brown have milk and eggs?* No, he cannot. Display page 283. Point to Farmer Brown. *How does Farmer Brown feel about this?* He feels very angry.

Intermediate Point to the letter on page 280. *What do the cows and hens write to Farmer Brown?* He cannot have milk and eggs. Display page 283. *How does Farmer Brown feel about this?* He feels furious.

Advanced/Advanced High Have partners add details to their responses. *What does Farmer Brown say that helps you know he is furious?* ("Cows that type. Hens on strike! Whoever heard of such a thing?")

Page 292

Page 292 Read the text. *Farmer Brown gets another note. Whom is the note from?* The note is from the ducks. *They want a diving board. People use a diving board to jump into a swimming pool. Why might the ducks like a diving board?* They like to be in water.

What do the repeating words show? Discuss with a partner.

Beginning Point to the repeated words. *Which words does the author repeat?* (click, clack, quack) *What does the sound* click clack *go with?* It goes with the typewriter. *Who is using the typewriter?* The ducks are using the typewriter.

Intermediate Help partners review to respond. *Who makes the* click clack *sound at the beginning of the story?* (the cows) *What does the sound show?* It shows they are typing. *Who is typing now?* The ducks are typing now.

Advanced/Advanced High Extend the discussion by having partners discuss why the author might use the same words as at the beginning of the story. The author might want to show that the same story is going to repeat again.

FORMATIVE ASSESSMENT

❯ STUDENT CHECK IN

Have partners retell what messages the cows have in the story. Then have children reflect, using the Check-In routine

Independent Time

Write a Dialogue Have pairs of mixed proficiency levels imagine what it might be like if the cows and chickens talked with Farmer Brown instead of writing notes. Have children collaborate on a dialogue between Farmer Brown and the cows or between Farmer Brown and the chickens. Remind children to include both the animals' and Farmer Brown's point of view. Provide sentence frames for support: Farmer Brown, we are cold. We would like electric blankets. Cows, I am not going to give you electric blankets. If you don't give us electric blankets, we won't give you milk. Have pairs rehearse their dialogues. Then encourage pairs to present their dialogues to another pair, a small group, or the whole class.

ENGLISH LANGUAGE LEARNERS **265**

READING • LEVELED READER • ACCESS THE TEXT

LESSONS 4-5

LEARNING GOALS

We can reread to better understand a fantasy story.

OBJECTIVES

Ask and answer questions about key details in a text.

Explain major differences between books that tell stories and books that give information, drawing on a wide reading of a range of text types.

Compare and contrast the adventures and experiences of characters in stories.

Ask and answer questions about key details in a text read aloud or information presented orally or through other media.

LANGUAGE OBJECTIVES

Children will narrate how the animals share, using plural nouns and complete sentences.

ELA ACADEMIC LANGUAGE

- fantasy, expression, respond, theme
- Cognates: *fantasía, expresión, responder, tema*

MATERIALS

ELL Leveled Reader: *What a Feast!*

Online Differentiated Texts, "Mouse Is Cold"

Online ELL Visual Vocabulary Cards

DIGITAL TOOLS

Have children listen to the selection as they follow along to develop comprehension and practice fluency and pronunciation. Use Graphic Organizer 12: Theme to enhance the lesson.

What a Feast!

Prepare to Read

Build Background

- Remind children of the Essential Question. *Let's read to find out how the animals in this story work together to help each other.* Tell children to seek clarification when they do not understand by asking "What does ___ mean?"

- Point to and read the title, and have children repeat it. Explain that this is a fantasy story because it has animal characters that act like people. Point to the illustrations to name things and actions; for example: *These are berries. Bird eats berries. What do you eat?*

Lexile 350L

Focus on Vocabulary Use **ELL Visual Vocabulary Cards** to preteach the words *collecting* and *wrong*. Then use gestures or visuals to clarify key terms, such as *feast, emergency,* and *gathered*.

Read the Text

Use the Interactive Question-Response routine to help children understand the story.

Pages 2–6

Read pages 2–5 as children follow along. Ask: *What problem do Squirrel and Bird have?* Have children **reread** page 5. They eat the same thing every day.

Beginning Help partners point to the pictures. *What does Squirrel eat?* Squirrel eats nuts. *What does Bird eat?* Bird eats seeds and berries.

Advanced/Advanced High Ask and have partners discuss: *How do you know that Squirrel and Bird want something else?* (They talk about it.)

Pages 7–9

Read pages 7–9 as children follow along. Point to *our bellies demand*. "Our bellies demand something different" means they are hungry for another kind of food.

Beginning *What food does Squirrel have a lot of?* Squirrel has a lot of nuts. *What food does Bird have a lot of?* Bird has a lot of berries and seeds.

Intermediate Have partners ask and answer: *What might be Bunny's idea?* Bunny's idea might be to say they should share their food.

266 UNIT 6 WEEK 1

Pages 10–12

Read pages 10–11 aloud. Ask questions to help discuss Bunny's idea.

Intermediate Help children discuss what happens when the animals share food. They try different foods and are happy.

Advanced/Advanced High Have partners discuss why the characters are happy. They are happy because they shared a meal and tried different foods.

Theme Help children identify the theme, or message, of the story. (We can help each other when we share what we have.)

Respond to Reading Have partners work together to retell the story and respond to the questions on page 12.

Focus on Fluency

Read pages 10–11 to model appropriate expression. Read the passage again, and have children repeat after you. For more practice, record children reading the passage, and select the best recording.

Paired Read: "Helpers Bring Food"

Analytical Writing — Make Connections: Write About It

Echo-read each page with children. Discuss people who need help getting food: *Whom do the helpers take food to?* They take food to older people in New York City. Help children make connections between texts by using the question on page 15. In both texts, characters work together to help others have food.

Leveled Reader

Build Knowledge: Make Connections

Talk About the Text Have partners discuss how the texts show that working together can make lives better.

Write About the Text Have students add their ideas to the Build Knowledge pages of their reader's notebooks.

Self-Selected Reading

Help children choose a fantasy selection from the online **Leveled Reader Library** or read the **Differentiated Text,** "Mouse Is Cold."

WEEK 1

FOCUS ON GENRE

Children can extend their knowledge of fantasy by completing the genre activity on page 16.

LITERATURE CIRCLES

Lead children in conducting a literature circle using the Thinkmark questions to guide the discussion. You may wish to discuss what children have learned about how sharing helps make lives better from both selections in the **Leveled Reader**.

FORMATIVE ASSESSMENT

STUDENT CHECK IN

Have partners share their Respond to Reading. Have children reflect, using the Check-In routine.

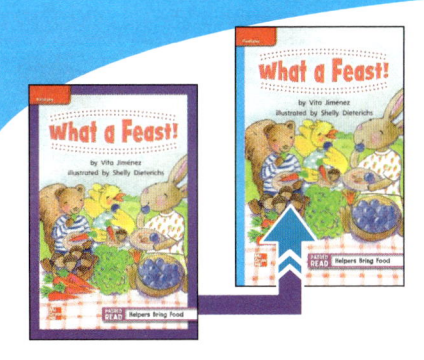

LEVEL UP

IF children can read *What a Feast!* **ELL Level** with fluency and correctly answer the Respond to Reading questions,

THEN tell children they will read a more detailed version of the story.

- Use pages 9–11 of *What a Feast!* **On Level** to model using Teaching Poster 37 to identify clues to the theme.

- Have children read the selection, checking their comprehension by using the graphic organizer.

ENGLISH LANGUAGE LEARNERS **267**

READING • GENRE PASSAGE • ACCESS THE TEXT

LESSONS 4-5

LEARNING GOALS

We can apply skills and strategies to a fantasy story.

OBJECTIVES

Ask and answer questions about key details in a text.

Explain major differences between books that tell stories and books that give information, drawing on a wide reading of a range of text types.

Compare and contrast the adventures and experiences of characters in stories.

Ask questions to clear up any confusion about the topics and texts under discussion.

LANGUAGE OBJECTIVES

Children will discuss the theme of the story, using verbs.

Children will reread to understand synonyms in context.

ELA ACADEMIC LANGUAGE

- fantasy, theme
- Cognates: *fantasía, tema*

MATERIALS

Online ELL Genre Passage, "Maria Mouse's Good Idea," pp. E1–E3

"Maria Mouse's Good Idea"

Prepare to Read

Build Background Review what children have learned about how people work together. *How can working together make our lives better?* We can ____ more easily. Allow children to share ideas about other ways that working together makes our lives better. Tell children they will be reading about animals who work together to gather food for the winter.

Lexile 450L

Vocabulary Use the Define, Example, Ask routine to preteach difficult words or unfamiliar concepts, such as *forest, vote, race* (verb, noun), *pile,* and *huge.* Invite children to add new vocabulary to their glossaries.

Read the Text

Use the Interactive Question-Response routine to help children understand the story.

Page E1

Paragraphs 1–3 Read the text aloud as children follow along. Point to the trees. *Where does the story take place?* It takes place in a forest. Point to the text. *What do the animals talk about?* They talk about finding food for the winter.

Intermediate Have children talk with a partner about the details from the story that tell them it is fantasy. Help children respond: I know the story is fantasy because it has talking animals.

Paragraphs 4–5 Read the text aloud as children follow along. Help children figure out the story's **theme.** Point to the word *vote.* Remind children that voting is a way to tell what you want. *What two choices do the animals have?* They can vote to play or to find food.

Advanced/Advanced High Have children ask and answer with a partner: Based on what we read about the animals' votes, what do you think the story's main message, or **theme,** might be about? The story's theme might be about choosing whether to work or play.

Page E2

Paragraphs 1–2 Read the text aloud. Have children *reread* to confirm the following information. *Which activity got the most votes?* Finding food got the most votes. *What is Maria Mouse's idea?* Her idea is to have a race.

Advanced Have partners ask and answer: Why is it a good idea for Maria Mouse to suggest a race? The animals who voted to play will be happy too.

268 UNIT 6 WEEK 1

WEEK 1

Advanced High Have partners discuss: *How might the animals who voted to play react to what Chad says?* They might be frustrated and not want to work. *How might they react to Maria's suggestion?* They might be glad they can play while finding food.

Paragraph 3 Read the text aloud as children follow. *What do the animals think of the race?* They have fun. Point to the picture. *What do the animals have after the race?* (a huge pile of seeds, nuts, and acorns)

Beginning Point to the illustration. *What are the animals doing? Point to them.* The animals are carrying food. Point to the pile. *What does the illustration show?* It shows the animals' pile of food.

Paragraph 4 Read the text aloud as children follow along. *Chad is happy. Why is Chad happy?* Chad is happy because he found food and still had fun.

Intermediate Have partners ask and answer: *How does the illustration show how the animals worked together?* The illustration shows all the animals carrying a little bit of food to make a huge pile.

Synonyms Have children *reread* paragraphs 2–3. Ask: *Which two words have the same meaning?* Help them describe: The words big and huge are synonyms. Synonyms have similar meanings. Then help children use *big* and *huge* to describe the pile. Everyone thinks they will have a big pile. Chad says the pile is huge.

Respond to Reading

Use the following instructions to help children answer the questions on page E3.

1. **Fantasy** Have children describe what they see in the illustrations. Ask questions to help them complete the sentence. For example: *Where do Maria and Chad stand?* (They stand on the stump.) *How can you tell this story is a fantasy?* (The animals are wearing clothes.)

2. **Theme** Discuss with children how the title relates to theme. Ask: *What is the story mostly about?* The story is about a vote for two ideas. Maria Mouse's good idea wins the vote.

3. **Fluency** Have children take turns reading the first paragraph to a partner. As they read, fill in the chart on page E3.

Build Knowledge: Make Connections

Talk About the Text Have partners discuss how the animals in the story work together to make their lives better.

Write About the Text Have students add their ideas to the Build Knowledge pages of their reader's notebooks.

FORMATIVE ASSESSMENT

STUDENT CHECK IN

Have partners share their Respond to Reading. Then have children reflect, using the Check-In routine.

LEVEL UP

IF children read the ELL Level fluently and answered the questions,

THEN pair them with children who have proficiently read the On Level. Have them

- partner-read the On Level passage.
- determine the theme of the text.

ENGLISH LANGUAGE LEARNERS **269**

LESSONS 1-5

WRITING

MODELED WRITING

LESSON 1

LEARNING GOALS

We can learn to write a paragraph.

OBJECTIVES

Write informative texts in which they provide some sense of closure.

LANGUAGE OBJECTIVES

Children will inform by writing a paragraph, using a strong verb.

ELA ACADEMIC LANGUAGE

- paragraph
- Cognate: *párrafo*

Writing Practice Have children choral read p. 24 of the **Reading/Writing Companion.** Help them analyze the sentences using the Actor/Action routine: *Who is the actor?* (I) *What is the action?* (garden) Check that children understand that *garden* can be either a noun or a verb. Then read the prompt on p. 25, and ask children to answer it as a group. Write their paragraph on the board and ask children to choral read. Then help children write their own paragraph.

Beginning Provide sentence frames to help partners create their opening sentence and concluding statement: *My favorite hobby is painting. Painting is fun!* Help partners name an actor and action for each detail sentence.

Intermediate Have partners ask and answer *who/what* questions to create their sentences. Remind them to include an opening sentence and concluding statement.

Advanced/Advanced High Have children exchange sentences, identify verbs, and suggest stronger verbs to replace them.

FORMATIVE ASSESSMENT ▸ **STUDENT CHECK IN** Partners share their sentences. Ask children to reflect, using the Check-In routine.

INTERACTIVE WRITING

LESSON 2

LEARNING GOALS

We can read and write about a Student Model.

OBJECTIVES

With guidance and support from adults, focus on a topic.

LANGUAGE OBJECTIVES

Children will discuss and write sentences about the Student Model, identifying the opening sentence.

ELA ACADEMIC LANGUAGE

- letter, pronoun
- Cognate: *pronombre*

Analyze the Student Model Have children chorally read the Student Model on p. 32 of the **Reading/Writing Companion.** Use the Actor/Action routine to analyze the first sentence: *Who are the actors?* (We) *Whom does we refer to?* (the writing tools) *What is the action?* (loved working) *Is this the opening sentence, a detail, or the concluding statement?* (the opening sentence) Help children complete p. 33.

Beginning Have partners point to examples of pronouns and say whom or what each one refers to.

Intermediate Have partners ask and answer questions: *What do you notice about Billy's writing?* He uses strong verbs like *loved* and *created*.

Advanced/Advanced High Challenge children to write their own sentences about the text. Encourage children to share their ideas.

FORMATIVE ASSESSMENT ▸ **STUDENT CHECK IN** Partners share their responses. Ask children to reflect, using the Check-In routine.

WEEK 1

INDEPENDENT WRITING

LESSONS 3-4

LEARNING GOALS

We can respond to a fantasy story by writing a new story.

OBJECTIVES

Write narratives in which they include some details.

LANGUAGE OBJECTIVES

Children will narrate by writing sentences with the pronoun *we*.

ELA ACADEMIC LANGUAGE

- letter
- Cognate: *letra*

Find Text Evidence Follow the Independent Writing routine. Help children orally retell the anchor text. Ask questions, such as: *What do Farmer Brown's cows type?* (letters) *What do they ask for?* (electric blankets for themselves and the hens) Read the prompt on **Reading/Writing Companion** p. 38: *Imagine the farmer wouldn't give the ducks a diving board. Write a letter that he might receive from the animals after he says no.* Ask: *What do the ducks reply? We need to write a letter from the ducks to the farmer.*

Write a Response Distribute My Writing Outline 26, and work with children to complete it. Then have them use the sentences to complete p. 38.

Writing Checklist Read the checklist with students, and have them check for these items in their writing.

Beginning Provide sentence frames to help children talk about their sentences: I used the pronoun *we*. It takes the place of the ducks.

Intermediate Encourage partners to read each other's letters and look for at least one strong verb.

Advanced/Advanced High Have children use the sentence starters on p. T48 of the **Teacher's Edition** to create new sentences.

FORMATIVE ASSESSMENT ▸ **STUDENT CHECK IN** Partners share their sentences from My Writing Outline. Ask children to reflect, using the Check-in routine.

SELF-SELECTED WRITING

LESSON 5

LEARNING GOALS

We can revise our writing.

OBJECTIVES

Use personal, possessive, and indefinite pronouns.

LANGUAGE OBJECTIVES

Children will inquire about their writing by checking their pronouns.

ELA ACADEMIC LANGUAGE

- pronoun
- Cognate: *pronombre*

Work with children to revise the group writing activity. Point to each word as you read the sentences. Stop to ask questions, such as: *What/Whom is this pronoun referring to?* If needed, write a sentence with a pronoun used incorrectly, and work together to revise the sentence. Then have partners revise each other's sentences before publishing them.

For support with grammar and pronouns, refer to the **Language Transfers Handbook** and **Language Development Card** 16A.

FORMATIVE ASSESSMENT ▸ **STUDENT CHECK IN** Partners tell what revisions they made. Ask children to reflect, using the Check-in routine.

READING • SHARED READ • ACCESS THE TEXT

LESSONS 1-2

LEARNING GOALS

We can read and understand a nonfiction text.

OBJECTIVES

Ask and answer questions about key details in a text.

Identify the reasons an author gives to support points in a text.

With prompting and support, read informational texts appropriately complex for grade 1.

Ask questions to clear up any confusion about the topics and texts under discussion.

LANGUAGE OBJECTIVES

Children will inform about how people help, using verbs and complete sentences.

ELA ACADEMIC LANGUAGE

- author's purpose, summarize
- Cognate: *propósito del autor*

MATERIALS

Reading/Writing Companion, pp. 50–59

Visual Vocabulary Cards

DIGITAL TOOLS

MULTIMODAL

Have children listen to the selection as they follow along to develop comprehension and practice fluency and pronunciation.

Use the ELL Vocabulary Practice for additional support.

"All Kinds of Helpers"

Prepare to Read

Build Background Read aloud the Essential Question on page 50. *Who helps you?* Have children think about who helped them from the moment they woke up until now. Use the photographs on pages 50–53 to generate ideas. Point to the title on page 51, and read it aloud. *We are going to learn about helpers at home, at school, in sports, and in our community. Which one does this picture show? These adults are helping the children _____.*

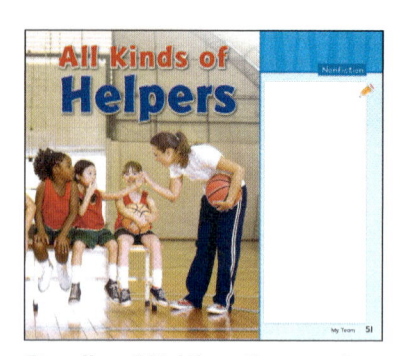

Reading/Writing Companion, Lexile 530L

Focus on Vocabulary Use the **Visual Vocabulary Cards** to review the high-frequency words *brother, father, friend, love, mother,* and *picture* and the oral vocabulary words *decision, distance, inspire, respect,* and *swiftly*. As you read, use gestures and visual support to teach important selection words, such as *family, teacher, coach, doctor, bus driver, police officer,* and *firefighter*. Use the following routine for each new word: Point to the picture of the doctor. Say the word *doctor* for children to repeat as they point to the picture. *The doctor helps you stay healthy. Who helps you stay healthy?* The doctor helps me stay healthy.

Summarize the Text Before reading, say the summary and point to the photographs. *This text tells about the people who help you: your family, your teachers, your coaches, your doctor, and other people in your community.*

Read the Text

Use the Interactive Question-Response routine to help children understand the text.

Pages 52–55

Pages 52–53 Read the text aloud. *What does* help *mean?* (to give what is needed and useful) Elicit examples of things children need and use. Then have children look at the picture on page 52. *Look at the boy in the red shirt. How is he helping?* He is helping his mom cut vegetables. Have children turn to page 53. *How is the older brother helping?* He is helping his brother do homework.

Pages 54–55 Read the text aloud as children follow. Say the word *subject* for children to repeat. *What two subjects did you read about?* (math, social studies)

What do you learn in math/social studies? Have volunteers draw their answers, which might be numbers or a map. Say the word *subjects* for children to repeat. *What other subjects do you study?* (reading, science)

COLLABORATE *Who helps you learn how to play a sport? How does the person help? Discuss with a partner.*

272 UNIT 6 WEEK 2

WEEK 2

Beginning Provide sentence frames to help children answer based on the text: *A coach helps you learn a sport. A coach talks to you and shows you what to do.*

Intermediate Have pairs add details to their answers by describing the picture: *This coach is teaching the boys how to play baseball. He is showing them how to hold a ball.*

Advanced/Advanced High Have pairs ask and answer based on their own experience: *Who taught you how to play a sport? [My coach/Mr. Brown] taught me how to play [soccer]. He/She taught me how to [kick the ball].* Encourage children to draw their answers to help them think about what they learned in the sport.

Pages 56–59

Page 56 Read the text as children follow along. *Are you healthy or sick when you visit the doctor for a checkup? You are healthy.* Explain that the doctor "checks" to see if you are healthy. Help children understand both meanings of *cold*. Say and demonstrate: *Brrr! It's winter. You are cold. I'm coughing and sneezing. You have a cold.* Explain that when you "get better," you go from *sick* to *healthy*.

Page 57 Read the text as children follow along. Pace back and forth across the classroom, and have children repeat the phrase *back and forth*. Have children take a few steps to one side and then to the other. *You're stepping back and forth. How does the bus driver take you back and forth? The bus driver takes us back and forth between school and home. What does protect mean?* (keep safe)

Pages 58–59 Read the text as children follow along. Use the cognate *adulto* to help children understand that a grown-up is an adult. *What will you be when you grow up?* (a grown-up) Ask children if they know about the Big Brothers Big Sisters organization. *Are these real brothers and sisters? No, they are friends/helpers.* Have children look at the photo. *How is this grown-up helping the boy? He is playing soccer with the boy.* Discuss the idea that it is helpful to spend time with someone. Remind children that *help* can mean "make something better."

What is the purpose of the text on page 59? Discuss with a partner.

Beginning To help children understand that the author's purpose, or reason, for including this page is to summarize the text, have them find pictures of the helpers mentioned on this page. If needed, point out that police officers and firefighters are *safety helpers* because they keep us safe. If children have trouble finding a "special group," encourage them to read the caption on page 58.

Intermediate To help children understand that this page summarizes the rest of the text, have pairs flip back through the article and find the pages where families, teachers, doctors and nurses, safety helpers, and special groups are described.

Advanced/Advanced High Have children answer in their own words: *Why is this page a good ending for the article? Is it a summary, or is it new information? It is a summary. What does it tell about? It tells about the helpers.* Have pairs support their answers by reading aloud sentences from the text.

FORMATIVE ASSESSMENT

❯ STUDENT CHECK IN

Have partners retell how different people can help each day. Then have children reflect, using the Check-In routine.

Independent Time

Describing Helpers Form pairs of mixed proficiencies. Assign or have pairs choose one type of helper: families, teachers, doctors and nurses, safety helpers, or special groups. Have partners make and illustrate a list of tasks to answer this question: *How do these helpers help you? They keep me safe.* Tell children to think about their own experiences. Have each pair share their responses with the rest of the group.

ENGLISH LANGUAGE LEARNERS **273**

LESSON 3

READING • ANCHOR TEXT • ACCESS THE TEXT

Meet Rosina

Prepare to Read

Build Background Point to the girl on the title page. *We are going to read about a girl named Rosina. She is deaf.* Write *deaf,* and read it for children to repeat. Have them point to their ears and say: *A person who is deaf cannot _____. What do you think Rosina likes to do?* She likes to ___. Then point to the signs and say: *Let's make these shapes with our hands.* Guide children in using their hands to make the signs.

Literature Anthology, Lexile 420L

Focus on Vocabulary Use the **Visual Vocabulary Cards** to review the high-frequency words *brother, father, friend, love, mother,* and *picture* and the oral vocabulary words *decision, distance, inspire, respect,* and *swiftly.* As you read, use gestures and pantomime to teach important selection words, such as *sign language* and *sign.* Say the words for children to repeat. Point to the signs on page 303. *This is* American Sign Language. Show a sign with your hand. *This is a* sign. *When I use signs for words, I am* signing. *What am I doing?* You are signing.

Summarize the Text Before reading, say the summary while pointing to the photos. *This text is about a girl named Rosina. She is deaf, so she uses sign language. She goes to school and spends time with her family, just like you.*

Read the Text

Use the Interactive Question-Response routine to help children understand the text.

Pages 304–305

Pages 304–305 Read the text on page 304, and have children make the signs with you. Then read the text on page 305, and point to the photo. *What is her name?* Her name is Rosina. *What have you learned about her?* She is deaf. She talks with her hands. *Another word for* talk *is* communicate. *Say* communicate.

Why does the author include the feature at the beginning of the text? Discuss with a partner.

Beginning Point to the feature on page 304. Help children mimic the signs as they chorally read the words under the signs. *Do these pictures show how Rosina talks?* (yes) *How does she talk?* She talks with her hands.

Intermediate Help partners summarize the feature: Rosina uses her hands to say, "Hi! I'm Rosina." *What does the author want us to know?* The author wants us to know how Rosina talks/communicates with her hands.

Advanced/Advanced High Have partners read the words for the signs and explain the author's purpose for the feature: The author uses pictures and words to show how Rosina talks/communicates with her hands.

LEARNING GOALS

We can read and understand a nonfiction text.

OBJECTIVES

Ask and answer questions about key details in a text.

Know and use various text features (e.g., headings, tables of contents, glossaries, electronic menus, icons) to locate key facts or information in a text.

Identify the reasons an author gives to support points in a text.

Ask questions to clear up any confusion about the topics and texts under discussion.

LANGUAGE OBJECTIVES

Children will discuss Rosina's daily habits, using key vocabulary and complete sentences.

ELA ACADEMIC LANGUAGE

• feature, text, author, photo
• Cognates: *texto, autor, foto*

MATERIALS

Literature Anthology, pp. 302–323

Visual Vocabulary Cards

DIGITAL TOOLS

Have children listen to the selection as they follow along to develop comprehension.

Use the additional grammar video.

Grammar Video

274 UNIT 6 WEEK 2

WEEK 2

Pages 306–319

Pages 306–315 Read the text aloud. At the end, ask: *What is this part of the text about?* It tells about Rosina's school. Help children compare Rosina's school day with their own. *How is Rosina's day similar to yours?* She studies math/plays sports/paints/writes stories. Then help children think about how Rosina's day is different. *How do the teachers and students talk to one another?* They don't speak. They sign.

Pages 316–317 Read the text aloud. Help children describe what is happening in each picture. Rosina's mom is fixing her hair. *How do Rosina's family members help?* Mom cooks. Rosina chops lettuce. Emilio cuts cheese. Dad makes guacamole.

Pages 318–319 Read the text. Have children point to the chessboard and chess pieces. *Who is playing?* Rosina and Dad are playing. *What is Emilio doing?* He is cheering for Rosina. Have children identify Rosina's family members in the picture on page 319. Point out that Rosina says "there are many more" people in her family. *Who else in Rosina's family have we learned about?* (Aunt Carla) Have children turn back to pages 308–309 to help them recall Rosina's family members.

COLLABORATE *How does the author show that this part of the text is about Rosina's home life? Discuss with a partner.*

Beginning Have partners use the pictures on pages 316–319 to respond: *Do the pictures show Rosina and her family at home?* (yes) *What are Rosina and her family doing?* Her mom is fixing her hair. They are making dinner. Rosina and her dad are playing chess.

Intermediate Have pairs look at each picture on pages 316–319 and answer: *When is this?* (after school, at dinner, after dinner) Encourage them to look at the first phrase on each page for help. *Where are Rosina and her family in these pictures?* They are at home.

Advanced/Advanced High Provide sentence frames to help pairs add details based on the text. Rosina's mom fixes her hair after school. Rosina's family makes dinner. Rosina and her dad play chess after dinner. *Where are Rosina and her family?* They are at home.

Pages 320–321

Pages 320–321 Read the text. Explain that when Rosina says her family is *big*, she means that there are a lot of people in her family. Present or review vocabulary for extended family: *aunt, cousin, grandpa, grandma*. Challenge children to point to members of Rosina's family they have already learned about.

COLLABORATE *What do the photo and text tell you about what's important to Rosina? Discuss with a partner.*

Beginning Have children look at the picture and infer: *Do you think Rosina likes having a big family?* (yes) *How do you think she talks to her family?* She uses sign language.

Intermediate Help children answer each part of the question. *What does the photo tell you about Rosina?* She has a big family. Reread the last sentence. *What does the text tell you that would be important to Rosina?* People in her family use sign language to talk to each other.

Advanced/Advanced High Help children extend their thinking. *Are all the people in Rosina's family deaf?* No, some people can hear. *Why do you think they know sign language?* It's important for them to be able to talk to Rosina and the others who are deaf.

FORMATIVE ASSESSMENT

> **STUDENT CHECK IN**

Have partners retell what Rosina likes to do each day. Then have children reflect, using the Check-In routine.

Independent Time

Asking and Answering Questions Remind children of the Essential Question. Form pairs of mixed proficiencies, and have them flip back in the reading to find people who help. To get pairs started, ask questions: *How do Rosina's teachers/family members help her? How does Rosina's mom help at school? How do the players on Rosina's rugby team help each other?* Have pairs present their findings to the group.

ENGLISH LANGUAGE LEARNERS

LESSONS 4-5

READING • LEVELED READER • ACCESS THE TEXT

LEARNING GOALS

We can reread to better understand a nonfiction text.

OBJECTIVES

Know and use various text features (e.g., headings, tables of contents, glossaries, electronic menus, icons) to locate key facts or information in a text.

Identify the reasons an author gives to support points in a text.

Identify basic similarities in and differences between two texts on the same topic (e.g., in illustrations, descriptions, or procedures).

Ask and answer questions about key details in a text read aloud or information presented orally or through other media.

LANGUAGE OBJECTIVES

Children will inform about how people help each other, using key vocabulary and complete sentences.

ELA ACADEMIC LANGUAGE

- chapter, table of contents, captions, intonation
- Cognate: *entonación*

MATERIALS

ELL Leveled Reader: *Helping Me, Helping You!*

Online Differentiated Text, "Morning Helpers"

Online ELL Visual Vocabulary Cards

DIGITAL TOOLS

Have children listen to the selection as they follow along to develop comprehension and practice fluency and pronunciation. Use Graphic Organizer 4: Author's Purpose to enhance the lesson.

Helping Me, Helping You!

Prepare to Read

Build Background

- Remind children of the Essential Question. *Let's read about people in your family and neighborhood who help you.* Encourage children to ask for help when they do not understand a word or phrase. Provide language to help them seek clarification, such as: What does that mean? Could you please explain?

Lexile 290L

- Read the title and the table of contents. *This is a table of contents. It lists each part of the book. What are the two parts called?* ____ Read the title of each chapter. *What is the author's purpose for a table of contents?* The author's ____ is to show where the chapters ____. *Where does Chapter 1 start?*

Focus on Vocabulary Use **ELL Visual Vocabulary Cards** to preteach the words *helpers* and *knit*. Then use gestures or visuals to clarify key terms, such as *dentist, librarian, library, sitter, firefighter, builder, office, hospital,* and *playground*.

Read the Text

Use the Interactive Question-Response routine to help children understand the text.

Pages 2–6

Read pages 2–6 as children follow along. On page 2, help children look at the pictures and predict who the helpers will be. On page 6, explain that when someone *accepts* you, that person likes you the way you are.

Beginning Have pairs point to the corresponding parts of each picture as they *reread* the captions and labels aloud.

Intermediate Have partners ask and answer questions about the pictures. For example, Who helps him/her ride a bike? His/Her dad helps him/her ride a bike.

Pages 7–9

Read pages 7–9 as children follow along. *What does a dentist do?* A dentist cleans your teeth. *How do you clean your teeth at home?* I brush my teeth. Have children mime the action of brushing teeth.

Intermediate Have pairs *reread* page 9, and then ask and answer: Do you have a sitter? How can a sitter help you?

Advanced/Advanced High Have children use the text and caption on page 8 to explain different ways a librarian helps them find books.

276 UNIT 6 WEEK 2

WEEK 2

Pages 10–12

Read pages 10–11, and have children follow along. Ask children if they have seen firefighters, fire trucks, or builders in their neighborhoods.

Beginning Help children connect related words. *Who puts out fires?* Firefighters put out fires. *What do they drive?* They drive fire trucks.

Advanced/Advanced High Have partners explain to each other what to do if there is a fire. *Who can help you?*

Author's Purpose Remind children that the author's purpose is the reason an author writes a text. *What is the author's purpose of this text?* (The author's purpose is to inform about how people of the community can help each other.)

Respond to Reading Have partners work together to retell the story and respond to the questions on page 12.

Focus on Fluency

Read pages 10–11 to model appropriate intonation. Read the passage again, and have children repeat after you. For more practice, record children reading the passage, and select the best recording.

Paired Read: "Fire!"

Analytical Writing — Make Connections: Write About It

Echo-read the poem with children two lines at a time. Discuss what is happening in each pair of lines: *What do they hear?* They hear bells. Help children make connections between texts by using the question on page 15: Firefighters are helpers who put out fires to keep us safe.

Leveled Reader

Build Knowledge: Make Connections

Talk About the Text Have partners discuss how people in the texts help others.

Write About the Text Have students add their ideas to the Build Knowledge pages of their reader's notebooks.

Self-Selected Reading

Help children choose a nonfiction selection from the online **Leveled Reader Library,** or read the **Differentiated Text,** "Morning Helpers."

🌍 FOCUS ON SOCIAL STUDIES

Children can extend their knowledge of people who help them by completing the social studies activity on page 16.

LITERATURE CIRCLES

Lead children in conducting a literature circle using the Thinkmark questions to guide the discussion. You may wish to discuss what children have learned about different ways people help them from both selections in the **Leveled Reader.**

▶ FORMATIVE ASSESSMENT

❯ STUDENT CHECK IN

Have partners share their Respond to Reading. Have children reflect, using the Check-In routine.

LEVEL UP

IF children can read *Helping Me, Helping You!* **ELL Level** with fluency and correctly answer the Respond to Reading questions,

THEN tell children they will read a more detailed version of this selection.

- Use pages 2–3 of *Helping Me, Helping You!* **On Level** to model using Teaching Poster 38 to list clues about the author's purpose.

- Have children read the selection, checking their comprehension by using the graphic organizer.

ENGLISH LANGUAGE LEARNERS 277

READING • GENRE PASSAGE • ACCESS THE TEXT

LESSONS 4-5

LEARNING GOALS

We can apply skills and strategies to a nonfiction text.

OBJECTIVES

Describe the connection between two individuals, events, ideas, or pieces of information in a text.

Explain major differences between books that tell stories and books that give information, drawing on a wide reading of a range of text types.

Identify the reasons an author gives to support points in a text.

Build on others' talk in conversations by responding to the comments of others through multiple exchanges.

LANGUAGE OBJECTIVES

Children will discuss the author's purpose, using key vocabulary.

Children will reread to understand the author's purpose.

ELA ACADEMIC LANGUAGE

- describe, author's purpose, nonfiction, reread
- Cognates: *describir, propósito del autor, no ficción*

MATERIALS

Online ELL Genre Passage, "Good Helpers," pp. E1–E3

"Good Helpers"

Prepare to Read

Build Background Read the title aloud. *Who are some good helpers you have learned about?* Elicit home, school, and community helpers, such as family members, teachers, doctors, and firefighters. *How do these helpers keep you safe?* Elicit, for example, that doctors help you be healthy and firefighters put out fires. *Do you think good helpers are important in your community?*

Lexile 450L

Focus on Vocabulary Use the Define, Example, Ask routine to preteach difficult words or unfamiliar concepts, such as *citizen, crossing guard, wait, cross the street, drive carefully,* and *lost*. Explain that each member of a community is a *citizen*. Invite volunteers to describe situations where they have to *wait*, such as in line at the cafeteria, and times they have gotten *lost*. Ask questions to elicit their prior experiences: *Where were you? How did you feel? Who helped you?* Invite children to add new vocabulary words to their glossaries.

Read the Text

Use the Interactive Question-Response routine to help children understand the text.

Page E1

Paragraph 1 Read the text aloud, and have children answer questions to find the **author's purpose**. *Who are citizens?* Citizens are people who live in a city or town. *What kind of person is a good citizen?* A person who helps is a good citizen.

Beginning Have pairs agree on an answer to this question: *Are you citizens of our city/town?* (yes) *Why?* We live in this city/town.

Advanced/Advanced High Help children use prior experiences to help them understand. *Who is a "good citizen" you know?* Have partners share an example. *How do you know this person is a good citizen?* The person helps me stay safe.

Paragraph 2 Read the text aloud as children follow along. *Point to the crossing guard. What is she holding?* She is holding a stop sign. *What does the sign say?* The sign says stop. *What is the sign for?* The sign is for cars. It tells cars to stop and wait. *How does that help the children?* They can cross the street safely.

Antonyms Help children think about an antonym for the word *stop. When cars see a stop sign, should they go or stop?* (stop) *Go* is the opposite of *stop. What do cars do when they don't see a stop sign?* (They go.) Have children mimic stopping and going when driving a car.

278 UNIT 6 WEEK 2

Beginning Have pairs point to and describe what they see in the picture. *She is a crossing guard. That is a stop sign. They are crossing the street.*

Advanced/Advanced High Have children describe their experiences with a crossing guard. *Our crossing guard's name is [Ms. Bell]. She wears an orange vest. She holds up a stop sign. She says, "It's OK to cross."*

Page E2

Paragraph 1 Read the text aloud. Have children *reread* to find the answer to this question: *Which kind of helper is this paragraph about?* (bus drivers)

Intermediate Have pairs identify two ways bus drivers keep people safe. *Bus drivers make cars wait. Bus drivers drive carefully.*

Advanced Have pairs compare crossing guards and bus drivers. *How do both of these helpers help you?* (They make cars wait.) *What else do bus drivers do?* (They drive us to school.)

Paragraph 2 Read the text aloud as children follow along. *What can you do if you get lost?* I can ask a police officer for help.

Advanced High Have pairs briefly role-play a child asking a police officer for help: *I'm lost. I can't find my family. Can you help me?*

Paragraph 3 Read the text aloud as children follow along. Guide children to understand the *author's purpose* in writing this concluding paragraph.

Beginning Have pairs point to the paragraph about each helper. *Which three helpers is this article about?* (crossing guards, bus drivers, and police officers)

Intermediate *How are crossing guards, bus drivers, and police officers alike?* They are good citizens. They help people. They keep us safe.

Respond to Reading

Use the following instructions to help children answer the questions on page E3.

1. **Nonfiction** Remind children that nonfiction describes real people, things, and events. *What three people does this text describe?* (crossing guards, bus drivers, police officers) *Do you have these helpers in your community in real life?* (yes)

2. **Author's Purpose** Help children *reread* pages E1 and E2. Ask: *What is the author's purpose in the text? The author's purpose is to inform us about helpers where we live.* Have children find the definition of good citizen. (page E1) *A citizen is a member of a city or town, and a good citizen is a citizen who helps others.*

3. **Fluency** Have children take turns reading the first paragraph to a partner. As they read, fill in the chart on page E3.

Build Knowledge: Make Connections

Talk About the Text Have partners discuss how the helpers in the text help people.

Write About the Text Have students add their ideas to the Build Knowledge pages of their reader's notebooks.

FORMATIVE ASSESSMENT

▶ STUDENT CHECK IN

Have partners share their Respond to Reading. Then have children reflect, using the Check-In routine.

LEVEL UP

IF children read the ELL fluently and answered the questions,

THEN pair them with children who have proficiently read the On Level. Have them

- partner-read the On Level passage.
- determine the author's purpose for writing.

ENGLISH LANGUAGE LEARNERS

LESSONS 1-5

WRITING

MODELED WRITING

LESSON 1

LEARNING GOALS

We can learn how to use our own voice in our writing.

OBJECTIVES

Write informative texts in which they supply some facts about the topic.

LANGUAGE OBJECTIVES

Children will inform by writing a paragraph, using a word that tells how they feel.

ELA ACADEMIC LANGUAGE

- voice

Writing Practice Have children chorally read p. 60 of the **Reading/Writing Companion**. Use the Actor/Action routine to help children analyze sentences: *Who is the actor?* (the crossing guard) *What is the action?* (helps me) *When does she help?* (every day) Then read the prompt on p. 61, and ask children to answer it as a group. Write their paragraph on the board, and ask children to chorally read it. Then help children write their own paragraphs.

Beginning Provide a sentence frame to help partners introduce their topics and tell what they think: The coach helps me. He is an important helper!

Intermediate Have partners ask and answer *who/what* questions to create their paragraphs. Remind children to use their own voice. *How do you feel about this helper?*

Advanced/Advanced High Have children exchange sentences and identify a topic sentence and a sentence where the writer uses his or her voice.

FORMATIVE ASSESSMENT ▶ **STUDENT CHECK IN** Partners share their sentences. Ask children to reflect, using the Check-In routine.

INTERACTIVE WRITING

LESSON 2

LEARNING GOALS

We can read and write about a Student Model.

OBJECTIVES

Add details to strengthen writing as needed.

LANGUAGE OBJECTIVES

Children will discuss and write sentences about the Student Model, identifying possessive pronouns.

ELA ACADEMIC LANGUAGE

- topic, possessive pronoun
- Cognate: *pronombre posesivo*

Analyze the Student Model Have children chorally read the Student Model on p. 68 of the **Reading/Writing Companion**. Use the Actor/Action routine to help children analyze the sentence: *Who is the actor?* (Miss Potter) *How does the writer describe her?* (as a great helper) Point out the possessive pronouns. *What do possessive pronouns tell us?* (who or what has something) Then help children complete p. 69.

Beginning Have partners point to examples of possessive pronouns. Provide a sentence frame: I notice the word our. It shows that we have a librarian.

Intermediate *What do you notice about Farah's writing?* She uses her voice in the last sentence, "Miss Potter is the best!"

Advanced/Advanced High Challenge children to write their own sentences about the text. Encourage children to share their ideas.

FORMATIVE ASSESSMENT ▶ **STUDENT CHECK IN** Partners share their responses. Ask children to reflect, using the Check-In routine.

WEEK 2

INDEPENDENT WRITING

LESSONS 3-4

LEARNING GOALS
We can respond to a nonfiction text by writing a new text.

OBJECTIVES
Write informative texts in which they supply some facts about the topic.

LANGUAGE OBJECTIVES
Children will inform by writing a sentence with a feeling word.

ELA ACADEMIC LANGUAGE
- *evidence*
- Cognate: *evidencia*

Find Text Evidence Follow the Independent Writing routine. Help children orally retell the anchor text. Ask questions, such as: *Why does Rosina talk with her hands?* (She is deaf.) *At her school, how do the teachers talk with students?* (They use American Sign Language.) Then read the prompt on p. 74 of the **Reading/Writing Companion**: *Rosina has a special community that works together. How do the people in your community work together to help you? We need to write about the helpers in our community.*

Write a Response Help children complete My Writing Outline 27. Then have them use the sentences from their outlines to complete p. 74.

Writing Checklist Read the checklist with students, and have them check for these items in their writing.

Beginning Provide sentence frames to help children talk about their sentences: I used the word *thankful* to *tell about my feelings*.

Intermediate Have partners explain how they use possessive pronouns in their writing: The word *my* shows that *I have a community*.

Advanced/Advanced High Have partners use the sentence starters on p. T138 of the **Teacher's Edition** in their writing.

FORMATIVE ASSESSMENT ▸ **STUDENT CHECK IN** Partners share their sentences from My Writing Outline. Ask children to reflect, using the Check-in routine.

SELF-SELECTED WRITING

LESSON 5

LEARNING GOALS
We can revise our writing.

OBJECTIVES
Use personal, possessive, and indefinite pronouns.

LANGUAGE OBJECTIVES
Children will inquire about their writing by checking their pronouns.

ELA ACADEMIC LANGUAGE
- *pronoun*
- Cognate: *pronombre*

Work with children to revise the group writing activity. Point to each word as you read the sentences. Stop to ask questions, such as: *What/Whom is this pronoun referring to?* If needed, write a sentence with a possessive pronoun used incorrectly, and work together to revise the sentence. Then have partners revise each other's sentences.

For support with grammar and possessive pronouns, refer to the **Language Transfers Handbook** and **Language Development Card** 17B.

FORMATIVE ASSESSMENT ▸ **STUDENT CHECK IN** Partners tell what revisions they made. Ask children to reflect, using the Check-in routine.

ENGLISH LANGUAGE LEARNERS

READING • SHARED READ • ACCESS THE TEXT

LESSONS 1-2

LEARNING GOALS

We can read and understand a realistic fiction story.

OBJECTIVES

Retell stories, including key details, and demonstrate understanding of their central message or lesson.

Identify words and phrases in stories or poems that suggest feelings or appeal to the senses.

Use illustrations and details in a story to describe its characters, setting, or events.

Produce complete sentences when appropriate to task and situation.

LANGUAGE OBJECTIVES

Children will narrate how the characters spend time during an ice storm, using descriptive words and complete sentences.

ELA ACADEMIC LANGUAGE

- realistic fiction, illustration, details
- Cognates: *ficción realista, ilustración, detalles*

MATERIALS

Reading/Writing Companion, pp. 86–95

Visual Vocabulary Cards

DIGITAL TOOLS

Have children listen to the selection as they follow along to develop comprehension and practice fluency and pronunciation.

Use the ELL Vocabulary Practice for additional support.

"Wrapped in Ice"

Prepare to Read

Build Background Read aloud the Essential Question on page 86. Have children share ideas about how weather can affect them. Use the illustrations on pages 86–87 to generate ideas. Point to and read aloud the title. *We are going to read a realistic fiction story about a winter storm and how it affects a neighborhood.* Realistic fiction *is a made-up story with events that could happen in real life.* Point to the ice on the trees, houses, and street. *This is ice. Say* ice *with me. An ice storm is a type of winter storm. Say* winter storm *with me.*

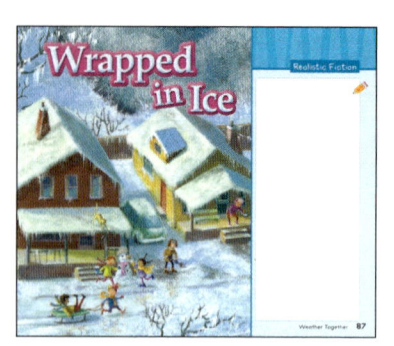

Reading/Writing Companion, Lexile 320L

Focus on Vocabulary Use the **Visual Vocabulary Cards** to review the high-frequency words *been, children, month, question, their,* and *year* and the oral vocabulary words *creative, cycle, frigid, predict,* and *scorching.* As you read, use gestures and visual support to teach important story words, such as *coated, sparkled, freeze, branches,* and *reporter.* Use this routine for each new word: Point to the ice covering the car. Say the word *coated.* Have children point to the picture and repeat the word. *The car is coated with ice. What is the car coated with?* Have children respond: The car is coated with ice.

Summarize the Text Before reading, say the summary and point to the illustrations. *This story tells about an ice storm and how it affects one community.*

Read the Text

Use the Interactive Question-Response routine to help children understand the story.

Pages 88–89

Pages 88–89 Read the text aloud. Point to the illustration on page 88. *This is Kim. What does she see outside?* She sees ice that covers the yard, the car, and the trees. Point to the italicized words. *These words tell how the ice sounds on Kim's window: "Ping! Ping, ping!" Say these sound words with me. Kim asks why everything is covered in ice. What does Mom say about the air?* Mom says the air is very cold. *What happens to raindrops when the air is very cold?* When the air is very cold, raindrops freeze.

What does Kim see outside? Discuss with a partner.

Beginning Use the illustrations to review the words *ice, freeze, tree branches,* and *coated.* Point to the picture of Kim and say: *Kim is looking out the window.* Point to the ice on the tree branches. *What does Kim see?* Kim sees ice covering the tree branches.

282 UNIT 6 WEEK 3

WEEK 3

Intermediate Help partners give a more specific answer. *What does Kim see? Point to each thing.* Kim sees ice on the trees, on the driveway, and on the car. Guide children to point to the tree branch and the car. *What does the ice look like?* The ice sparkles.

Advanced/Advanced High Help partners add details to their responses. Point to the scene outside the window. *What details tell you that Kim thinks what she sees is beautiful?* The author uses words like sparkle and icy design.

Pages 90–91

Pages 90–91 Read the text aloud as children follow along. *Look at the illustration. What do you see on the TV?* I see a reporter and a map. The map is a weather map. The reporter tells people to stay inside. Even school is closed! Point to page 90. *What happens to Kim's house because of the storm?* The lights go out. *Is Kim worried?* (yes) Say *worried* with me.

How does Kim feel when the lights go out? Discuss with a partner.

Beginning Guide children to use the illustrations to help them respond. Point to Kim. *How does Kim look?* Kim looks worried. *Show me the face you make when you are worried.* Share your worried expression, and have children do the same.

Intermediate Help partners give details about their answers. *How does Kim feel?* She feels worried. *How do you know?* I know because the story says "Kim looked worried." Her face also looks worried.

Advanced/Advanced High Encourage partners to elaborate on their responses. *What details tell you Kim is worried?* The story says "Kim looked worried." Her face also looks worried. *Why might Kim be worried about the lights being out?* She might be scared because the house will be very dark.

Pages 92–95

Page 92–93 Read the text aloud as children follow along. Point to the word *neighbors,* and say it aloud for children to repeat. *Who comes to Kim's house?* The neighbors come to Kim's house. Point to the snacks and cider. *What does everyone do together?* Everyone eats snacks and drinks cider. *Do they have a good time?* Yes, they have a good time.

How does the winter storm affect Kim, Mom, and their neighbors? Discuss with a partner.

Beginning Point to the two children and two adults. Explain that these are Kim and Mom's neighbors. *Who comes to Kim's house?* The neighbors come to Kim's house. *What do they do at Kim's house? Point to the pictures.* They eat. They drink. They have fun.

Intermediate Help partners give details with their answers. *What do the neighbors do at Kim's house?* The neighbors eat, laugh, and have fun together with Kim and Mom. *Does everyone enjoy the ice day?* Yes, everyone enjoys the ice day.

Advanced/Advanced High Help partners elaborate on their answers. Ask: *Why does Mom say that it's nice when everyone gathers together?* Mom says it's nice because they eat, laugh, and have fun.

FORMATIVE ASSESSMENT

▶ STUDENT CHECK IN

Have partners retell what the characters do during an ice storm. Then have children reflect, using the Check-In routine.

Independent Time

Write a Song or Poem Have pairs of mixed proficiency levels write a song or poem about what happens to Kim, Mom, and their neighborhood during the winter storm. Before beginning, have pairs review some of the key words from the story, including *advise, coat, cozy,* and *sparkle.* Have pairs repeat the words to one another and tell their meanings. Challenge pairs to include these words from the story in their song or poem. After pairs have written their song or poem, encourage them to practice it. Then have them present their song or poem to another pair, a small group, or the whole class.

ENGLISH LANGUAGE LEARNERS **283**

LESSON 3

READING • ANCHOR TEXT • ACCESS THE TEXT

LEARNING GOALS

We can read and understand a realistic fiction story.

OBJECTIVES

Describe characters, settings, and major events in a story, using key details.

Identify words and phrases in stories or poems that suggest feelings or appeal to the senses.

Use illustrations and details in a story to describe its characters, setting, or events.

Describe people, places, things, and events with relevant details, expressing ideas and feelings clearly.

LANGUAGE OBJECTIVES

Children will narrate how the children build and use their school, using descriptive words and complete sentences.

ELA ACADEMIC LANGUAGE

- author, title
- Cognates: *autor, título*

MATERIALS

Literature Anthology, pp. 326–357

Visual Vocabulary Cards

DIGITAL TOOLS

Have children listen to the selection as they follow along to develop comprehension and practice fluency and pronunciation.

Use the additional grammar song.

Grammar Song

Rain School

Prepare to Read

Build Background *We are going to read a story about children in the African country of Chad. The children want to go to school.* Show the title page, and ask children to tell what they see. Point to the *children*, *rain*, and *notebooks*. Say the words, and have children repeat them. Point to the girl in the blue dress. *This girl is running. She is trying to cover her head. It is raining hard. What do you do when you get caught in the rain? I ___ to get inside.*

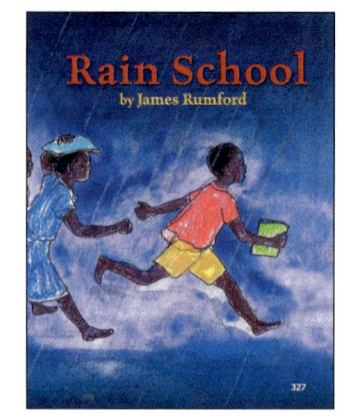

Literature Anthology, Lexile 440L

Focus on Vocabulary Use the **Visual Vocabulary Cards** to review the high-frequency words *been, children, month, question, their, year, country,* and *gathers* and the oral vocabulary words *creative, cycle, frigid, predict,* and *scorching*. As you read, use gestures and pantomime to teach important story words, such as *build, bricks, roof, stool,* and *blackboard*.

Summarize the Text Before reading, say the summary while pointing to the illustrations. *The story tells about children in Chad who want to go to school. First, they must build their school. When the rain starts, the school is gone again.*

Read the Text

Use the Interactive Question-Response routine to help children understand the text.

Pages 332–341

Pages 332–333 Read the text. Point to the children on page 332. *The children arrive at the schoolyard. A* schoolyard *is the ground around a school. Do the children see a school?* (no) *Do you see a school in the picture?* (no) Point to the words *It doesn't matter*. *These words are another way to say something is not important.* Point to the teacher on page 333. *This is the teacher. She has materials and tools. What are the children and the teacher going to do?* They are going to build *their school.*

Pages 340–341 Read the text. Point to the children. *What have the children built?* They have built their school. Point to the word *earth*. *Here, the word* earth *means "dirt." Why does the school smell like dirt?* Its walls are made of mud. Point to the stools. *The children brought stools. What do the children do with the stools?* The children sit *on the stools. They are waiting for school to start.*

Why did the author include words that tell what the room smells like? Discuss with a partner.

284 UNIT 6 WEEK 3

WEEK 3

Beginning Say *cool*, and act it out. Have children imitate you and repeat *cool*. Ask: *Does the room smell like earth?* (yes) *How do you know? Point to it in the text.* Guide children to point to the last sentence.

Intermediate Ask partners whether they think it is hot outside the room. (yes) *How do you know?* The text says, "Inside it is cool." Ask them to tell what the author says the room smells like. (earth, fields)

Advanced/Advanced High Extend the discussion by having partners discuss other details the author includes that help them know what being in a school made of mud and grass is like. It smells like earth. It smells like the fields ready for planting.

Pages 346–349

Pages 346–349 Read the text. Point to the children on pages 346–347. *What are the children looking at?* (a map) *The children are learning about Africa.* Display pages 348–349. *The school year is over. What do the children say to their teacher?* They say, "Thank you, Teacher."

How does the author show how the children feel? Discuss with a partner.

Beginning Help partners point to the pictures as they respond. Point to the boy holding the green notebook on page 348. *Does this boy look happy?* (yes) *The children say* thank you *to the teacher. Why?* They are happy to be at school. They are happy to learn.

Intermediate Point to the picture on pages 348–349. *How do the children feel?* They feel happy. *How do you know?* The children's faces look happy. They look excited. They tell their teacher thank you.

Advanced/Advanced High Extend the discussion by having partners talk about why the children are happy to be at school. Encourage pairs to give details from the text. They are happy because they learned a lot. Their minds are fat with knowledge.

Pages 350–355

Pages 350–351 Read the text. Point to and say *slump*. Have children repeat. Slump *means "fall down."* Point to the school. *It is raining. What does the rain do to the school?* The rain makes the school start to fall down.

Pages 354–355 Read the text. Point to the children. *A new school year is going to begin. The children come back. What will the children do?* The children will build their school again.

Why is Rain School *a good title for this book? Discuss with a partner.*

Beginning Display pages 334–335. *Is it raining when the school year starts?* (no) Display pages 350–351. *Is it raining when the school year ends?* (yes) *Can the children go to school when it rains?* No, the children cannot go to school when it rains.

Intermediate Help partners review to respond. *Is there a school when it rains?* No, the school falls down when it rains. *When do the children build their school?* They build their school when the weather is dry.

Advanced/Advanced High Extend the discussion by having partners discuss what might be another good title for the story. (Possible response: *Working Together* might be a good title because the students have to work together to build the school.)

FORMATIVE ASSESSMENT

› STUDENT CHECK IN

Have partners retell how the children build their school. Then have children reflect, using the Check-In routine

Independent Time

Art Project Pair children of mixed proficiency levels. Have pairs work together to create a sign for the school in the story. Explain that the sign would go outside the school and tell everyone what kind of school it is. As children plan and create their signs, they should consider what makes this school different and what the students in the story like about it. When pairs have finished creating their signs, encourage them to present their work to another pair, a small group, or the whole class. They should show the signs and explain what they represent.

ENGLISH LANGUAGE LEARNERS **285**

LESSONS 4-5

READING • LEVELED READER • ACCESS THE TEXT

LEARNING GOALS

We can visualize what happens in a realistic fiction.

OBJECTIVES

Retell stories, including key details, and demonstrate understanding of their central message or lesson.

Identify words and phrases in stories or poems that suggest feelings or appeal to the senses.

Identify basic similarities in and differences between two texts on the same topic (e.g., in illustrations, descriptions, or procedures).

Describe people, places, things, and events with relevant details, expressing ideas and feelings clearly.

LANGUAGE OBJECTIVES

Children will narrate what people do in hot weather, using key vocabulary and verbs that end with -ing.

ELA ACADEMIC LANGUAGE

- cause, effect, visualize
- Cognates: causa, efecto, visualizar

MATERIALS

ELL Leveled Reader: *Heat Wave*

Online Differentiated Texts, "A Rainy Day"

Online ELL Visual Vocabulary Cards

DIGITAL TOOLS

Have children listen to the selection as they follow along to develop comprehension and practice fluency and pronunciation. Use Graphic Organizer 10: Cause and Effect to enhance the lesson.

Heat Wave

Prepare to Read

Build Background

- Remind children of the Essential Question. Write and say the temperature. *It's warm/hot here. Let's read to find out what some kids do in hot weather.* Encourage children to ask for help when they do not understand a word or phrase.

Lexile 370L

- Point to and read the title aloud and have children repeat. Have children turn to the table of contents and read the chapter titles chorally. Then point to the illustrations to name things and actions; for example: *This is a pool. You swim in a pool. Where else can you swim?*

Focus on Vocabulary Use **ELL Visual Vocabulary Cards** to preteach the words *cool* and *sunscreen*. Then use gestures or visuals to clarify key terms, such as *pretend, floating,* and *gathers*.

Read the Text

Use the Interactive Question-Response routine to help children understand the story.

Pages 2–5

Read the chapter title and the text on pages 2–3 as children follow along. Ask questions to help describe what the characters do on a hot day.

Beginning Help partners point to the pictures as they respond: *Is it hot or cold?* It is hot. *What do the people do when it's hot?* When it's hot, the people go swimming.

Intermediate *What causes Ty, Jamal, and Martin to go swimming?* They go swimming because it is hot. They want to stay cool.

Pages 6–9

Read the chapter title and text on pages 6–7 as children follow along. Have children look at the pictures. Ask questions to help them explain how the author helps them visualize what the boys are thinking about as they try to stay cool.

Intermediate Help partners respond: *What do the text and pictures help you visualize?* They help me visualize the boys floating on ice cubes.

Advanced/Advanced High Have partners discuss: *What do the boys pretend to do?* (float on ice cubes) *What helps you visualize it?* They talk about it, and a picture shows they are thinking about it.

286 UNIT 6 WEEK 3

WEEK 3

Pages 10–11

Read the chapter title and pages 10–11 aloud as children follow along. *The boys try to think of more ways to stay cool. Ty's mom has an idea.*

Beginning Point to Ty's mom. *This is Ty's mom. What does she tell the boys to do?* She tells them to drink water.

Advanced/Advanced High *What suggestion does Ty's mom make?* She suggests that the boys drink water.

Events: Cause and Effect Remind children that a cause is what makes an event happen. An effect is the event that happens. Help children identify cause and effect relationships in the story. (A cause is the hot weather. An effect is that people go to the pool.)

Respond to Reading Have partners work together to retell the story and respond to the questions on page 12.

Focus on Fluency

Read pages 10–11 to model appropriate intonation. Read the passage again and have children repeat after you. For more practice, record children reading the passage and select the best recording.

Paired Read: "Stay Safe When It's Hot"

Analytical Writing Make Connections: Write About It

Echo-read each page with children. Discuss how animals stay safe in hot weather: *How do turtles stay safe?* Their shells cover them. Help children make connections between texts using the question on page 15. You can be safe by drinking lots of water.

Leveled Reader

Build Knowledge: Make Connections

Talk About the Text Have partners discuss how the weather in the texts affects people.

Write About the Text Have students add their ideas to the Build Knowledge pages of their reader's notebooks.

Self-Selected Reading

Help children choose a fiction selection from the online **Leveled Reader Library** or read the **Differentiated Text,** "A Rainy Day."

FOCUS ON SCIENCE

Children can extend their knowledge of weather by completing the science activity on page 16. **STEM**

LITERATURE CIRCLES

Lead children in conducting a literature circle, using the Thinkmark questions to guide the discussion. You may wish to discuss what children have learned about hot weather from both selections in the Leveled Reader.

FORMATIVE ASSESSMENT

▶ STUDENT CHECK IN

Have partners share their Respond to Reading. Have children reflect using the Check-In routine.

LEVEL UP

IF children can read *Heat Wave* **ELL Level** with fluency and correctly answer the Respond to Reading questions,

THEN tell children that they will read a more detailed version of the story.

- Use page 5 of *Heat Wave* **On Level** and Teaching Poster 32 to list causes and effects.

- Have children read the selection, checking their comprehension by using the graphic organizer.

ENGLISH LANGUAGE LEARNERS **287**

LESSONS 4-5

READING • GENRE PASSAGE • ACCESS THE TEXT

LEARNING GOALS

We can apply skills and strategies to a realistic fiction text.

OBJECTIVES

Describe characters, settings, and major events in a story, using key details.

Identify words and phrases in stories or poems that suggest feelings or appeal to the senses.

Explain major differences between books that tell stories and books that give information, drawing on a wide reading of a range of text types.

Identify the reasons an author gives to support points in a text.

LANGUAGE OBJECTIVES

Children will discuss cause and effect using key vocabulary.

Children will visualize and use descriptive words.

ELA ACADEMIC LANGUAGE

- realistic fiction, visualize
- Cognates: *ficción realista, visualizar*

MATERIALS

Online ELL Genre Passage, "My Sick Day," pp. E1–E3

"My Sick Day"

Prepare to Read

Build Background Review what children have learned about how the weather affects people. *What are some ways weather can affect people?* When it's too hot, people need to drink _____. Allow children to share additional ideas. Ask children if it is rainy today. Guide them to write a sentence about today's weather: It is _____ today. Then tell children they will be reading about a girl who has a lucky experience with the rain.

Focus on Vocabulary Use the **Define, Example, Ask** routine to preteach difficult words or unfamiliar concepts, such as *sick, fever, giraffes, clouds, thunder, boomed, stomping,* and *storm*. Invite children to add new vocabulary to their glossaries.

Lexile 450L

Read the Text

Use the Interactive Question-Response routine to help children understand the story.

Page E1

Paragraphs 1–3 Read the text aloud as children follow along. Point to the illustration. *What is wrong with the girl?* The girl feels sick. She has a fever. Mama tells the girl she has to stay home for the day.

Beginning Point to the girl in the illustration. Have partners answer the questions and visualize what the text says. *How does the girl look?* The girl looks sad. *Why does the girl look sad?* She looks sad because she is sick. *What will happen because she is sick?* She will not go to school because she is sick.

Paragraphs 4–5 Read aloud as children follow along. Help children discuss cause and effect. *The girl is sick.* This is the cause. *She cannot go on the school trip.* This is the effect. *Where will the children go on the school trip?* The children will go to the zoo. *What animal does the girl want to see?* The girl wants to see giraffes.

Intermediate Have partner s discuss: *What details in the text and illustrations tell you that the girl was very excited to see the giraffes?* The girl says, "I wanted to see the giraffes." The girl also has a giraffe toy in her bed.

Page E2

Paragraph 1 Read the text aloud as children follow along. *What does the girl do?* The girl falls asleep. *What does the girl dream about?* She dreams about giraffes.

Advanced/Advanced High Have partners discuss: *Why did the author write the detail that the girl dreams about giraffes?* The author wrote this detail to show how much the girl likes giraffes.

288 UNIT 6 WEEK 3

WEEK 3

Paragraph 2 Read the text aloud as children follow along. Point to the trees in the illustration. *What do you see in the illustration?* I see rain. It looks windy. *When the girl wakes up, she sees dark clouds. She hears thunder. What is happening?* There is a storm.

Intermediate Guide partners to notice text details: *How does the author show you what the storm is like?* The author says the clouds are dark. The author says the thunder sounds like stomping.

Paragraphs 3–4 Read the text aloud as children follow along. Point to Mama. *Mama tells the girl that her class did not go to the zoo. Another way to say this is* the trip was canceled. *Why didn't the class go to the zoo?* The class didn't go because of the storm. *Is the girl happy?* (yes)

Simile Reread paragraph 2. Explain that a simile is a phrase or sentence that compares two things and uses the word *like* or *as*. *What does the girl hear when she wakes up?* She hears thunder. *Is thunder noisy or quiet?* (noisy) *What does the girl say about the sound of thunder?* She says it sounds like a giant stomping in the sky. Explain that to stomp means to walk, making noisy steps. Have children pantomime a giant stomping on the floor.

Advanced Have partners ask and answer: *How does the girl change?* She feels better. *Why?* Mama tells her the trip will be next week, so she will go on it.

Advanced High Have partners talk about what causes the girl to be able to go on the zoo trip. The trip was canceled because of the storm. The zoo trip will be next week, and the girl will be well by then.

Respond to Reading

Use the following instructions to help children answer the questions on page E3.

1. **Realistic Fiction** Have children describe what they see in the illustrations. (Possible answers: I see a girl sick in bed. I see a storm outside the window.) Ask children how they know it is a realistic fiction. The events could happen in real life.

2. **Events: Cause and Effect** Discuss causes and effects in the story. *Why does the girl stay home from school?* (She is sick.) *Why does she start to feel better?* (She rests in bed. She hears good news.)

3. **Fluency** Have partners take turns reading the first paragraph. As they read, fill in the chart on page E3.

Build Knowledge: Make Connections

Talk About the Text Have partners discuss how the weather in the text affects characters.

Write About the Text Have students add their ideas to the Build Knowledge pages of their reader's notebooks.

FORMATIVE ASSESSMENT

▶ STUDENT CHECK IN

Have partners share their Respond to Reading. Then have children reflect using the Check-In routine.

LEVEL UP

IF children read the ELL Level fluently and answered the questions,

THEN pair them with students who have proficiently read the On Level. Have them

- partner read the On Level passage.
- use details to visualize the text.

ENGLISH LANGUAGE LEARNERS **289**

LESSONS 1-5

WRITING

MODELED WRITING

LESSON 1

LEARNING GOALS

We can learn how to write a main idea.

OBJECTIVES

Write narratives in which they include some details.

LANGUAGE OBJECTIVES

Children will narrate by writing a paragraph with a descriptive detail.

ELA ACADEMIC LANGUAGE

- *paragraph*
- Cognate: *párrafo*

Writing Practice Have children choral read the sample on p. 96 of the **Reading/Writing Companion.** *What is the event?* (a big storm) Then use the Actor/Action routine for the remaining sentences: *Who is the actor?* (the strong wind) *What is the action? What did it do?* (knocked down trees) Read the prompt on p. 97 and ask children to answer it as a group. Write the paragraph on the board for children to choral read. Then help children write their own paragraph on p. 97.

Beginning Provide a sentence frame for the main idea: There was a storm. Prompt partners to come up with descriptive details by asking questions: *What was the storm like?* Provide vocabulary as needed.

Intermediate Have partners ask and answer questions to create their sentences: *What happened? What was the event?*

Advanced/Advanced High Have children include at least two descriptive details in their sentences. Invite them to share their sentences with the group.

FORMATIVE ASSESSMENT ❯ **STUDENT CHECK IN** Partners share their sentences. Ask children to reflect, using the Check-In routine.

INTERACTIVE WRITING

LESSON 2

LEARNING GOALS

We can read and write about a Student Model.

OBJECTIVES

Respond to questions and suggestions from peers.

LANGUAGE OBJECTIVES

Children discuss and write sentences about the Student Model and identify the main idea.

ELA ACADEMIC LANGUAGE

- *paragraph, main idea*
- Cognate: *párrafo*

Analyze the Student Model Have children choral read the Student Model on p. 104 of the **Reading/Writing Companion.** Use the Actor/Action routine to analyze the sentence: *Who is the actor?* (everyone from town) *What is the action?* (worked together to clean up) *Which words describe the storm?* (*big* and *ice*) Provide a sentence frame: These words are descriptive details. Then help children complete p. 105.

Beginning Have partners point to descriptive details in the text. Provide a sentence frame: I noticed descriptive details like *big* and *ice*.

Intermediate Have partners ask and answer questions: *What did you notice about Hector's writing?* He used a main idea sentence at the beginning.

Advanced/Advanced High As partners discuss the descriptive details that Hector used, have them suggest other words that could be used.

FORMATIVE ASSESSMENT ❯ **STUDENT CHECK IN** Partners share their responses. Ask children to reflect, using the Check-In routine.

WEEK 3

INDEPENDENT WRITING
LESSONS 3-4

LEARNING GOALS
We can use text evidence to respond to realistic fiction.

OBJECTIVES
Write informative texts in which they supply some facts about the topic.

LANGUAGE OBJECTIVES
Children will inform by writing a paragraph that includes a special pronoun.

ELA ACADEMIC LANGUAGE
- *main idea, detail, pronouns*
- Cognates: *detalle, pronombres*

Find Text Evidence Use the Independent Writing Routine. Have children retell the shared read by asking questions, such as: *What country do the children live in?* (Chad) *How do they go to school?* (walk with their brothers and sisters) Then read the prompt on p. 110 of the **Reading/Writing Companion:** *What do the children in* Rain School *learn from their first lesson? What do the children learn when they first arrive at school? We need to write about what they learned to do.*

Write a Response Help children complete My Writing Outline 28. Then have them use the sentences from their outline to complete p. 110.

Writing Checklist Read the checklist with children and have them check for these items in their writing.

Beginning Provide sentence frames to help partners talk about their paragraph: I used the word *everyone* to refer to all the students in the school.

Intermediate Have partners identify each other's main idea: The first sentence is the main idea. It tells what the paragraph is about.

Advanced/Advanced High Have partners trade paragraphs and check for the main idea.

FORMATIVE ASSESSMENT ▶ **STUDENT CHECK IN** Partners share their sentences from My Writing Outline. Ask children to reflect, using the Check-in routine.

SELF-SELECTED WRITING
LESSON 5

LEARNING GOALS
We can revise our writing.

OBJECTIVES
Use indefinite pronouns.

ELA LANGUAGE OBJECTIVES
Children will inquire about their writing by checking the special pronouns.

ELA ACADEMIC LANGUAGE
- *pronoun*
- Cognate: *pronombre*

Work with children to revise the group writing activity. Point to each word as you read. Stop to ask questions, such as: *Can we use the special pronoun* everything *here?* If needed, write a sentence using an indefinite pronoun incorrectly, and then work together to revise the sentence. Then have partners revise each other's sentences before publishing them.

For support with grammar and indefinite pronouns, refer to the **Language Transfers Handbook** and **Language Development Card** 17A.

FORMATIVE ASSESSMENT ▶ **STUDENT CHECK IN** Partners tell what revisions they made. Ask children to reflect, using the Check-in routine.

ENGLISH LANGUAGE LEARNERS 291

READING • SHARED READ • ACCESS THE TEXT

LESSONS 1-2

LEARNING GOALS

We can read and understand a realistic fiction story.

OBJECTIVES

Retell stories, including key details, and demonstrate understanding of their central message or lesson.

Describe characters, settings, and major events in a story, using key details.

Compare and contrast the adventures and experiences of characters in stories.

Describe people, places, things, and events with relevant details, expressing ideas and feelings clearly.

LANGUAGE OBJECTIVES

Children will narrate the character's birthday celebration, using subjective and objective pronouns.

ELA ACADEMIC LANGUAGE

- theme, vocabulary
- Cognates: *tema, vocabulario*

MATERIALS

Reading/Writing Companion, pp. 122–131

Visual Vocabulary Cards

DIGITAL TOOLS

Have children listen to the selection as they follow along to develop comprehension and practice fluency and pronunciation.

Use the additional grammar video.

Grammar Video

"A Spring Birthday"

Prepare to Read

Build Background Read aloud the Essential Question on page 122. Then point to the title and read it aloud for children to repeat. *People turn one year older on their birthdays. When is your birthday? How old will you be on your next birthday?* Invite several volunteers to answer and write their answers on the board. *Whose birthday is in spring? Name the other seasons. We are going to read about how a boy celebrates his birthday in spring. His name is Marco. Say the name* Marco *with me.*

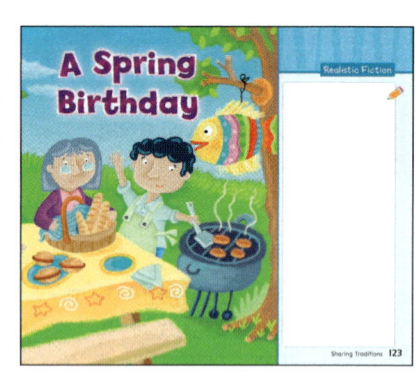

Reading/Writing Companion, Lexile 380L

Focus on Vocabulary Use the **Visual Vocabulary Cards** to review the high-frequency words *before, front, heard, push, tomorrow,* and *your* and the oral vocabulary words *ancient, drama, effort, movement,* and *tradition.* As you read, use gestures and visual support to teach important story words, such as *birthday cake, party, empanadas, hot dogs, burgers, gift,* and *baseball mitt.* Use this routine for each new word: Point to the birthday cake. Say the term for children to repeat as they point to the picture. *It's a cake for Marco's birthday. When do you eat birthday cake?* You eat birthday cake on someone's birthday.

Summarize the Text Before reading, say the summary and point to the illustrations. *This story tells how Marco's family celebrates his birthday. Marco's family is Mexican. They celebrate it with Mexican traditions and in new ways.*

Read the Text

Use the Interactive Question-Response routine to help children understand the story.

Pages 124–126

Pages 124–125 Read the text aloud as children follow along. Have children point to Marco. *Who are the other three people?* (Marco's parents and Gram) Point to the calendar. *What month is it?* (May) *What happens in May?* Marco's birthday is in May. *Marco's family has traditions. One of them is a birthday dinner. What traditional food does Gram make?* (empanadas) Explain that *empanadas* is a Spanish word. Marco's family uses Spanish words for their Mexican traditions.

Page 126 Read the text aloud. Explain that *spot* is another word for *place.* Say the term *ball field* for children to repeat. *Where can you play baseball?* You can play baseball on a ball field. Have children point to and identify each food in the picture as they repeat the name after you.

Does Marco want a traditional celebration? Discuss with a partner.

292 UNIT 6 WEEK 4

WEEK 4

Beginning Provide sentence frames to help pairs respond. *Marco doesn't want a traditional birthday dinner. He wants a party.*

Intermediate Help children add details. *Marco wants a party instead of a traditional dinner. Marco's dad says he can have a picnic in the park.*

Advanced/Advanced High Help children extend their thinking. *What part of Marco's celebration will still be traditional? They will eat Gram's empanadas.*

Pages 127–129

Page 127 Read the text aloud as children follow along. Explain that the word *sprang* means "jumped quickly." *What is today? It's Marco's birthday. What tradition do we learn about on this page? Marco's family sings the Mexican birthday song, "Las mañanitas."* Have children look at the picture and name the characters. *Where are they? They are in Marco's bedroom.*

Pages 128–129 Read the text aloud. Point out the italicized Spanish words. *What do Mom and Dad buy before the party? They buy a baseball mitt, a birthday cake, and a piñata. A piñata has treats, or candies, inside it.* Point to the birthday cake and the piñata. Guide children to make an inference. *Where do you think the baseball mitt is? It's in a box on the table. It is a gift.* Have children name the foods in the picture.

What is a piñata? What do Marco and his friends do with it? Discuss with a partner.

Beginning Have pairs complete these sentences: *A piñata has treats inside. Marco and his friends hit it three times until it breaks. Then they get the treats.*

Intermediate Help children add details. *Marco's mom hangs the piñata. The children hit the piñata with a stick. When it breaks, they grab the treats.*

Advanced/Advanced High Help pairs extend their thinking. *Look at the picture. Why do you think the piñata is "difficult to hit"? The children cover their eyes. They can't see the piñata.*

Pages 130–131

Pages 130–131 Read the text aloud as children follow along. Say the words *sing* and *hum* for children to repeat. *When you sing, you use words. When you hum, you say "mmm."* Lead children in singing and then humming the beginning of "Happy Birthday."

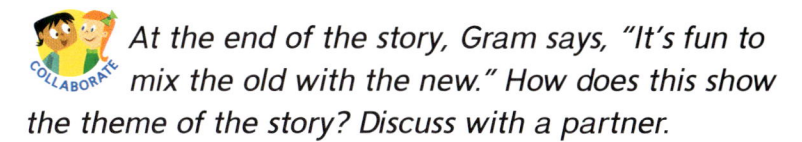

At the end of the story, Gram says, "It's fun to mix the old with the new." How does this show the theme of the story? Discuss with a partner.

Beginning Tell children that the theme is the central message or lesson of a story. Help children tell about this story's theme: *An old tradition is eating empanadas. A new tradition is a birthday picnic.*

Intermediate Help pairs answer by sorting details from the story into two categories: Old Traditions, New Traditions. Provide these details: *birthday song, empanadas, hot dogs, burgers, park, picnic, piñata.*

Advanced/Advanced High Have pairs brainstorm at least two old traditions and two new things at Marco's birthday party; for example: *They sing the Mexican birthday song. That's an old tradition. They are at the park. That's new.*

FORMATIVE ASSESSMENT

STUDENT CHECK IN

Have partners retell what Marco does for his birthday celebration. Then have children reflect using the Check-In routine.

Independent Time

Connecting to Personal Experience Form pairs of mixed proficiencies. Have partners each draw themselves on their last birthday. Have them describe who was there, what they did, and any family traditions. Encourage children to use vocabulary from the story to help them use the new language they learned. Have partners discuss how their birthday traditions are similar or different. Then have pairs share their comparisons with the group.

ENGLISH LANGUAGE LEARNERS 293

LESSONS 3

READING • ANCHOR TEXT • ACCESS THE TEXT

LEARNING GOALS

We can read and understand a realistic fiction story.

OBJECTIVES

Retell stories, including key details, and demonstrate understanding of their central message or lesson.

Compare and contrast the adventures and experiences of characters in stories.

Identify the reasons an author gives to support points in a text.

Describe people, places, things, and events with relevant details, expressing ideas and feelings clearly.

LANGUAGE OBJECTIVES

Children will narrate how the character makes a new friend, using adjectives, verbs, and key vocabulary.

ELA ACADEMIC LANGUAGE

- text, illustration, author
- Cognates: *texto, ilustración, autor*

MATERIALS

Literature Anthology, pp. 362–393

Visual Vocabulary Cards

DIGITAL TOOLS

Have children listen to the selection as they follow along to develop comprehension and practice fluency and pronunciation.

Use the online ELL Vocabulary Practice for additional support.

Lissy's Friends

Prepare to Read

Build Background *We are going to read a story about a girl who is new in school. She doesn't know anybody. She doesn't have any friends.* Ask children if they have ever been the new student in school. *How did you feel?* I felt ____. Display and read the title aloud. *Who is Lissy? Who are her friends? Are Lissy's friends people? What do you think they are?* Children may guess that they are animals, toys, or objects made of paper.

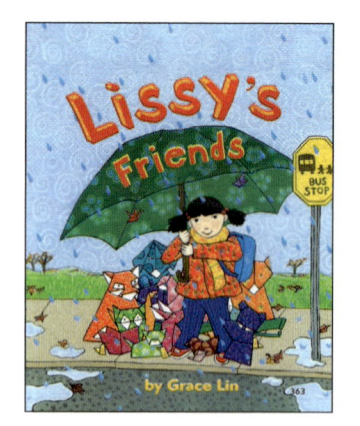

Literature Anthology, Lexile 460L

Focus on Vocabulary Use the **Visual Vocabulary Cards** to review the high-frequency words *before, front, heard, push, tomorrow,* and *your,* and the oral vocabulary words *ancient, drama, effort, movement,* and *tradition.* As you read, use pictures and pantomime to teach important story words, such as *merry-go-round* and *playground.* Sketch or display pictures of these animals on the board: *crane, dragonfly, elephant, fox, giraffe, rabbit.*

Summarize the Text Before reading, say the summary while pointing to the illustrations. *The story tells about a girl named Lissy. She is new and doesn't have any friends yet. But she makes her own friends out of paper.*

Read the Text

Use the Interactive Question-Response routine to help children understand the story.

Pages 364–377

Pages 364–373 Read the text. Point to Lissy in the picture on page 366. *Does Lissy have any friends?* (no) *How do you know?* The other children aren't eating lunch with her. Then point to Lissy on page 377. *Does Lissy have a friend now?* (yes) *What is it?* It's a crane. *Yes, she imagines that the paper crane is her friend. What other imaginary friends does Lissy have?* (owl, rabbit, bird)

Pages 374–375 Read the text. *Where does Lissy take her paper friends?* She takes them to the bus stop/to school/on the bus/to the library.

Pages 376–377 Read the text. Point to the paper animals and have children identify as many as they can. *Where does Lissy put her paper friends at night?* She puts them in her bedroom. Ask children if they have a teddy bear or other stuffed animal they sleep with at night. *How do you feel when you have it?* I feel happy. I don't feel lonely/scared.

COLLABORATE *How does the author help you know how Lissy feels?*

294 UNIT 6 WEEK 4

WEEK 4

Beginning Have pairs focus on the illustration on pages 376–377 in their answer. *I think Lissy feels happy. She is smiling.*

Intermediate Have pairs describe Lissy's expression in the illustration: *Lissy looks happy.* Then have them explain why, based on the text. *She is "never alone" because she has paper friends.*

Advanced/Advanced High Help children extend their thinking: *At the beginning, Lissy feels lonely because she has no friends. In this picture, she is happy because she has many paper friends. The text says she is "never alone."*

Pages 378–379

Pages 378–379 Read the text. Have children point to the kids and the house outside. Then have them identify as many of Lissy's paper animals as they can.

How does the author show how Lissy feels when she looks outside? Discuss with a partner.

Beginning Help pairs answer. *Look at the illustration. What is Lissy doing? She is looking outside. Does Lissy look happy or sad in the illustration? She looks sad.*

Intermediate Help pairs add details. *What does the illustration show Lissy looking at? She's looking at some kids. What does the text say the kids are doing? They are laughing/going to other houses. How do you think that makes her feel? She feels lonely.*

Advanced/Advanced High Help children extend their thinking. *Who does the text say Lissy sees? She sees a group of kids. Are they Lissy's friends?* (no) *How do you know? The text says they don't stop at Lissy's house. Look at the picture. Who are Lissy's friends? Her friends are her paper animals. Do you think Lissy wants to be friends with the other kids?* (yes)

Pages 380–389

Pages 380–385 Read the text aloud. Help children summarize what happens at the playground: *Lissy puts her paper animals on the merry-go-round. She pushes it. The wind blows the paper animals away.*

Pages 386–387 Read the text. Say the name *Paige* for children to repeat as they point to Paige in the picture. *What does Paige do? She finds Lissy's crane/talks to Lissy.* Help children make a prediction. *What will happen next? I think Paige will be Lissy's friend.*

Pages 388–389 Read the text. *What do Paige and Lissy do? They make more paper animals. Why? They are friends. Look at the picture. Find the window. Who is looking inside? Other children are looking inside.*

How do you know that things are different now? Discuss with a partner.

Beginning Help pairs use the illustration on pages 388–389 to respond. *I see in the picture that Lissy has a new friend. Lissy is smiling.*

Intermediate Help pairs add more details based on the illustration on pages 388–389. *Lissy and Paige are making paper animals together. The other kids are looking in the window.*

Advanced/Advanced High Have children compare the illustrations on pages 378–379 and 388–389. *Before, Lissy was lonely. She looked out the window at the other kids. Now, Lissy has a new friend. The other kids aren't going to other houses. They are looking in the window at her.*

FORMATIVE ASSESSMENT

STUDENT CHECK IN

Have partners retell how Lissy makes a new friend. Then have children reflect using the Check-In routine.

Independent Time

Make Your Own Paper Animal Have children make a simple paper animal like one of Lissy's by cutting, folding, and drawing eyes/ears. Have them write a few sentences about their animal: *This is my friend Rabbit. He goes to school/plays on the playground/sleeps in bed with me.* Have children present their animals and have group members ask questions; for example: *Can you show me how to make it?* (Possible response: *You fold the paper here. You cut it here. Then you draw eyes/ears on it.*)

ENGLISH LANGUAGE LEARNERS 295

LESSONS 4-5

READING • LEVELED READER • ACCESS THE TEXT

LEARNING GOALS

We can visualize what happens in a realistic fiction story.

OBJECTIVES

Retell stories, including key details, and demonstrate understanding of their central message or lesson.

Use illustrations and details in a story to describe its characters, setting, or events.

Identify basic similarities in and differences between two texts on the same topic (e.g., in illustrations, descriptions, or procedures).

Describe people, places, things, and events with relevant details, expressing ideas and feelings clearly.

LANGUAGE OBJECTIVES

Children will inform about foods from different cultures, using key vocabulary and complete sentences.

ELA ACADEMIC LANGUAGE

- theme, visualize
- Cognates: *tema, visualizar*

MATERIALS

ELL Leveled Reader: *Latkes for Sam*

Online Differentiated Texts, "A Special Lesson"

Online ELL Visual Vocabulary Cards

DIGITAL TOOLS

Have children listen to the selection as they follow along to develop comprehension and practice fluency and pronunciation. Use Graphic Organizer 12: Theme to enhance the lesson.

Latkes for Sam

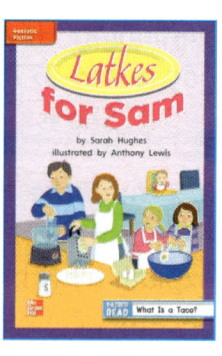

Prepare to Read

Build Background

- Remind children of the Essential Question. *Let's read about two traditional foods.* Encourage children to ask for help when they do not understand a word or phrase.

- Point to and read the title. *Latkes are a traditional Jewish food. What food are they making?* They're making ____. *What ingredients do you need to make latkes?* Have children look at the picture and name any they recognize. *Whom are they making latkes for?* They're making latkes for ____.

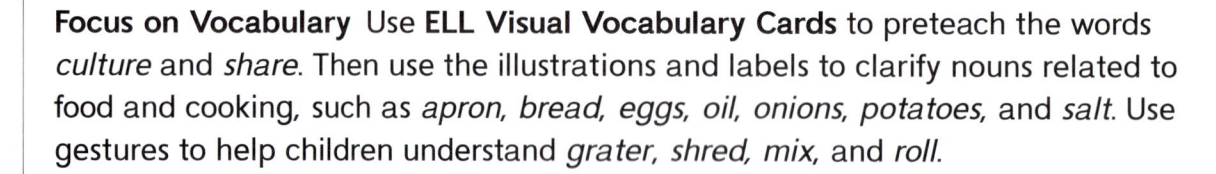

Focus on Vocabulary Use **ELL Visual Vocabulary Cards** to preteach the words *culture* and *share*. Then use the illustrations and labels to clarify nouns related to food and cooking, such as *apron, bread, eggs, oil, onions, potatoes,* and *salt*. Use gestures to help children understand *grater, shred, mix,* and *roll*.

Lexile 370L

Read the Text

Use the Interactive Question-Response routine to help children understand the story.

Pages 2–5

Read the chapter title and then the text on pages 2–5 as children follow along. Ask questions to help children retell the details in this chapter. *Who is visiting?* (Sam) *Sam is at Emma's house. What does Sam bring?* She brings bread. *What is Emma's family making?* They are making latkes.

Beginning Help partners take turns pointing to and naming ingredients in a latke.

Advanced/Advanced High Help pairs use text evidence to infer. *Do you think Sam's family is from the same culture as Emma's family?* (no) *Why?* She has not heard the word *latke*, so her family probably does not make them.

Pages 6–9

Read the chapter title and then the text on pages 6–9 as children follow along. Have children mimic the motions as you read to help them visualize, or create a mental image of, each step. *Who makes the latkes?* Everyone has a job.

Beginning Provide pairs with the steps on page 7 out of order and have them put the steps in the correct sequence.

Intermediate Have partners ask and answer about each step; for example: *What do they do* first? First, they shred potatoes.

296 UNIT 6 WEEK 4

Pages 10–11

Read the chapter title and text on pages 10–11 as children follow. Say *Irish* and *Ireland* for children to repeat. *What is Sam's culture?* It is Irish. *In what country do people eat Irish soda bread?* (Ireland)

Intermediate Help pairs retell this chapter. Sam brings Irish soda bread. She wants to share food from her culture. Emma's family eats it the next morning. They all like it.

Advanced/Advanced High Help partners add more details. (The next day, Sam shares Irish soda bread that she and her mother made.)

Theme Help children identify the message that the author wants to share. People can share food to learn about each other's culture.

Respond to Reading Have partners work together to retell the story and respond to the questions on page 12.

Focus on Fluency

Read pages 4–5 to model appropriate phrasing. Read the passage again and have children repeat after you. For more practice, record children reading the passage and select the best recording.

Paired Selection: "What Is a Taco?"

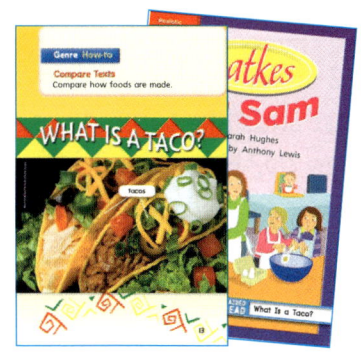

Analytical Writing **Make Connections: Write About It**

Echo-read each page with children. Point out the steps for making a taco. *What is step 1?* In step 1, you put meat and beans in a taco shell. Help children make connections between texts, using the question on page 15. To make both foods, you follow steps in order.

Leveled Reader

Build Knowledge: Make Connections

Talk About the Text Have partners discuss how the traditions are similar to and different from other traditions they have learned about.

Write About the Text Have students add their ideas to the Build Knowledge pages of their reader's notebooks.

Self-Selected Reading

Help children choose a fiction selection from the online **Leveled Reader Library,** or read the **Differentiated Text,** "A Special Lesson."

WEEK 4

FOCUS ON GENRE

Children can extend their knowledge of realistic fiction by completing the genre activity on page 16.

LITERATURE CIRCLES

Lead children in conducting a literature circle using the Thinkmark questions to guide the discussion. You may wish to discuss what children have learned about traditional foods from both selections in the Leveled Reader.

FORMATIVE ASSESSMENT

▸ STUDENT CHECK IN

Have partners share their Respond to Reading. Have children reflect using the Check-In routine.

LEVEL UP

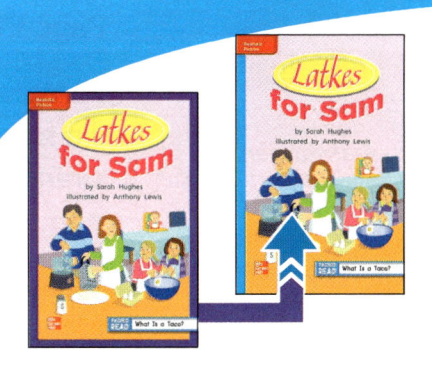

IF children can read *Latkes for Sam* **ELL Level** with fluency and correctly answer the Respond to Reading questions,

THEN tell children that they will read a more detailed version of the story.

- Use pages 7–10 of *Latkes for Sam* **On Level** and Teaching Poster 37 to list clues to the theme.
- Have children read the selection, checking their comprehension by using the graphic organizer.

ENGLISH LANGUAGE LEARNERS **297**

READING • GENRE PASSAGE • ACCESS THE TEXT

LESSONS 4-5

LEARNING GOALS

We can apply skills and strategies to a realistic fiction.

OBJECTIVES

Retell stories, including key details, and demonstrate understanding of their central message or lesson.

Explain major differences between books that tell stories and books that give information, drawing on a wide reading of a range of text types.

Compare and contrast the adventures and experiences of characters in stories.

Ask questions to clear up any confusion about the topics and texts under discussion.

LANGUAGE OBJECTIVES

Children will discuss the theme of the text, using complete sentences. Children will visualize, using verbs and key vocabulary.

ELA ACADEMIC LANGUAGE

- realistic fiction, theme
- Cognates: *ficción realista, tema*

MATERIALS

Online ELL Genre Passage, "A Growing Tradition," pp. E1–E3

"A Growing Tradition"

Prepare to Read

Build Background Read the title aloud. Provide prereading support by having children preview the pictures and make predictions. *Who do you see?* I see ____ and ____. *Do you think they are in the same family?* Yes, the old man is a ____. The boys are his ____. *Where are they?* They are in a ____. *What can you grow in a garden?* You can grow ____, ____, and ____.

Lexile 450L

Focus on Vocabulary Use the Define/Example/Ask routine to preteach difficult words or unfamiliar concepts, such as *come back, having fun, dirt, signs,* and *rather*. Help children understand that the words *garden* and *plant* can be either nouns or verbs. Ask these questions one at a time and have children share their answers in complete sentences: *Do you have a garden at home? Do you garden? Do you have a lot of plants in your garden? Do you plant seeds?* Invite children to add new vocabulary to their glossaries.

Read the Text

Use the Interactive Question-Response routine to help children understand the text.

Page E1

Paragraphs 1–2 Read the text aloud as children follow along. Explain that when Jin says, "That sounds like fun!" he means, "I think it will be fun!" *What does Grandpa want to do?* He wants to teach the boys to garden. *How do the boys feel about it? Are their responses similar or different?*

Compound Words Remind children that a compound word is made of two or more smaller words. *What does Joon want to play?* Joon wants to play baseball. *What are the two small words in baseball?* (base and ball) Invite volunteers to tell how they play the game. Help them use the words *base* and *ball* in their explanations.

Beginning Have partners each describe one boy. Jin/Joon wants/doesn't want to learn. Then have pairs decide: The boys are different.

Paragraphs 3–4 Read the text. Explain that we sometimes use *can* to ask for permission to do something. *What does Joon want permission to do?* Joon wants to play baseball at the park. *How does Grandpa feel?*

Intermediate Have children look for a word in *sadly*. (sad) Have pairs complete this sentence frame: Grandpa feels sad, but he says Joon can go play baseball.

298 UNIT 6 WEEK 4

Page E2

Paragraphs 1–5 Read the text aloud as children follow along. *Where was Joon?* He was at the park. *What was he doing?* (playing baseball) *What were Jin and Grandpa doing?*

Intermediate Have partners work together to find phrases that help them visualize, or create mental images of, what Jin and Grandpa were doing. (signs in the dirt, planted vegetables)

Advanced Guide children to infer, based on text evidence: *Does Jin like gardening?* (yes) *How do you know?* (He is "having fun in the dirt.")

Paragraphs 3–4 Read the text aloud. Explain that when Joon asks, "Can I help?" he is offering to help.

Advanced/Advanced High Help pairs make an inference: *Why does Grandpa smile?* He is happy because Joon wants to learn to garden.

Paragraphs 5–6 Read the text aloud as children follow along. Help children understand the **theme** of the story. *What lesson can you learn from this story?*

Beginning *What can the boys learn from Grandpa?* They can learn to garden. Help children rephrase this idea as a theme. Children can learn from their grandparents.

Advanced High Help pairs extend their thinking. *Why was it important to Grandpa to teach the boys to garden?* Encourage children to look at the title to help them. Gardening is his tradition. Help children rephrase this idea as a theme. It is important for children to learn family traditions.

Respond to Reading

Use the following instructions to help children answer the questions on page E3.

1. **Realistic Fiction** Help children recall the characteristics of realistic fiction. The story is made up, but the events can happen in real life. *Can real grandparents garden/teach people to garden? Can children help them/play baseball?*

2. **Theme** Remind children that the theme is the big idea or message. *What is the theme of this story?* Families have traditions that they share with each other. *Why doesn't Joon want to play baseball when Grandpa asks.* Joon wants to learn about his family's tradition of gardening.

3. **Fluency** Have children take turns reading the first paragraph to a partner. As they read, fill in the chart on page E3.

Build Knowledge: Make Connections

Talk About the Text Have partners discuss the traditions described in the text.

Write About the Text Have students add their ideas to their Build Knowledge pages of their reader's notebooks.

FORMATIVE ASSESSMENT

❯ STUDENT CHECK IN

Have partners share their Respond to Reading. Then have children reflect using the Check-In routine.

LEVEL UP

IF students read the ELL fluently and answered the questions,

THEN pair them with students who have proficiently read the On Level. Have them

- partner read the On Level passage.
- identify the theme or lesson of the story.

LESSONS 1-5

WRITING

MODELED WRITING

LESSON 1

LEARNING GOALS

We can learn how to vary the sentence types in our writing.

OBJECTIVES

Produce and expand complete simple interrogative and exclamatory sentences.

LANGUAGE OBJECTIVES

Children will narrate by writing a paragraph with a question, a statement, and an exclamation.

ELA ACADEMIC LANGUAGE

- question, statement, exclamation

Writing Practice Have children choral read the sample on p. 132 of the **Reading/Writing Companion**. Help children analyze the third sentence using the Actor/Action routine: *Who is the actor?* (We) *What is the action?* (care for it all year) Then read the prompt on p. 133 and ask children to answer it as a group. Write their sentences on the board and ask them to choral read. Then help them write their own sentences.

Beginning Provide sentence frames to help partners write a question, a statement, and an exclamation: Have you ever celebrated Earth Day? My family's tradition is to work in our community garden. It's fun!

Intermediate Have partners ask and answer questions to write their question, statement, and exclamation.

Advanced/Advanced High Have children exchange sentences and identify a question, a statement, and an exclamation. If one is missing, have partners make suggestions.

FORMATIVE ASSESSMENT ▶ **STUDENT CHECK IN** Partners share their sentences. Ask children to reflect, using the Check-In routine.

INTERACTIVE WRITING

LESSON 2

LEARNING GOALS

We can read and write about a Student Model.

OBJECTIVES

Respond to questions and suggestions from peers.

LANGUAGE OBJECTIVES

Children will discuss and write sentences about the Student Model and identify pronouns.

ELA ACADEMIC LANGUAGE

- letter, pronoun
- Cognates: *pronombre*

Analyze the Student Model Have children finger point as they choral read the Student Model on p. 140 of the **Reading/Writing Companion**. Use the Actor/Action routine to review the sentences: *Who is the actor?* (I) *What is the action?* (want to start a new tradition) *What is the pronoun in this sentence?* (I) *Is I the subject or is it part of the predicate?* (the subject) Then help children complete p. 141. Provide sentence frames as needed.

Beginning Have partners point to examples of pronouns and describe them. Provide a sentence frame: I noticed the word me. It is a(n) object pronoun.

Intermediate Have partners ask and answer questions: *What did you notice about Kate's writing?* She used a question at the end of her letter.

Advanced/Advanced High Have children discuss the sentence types used in the letter. Challenge children to write about the text using their own sentences. Encourage them to share their ideas.

FORMATIVE ASSESSMENT ▶ **STUDENT CHECK IN** Partners share their responses. Ask children to reflect, using the Check-In routine.

300 UNIT 6 WEEK 4

WEEK 4

INDEPENDENT WRITING
LESSONS 3-4

LEARNING GOALS

We can respond to realistic fiction by extending the story.

OBJECTIVES

Write narratives in which they provide some closure.

LANGUAGE OBJECTIVES

Children will narrate by writing a letter with a greeting.

ELA ACADEMIC LANGUAGE

- *prompt, letter, comma*
- Cognate: *letra*

Find Text Evidence Use the Independent Writing Routine. Help children retell the shared read by asking guiding questions. Then read the prompt on p. 146 of the **Reading/Writing Companion**: *Write a letter from Lissy to her paper friends, telling them how things are going now. Let's imagine what Lissy wants to tell her paper friends what happened after they blew away.*

Write a Response Have children complete My Writing Outline 29. Then have them use the sentences from their outline to complete p. 146.

Writing Checklist Read the checklist with children and have them check for these items in their writing.

Beginning Have partners take turns reading their sentences to each other and identifying sentence type: That sentence is a question.

Intermediate Have partners identify pronouns in their writing and explain how they are used: The word *I* is a subject pronoun. It is part of the subject "My new friends and I."

Advanced/Advanced High Have children use the sentence starters on p. T326 of the **Teacher's Edition** to create new sentences.

FORMATIVE ASSESSMENT ▸ **STUDENT CHECK IN** Partners share their sentences from My Writing Outline. Ask children to reflect, using the Check-in routine.

SELF-SELECTED WRITING
LESSON 5

LEARNING GOALS

We can revise our writing.

OBJECTIVES

Use personal, possessive, and indefinite pronouns.

LANGUAGE OBJECTIVES

Children will inquire about their writing by checking pronouns.

ELA ACADEMIC LANGUAGE

- *pronoun*
- Cognate: *pronombre*

Work with children to revise the group writing activity. Point to each word as you read the sentences. Stop to ask questions, such as: *Can we replace this word with a pronoun?* Then have partners revise each other's sentences before publishing their writing.

For support with grammar, refer to the **Language Transfers Handbook** and review object and subject pronouns using **Language Development Cards** 16A and 16B.

FORMATIVE ASSESSMENT ▸ **STUDENT CHECK IN** Partners tell what revisions they made. Ask children to reflect, using the Check-in routine.

ENGLISH LANGUAGE LEARNERS

READING • SHARED READ • ACCESS THE TEXT

LESSONS 1-2

LEARNING GOALS

We can read and understand a nonfiction text.

OBJECTIVES

Ask and answer questions about key details in a text.

Ask and answer questions to help determine or clarify the meaning of words and phrases in a text.

Use the illustrations and details in a text to describe its key ideas.

Ask questions to clear up any confusion about the topics and texts under discussion.

LANGUAGE OBJECTIVES

Children will inform about holidays, using common nouns, proper nouns, and complete sentences.

ELA ACADEMIC LANGUAGE

- photograph
- Cognate: *fotografía*

MATERIALS

Reading/Writing Companion, pp. 158–167

Visual Vocabulary Cards

DIGITAL TOOLS

MULTIMODAL

Have children listen to the selection as they follow along to develop comprehension and practice fluency and pronunciation.

Use the additional grammar song.

🎵 Grammar Song

"Share the Harvest and Give Thanks"

Prepare to Read

Build Background Read aloud the Essential Question on page 158. Have children share ideas about holidays they celebrate. Use the illustrations to generate ideas. Point to and read the title aloud. *We are going to read a nonfiction text about different ways to celebrate the harvest.* Point to the fruits and vegetables on pages 158–159. *A harvest is when many foods people grow are picked. Say* harvest *with me.* Invite children to name the foods they see in the photograph.

Reading/Writing Companion, Lexile 680L

Focus on Vocabulary Use the **Visual Vocabulary Cards** to review the high-frequency words *favorite, few, gone, surprise, wonder,* and *young* and the oral vocabulary words *design, display, pride, purpose,* and *represent.* As you read, use gestures and visual support to teach important story words, such as *celebrate, feast, costumes,* and *nation.* Use this routine for each word: Point to the family at the table on page 162. Say the word *celebrate.* Have children point to the picture and repeat the word. *The family celebrates a holiday together. What holidays do you and your family celebrate?* Help children respond: We celebrate [New Year's Day].

Summarize the Text Before reading, say the summary and point to the images. *This text tells about different harvest celebrations people have in the United States. People like to celebrate the harvest in different ways.*

Read the Text

Use the Interactive Question-Response routine to help children understand the text.

Pages 160–161

Page 160 Read the text aloud as children follow along. Point to the family with the bushel baskets of apples. *People in the United States give thanks for the fall harvest. They give thanks on a holiday called Thanksgiving. Say* Thanksgiving *with me. Thanksgiving is on the fourth Thursday in November. In what season is November?* November is in the fall. *What is the weather like in fall?* The weather is cool.

COLLABORATE *How do people celebrate Thanksgiving? Discuss with a partner.*

Beginning Use the picture on page 160 to review the words *harvest* and *crop. What do people give thanks for on Thanksgiving?* They give thanks for the harvest. Point to the photograph on page 161. *What is one food that you can eat in the fall?* You can eat apples.

Intermediate Help partners give a more specific answer. *What do people give thanks for at Thanksgiving?* They give thanks for the fall harvest. *How do they celebrate?* They celebrate by eating together.

302 UNIT 6 WEEK 5

WEEK 5

Advanced/Advanced High Help partners add details to their response. *What do families want to show that they are thankful for?* Families want to show that they are thankful for the harvest.

Pages 162–163

Page 163 Read the text aloud as children follow along. Point to the family in the photograph. *These people are lighting candles. They are celebrating Kwanzaa. Say Kwanzaa with me. What are the symbols of Kwanzaa?* Corn and fruit are symbols of Kwanzaa. *What do families do to celebrate?* (They have a feast.)

How do people celebrate Kwanzaa? Discuss with a partner.

Beginning Guide children to use the photograph to respond. Point to the family. *What holiday is the family celebrating?* They are celebrating Kwanzaa. *What are they doing?* (lighting candles) Reread the caption. *When does Kwanzaa begin?* It begins on December 26.

Intermediate Help partners give details with their answers. *What ways of celebrating Kwanzaa do you see?* People celebrate Kwanzaa by lighting candles. *What way of celebrating did you read about?* People can celebrate by eating a feast with family.

Advanced/Advanced High Encourage partners to elaborate on their response. *Look at the photo and read the text. What are the different ways that people can celebrate Kwanzaa?* People can light candles, have a big feast with family, and eat corn and fruit.

Pages 164–167

Page 166 Read the text aloud as children follow along. Help children listen actively. Point to the people in the pumpkin boats. *People celebrate the harvest in other ways. What are these people doing?* They are using big pumpkins as boats.

What is one way people in Oregon celebrate the harvest? Discuss with a partner.

Beginning Point to the people paddling pumpkin boats. *What harvest vegetable are people celebrating?* They are celebrating pumpkins. *What do they do after the race?* They make compost.

Intermediate Help partners give details with their answers. *What is another way people celebrate the harvest?* People celebrate by racing boats made from large pumpkins. Reread the caption. *Where does the race take place?* It takes place in Oregon.

Advanced/Advanced High Help partners elaborate on their answers. *Why do you think pumpkin racing is a fun way to celebrate the harvest?* Provide a sentence frame: I think it is a fun way to celebrate the harvest because the race uses a harvest food. People use it after the race to make dirt.

Page 167 Point to the map and explain the key. Match the icons in the key to places on the map. *Two states have corn festivals. What do people there eat to celebrate the harvest?* They eat corn.

FORMATIVE ASSESSMENT

STUDENT CHECK IN

Have partners retell how people celebrate different holidays in the text. Then have children reflect using the Check-In routine.

Independent Time

Asking and Answering Questions Have children ask and answer: *Why do we celebrate holidays?* Pair children of mixed proficiency levels. Have partners discuss why people celebrate holidays like Thanksgiving and Kwanzaa. Have them take turns asking and answering questions. Then have each pair tell the rest of the group. Provide sentence frames to help children respond to questions: *What do people do on Thanksgiving?* People eat foods like turkey, corn, and green beans. *Why do people celebrate Thanksgiving?* They want to say thanks for the harvest. *What foods are symbols for Kwanzaa?* Corn and fruit are symbols for Kwanzaa.

ENGLISH LANGUAGE LEARNERS 303

LESSON 3

READING • ANCHOR TEXT • ACCESS THE TEXT

LEARNING GOALS

We can read and understand a nonfiction text.

OBJECTIVES

Distinguish between information provided by pictures or other illustrations and information provided by the words in a text.

Identify the reasons an author gives to support points in a text.

With prompting and support, read informational texts appropriately complex for grade 1.

Produce complete sentences when appropriate to task and situation.

LANGUAGE OBJECTIVES

Children will inform about the history of the Fourth of July, using common nouns, proper nouns, and complete sentences.

ELA ACADEMIC LANGUAGE

- organize, information, dates
- Cognates: *organizar, información*

MATERIALS

Literature Anthology, pp. 398–405

Visual Vocabulary Cards

DIGITAL TOOLS

Have children listen to the selection as they follow along to develop comprehension and practice fluency and pronunciation.

Use the online ELL Vocabulary Practice for additional support.

Happy Birthday, U.S.A.!

Prepare to Read

Build Background *We are going to read a text about how and why people celebrate the Fourth of July. The Fourth of July is a special holiday for people in the United States.* Show the title page and invite children to tell what they see. Point to the *fireworks, parade, drums,* and *trumpet.* Say the words and have children repeat. Then point to the children on page 399. *These children are in a parade. They are wearing special clothes. They are marching. They are playing music. This is the way they celebrate the Fourth of July. What are other ways people might celebrate?* People might celebrate by looking at _____. Invite children to think of holidays they know and tell how they celebrate them.

Literature Anthology, Lexile 490L

Focus on Vocabulary Use the **Visual Vocabulary Cards** to review the high-frequency words *favorite, few, gone, surprise, wonder,* and *young,* and the oral vocabulary words *design, display, pride, purpose,* and *represent.* As you read, use gestures and pantomime to teach important selection words, such as *light up, crowds, ruled, laws, declaration,* and *blared.*

Summarize the Text Before reading, say the summary while pointing to the illustrations. *The text tells how people celebrate the Fourth of July. It also tells how the United States became a new country.*

Read the Text

Use the Interactive Question-Response routine to help children understand the text.

Pages 398–401

Pages 398–399 Read the text. Point to and say the sound words *Whiz! Boom! Bang!* Have children repeat. *What makes these sounds?* (fireworks) Point to the children on page 399. *The children are celebrating in a parade. What holiday do they celebrate?* They celebrate the Fourth of July. Help children practice pronouncing the word *Fourth,* focusing on the voiceless *th* sound. *The Fourth of July is the birthday of which country?* The Fourth of July is the birthday of the United States. *People do different things to celebrate this holiday. They watch fireworks, go to parades, and have picnics. People have been celebrating the Fourth of July for a long time. How long have people celebrated this holiday?* People have celebrated it for more than 200 years.

Page 400 Read the text. Point to the picture of the horse and carriage. *Does this picture show something from life today or from long ago?* It shows something from life long ago. Point to *In 1775* in the text. *The text tells what our nation was*

304 UNIT 6 WEEK 5

like in 1775, a date long ago. Was it big or small? It was small. *Who was the leader?* The king of England was the leader. *Did people like the king?* No, people did not like the king.

Page 401 Read the text. Point to *On June 11, 1776. This date tells us that the event described on this page happened long ago. The leaders of the colonies met. What did they want to do?* They wanted to make their own rules and laws.

How does the author organize the information in the text? Discuss with a partner.

Beginning *What information does the author give first?* The author tells how people celebrate the Fourth of July. Point to *1775* and then *1776: What do both pages 400 and 401 begin with?* They begin with dates. *Do the pages tell about things that happen today or that happened in the past?* (the past)

Intermediate *What information does the author give first?* The author tells how people celebrate the Fourth of July. Guide partners to point to the dates as they discuss. *Do the pages tell what's happening today or what happened in the past?* They tell about what happened in the past. *How do you know?* The pages start with dates. The pages tell about the past.

Advanced/Advanced High Extend the discussion by having partners talk about the type of information they learn on pages 400 and 401 and how it differs from what they learn on page 399. The author tells about events that happened before the holiday began.

Pages 402–403

Page 402 Read the text. Point to the statue and read the caption. *Whom is this a statue of?* (Thomas Jefferson) *What did he write?* (the Declaration of Independence) *To declare is to say something loud and strong. What did Thomas Jefferson declare?* He declared that people wanted to be free. *This way people could choose their own government. A government makes rules for a country.*

Page 403 Read the text. Point to the painting. *The leaders are signing the Declaration of Independence. Whom did they send the declaration to?* They sent it to the king of England. *What happened one year later?* People celebrated with fireworks.

Pages 404–405 Read the text. *Why does the text say the Declaration of Independence was just the beginning?* People had to fight to get freedom. *What makes the Fourth of July fun?* (picnics, parades)

Why does the author use dates in the text? Discuss with a partner.

Beginning Help partners review page 403. *Point to where you see dates on this page.* Guide children to point to *July 4, 1776* and *July 4. Does the date 1776 tell you this page is about today or the past?* The date 1776 tells me this page is about the past.

Intermediate *Point to dates in the text.* Check that children point to *July 4, 1776* and *July 4. What do you know when you read the date 1776?* I know that the author is talking about events in the past.

Advanced/Advanced High Extend the discussion: *How would the text be different if the author did not tell the dates?* If the author did not tell the dates, you might not be sure of when the events happened. You might get confused.

FORMATIVE ASSESSMENT

❯ STUDENT CHECK IN

Have partners retell why the Fourth of July is a holiday. Then have children reflect using the Check-In routine

Independent Time

Make a Birthday Card Pair children of mixed proficiency levels. Have pairs work together to create a birthday card for the United States. Explain that children should include details about how the United States was formed long ago. They should also include details about how the Fourth of July is celebrated today. When pairs have finished creating their birthday card, encourage them to present their work to another pair, a small group, or the whole class. They should show the card and explain why they included the details they did.

ENGLISH LANGUAGE LEARNERS **305**

LESSONS 4-5

READING • LEVELED READER • ACCESS THE TEXT

LEARNING GOALS

We can reread to better understand a nonfiction text.

OBJECTIVES

Identify the reasons an author gives to support points in a text.

Identify basic similarities in and differences between two texts on the same topic (e.g., in illustrations, descriptions, or procedures).

Build on others' talk in conversations by responding to the comments of others through multiple exchanges.

Describe people, places, things, and events with relevant details, expressing ideas and feelings clearly.

LANGUAGE OBJECTIVES

Children will inform about Labor Day traditions, using compound words and proper nouns.

ELA ACADEMIC LANGUAGE

- author, purpose, reread
- Cognate: *autor*

MATERIALS

ELL Leveled Reader:
It's Labor Day!

Online Differentiated Texts,
"Memorial Day"

Online ELL Visual Vocabulary Cards

DIGITAL TOOLS

Have children listen to the selection as they follow along to develop comprehension and practice fluency and pronunciation. Use Graphic Organizer 4: Author's Purpose to enhance the lesson.

It's Labor Day!

Prepare to Read

Build Background

- Remind children of the Essential Question. *Let's read a nonfiction text to learn about why people celebrate Labor Day.* Encourage children to ask for help when they do not understand a word or phrase.

- Point to and read the title aloud and have children repeat. Ask: *What is the title?* Point to the table of contents. *What are the titles of Chapter 1 and Chapter 2?* Point to the images to name things and actions; for example: *This is a factory. These people are working in a factory. What are some other places that people can work?*

Focus on Vocabulary Use **ELL Visual Vocabulary Cards** to preteach the words *honor* and *relax*. Then use gestures or visuals to clarify key terms, such as *work, parade, concert, picnic,* and *beach*.

Lexile 360L

Read the Text

Use the Interactive Question-Response routine to help children understand the text.

Pages 2–5

Read pages 2–5 as children follow along. Ask questions to help children discuss the history of Labor Day.

Beginning Point to the bottom of page 5. *What does the question ask?* It asks why we celebrate Labor Day. *Did the text answer this?* (yes)

Advanced/Advanced High Have pairs discuss: *What is the purpose of Labor Day?* The purpose is to honor workers.

Pages 6–7

Read pages 6–7 as children follow along. Point to the visuals for *parade, flag, outdoor,* and *concert*. Have children point to and repeat the words.

Intermediate *What are two ways that cities celebrate Labor Day?* Cities celebrate Labor Day with parades and outdoor concerts.

Advanced/Advanced High Have partners discuss why cities celebrate Labor Day with events like parades and outdoor concerts. Parades and outdoor concerts give workers something fun to do.

306 UNIT 6 WEEK 5

WEEK 5

Pages 8–11

Read pages 10–11 aloud as children follow along. Guide children to reread the text to monitor their comprehension.

Beginning Help partners work together to respond. *What is Labor Day the end of?* Labor Day is the end of summer. *What do children do the next day?* They go to school.

Intermediate *Why else is Labor Day important?* Labor Day is the end of summer. Children go to school the next day.

Author's Purpose Help children identify the author's purpose for writing this text. (The author wants to inform about why we celebrate Labor Day. The author also informs about how we celebrate.)

Respond to Reading Have partners work together to retell the text and respond to the questions on page 12.

Focus on Fluency

Read pages 10–11 to model appropriate phrasing. Read the passage again and have children repeat after you. For more practice, record children reading the passage and select the best recording.

Paired Read: "A Celebration of Trees"

Make Connections: Write About It

Echo-read each page with children. Discuss what Arbor Day is: *How can people celebrate Arbor Day?* They can plant trees and flowers. Help children make connections between texts using the question on page 15. It is important to celebrate how both workers and trees help us.

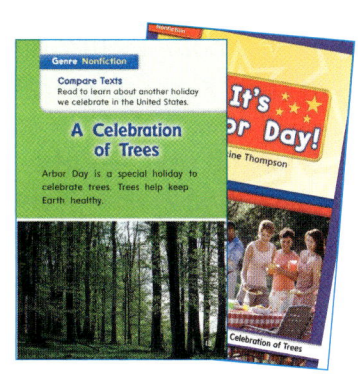

Leveled Reader

Build Knowledge: Make Connections

Talk About the Text Have partners discuss why we celebrate the holidays discussed in the text.

Write About the Text Have students add their ideas to the Build Knowledge pages of their reader's notebooks.

Self-Selected Reading

Help children choose an informational text from the online **Leveled Reader Library,** or read the **Differentiated Text,** "Memorial Day."

FOCUS ON SOCIAL STUDIES

Children can extend their knowledge of workers they know by completing the social studies activity on page 16.

LITERATURE CIRCLES

Lead children in conducting a literature circle, using the Thinkmark questions to guide the discussion. You may wish to discuss what children have learned about holidays from reading the two selections in the Leveled Reader.

FORMATIVE ASSESSMENT

STUDENT CHECK IN

Have partners share their Respond to Reading. Have children reflect using the Check-In routine.

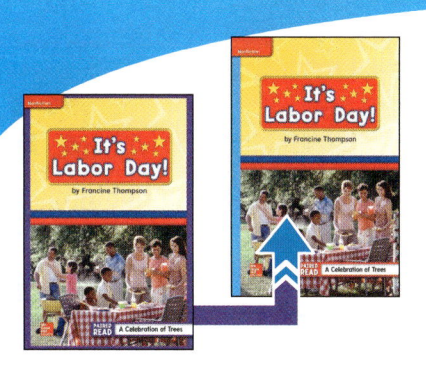

LEVEL UP

IF children can read *It's Labor Day!* **ELL Level** with fluency and correctly answer the Respond to Reading questions,

THEN tell children that they will read a more detailed version of the selection.

- Use pages 2–3 of *It's Labor Day!* **On Level** and Teaching Poster 38 to list clues about the author's purpose.
- Have children read the selection, checking their comprehension by using the graphic organizer.

ENGLISH LANGUAGE LEARNERS 307

READING • GENRE PASSAGE • ACCESS THE TEXT

LESSONS 4-5

LEARNING GOALS

We can apply skills and strategies to a nonfiction text.

OBJECTIVES

Explain major differences between books that tell stories and books that give information, drawing on a wide reading of a range of text types.

Identify basic similarities in and differences between two texts on the same topic (e.g., in illustrations, descriptions, or procedures).

With prompting and support, read informational texts appropriately complex for grade 1.

Produce complete sentences when appropriate to task and situation.

LANGUAGE OBJECTIVES

Children will reread to inform about the text, using key vocabulary. Children will discuss the author's purpose and use a metaphor.

ELA ACADEMIC LANGUAGE

- photo, caption, reread
- Cognate: *foto*

MATERIALS

Online ELL Genre Passage, "Earth Day: Then and Now," pp. E1–E3

"Earth Day: Then and Now"

Prepare to Read

Build Background Review what children have learned about different holidays. *What are some reasons people celebrate holidays?* People celebrate the independence of their _____. People celebrate to remember _____. Allow children to share additional ideas. Tell children they will be reading about a holiday where people celebrate Earth and the environment.

Lexile 450L

Focus on Vocabulary Use the **Define, Example, Ask** routine to preteach difficult words or unfamiliar concepts, such as *remind, air, water, plant, trash, recycling,* and *gift*. Invite children to add new vocabulary to their glossaries.

Read the Text

Use the Interactive Question-Response routine to help children understand the text.

Page E1

Paragraph 1 Read the text aloud as children follow along. Point to the phrase *take care of*. To take care of something *is to make sure it has what it needs to survive. How can we take care of Earth?* Remind children that they can reread when they do not understand text. We can take care of Earth by keeping air and water clean.

Advanced/Advanced High Point to the people in the photo. *What are these people doing?* They are picking up trash. *How is picking up trash related to Earth Day?* Picking up trash is a way to take care of Earth.

Paragraph 2 Read the text aloud as children follow along. Point to the date. *The first Earth Day was celebrated on April 22, 1970. What did people do on the first Earth Day?* People helped clean up Earth. Point to the photo. *Who were many of the people who helped?* Many of the people who helped were children.

Have partners discuss: *What do the photo and caption help you learn about the first Earth Day?* Encourage children to **reread** text. The photo and caption help me learn that many children/students helped on Earth Day. They also help me understand some of the activities people did.

Page E2

Paragraph 1 Read the text aloud as children follow along. *People around the world celebrate Earth Day. What do they do?* They learn new ways to help Earth, like using less water.

Advanced Have children ask and answer with a partner: *Why is learning to use less water a good way to celebrate Earth Day?* It's a good way to celebrate Earth Day because it helps the Earth.

308 UNIT 6 WEEK 5

WEEK 5

Advanced High Have partners discuss: *Why do you think that using too much water could be a problem? If we don't use less water, there* might not be enough water left for people to survive.

Paragraphs 2–3 Read the text aloud as children follow along. *Some people plant trees.* Point to the photo. *What are these children doing?* They are recycling trash. *Recycling is another way that people help Earth.*

Beginning Guide children to point to the photo as they respond. *What are the children doing?* The children are recycling trash. *What is one way people help Earth?* People help by recycling.

Paragraph 4 Read the text aloud as children follow along. *Earth Day is a day when people work together. Why do they work together?* They work together to help Earth. Point to the word *gift*. *A gift is something special that you are given. Earth is something special.*

Intermediate Have children discuss the *author's purpose* with a partner: *Why does the author include the last sentence,* Earth is a gift*?* The author wants to remind us of why people work to take care of the Earth.

Metaphors Remind children that a metaphor is a figure of speech that compares one thing to another. *Authors use metaphors to help describe something for the reader. Similes use the word* like *or* as, *but metaphors do not.* Have children look at the last sentence on E2. *What is the metaphor?* (Earth is a gift!) *What two things are being compared?* (Earth, a gift) *What is the author trying to tell us?* (Possible response: Earth is special. We should take care of it.)

Respond to Reading

Use the following instructions to help children answer the questions on page E3.

1. **Nonfiction** Have children describe what they see in the photos and captions. Ask questions to help them complete the sentence; for example: *What are the people in the photo doing?* (The people are picking up trash on the first Earth Day. The children are recycling at home.)

2. **Author's Purpose** Help children reread pages E1 and E2. Ask: *What is the author's purpose in the text?* The author's purpose is to inform us about the holiday Earth Day. *What does the author want to persuade you to do?* The author wants people to take care of Earth.

3. **Fluency** Have children take turns reading the first paragraph to a partner. As they read, fill in the chart on page E3.

Build Knowledge: Make Connections

Talk About the Text Have partners discuss why we celebrate Earth Day.

Write About the Text Have students add their ideas to their Build Knowledge pages of their reader's notebooks.

FORMATIVE ASSESSMENT

STUDENT CHECK IN

Have partners share their Respond to Reading. Then have children reflect using the Check-In routine.

LEVEL UP

IF students read the **ELL** fluently and answered the questions,

THEN pair them with students who have proficiently read the **On Level.** Have them

- partner read the **On Level** passage.
- reread to increase understanding of the text.

ENGLISH LANGUAGE LEARNERS **309**

LESSONS 1-5

WRITING

MODELED WRITING

LESSON 1

LEARNING GOALS

We can learn how to write a paragraph.

OBJECTIVES

Write opinion pieces in which they supply a reason for the opinion.

LANGUAGE OBJECTIVES

Children will argue by writing a paragraph using words that show feeling.

ELA ACADEMIC LANGUAGE

- opinion
- Cognate: *opinión*

Writing Practice Have children choral read the sample on p. 168 of the **Reading/Writing Companion**. Use the Actor/Description routine: *What is this sentence about?* (my favorite holiday) *How can we describe it?* (is Earth Day) Then read the prompt on p. 169 and ask children to answer it as a group. Write their paragraph on the board and ask them to choral read. Then help children write their own paragraph.

Beginning Provide a sentence frame to help children write their opinion: *My favorite holiday is* Thanksgiving. Ask questions to help children support their opinion: *Who do you celebrate with? What do you do? Why do you like it?*

Intermediate Have partners ask and answer questions to create their sentences: *What is your favorite holiday? Why do you like it?*

Advanced/Advanced High Have children exchange sentences and identify the opinion, reason(s), and words that show feelings.

FORMATIVE ASSESSMENT ▸ **STUDENT CHECK IN** Partners share their sentences. Ask children to reflect, using the Check-In routine.

INTERACTIVE WRITING

LESSON 2

LEARNING GOALS

We can read and write about a Student Model.

OBJECTIVES

With guidance and support from adults, focus on a topic.

LANGUAGE OBJECTIVES

Children will discuss and write sentences about the Student Model and identify reasons for an opinion.

ELA ACADEMIC LANGUAGE

- opinion, adverb
- Cognates: *opinión, adverbio*

Analyze the Student Model Have children finger point as they choral read the Student Model on p. 176 of the **Reading/Writing Companion**. Check comprehension of the first sentence. *What is the author's opinion?* (It is very important to give thanks for a harvest.) Use the Actor/Action routine to review the remaining sentences. Discuss the adverb at the end. *What adverb do you see in the last sentence?* (yearly) *What action does it describe?* (giving thanks) Then help children complete p. 177.

Beginning Have partners point to reasons for Grace's opinion in the text.

Intermediate Have partners identify the words that tell feelings: Grace used the word *thankful* to tell how she feels.

Advanced/Advanced High Challenge children to write about the Student Model using their own sentences. Encourage them to share their ideas.

FORMATIVE ASSESSMENT ▸ **STUDENT CHECK IN** Partners share their sentences. Ask children to reflect, using the Check-In routine.

310 UNIT 6 WEEK 5

WEEK 5

INDEPENDENT WRITING

LESSONS 3-4

LEARNING GOALS

We can write an opinion about nonfiction text.

OBJECTIVES

Write opinion pieces in which they supply a reason for the opinion.

LANGUAGE OBJECTIVES

Children will argue by writing a paragraph and giving reasons to support their opinion.

ELA ACADEMIC LANGUAGE

- *opinion, adverb*
- Cognates: *opinión, adverbio*

Find Text Evidence Use the Independent Writing routine. Help children retell the anchor text. Ask questions, such as: *When is the birthday of the United States?* (July 4th) *In 1775, who ruled the 13 colonies?* (the king of England) Then read the prompt on p. 181 of the **Reading/Writing Companion:** *Which part of the Fourth of July celebration is the most important to you? Use text evidence. We need to give our opinion about the Fourth of July celebration. Then we need to write reasons why.*

Write a Response Work with children to fill out My Writing Outline 30. Then have them use the sentences from their outline to complete p. 181.

Writing Checklist Read the checklist with students and have them check for these items in their writing.

Beginning Provide sentence frames to help partners talk about their paragraph: I used the word *thankful* to tell about my feelings.

Intermediate Have partners identify reasons and then identify an adverb and explain how it is used: The word *together* tells how we have picnics and watch fireworks.

Advanced/Advanced High Have children use the sentence starters on p. T408 of the **Teacher's Edition** to write their own sentences.

FORMATIVE ASSESSMENT ❯ **STUDENT CHECK IN** Partners share their sentences from My Writing Outline. Ask children to reflect, using the Check-in routine.

SELF-SELECTED WRITING

LESSON 5

LEARNING GOALS

We can revise our writing.

OBJECTIVES

Produce and expand complete simple declarative sentences.

LANGUAGE OBJECTIVES

Children will inquire about their writing by checking adverbs.

ELA ACADEMIC LANGUAGE

- *adverb*
- Cognate: *adverbio*

Work with children to revise the group writing activity. Point to each word as you read the sentences. Stop to ask questions, such as: *Can we add an adverb here that tells how or when?* Then have partners revise each other's sentences before publishing their writing.

For support with grammar and adverbs that tell how, refer to the **Language Transfers Handbook** and **Language Development Card** 15B.

FORMATIVE ASSESSMENT ❯ **STUDENT CHECK IN** Partners tell what revisions they made. Ask children to reflect, using the Check-in routine.

ENGLISH LANGUAGE LEARNERS **311**

UNIT 6

Summative Assessment
Get Ready for Unit Assessment

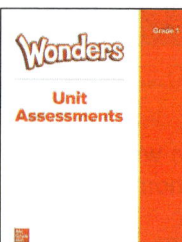

Unit 6 Tested Skills

LISTENING AND READING COMPREHENSION	VOCABULARY	GRAMMAR	SPEAKING AND WRITING
• Listening Actively • Details	• Words and Categories	• Pronouns • Adverbs	• Presenting • Composing/Writing • Supporting Opinions • Retelling/Recounting

Create a Student Profile

Record data from the following resources in the Student Profile charts on pages 356–357 of the Assessment book.

COLLABORATIVE	INTERPRETIVE	PRODUCTIVE

• Collaborative Conversations Rubrics
  • Listening
  • Speaking
	• Leveled Unit Assessment
	  • Listening Comprehension
	  • Reading Comprehension
	  • Vocabulary
	  • Grammar
	• Presentation Rubric
	  • Listening
	• *Wonders* Unit Assessment
		• Weekly Progress Monitoring
		• Leveled Unit Assessment
		  • Speaking
		  • Writing
		• Presentation Rubric
		  • Speaking
		• Write to Sources Rubric
		• *Wonders* Unit Assessment

The Foundational Skills Kit, Language Development Kit, and Adaptive Learning provide additional student data for progress monitoring.

Level Up

Use the following chart, along with your Student Profiles, to guide your Level Up decisions.

LEVEL UP	If **BEGINNING** level students are able to do the following, they may be ready to move to the **INTERMEDIATE** level:	If **INTERMEDIATE** level students are able to do the following, they may be ready to move to the **ADVANCED** level:	If **ADVANCED** level students are able to do the following, they may be ready to move to **ON** level:
COLLABORATIVE	• participate in collaborative conversations using basic vocabulary and grammar and simple phrases or sentences • discuss simple pictorial or text prompts	• participate in collaborative conversations using appropriate words and phrases and complete sentences • use limited academic vocabulary across and within disciplines	• participate in collaborative conversations using more sophisticated vocabulary and correct grammar • communicate effectively across a wide range of language demands in social and academic contexts
INTERPRETIVE	• identify details in simple read alouds • understand common vocabulary and idioms and interpret language related to familiar social, school, and academic topics • make simple inferences and make simple comparisons • exhibit an emerging receptive control of lexical, syntactic, phonological, and discourse features	• identify main ideas and/or make some inferences from simple read alouds • use context clues to identify word meanings and interpret basic vocabulary and idioms • compare, contrast, summarize, and relate text to graphic organizers • exhibit a limited range of receptive control of lexical, syntactic, phonological, and discourse features when addressing new or familiar topics	• determine main ideas in read alouds that have advanced vocabulary • use context clues to determine meaning, understand multiple-meaning words, and recognize synonyms of social and academic vocabulary • analyze information, make sophisticated inferences, and explain their reasoning • command a high degree of receptive control of lexical, syntactic, phonological, and discourse features
PRODUCTIVE	• express ideas and opinions with basic vocabulary and grammar and simple phrases or sentences • restate information or retell a story using basic vocabulary • exhibit an emerging productive control of lexical, syntactic, phonological, and discourse features	• produce coherent language with limited elaboration or detail • restate information or retell a story using mostly accurate, although limited, vocabulary • exhibit a limited range of productive control of lexical, syntactic, phonological, and discourse features when addressing new or familiar topics	• produce sentences with more sophisticated vocabulary and correct grammar • restate information or retell a story using extensive and accurate vocabulary and grammar • tailor language to a particular purpose and audience • command a high degree of productive control of lexical, syntactic, phonological, and discourse features